The International Handbook of Corporate and Personal Taxes

Sixth Edition

NEXIA INTERNATIONAL

Edited by John Cooney

Tolley
A Member of the LexisNexis Group

Members of the LexisNexis Group worldwide

United Kingdom	Butterworths Tolley, a Division of Reed Elsevier (UK) Ltd, Halsbury House, 35 Chancery Lane, London, WC2A 1EL, and 4 Hill Street, Edinburgh EH2 3JZ
Argentina	Abeledo Perrot, Jurisprudencia Argentina and Depalma, Buenos Aires
Australia	Butterworths, a Division of Reed International Books Australia Pty Ltd, Chatswood, New South Wales
Austria	ARD Betriebsdienst and Verlag Orac, Vienna
Canada	Butterworths Canada Ltd, Markham, Ontario
Chile	Publitecsa and Conosur Ltda, Santiago de Chile
Czech Republic	Orac sro, Prague
France	Editions du Juris-Classeur SA, Paris
Hong Kong	Butterworths Asia (Hong Kong), Hong Kong
Hungary	Hvg Orac, Budapest
India	Butterworths India, New Delhi
Ireland	Butterworths (Ireland) Ltd, Dublin
Italy	Giuffré, Milan
Malaysia	Malayan Law Journal Sdn Bhd, Kuala Lumpur
New Zealand	Butterworths of New Zealand, Wellington
Poland	Wydawnictwa Prawnicze PWN, Warsaw
Singapore	Butterworths Asia, Singapore
South Africa	Butterworths Publishers (Pty) Ltd, Durban
Switzerland	Stämpfli Verlag AG, Berne
USA	LexisNexis, Dayton, Ohio

A CIP Catalogue record for this book is available from the British Library.

ISBN 0 406 94627 2

Typeset by YHT Ltd, London
Printed and bound in Great Britain by The Bath Press, Bath

Introduction

This book has been produced by Nexia International, the twelfth largest international network of accounting firms in the world. It is represented by more than 3000 in over 76 countries worldwide. My thanks go to all the contributors.

Each chapter in the Handbook has been compiled by a Nexia member firm in the country concerned and describes in outline the tax system of that country. A unique feature of this publication is that it includes information on both corporate and personal taxes. A table of withholding taxes, applicable under each country's double taxation treaties with its major trading partners, is included in each chapter.

A standard format is followed throughout the book so that whichever country is involved, the reader will know exactly where to look for the information he or she requires.

The book will be useful to businessmen, finance directors, lawyers and accountants who are either already involved in trading internationally or are contemplating looking beyond their own borders for the first time. It will also prove to be an invaluable reference work for professional advisers whose clients are operating in foreign countries.

Individual employees taking up employment in foreign countries will be able to obtain some idea of their future tax liabilities and to compare them with liability in their own country.

Tax is a cost of doing business just like any other cost. It is vitally important for any business to know the additional tax costs of operating outside its own country. Skilled professional advice is essential to ensure that businesses are structured in such a way that overall tax liability is kept to an absolute minimum.

While the Handbook aims to provide accurate and up-to-date information at the time of publication, it is no substitute for international tax advice, which should be sought from an international tax practitioner before any action is taken or a decision is made.

Every effort has been taken to ensure the accuracy of the contents of this book. However, neither the authors nor the publishers can accept any responsibility for any loss occasioned to any person acting or refraining from action in reliance on any statement contained in the book.

The reader should contact, in the first instance, his nearest Nexia office (details are shown at the end of the book) or by using the facilities in the Nexia website www.nexia.com. Alternatively, he may obtain direct access to the Nexia International Tax Committee, a team of international tax experts from all over the world, by writing or emailing to the Chairman:

John Cooney
Tax Committee Chairman
Smith and Williamson
No.1 Riding House Street
London
W1A 3AS
United Kingdom

Email: JCC1@smith.williamson.co.uk

John Cooney
Editor
August 2001

Contents

Argentina

Estudio Giordano & Asociados

Introduction

Taxation in Argentina is applied at Federal, Provincial, and Municipal level.

The main taxes are based on income, on sale of goods and services, and on estates. The main tax collector is the federal government acting through its tax bureau, the Administracion Federal de Ingresos Públicos (AFIP) and its agent, the Dirección General Impositiva (DGI).

All taxpayers are issued with an identification number by the DGI. This number applies for all taxes payable to the Federal Government and must be printed on invoices, delivery notes and receipts.

Taxes are paid mainly on the basis of self-assessment. Every year individuals and all other taxable entities prepare and file a return for each tax for which they are liable and compute the amount payable; VAT (Federal tax) and turnover tax (Provincial tax) are paid on a monthly basis.

Payments are made through the use of personalised payslips prepared by the tax administration. According to the statute of limitations, the tax administration has the authority to revise the returns within five years, on 1 January of the year following the year in which the return is filed. For example, 2000 income tax for individuals due in April 2001 is subject to review until December 2006.

The taxpayer may file a rectifying return during this period. If there is a balance to be paid, interest will be applicable and the tax bureau may impose penalties.

If tax has been overpaid, it is the taxpayer who must initiate the administrative procedure to obtain recognition from the tax bureau of the balance in his favour. If the claim is accepted, it may be offset against any other tax payable to the DGI.

Regarding income tax, the tax bureau has a withholding scheme, which classifies taxpayers into two groups, as follows:

- for resident individuals or corporations, a withholding income tax is applicable on the payment of rentals, fees, interests, royalties, services, and commercial transactions if the amount paid exceeds a given limit. The limits and rates of tax applicable vary according to the type of payment. The amounts withheld are offset against the annual tax liability;
- for foreign beneficiaries, individuals or corporations, flat allowances for expenses are fixed for each type of income without any proof to the contrary. A tax rate of 35% is then applied to the net income, as full and final payment.

Profits from local transactions in shares and bonds made by individuals or corporations not domiciled in Argentina are income tax free.

Corporate taxes

Taxable entities

Resident companies

Resident companies are liable to income tax on their worldwide income, including capital gains. A company is considered resident if it is incorporated under Argentine law. Branches of foreign companies are treated as resident companies and are required to carry complete and separate accounting records to determine their Argentine source income. Resident companies are taxed on worldwide income.

Non-resident companies

Non-resident companies are liable to income tax on Argentine source income including capital gains (with the exception of income from shares and bonds). They are generally taxed through withholding taxes applied at a 35% rate.

Fiscal year and filing requirements

The fiscal year is normally the financial year of the company.

The taxpayer must prepare a return determining taxable income and assessing the tax. One part of the return provides figures from the taxpayer's financial statements and must be signed by an independent accountant. It is not mandatory that this professional be the same person who has audited the financial statements. The due date for the return is the fifth month after the financial year end. Payment of tax is due on the same day.

Ten monthly advance payments, based on the previous year's tax payable, are due commencing on the sixth month of the financial year.

Taxes imposed

Tax on income is levied only at the Federal level by the DGI.

Income tax rate

The rate applicable is 35% on taxable profit for resident and non-resident corporations.

Income subject to tax

General rules

Income subject to tax is based on the profits obtained from the activity of the company determined on a consistent basis year to year. Profits or losses from the sale of fixed assets must be included as well as profits from the sale or disposal of any other assets of the company.

Stock/ inventory valuation

As a general rule, commercial and industrial year end inventories are to be valued at the latest purchase price or the production cost within the last two months of the financial year. If there has been no purchase or production in the period, earlier costs must be updated at the period end on the basis of the wholesale price index.

Production costs include indirect costs. Specific industries such as cattle breeding, construction, etc., are subject to special treatment.

Unit prices cannot be higher than market value and obsolete or depreciated items may be written down to their probable market value but a general reserve is not allowed.

Capital gains and losses

Capital gains and losses have no special treatment, with the exception of losses from the sale of shares, which may only be offset against profits of the same type.

Dividends

Dividends paid by local companies are not taxable, however, when dividends paid on a book profit are higher than the taxable income for the same period, a withholding at a rate of 35% as full and final payment is applicable on such excess.

Deductions

General rules

All expenses incurred in order to obtain and maintain taxable income are deductible. Where a company has both taxable and non-taxable income, expenses must be apportioned.

Depreciation and amortisation

In general, all fixed assets which are related to the activity of a company are subject to depreciation. The depreciation rates are generally applied on a straight line basis. The most common rates are the following:

Buildings	2%
Machinery and furniture	10%
Vehicles	20%

Other depreciation rates or methods may be applied if technically justified in accordance with the nature of the activity.

These expenses are adjusted for inflation between the date of purchase and March 1992. For fixed assets, the depreciation is not adjusted for inflationary increases after that date.

Goodwill, trademarks and similar intangible assets cannot be amortised for income tax purposes.

Organisation costs and research and development expenses may be deducted at the taxpayer's option, as follows:

- in the year they are expensed; or
- in the first five years.

Royalties

Royalty expenses are deductible. If the recipient is a foreign parent company, royalty expenses are deductible provided withholding tax has been paid to the tax bureau.

Interest

Interest paid or accrued is deductible. If the beneficiary is not a local bank, income tax must be withheld. As with royalties, interest paid to a foreign parent company is deductible as long as the withholding tax has been paid to the tax bureau. Since 1 January 1999, some limitations on the deduction of interest may be applied where unacceptable debt to equity ratios applies.

Dividends

Dividends paid are not deductible.

Bad and doubtful accounts

A reserve for doubtful accounts or a straight write-off is deductible up to justifiable amounts and in accordance with consistent business practice.

Employees' and directors' remuneration and benefits

These items are fully deductible, as are the following:

- dismissal indemnities (termination payments) at the time of payment;
- directors' fees are deductible up to a maximum of 25% of book profits.

Specifically non-deductible expenses

These include:

- goodwill and trademark amortisation;
- in general, any expense related to non-assessable income;
- taxes on undeveloped real estate;
- remuneration and fees paid to foreign advisors and to directors who work abroad when these are in excess of given limits;
- donations made in amounts exceeding 5% of the year's profits or which are made to Federal, Provincial or Municipal treasuries or legally recognised public benefit institutions.

Foreign source income

Since 1 April 1992, resident corporations and the branches of foreign corporations have been assessable on worldwide income (see above under taxable entities). A credit may be given for foreign tax paid.

Investment incentives and special benefits

Some companies continue to enjoy benefits from laws, which were established to promote investment in certain provinces for a limited period. However, it is considered unlikely that the government will establish new incentives or benefits of this kind.

Incentives established to encourage non-traditional exports are tax exempt.

Mining activity enjoys some special tax benefits as well as forestry activity, and also wind and sun power generation.

Specific schemes of financing or reimbursement – under certain circumstances – of VAT paid at the time of purchase or importation are granted to investments in capital goods.

Related party transaction and transfer pricing

Since December 1998, in accordance with OECD international rules, transfer pricing regulations have been adopted. Related party transactions must be on an arm's length basis. Consequently, the transfer prices must be evaluated under the terms of various methods defined in income tax law. Taxpayers must keep supporting documentation and reporting requirements must be fulfilled.

Losses

Losses may be carried forward for five years to offset future profits. No carry back is allowed.

Losses arising from the sale of shares and trading in investment funds can only be offset against profits of the same type. Foreign source losses are treated in the same way.

Corporate groups

Each company must prepare an individual return. Group filing is not allowed.

Tax free mergers and disposals

Mergers and reorganisations are authorised by Argentine law. For tax purposes, the assets and liabilities of the merged corporation maintain the same values in the surviving company.

Tax losses may be carried forward.

If a merger complies with the rules established by income tax law, there is no taxable effect for the shareholders.

Liquidation of a company

Upon liquidation of a corporation, the final difference between funds available and paid up share capital is treated as the company's taxable profit.

Capital distributions are not taxable in the hands of the shareholder (both company and individuals).

Capital taxes

Capital duty

Under stamp tax regulations, a 1% duty was levied on the capital of any type of company at the time of its formation and on future increases in the capital. This duty has been discontinued at federal level, but still exists in several provinces.

Minimum presumed income tax

This tax is calculated on total of assets less investment in other corporations.

Fixed assets are not taxable during the two years subsequent to purchase. Cars are excluded from this relief.

Under certain conditions similar taxes paid to foreign countries are treated as prepayments.

The rate is 1%. Income tax assessed for same fiscal year is computable as a payment on account of this tax. However, if payment is due (income tax is less than 1% of valuation of assets) then, this payment may be carried forward for ten years to be offset against future income tax liability if certain requirements are fulfilled.

Banks and insurance companies are entitled to a reduced rate of tax.

Treatment of branches (branch profits tax)

The profits of foreign branches of resident corporations are assessable. The profits of branches of foreign corporations are assessable on the same basis as resident corporations. Consequently, when the transfer of a branch book profits is higher than the taxable income a withholding at a rate of 35% is applicable on such excess (see 'Dividends' above).

Personal taxes

Taxes on income

The federal government collects tax on income.

The tax bureau is entitled to revise tax returns within a five year period (as described above for corporations).

Taxable individuals

Residents

Income tax law establishes the conditions under which an individual is considered resident for tax purposes. As a general rule, individuals with Argentine nationality and foreigners with permanent residence in Argentina are considered residents.

In the case of residents, worldwide income is subject to taxation.

Non-residents

For individuals who do not qualify as resident, only Argentine income is subject to tax through withholding.

Tax year and filing requirements

An individual's tax year is the calendar year. Returns must be filed in April of the following year. Residents whose income is solely from employment and who have been subject to withholding tax on that income are not required to file tax returns.

Sources of income

An individual's income is classified in four ways, as follows:

- income from real estate (usually rental);

- income from capital investment (interest, sale of goodwill, dividends, royalties, annuities);
- income from business activities;
- income from personal services or pensions.

Employment income and directors' fees

All remuneration and benefits paid to residents is subject to tax. Withholdings for social security contributions must be declared and deducted by the employer. The employer must prepare a tax return to calculate the income tax he must withhold from the employee's monthly salary. At year end, the employer prepares and files a final return with the tax bureau.

Business income

For income tax purposes, trading profits are calculated in accordance with generally accepted accounting principles. Yearly income is included in the calendar year in which the financial year of the business ends.

Capital gains

As a general rule, capital gains are not taxable for individuals, although capital gains made in the course of business are taxable.

Individuals must pay a transfer tax of 1.5% on the sale price of non-business related real estate. This exempts the transfer from income tax.

Dividends

Dividends are tax-free since corporations pay a straight 35% on their taxable income (see 'Dividends' under 'Corporate taxes').

Interest

Interest from deposits in banks and finance companies are tax-free. All other interest is taxable.

Rentals

All rental income is taxable. A deduction of 5% of the total rent received is allowed for maintenance and other expenses. Taxes on property and depreciation are also deductible.

Royalties

Royalties received are taxed as normal income, subject to deductions for expenses and depreciation of the cost of the rights.

Social security benefits and pensions and annuities

These two groups of income are taxable in the same way as earnings from employment.

Exempt income

The main exemptions from income tax are:

- interest income from deposits in banks and finance companies;
- dividends;
- copyright income received by individuals domiciled in Argentina, up to $10,000 per year;
- profits from trading in shares, bonds, and investment funds.

Foreign source income

The foreign source income of resident individuals is taxable. Income tax paid or withheld abroad may be credited against the amount of higher local income tax payable on foreign income.

Personal allowances and deductions

Resident taxpayers are granted tax free allowances. These allowances are as follows:

	ARP
Personal basic allowance	4,020
Additional allowance for pensioners or employees	13,500
Additional allowance for workers not pensioners or employees	4,500
Allowance for spouse	2,040
Allowance for each child under 24	1,020
Allowance for each other family dependant (parents or grandchildren)	1,020

These allowances are only permitted where the spouse, children or other family members do not have a yearly income higher than ARP 4,020 per head.

A rebate in these allowances is applicable, ranging from 0% to 100%

depending on a graduated scale of net taxable income of the year ranging from ARP 39,000 to ARP 221,000.

As a general rule, any expense incurred in obtaining or maintaining taxable income is deductible, including the following:

- interest (related to loans applied to the taxable activity);
- charitable gifts (within determined limits);
- social security contributions (within determined limits in the case of private pension funds);
- health and medical care insurance (within determined limits);
- life insurance premiums (within determined limits).

Losses

Losses cannot be carried back. They may be carried forward for five years. Foreign source losses can only be offset against the same kind of income. Losses incurred on trading in shares, bonds and investment funds are not deductible for individuals.

Special family rules

Spouse's incomes are taxed separately. In addition to his personal income, a husband must include the income from assets belonging to the marital partnership and the income of dependant children.

Special treatment for expatriates

Expatriates working on contract for less than six months are allowed to deduct a straight 30% of the amount earned and must pay a 35% income tax on the remaining 70% (effective rate 24.5% of the amount earned).

An expatriate with work permit residence, living in Argentina during 12 months, has resident status and is taxed on worldwide income.

Rates of tax

There are no provincial and local taxes on income for either resident or non-resident individuals.

Income tax rates assessable on taxable income are as follows:

Taxable income		*Basic Tax*	*Plus*	*On the excess of*
From ARP	*To ARP*	*ARP*	*%*	*ARP*
0	10,000	0	9	0
10,000	20,000	900	14	10,000
20,000	30,000	2,300	19	20,000
30,000	60,000	4,200	23	30,000
60,000	90,000	11,100	27	60,000
90,000	120,000	19,200	31	90,000
120,000	No limit	28,500	35	120,000

Tax credits

Income tax withheld is credited against the final amount payable as per the annual return.

Payment of tax

The return for the calendar year must be filed by the end of April of the following year. The balance due to the tax bureau must be deposited in the bank on the same day or beforehand.

Payroll deductions

Income tax on wages must be withheld by the employer. If an employee has no income other than his wages he is not obliged to file a personal return.

If an employee has other sources of taxable income he must file a personal return, and is allowed to offset withholdings against the amount of income tax payable.

Prepayments

Five bi-monthly prepayments must be made, commencing in June. The amount payable is based on the previous year's income tax payable.

Estate and gift tax

There are no gift or inheritance taxes in Argentina.

Wealth tax

Resident individuals are taxed on worldwide assets in excess of ARP 102,300 and the rate of tax rise from 0.50% up to 0.75% when taxable assets exceed ARP 200,000. Similar taxes paid abroad may be credited against tax. Individuals domiciled abroad are taxed on their assets located in Argentina at a rate of 0.75%, excluding investments in bonds and shares under certain provisions.

Social security contributions

State Pension Funds

Employers and employees contribute on the employee's full earnings (whether in cash or fringe benefits). The rates applicable vary in accordance with the activity or location.

Under certain conditions, a two-year exemption is available for expatriates, provided they are covered for old age, disability, or death in the country of nationality or permanent residence.

Family allowances

Employers contribute to a family allowance fund on the same basis as they contribute to state pension funds but need only deposit the difference between the family allowances of their personnel and the contributions due to the fund. If family allowances are higher than the employer's contribution, the balance is reimbursed.

If the average salary of an employee is higher than US$ 1,500, family allowances will not be credited to the employee and the employer must pay contributions to the family allowance fund in full.

Unemployment fund

Employers must contribute 1.5 % of all remuneration.

Social security and medical care

Employers and employees contribute on the same basis as for state pension funds.

Medical care organisations are established by business activity and mainly managed by unions; therefore only limited possibilities exist for the employee to choose a medical organisation. Some minor additional contributions may be applicable in accordance with location or collective contracts.

Since September 1995, a rebate has applied on the charges to the employer (except in the case of medical care) provided that the employer has paid all social security and VAT.

This rebate varies according to the location of the beneficiary, from 30% in the most industrialised areas to 80% for highly undeveloped areas. An additional rebate is granted in respect of employer's contributions for each new employee that increases the payroll as at April 2000 thereon.

Employer's social security contributions must only be applied up to a limit of ARP 6,000 per month for each employee, while employee's contributions have a limit of ARP 4,800. Thus, any monthly amount above that figure will be free from social security taxes.

The employer must pay insurance to cover labour risks. Premium rates depend on the type of work performed by the employee and its attendant risks. The rate varies between 1% and 1.5% of the employee's salary plus a fixed amount per employee of approximately US$ 1.

The first month of the labour relationship is regarded as a testing period, so an employee is not entitled to severance indemnities if dismissed.

A summary of employer and employee contributions (excluding the rebate) is shown below:

	Employer %	*Employee* %
Pension fund	18	14
Family allowances fund	7.5	–
Unemployment fund	1.5	–
Medical care	5	3
	32	**17**

Other taxes

Treatment of partnerships

Partnerships must file their income tax returns during the fifth month following their financial year end.

Partnerships are subject to the same fiscal treatment as corporations and are therefore taxable in their own right.

VAT and sales taxes

VAT (known in Argentina as IVA) is a general tax on the consumption of goods and services. The standard rate is 21%. Certain essential goods are not taxed at the retail level.

Gas, electricity, telecommunication, the provision of running water and sewage treatment are taxed at 27% when invoiced to industry, commerce and service providers.

Exports of goods and services are tax exempt and the exporter can compute as a fiscal credit the VAT transferred to them by their suppliers.

The other main exemptions are on the following:

- books, publishing, newspapers;
- life insurance and annuities;
- educational services provided by authorised institutions.

IVA must be paid in the month following purchase. The IVA invoiced to the receiver by suppliers of goods and services is offset against IVA amounts invoiced to clients. If there is a balance in favour of the taxpayer, it is not reimbursable, but can be carried forward as a credit to the following month. Withholding schemes on IVA amounts invoiced are applicable at the time of payment by clients and then offset by the taxpayer in its monthly return.

Reimbursement of IVA is only available in the case of exports.

Excise tax

This tax is applicable to specific products such as wines and spirits, soft drinks, tobacco, cigarettes, gasoline and lubricants. The basis of assessment and the rates applicable vary from item to item.

Exports are not taxed.

Stamp duty

The provinces apply a stamp tax on contracts, promissory notes, banker's drafts, etc. The most common rate is 1%.

In the city of Buenos Aires (federal district) stamp duty has been discontinued except on the transfer of real estate where the rate applicable varies in accordance with the value of the transaction (with a maximum rate of 2.5%).

Local and provincial taxes

Turnover tax

Provincial governments and the federal district impose a tax on turnover applicable to the gross income at rates that vary according to activity and jurisdiction. Exports of goods are tax-exempt.

The most common rates are:

Farming, cattle breeding, mining, other primary activities	1%
Industrial activities	1.5%
Commerce and services in general	3%
Financial and intermediary activities	4.9%

Although based on the calendar year, tax becomes payable in the first few days of the following month.

An agreement between the federal district and the provinces avoids multiple taxation.

Real estate taxes

Real estate is taxed by the provinces and the Federal District on the basis of assessable values calculated by the corresponding administrations.

Municipal taxes

Lighting and cleaning tax

Based on the same valuation as that used for real estate tax, the rate normally applied is 0.5%. The revenue from this tax is used to pay for the services rendered.

Sanitary and safety tax

Revenue from this tax pays for the municipal control of industry and commerce and is normally assessed on the basis of gross income less IVA and turnover tax, at a rate of around 0.5%.

Exchange controls

There are no exchange controls in Argentina.

Tax treaties and withholding taxes

Dividends

Dividends paid to local as well as foreign stockholders are not subject to withholding taxes except when dividends paid on a book profit are higher than the taxable income of same period and then a withholding, as full and final payment, at a rate of 35% is applicable on such excess.

Interest payments on offshore loans

The general withholding rate is 15.05%, provided that the creditor is a financial institution of a country whose Central bank has adhered to the international standards set by the Basilea Banks Committee. Otherwise, the withholding rate is 35%.

Royalty payments

The general withholding rate is 31.5%. In the case of patents and trademarks, the rate is reduced to 28%. For technology transfer contracts, the applicable rate is 21% provided that the technology is not available in Argentina. In both cases, to qualify for the rate reduction the contracts must be registered with the corresponding Government agency.

When treaties to avoid double taxation establish limits that are below the above general rates, the maximum rate set by such treaties prevails.

Country	*Interest tax rate (%)*	*Royalties tax rate (%)*	*Dividends tax rate (%)*
Selected treaty countries:			
Australia	12.0	15.0	15.0
Austria	12.5	15.0	15.0
Belgium	12.0	15.0	15.0
Canada	12.5	15.0	15.0
Denmark	12.0	15.0	15.0
Finland	15.0	15.0	15.0
France	20.0	18.0	15.0
Germany	15.0	15.0	15.0
Italy	20.0	18.0	15.0
Netherlands	12.0	15.0	15.0
Spain	12.5	15.0	15.0
Sweden	No limits	15.0	No limits
United Kingdom	12.0	15.0	15.0

Other treaty countries

Treaties with the following countries avoid double taxation only in the case of international transport:

Belgium, Brazil, Canada, C.I.S. (Ex–USSR), Colombia, Cuba, Chile, Denmark, Ecuador, Finland, France, Germany, Iran, Israel, Italy, Japan, United Kingdom, Netherlands, Norway, Paraguay, Peru, Poland, Portugal, Spain, United States, Sweden, Switzerland, Uruguay, Venezuela, Yugoslavia.

Anti-avoidance measures

Although there is no specific anti-avoidance legislation in Argentina, some measures are enforced in relation to the pricing of imports and exports and to disallow exemptions or allowances that could ultimately unfairly benefit the tax administrations of foreign countries.

Australia

Lord & Brown

Introduction

Income tax, fringe benefits tax, goods and services tax, superannuation surcharge and superannuation guarantee charges are levied at the National level whilst land tax, pay-roll tax, stamp duty and workcare levies are levied at the State level.

At the time of publication, Australia is currently undergoing major tax reform which has seen the introduction of a Goods and Service Tax (GST) and the abolition of Wholesale Sales Tax, with effect from 1 July 2000. The reforms also include the ultimate abolition of a range of other business imposts and a significant review of the way income derived by business entities are taxed. Significant in the changes to business entity taxation is the intention to tax income derived through trusts in the same way as companies. These amendments, if implemented, will also become effective from a date yet to be announced.

Unless otherwise stated, this summary of taxation in Australia does not reflect any of the proposed tax reform measures and is a summary of the laws as they currently exist.

Corporate taxes

Resident companies

Resident companies are liable to income tax on their worldwide income and gains. Australia operates under a comprehensive Controlled Foreign Corporation regime.

Companies are resident in Australia if incorporated in Australia, or if they carry on business in Australia and have either their central management and control in Australia or their voting power controlled by Australian resident shareholders.

Non-resident companies

Non-resident companies are liable to income tax on income and gains derived directly and indirectly from all sources in Australia.

The existence of double taxation treaties will often reduce the Australian tax liability of non-resident companies.

Tax year and filing requirements

The statutory tax year for corporate taxpayers ends on 30 June. It is possible to apply to the Taxation Office to substitute a year end other than 30 June in appropriate circumstances, e.g. to match the year end of an overseas parent.

The due date for the lodgment of the annual tax return is determined by the tax level of the company. Generally the tax return is required to be filed within seven to ten months of the end of the year. Companies operate under a full self-assessment system whereby they must calculate their own tax liability and pay the assessment accordingly.

Rate of tax

The rate of income tax applicable to companies is currently 34% and will reduce to 30% effective from 1 July 2001.

Income subject to tax

General rules

Gross income from all sources, such as trading receipts, rents, investment income, taxable capital gains etc, which arise in a fiscal period are aggregated to form the assessable income. Expenses incurred in earning this income are then deducted to calculate taxable income.

Stock/inventory rules

Inventories held at year end may, at the option of the taxpayer, be valued at either cost price, market selling value or replacement cost. The taxpayer has this option in respect of *each item* included in stock or inventory. FIFO, average costs, standard cost and retail inventory method (in certain circumstances) are acceptable methods of stock valuation; LIFO and the base stock method are not permitted.

Capital gains and losses

Profit arising on the sale of any property acquired prior to 20 September 1985 for the purpose of profit making by sale is included in assessable income. In addition (and if not otherwise taxable), the amount of any net capital gain (gains and losses are netted off) arising on the disposal of assets acquired or deemed to have been acquired after 19 September 1985 is also included in assessable income.

If there is a net capital loss for a year, it is carried forward to subsequent years for offset against future taxable capital gains. Such losses can also be transferred to another company within the same group. Capital losses cannot otherwise be used to reduce assessable income.

Losses from a company's trading activities can be offset against taxable capital gains.

In certain circumstances, capital gains can be rolled over and the tax deferred.

Dividends

An imputation system applies in the assessment of dividend income. Under this system, dividends are franked (i.e. have franking credits attached) to the extent to which they are paid out of taxed company profits or franked dividend income.

Dividends are included in assessable income, but resident companies are generally entitled to a rebate of the tax on dividends, received from other resident companies. From 1 July 2000, the dividend rebate has been removed for unfranked dividends, except where those dividends have been received from members of the same wholly owned group.

A rebate is not given for dividends received from non-resident companies (see also corporate groups). However, it is proposed (effective from 1 July 2001) that imputation credits of up to 15% are to be granted for foreign dividend withholding taxes on repatriated dividends.

Franking credits cannot be used to reduce the tax liability of a corporate shareholder but rather are passed on to its own shareholders as franked dividends. From 1 July 2000, excess imputation credits are refundable to individuals, superannuation funds and other taxpayers.

Anti-avoidance rules are included in the legislation to prevent unintended benefits being exploited, e.g. through dividend and franking credit streaming.

The section on 'double tax relief' below covers the system of taxing foreign source income and dividends.

Partnership income

Generally partnerships are not taxable entities. A share in the income of the partnership is assessable.

Trust income

Tax laws encourage distribution of income each year. Distributed income is assessable. Undistributed trust income is assessed to the trustee. Proposed tax reforms will result in certain trusts being taxed in the same way as companies.

Foreign source income

Foreign source income derived by residents is generally subject to tax and a credit is given for foreign taxes paid. A comprehensive system of accruals taxation dealing with controlled foreign companies, foreign investment funds and transferor trusts exists. This may affect the assessability of foreign sourced income.

Deductions

General rules

Deductions are allowed in respect of expenditure incurred in earning assessable income or necessarily incurred in carrying on a business for that purpose, other than expenditure of a capital, private or domestic nature. Special requirements must be fulfilled to obtain deductions for bad debts, expenses of borrowing, contributions to superannuation funds, depreciation, gifts and losses of previous years. There are also some limits on the immediate deductibility of prepaid expenses.

Deductibility may also be affected where the company is the beneficiary of commercial debt forgiveness.

Depreciation and amortisation

From 1 July 2001, a uniform capital allowance regime will be operating. The regime will be based on effective life of assets and will apply to most depreciable assets. Depreciation will be allowed by using either the straight-line method or the diminishing value method from the date of acquisition.

A deduction in certain circumstances is available on the cost of construction, extension, alteration or improvement of buildings.

From 1 July 2000, most taxpayers are no longer entitled to an immediate depreciation deduction for items of plant costing A$ 300 or less. This concession will continue for small business taxpayers until 1 July 2001. Small business taxpayers will be able to calculate depreciation under the simplified tax system, which is operative from 1 July 2001.

Partnership losses

Partners are entitled to a deduction for their share of losses in the year in which the loss is incurred.

Trust losses

Beneficiaries/unit holders of trusts are not entitled to deductions in respect of losses incurred by the trust.

Royalties

Royalties, to the extent that they are of a non-capital nature, are deductible when incurred.

Interest

Interest incurred by corporate entities in the production of assessable income is deductible. However, interest paid to a non-resident which holds at least a 15% interest in the Australian paying company may be subject to the thin capitalisation rules. Under these provisions, interest is not deductible to the extent that the debt exceeds a defined debt/equity ratio, currently 2:1 (6:1 for financial institutions). Proposed tax reforms, to be effective from 1 July 2001, will strengthen the application of the thin capitalisation provisions and introduce safe harbour gearing ratios.

In addition, interest deductions are not allowed on debt used to finance the transfer of assets from one related company to another where the buyer and seller are at least 50% controlled by a non-resident.

Dividends

Generally, dividends paid are not deductible. However, dividends, which fall within the definition of a 'debt dividend', are allowable deductions.

Bad debts

Bad debts are deductible in the year they become bad and are physically written off. However, certain anti-avoidance provisions also exist to limit the deductibility of bad debts.

Reserves and provisions

Reserves and provisions are normally not deductible.

Employees' and directors' remuneration and benefits

Employees' and directors' remuneration and benefits are generally deductible.

Excessive directors' remuneration in private companies can be deemed to be a dividend and not deductible.

Whilst benefits are deductible to the employer, they may also be subject to fringe benefits tax.

Non-deductible expenses

Certain items of expenditure such as recreational club fees, entertainment expenses and expenditure relating to leisure facilities are normally non-deductible.

In situations where these expenses form part of an employee's remuneration package, the payment of the expense by the employer will be tax deductible to the employer but will be subject to fringe benefits tax.

Investment incentives and special benefits

Mining industries

Complex provisions exist for the allowance of deductions to companies engaged in mining minerals and oil and gas, and for those engaged in prospecting and exploration. In general terms, capital expenditure related to the mining and treatment of minerals is deductible over the estimated life of the mine or ten years, whichever is the lesser. Expenditure on prospecting is deductible in the year of expenditure.

Primary production

Companies involved in primary production (e.g. agriculture and fishing) receive a number of special tax concessions.

Research and development

Companies which incur expenditure on research and development on or after 20 August 1996 may claim a number of concessions. These include a 125% deduction for expenditure on salaries and other eligible expenditure of a revenue nature exclusively incurred for research and development activities, a deduction of 41.67% per year over the first three years for the cost of plant and a deduction limited to 100% for expenditure on acquiring the right to use 'core' technology. Under proposed tax reforms, the eligibility criteria for obtaining research and development concessions will be strengthened and a number of additional concessions will be introduced.

Related party transactions

Numerous provisions exist in the tax legislation enabling the Taxation Office to restructure, for tax purposes, transactions between parties deemed not to be at arm's length when it is considered that there would otherwise be a loss of revenue.

Company losses

Subject to satisfying certain continuity of ownership or same business tests, losses incurred by a company in a current and prior period can be carried forward indefinitely as a deduction against future assessable income.

The same criteria exists in relation to a non-resident company applying Australian losses against income derived in Australia.

Losses may be transferred between companies within the same 100% common ownership group, provided that the transferring and recipient companies are both resident in Australia and the transferring company is not a dual resident company. A net capital loss can similarly be transferred within a company group (see also corporate groups).

Trust losses

Similar to companies, trusts must satisfy specific tests in order to utilise prior year tax losses. In addition, the trust must satisfy the income injection test. 'Family trusts' will not be subject to this test, providing they are closely held family trusts.

Proposed tax reforms will result in certain trusts being taxed in the same way as companies.

Corporate groups

Companies are taxed on a separate, non-group basis. At present there is no provision for taxing companies on a group basis. Proposed tax reforms may, however, result in corporate groups, which satisfy certain conditions, being entitled to consolidate their group position. If the consolidated regime is introduced as proposed, the group loss transfer mechanism and the intercorporate dividend rebate will be abolished. The effective date for the introduction of the consolidation regime is 1 July 2002.

Mergers and disposals

Gains made as a result of disposals of assets in the course of corporate reconstructions, such as mergers, are normally taxable in the year in which the gain arises. The tax can be deferred and the gains rolled over to a later year in certain circumstances, mostly restricted to the preservation of beneficial ownership of the particular asset.

Liquidation of companies

Distributions by liquidators are deemed to be dividends and are treated as assessable income, to the extent that the distributions represent income derived by the company. Shareholders may also be subject to tax as the cancellation of shares on liquidation represents a disposal of the shares.

Capital taxes

There is no capital duty on any contribution to the capital of a company in exchange for shares, including share premium and informal capital.

Net worth tax

There is no annual net worth tax levied on companies.

Treatment of branches (branch profits tax)

Profits of a branch of resident companies, derived from a business carried on in another country, are treated as foreign source income and may be exempt in certain circumstances.

Profits of a branch of a foreign company from a business carried on in Australia will normally be subject to corporate income tax. There is no separate branch profits tax imposed on remittance of profits out of Australia.

Personal taxes

Taxable individuals

Residents

Australian resident individuals are normally subject to income tax on their worldwide income from all sources.

The term 'resident' is a defined term and means an individual who resides in Australia and includes an individual:

- whose domicile is in Australia, unless the Commissioner of Taxation is satisfied that his permanent place of abode is outside Australia; or
- who has actually been in Australia, continuously or intermittently, during more than one half of the year of income, unless the Commissioner of Taxation is satisfied that his usual place of abode is outside Australia and that he does not intend to take up residence in Australia.

A person's domicile for the purposes of the tests of residency is briefly either that of origin, choice or as ascribed by law. It is not defined by statute, but is a question of fact or degree.

Part-year resident

An individual who is a resident of Australia for only part of the year of income is only taxable as a resident for that part-year.

Non-residents

The assessable income of non-resident individuals is their gross income derived from sources within Australia. The 'source' or place where income is derived is determined as a question of fact and is not defined by statute.

The existence of a double taxation treaty with another country may modify the general rules.

Tax year and filing requirements

The statutory year of tax is the 12 months ended on 30 June. Substituted accounting periods are rarely granted for individuals.

Resident individuals may not be required to file a tax return if their taxable income does not exceed the tax-free threshold (2000/01 – A$ 6,000).

Tax returns must be filed by 31 October following the year concerned. Where a tax agent is engaged, the filing requirement may be extended.

Non-residents are required to file a return if they derive any Australian source income.

Non-residents in receipt of interest, unfranked dividends or royalty income are generally subject to withholding tax. This is a final tax and the non-resident is not required to include this income in an income tax return.

Franked dividends, generally, are not subject to withholding tax.

Taxes on income

Income tax is levied solely by the Australian Federal Government. The taxable income of an individual is his gross assessable income derived during the fiscal year, other than exempt income less allowable deductions. Australian residents are also subject to tax on their proportionate share of undistributed profits accruing from lowly taxed, non-resident companies and trusts in which they have interests at prescribed levels.

Employees are not generally taxed on non-cash fringe benefits, such as the provision of motor vehicles, free and low interest loans, residential accommodations, goods and services etc. However, the employer is liable to pay Fringe Benefits Tax ('FBT') at the maximum personal tax rate of 48.5% (including medicare levy) on the grossed-up amount of the taxable value of fringe benefits. Employers will generally be allowed a tax deduction for the FBT payable.

Employment income

Employment income is generally regarded as having a source where the services are performed. However, where special skills or creative talents are being exercised, factors such as the place of negotiation and conclusion of the contract and the place of payment are considered relevant.

Australian residents are generally taxed on all employment income, but there is an exemption for foreign source employment income if the continuous foreign service period exceeds 91 days and the income is taxed in the country of source. Non-resident individuals are taxed on income arising (wherever paid) from employment in Australia, unless exempt by reason of a provision in a double tax treaty.

Business income

Business income is included in an individual's gross assessable income. Except where specific source deduction rules apply, most taxpayers who derive business or investment income must pay a quarterly instalment of tax after the end of the quarter to which it relates, based on the income derived during that quarter. Some taxpayers may pay annually rather than quarterly.

Capital gains

Gains on the sale or disposal of property acquired or deemed to have been acquired after 19 September 1985 are included in assessable income. Gains are calculated by deducting the original cost, improvement costs and incidental expenses of sale, such as commissions and fees, from the proceeds on disposal. Where the asset has been held for a period greater than 12 months, only 50% (33% for superannuation funds) of the gain is included in assessable income. This concession is not available to companies.

Capital losses may be offset against capital gains of the same or subsequent years.

A capital gain or loss will only occur if a capital gains tax (CGT) event happens. A CGT event includes the disposal of property acquired after 19 September 1985, granting an option or creating contractual or other rights.

Gains made by non-residents of Australia on the disposal of certain Australian assets acquired after 19 September 1985 are subject to Australian tax. These are assets which have the necessary connection with Australia and comprise Australian real estate, shares in an Australian private company, assets used in carrying on a business in Australia, an interest in an Australian trust estate, shares in a public company or units in a unit trust where at any time in the five years preceding disposal the non-resident (together with associates) beneficially owned 10% or more of the public company or unit trust.

For CGT purposes, and where the asset is other than an asset which has the necessary connection with Australia, a person who becomes a resident of Australia is deemed to have acquired, before taking up such residence, any asset which was acquired after 19 September 1985 at a value equal to the market value of that asset at that time. This rule does not apply where the person ceases to be an Australian resident and has been resident for less than five out of the ten years immediately preceding departure.

Subject to the 'less than five years residence rule' mentioned above, when a person ceases to be a resident he is deemed to have disposed of his assets, other than those assets which have the necessary connection with Australia for the market value at the time. However, an election is available to treat those assets as having the necessary connection with Australia in order to avoid the deemed disposal rules.

Dividends

Gross dividends derived by resident individuals from all sources are subject to income tax and a credit is allowed for the foreign tax paid or deducted from those dividends. Generally, credit is not allowed for underlying company tax. The amount of tax credit may not exceed the Australian liability.

Australia operates a full imputation system for dividends from Australian companies. Such dividends have 'franking credits' attached, to the extent that they are paid out of company income which has suffered tax at the full company rate. Dividends with credits attached are called 'franked dividends'.

Anti-avoidance rules are included in the legislation to prevent unintended benefits being exploited, e.g. through dividend and franking credit streaming.

In the hands of a resident individual, dividends are grossed up by the amount of any franking credit, but the tax payable on the grossed up amount is reduced by the amount of the credit. A taxpayer whose marginal tax rate is equal to or less than the company tax rate will therefore not have any further tax to pay on the dividend. Any excess credit can be used to reduce the tax on other income.

From 1 July 2000, excess franking credits are refundable to individuals, superannuation funds and certain other taxpayers.

In certain circumstances payments, forgiveness of debt and loans to shareholders and associates may be deemed to be dividends. Such dividends will be unfranked although the company will suffer a reduction in its franking account of an amount equal to the deemed dividends.

Non-residents benefit from franking credits, as franked dividends paid to non-residents are exempt from withholding tax. Unfranked dividends paid to non-residents are subject to withholding tax at the rate of 30% of the gross payment. A double tax treaty may limit the rate to a lesser specified percentage.

Interest

Interest derived by Australian residents is taxable. Credit is given against Australian tax for any foreign tax paid.

Australian source interest derived by a non-resident is generally subject to withholding tax of 10%.

Rentals

Rental income is taxed in the same way as business income. Land tax on a rental property, imposed under State or Territory laws, is deductible for income tax purposes. Interest on borrowings to acquire a rental property may also be deductible.

Royalties

Royalties derived by Australian residents are taxable with credit given for any foreign tax paid. Deductions are available in respect of the acquisition of rights giving rise to royalties. Non-residents are subject to withholding tax on Australian royalty income at a rate of 30% of the gross royalty payment. The person remitting the royalty to the non-resident withholds tax at source.

A double tax agreement may reduce the withholding tax rate to a lesser specified percentage.

Social security benefits

Social security benefits are normally taxable.

Pensions and annuities

Pensions and annuities received from a former employer or a superannuation fund are generally taxed as income, although subject to a 15% tax rebate. Pensions and annuities are tax-free to the extent that they do not exceed the amount paid for them out of taxed income.

Foreign source income

Foreign source income is generally taxable and a credit for withholding or other foreign tax is generally given. A comprehensive system of accruals taxation dealing with controlled foreign companies, foreign investments funds and transferor trusts also exists. This will alter the assessability of foreign source income.

Exempt income

There are certain limited circumstances in which Australian sourced income derived by non-resident individuals will be exempt. For instance, the remuneration paid by the Government to a non-resident individual for expert advice to the Government is exempt.

Alimony, maintenance or other periodic payments made to a person who is or has been the spouse of the payer are exempt.

Particular components of termination payments may be exempt from tax or taxed at concessional rates.

Personal allowances and deductions

As mentioned above, allowable deductions are taken from assessable income to determine an individual's taxable income.

Generally, expenditure incurred in deriving assessable income is an allowable deduction to the extent that the expenditure is not of a capital, private or domestic nature.

Losses

When an individual sustains a loss he may offset it against the taxable income in the current year. Unrecouped losses can be carried forward indefinitely. Capital and foreign sourced losses can only be offset against capital gains and foreign sourced income respectively.

Special family rules

Income is taxed in the hands of each taxpayer that earns the income. There are no special rules in respect of married taxpayers or families.

Rates of tax

Income tax

The following rates are applicable to the taxable income derived by residents:

Band (A$)	*Resident* (%)*	*Band (A$)*	*Non-Resident* (%)*
0 – 6,000	Nil		
6,001 – 20,000	17	1 – 20,000	29
20,001 – 50,000	30	20,001 – 50,000	30
50,001 – 60,000	42	50,001 – 60,000	42
60,001 +	47	60,001 +	47

* Rates applicable for the 2000/01 financial year.

The tax-free threshold is available only on a pro rata basis to a taxpayer first joining the Australian workforce on a full-time basis or taking up or ceasing Australian residence during a tax year. Resident tax rates will apply to a person who is resident at any time during a tax year.

Provincial and local taxes

There are no provincial or local Government taxes imposed on income.

Withholding tax

Australian sourced interest, unfranked dividends and royalties derived by non-resident individuals are taxed at a flat rate of 10%, 30% and 30% respectively, except where the rate applicable to interest, dividends or royalties is limited by the double tax treaties. Withholding tax is a final tax and the income is not aggregated with income from other sources. Franked dividends are generally not subject to withholding tax.

Rebates of tax

A resident individual is allowed rebates of tax for the 2000 and 2001 financial years as follows:

Rebates	*2000 (A$)*	*2001 (A$)*
Spouse rebate		
– Dependant child	1,452	1,637
– No dependant child	1,340	1,365
Invalid relative	603	603
Parents and parents-in-law	1,204	1,204
Sole parent	1,258	1,258
Net medical expenses exceeding A$ 1,250		20% of excess

Reduction in rebates

The spouse rebate is reduced by A$ 1 for every A$ 4 of net income of the dependant that exceeds A$ 282. The parenting allowance and the dependant child's income may reduce the rebate.

The invalid relative and parents and parents-in-law rebates are reduced by A$ 1 for every A$ 4 of separate net income of the dependant that exceeds A$ 282.

The availability of the sole parent rebate is subject to a dependant's income test and to the time the dependant is under the care of the parent.

Payment of tax

Payroll deductions – Pay-As-You-Go – Withholding (PAYG – Withholding)

An employer is obliged to deduct tax instalments (PAYG – withholding deductions) from the salary or wages paid to each employee.

Pay-As-You-Go – Instalments (PAYG – Instalments)

Individuals who derive income, other than salary or wages, greater than A$ 1,000 will normally pay PAYG instalments.

Specific tax payment rules

There are specific payment rules to prevent tax avoidance which apply in certain industries and which in certain circumstances impose a withholding tax responsibility on the payer of income.

Other taxes

Federal

Fringe benefits tax

Fringe benefits tax is payable by employers on the value of non-cash benefits (e.g. company cars) provided to employees. The rate of tax is 48.5%.

Goods and services tax – (GST)

From 1 July 2000, Australia introduced a GST. The GST is a value added tax, its basic structure being similar to those currently operative in New Zealand, Singapore, Canada, South Africa, the United Kingdom and other European countries.

The GST replaced the wholesale *sales tax regime*, and is levied at a flat rate of 10% on the supply of goods and services connected with Australia.

GST registration, if required, must be made to the Australian Taxation Authorities.

As not all supplies of goods and services are subject to GST, it is imperative that companies or other entities conducting business operations in Australia review their current activities to determine where the activities fit within the GST framework and consider the GST impact on the accounting, record keeping and cashflow needs of the enterprise.

Bank transactions

Each debit to a bank account is subject to a duty of between 30 cents and A$ 4. Proposed tax reforms will result in the abolition of this duty from 1 July 2005.

Most states also levy a duty on credit entries of up to 0.06% of the transaction. Proposed tax reforms will result in the abolition of this duty from 1 July 2001.

Customs and excise duties

These duties are imposed on a comprehensive range of goods imported into or manufactured in Australia.

Superannuation guarantee charge

The government requires employers to provide a minimum amount of superannuation for the behalf of their employees (8% for 2000/01) or alternatively pay a 'charge' to the Taxation Office which equals the amount of superannuation the employer should have provided plus an administration fee.

Superannuation surcharge

Effective from 20 August 1996, a 15% surcharge will apply to tax deductible superannuation contributions made by employers on behalf of employees or by self-employed individuals on their own behalf where the total annual income (being the taxable income plus any tax deductible employer/self-employed superannuation contributions) exceeds A$ 85,000 indexed. The surcharge will phase in where the annual income is in the range of A$ 75,000–A$ 85,000 indexed. For the 2000–2001 year, the surcharge will phase in where the annual income is in the range of A$ 81,493–A$ 98,955.

Estate and gift tax

There are no death or gift taxes levied in Australia.

Wealth tax

There is no wealth tax in Australia.

State and territory

Payroll tax

Payroll tax is levied on employers by state or territory governments on gross salaries and wages of each respective state or territory. The rate varies – the minimum rate is 3.65% and the maximum rate is 6.85% of the payroll, with exemptions being available to smaller employers (approximately A$ 500,000 payroll).

Land tax

Land tax is levied annually by each state or territory government on the unimproved value of the freehold land held within the State. The rates vary from state to state. Exemption from land tax is usually available where the land is used for:

- charitable, educational or religious purposes;
- primary production;
- the principal residence of the land owner (in some states only and subject to the land value).

Stamp duty

Certain documents, legal and other, are subject to stamp duty. Deposits to bank accounts and certain credit transactions also incur duty. The rates of duty vary between the various states and territories. Proposed tax reforms will result in stamp duty on marketable securities being abolished from 1 July 2001. From a date unknown at the time of publication, it is also proposed that conveyance duties on business property, stamp duties on credit arrangements, instalment purchase arrangements and rental (hiring) agreements, stamp duties on leases, stamp duties on mortgages and other loan securities will be abolished.

Local government taxes

Local councils and other semi-government authorities charge rates for the provision of various domestic services, e.g. local roads, water, sewerage and drainage. The amount of rates paid varies depending on the locality, value of the property and the degree of use of the services.

Miscellaneous

Workers' compensation

A business is obliged to pay compensation to employees injured whilst working. Each state administers a scheme funded by levies payable by employers.

Social security

There are no social security contributions in Australia, although a medicare levy of 1.5% (2000-01) of taxable income is levied on all resident taxpayers. The levy is in addition to the rates of tax mentioned above and is collected with income tax.

In addition to the medicare levy, a further 1% surcharge is payable for singles with taxable income in excess of A$ 50,000 and couples and families with taxable incomes in excess of A$ 100,000 without private health cover.

Higher education contribution scheme

A higher education contribution scheme fee is charged for enrolment in a non-fee paying higher education award course. Students who do not pay the fee 'up front' have several options available to progressively pay off their debt.

Foreign investment and exchange controls

Generally the rules and regulations governing foreign investments have been relaxed. The exclusions to this are:

- urban real estate;
- banking;

- civil aviation; and
- media.

The Reserve Bank of Australia administers the exchange controls regulations within Australia. However, most exchange controls have also been relaxed in recent years.

The Financial Transaction Reports Act 1988 (formerly the Cash Transaction Reports Act 1988) was introduced by the Federal Government to counter tax evasion, the cash economy and money laundering. Under the legislation, the Australian Transactions Reporting and Analysis Centre ('AUSTRAC') was formed to compile, analyse and disseminate information it receives in consultation with the Commissioner of Taxation. Effectively all transactions, other than exempt transactions, must be reported.

Reportable transactions which the Act encompasses include:

- cash dealings – currency transactions exceeding A$ 10,000;
- transfers of A$ 10,000 or more of Australian or foreign currency in or out of Australia; and
- receipts of A$ 10,000 or more of Australian or foreign currency from outside Australia.

Cash dealers are under further obligations to report transactions where there are reasonable grounds to suspect that the information may be relevant to an offence against a Commonwealth law.

Non-bank cash dealers in Australia must also report details of international funds transfer instructions that they remit and receive.

Double tax relief

Since 1 July 1987, when a comprehensive foreign tax credit system came into effect, Australian resident companies have been taxable on their worldwide income and gains. For the period 1 July 1987 to 30 June 1990, the foreign tax credit system was operative such that Australian tax was levied on foreign source income with a credit given for foreign taxes paid, including underlying corporate tax where an Australian resident company received dividends from a foreign company in which it had a 10% voting interest.

From 1 July 1990, the foreign income accruals legislation entered into force, which subjects Australian residents to tax on their proportionate share of profits accruing to lowly taxed non-resident companies and trusts in which they have interests. However, income will not be attributed where it is derived by a company resident in a country with a tax system comparable to Australia's or where the company is predominantly (95%) engaged in active business. Where income is attributed to an Australian resident, it will be derived, for Australian tax purposes, when derived by the foreign company and not when dividends are declared.

Dividends will be exempt from tax where they are dividends received from a company that is resident in a country with a tax system comparable to Australia's and the Australian resident has a voting interest of at least 10% in the non-resident company. Dividends will also be exempt from tax where they are paid out of previously attributed income.

Tax treaties and withholding taxes

Withholding taxes are imposed under Australian tax laws on royalties, interest and dividends paid to non-residents of Australia. Where appropriate, a double tax treaty will reduce the rate imposed to a lesser extent.

The following table illustrates the maximum rates currently in force:

Country of residence	*Royalties (a)(b)*	*Interest (c)*	*Dividends (d)*
	%	%	%
Non-treaty countries	30	10	30
Treaty countries:			
Argentina	10-15 (k)	12	10-15
Austria	10	10	15
Belgium	10	10	15
Canada	10	15	15
China	10	10	15
Czech Republic	10	10	15 (l)
Denmark	10	10	15
Fiji	15	10	20
Finland	10	10	15
France	10	10	15
Germany	10	10	15
Hungary	10	10	15
India	10-15 (g)	15	15
Indonesia	10-15 (h)	10	15
Ireland	10	10	15
Italy	10	10	15
Japan	10	10	15
Kiribati	15	10	20
Korea	15	15	15
Malaysia	15	15	15
Malta	10	15	15

Netherlands	10	10	15
New Zealand	10	10	15
Norway	10	10	15
Papua New Guinea	10	10	15
Philippines	25	15	25 (e)
Poland	10	10	15
Romania	10	10	5-15
Russia	10	10	5-15
Singapore	10	10	15
Slovak Republic	10	10	15
Spain	10	10	15
Sri Lanka	10	10	15
South Africa	10	10	15
Sweden	10	10	15
Switzerland	10	10	15
Taiwan	12.5	10	15 (j)
Thailand	15	10-25	15-20 (f)
United Kingdom	10	10	15
United States	10	10	15
Vietnam	10	10	10-15

(a) Rate indicated is maximum tax as a percentage of gross royalty.

(b) Royalties have an extended meaning in the legislation and are also deemed to have an Australian source.

(c) Interest paid to non-residents may be exempt in certain circumstances, such as when paid on qualifying debentures issued by an Australian company outside Australia. In circumstances where the withholding tax is greater than 10%, Australian domestic laws will limit the withholding tax rate to 10%.

(d) Except where double tax treaties override, a full company rate of tax is payable where dividends are received by a non-resident corporation carrying on business in Australia at or through a permanent establishment. It should be noted that withholding tax does not apply to the extent that the dividend is franked (refer to '*Dividends*' above).

(e) 15% if the recipient satisfies certain conditions giving a rebate of Australian tax on the dividend or relief for underlying tax.

(f) May be reduced to 15% when the recipient of the dividend is a company holding at least 25% of the issued capital.

(g) This may be increased to 15% in certain circumstances.

(h) Certain royalties have a concessional rate of 10%.

(i) May be reduced to 5% in certain circumstances.

(j) May be reduced to 10% in certain circumstances.

(k) May be reduced to 10% in certain circumstances.

(l) May be reduced to 5% in certain circumstances.

Austria

EWB Wirtschaftsprüfungs und Steuerberatungsgesellschaft MBH

Corporate taxes

Taxable entities

Taxable entities are:

- public limited companies;
- limited liability companies;
- private foundations;
- associations, institutions.

Resident companies

Resident companies are liable for corporate income tax on their worldwide income including capital gains. A company is resident if it is incorporated under Austrian law and a company which has its central management located within Austria will also be subject to Austrian taxation as a resident company.

Non-resident companies

Non-resident companies are liable to corporate income tax only on certain Austrian sourced income. The most important components of income are the profits of a business carried out in Austria through a permanent establishment or representative, and income from immovable property in Austria.

Rate of tax

Corporate tax rate is 34%. Minimum corporate tax is EUR 1,750 for private limited companies and EUR 3,500 for public limited companies.

Taxes imposed

All taxes on income are imposed at national level. The Austrian tax system grants no special advantages or disadvantages to foreign companies or branches of foreign companies regarding rates of tax payable. The tax year is the calendar year, but the financial year of a company may be any fixed 12 month period provided for in the company's articles of association. Tax is payable in advance in instalments in the middle of each quarter and the residual tax is payable within one month of receipt of an assessment.

Income subject to tax

General rules

Income subject to tax is based on commercial profits less losses. The determination of the taxable income is governed by the 'substance-over-form' principle, meaning that a transaction must be assessed according to its economic effect and not according to the legal form it takes (e.g. tax treatment of lease: under certain conditions the lease object is attributed, for fiscal purposes, to the lessee contrary to the formal stipulation of the lease contract).

Commercial profits are defined as the total sum of all profits, including capital gains, realised through the conduct of business corporations and are measured in Schillings or (from the 1 January 2002) in EURO.

The method of determining commercial profits should be consistent from year to year and may be changed only if justified by sound business practice, provided the purpose of the change is not to gain an incidental tax benefit.

Capital gains and losses

There is no special treatment for capital gains or losses (except those falling under the participation exemption, see below): they are treated as normal income and taxed or relieved at the applicable rate.

On disposal of a business asset, any capital gain may be transferred tax free to a replacement reserve. The tax book value of the new asset must be reduced by the amount of the reserve.

Dividends

General participation exemption

Any dividends *received* by Austrian (resident) companies from Austrian (resident) subsidiaries remain exempt from corporate income tax with the recipient irrespective of the percentage of stock holding.

International participation exemption

Dividends and capital gains arising from qualified investments in other foreign companies are exempt from corporate income tax in the hands of the recipient provided the shareholding is at least 25% of the nominal share capital and is held longer than two years (international participation exemption).

Dividends *paid* are not deductible in arriving at taxable income. Dividends are subject to a withholding tax of 25% or to a lower rate if prescribed by a double taxation agreement. According to the parent-subsidiary directive there is no withholding tax where both parent and subsidiary are located in EU countries.

The tax is final for residents and for partnerships. This means that the tax is not creditable or refundable against the individual income tax.

Stock/inventory valuation

Stock should be valued in accordance with 'sound business practice', in most cases at the lower of cost or market value. The FIFO and average cost methods are most common.

Deductions

General rules

Expenses directly or closely connected with the conduct of the business are generally wholly or partly tax deductible. Many expenses considered to contain a personal element (such as food and drink) are only partly deductible. Certain expenses are subject to maximum limits.

Depreciation and amortisation

Only one method of depreciation is permitted, i.e. straight-line depreciation. The depreciation basis of an asset is its historic cost and the duration of the useful life of an asset is taken into account.

Acceptable rates are as follows:

• Buildings	2%-3%
• Plant, machinery, office equipment	10%-20%
• Vehicles	12.5%

Certain assets, such as land, are not depreciable.

Only in case of proving a shorter utilisation period, higher depreciation rates can be used.

Goodwill

Purchased goodwill is treated as a capital asset and written-off, generally over a period of 15 years.

Self-created goodwill cannot be capitalised, and amortisation is not allowed. Patents purchased for a lump sum are valued in the same manner as other depreciable capital assets.

Royalties

Royalties are deductible as business expenses to the extent that they are at arm's length rates.

Interest

In principle, all interest payments on loan stock and other debts of a company are considered to be business expenses and are, therefore, deductible.

Dividends

Dividends paid are not deductible.

Doubtful debts

Debts can only be valued on a specific basis.

Non-deductible expenses

- Donations for purposes of public benefit, charitable or religious purposes.

- 50% of business-related meal expenses.
- Expenditure on business entertainment and amusement including entertainment of guests at theatres, night clubs, sporting events, etc.
- Gifts to non-employees.
- Improper payments, such as bribe money.
- Expenses incurred in connection with non-taxable income (e.g. interest expenses on debt funded acquisition of shares qualifying for the participation exemption are therefore not deductible for corporate income tax purposes).
- Corporate income tax itself.

Investment incentives and special benefits

Until 31 December 2000 there is relief on costs incurred on the acquisition or production of depreciable fixed assets. The taxpayer has been allowed to reduce the taxable profit by an investment allowance of up to 9% of the acquisition or production costs.

This investment allowance was abolished with effect from 1 January 2001.

Regional grants are available for investments in under-developed areas. Other grants can be obtained for certain types of investments which improve the environment.

Related party transactions

Non-arm's length transactions may be treated as informal capital (resulting in capital duty) or as a deemed dividend distribution (subject to dividend tax of up to 25%).

Losses

In 1998, losses incurred may be carried forward without time limit. However, from 2001 onwards, the extent to which losses carry forwards may be offset against current profits has been reduced.

From 2001 onwards, loss carry forwards can only be deducted to cover a maximum of 75% of the taxable profit (until 31 December 2000–100 %).

Losses should be offset in the order in which they arise. Losses may lapse on a major change of shareholders and business, i.e. they may not be deducted at all if the ownership of a corporation changes materially and if the nature of the business carried out alters dramatically.

No carry-back of losses to previous years is allowed.

Provisions

Individual accruals may be set up provided the underlying circumstances, which may lead to future charges/losses, result from a period prior to the balance sheet date. The following provisions may be set up for tax purposes:

- severance payments (tax deductible accruals for severance payments may be made up to a maximum amount of 50% of the payments theoretically due at the balance sheet date, for employees older than 50 years, the percentage increases up to 60%);
- current pensions and future pension payments (securities have to be held by an employer if he accounts for pension and severance payment accruals);
- other contingent liabilities, including anniversary payments to employees in the future (anticipated losses related to incomplete contracts, etc.).

Capital taxes

Capital duty

A one-off 1% of any contribution to the capital of a company in exchange for shares, including share premium and informal capital.

Corporate groups

An Austrian parent company and its resident subsidiary may be considered as one entity (a fiscal unit) for tax purposes, provided a number of requirements have been met.

Within a fiscal unit, the assets and liabilities of the subsidiary are considered, for tax purposes, to belong to the parent company. The principal advantage of opting for fiscal unity is that the taxable profits and losses of all companies within the fiscal unit are pooled. Moreover, losses of the subsidiary prior to the set-up of the fiscal unit can be carried forward.

The most important conditions are as follows:

- the holding company must hold at least 75% of the subsidiary;
- the financial years of the parent and subsidiary must be the same;

- the shares must be held throughout the financial year concerned;
- the companies must be Austrian;
- an agreement excluding gains or losses must have been made between the group companies.

Certain reorganisations are possible on a capital tax-free basis.

Personal taxes

Taxable individuals

The extent to which the income of an individual is subject to Austrian tax depends on whether or not the person is resident in Austria.

Residents (unlimited liability for tax)

Residence is determined according to circumstances. Major factors are physical presence, having a home at one's disposal, location of family and the centre of an individual's economic and social activities. An individual who leaves Austria and returns within one year without having been resident elsewhere will be considered a resident of Austria for the intervening period.

A person who arrives in Austria in the course of a year will be considered a resident from the date of arrival if it is his intention to stay.

An individual who is resident in Austria is subject to income tax on his worldwide income.

Non-residents (limited liability for tax)

Non-residents are normally subject to income tax on income arising in Austria. This limited liability for tax of non-residents is often reduced by a network of double taxation agreements.

Taxes on income

The most important taxes on income are wage tax (deducted at source from wages and salaries and offsettable against the final income tax liability) and income tax.

In principle, employees and pensioners pay wage tax; self-employed persons pay income tax, whereby wage tax and income tax only differ in the method by which they are levied. The tax rate is fundamentally the same. For employees there are, however, additional deduction amounts and special stipulations for the taxation of certain components of wage.

Wage tax has to be deducted by every employer and transferred on the fifteenth of the following month to the tax office. Income tax is collected through an assessment procedure. This necessitates making a declaration of income to the tax office. Income tax is then assessed on the basis of this declaration and a notice of assessment issued. An assessment also incorporates income from employment in which case wage tax already withheld by the employer is credited to the income tax. Even if only employment income has been achieved, an income tax assessment is, nevertheless, made in order to make allowance for deductions or for several employers.

Social security contributions are payable by both employers and employees and are levied in part by the tax authorities and in part by independent bodies.

A certain basic income (existence minimum) remains tax-free for every person with unlimited tax liability. This amounts to at least EUR 8,720 p.a. for persons only liable to wage tax and EUR 6,975 p.a. for self-employed persons.

Categories of income

The object of income tax is revenue. It comprises several types of income. All the categories of income, which are subject to income tax, are listed in the Income Tax Law. Moreover, only those types of income are subject to income tax, which are actually listed in this law (for example, gambling and lottery wins are not liable to tax).

The Income Tax Law embraces the following categories of income:

- agriculture and forestry;
- self-employment;
- trade;
- employment;
- investment;
- renting and leasing; and
- other income.

= *total amount of income*
– special expenses
– extraordinary burdens

= *income (tax assessment basis)*

Austria

Employment income

An employee (also including directors) who is resident in Austria is normally taxed on all his emoluments for a tax year (earnings and benefits from an existing or earlier employment status, sickness benefits, etc.). Employment income consists of wages, salaries and all other remuneration of benefits derived directly or indirectly from employment.

Most benefits in kind are taxable.

Deductions are available for employees' social security contributions. Travelling expenses to and from work (fixed amounts) and other employment expenses are also deductible.

Social security benefits

Where social security contributions are deductible, the benefits arising from contributions are normally taxable.

Pensions

Pensions received from a former employer are generally taxed as income from the former employment.

Business income

For income tax purposes, trading profits are calculated in accordance with generally accepted accounting principles. Accounts must normally be prepared for the calendar year but other tax years may be permitted by the tax authorities.

Where an individual sustains a loss in his business, he may offset the loss against the profits of the following years (up to 75%).

Profits made by a partnership are allocated to the partners in accordance with their profit shares and taxed in their hands.

Capital gains

Taxable capital gains include gains from the sale of the following:

- business assets;
- non-business property held for short periods (up to ten years for real estate and up to one year for other assets);
- shares in a company in which the taxpayer has had more than a 1% shareholding within the last five years.

Gains in the last category are taxed at half the normal rate. The capital gains on shares, which belong to business assets, are also taxed at half the normal rate.

Dividends

Dividends paid by an Austrian (resident) company are subject to a 25% withholding tax whether the recipient is a non-resident, a resident individual, or a resident company. For non-resident as well as for resident shareholders, the withholding tax is final. Double taxation treaties often reduce the rate for non-residents.

Interest

A 25% withholding tax is deducted from interest paid on bank deposits and other banking debts. It is a final tax for both non-residents and residents. A 25% withholding tax may also be deducted from bond interest paid in Austria, but this tax is usually refunded to non-residents, whether or not a treaty applies. Interest on ordinary inter-company loans is not subject to withholding tax.

Expenses relating to dividends and interest cannot be deducted.

Rentals

Rents received from letting real estate are subject to income tax. Deductions are allowed for expenses, including a notional figure for depreciation and interest.

Royalties

Royalties paid to non-residents are subject to a 20% withholding tax, which may be reduced or eliminated under a treaty.

Where payable, this tax is usually a final tax. Royalties paid to residents are not subject to withholding tax.

Personal allowances and deductions

Personal allowances

Income tax payable by a resident taxpayer is reduced by various lump sum credits. These include a general credit of up to EUR 866 and a credit of EUR 363 for a married taxpayer whose spouse does not work or for a single person with children. A precondition is that the spouse does not earn more than EUR 4,360 a year if they have at least one child, otherwise only EUR 2,180 per year is credited. Taxpayers who receive family allowance have the right to an additional credit for children. This credit amounts to a monthly EUR 25 for the first dependant child, EUR 38 for a second child and EUR 51 for each additional child. There is a further credit of EUR 291 given as relief on travel expenses to work and EUR 55 for a taxpayer with employment income subject to wage tax.

Deductions

Expenses relating to income are generally deductible (although some types of expense may be deductible only up to a certain amount or percentage).

Within limits, residents may deduct so called 'special personal expenses' and 'extraordinary charges' in arriving at taxable income. Special personal expenses include life insurance premiums, home construction and improvement expenses, and subscriptions to new issues of qualifying shares. Extraordinary charges are unusually burdensome personal expenses such as those arising from an accident or illness.

Special treatment for expatriates

In general, apart from the rules normally included in double taxation treaties, there are no specially favourable tax rules that apply to expatriates seconded to Austria for limited periods.

Rates of tax

Tax rates since 1 January 2000 are as follows:

Band of Taxable income (AS)	*Rate of Tax Applicable to Band (%)*
0–50,000	0
50,100–100,000	21
100,100–300,000	31
300,100–700,000	41
over 700,000	50

Taxable income is determined by aggregating net income (after deducting expenses incurred in earning the income of each category) and deducting from the net total special personal expenses and extraordinary charges (see above). A deduction of income related expenses is allowed of either EUR 131 or the amount of actual income connected expenses incurred, whichever is the greater.

Payment of tax

Employers must withhold wage tax, a form of income tax, at varying rates from wages and salaries paid to their employees, whether the employees are resident or not. This is usually a final tax on employment income unless for some reason an income tax assessment is required. Residents need not file tax returns if their income consists solely of employment income or employment income plus other income of EUR 727 or less. Non-residents with Austrian source income must file tax returns unless their income is taxed by way of final withholding taxes.

Where relevant, rules regarding the tax year, due dates for filing tax returns, assessments and payments are substantially the same as those described for companies.

Estate and gift tax

Individuals are liable for inheritance and gift tax on property acquired by reason of death or by way of gift. The tax applies to property located in Austria and abroad unless the beneficiary and the deceased individual or donor are both non-resident, in which case the tax applies only to specific types of Austrian property. Rates of tax vary from 2% to 60%, depending on the recipient's relationship to the donor or deceased and the value of the property transferred.

To avoid international double taxation there are certain estate and gift tax treaties in force.

Social security

Employers and employees must both pay social security contributions. These are calculated as a percentage of the employee's monthly gross earnings (including the usual thirteenth-month vacation bonus and fourteenth-month Christmas bonus) up to a maximum of EUR 3,227 per month. Contribution rates vary from 17% to 25%. Exemption from, or a refund of, contributions may be available in the case of foreign employees under the terms of a relevant social security treaty.

Most municipalities levy a payroll tax on total payroll. The maximum effective rate is 3%.

Other taxes

Transfer tax

3.5% on transfers of real estate.

Austria

Value added tax

Most goods and services within Austria are taxed at 20%, but certain essential goods and services are taxed at 10%.

A zero rate applies to the export of goods and services.

Double taxation relief

Foreign source income, other than dividends, interest and royalties, is generally exempt from Austrian tax (subject to progression, which is not material for corporate income tax) provided a treaty applies or the income has been taxed in the other country.

For dividends, interest and royalties from treaty countries and from listed developing countries a credit for withholding tax is generally given. Where the participation exemption applies, no credit is given, as the income is exempt.

Withholding taxes

The following treaties are in force between Austria and other countries, and the following taxes are withheld (%) in Austria on sample outward remittance.

Withholding tax rates under selected tax treaties currently in force are:

Country of residence	*Dividends (%)*	*Interest (%)*	*Royalties (%)*
Non-treaty countries	25	25	20
Treaty countries:			
Argentina	15	12.5	15
Australia	15	10	10
Belgium	nil-15	15	nil-10(a)
Brazil	15	15	10-15-20
Bulgaria	nil	nil	nil
Canada	15	15	nil-10(f)
China	10-7	10	10
Czech Republic	10	nil	5
Denmark	nil-10	nil	nil-10(c)
Egypt	nil-10	nil	nil
Finland	nil-10	nil	nil-10(d)
France	nil-15	nil	nil-10(d)
Germany	nil-5-15(e)	nil(g)	nil
Greece	nil-25	nil	nil-10(a)
Hungary	10	nil	nil
India	25(b)	25	25

Indonesia	10-15(b)	10(h)	10
Ireland	nil-10(b)	nil	nil-10(a)
Israel	25	15	nil-10(f)
Italy	nil-15	10	nil-10(f)
Japan	10-20(b)	10	10
Korea	10-15	10	10
Liechtenstein	15	10	5-10(c)
Luxembourg	nil-5-15(b)	nil	nil-10(a)
Malta	15	5	nil-10(f)
Netherlands	nil-5-15(b)	nil	nil-10(d)
Norway	nil-15(b)	nil	nil-10(a)
Pakistan	10-25(b)	25	20
Philippines	10-25(e)	15	5-10(a)
Poland	10	nil	nil
Portugal	nil-15	10	5-10
Romania	15	10	10
Russia	nil	nil	nil
Slovak Republic	10	nil	10
Spain	nil-10-15	5	10
Sweden	nil-5-10	nil	nil-10(a)
Switzerland	5	5	5
Thailand	10-25	25	15
Tunisia	10-20(b)	10	10-15(f)
Turkey	25	15	10
United Kingdom	nil-5-15(b)	nil	nil-10(a)
United States	5-15(d)	nil	nil

Notes

(a) Higher rate if recipient owns over 50% of shares;
(b) Lower rate applies if recipient owns 25% or more;
(c) Lower rate applies to industrial companies;
(d) Lower rate generally applies if foreign recipient has no branch and owns 95% or more;
(e) Lower rate applies if recipient owns 10% or more;
(f) Lower rate applies to special rights;
(g) Nil/only applied to bonds;
(h) Nil if interest paid to public sector;
(i) Nil in case of export credits, dividends 7 for holdings, i.e. note (b).

Belgium

Delvaux, Fronville, Servais & Co

Introduction

Taxable entities

Belgian income tax laws and regulations apply to both resident and non-resident individuals and corporate entities.

Non-profit making entities which are not set up in the incorporated form provided for by Belgian company law are subject either to a special 'legal entity tax' or to a corporate tax, depending on the nature of their activities.

For non-incorporated partnerships or entities with no legal status of their own, partners may be treated either as individuals or as corporate entities in accordance with their own legal status.

Income tax is levied on the basis of annual tax returns filed by the taxpayer at the end of the relevant taxable period. In some cases, it may also be levied during the taxable year via withholdings which will either constitute the final tax, be deductible as professional charges from the income, or be credited in whole or part against the tax assessed.

It may be necessary to distinguish between income from real estate (land, buildings, etc.) income from personal property (dividends, interests, etc.), income from professional activities, (salaries, fees, profits from trading activities, etc.) and miscellaneous income.

Euro

The tax authorities have stated that for a transitional period following the introduction of the Euro from 1 January 1999, the Belgian taxpayer may report either in BEF or in Euro. This is on the understanding that once reporting in Euro has begun, there may be no reversion to reporting in BEF. All matters arising prior to 1 January 1999 must be handled in BEF. As from 1 January 2002, only the Euro will be allowed.

Corporate taxes

All entities incorporated in accordance with the rules fixed by Belgian company law or relevant foreign legislation are liable for corporate income tax.

Resident companies

Companies formed under Belgian law or foreign legislation, which have their registered office, their main office or main management centre in Belgium, are treated as resident companies.

Resident companies are taxable on their net profit from all and any source, including capital gains and distributed dividends. Special rules may apply to foreign source income.

Non-resident companies

Non-resident companies with a Belgian permanent establishment are, whether registered or not, taxable on all income derived from such establishment, including foreign source income. Tax also applies on the income of all immovable property located in Belgium, even where there is no fixed establishment or office.

While dividends paid out by resident companies from the net profit after corporate tax are usually subject to a withholding tax, the taxed branch profits which are transferred to the head office abroad are not subject to any further taxation in Belgium.

Tax year and filing requirements

The usual tax year coincides with the calendar year, but the financial year of a company may be fixed for any 12 month period provided for in the company's articles of association.

Tax returns must be filed within six months of the financial year end and taxation normally follows within the twelve subsequent months.

For corporations with financial years ending on 31 December, the 'tax year' is the following calendar year. When the financial year ends at another date, the tax year is the calendar year in which the financial year ends.

If the tax is not prepaid during the financial year itself (usually in quarterly instalments) a surcharge will apply to the final tax liability, the rate of which will vary from one year to another based on rates referred by the National Bank of Belgium.

For tax year 2001 (financial year end at 31 December 2000 or during 2001), this surcharge has been fixed at 9% of the main tax rate – in the past increases of up to 22.5% have been applied.

Taxes imposed

Withholding taxes and final tax

In the course of the financial year, some withholding taxes may be levied and where in excess, may be either credited against the main tax assessed or reimbursed. In certain cases, however, excess withholdings may only be credited against a future tax liability or even be neither credited nor reimbursed.

Real estate withholding tax ('précompte immobilier' – 'Onroerende voorheffing')

The annual *'précompte immobilier'* tax is based on the assumed net annual income (*'revenu cadastral'*) from land, buildings and industrial equipment. The effective rate varies between 18% and 50% of the *cadastral income*, depending on the municipality where the property is located.

The *'précompte immobilier'* is a deductible professional expense, but no refund or tax credit is available.

Temporary exemptions may be obtained, subject to certain conditions for new industrial investments.

Personal property withholding tax ('précompte mobilier' – 'Roerende voorheffing')

The *précompte mobilier* tax is deducted at source at a basic rate of 25% from payments of dividends and 15% on interests (some dividends are also fixed at 15%). The tax can be offset against corporate income tax due, and any excess is refundable.

Many tax treaties provide for a reduction in withholding taxes. Rates generally vary between 5% and 15%.

As a result of the implementation of the EC Parent-Subsidiary Directive, no withholding tax is levied on dividend distributions made to a parent company resident in an EU member state, provided that a substantial interest (i.e. 25% or more) has been held for at least 1 year by the parent company which must be subject to a tax comparable to Belgium income tax. Since 1997, an exemption from the transfer of the withholding tax to the tax authorities also applies where an interest has not been held for a full year, provided the beneficiary undertakes to maintain an interest for at least one full year. The paying company must reserve sufficient funds until this period expires but need not then transfer the funds to the tax authorities provided this condition is met.

Holding companies benefiting from tax exempt status (such as in Luxembourg), or companies located in tax havens, cannot benefit from reduced rates or exemption.

Tax rates

Resident companies

The standard corporate income tax rate is presently fixed at 39%. Since 1993, a special 'temporary' crisis tax of a further 3% of the original 39% has been added which brings the tax rate to 40.17%. Resident companies with taxable profits below BEF 13,600,000 are taxed (subject to certain conditions) at rates between 28% and 41% (to which the 3% crisis tax must be added).

The reduced rates are *not* applicable to:

- financial companies in which financial assets form more than 50% of the equity and taxed reserves, unless these represent at least 75% of the paid up capital of the affiliation;
- companies 50% owned by one or more other companies;
- companies which distribute more than 13% of their paid up capital;
- companies which do not distribute to a director a remuneration of at least BEF 1,000,000 or at least equal to the net taxable profit if the latter is under BEF 1,000,000;
- companies which are part of a group which includes a Belgian co-ordination centre; or
- co-ordination centres.

Income BEF	*Percentage on the excess over the lower amount (+3% crisis surtax)*
Under 1,000,000	Tax = 28%
1,000,000 – 3,600,000	Tax = 280,000 + 36% on the income exceeding 1,000,000 BEF
3,600,000 – 13,000,000	Tax = 1,216,000 + 41% on the income exceeding 3,600,000 BEF

Belgium

Since 1 January 1990, there has been no specific taxation on the winding up of companies as these remain subject to corporate income tax until wound down. Withholding tax is not normally due on the amounts distributed where these constitute capital paid up, reserves or retained earnings, which have been subjected to taxation (including tax exempt income such as capital gains on financial assets). This regime favours, therefore, the reservation of profits over the distribution of dividends.

Non-resident companies

Since the end of fiscal year 1996, the basic corporate income tax rate applicable to branches of non-resident companies has been fixed at 39% (+3% crisis tax). In principle, this lower rate applies under the same conditions as for Belgian resident companies.

Profit subject to tax

General rules

Financial statements approved by the annual general meeting of shareholders form the basis for a Belgian company's computation of its taxable income. A number of disallowed expenses must be added to this taxable income, while certain deductions are allowed.

Stock/inventory rules

The law prescribes no specific system but rather refers to the accounting laws. Normally, inventories must be valued at the lower of cost or market value. The methods generally used are actual cost for identifiable items, FIFO, average cost or LIFO.

The standard cost method is not allowed.

Capital gains and losses

Capital gains on both intangible and tangible assets are generally treated as ordinary taxable income, except for gains on fixed assets held for more than five years. The taxation of these may be spread in accordance with the depreciation of new assets which are acquired as reinvestment. Since the 1992 tax year, capital gains realised on financial fixed assets (shares) have not generally been taxable and capital losses on such financial assets not deductible. This applies solely to financial assets, which are liable to produce income that is at least 95% exempt, known as '*revenus définitivement taxés*'.

Dividends received

Dividends from financial investments received by Belgian commercial or industrial companies are 95% tax exempt, provided the company's interest amounts to at least 5% of the capital or BEF 50,000,000 and the paying company is subject to a 'normal' corporate income tax.

For domestic dividends, this exemption is computed on the amount of dividends received (grossed up by the 25% withholding tax if levied). The 25% withholding tax may then be credited against the parent company's tax liability or refunded.

The 95% deduction is also available on dividends of foreign origin, unless the foreign paying company is not subject to income tax.

Since 1995, withholding tax on dividends paid has been fixed at 25%, reducing to 15% on certain types of newly issued registered shares or newly issued shares of quoted companies.

For financial assets representing at least 25% of the capital of a company and which have been held for more than one year, there is no withholding tax between Belgian companies.

The same rule applies between an EU parent company and a Belgian subsidiary.

Where shares have not been owned for the preceding 12 months, the withholding tax exemption may nevertheless apply provided a statement is made by the beneficiary that the shares will be retained for at least 12 months. The paying company is required to retain sufficient funds during the 12 month period and provided this requirement is met, no transfer of these funds to the tax collector is necessary.

Deductible charges and expenses

General rules

Expenses are deductible provided they are incurred in 'obtaining or maintaining the company's income'.

However, the following items are generally not deductible:

- 25% of car expenses (except fuel, financial charges and car phone);
- 50% of entertainment/restaurant expenses incurred in Belgium;
- 100% of so-called 'social benefits' (restaurant bills, etc.);

- donations to officially recognised charities, over and above 5% of taxable income or exceeding BEF 20,000,000;
- commissions and other payments to undisclosed recipients (special tax of 300%);
- Belgium corporate income taxes (foreign income taxes are deductible);
- fines;
- clothing (except specific professional clothing required by safety regulations etc.);
- gifts; and
- losses on fixed financial assets such as shares, albeit with the exception of losses relating to capital paid up in case of liquidation or bankruptcy.

Depreciation and amortisation

The straight-line or the declining balance methods of depreciation are both acceptable in calculating depreciation for accounting and tax purposes. Depreciation is based on the cost or acquisition value price and is allowed for the whole year, even if the asset is acquired only in the course of, or at the end of, a specific year. In principle, depreciation rates are determined on the basis of the expected useful economic life of the assets. Although there are no prescribed rates, the following rates may be considered as representative:

Type of asset	*Rate per annum*
Office buildings	3 %
Industrial buildings	4-5%
Industrial machinery and equipment	10%
Office machines and equipment	20%
Vehicles	20-25%
Electronic data processing equipment	20-50%

In the declining balance method, the rate may not exceed twice the above rates or a maximum of 40%. This method cannot be applied to vehicles.

Accelerated depreciation is granted for:

- ships (write-off over eight years);
- plant and machinery for scientific research (33.3% annually); and
- new qualifying assets acquired by industries considered particularly important to the Belgian economy (33.3%).

As an incentive, industrial buildings, machinery and equipment for which a grant was made by the State may be depreciated at a rate, which is twice the straight-line depreciation rate, but only over a maximum period of three years.

The depreciation allowed will be pro-rated (*'prorata temporis'*) for companies which are formed in the course of a year. No depreciation is to be computed on assets sold in the course of the year.

Royalties

Royalty expenses are deductible where the Belgian company can prove that these constitute payment for the receipt of reasonable value or services.

A withholding tax may be levied, unless exemption is indicated by a double taxation treaty.

Pension contributions

Contributions made under a contractual obligation to a recognised pension fund located in Belgium are deductible within certain limits.

Commissions and fees

Commissions, fees and similar payments are deductible only if the amounts and recipients are clearly specified.

Commissions paid to unidentified beneficiaries are not tax-deductible. A special tax rate is applied, equaling 300% (+3%) of the value of the 'secret commission' (this special tax is, however, a deductible expense).

Interest

Interest is allowed for tax purposes when it is paid to Belgian banks and recognised savings associations. It is also allowed when paid to other lenders, unless it is paid at rates exceeding the usual market rates. Interest paid to a foreign holding company taxed at a lower rate or to an entity in a tax haven, will be disallowed unless the Belgian company can furnish proof that the interest payments are not made in order to avoid Belgian taxation.

Thin capitalisation

The re-classification of interest as dividends may apply where:

- loans are granted to a company by individual shareholders or directors, which exceed the sum of the company's paid in capital and taxed reserves (the re-classification applies to the interest on the excess);
- loans are granted by the same individuals at an interest rate which exceeds the usual market rates; or where
- loans are granted by a foreign company having director's functions which exceed a 1:1 loan/equity ratio.

Since 1 January 1997, interest is no longer deductible on loans granted by a foreign company which is not subject to income tax or which is located in a country granting a privileged tax regime, or on that part of a loan which exceeds the 7:1 debt/equity ratio. In such a case, no re-classification of interest as dividends applies, but the interest is treated as a non-deductible expense.

Dividends

Dividends paid are not deductible and must be included in taxable profit.

Part of the price paid by a company when acquiring its own shares may be treated as distributed dividends.

Bad and doubtful debts

Reserves for bad and doubtful debts are deductible provided they can be satisfactorily substantiated by court proceeding, recourse through lawyers, etc. Special schedules are required to detail these provisions as well as an annual follow-up.

In case of bankruptcy, the amount receivable may be written off immediately in the year in which the bankruptcy is pronounced by the Court, without providing further evidence.

Employers' and directors' remuneration and benefits

These will be deductible, provided they are listed at year end on special forms.

Reserves and provisions

Provisions for expected charges are acceptable as far as they relate to foreseeable expenses in the relevant financial year. Under certain conditions, provision may be made for heavy repairs or replacement, such as a furnace used in the glass or steel industry.

Such provisions must be listed on special schedules with an annual follow-up.

Foreign source income

Unilateral relief is granted on:

- the foreign source income of a foreign establishment which is subject to foreign tax; and
- the foreign source income from foreign real estate.

The relief takes the form of a 75% reduction of the income tax on net income from such sources (after deduction of foreign tax).

Full relief will generally be granted under the double taxation treaties.

Investment incentives and special benefits

Both tax and non-tax incentives are available to encourage investment in certain industries throughout the country and in special development areas.

These incentives, subject to certain conditions, include capital and interest subsidies, exemptions from real estate tax and, in development areas, accelerated (double) depreciation on industrial buildings and equipment and exemption from capital registration tax.

Employment zones

Special incentives are granted to enterprises in employment zones which do not employ more than 200 employees, are engaged in certain areas of high technology and create new employment. The incentives comprise:

- a temporary exemption from corporate income tax on retained and distributed profits;
- a temporary exemption from withholding tax on dividends, interest and royalties; and
- a temporary exemption from real estate tax (up to five years) and from registration duty on contributions in capital (0.5%).

Belgium

Innovative companies

Innovative companies are those incorporated between 1984 and 1993 and involved in the production and development of innovative high technology processes. Limits are placed on the number of employees and the extent of overseas operations. There are numerous incentives for recognised innovative companies, including:

- a ten year exemption from corporate income tax on distributed profits of up to 13% of paid up capital;
- higher rates of investment allowance; and
- a ten year exemption from the real estate prepayment and registration duty on contributions of capital.

Reconversion companies

Various benefits are available to reconversion companies aimed at research, development, manufacture or sale of new products, new technologies and energy-saving processes. The detailed requirements and benefits are fairly complex.

Co-ordination centres

Co-ordination centres set up in Belgium to provide certain defined services to member companies of an international group are taxed on a notional profit calculated as a percentage of part of their overheads during the first ten years (8% of overhead, excluding such costs as salaries, accounting costs, etc.).

Further benefits include exemption from registration tax on share capital and exemption from withholding tax on dividends, interests and royalties as well as from real estate tax. An application must be filed in order to obtain recognition as a co-ordination centre and the centre must fulfill certain requirements, for example, it must employ at least ten people. A special levy of BEF 400,000 per employee on the payroll to a maximum of BEF 4,000,000 must be paid by the centre.

Foreign sales corporation

The US Deficit Reduction Act 1984 recognised a new type of corporation in order to help US corporations to stimulate exports. The Belgian tax authorities created special rules for these foreign sales corporations ('FSC's') in order to make Belgium more attractive as a location for such entities. The profit of these establishments will be determined at 8% of expenditure incurred in obtaining orders, organising of deliveries, preparation and dispatch of invoices, and receipt of payment. Costs of publicity, promotion and transportation of exported merchandise, as well as the burden of credit risk, are not taken into consideration.

An application must be filed in order to obtain this special status.

A Belgian co-ordination centre cannot act as an FSC.

Distribution centres

These are formed for buying, storing and delivering goods on behalf of a member of a group. Taxation is on a cost-plus basis.

Service centres

These provide introductory services to members of a group (for example information centres) and also benefit from special tax regimes (usually on a mark-up or cost-plus basis).

An application must be filed with the tax authorities.

Investment allowances and special benefits

Investment allowances are deductible as a percentage of the cost price of qualifying investments, as follows:

- between 20% and 13% for investments in connection with energy conservation and/or new technology;
- between 5% and 3% for all other investments.

Qualifying investments are new depreciable assets (tangible or intangible) used in Belgium. Cars do not qualify.

An investment allowance is granted in addition to normal depreciation and does not decrease the base cost of the asset for depreciation purposes.

These deductions are only available to companies which are at least 50% owned by individuals. Allowances can be carried over into subsequent years where the profit available in the current year is insufficient. There is, however, an annual fixed limit.

Some investments will not qualify as deductible, such as buildings which are not used in industrial or trading activities but are merely rented out, nor will certain activities qualify.

Related party transactions

Transactions between related parties must be at fair market value to be accepted for tax purposes. Generally, fair market value means the value that would be obtained if the parties were not related to each other (in accordance with the 'arm's length' rule).

Transfer prices will become more and more subject to control in the future, as the introduction of the Euro allows greater transparency as described below:

- unusual advantages granted to foreign entities will be disallowed and added to the profit of the Belgian company which supports the burden;
- unusual advantages granted to Belgian entities will be allowed provided they form part of the taxable basis of the beneficiaries.

The taxpayer may have to provide legitimate economic and financial justification for certain transactions.

Transactions with entities located in tax havens or which are not subject to a 'normal' taxation, may be closely investigated and any unusual advantages will be disallowed and taxed.

Losses

Generally, losses may be carried forward for deduction from profits in subsequent financial periods. There is no carry-back of losses.

Restrictions may apply however, in cases where a change of company control takes place which does not answer 'legitimate financial or economic needs'. In such cases, existing prior losses may be completely lost for the future.

The notion of 'control' is defined by accounting legislation as including both the formal and de facto decision-making power which may interfere with the appointment of the majority of the Board members, or with management policy in general.

Some exceptions are provided for explicitly, as follows:

- the regulation does not apply to companies in difficulty provided the continuity of its activities is ensured through the change of control;
- changes which take place within an existing group of companies;
- changes due to inheritance.

A ruling may be requested from the tax authorities in the case of doubt as to what constitutes 'legitimate' needs.

The deduction of existing losses is also restricted in the case of a merger or the reconstruction of a company.

Corporate groups

There is no provision for the treatment of a group as a single taxable entity or for loss relief to be transferred between group companies.

In the case of a merger or reconstruction of a legal status company, part of the existing losses may be lost.

Tax-free mergers and disposals

Capital gains resulting from mergers are tax-free if:

- the transfer is totally remunerated by attribution of shares;
- the absorbing company is a Belgian resident;
- the merger can be financially and economically justified (transnational mergers are not yet recognised in Belgian tax law).

Liquidation of company

- The normal tax rate is applicable on profits up to the closing date.
- There is no withholding tax on distributions that exceed paid-up capital, provided ordinary taxation has applied.

Capital taxes

Capital duty

Company formations and increases in capital are subject to a 0.5% registration tax on subscribed capital and any capital increases. The registration of a branch of a foreign company is subject to a nominal registration fee.

In some cases, the registration duty is 12.5% (e.g. the contribution-in-kind of a personal dwelling to the capital of the company – the contribution of real estate combined with some debt such as a mortgage).

Net worth tax

There is no annual net worth tax levied on companies.

Treatment of branches (branch profit tax)

The same rules normally apply to branches as to Belgian companies, as branches must keep complete accounts in Belgium. If the branch records no income – i.e. it operates as a cost centre – profit will be assessed either by comparison with similar entities or on a notional basis (number of employees, percentage of expenses etc.). The taxable basis of a service company is generally fixed at 10% of overhead costs with a minimum of BEF 300,000 per employee on the payroll.

Personal taxes

Taxable entities

Residents

Resident individuals are subject to personal income tax on their net worldwide income from all sources, after deduction of allowed charges and expenses.

A resident is defined as a person whose family home or place from which he manages his fortune, his business or his occupation is located in Belgium. The place or residence of the household may be conclusive.

Non-residents

Non-resident individuals are taxable on income from Belgian sources.

A non-resident is defined as a person whose family home, or place from which he manages his fortune, his business or his principal occupation, is located abroad.

Residency does not depend only on physical presence but is a question of where the taxpayer has his or her customary abode after considering factors such as family and patrimony.

Some of the deductions or allowances granted to a resident taxpayer may be disallowed for non-residents. A special regime may apply to foreign expatriates.

Tax year and filing requirements

An individual's tax year is the calendar year.

A personal income tax return must be filed annually within the period given on the form received by the taxpayer.

Where no form is received by 30 June of the year following the calendar year during which the income is earned, the taxpayer must ask the authorities to send a form. Taxes assessed are payable within two months.

Taxes on income

Belgian personal income tax law generally provides for taxation at progressive rates on total personal taxable income. However, certain types of income, such as interest, dividends, capital gains from disposal of certain land holdings and occasional profits are taxed separately at fixed rates, and are excluded from income subject to progressive rates of taxation.

Municipalities are entitled to levy an additional tax on taxpayers residing in their area which usually varies from 0% to 10% of the income tax payable.

Taxes may also be levied by way of the following withholding taxes which may or may not be credited against the final tax:

- real estate withholding tax;
- personal property withholding tax;
- payroll withholding tax.

In some cases, the withholding tax will also constitute the final tax.

Sources of income

Employment and business income

This income includes salaries, wages, pensions and other remuneration and taxable benefits.

The salaries and wages of 'border workers' also fall under 'employment and business income'. Border workers are individuals who reside in Belgium and commute, usually daily, to bordering places of employment in France, Germany, Luxembourg and the Netherlands. By special agreement with these countries, such income is taxable only in Belgium and not in the country of source.

Fees and other remuneration of professional persons and business profits are taxed as business income.

Personal property income

All dividends, interest, royalties and other income from personal property are treated as income for tax purposes and are subject to withholding tax. However, there is a tax exemption for income from savings deposits by individuals of up to BEF 56,000 (indexed each year).

Since tax year 1985, withholding tax on interest and dividends received has been the final tax for resident individuals, although they may opt to aggregate this income, in which case the withholding tax will be credited or possibly reimbursed.

Real estate income

This income includes assumed real estate net income ('cadastral income') which is periodically determined for all real estate in Belgium. Reductions are available for the house which the taxpayer occupies. If the property is leased for business purposes, the taxable amount is the cadastral income plus the amount by which the 'net rent' (being 60% of the gross rent) exceeds the cadastral income.

The deduction of 40% is meant to cover maintenance and repair expenses and is limited to two-thirds of the cadastral income multiplied by a coefficient (3.19 for tax year 2001).

The rent or rental value of real estate located abroad must be included in income. Such foreign income will, however, usually be tax exempt where double taxation treaties apply.

Social security benefits

These include retirement benefits, sickness indemnities and unemployment indemnities which are taxable but subject to a special allowance.

Indemnities for material or bodily damage suffered are not taxable.

Miscellaneous income

Other types of receipts that must be included in income are:

- net revenues from casual services and operations;

- net revenues from sub-leasing personal property;
- certain prizes and subsidies;
- pensions or annuities paid to scientists, authors or artists;
- alimony or support receipts in accordance with certain legal provisions (include 80% of gross income); and
- special lottery prizes on public bonds, except for those specifically exempt from tax.

Capital taxes

In general, gains on the sale of an individual's assets are not taxable unless they arise on business assets resulting from a regular activity of the taxpayer. Always taxable are:

- capital gains on undeveloped Belgian real estate owned for less than eight years and land which includes real estate where the sale proceeds of the buildings are less than 30% of the total (the tax rate is 33% if owned less than five years and 16.5% if owned more than five years but less than eight years);
- capital gains on the sale of built properties resold within a five year period following acquisition there are certain exceptions, such as the sale of a main place of residence or property received through inheritance – rate : 16.5%; and
- capital gains made on the sale of shares to a foreign company or organisation by a substantial shareholder in a Belgian corporation if the transferor (alone or with his family) has owned more than 25% of the share capital, directly or indirectly, at any time during the five years preceding the transfer – rate : 16.5%.

Foreign source income

Foreign source income must be declared by Belgian residents at least in respect of the effect it may have on the progressive income tax rates applicable to the Belgian taxable income.

Foreign income may be tax exempt (depending upon any applicable tax treaty) or subject to a reduced taxation (where no treaty exists).

Dividends and interests cashed outside Belgium must be declared in the income tax return and will be subject to a 25% or 15% tax (plus local tax). This income will not be grossed up with the other income. The taxpayer must state in his tax return whether or not he has opened a bank account in a foreign country.

Personal allowances and deductions

Deductions

Individuals may deduct actual expenses incurred during the taxable period for the purpose of acquiring or preserving income from an occupation or business.

Deductions on the following expenses will be restricted:

- car expenses to a maximum of 75% (except on fuel and on car phone charges which are fully deductible); and
- restaurant and entertainment expenses incurred in Belgium, to a maximum of 50%.

Alternatively, standard deductions may be claimed for salary and wage-earners on gross salary less social security contribution as follows (all rates as applicable to tax year 2001 – income of 2000):

Income–(BEF)	*Euro (€)*	*Marginal rate*
0 – 168,000	0 – 4,164,61	20%
168,001 – 337,000	4,164,61 – 8,354,01	+10% on the amount above 168,000 BEF
337,001 – 561,000	8,354,01 – 13,906,83	+5% on the amount above 337,000 BEF
564,001 – 2,218,333	13,906,83	+3% on the amount above 564,000 BEF

Maximum allowance: BEF 112.000 or € 2.776,41.

Similarly, directors, statutory auditors and the partners of firms (provided the partnership is subject to corporate income tax) are allowed to deduct only 5% up to a maximum of BEF 112,000. In addition they may claim a deduction for social security contributions if they have personally made such payments.

Non-residents

Unless the non-resident has a place of residence in Belgium or receives a major part (at least 75%) of his total professional income from Belgium, no standard deductions for dependants or allowances will be granted. Special rules will apply to non-residents of some countries such as France.

Other deductions

Certain items are specifically deductible in determining the net employment income, as follows:

- additional insurance premiums paid by self-employed tax payers and their dependants against illness or disability (where the insurance organisation is recognised in Belgium);
- contributions paid through the intermediary of an employer to a group insurance or pension plan;
- individual life insurance premiums, subject to certain conditions and provided the payments are made in Belgium (limited to BEF 66,000); and
- capital reimbursements on certain small mortgages, provided certain conditions are met.

The following additional items are deductible against any source of income:

- alimony or support payments to family members in accordance with certain legal provisions (80% of gross amount);
- charitable donations to Belgian universities and to organisations in developing countries (up to 10% of the total net income);
- donations to companies which finance political parties and to museums (up to specific limits);
- expenses for the renovation of houses at least 15 years old;
- cost of the acquisition of shares of an employer (up to BEF 22,000);
- premiums paid to savings linked pension schemes up to BEF 22,000, increased by BEF 22,000 for a spouse (this deduction cannot be accumulated with the deduction for acquisition of shares); and
- losses incurred by an individual with respect to earned income may be offset against other earned income of the same year, or carried over (without time limit), against a spouse's earned income.

Special family rules

Joint filing

In general, the income of husband and wife is reported on a joint basis, regardless of the type of matrimonial contract between them, although there are certain provisions in the law for income splitting. The professional income of the wife (or the husband if he earns the lower professional income) will be taxed separately. Where one spouse has no professional income, a 'deemed' professional income will be allocated and deducted from the professional income of the working spouse. This amount will then be taxed separately. Where the parents are the legal beneficiaries of the income of children, such income must be included in the parent's tax return. Professional income earned and alimony received by children are exceptions to this rule.

Standard deductions are allowed for the taxpayer and spouse (BEF 167,000 for each spouse or BEF 210,000 for a single tax payer) as well as for children (BEF 44,000 for 1 child, BEF 115,000 for 2 children, BEF 258,000 for 3 children, etc.).

Special treatment applicable to foreign personnel temporarily assigned to Belgium by international companies (expatriates)

In the 1960's, the Belgian authorities looked for incentives to induce foreign and multinational companies to invest in Belgium.

As Belgian income tax compared unfavourably with many of the systems existing in other countries, the Belgian authorities decided to grant a special benefit to those foreign employees who were temporarily assigned to Belgium by their employers, in the hope that this policy would encourage foreign companies to transfer new technology and know-how to Belgium.

Originally, it was intended that this special benefit would apply for five years. However, in many cases expatriates were assigned for longer than the five year period which led to the Belgian authorities renewing the regulation several times. This in turn created legal difficulties which culminated in the issuing of a new set of regulations in August 1983. The legality of these regulations is doubtful as they create special rules for a special category of taxpayer. This has not been addressed by the Courts beyond their declaration that they are not competent to deal with cases of litigation against the tax authorities.

The regulations are restricted to foreign executives as follows:

- an employee is not taxable on amounts which his employer pays to him/her in order to reimburse expenses which are in fact, 'expenses attributable to the employer'; and
- as a non-resident, the foreign executive will not be taxable on foreign source income or on remuneration for activities carried out abroad.

Four categories of persons qualify for this special treatment:

- executive personnel requiring special knowledge and entrusted with responsibilities;
- corporate directors exercising permanent functions;
- special non-executive personnel whose recruitment in Belgium is very difficult; and
- foreign research workers operating in scientific research centres or laboratories.

The rules expressly exclude personnel whose recruitment abroad or assignment to Belgium is not indispensable and who could be replaced by Belgians.

In the case of research centres, there is no requirement that there is a corporate link between the research centre in Belgium and the foreign organisation, and it is sufficient that the individuals concerned are recruited directly or that the assignment in Belgium is temporary.

It must be shown that an executive has been assigned by a foreign enterprise to work temporarily in Belgium, either in a branch of the enterprise or for a company under the control of the enterprise, or in a co-ordinating and control office operating with the group.

Questionnaires must be completed and forwarded to the Ministry of Finance in order to determine whether these criteria are satisfied.

The regulations treat certain expenses as 'employer's expenses' if they are incurred because the expatriate is living in Belgium rather than in his country of origin.

These may include recurring and non-recurring expenses, the significance of this distinction being that recurring expenses (other than school fees) are limited to BEF 450,000 per annum, while non-recurring expenses (and school fees) are not subject to this limitation.

There is an exclusion from Belgian tax under the regulations for that part of an individual's remuneration which relates to duties performed outside Belgium.

It should be noted that the Belgian Social Security Office has different rules. It usually requires that Social Security contributions be paid on amounts which are treated as tax-free by the fiscal authorities.

The various rules mentioned above result from the execution of Belgian internal law and can be considered as 'common law'.

The application of these rules should not normally interfere with the articles of the treaties for avoidance of double taxation which have been signed between Belgium and certain other countries.

Some difficulties may arise due to the fact that, in Belgium, an expatriate is technically considered to be a fiscal 'non-resident', but the expatriate's country of origin may take a different view.

Tax rates

Income tax applicable to residents and non-residents

Residents and non-residents alike are subject to the same tax rates on net taxable income after deduction of personal allowances:

Tax year 2001 (2000 income)
(the amounts are reviewed annually on the basis of cost of living)

BEF '000 from – up to	*Euro €*	*Rate (BEF 000)*	*Euro €*
1 – 258	0 – 6,395,65	25%	
258 – 342	6,395,66 – 8,477,96	+ 30% on amount over 258	6,395,65
342 – 488	8,477,96 – 12,097,20	+ 40% on amount over 342	8,477,96
488 – 1,123	12,097,20 – 27,838,44	+ 45% on amount over 488	12,097,20
1,123 – 1,684	27,838,44 – 41,745,27	+ 50% on amount over 1.164	41,745,27
1,684 – 2,470	41,745,27 – 61,229,70	+ 52,5% on amount over 1684	41,745,27

Notes

- 2.470 and over 61.229,70 + 55% on amount over 2.47061.229,70;
- All rates to be increased with a crisis surcharge of 3% plus a variable local tax;
- The 3% surcharge should progressively disappear over the next year, starting from the lower salaries as from tax year 2001.

Surcharge applicable for independent workers

Tax payable by directors and similar officers of companies, self-employed workers, businessmen and partners is subject to a surcharge unless sufficient advance payments are made. During the calendar year, however, individuals who start an independent business or profession for the first time are exempt from surcharges for the first three years. For the tax year 2001 (i.e. income for 2000), the surcharge was still fixed at 9%.

Payment of tax

Withholding taxes

Income from real estate is subject to an annual real estate withholding tax (*'précompte immobilier'*), part of which – equal to 12.5% of the 'revenu cadastral' for the house personally occupied – may be used as a tax credit but is not refundable. In the event that the real estate withholding tax applies to a building used in the professional activity, it will however, be a deductible expense in the same way as for a company.

Income from personal property withholdings are made at source (*'précompte mobilier'*). Since 1 January 1996, they have amounted to 25% on dividends and 15% on interest and royalties. Usually, they constitute a final tax, however, the individual taxpayer may recover these withholdings where he declares the income in his annual tax return. The withholding tax may be offset against personal income tax or reimbursed if it exceeds these.

Dividends or interest cashed outside Belgium by a Belgian resident, and on which no Belgian withholding tax has been levied, must be reported in the annual tax return and will be subject to a 25% or 15% taxation plus local surcharge.

Payroll deductions ('Précompte professionnel')

Income tax is withheld at source on salaries and wages (including directors' fees) and credited against the final income tax due. The deductions are calculated on the basis of schedules fixed by the tax authorities. Withholding tax is credited against the final tax liability.

Estimated advance payments ('Versements anticipés')

In order to avoid surcharges, advance payments should be made every quarter by individuals who earn income from a business or self-employed activity. Quarterly prepayments may also be made by other taxpayers and result in tax reduction.

Belgium

Final tax

This is paid upon assessment.

Estate, inheritance and gift taxes

Article 1 of the inheritance tax code provides that an inheritance tax is to be levied on the net value of all assets in the estate of a resident of Belgium, as well as on the value of any real estate located in Belgium which is part of the estate of a non-resident of Belgium.

Any person is treated as resident who, at the time of his death, has a domicile in the country. The tax will apply whether or not the individual concerned dies intestate.

If the estate includes real estate located outside Belgium which will be subject to local inheritance taxes, the taxes are deducted from Belgian inheritance tax. For this purpose, the relevant vouchers relating to taxes paid abroad must be provided.

Inheritance tax is computed on total assets after deduction of charges and liabilities and, for non-residents, on the net value of real estate located in Belgium (without any deduction of charges or liabilities).

Valuation

The valuation is normally based on the market value at the date of the death; the value is estimated by the individuals who declare the estate. For buildings located outside the country for which no evidence can be provided the market value is obtained by multiplying the rental value by 20 or 30, according to whether it is built or unbuilt property. The value will never be lower than that which has been used for fixing the foreign tax.

Capital, interest and debts due are valued at their nominal amount with a possible deduction for bad debts or depreciation.

Securities (shares, bonds, etc.) are valued at their official quoted value or on net assets value in the absence of a quote.

Life insurance is valued on the basis of annual income calculated at 4% of the full property value, multiplied by a factor included in published tables.

Deductible charges include funeral expenses and the debts of the deceased person at the time of death. Evidence must be available as to the amount of these charges and expenses.

Formalities

A statement must be filed with the registration office in respect of the inheritance of the deceased person's domicile by their heirs and legatees. In the case of death of non-residents, this statement must be filed with the registration office appropriate to the locality of the real estate.

The statement must be made within five months of the death if it occurs in Belgium, six months if it occurs in another European country and seven months if it occurs outside Europe.

Inheritance tax matters are no longer governed by State law but by the three Regions (Flanders, Brussels and Walloon region) which employ different schedules.

In general, a reduced rate will apply on the transfer of a family business (only applicable to small and medium sized enterprises) provided the business will be continued by the beneficiary and subject to some strict conditions, such as maintaining employment, etc. These conditions also vary according to the region in which the late person was domiciled (Flemish region, Brussels, Walloon region).

Inheritance tax rates

These usually vary from 3% to 30% between parents and children or between spouses, and may reach 80% for non-related persons.

The tariffs applicable will depend on the latest residence of the deceased.

Gifts and donations

Gift and donation taxes are presently levied at national level but will also become regional in the near future.

Rates vary between 3% and 80%, depending on the nature of the relationship existing between the parties and the amounts concerned.

Belgium

Exception

Gifts of tangible assets (including bearer shares, money, etc.) made at least three years before the death of the donor, are not subject to gift tax provided no written contract or notarised deed is established (*'Don manuel'*).

Special rules also apply to donations transferring family business (only applicable to small and medium sized enterprises).

Inheritance, gift tax and non-residents

Difficulties may arise upon the death in Belgium of a foreign resident or domiciled individual. Rules vary according to whether real estate or movable property is concerned.

An example is the death of a French citizen with a domicile in Belgium owning movable property, bank accounts and credits in France, Belgium and Spain, as well as real estate in France and the United Kingdom. Belgian law normally applies to movable property as a whole, but (in this example) French and UK laws also apply to the real estate. The heir's rights are therefore different for each of the three estates.

The Hague Treaty of 5 October 1961 will normally settle conflicts of law as far as wills are concerned as this convention was adopted as Belgium Law in 1971.

Wealth tax

There is currently no wealth tax in Belgium.

Social security contributions

The Belgian social security system is compulsory for all individuals, including foreigners who are employed in Belgium. The system covers the following benefits: unemployment, sickness and disability, pension, child allowances and (for workmen only) annual vacation. In addition, a special insurance is implemented for accidents at work.

EU workers who are temporarily assigned to Belgium may, however, opt to remain subject to the social security regime applicable in the country of origin for a limited time (E101 regulations). The same applies to workers from some other countries with which bilateral social security treaties have been agreed.

Monthly contributions are calculated as a percentage of gross income. The following rates apply:

Employees	Gross income	13.07%
Workmen	Gross income x 1.08%	13.07%
Employers	For employees ('white collar')	+/− 33%–35%
	For workmen ('blue collar')	+/− 54%

When giving an annual budget for the salary of an employee, the employer should consider:

- monthly gross salary (12 times a year);
- additional holiday pay in respect of four weeks annual vacation leave (this equals 92% of a normal monthly salary and is to be paid on top of the monthly salary); and
- a year end bonus payable in December and equaling at least one month's salary.

A minimum budget is, therefore, to be computed on the basis of 14 times the gross monthly salary.

Also to be added is the employer's social security contributions at a rate of +/− 35%.

Other taxes

Partnerships

No special treatment applies to non-incorporated partnerships. The partners will be subject to taxation according to their personal status (corporate or personal income tax).

VAT and sales taxes

Value added tax is levied at the following rates on sales of all goods and services:

Standard rate:		21%
Reduced rates:	Newspapers	0%
	Gold	1%
	Food & some listed items	6%
	Some other listed items	12%

Registration and stamp taxes

Real property

A registration tax of 12.5% is generally applicable to sales or exchanges of real estate located in Belgium. Mortgages on real estate located in Belgium are subject to stamp and registration taxes of 1%. Stamp taxes are payable on certain documents such as documents of title, bills of exchange and documents issued by the courts.

Customs & excise duties

Customs duties are levied at various rates at the time of importation of goods from outside the EU in accordance with EU rules.

Excise duties are levied on the production or importation of certain goods such as sugar, tobacco, alcohol, beer, wine, mineral water and fuel.

Exchange control

Exchange control regulations concern the provision of statistical information.

There are no restrictions on foreign ownership and all foreign investments can be freely repatriated.

Withholding taxes

Withholding tax (*précompte mobilier*) is deducted at source at a basic rate of 25% from payments of dividends and 15% on interest (rates as from 1 January 1996). It may be offset against the corporate income tax due, and any excess is refundable. If the recipient is a resident individual, the withholding tax is (in principle) a final tax.

Interests on some types of loans or bonds issued prior to 1 March 1990 may be subject to a 25% withholding tax.

Dividends on some types of shares issued after 1 January 1994 may be subject to a reduced 15% rate.

Reduction provided for by tax treaties

Many tax treaties provide for an exemption or a reduction in withholding taxes on royalties interests and dividends payable. The reduced rates are generally set at between 5% and 15%.

Country of Residence	*Royalties* (%)	Interest (%)	*Dividends* (%)
Non-treaty countries	25	15	25
Selected treaty countries:			
Australia	10	10	15
Austria	10	0/15	15
Brazil	25/15/10	0/10/15(f)	15
Canada	10	0/15	15
China Rep.	10	10	10
Korea	10/15	0/15	15
Denmark (e)	0	0/15	15
France (e)	0	10	10/15(a)
Finland (f)	0/5	0/10	15/10
Germany	0	0/15(b)	15
Greece	5	10	15
Hungary (f)	0	0/15	10
India	No special rates		
Indonesia	10	10/15	15
Ireland (e) (f)	0	0/15	15
Israel (f)	10	0/15	15
Italy (e)	0	15	15
Ivory Coast	10	16	15
Japan	10	15/10	15
Luxembourg (d) (e)	0	0/15(b)	15/15(a)
Malaysia	25/10	0/10	15
Malta	0/10	0/10	15
Morocco	5/10	15	15
Netherlands (e)	0	0/10(b)	5/15(a)
New Zealand	10	10	15
Norway (f)	0	0/15	5/15(a)
Pakistan (f)	0/15	0/15	15
Philippines (f)	25	0/15	15/20
Poland	10	0/10	10
Portugal	5	0/15	15
Romania (f)	10	0/15	10
Singapore	0	15	0
Singapore (f)	25/0	0/15	15
Spain (e)	5	15	15
Sweden	0	15	15
Switzerland	0	10	10/15(a)
Thailand	5/15	0/15	20/15
Tunisia	25/15/5	0/15	15
UK (e)	0	15	5/10(a)
USA	0	15	5/15(a)

Notes

(a) The lower rate usually applies if the foreign company owns, directly or indirectly, more than 25% of the capital of the Belgian company. In some cases the reverse rule may apply.

(b) In certain cases, royalties are not subject to withholding tax but only to the corporate income tax for their net amount.

(c) Holding companies benefiting from tax-exempt status (such as in Luxembourg) can (usually) not benefit from reduced rates of exemption.

NB: The Luxembourg SOPARFI entity would normally not be concerned by this rule.

The SOPARFI is a Luxembourg company form (*'Société de Participation et de Financement'*) which has a trading activity but mainly deals with investments and participations. This company form is adopted in order to avoid the fiscal restrictions applicable to pure holding companies. The SOPARFI is taxable only on the trading activity.

(d) Following the implementation of the EC Parent-Subsidiary Directive, no withholding tax is levied on dividend distributions made to a parent company resident in an EU member state, provided that a substantial interest (25% or more) has been held for at least one year by the parent company, which is subject to a tax comparable to Belgium income tax, and the dividends are paid by a company subject to 'normal' corporate income tax.

(e) Zero or reduced rates on interest may apply on loans to foreign governments or authorities. Therefore, where several rates are given, please check in detail.

All the above rates are indicative and many exceptions exist, so professional advice is always recommended (for example, several new treaties have also been signed which are not included in the above).

Anti-avoidance legislation

Most tax treaties provide for the exchange of information between the authorities of concerned countries albeit with some exceptions, such as the treaty between Belgium and Switzerland where information may be obtained only if the tax payer requests the application of the treaty.

In some cases, information may be transmitted automatically from one country to another i.e. France, Netherlands and Italy.

In the case of:

- registration of acquisition of real estate; or
- commission fees;

certain regulations exist to prevent money laundering.

Brazil

Villas Rodil Auditores
ARC & Associados
Fonteles & Associados
Gelman Consultores Associados (Tax)

Introduction

Major changes were made to the tax system in Brazil in 1997 and a broader tax reform is expected in the next few years. Although the trend and community pressures are towards simplification and an increase in the number of taxpayers (leading to a lessening of the tax burden), the addition or exclusion of taxes is substantially tied to the measures introduced by the General Constitution Amendment which took place in 1995. Congressional work will continue for at least the next two years.

The principle changes were as follows:

- prohibition of any sort of monetary correction;
- option for a company to credit or to pay its shareholders interest on their shareholdings, provided the rate does not exceed certain limits and the company has obtained net income (excluding such interest) or has retained earnings equivalent to twice the amount to be credited or paid to the shareholders (this is a particularly important element of tax planning for the investor as these amounts are deductible for income tax purposes);
- inclusion of foreign source income in the basis of calculation of the income tax of Brazilian corporations and individuals;
- restrictions on the deductibility of certain expenses, including almost all accounting provisions and reserves, leasing instalments and depreciation of fixed assets not related to manufacturing, selling and delivering operations and meals when not extended to all employees and donations (with some exceptions);
- no income tax to be paid on dividend distributions to individuals and companies, resident or non-resident, based on net income generated as from 1996;

- regulation of transfer pricing rules (similar to those in the USA) to avoid profit manipulation among related parties; and
- taxation on loans between related parties (IOF – after the initials in Portuguese).

Corporate taxes

Taxable entities

Resident companies

Resident companies (both corporations and limited liability partnerships) are liable to corporate income tax on income derived from Brazilian and foreign sources (including capital gains) on an annual basis.

A company is considered 'resident' if it is incorporated under Brazilian laws, even where it is a single representative office.

Non-resident companies

Non-resident companies are subject to corporate income tax on certain Brazilian source income, namely:

- royalties;
- technical assistance and know-how; and
- interest.

The level of corporate income tax on non-resident companies is determined by the relevant tax treaty with Brazil (see 'Tax treaties and withholding taxes' below). However, income tax is withheld on dividends remitted to corporations incorporated in tax havens.

Calculation criteria

A company may opt to apply the following alternative calculation methods:

- actual income, calculated either quarterly or annually;
- deemed income; or
- assessed income.

'Actual income' represents pre-tax income as per the company's accounting records, adjusted in accordance with tax regulation provisions. The actual income method is the most extensively used and the one that is described in detail in the following pages.

The 'deemed' or income method is only applicable to enterprises that meet all of the following criteria:

- having an annual gross income up to R$ 24,000,000 (equivalent to US$ 12,000,000, as at April 2001) – the limits are pro-rated to reflect the numbers of months of operations since inception to year end in the first year;
- not being a publicly held company
- not being a financial institution (commercial bank, savings and loans, investment bank, insurance company, pension fund or security broker); and
- understanding the fact that government or government-owned companies are not shareholders.

'Assessed income' is a calculation system that may be adopted by enterprises ineligible for the deemed income method. The assessed basis is lower than the actual income. Under this method, taxable income is assessed at 1.2 times a certain percentage of the gross income (1.45 times where the company is a financial institution). These percentages are used to calculate the estimated monthly advances and are determined by the industry category into which the enterprise falls, as follows:

Industry	*Percentage*
Resale of fuel in general	1.6 %
Transportation, except cargo	16.0 %
Financial institutions, except factoring (below)	16.0 %
Services in general, except hospitals	32.0 %
Brokerage	32.0 %
Realtors, real estate management and rental	32.0 %
Factoring	32.0 %
All other	8.0 %

Tax year and filing requirements

In general the system consists of monthly payments based on the previous month's taxable income, subject to an annual or quarterly 'adjustment' return, which is intended to consolidate monthly results compared to taxes paid. At the year or quarter end, the difference between the tax effectively due and the cumulative payments made during the period (elected by the taxpayer) must be either supplemented by the company (where tax due is higher) or carried forward for offset against income tax payable in subsequent periods (where tax paid is higher).

The fiscal year for companies is the calendar year. As a general rule, companies close their financial years at 31 December in order to avoid the administrative burden of preparing two sets of financial statements per year, but they may have a financial year over any 12 month period.

Where a company merges, consolidates or splits during a fiscal year it must calculate income tax due from 1 January of the year of merger, consolidation or division, up to the date of any of these events. An adjustment return must be prepared for that period and the resulting income tax must be paid or offset.

Taxes imposed

The following taxes are levied prior to income taxes on taxable income:

- social contribution;
- basic income tax; and
- additional income tax.

Rates

Income tax rate for corporations

The general income tax rate for corporations is 15% on the first R$ 240,000 of annual pre-tax income (or R$ 60,000 of quarter pre-tax income for taxpayers that elected this period) with the excess subject to tax at a rate of 25%.

Social contribution

Social contribution is calculated (based on a rate of 9%) before the determination of pre-tax income.

Income subject to tax

General rules

The income which is subject to taxes is calculated based on an entity's profits, both operating and non-operating (including capital gains), and is measured in local currency (Real – R$).

The accounting criteria applied in determining taxable income should be consistent from year to year and may only be changed to alternative acceptable criteria where the change is not intended to gain an incidental tax benefit.

Inventory valuation

Inventories are stated at the lower of cost or market value in the accounting records. Provisions reducing inventories to market value, if lower, are not deductible for income tax purposes. Either average or FIFO cost systems may be used, the LIFO method is not acceptable, but valuation at selling price, less mark-up, is permitted.

Capital gain and losses

Capital gains and losses have no special treatment for income tax purposes, being included within non-operating revenue and expenses and normally accounted for in the income tax calculation. Capital losses must be separately controlled as they are offset able against capital gains only.

Dividends

Dividends received are not subject to income tax and dividends paid are not deductible in arriving at taxable income.

Deductions

General rules

Expenses directly or closely connected with the conduct of the business that are necessary to obtain income and to maintain income sources are deductible.

Depreciation, amortisation, depletion

Deductibility of these charges is acceptable if:

- the relevant assets are being used for manufacturing, selling or distributing the products or for rendering the services of the company; and
- the rates applied to calculate the charges, applying the straight-line method, are equal to or lower than the following limits:

Type of asset	*Rate (%)*
Land	N/A
Buildings	4%
Machinery, equipment, furniture and fixtures	10%
Tools	15%
Vehicles and computer equipment	20%

Disbursements or accrued expenses relating to maintenance, repairs, taxes and the insurance of assets not used for the activities referred to above, are not deductible under the new regulations. Accelerated depreciation is admitted under certain conditions.

Royalties

As a general rule, royalties are deductible as business expenses to the extent that they are covered by a formal agreement duly registered with, and approved by, the Federal Agency on Technology Issues. Certain limitations apply to the deductibility of royalties – this is based upon the percentage of revenue generated relating to the royalty.

Interest

Interest paid on loans and debts, either to banks or to other entities (including a related party, provided there is a formal agreement) is deductible as an operating expense. Interest expense may not be deductible if foreign subsidiaries have retained earnings at the date of the loan.

Reserves and provisions

Provisions and reserves are not deductible, with the following exceptions:

- technical and mathematical reserves accounted for by insurance and capitalisation companies;
- provision for employees' salary for month 13, as well as paid vacations to employees; and
- allowance for bad debts, subject to certain limits.

Leasing agreements

Instalments paid under lease agreements on buildings, vehicles, machinery, equipment or furniture may only be deducted as operating expenses if the relevant assets are used for manufacturing, selling or distributing the company's products or for the business of the company. Most lease contracts in Brazil are for capital rather than for operating leases.

Non-deductible expenses

In principle, expenses not related to the business, or not necessary to maintain its source of income, are not tax deductible. Expenses which are subject to limits or conditions are not deductible where the conditions are not met (or the portion that exceeds specified limits is not tax deductible). The following expenses are also not tax deductible:

- non-mandatory contributions, except when the objective is the insurance, healthcare or pension plans of the business's employees and officers;
- gifts to clients or suppliers;
- meals paid to partners, shareholders and officers, except in the case of food provided to all employees; and
- donations, except when certain conditions are met.

Investment incentives

Investment incentives are presently restricted to investment in certain underdeveloped and developing regions, as follows:

- the amazonian region;
- the north east region; and
- the Manaus free trade zone

Related party transactions and transfer price

Related party transactions which are not carried out on an arm's length basis may be considered a dividend distribution or an attempt to improperly transfer expenses or profits. As such, these operations are subject to certain limits and rules.

Tax losses carry-forward

Tax losses may be carried forward and offset against gross income up to an annual limit of 30% of that income. Non-operating revenue and losses, subject to identical limits, must be controlled separately.

Personal taxes

Taxable individuals

Residents

Residents pay income tax under a general system known as 'current basis', which consists of paying tax on monthly income and preparing an adjustment return at each year end. Tax is paid on the individual's worldwide income, but income taxes paid abroad may be offset, subject to certain restrictions and conditions.

Non-Residents

Non-residents pay income tax on their Brazilian source income. Aliens pay income tax on income received from Brazilian sources as from the seventh month of residence or as from when a permanent visa is obtained.

Sources of income

Employment income

An employee, including a director or manager who is a Brazilian resident, is normally taxed on all of his or her emoluments for a fiscal year. Deductions are restricted to social security contributions, family allowances and education (certain limits apply) and medical expenses.

Business income

For income tax purposes, business profits received from corporations are, as stated above, free of further income tax. Profits obtained in the conduct of other non-corporate business are taxed on the following basis:

- profits from a personally owned enterprise (known as a 'unipersonal company') are taxed at corporate level;
- profits from a so-called 'microcompany', where taxation is similar to that of an employee, are taxed at an income tax level (calculated and paid on monthly income).

Social security benefits

Subject to certain limits, social security benefits are (in general taxable), except for those that have an indemnity nature.

Capital gains

An individual's capital gains are taxable, although capital losses are not deductible or in any way offsettable. Income tax on capital gains is due on a monthly basis at a 15% rate.

Interest

Interest earned from financial institutions or corporations is usually subject to withholding tax. Interest on shareholdings, as described in the section above dealing with corporate income tax, is subject to a 15% withholding tax which is the final tax.

Rentals

Rental income from real estate, net of certain deductible expenses, is subject to income tax – both at the corporate level and the individual level.

Personal allowances and deductions

The most common permittable deductions are social security contributions (both the mandatory government managed system and private pension plans), family allowances, alimony payments imposed by the Courts, education expenses and certain charitable gifts and medical expenses. Certain items are subject to maximum deductible amounts.

Applicable rates

Rates for the 2001 calendar year

Taxable Income (A)	*Rate (B)*	*Amount to deduct from (A)×(B)*
Monthly calculation/payment:		
Up to R$ 900	0	Exempt
From R$ 900 to R$ 1,800	15.0%	R$ 135
More than R$ 1,800	27.5 %	R$ 360
Adjustment/annual basis:		
Up to R$ 10,800	0	Exempt
From R$ 10,800 to R$ 21,600	15.0 %	R$1 620
More than R$ 21,600	27.5 %	R$4 320

Other taxes

Sales and service tax

This operates in a similar way to value added tax (VAT) and is levied on almost all domestic products as well as some services (transport and certain utilities). Rates range from 7% to 25% and the tax is administered at state level.

Excise tax

Excise tax is imposed by the federal government on industrialised and imported products. The tax is non-cumulative and has the effect of targeting certain social groups, e.g. alcohol, tobacco and luxury goods are heavily taxed.

General rates range from 10% to 25%, the highest tax is on tobacco at 360%.

Social programmes

Social programmes are funded by two contributions (taxes in practical terms) levied on gross revenues, as follows:

- SIP (Social Integration Program) – 0.65%
- COFINS (Contribution for Social Security Programmes) – 3% from 1999.

Salary taxes

Salary taxes are intended to provide for pension payments on retirement and to fund the healthcare system and are levied as follows:

- Employees – 8% to 11% of salary
- Employer – 27% to 29% with no limit

An employer must contribute payments on the basis of a percentage of gross salary to a fund for severance indemnities. This fund is managed by the federal government.

Temporary tax on bank account withdrawals

This is known as CPMF (after the initials in Portuguese) or 'cheque tax' and it is withheld by the bank on any kind of withdrawal by means of cheque, debit order, payment order, ATM operations, etc. (with the exception of funds transferred between accounts of the same person or company). CPMF is taxed at 0.38% and is paid weekly.

Exchange control

Exchange control mechanisms have been substantially removed. One remaining requirement is that foreign currency remittances, both outbound and inbound, be electronically registered before the Central Bank.

Tax treaties and withholding taxes

The percentage of tax on interest and royalties for non-treaty countries is 15%.

The percentage of tax on interest and royalties for most treaty countries is also 15%, including: Argentina, Austria, Belgium, Canada, China, Czech Republic, Denmark, Ecuador, Finland, France, Germany, India, Italy, Korea, Luxembourg, Netherlands, Norway, Philippines, Portugal, Spain and Sweden. An exception is Japan, where tax is levied at 12.5%.

Usually, income tax withheld in Brazil is taken as an advance against the payment of the income tax by the parent company in the investor country, where both countries have a treaty to avoid double taxation.

Where the parent company is incorporated in a country that does not have such a treaty, the amount withheld in Brazil is normally taken as a deductible expense in the parent company's income tax return.

Canada

Campbell Saunders & Co.
Friedman & Friedman
Hudson & Company
Lyle Tilley Davidson
Shimmerman Penn Burns Becker

Introduction

For every taxation year for a corporation and for each taxation year for which tax is payable (and in a few other cases) for an individual, a federal tax return shall be filed without notice or demand.

For corporations, a tax return also has to be filed with the provincial authorities when the corporation has a permanent establishment in the specified province. This filing requirement applies to Alberta, Ontario, British Columbia and Quebec.

At an individual level, a separate tax return has to be filed only for the province of Quebec if the taxpayer was a resident of Quebec on 31 December of the taxation year.

For all other provinces, the federal government acts as a collection agent. The provincial tax is calculated on the federal tax return.

Corporate taxes

Taxable entities

Resident companies

Resident companies are taxable on their world income from all sources, including 50% of all realised capital gains net of capital losses, as discussed further below. Companies are resident in Canada if incorporated in Canada or if their central management and control is situated in Canada. Additionally, companies incorporated outside of Canada can obtain 'continuance' to their incorporated status within Canada either to a federal or provincial level of incorporation, resulting in residency status.

Non-resident companies

Non-resident companies are taxable on the net income from a business carried on in Canada. Net income also includes 50% of realised capital gains net of capital losses on certain classes of Canadian capital property including business assets and all real estate located in Canada. There is also a 25% branch tax on Canadian business profits, capital gains resulting from the sale of taxable Canadian property, and royalties, which is similar to the withholding tax on dividends paid by resident companies to non-residents.

Non-resident companies are also subject to withholding tax on most types of Canadian source investment income.

These general rules are modified in many cases by tax treaties between Canada and a particular country.

Tax year and filing requirements

The tax year is the calendar year, but the financial year of a company may be any fixed 12 month period provided for in the company's articles of incorporation. In principle, the tax return has to be filed within six months after the termination of the financial year of the company.

Taxes imposed

Income taxes are levied by the Federal government and by the governments of the provinces where business is carried on. There are no municipal income taxes but municipalities do levy taxes on real estate.

Income taxes are paid in monthly instalments based on the lower of the previous fiscal year's income tax or the current fiscal year's estimated tax. Any balance of tax is due generally two months after the end of the fiscal year. A fiscal year can be any 12 month period but, once chosen, cannot generally be changed without the permission of the income tax authorities.

Rates of tax

The basic Federal income tax rate is 28%. A 4% surtax upon the basic rate, increases it to 29.12%. There are several rate reductions available for certain types of income in certain corporations. A 7% reduction is allowed for manufacturing and processing profits, which are taxed at 22.12%. A special 16% rate reduction is available upon the first CAN$ 200,000 of the active business income of Canadian-controlled private corporations and a 7% reduction is available on the active business income of Canadian-controlled private corporations between CAN$ 200,000 and CAN$ 300,000. Also, a 1% rate reduction to 28.12% is available in 2001 to all active business income of all Canadian corporations in excess of the amounts subject to the deductions just discussed. This 1% rate reduction will become 3% in 2002 (effective rate of 26.12%), 5% in 2003 (effective rate of 24.12%), and 7% in 2004 and later years (effective rate of 22.12%). An additional 6.66% refundable tax applies on investment income (other than dividends) of Canadian-controlled private corporations. Provincial rates vary from 4.5% to 17% depending on the province in which the business is carried on and the source of the revenue. Provincial income taxes are not tax deductible.

Income subject to tax

General rules

Income for tax purposes is calculated in accordance with generally accepted accounting principles adjusted by specific rules.

All but three provinces use the Federal basis of determining taxable income. Alberta, Ontario and Quebec permit some limited variations, particularly in the case of mining and oil and gas income.

Stock/inventory rules

Each property described in the inventory may be valued for tax purposes at the lower of cost and market value or at market value for all inventories. Various methods of inventory costing are permitted except for LIFO which may only be used in the very rare cases where it corresponds with the physical flow of goods. The valuation of inventory at the lower of cost or market value may apply to inventory consisting of real estate.

Capital gains and losses

50% of all realised capital gains are taxable. The remaining portion of the gain is tax-free. A capital gain is generally the excess of the proceeds of disposal over the sum of original cost, improvements, and expenses of disposal such as commissions and fees. A capital loss is similarly determined. Accrued gains and losses are not generally recognised for income tax purposes.

While the treatment of gains is the same for all classes of capital assets, the treatment of losses is not.

In the case of non-depreciable assets (such as land, and investments in the securities of other companies including subsidiaries), 50% of all capital losses realised in a year must be fully deducted to the extent of 50% of all capital gains realised in the same year. If capital losses exceed capital gains, 50% of the excess may, at the corporation's option, either be carried back for one, two or three years or forward indefinitely to subsequent years. In turn, the only limitation in each of these years is that the maximum portion of the loss that can be used may not exceed the lesser of that year's taxable income before the deduction and 50% of the net capital gains realised in that year.

For depreciable assets (such as buildings, machinery and equipment), the capital loss concept does not apply. Instead, losses on such property are deductible through the tax depreciation system (see 'Depreciation' below).

Dividends

Canadian dividends are not taxable when received by a Canadian public company. For a Canadian private company, Canadian dividends are tax-free if received from a connected corporation that did not receive a dividend refund in the year (otherwise a refundable tax of 33.33% will apply). A connected corporation is one that is either controlled directly or indirectly by the recipient of the dividend or the recipient has a certain shareholding interest being generally greater than 10% of votes and value of the paying corporation. The refundable tax is returned to the private company at the rate of CAN$ 1 of refund for every CAN$ 3 of dividend paid out.

Foreign dividends are not taxable until received by the Canadian corporation. Once the foreign dividends are received, Canada uses a combination of an exemption and a tax credit system to determine their taxation.

Foreign dividends are received by a Canadian corporation tax-free, if they are paid out of business income earned in a treaty country by a connected foreign corporation resident therein.

Foreign dividends received from non-treaty countries or from non-connected foreign corporations are taxable at the rates noted herein (above) under Rates of Tax. A foreign tax credit will be allowed for any withholding taxes. In addition, for foreign dividends received from connected corporations, a foreign tax credit is permitted for foreign income taxes paid on the underlying foreign income.

In the case of a controlled foreign affiliate, passive investment income (including capital gains) will be imputed as income to the Canadian corporation when earned by the foreign corporation. The rules for determining passive investment income were substantially amended during 1995, broadening the definition of passive investment income.

Deductions

General rules

Expenses are deductible to the extent that they are: incurred to earn income, are reasonable in the circumstances, are not on account of capital, and relate to the period in question. However, there are numerous exceptions, some of which are set out below.

Depreciation and amortisation

The cost of depreciable assets is deductible at varying rates under the capital cost allowance (CCA) system. Generally, the CCA system operates on a pool or class basis with each item of depreciable property being included in one of a limited number of classes.

Each class has its own CCA rate which is used to determine each year's maximum claim. There is no requirement to make a claim. The rate is applied (generally on a diminishing balance basis) to the balance in the class at the end of the year. In the year an asset is acquired, the CCA on that addition is generally limited to half that otherwise permitted, regardless of when in the year the asset is acquired. Available-for-use rules apply, so that CCA will not generally be deductible until the asset is placed in service. Subject to these rules, CCA is computed on the acquisition costs of all property included in the class less the sum of:

- the proceeds of disposal (not exceeding original cost) of any property previously included and since disposed of; and
- the total of prior years' CCA claimed on that class.

If a pool's balance at the end of a year is negative, this amount is added to income. Conversely, if there is a balance in a pool and no underlying assets, the balance is classified as a 'terminal loss' and is generally deductible in full. Special CCA rules apply to certain industries, most notably real estate.

Goodwill

When goodwill is purchased, 75% of the expense goes in a special CCA class with a 7% depreciation rate. When it is sold, 50% of the proceeds are removed from the class. If there is still a balance left, it stays in the class and keeps on being depreciated at the same rate until there is no balance left. Otherwise, the negative amount is taxed as regular business income. Self-created goodwill cannot be capitalised or expensed in any way.

Royalties

Mining and oil and gas royalties and taxes payable by producers to the federal and provincial governments are not deductible. However, some compensatory relief is available through special 'resource allowance' deductions and provincial tax credits.

All other royalties are deductible in the normal way.

Interest

While interest is generally deductible, it is not deductible by a resident Canadian company on excess debt owing to a non-resident shareholder who, together with any related persons, owns 25% or more of the shares of any class. For taxation years commencing before 2001, excess debt is that portion of the debt that at any time during a tax year exceeds three times the sum of:

- the greater of the paid-up capital at the commencement of the year and the paid-up capital at the end of the year of all shares of the company owned by the non-resident;
- contributed surplus at the commencement of the year related thereto;
- the company's retained earnings at the beginning of the particular year.

For taxation years beginning after 2000, excess debt is that portion represented by the amount by which the monthly average of the debt during the tax year exceeds twice the sum of:

- the monthly average amount of the paid-up capital of all shares of the company owned by the non-resident;
- the monthly average amount of contributed surplus related thereto;
- the company's retained earnings at the beginning of the particular year.

Dividends

Dividends paid are not deductible but may trigger a tax refund (see 'Dividends' in the 'Income Subject to Tax' section).

Bad and doubtful debts

Debts can be valued on a specific or a general basis or a combination of the two. Write-offs and provisions are deductible.

Deductible reserves

The principal reserve that is deductible is the allowance for doubtful accounts receivable. Reserves are also deductible, up to certain maxima, on gains arising from dispositions of real estate (both trading and capital) and on other capital property which is sold subject to a debt instrument whereby the receipt of the proceeds is deferred.

Exploration and development expenses

In both the oil and gas and the mining industries, special deductions apply for acquisition costs and for exploration and development expenses that would otherwise be non-deductible as outlays on account of capital. Conversely, the full proceeds on the disposal of wells, mines, petroleum leases and mining claims are taxable as income – not just the profit component.

Scientific research and experimental development (SR&ED)

Besides current expenditures, capital expenditures (excluding land and building) are fully deductible in the year incurred if directly connected to SR&ED and incurred in Canada. The cost of a building is expendable by way of the depreciation deductibility rule as the building is deemed to be of a separate prescribed class. The rules concerning what constitutes SR&ED are quite restrictive and generally exclude such things as product development beyond the prototype stage, style changes, and any research or development which does not have technological uncertainty.

Other non-deductible expenses

Provincial income taxes are not deductible in computing Federal income taxes, and vice versa. Other expenses such as warranty reserves, contingencies, recreational club dues, and interest and property taxes on vacant land are also not deductible.

Certain expenses are not fully deductible (e.g. meals and entertainment are only 50% deductible, certain automobile expenses have deductibility restrictions, etc.).

Foreign source income

Foreign source income, other than dividends, interest and royalties, is generally exempt from Canadian tax, provided a treaty applies. For dividends, interest and royalties from treaty countries and from listed developing countries, a credit for withholding tax is generally given.

Investment incentives and special benefits

Investment tax credits (ITCs)

ITCs are given, as a reduction of tax payable, for acquisition of manufacturing equipment, SR&ED expenditure and investment in equipment and industrial buildings in more remote areas. Rates are 10% for manufacturing equipment to be used in prescribed areas and 20% to 35% for SR&ED (Quebec provides ITCs of 20% to 40% for Quebec SR&ED wages). To the extent these ITCs are not utilised by the corporation against taxes payable, they may be refunded or carried forward. ITCs relating to the acquisition of manufacturing equipment have been substantially eliminated since 1 January 1995.

Government grants

Grants are available from the Federal government and most provincial governments to encourage investment in certain industries and regions of the country. These grants are normally either taxable as income or reduce the depreciable cost of property acquired with the grants. In many cases the amount of a grant depends on the degree of Canadian ownership.

Other investment incentives and special benefits

Private companies not controlled by non-residents (termed Canadian-controlled private corporations) are eligible for a 13.12% rate of Federal tax on the first CAN$ 200,000 of Canadian active business income per year, as well as a 22.12% rate of Federal tax on the next CAN$ 100,000 of Canadian active business income per year. These amounts are allocated amongst corporations within an 'associated' group. Corresponding provincial rates vary from 4.5% to 9% depending upon the provinces in which the business is carried on and certain other factors. Corporations with taxable capital in excess of CAN$ 10 million (see 'Large Corporation Tax', below) will see reduced access to the CAN$ 200,000 small business deduction and the deduction on the next CAN$ 100,000 with both being eliminated when taxable capital exceeds CAN$ 15 million.

Large corporation tax

This tax applies at the rate of 0.225% to corporations whose taxable capital employed in Canada at the end of a taxation year exceeds CAN$ 10 million. This CAN$ 10 million deduction has to be shared among related corporations (associated corporations, where all corporations in a related group are Canadian-controlled private corporations). The 4% surtax paid by a corporation reduces this tax. This tax only applies to a related group of corporations whose aggregate taxable capital employed in Canada is in excess of CAN$ 10 million.

Related party transactions

Transactions between related parties must occur at fair market value for tax purposes. Generally, fair market value means the value that would be obtained if the parties were not related to each other.

Losses

Business losses must be fully deducted against any income arising in the same year. If a net loss results for the year, it may, at the corporation's option, be carried back for one, two or three years and deducted to the extent of income in any of those years. Any portion not claimed in those years can be carried forward and claimed to the extent of income in any of the next seven years.

Corporate groups

Special rules allow groups of commonly-controlled Canadian corporations to reorganise on a tax-free basis. This includes the movement of shares and assets and in some cases, capital losses and business losses. Certain reorganisations of a company's own debt and share capital can also be done on a tax-free basis. However, consolidated tax returns are not permitted.

Tax free mergers and disposals

Mergers can be tax exempt if certain conditions are met, particularly where assets or shares are exchanged for shares.

If the participation exemption is applicable, the disposal of subsidiaries is tax-free (which is generally preferable to a disposal of assets since any gain is not realised for tax purposes).

Liquidation of the company

An individual shareholder will, in principle, be subject to income tax on liquidation distributions to the extent that these exceed the paid-up capital of the shares held by the shareholder.

If the shareholder is a company, then it may be possible to accomplish the wind-up tax-free if the shareholder owns at least 90% of all classes of shares issued and outstanding of the subsidiary company and where both the parent and subsidiary are 'taxable Canadian corporations'.

Capital taxes

Many provinces levy capital taxes similar to the large corporation tax discussed earlier. However, provincial capital taxes do not reduce provincially levied income surtaxes.

Treatment of branches (branch profits tax)

Profits of foreign branches of Canadian corporations are generally treated as foreign source income and subject to tax in Canada. Profits of Canadian branches of foreign corporations are subject to tax in Canada. In addition, branch tax could apply over and above the regular income tax. The application of branch tax to the Canadian branches of foreign corporations may, in certain circumstances, be modified or reduced by the various international tax treaties into which Canada has entered.

Personal taxes

Taxable individuals

Residents

Resident individuals are taxed in Canada on their worldwide income from all sources. Income is computed on a calendar year basis (subject to a fiscal year basis prior to 1995 for business income, see below) and includes one half of all realised capital gains net of capital losses (subject to a lifetime exemption of CAN$ 500,000 for gains realised in certain specific cases, see below). Residency for Canadian tax purposes is a question of fact. The courts have held that an individual is a resident of Canada if Canada is where, in the 'settled routine of his life, he regularly, normally or customarily lives'. In addition, an individual is deemed to be a resident of Canada for any year in which he 'sojourns' (i.e. temporarily stays) in Canada for 183 days or more.

Part-year residents are taxed in Canada on their world income that arises during the part of the calendar year that they are resident in Canada and on certain Canadian source income during the part that they are non-resident (see Non-residents below).

Non-residents

Non-resident individuals who are employed in Canada, carry on business in Canada or dispose of 'taxable Canadian property' are taxed in Canada on the income and the taxable portion of net realised capital gains arising from those sources in a calendar year. 'Taxable Canadian property' comprises certain Canadian property, for example, real estate located in Canada, shares of Canadian private companies, etc. Further, the sale of foreign corporation shares whose value is principally derived from 'Taxable Canadian Property' would be subject to Canadian taxation, except as modified by a bilateral income tax treaty.

Tax year and filing requirements

For individuals, the taxable period is the calendar year. The due date for filing the tax return is 30 April of the following year. Individuals with businesses and their spouses have until 15 June to file, but all taxes are due by 30 April. Non-residents are required to file a return if they earn employment or business income in Canada or dispose of taxable Canadian property.

Taxes on income

Income taxes are paid to the Federal government and the governments of each of the ten provinces and three territories. The Federal government acts as collection agent for the provinces (with the exception of Quebec), collecting tax at various rates established under provincial law. Provincial tax is paid to the province in which the individual is resident on 31 December in the year, except for the tax on business income which is payable (by both residents of Canada and non-residents) to the province or provinces where the business is carried on through a permanent establishment.

In the case of employment income earned in Canada by non-residents, provincial tax is payable to the province or provinces where the employment is carried on. In the case of capital gains realised by non-residents on 'taxable Canadian property', a Federal surtax of 48% may apply in lieu of provincial tax.

There are no municipal income taxes.

Sources of income

Employment Income

Employment income, including most benefits and directors' fees, is taxable when received. Certain deductions are permitted, the most common being:

- salesmen's expenses incurred to earn commission income (up to the level of the commissions earned);
- certain travelling expenses;
- professional membership fees and union dues;
- contributions to employer-sponsored registered pension plans and to private registered retirement savings plans.

Residents employed overseas by Canadian businesses in connection with resource exploration or exploitation, construction, agriculture or engineering projects, are granted a special tax credit. It is the portion of their tax otherwise payable which is attributed to the lesser of 80% of their income for the period while employed outside Canada or CAN$ 80,000 (pro-rated if the foreign employment is less than the full year). To qualify, the foreign employment term must exceed six consecutive months.

Business income

Prior to 1995, individuals were permitted to report income from a business (normally a proprietorship or share of income from a partnership) for any twelve-month fiscal period ending in a calendar year (once a fiscal year end date is chosen for the business, normally it cannot be changed). However, for 1995 and subsequent years, rules have been enacted requiring individuals to recognise business income on a calendar year basis subject to a complex system of reserves.

Business income for tax purposes is usually determined according to generally accepted accounting principles as adjusted by the specific rules of the Income Tax Act of Canada. These rules are essentially the same for unincorporated as well as for incorporated businesses.

Business losses are fully deductible against other income (including non-business income) that arises in the same year. If a net loss arises, it may be carried back three years or forward for the next seven years and deducted in such amounts as the taxpayer may choose from the income of those years.

Partnership income

Each partner is taxed on his share of the partnership income and the partnership itself is not taxed. Once determined, the partner's share is added to any other income derived by the partner and the total becomes his taxable income. If a loss is incurred for any particular year, the individual taxpayer will generally be allowed to deduct his share of that loss from his other income. Losses which result in a partner having a negative capital account may, in certain circumstances, result in the recognition of capital gains in the year of the loss.

Capital gains

One half of a realised capital gain is taxable. The remaining portion is tax-free. A capital gain is generally the excess of the proceeds of disposition over the sum of original cost, improvement costs, and expenses of disposition such as commissions and fees. A capital loss is similarly determined. Accrued gains and losses are generally not recognised for income tax purposes, except on death or emigration.

A deferral can be claimed for the portion of a gain that has not been realised due to part of the proceeds being outstanding in the form of a mortgage or other deferred payment arrangement. Regardless of the amount of proceeds outstanding at any year end, at least 20% of the gain must be recognised each year. In order to claim such a deferral, the taxpayer has to be a resident in Canada at the end of the year or at any time in the immediate following year. Other limitations can apply in special cases.

While almost all capital gains are taxable, one notable exception is the gain on the disposition of an individual's 'principal residence' (up to one per family).

There is an individual CAN$ 500,000 exemption for gains from qualified small business corporation shares or qualified farm property. However, the qualification requirements for these exemptions are quite complex.

If an individual has cumulative net investment losses (i.e. investment expenses greater than investment income) after 1987, this may limit the claiming of the capital gains exemption.

In addition, various 'rollover' rules are available whereby certain transfers of property can be effected on a tax-deferred basis. These are transfers to a Canadian corporation in exchange for its shares, or transfers between spouses (see 'special family rules' below).

While the treatment of gains is the same for all classes of capital assets, the treatment of losses differs between depreciable assets and non-depreciable assets.

In the case of non-depreciable assets (such as land and shares of corporations), one half of all capital losses are deductible in the year but only to the extent of one half of capital gains. Any losses remaining may be utilised at the taxpayer's discretion in the same way against capital gains of the three previous years and those of future years.

One half of losses on dispositions of shares or debts held in Canadian controlled small business corporations (an 'Allowable Business Investment Loss') are deductible from other income if certain conditions are met.

For depreciable assets (such as buildings, machinery and equipment) the capital loss concept does not apply. Instead, losses are deductible through the depreciation system (see same subject in corporate taxes for a description of the system).

Immigrants determine capital gains and losses on property which they owned at the time of becoming a resident in Canada (except 'taxable Canadian property') generally using a cost equal to the fair market value of the property at the time of immigration.

Emigrants are deemed to dispose of capital property which they own at the time of ceasing Canadian residence for deemed proceeds of disposition equal to the fair value of the property at that time. This rule does not apply to property owned by an individual when he became a resident of Canada (or which he subsequently inherited while resident) provided he was resident for not more than 60 months in the preceding ten years.

Goodwill

When goodwill is disposed of by an individual, the treatment of the negative balance (refer to 'Goodwill' in the deduction section for corporations) is taxed as business income to the extent of the total amount claimed as depreciation in the previous years. Any excess is taxed as a capital gain.

Dividends

Dividends are reported as income in the year paid. Foreign dividends are reported at their Canadian dollar equivalent (before deduction of foreign withholding taxes). Dividends from Canadian companies receive the following special tax treatment:

- the amount included in income is 125% of the actual dividend;

- a dividend tax credit is granted equal to 16.66% of the cash dividend.

Stock dividends from Canadian companies and non-resident companies are taxable. Stock splits are generally not taxable. However, stock splits of foreign companies may be treated as stock dividends (i.e. taxable).

Private companies can elect to pay special 'capital' dividends equal to the tax-free portion of their capital gains. These are not taxable when paid to residents but are taxable, by way of withholding tax, when paid to non-residents.

Interest

Interest income must be reported annually using the accrual basis method. If the investment was made before 1989, the individual could use the cash basis, receivable basis or accrual basis.

Rentals

Rental revenue and related expenses are reported by individuals on an accrual basis. Building depreciation may be claimed at the taxpayer's discretion, unless it creates or increases a net rental loss.

Non-residents deriving rental income in Canada are subject to withholding tax at a rate of 25% on the gross rents without deduction for expenses. An election may be filed in certain circumstances to reduce withholding tax to a rate of 25% of the net real estate rental income. Alternatively, for real estate rentals, a return may be filed reporting rental income net of related expenses and depreciation. Tax is then payable according to the progressive rate schedule for residents – including surtaxes and, if applicable, Alternative Minimum Tax. To the extent that the tax withheld from gross rents (and in some cases, from net rents) exceeds the tax based on the rate schedule, the excess is refunded.

Royalties

Royalties can be either investment income or business income, depending on the circumstances. Royalties also include proceeds received from the sale of a property, where the amounts received are dependent upon production or use from the property.

Other income

Resident individuals are also taxed on retirement income (including pensions), income distributions from trusts and estates, scholarships and bursaries in excess of CAN$3,000 per year and certain government training allowances, grants and social assistance payments.

Special income

Professionals: the income from the professional practice of an accountant, dentist, lawyer, medical doctor, veterinarian and chiropractor can be computed by excluding work in progress. Usually such an individual cannot incorporate a company to carry on a profession.

Farming: a farmer may calculate his income on the accrual basis or on the cash basis. Under the cash basis, revenue is recorded when received, expenses are recorded when paid and inventories are not generally taken into account. When farming is an individual's chief source of income (either alone or in combination with some other source), losses may be deducted in full from other income of the loss year. Undeducted losses may be carried back for three years or forwarded for the next ten years and deducted in such amounts as the taxpayer may choose from any income of those years. Deduction of farm losses is restricted when a farm represents only a secondary source of income. In that event, the deductible amount of the loss is limited to the first CAN$2,500 plus one half of the next CAN$12,500. Any undeducted loss may be carried back for three years or forwarded for the next ten years and deducted in such amounts as the taxpayer may choose from farming income of those years. The losses of 'hobby' farms (i.e. where there is no reasonable expectation of profit) are not deductible at any time.

Oil and Gas: generally, oil and gas income is taxed as business income, although special rules apply in its calculation. Government incentives are available in the form of grants, credits, accelerated exploration and development deductions and depletion. Royalties paid to the Crown are usually non-deductible, instead there is a 'resource allowance' deduction which is generally less than such royalties.

Estates and Trusts: estates and trusts are taxed as individuals without personal allowances but with deductions for income distributions or entitlements. They will be subject to the Alternative Minimum Tax (see below). They do not enjoy the capital gains exemption (see below), though beneficiaries might have claimed the exemption on gains allocated to them by the trust.

Exempt income

The following income items are not taxed:

- alimony, maintenance and child support payments if they are not deductible by the payer (see below);
- the first CAN$ 10,000 paid by an employer upon or after the death of any employee;
- casual betting and gambling profits, including lottery winnings;
- certain military pensions;
- certain payments related to personal injury;
- certain reimbursements such as for moving expenses.

Foreign source income

Foreign source income, other than dividends, interest and royalties, is generally exempt from Canadian tax, provided a treaty applies. For dividends, interest and royalties from treaty countries and from listed developing countries, a credit for withholding tax is generally given.

Personal allowances and deductions

Deductions

The following amounts are deductible by residents of Canada.

Registered Retirement Savings Plan: annual contributions up to the lesser of CAN$ 13,500 (for 2001) and 18% of the previous year's earned income which are made to a personal retirement income plan called an RRSP. In the case of an individual who is a member of an employer-sponsored pension plan, contributions are limited to the lesser of 18% of the preceding year's earned income and CAN$ 13,500 less a pension adjustment. The contribution limit for RRSPs for 2001, through 2003, will be CAN$ 13,500, CAN$ 14,500 for 2004 and CAN$ 15,500 for 2005.

Child Care Expenses: expenses for child care up to CAN$ 10,000 for each eligible child for whom anyone is entitled to claim a disability credit, CAN$ 7,000 for each eligible child who is under 7 at the end of the year or who is severely handicapped and up to CAN$ 4,000 for each other eligible child between the ages of 8 and 16. The total deduction is however, limited to two-thirds of the taxpayer's earned income (of the lower income earning spouse) and is subject to other further restrictions.

Alimony: for court orders and agreements entered into after 30 April 1997, child support payments are not be deductible to the payer, nor are they taxable to the recipient. Alimony, maintenance and child support payments are deductible if paid on a periodic basis (usually monthly) pursuant to a court order or a written agreement between separated spouses. Such amounts are also taxable to the recipient.

Moving Expenses: certain costs of an employee or student moving from one location to another within Canada, to the extent that the expenses are not reimbursed and the move causes the individual to be at least 40 kilometres closer to a new work location (in the case of an employee) or to a university-level educational institution (in the case of a student), are deductible. Costs of a move to or from Canada are not deductible (except for students).

Goodwill: for the deduction of goodwill, refer to the same topic in the corporation section, since the same rules apply.

Non-residents

Certain of the deductions above may be available to non-residents, depending on the nature of their Canadian income.

Losses

Where an individual sustains a loss he may offset it against the positive income in the preceding three years and then against the positive income for the next seven years.

Special family rules

Spouses' incomes are taxed separately. Thus, one spouse can deduct remuneration paid to the other where one is employed in the other spouse's business.

Transactions between family members must normally take place at fair market value. Accordingly, gifts and other transfers of property are treated as dispositions at fair market value (except between spouses where they are normally valued at cost).

Income or loss derived from property transferred to a spouse or to a child (until the year the child attains age 18) is attributed to the transferor. In the case of property transferred to a spouse, attribution also includes any capital gain or loss on a subsequent disposition of the property. A loan is treated as a transfer of property.

Investment income that is diverted by an individual to another connected individual through a low interest, or an interest-free, loan will be taxed in the first individual's hands.

Rates of tax

General

Federal income tax is calculated by applying the following rate schedule (2001) to taxable income. Taxable income is income less deductions and loss carryovers. The tax brackets below are increased annually by the percentage increase in the Consumer Price Index.

Band CAN$	*Rate*	*Tax on Band CAN$*	*Cumulative Tax CAN$*
0 – 30,754	16%	4,921	4,921
30,755 – 61,509	22%	6,766	11,687
61,510 – 100,000	26%	10,008	21,695
100,001 and up	29%	–	–

Provincial tax

Certain provinces and territories calculate income tax as a percentage of Basic Federal Tax. The remaining provinces (except for Quebec) calculate income tax using a rate scale applied to the federal taxable income. Quebec calculates income tax based on taxable income calculated according to its own rules.

Surtaxes

The Federal government applies no surtaxes on personal income tax.

Certain provinces add surtaxes ranging from 0.5% to 36% of their taxes otherwise payable.

Personal tax credits

Personal tax credits are allocated at the lowest personal tax rate of 16%. The effect is to provide the same tax benefit to taxpayers regardless of their tax bracket. The personal tax credits are increased annually by the percentage increase in the Consumer Price Index.

For 2001, some of the personal tax credits are:

	Personal Amount CAN$	*Tax Credit Equivalent CAN$*
Basic personal amount	7,231	1,157
Married amount (reduced if the dependant's income exceeds CAN$614)	6,140	982
Age 65 or over in the year	3,531	565

Other credits:

- there is a 16% tax credit for unemployment insurance premiums, contributions to government pension plans and university or college tuition fees;
- there is a 16% tax credit for up to CAN$ 1,000 of eligible private pension income; and
- there is a two-tiered Federal tax credit for donations to federally registered charities, certain non-profit organisations and certain foreign (mainly US) organisations. The credit for 2001 is 16% of the first CAN$ 200 of donations and 29% of donations in excess of CAN$ 200. Donations are ineligible for a credit in the current year to the extent that they exceed 75% of net income (income after claiming all deductions except for the capital gains exemption, loss carryovers of other years and certain other items). Unused donations (the portion exceeding 75% of net income or by election) can be carried forward for up to five years.

Other credits

Foreign taxes on foreign income are normally allowed as a credit not exceeding the equivalent Canadian tax on the foreign income. However, for foreign investment income (other than real estate income) the credit is limited to 15% of the foreign income and the excess is allowed as a deduction. At the taxpayer's option, the foreign tax on non-business foreign income (except employment income) may be claimed partially or fully as a deduction rather than a tax credit.

The dividend tax credit (see above) is deducted from 'basic Federal Tax' before the computation of the provincial income tax.

If a non-resident derives at least 90% of his world income from Canadian sources, he can claim all applicable Canadian tax credits. Otherwise, the tax credits are severely limited.

A part-year resident can claim a pro-rated portion of personal tax credits.

Alternative minimum tax

This minimum tax was introduced in an attempt to have all high income individuals pay some tax. The main features are as follows:

- the taxpayer will pay the greater of the ordinary income tax or the minimum tax;
- any excess of minimum tax over ordinary tax may be carried forward to offset ordinary tax payable over the following seven years to the extent that ordinary tax exceeds minimum tax in those later years;
- the Federal minimum tax rate is 16%, the combined marginal tax rate will be about 23 to 26% depending on the jurisdiction of residence;
- the tax base is the sum of taxable income for ordinary income tax plus the following amounts, less a special deduction of CAN$ 40,000;
- the non-taxable portion of capital gains;
- losses arising as a result of claiming certain resource related deductions;
- losses from claiming depreciation on certified Canadian films and multiple unit residential buildings;
- Canadian dividends will be included at 100% of the actual dividend rather than at 125% thereof as for ordinary income tax, the minimum tax is not reduced by the dividend tax credit;
- foreign tax credits, with certain adjustments, will be deductible from minimum tax;
- generally, the tax will only apply to taxpayers with gross income in excess of CAN$ 40,000;
- as a practical matter, the alternative minimum tax is not a problem for most individuals.

Quebec

Quebec, which levies and collects its own personal income tax, has its own form of minimum tax which is very similar to the Federal. The rate of Quebec minimum tax is 20.75% in 2001, 20% in 2002 and thereafter.

Payment of tax

Generally, tax is deducted at source from employment income and pension income.

Individuals who do not have tax deducted at source are required to pay quarterly tax instalments in some circumstances.

Individuals file an annual return, on a self-assessing basis, for each calendar year. The return, and any balance of tax owing, is due on 30 April of the following year. Compound interest is charged on deficiencies in payments. The rate is determined on a quarterly basis and the interest is non-deductible.

Estate and gift taxes

Canada has no inheritance duties, estate taxes or gift taxes.

Wealth tax

Canada has no wealth tax.

Social security

Canada Pension Plan (CPP): for 2001, employees and employers each contribute up to CAN$ 1,496.40 (self employed persons – CAN$ 2,992.80) to the CPP. Quebec has its own pension plan.

Employment insurance (EI): employees pay premiums to the EI fund (maximum CAN$ 877.50 for 2001) which is a government fund designed to compensate the unemployed. Employers generally pay 1.4 times the employee's premiums.

Other taxes

Federal

Goods and services tax: tax will apply at a rate of 7% on most goods and services and is similar to value added taxes currently applicable in many other countries.

Excise tax: this tax applies to a wide range of goods such as jewellery, tobacco, alcohol and gasoline.

Customs duties: are levied at various rates on the value of goods imported into Canada.

Provincial

Retail sales tax: all provinces, except Alberta, levy these taxes at rates varying from 5% to 12%. Quebec has converted its retail sales tax to a value added tax (7.5% as of 2001) similar in most cases to the Goods and Services Tax applied by the federal government. Further, on 1 April 1997, New Brunswick, Nova Scotia and Newfoundland established a 15% combined federal/provincial harmonised sales tax based upon the Federal Goods and Services Tax.

Land transfer taxes: some provinces levy a land transfer tax on acquisitions of real property. Rates are generally between 1% and 2% of fair market value but for non-residents of Canada they can be as high as 33% in certain restricted situations.

Medical & hospital insurance: Ontario, Alberta, and British Columbia require premium payments by individuals resident in the province.

Municipal

Property taxes: municipalities levy taxes on real estate.

Exchange control

Canada has no monetary exchange controls of any kind.

Double tax relief

Double tax relief is provided through three basic mechanisms. The first is the treatment of foreign dividends (see 'Dividends').

The second is the network of over 40 bilateral tax treaties that Canada has signed and ratified. The preamble to most treaties provides that they are for the avoidance of double taxation. Each treaty generally provides rules for determining residency (so-called 'tie-breaker' rules), rules for sourcing income, and rules determining which country has the right to tax. As well, there is a competent authority provision to which a taxpayer may apply to resolve a tax dispute.

The third is the foreign tax credit system whereby a Canadian resident may claim a credit against his Canadian taxes for taxes paid to a foreign government. Unused foreign tax credits in respect of foreign taxes paid on business income may be carried back three years and forward seven. There is no carry-over of foreign tax credits in respect of non-business income.

International aspects

Investment controls

Canada has a policy of reviewing proposed foreign takeovers of Canadian business enterprises and the establishment by foreigners of new business enterprises to determine if they would be of significant benefit to Canada. The review is performed by Investment Canada which can deny the takeover or establish criteria to be met before the investment would be permitted. However, there are broad exemptions from review which:

- exempt almost all new businesses from review and require only a notification of those investments;
- establish thresholds to limit review to larger acquisitions by non-Canadians and require only notification of acquisitions below the thresholds;
- provide that the thresholds for review are:
  - (i) direct acquisitions by non-Canadians of businesses in Canada with assets of CAN$ 5 million or more;
  - (ii) indirect acquisitions, resulting from the acquisition of parent companies outside Canada, when the Canadian subsidiary acquired has assets of CAN$ 50 million or more;
- give exceptional authority to review acquisitions below the thresholds, or investments to establish new businesses in culturally sensitive sectors such as book publishing and film production and distribution.

Canada has significant monopoly and competition legislation and proposed major acquisitions must always be reviewed from this perspective.

Certain industries, notably financial services, telecommunications, transportation, and publishing, are regulated by legislation that may restrict foreign investment. Resource industries have tax incentives biased towards Canadian ownership.

Withholding taxes and tax treaties

Most payments to non-residents, unless included in income subject to regular tax, are subject to withholding tax at 25% (usually reduced to 15% by treaty). Such payments are interest, dividends, rents, royalties, retirement income, management fees, alimony, maintenance and child support payments and entitlements to income from estates and trusts. However, certain types of interest, principally on specified government securities and certain medium and long-term loans to Canadian corporations, are exempt from withholding tax altogether.

Where a non-resident disposes of 'taxable Canadian property', he is liable to tax on the capital gain. If he does not pay the tax prior to the closing or settlement of the sale, the purchaser must withhold 33.33% from the purchase price on the non-resident's behalf. The following table illustrates the rates currently in force:

Country of Residence	*Natural Resource Royalties* (%)	*Other Royalties* (a) (%)	*Interest* (%)	*Dividends* (%)
Non-treaty countries	25	25	25	25
Selected treaty countries:				
Algeria	(l)	0/15	15	15
Argentina	25	3/5/10/15	12.5	10/15(g)
Australia	25	10	15	15
Austria	25	0/10(b)	10	5
Bangladesh	(l)	10	15	15
Barbados	(l)	10	15	15
Belgium	25	10	15(c)	15
Brazil	25	15/25(e)	15(c)	15/25(h)
Bulgaria*	(l)	0/10	10	10/15
Cameroon	(l)	15	15	15
Chile	(l)	15	15	10/15
China	25	10	10(c)	10/15(h)
Croatia	(l)	10	10	5/15
Cyprus	25	10	15(c)	15
Czech & Slovak Federal Republics	25	10	10(c)	10/15(h)
Denmark	15	0/10	10	5/10/15
Dominican Republic	(l)	18	18	18
Egypt	25	15	15(c)	15
Estonia	(l)	10	10	5/15
Finland	10	10	10	10/15(h)
France	25	0/10	10(c)	5/10/15
Germany	25	10	15(c)	15
Guyana	(l)	10	15/25	15
Hungary	25	10	10(c)	5/10/15
Iceland	(l)	0/10	10	5/15
India	25	10/15/20	15(c)	15/25(h)
Indonesia	25	10/15(b)	10	0/15
Ireland	15	0/15	15(c)	0/15
Israel	25	15(b)	15(b)	15
Italy	25	10	15(c)	15
Ivory Coast	25	10	15	15/18(i)
Jamaica	(l)	10	15	15

Japan	25	10	10(c)	15(c)
Jordan	(l)	10	10	10/15
Kazakhstan	(l)	10	10	5/15
Kenya	25	15(b)	15(b)	15/25(h)
Korea	25	15	15	15
Kyrgyzstan	(l)	0/10	15	15
Latvia	(l)	10	10	5/15
Lebanon*	(l)	5/10	10	5/15
Lithuania*	(l)	10	10	5/15
Luxembourg	25	0/10	10	5/15
Malaysia	25	15	15	15(b)
Malta	25	10	15(c)	15
Mexico	25	15	15(c)	10/15(j)
Morocco	25	10(d)	15(b)	15
Netherlands	25	0/10	10	5/10/15
New Zealand	25	15	15	15
Nigeria	(l)	12.5	12.5	12.5/15
Norway	25	10/15	15	15
Pakistan	25	15/20(i)	15/25(j)	15
Papua New Guinea	(l)	10	10	15
Philippines	25	10(b)	15(b)	15/25(h)
Poland	25	10	15	15
Portugal*	(l)	10	10	10/15
Romania	25	15(b)(c)	15(b)	15
Russian Federation	25	0/10	10	10/15(h)
Singapore	25	15(b)	15(b)	15
Slovenia*	(l)	10	10	5/15
South Africa	25	6/10(f)	10	5/15(h)
Spain	25	10(b)	15(b)	15
Sri Lanka	25	10(b)	15(b)(c)	15
Sweden	10	0/10	10	5/10/15
Switzerland	10	0/10	10	5/10/15
Tanzania	(l)	20	15	20/25
Thailand	25	15	15	15
Trinidad and Tobago	(l)	10	10	5/15
Tunisia	(l)	15/20	15	15
Ukraine	25	10	10	5/15
United Kingdom	25	10	10(c)	10/15(h)
United States of America	25	0/10	10(c)	5/10/15(k)
Vietnam	15	7.5/10	10	5/10/15
Zambia	25	15(b)	15(b)	15
Zimbabwe	25	10(c)	15(c)	10/15(j)

Notes

(a) 'Other' royalties do not include those in respect of the production or reproduction of any literary, dramatic, musical or artistic work, but do include payments for a right in or to the use of certain motion picture films and video tapes and payments for industrial know-how;

(b) The lower rates apply where royalties, interest and dividends are taxable in the country of residence of the beneficial owner, otherwise the rate is generally 25%;

(c) In some circumstances the rate may be lower (see the terms of the relevant convention);

(d) The lower rate applies to royalties of the production or reproduction of any literary, dramatic, musical or artistic work other than a motion picture film or videotape for use in connection with television;

(e) The rate is 25% arising on royalties arising from the use of the right to use trademarks, 15% in all other cases;

(f) The lower rate applies to patents, trademarks, and computer software;

(g) The lower rate applies to corporate shareholders owning at least 25% of share capital;

(h) The lower rate applies to corporate shareholders owning at least 10% of voting stock;

(i) The lower rate applies to amounts paid from Canada;

(j) The lower rate applies to shareholders owning at least 25% of voting stock;

(k) The 5% rate applies to corporate shareholders owning at least 10% of voting stock, the 10% rate applies to dividends from a non-resident owned investment corporation if the recipient is a corporation owning at least 10% of voting stock;

(l) Rate varies, consult treaty.

***Unratified treaties**

Until ratified, the withholding tax rate is generally 25%.

Anti-avoidance measures

There are special anti-avoidance rules to prevent strictly tax-motivated transactions that would have the effect of avoiding, reducing or deferring taxes that might otherwise have become payable. These rules seek to distinguish between legitimate tax planning and abusive tax avoidance. Therefore, they are not intended to interfere with legitimate commercial and family transactions.

Chile

Humphreys & Cía.
Auditores Humphreys
Humphreys Consultores
Clasificadora de Riesgo Humphreys Ltd.

Introduction

Current issues

Two areas of the tax system are currently being studied by Congress:

- elimination of some 'loopholes' in corporate taxation to preclude tax avoidance;
- reduced levels of personal taxation.

The first area of change, even though it is centred more on regulatory than law aspects, is being contested by the private corporate sector who argue that it involves a disguised tax increase, something that would never be passed by the legislature if presented as such. Notwithstanding ongoing discussions, some of the measures in this package of reforms may be approved during 2001.

The idea of scaling down the personal income tax rates has been at the forefront of the tax debate for over a year, and there is consensus about a substantial reduction that would take the top marginal rate of 45% to a maximum in the order of 30% to 35%. To compensate for this reduction, an increase in the corporate tax rate is being proposed from the current 15% to probably 17% or 18%. This reform could also take place during 2001.

Corporate taxes

General

Taxes in Chile are applied nationally. There are no regional, provincial or local taxes except for property taxes (a proportion goes to the municipality) and a municipal licence tax levied on professionals and business entities.

Company income tax is levied on accrued income on the basis of a single flat rate of 15%, regardless of size, type of business, amount of revenue or form of organisation.

An indexation system ('Monetary Correction') is incorporated into the tax structure. The indexation is applied by the use of 'indexed units', based on the month-to-month variation of the Consumer Price Index ('CPI'). Indexation is particularly important in the computation of taxable income and it is shown as a separate item in the financial statements under the heading 'Monetary Correction'.

Corporate tax base

All operating and non-operating income, including (among others) capital gains, revenue from investments, commissions of any sort, technical assistance fees earned, profit (loss) on the sale of fixed assets, are treated as taxable income.

All operating and non-operating expenses that are necessary to produce income, are tax deductible.

The following are disallowed expenses:

- compensation paid to partners in a limited liability company;
- charges made by a foreign parent company to its local subsidiary;
- interest payments arising from financial operations paid to partners or to the foreign parent company;
- travel, entertainment and advertising, considered by the tax authorities ('IRS') to be excessive or not directly related to the business.

Sources of income

All income originated or generated by goods located in the country or activities performed in Chile, whatever the domicile or residence of the taxpayer, are taxable. Corporate tax is levied on accrued Chilean source income and income from foreign sources received by Chilean residents.

Basic corporate residence rules

Business entities are deemed to be resident, for tax purposes, if they are incorporated or indentured in the country. Subsidiaries or branches of foreign companies are taxed on their Chilean source income as determined by their local accounting records.

Subsidiaries of foreign entities which have been set up in Chile as corporations are required to have a Board of Directors, at least three members of which must hold formal meetings in the company's official address within the country's borders.

Tax year

The fiscal year is the calendar year. All commercial entities are required to keep accounting books and prepare a balance sheet at 31 December for tax purposes. An annual tax return must be filed by the following 30 April. However, for financial accounting purposes, a company may close its year at any preferred date.

Dividends

Dividends paid by local companies to resident shareholders are not subject to withholdings. Dividends received by local business entities from other companies are excluded from their taxable income. If the dividend comes from a foreign source, however, it is included in taxable income.

Distributions to non-residents are subject to a withholding tax of 35%.

The 15% corporate income tax paid by the distributing company at the end of fiscal year is given as a credit against the receiving party's own taxable income.

Payment and penalties

Business entities are required to make monthly provisional payments against their year end tax liabilities. Such payments are computed as a percentage of total revenue which is adjusted every year on the basis of the last year's effective proportion. The annual net balance of the tax liability accrued after deductions of provisional payments is payable simultaneously with the filing of the return in April.

Postponing payment causes indexation based on the CPI and interest. The interest rate is 1.5% per month in addition to fines starting at 10% of the liability and rising at a rate of 2% per month to a maximum of 30%.

Consolidation

Publicly held corporations are required to prepare and publish audited, consolidated financial statements to include subsidiaries in which they hold 50% or more of the ownership. However, companies in the group must file and pay income taxes independently.

Depreciation

Depreciation is calculated on an economic basis over the life of the asset but may also be accelerated under certain circumstances.

Previous years' losses

These may be carried forward indefinitely.

Inventory valuation

Either FIFO or weighted average inventory valuation methods may be used, but must be applied on a consistent basis over a period of no less than five years. Change from one method to another requires prior approval from the tax authorities.

Similarly, significant inventory write-downs or write-offs must be approved by the IRS in order to qualify as deductions for tax purposes. The same approval is required for the dismantling or demolition of installations, buildings and equipment, but not for actual disposals.

Tax-free reserves

Except for the restatement reserves arising from the application of monetary correction, no taxfree reserves are allowed, either for inventory devaluation and/or obsolescence, depletion of natural resources, or doubtful debts. In the latter case, specific write-offs are allowed only if proof is provided that a specific account is deemed irrecoverable, as in bankruptcy cases or when all reasonable collection methods have been carried out without success.

Start-up costs

Organisational and start-up expenses may be charged to operations as they occur or may be deferred over a maximum period of six years.

Inter-company transactions

Purchases of goods from foreign associates are not subject to any special regulations other than payment of custom duties.

Commissions paid by foreign suppliers to their local representatives or agents are subject to VAT (see below). The local commercial bank making the remittance abroad in payment of goods imported will deduct the related commission due to the local representative from the remittance and place it at the local agent's disposal, net of value added tax.

Taxation of branches of foreign corporations

Income tax rates applied to branches of foreign companies do not differ from those relating to national entities. No proportion of the head office expenses attributed to a local branch is tax deductible for the branch.

Withholding taxes

Dividends paid to individual residents are not subject to withholding taxes. Remittances abroad are subject to different withholding rates as follows:

Dividends	35%
Interest (except when paid to a financial institution)	35%
Interest (paid to a foreign bank)	4%
Royalties	30%
Fees, in general	30%
Insurance premiums	22%
Technical assistance fees	20%

Local fees paid by a business entity for professional services are subject to a 10% tax withholding which the contractors may use as a credit against their respective income tax liability.

Assessments of taxable earnings

Taxable earnings from mineral mining, smelting and refining (not through corporations), may be assessed as a percentage of net sales ranging between 4% and 20%, depending on the net average price per ton of copper, or its equivalent in gold and silver, sold during the year. Other mineral businesses can opt for this scheme with a flat rate of 6%. Once the tax base has been determined as described, the general tax rules apply.

Other activities that enjoy special tax treatments are farming, in general, and land transportation, where taxable income is assessed as 10% of the (taxable) valuation of the businesses' net assets, and then the general tax rule is applied. These incentives have limits and conditions.

Regional incentives apply to business entities operating in the northern and southern regions of the country. They consist chiefly of the elimination of customs duties and exemption of VAT on goods imported into defined 'free zones', as long as they are warehoused or used within the exempt area.

Export incentives

Exports of goods that do not exceed a certain amount of dollar export value per classification chapter are subsidised with a 10% reimbursement of the value of the export.

Deferred custom duties

Customs duties on imported capital goods may be deferred over a maximum term of seven years. Duties can also be totally or partially amortised over the life of the goods if they are used to produce exports.

Foreign investment statute

The country's attitude to foreign investment is favourable and encouraged. Foreign investment is guaranteed equal treatment with local businesses.

Foreign capital investments of over US$ 25,000 may be entered through an investment contract between the investor and the Republic of Chile, which in summary stipulates the period within which the proposed capital must actually enter the country – normally three years, or eight years in the case of mining investments.

Capital contributions may consist of:

- freely convertible foreign currency;
- tangible assets in any form, valued by the same procedures applying to imports;
- technology, authorised by the authorities;
- loans relating to the foreign investment which may be capitalised if previously authorised by the Central Bank;
- capitalisation of loans and foreign debt in freely convertible currency and profits obtained from previous foreign investments which may be capitalised;
- the foreign investor is guaranteed access to foreign exchange, at the official rate for repatriation of capital, earnings, interest and dividends;

- the foreign investment is guaranteed a fixed single income tax rate of 42% during a ten year period, which will cover all taxes levied on income during that period. The investor may at any time waive this right and opt to be taxed at the prevailing tax rates, which currently total 35% (a net combination of income tax and withholding).

Personal taxes

Residence

Any foreign individual becomes a tax resident after a stay of six months or more in one year, or more than six months in total within two consecutive fiscal years.

Domicile

Domicile is governed by both tax residence and the intention to remain in Chile. Foreign nationals, therefore, can be domiciled in Chile from the first day of their stay in the country. Domiciled persons become members of Chilean society even when they maintain the status of foreign nationals.

Loss of domicile

The absence of residence in Chile is not sufficient cause for the loss of domicile (for the effects of tax law). This concept applies to persons that leave the country but maintain the principal seat of their affairs in Chile. However, the taxpayer may prove that he has effectively established domicile abroad and request to be considered as non-domiciled in Chile.

Scope of taxation for foreigners

As a general rule, any person domiciled or resident in Chile must pay taxes on all income, whether its origin is located in the country or abroad. However, if the individual is a foreign national, they will be subject to taxation only on Chilean source income during the first three years of their stay. After that, income from all sources is taxed.

The mere fact of rendering services in Chile implies that the related revenue is of Chilean source and subject to taxation. This is regardless of whether the payment is performed by a Chilean or a foreign entity, whether the resources are domestic or foreign or the service provider has or has not acquired residence or domicile in Chile.

Taxation of non-residents

Non-resident foreign nationals are subject to a withholding income tax rate of 30% on gross compensations, with no allowances or deductions. The rate is reduced to 20% in the case of individuals qualifying as technical personnel, artists, performers, and sport instructors, subject to approval by the tax authorities. The 30% (20%) tax covers the non-resident's entire liability and requires no personal filing.

Taxation of residents

Individuals whose income consists solely of salaries or wages are subject to a withholding income tax on their compensation net of social security payments. After an initial exemption, the tax rate is computed on a progressive marginal scale starting at 5% for income currently equivalent to US$ 17,000 each year and going up to 45% for income equivalent to US$ 70,000 or more each year.

The withholding tax covers all of the wage earner's tax liability and no additional filing is required provided that there are no other sources of income.

Individuals earning income from any other source, either in addition to or substitution of salaries or wages such as professional fees, dividends and distributions, interest, real estate rentals, profit sharing, income of the self-employed, are required to file an annual tax return covering all such aggregated income. Taxes paid during the year offset the resulting annual tax amount.

Social security contributions

Retirement fund financing is based on payments by the employees into individual accounts managed by private pension fund managing companies supervised by the government. For this reason, even though they are mandatory, social security contributions are not viewed as 'taxes' since each person's payments are that person's exclusive savings toward his retirement fund.

The retirement fund receives 10% of the monthly salary. Voluntary payments up to another 10% can be made to the fund. An additional amount between 2.16% and 2.95% (depending on the insurance company contracted by the pension fund) goes to cover disability and survivors' insurance. Health insurance is 7%, paid either to private health care institutions or to the National Health Fund.

All these percentages are calculated on the basis of each employee's salary with a limit that is US$ 1,650 (estimated on current exchange rates) and are applied before the calculation of income tax.

The employer pays only a small premium to cover insurance for work related accidents.

Allowances

The following are the main deductions from taxable income:

- social security contributions, as described above;
- such part of a sole proprietor's drawings from the profits of the business, or a partner's drawing against profits in a limited liability partnership, that is invested as fresh capital in any other business enterprise which, in turn, is subject to corporate income tax (this exemption is applicable only over the period during which the investment is maintained);
- 20% of the investment made by any individual taxpayer in stock of a publicly held corporation whose shares are quoted on a Stock Exchange, other registered securities and time deposits, provided such investment has been held for at least one year at 31 December;
- total investments qualifying as allowances may not exceed certain limits; in the case of securities (bonds, shares), they may not exceed 20% of taxable income (investment in pension fund voluntary deposits may not exceed 25% of said income);
- dividends of publicly held corporations and capital gains on sales of shares are allowed a reduction of 50% in the computation of taxable income, with a limit.

Capital gains tax

Gains from the sale of securities are normally taxed as income.

If transactions are occasional and not part of the taxpayer's business purpose, occurring no more than a few times a year, the capital gains are subject to tax at 15%. Gains are generally subject to 15% tax, and are also included in the annual tax filing. Gains on transactions in property, which are occasional, are tax exempt.

Value added tax (VAT)

Scope of the tax

Value Added Tax (VAT) consists of an 18% flat rate which is levied in broad terms on the price of the following:

- sales and other contracts whereby title to goods (except property) is transferred on a recurring basis (recurrence is presumed in connection with sales from an entity's line of business);
- services rendered which may be deemed commercial, industrial, financial, or pertaining to mining, constructions, insurance, advertising, data processing, and other business activities;
- imports, recurring or not.

Tax liability

As a general rule, the seller of goods or services is liable for the payment of the tax and the buyer bears the tax burden in the price paid. An exception occurs when the seller is not domiciled in Chile or is, for other reasons, not subject to control by the Chilean IRS. In such case the buyer is liable for withholding and paying VAT. Such exceptions to the general rule are established by law or may be determined by the IRS.

The tax is payable monthly, except for special situations such as imports, commented on below.

Credit and debit system

VAT charged by a company on its sales is called 'VAT debit'. VAT borne by a company on purchases of goods or services is called 'VAT credit'. The taxpayer deducts every month the tax credits from the tax debits and files a tax return paying the difference, if any. If in a given month credit exceeds debit, the difference may be carried forward and added to the credit of the next month.

VAT borne on the acquisition of goods or services which, in turn, the entity uses in operations not subject to VAT, is not deductible. In other words, such VAT borne is not recoverable and, therefore, constitutes an additional cost.

Specific cases of VAT applicability

- Imports whether recurring or not, are subject to VAT. The

importer must pay this tax before the imported goods are cleared from customs. VAT borne and paid as an importer may be credited against VAT charges as a seller.

- The rental of goods, as well as property used for industrial or commercial activities, is subject to VAT. A leasing contract is considered a rental and, therefore, subject to VAT.
- Life assurance is VAT exempt. General insurance purchased from insurance companies established in Chile is subject to VAT, except when the coverage is for goods for export, transportation risks in connection with imports and exports or damage caused by earthquakes.

  Insurance with companies not established in Chile is not subject to VAT. Reinsurance is VAT exempt.
- In the case of instalment sales, both interest and the price-level restatement adjustment (monetary correction), if any, are subject to VAT. Interest on financial loans and securities is not subject to VAT.
- Capital contributions in the form of goods to limited partnerships or corporations made by a recurring seller of such goods are subject to VAT.
- Exports are VAT exempt.
- Investors covered by the Foreign Investment Statute are not subject to VAT on the importation of capital goods, provided such goods are included in a list issued by the Government for this purpose.
- The sale of fixed assets by the user is not subject to VAT, provided the sale takes place after one year of ownership.
- Freight costs from Chile to a foreign country and vice versa are tax-exempt.
- Personal services rendered by employees or by independent contractors are not subject to VAT.

Custom duties

In the last ten years Chile has entered into several trade treaties with countries and trade blocks. As a result of this, the effective duties vary significantly from country to country.

The general uniform custom duty, as of 1 January 2001, is 9% and it will decrease 1% per year until it reaches 6% in 2004. The table below, however, illustrates the effective custom duties at December 2000.

Trade blocks

Mercosur	4.0%
Nafta	5.8%
Asia	8.3%
European EU	8.6%

Selected countries

Americas		*Rest of the World*	
Ecuador	0.1%	France	6.3%
Mexico	0.2%	Taiwan	7.4%
Colombia	1.4%	China	8.0%
Canada	1.6%	Spain	8.4%
Argentina	3.5%	Italy	8.7%
Peru	3.7%	UK	8.8%
Brazil	4.7%	Japan	8.8%
Venezuela	5.2%	South Korea	8.8%
Uruguay	5.4%	Germany	8.9%
United States	7.8%	Hong Kong	9.0%

Double taxation and tax treaties

The general rule to soften the impact of double taxation in the Income Tax Act provides for the taxation in Chile of the amount actually received from dividends, distributions, fees and royalties from foreign sources excluding taxes paid abroad, subject to certain limitations and conditions. The maximum credit allowed corresponds to the Chilean corporate tax rate of 15%. Where a double taxation treaty has been signed, the Income Tax Act provides for broader measures.

Chile has signed numerous tax treaties but they have a limited scope, mainly air, sea and land transportation. There are, however, three comprehensive treaties signed with Argentina, Mexico and Canada.

The treaty with Argentina (1986) provides for taxation solely in the country where the taxed assets or rights are located or where the taxable activities are carried out. The treaty covers taxes on profits, royalties, interest, dividends and distributions, capital gains, pensions, scientific, literary and artistic rights, and taxes such as licences, vehicle and property taxes, and others.

The treaties with Mexico and Canada (1998) cover a similar range of taxable revenues and equity but provide that taxes in these countries affecting income of Chilean residents can be fully credited against the taxpayer's corresponding Chilean taxes, according to the stipulations of the law.

Other taxes

Stamp tax

Certain documents that represent financial transactions are taxed at variable or fixed rates.

A tax of 0.1% per month, with a maximum of 1.2%, calculated on the par value of the document or 0.5% if the document is payable on sight, is applied to bills of exchange, promissory notes, import letters of credit, IOU's and, in general, to any document representative of a loan or credit operation.

Import licences are subject to a stamp tax of 3%, which can be used as a credit against the payment of customs duties.

Cheques are subject to a fixed stamp tax of approximately US$ 0.10 per cheque, which is charged by the bank at the time of withdrawal of the chequebook by the customer.

Property tax

Land and buildings, including housing that exceed a certain value, are taxed at 2% each year on the taxable valuation of the property. This annual tax is paid in four quarterly instalments. The property valuation is subject to indexation.

Gifts and inheritance taxes

Gifts and inheritances are subject to a progressive tax that ranges from 1% to 25% on the net amount, after deducting expenses.

Gifts to higher education entities, the National Fund for Scientific and Technological Development, and not-for-profit institutions that promote the arts, science or social activities in benefit of the poor, are deductible to a maximum of 10% of taxable income. Gifts to universities and professional institutes are deductible to a maximum of 50% of taxable income, with a limit that currently is equivalent to about US$ 670,000. Other gifts to institutions that provide free education are deductible to a maximum of 2% of taxable income.

Special excise taxes

Excise taxes of variable rates are applied, besides VAT, to certain items such as alcohol, non-alcoholic beverages, fuels, tobacco, furs, jewels, and the proportion of the CIF cost of motor cars that exceeds US$ 15,000.

The transfer or sale of used vehicles is subject to a tax of 1.5% on the sale value.

Municipal licenses

All independent professionals, stores, companies, branches of companies and, in general, any person or entity engaged in any kind of commercial activities for profit, must pay an annual licence to the Municipality where the person's or entity's place of business is located (that varies from 0.15% to 0.5% of their capital).

Export proceeds

All exports require registration with the Central Bank which periodically sets the maximum period for the sale of foreign exchange proceeds. As in the case of imports, unit prices are monitored by Customs and may be regulated.

China

Charles Mar Fan & Co., Hong Kong
Beijing Xingye Certified Public Accountants, PRC
Shanghai New Zhong Chuang Certified Public Accountants, PRC

Introduction

Since the introduction of China's open door policy in the late 1970s, various tax laws have been implemented. In order to eliminate inconsistency and inequality as well as to streamline the various taxes and rates, the State Council carried out a major tax reform in 1993.

The principal tax laws include the Law for Foreign Enterprise Income Tax and Individual Tax Law.

Corporate taxes

Taxable entities

Corporate tax in the form of Enterprise Income Tax is levied on organisations established in China which include state-owned enterprises, private enterprises, collective ownership enterprises, enterprises with foreign investment, foreign enterprises and organisations having income from production or business and other operations in China.

Foreign Investment Enterprises are Sino-foreign equity joint ventures, co-operative joint ventures and wholly foreign-owned enterprises established in China.

Foreign enterprises are foreign companies, enterprises and other organisations that have establishments or sites in China which are engaged in production or business operations, or foreign organisations that do not have such establishments or sites but nonetheless earn income from sources within China.

Tax year and filing requirements

Foreign investment enterprises and foreign enterprises which have an establishment in China are required to file quarterly returns and provisional income tax returns to their local tax bureau. These returns must be filed within 15 days after the relevant quarter end. A final annual income tax return together with the financial statements must be filed within four months after the end of each calendar year.

Income tax on enterprises is levied on an annual basis running from 1 January to 31 December each year. However, provisional income tax is collected in quarterly instalments and must be paid within 15 days after the end of each quarter. The final settlement must be paid within five months after the end of the tax year.

The filing of the income tax return is normally done by the accounting personnel of the enterprise, whereas the financial statements accompanying the tax return of the enterprise are required to be audited by a Certified Public Accountant registered in China.

Taxes imposed

Enterprises (including enterprises with foreign investment) shall be taxed on income from production and business and other operations derived within and outside of China.

For foreign enterprises, income tax shall be levied on income derived by them within China, regardless of whether or not workplaces or operations have been established in China.

Rates of tax

The tax rate for enterprises with no foreign investment is 33%.

Enterprises with foreign investment or foreign enterprises having established work places or operations in China are liable to Enterprise Income Tax at 30% and Local Income Tax at 3%.

A 20% income tax shall be levied on income derived from the profit, interest, rentals, royalties and other income originating in China of foreign enterprises which do not have work places or operations established in China, or whose establishments in China are not used to generate the aforementioned income.

Profits subject to tax

Taxable income includes:

- income from production and business operations;
- income from transfer of property;
- interest income;
- rental income;
- income from the supply or transfer of patents, know-how, trademarks and copyrights;
- dividend income;
- other income.

An assessment of income from production and business operations is arrived at in accordance with generally accepted accounting principles applicable in China.

Stock valuation

Stock is valued at original cost, which includes the cost of purchase, transportation, insurance, normal loss in the course of transportation, handling expenses and any related tax paid thereon. For self-manufactured stock, cost includes cost of materials, labour and other directly related expenses.

Enterprises may, according to their circumstances, elect to value stock using either the first-in first-out (FIFO), weighted average, moving average, specific identification, or last-in first-out (LIFO) method. Any change in the adopted stock valuation method must be approved by the tax bureau.

Capital gains and losses

The difference between the proceeds from the disposal of fixed assets and the residual value of the assets, and handling expenses, shall be included in the profit and loss account in arriving at the assessable income.

Dividends

Dividends received by foreign investors from a foreign investment enterprise are exempt from Chinese withholding tax. Dividends received by a foreign investment enterprise from its investments in China may also be exempt from foreign enterprise income tax.

Deductions

General rules

Reasonable expenses and losses incurred in production and business operations are generally tax deductible.

Depreciation

Depreciation, as an expense relating to production and business operations, is tax deductible. Depreciation on fixed assets is generally computed applying the straight line method. Use of the accelerated depreciation method may be permitted in special circumstances upon application to the tax bureau.

For foreign enterprises the minimum useful life used in calculating the depreciation of fixed assets is as follows:

Buildings and structures	*20 years*
Trains, ships, machinery and other production equipment	*10 years*
Electronic and other transportation equipment as well as appliances, tools, furniture, etc. related to production or business operations	*5 years*

The residual value of a fixed asset should be deducted from the original cost of the item in calculating depreciation. The residual value should generally be not less than 10% of its original cost.

Royalties

Royalties paid by enterprises relating to production or business operations are considered as production costs and are tax deductible. However, royalties paid to the head office of the enterprise are not tax deductible.

Interest

Interest paid to financial institutions on borrowings for production or business operations are tax deductible. Interest paid to non-financial institutions is only deductible up to an amount not exceeding the equivalent amount of interest which would be payable on borrowings of a similar nature from a financial institution over the same period.

Interest paid on long term borrowings for fixed or intangible assets is tax deductible upon the final purchase of the fixed assets.

Interest expenses are not otherwise tax deductible.

Bad and doubtful debts

Bad debt provisions calculated according to the rules laid down by the tax bureau are tax deductible. When bad debts are actually written-off, that portion of debt not previously provided for or claimed may be treated as a deductible expense.

Employees' and directors' remuneration and benefits

Wages and salaries are deductible as production expenses. The amount deductible is calculated based on the taxable income of the earner. The scale of wages and salaries is determined by the local government with authority delegated by the Ministry of Finance. Wages and salaries paid in excess of this standard scale are not tax deductible.

Specifically non-deductible expenses

Non-deductible expenses include:

- expenditure incurred on the purchase or construction of fixed assets;
- expenditure on the acquisition or development of intangible assets;
- fines for illegal operations and losses in the form of confiscated property;
- delinquent tax payment and penalty;
- losses from natural calamity or accident covered by indemnity;
- royalties paid to head office;
- interest on capital;
- income tax;
- donations and contributions other than for public welfare or relief in China;
- other expenses not relevant to production and business operations.

Foreign income tax paid on income derived outside China can be deducted within limits not exceeding the tax payable on the foreign income calculated according to the tax law in China.

Investment incentives and special benefits

Production oriented foreign investment enterprises with terms of operation of ten years or more are entitled to full tax exemption for two years, commencing with the first profit making year, and to a 50% tax reduction in the subsequent three years.

Enterprises with foreign investment in Special Economic Zones, foreign enterprises which establish organisations that are engaged in production and business operations in Special Economic Zones and manufacturing enterprises with foreign investment operating in Economic And Technological Development Areas of coastal cities and Pudong New Development Zone of Shanghai are charged at a reduced income tax rate of 15%.

Manufacturing enterprises with foreign investment operating in the original districts of cities which are Special Economic Zones or within the city limits of the Economic and Technological Development Zones of the Coastal Cities Areas, are charged at a reduced income tax rate of 24%.

Following the expiration of the period for the reduction or exemption of Enterprise Income Tax, export oriented enterprises invested and set up by foreign investors will, if the value of their export products amounts to 70% or more of the value of their total production in a year, be entitled to a 50% reduction in income tax for that year. The minimum income tax rate is 10%.

Those technologically advanced enterprises invested and set up by foreign investors which remain technologically advanced after the expiration of the period of reduction or exemption of Enterprise Income Tax, may benefit from a three-year extension of such preferential treatment at a rate reduced by 50%.

Foreign investors in an enterprise with foreign investment who reinvest their share of profit in that enterprise and hence increase its registered capital or who establish other enterprises with foreign investment as capital and operate for a period not less than five years may, upon approval by the tax bureau, obtain a refund of 40% income tax levied on the reinvested amounts.

Related party transactions

The tax bureau has the right to make reasonable adjustments in accordance with arm's length principle where an enterprise receives or pays prices and fees which result in an abnormal decrease of taxable income.

Losses

Trading losses may be offset against all taxable income received in the same accounting period or may be carried forward to offset against the taxable income of future periods. The limitation period for carry-forward of losses is five years.

Liquidation of a company

Upon the liquidation of an enterprise, any amount realised in excess of the registered capital after settlement of debts and liquidation charges is regarded as profit and is subject to income tax.

Taxes on capital

Capital duty

There is no capital duty in China.

Net worth tax

There is no net worth tax in China.

Personal taxes

Basis of taxation of individuals

In practice, in determining whether income is sourced in China, the Chinese tax authorities mainly look at whether the work or services from which the income is derived is performed while the individual is working inside China. In addition to the source rule, whether an income is paid by a Chinese establishment also has a bearing on China's power to tax that income.

Chinese establishment generally means an enterprise, company, or other economic organisation or individual in China. In practice, Chinese establishments include those entities that are required to be registered for tax with the Chinese authorities, or persons domiciled in China.

Residing in China for 90 days or less (183 for tax residents of treaty countries)

For employment income, an individual's Chinese sourced income would *not* be subject to Individual Income Tax (IIT) if:

- the individual resides in China for 90 (or 183) days or less;
- his remuneration is borne by an employer who is not a Chinese establishment;
- the remuneration is not recharged by a foreign employer to a Chinese entity or Chinese permanent establishment of the foreign employer.

Residing in China for more than 90 (or 183) days but less than one year

If an individual resides in China for 90 (or 183) days or more but less than one year, his income earned within China would be subject to IIT regardless of whether he were a Chinese or foreign person. His income earned from outside China would normally not be subject to IIT.

Residing in China for more than one year but less than five years

If an individual resides in China for one year or more but for less than five years, all his income earned from within China would be subject to IIT. In addition, income earned from outside China, to the extent it is paid by a Chinese entity or a permanent establishment of a foreign corporation in China, would also be subject to IIT.

Residing in China for more than five years

If the person resides in China for five years or more, he will be subject to IIT on his worldwide income. However, any taxes paid to other governments on income could be credited against the IIT liability.

Tax year and filing requirements

The income earner shall be the party responsible for paying the IIT and the paying unit shall be the withholding agent. Taxpayers not covered by this arrangement are required personally to file declarations of their income and pay tax themselves.

Taxes withheld each month by a withholding agent and those to be paid each month by taxpayers filing personal returns, shall submit the tax return to the tax bureau within the first seven days of the following month.

Business owners shall account for business income annually and monthly tax payments shall be prepaid to the state treasury based on estimated income within the first seven days of the following month.

A final annual tax return shall be filed within three months following the end of each year.

Contractors shall pay tax due to the state treasury and submit a tax return to the tax bureau within 30 days of the end of each year. Contractors who receive income by instalments during the year shall pay tax to the state treasury within the first seven days following receipt of the income.

A person who earns income outside China shall submit a tax return to the tax bureau within 30 days of the end of each year or at the end of the tax year of the country where the income is derived and pay the appropriate tax due.

Taxes on income

IIT shall be levied on the following income:

- wages and salaries;
- compensation for personal services;
- royalties;
- interest, dividends and bonuses;
- income from lease of property;
- other income as specified by the Ministry of Finance.

Sources of income

Employment income

Employment income refers to wages, salaries, allowances and bonuses earned from work in offices, organisations and other entities. Employment income in excess of a specific amount (i.e. Rmb 800 per month for Chinese individuals and Rmb 4,000 per month for foreign individuals) shall be taxed at progressive rates ranging from 5% to 45%.

The tax status of various kinds of remuneration normally received by an employee are summarised as follows:

Wages and salaries	*taxable*
Foreign service and hardship allowances	*taxable*
Cost of living allowances	*taxable*
Tax reimbursement	*taxable*
Bonuses	*taxable*
Housing provided by employer	*non-taxable*

Paid home leave	*non-taxable*
Relocation and moving expenses	*non-taxable*
Meals provided or reimbursements of meal cost by employer	*non-taxable*
Cost of children's education	*non-taxable*

Business profits and losses

Business income from owners who undertake production and trade includes:

- income from industry, craft, construction, transport, commerce, food and beverage, service, repairs and other trades;
- income earned by individuals who have obtained approval from the authorities to provide education, medical treatment, consultancy and other related services;
- other income earned by business owners from production and business operations.

Business profit is calculated by deducting the cost of sales, operating expenses and losses from the gross revenue for the year and is taxed at progressive rates ranging from 5% to 35%.

Contractor income means income from undertaking of contracts or sub-contracting income. Income on contracts is taxed at progressive rates ranging from 5% to 35% after deduction of the personal allowance of Rmb 800.

Income and remuneration for the provision of services in designing, installation, draughtsmanship, medical treatment, law practice, accounting, consultancy, entertainment, sport, advertising and technical services shall be taxed at a flat rate of 20% after a deduction of Rmb 800 for income between Rmb 4,000 to Rmb 10,000. For a disproportionately high income, a surcharge is levied. For income from Rmb 20,000 to Rmb 50,000, a 30% surcharge is levied. Any assessable income over Rmb 50,000 shall have a 40% surcharge.

Dividends

Dividends and interests from investments are taxed upon receipt at a flat rate of 20%.

Interest

Interest on deposits is taxed, upon receipt, at a flat rate of 20%.

Rentals

Income from the leasing or sub-leasing of premises, land use rights, machinery and equipment, motor vehicles, ships and other kinds of property is taxed at a flat rate of 20%.

Royalties

'Royalties' refers to income from the provision or transfer of patents, copyright, the right to use technical know-how and other rights. An allowance of Rmb 800 is given for royalties of less than Rmb 4,000. An allowance of 20% is given for royalties above Rmb 4,000 and the balance is taxed at a flat rate of 20%.

Pension and annuities

Pension and annuities provided by the government are exempted from tax.

Exempt income

The following income shall be exempted from IIT:

- prizes and awards for scientific, technological or cultural achievements;
- welfare benefits, survivors' pensions and relief payments;
- insurance indemnities;
- subsidies and allowances received under the state uniform provisions;
- military severance pay, decommission or demobilisation pay for cadres and rank and file of the armed forces;
- severance pay or retirement pay for cadres, staff members and workers;
- salaries of the diplomatic officials of foreign embassies and consulates in China;
- tax-free income as stipulated in international conventions to which China is a party, or as stipulated in agreements which China has signed;
- income approved as tax-free by the Ministry of Finance.

Capital gains

Capital gain refers to gain from transfer of securities, shares, property, land use right, machinery and equipment, motor vehicles, ships and other kinds of property.

Capital gains are taxed at a flat rate of 20% (except for land and property, which is governed by the Land Appreciation Tax) on the proceeds from the transfer less the original cost of the asset and expenses related to the transfer.

Losses

Where individuals incur losses in their business, the losses cannot be carried forward to set off against future assessable income.

Special family rules

Taxpayers are treated as individuals and are assessed separately.

Special treatment for expatriates

Expatriates are taxed according to their length of residency in China, (see above, under the section entitled 'Basis of taxation of individuals').

Rates of tax

Wages and salaries

Monthly taxable income *(after deducting personal allowances)*	*Tax rate* (%)
Less than Rmb 500	5
Rmb 501 to 2,000	10
Rmb 2,001 to 5,000	15
Rmb 5,001 to 20,000	20
Rmb 20,001 to 40,000	25
Rmb 40,001 to 60,000	30
Rmb 60,001 to 80,000	35
Rmb 80,001 to 100,000	40
Over Rmb 100,000	45

China

Business income, contracting and leasing income

Annual taxable income	*Tax rate (%)*
Less than Rmb 5,000	5
Rmb 5,001 to 10,000	10
Rmb 10,001 to 30,000	20
Rmb 30,001 to 50,000	30
Over Rmb 50,000	35

Provincial and local taxes

There is no provincial and local individual income tax.

Withholding taxes

Withholding tax is imposed at a rate of 20% on dividends, interest, rentals, royalties and other income when these are paid to a foreign enterprise which does not maintain a permanent establishment in China.

Tax credits

Income tax paid to foreign tax authorities by taxpayers for income earned outside China may be credited against the amount of income tax assessed according to the rate prescribed by the tax law in China.

Estate tax and gift tax

There is no estate tax and gift tax in China.

Wealth tax

There is no wealth tax in China.

Other taxes

VAT and sales taxes

Entities or individuals who sell or provide processing, repairing or installation services within China or import goods into China shall pay VAT at a rate of 17%. Certain goods enjoy a reduced rate of 13%.

Other taxes

Business tax

Business tax is payable by entities or individuals who provide services, transport and construction or transfer intangible assets or immovable properties within China. Business tax is levied on gross turnover. The tax rates are 3% or 5% for services other than entertainment. Entertainment services are taxed at rates ranging from 5% to 20%.

Consumption tax

Consumption tax applies to entities or individuals who manufacture, sub-contract for processing work or import consumer goods within China. Consumption tax is determined on the basis of the sales revenues of the taxable goods at rates ranging from 3% to 45%.

Land appreciation tax

The detailed rules for implementation of Provisional Regulations on Land Appreciation Tax of the People's Republic of China came into effect on 27 January 1995. Under these rules, all units and individuals (including enterprises with foreign investments) receiving proceeds from the transfer of State owned land use rights, buildings and their attached facilities, shall be subject to Land Appreciation Tax. Proceeds on the transfer of real estate shall include monetary proceeds, proceeds in kind and other proceeds.

The following items are deductible when computing liability for land appreciation tax:

- the sum paid for the acquisition of land use rights;
- costs for the development of land;
- costs for the construction of new buildings and facilities or the assessed value for used properties and buildings;
- the tax related to the transfer of real estate;
- other deductible items as stipulated by the Ministry of Finance.

Gain in excess of cost basis	*Tax rate*
Less than 50%	30%
Portion between 50–100%	40%
Portion between 100–200%	50%
Portion over 200%	60%

Land Appreciation Tax shall be exempted under either of the following conditions:

- for taxpayers constructing ordinary standard residences for sale, where the appreciation amount does not exceed 20% of the sum of deductible items;
- where real estate is taken over and repossessed according to laws due to the construction requirements of the State.

Stamp duty

Stamp Duty is levied on stipulated documents which are concluded and received by any entity or individual. These stipulated documents include documents for purchases and sales, processing agreements, building and construction projects, properties leasing and other documents of a contractual nature. The rates of stamp duty vary with contracts, ranging from 0.003% to 0.1%.

Urban real estate tax and land use tax

Urban Real Estate Tax is a local tax imposed on the beneficial owners of land and buildings in cities and provinces which is charged at 1.2% annually on the assessed property value of the building (original value less 20% to 30% residual amount) or 18% of rental income. Land Use Tax is charged at Rmb 0.2 to Rmb 10 per square metre annually. Any houses purchased or constructed by foreign investment enterprises, foreign enterprises and expatriates are subject to Urban Real Estate Tax in respect of the housing element only.

Exchange control

There are various exchange control regulations formulated for the purpose of strengthening exchange controls in order to expedite national economic growth and to safeguard the rights and interests of the country. These are formulated in the Provisional Regulations for Exchange Control of the People's Republic of China.

Tax treaties and withholding taxes

China has concluded tax treaties with most European and Asia Pacific countries, Canada and the United States of America. The terms of most treaties are patterned after the United Nations Double Taxation Convention Between Developed and Developing Countries which encourages investment by industrialised countries in less developed ones.

The following rates of Chinese withholding tax apply to dividends, interest and royalties received by residents of the following countries under tax treaties concluded by China:

	Dividend (%)	*Interest* (%)	*Royalties (general)* (%)	*Royalties (use of equipment)* (%)
Australia	15	10	10	10
Austria	7/10	7/10	10	6
Belgium	10	10	10	6
Brazil	15	15	15	15
Bulgaria	10	10	10	7
Canada	10/15	10	10	10
Cyprus	10	10	10	10
Czechoslovakia	10	10	10	10
Denmark	10	10	10	7
Finland	10	10	10	10
France	10	10	10	6
Germany	10	10	10	10
Italy	10	10	10	7
Japan	10	10	10	10
Kuwait	5	5	10	10
Malaysia	10	10	10/15	10
Malta	10	10	10	10
Netherlands	10	10	10	6
New Zealand	15	10	10	10
Norway	15	10	10	10
Pakistan	10	10	12.5	12.5
Poland	10	10	10	7
Romania	10	10	7	7
Russia (Commonwealth of Independent States)	5	10	10	10
Singapore	7/12	7/10	10	10
Spain	10	10	10	6
Sweden	10	10	10	7
Switzerland	10	10	10	6
Thailand	15/20	10	15	15
United Kingdom	10	10	10	7
United States of America	10	10	10	7
Yugoslavia	10	10	10	10

Colombia

Amezquita & Cia. – Auditores Independientes

Introduction

The tax system in Colombia changes at least every two years. The changes do not substantially alter the system, but focus on new taxpayers, adding or omitting exclusions or the deductibility of certain expenses, increasing sales tax rates and income tax withholding rates.

The last tax reform was on 29 December 2000 (Law 633) with the major changes having taken place since January 2001. The most important changes are as follows:

- profits from stocks sold on the stock market are not taxable if the sale is less than 10% of the relevant corporation's issued stock in one given fiscal year; the same treatment is applied if the assignment of stock is pursuant to a 'democratisation' or Government sponsored process;
- the presumptive income rate is 6% on the net assets of the previous year (see later for a definition of the fiscal year); the term within which the excess of presumptive income over ordinary liquid income may be subtracted from gross income has been reduced from five to three fiscal years;
- the Law reduces the exemption for residential public services enterprises;
- taxpayers who, for a given fiscal year, increase the amount of income tax paid by a percentage equal to twice the inflation rate in Colombia, may only be audited by the Colombian tax administration within 12 months from the date of filing returns;
- as from 1 January 2001, Colombia has brought in by law the Financial Operations Tax (FOT); this is charged on all withdrawals made from cheque and saving accounts, including accounts held at the Central Bank (the rate is charged at 0.003%);
- the Law also increases the Colombian valued added tax (VAT) general rate by one point, up to 16%, for all products and services;
- another indirect tax is a 1.2% levy on the value of imports, this is

in respect of the cost of the service provided by customs authorities;

- deductibility of VAT paid on the purchase of fixed assets no longer applies; and
- tax stability agreements cease to exist; these agreements used to exist for a ten-year term, with the taxpayer and government agreeing to pay a stable 2% above the income tax rate at the time the contract was entered into.

Corporate taxes

Taxable entities

Resident companies

Colombian companies, regardless of whether ownership is in the hands of non-Colombian residents, pay tax on income derived from all sources, with some activities and services performed outside Colombia being taxable.

Taxes paid abroad on income from foreign sources may be deducted from Colombian income taxes on the same income up to the level of the Colombian income tax payable.

There are no consolidation arrangements for the taxation of corporate groups.

Non-resident companies

Foreign companies are subject to income tax on income derived in Colombia through withholding rates determined for each activity.

Branches of foreign companies are taxed at a rate of 35% on domestic income.

Tax year and filing requirements

The tax year runs from 1 January to 31 December. Tax is payable in two or five instalments depending on how the National Tax Administration has classified the taxpayer. As a general rule, companies close their financial year on 31 December in order to avoid administrative overload. However, the banking sector prepares two sets of financial statements per year.

Rates of corporation tax

The general income tax rate for corporations is 35%.

Presumptive income

The law established a presumptive income of 6% on the value of net assets of the previous year. This was based on the presumption that the net assets of the taxpayer at the end of one year must generate income of the same percentage of their value in the course of the following year.

Income subject to tax

Taxable net income is calculated by adding all income that increases net worth and is not specifically exempt by law. Any costs and expenses attributed to such income are then deducted from this amount to arrive at the gross income. Deductions are subtracted from gross income to obtain the net income. Income expressly determined as tax exempt is then deducted from net income to obtain the taxable net income. The tax rate is applied to obtain the payable tax. Any tax credits or withholdings are deducted from the Colombian tax on the income, to which the credit relates, to give the amount of tax due.

Inflation adjustments are made which are reflected in the computation of their taxable income to avoid tax being paid on accounting income generated by inflation.

Branches affiliated to foreign companies are allowed to deduct payments to their home offices or commissions, administration fees and royalties or rental of intangible assets, provided the payment is subject to withholding tax (subject to certain limits).

Earnings not subject to income tax

The following are the primary examples of earnings not subject to income tax, as stipulated by law:

- premiums or margins over par from public stock offerings when retained as part of the surplus or capitalised;
- profits accrued from the sale of stock registered with Colombian exchanges; they are not taxable if the same real beneficiary assigns less than 10% of the relevant corporation's outstanding stock in one given fiscal year; the same treatment applies if the assignment is performed pursuant to a 'democratisation' process (this process requires that shares be placed according to procedures set by the Colombian securities authority, ensuring

competitive participation by the general public); this exception only applies if 10% or more of a corporation's outstanding shares are offered for sale in the same public offering;

- profits distributed in the form of stock resulting from a revaluation of assets or premiums left over from public stock offerings; the revaluation of assets is a capital account comprised of increases from inflationary adjustments in the value of assets and constituting equity;
- distribution of profits in stock due to capitalisation of corporate reserves with earnings that do not constitute income or windfall profits, exempt income or inflation adjustments;
- dividends or distributed earnings, provided the company has paid all relevant taxes prior to distribution; and
- compensation for damages.

Deductions

As a general rule, deductible business costs and expenses are acceptable according to what is customary and proportionate in connection with income-producing activities, according to business criteria.

Stock/inventory

Colombian tax regulations do not establish which specific methods of inventory valuation must be used or how inventory flows must be determined. Currently, any of three bases (average, FIFO or LIFO) are permitted by tax rules.

Reserves for inventory shortages and obsolescence are not allowable for tax purposes.

Provisions reducing inventories to market value are not deductible for income tax purposes.

Depreciation and amortisation

All fixed and tangible assets, except land, that are used for the production of income are fully depreciable to zero (i.e. no residual value is applied). The normally accepted estimated useful life for a building is 20 years. For plant, equipment, furniture and fixtures, ten years, and for vehicles, five years. However, these general guidelines may be modified by the taxpayer on the basis of depreciation concepts or tables of recognised technical value (subject to prior approval by the Director of National Taxes).

Colombia

Since 1992, the cost of assets has been adjusted for inflation. Adjustments for inflation maybe depreciated for tax purposes if recorded in the books.

An annual deduction is available for amortisation of investments (other than those in depreciable equipment) that may be calculated for a minimum of five years.

Dividends

Dividends and profit participation from Colombian companies received by or credited to Colombian companies are not taxable.

Interest

Interest on certain government and mortgage bonds is exempt from income tax. In some cases, non-domiciled corporations are also exempt from paying tax on interest received.

Interest paid to authorised local banks or other authorised financial institutions is deductible in full, if certified by the recipient. Tax deductibility of interest paid to entities or persons other than local banks and credit institutions is limited to the highest banking rate used for calculating deductible financial costs, as certified by the Banking Superintendence.

Losses

Companies may offset losses suffered in one year against the income earned over the following five years. Losses are adjusted for inflation from year to year at the time they are offset.

Provisions

Provisions are not deductible. However, exceptions are made to the following:

- technical and mathematical (actuarial) reserves accounted for by insurance companies;
- allowance for bad debts which are subject to certain limits.

Excess of presumptive income over ordinary liquid income

The excess of presumptive income over ordinary liquid income may be subtracted from gross income adjusted for inflation over the following three fiscal years.

Donations

Donations to scientific or technological research are deductible up to a limit of 20% of the taxpayer's net income.

Exempt income

As from 1993, publishing companies that print books, magazines, pamphlets or collectible supplements of a scientific or cultural nature are exempt from income and related tax for 20 years.

Colombian public service enterprises are exempt if profits are capitalised or appropriated as a reserve to refurbish, extend or replace systems (gradually in certain percentages, the profits will be fully taxable by the year 2003).

Income from activities within free trade zones, and legally established entities using such zones, are considered tax exempt.

Tax credits

Tax credits are deducted directly from the taxpayer's assessed income tax. The following are the major tax credits:

Credits to avoid dual taxation

- Taxes, which are paid abroad by national taxpayers who have earned income from foreign sources, provided the credit does not exceed the amount of income tax payable in Colombia on the same income.
- Dividends or earnings distributed to companies domiciled in any country with which Colombia has a taxation agreement. These must be equivalent to the dividend or earning multiplied by the income tax rate applicable to the company's profits.

Tax credits as incentives to produce activities

- 35% of the value of Tax Rebate Certificates ('CERT') issued by the Central Bank on exports.
- 20% of a reforestation investment certified by the Ministry of Environmental Affairs.
- Companies registering a 5% increase in the number of people they employ directly, compared with 31 December of the previous year, are entitled to a tax credit equal to the labour costs related to these new jobs. However, the credit may not

exceed 15% of the tax due for the year when the increase occurred.

- In no case may tax credits apply to more than 75% of the total amount of tax due, whenever it is determined under the presumptive income tax system. The credit limit for CERTs is 70%.

Donations

60% of donations to Education Institutions can be deducted from tax. This cannot exceed the limit of 30% of the payable tax.

Capital gains tax

Capital gains from raffles, lotteries, gambling or similar activities are subject to 20% tax, which is withheld by the payer.

Inflation adjustments are applied to capital gains to enable them to be assimilated into ordinary income.

Remittance tax

The transfer abroad of regular income and capital gains is subject to remittance tax. The base rate which applies depends on the type of income remitted, with the most common rate being 7%.

In the case of foreign companies not domiciled in Colombia or foreign individuals not residence in Colombia, all perceived dividends or profits are subject to 7% income and remittance tax, which is withheld at the time of payment or deposit. If the distributing company has not been taxed on dividends or profits, the applicable tax rate is 35%. The additional 7% charged to foreigners is calculated after applying the 35%.

However, if these dividends or profits are reinvested in the country, tax payment is deferred while the investment is maintained. If the investment is maintained for a period of no less than five years, such dividends or yields are exempt from income tax. For this purpose, reinvestment is also taken to mean the retention of profits in the company.

Value added tax –VAT

The value added tax is a national levy on services and the sale of imported goods. The rate is normally 16%, however this varies depending on the type of goods and services.

There is a special 10% rate on passenger airfares inside Colombia, except during the high season and to destinations not accessible by land.

Differential rates of 10%, 20%, 35%, 45% or 48% on these goods depend on special circumstances described in the Tax Code as follows:

- vehicles;
- motorcycles;
- private aircraft;
- sporting and pleasure boats;
- oil and motor gasoline; or
- beers, soft drinks and alcoholic beverages.

Exemptions from VAT are:

- export of movable goods;
- scientific and cultural books and magazines; and
- services rendered in Colombia and used exclusively abroad by companies without businesses or activities.

Some activities, goods and services excluded from VAT are:

- medical services;
- public or private shipping inside Colombia and internationally;
- public passenger transportation in Colombia, by land, sea or air;
- interest;
- stockbroker's commissions;
- leasing payments;
- public utilities;
- electricity;
- water and sewer systems;
- sanitation services;
- natural gas for residential use;
- real estate rental;
- hotel accommodations; and
- some food.

Industry and trade tax

This is a local tax raised and regulated by municipalities within limits set by national laws.

This tax is generated by having commercial, industrial or service operations in each municipality.

The tax is on the total income received in the municipality in which the plant or factory is located.

The law authorises the application of a tax rate ranging between 0.002% and 0.007% to industrial activities and between 0.002% and 0.01% to commercial activities and services.

Property taxes

Municipalities assess taxes on real estate based on valuations. This is revised from time to time and is generally adjusted annually for inflation.

The rates of tax in urban areas are a maximum of 0.016% and a minimum of 0.001%.

In some municipalities, all the property taxes have been combined since 1990. This tax is known as the Unified Property Tax.

In Bogotá D.C. as from 1994, property owners are required to submit an annual return for this tax. Property tax is estimated based on a self appraisal of the property value, that should not be less than the self appraised value determined for the previous year plus the inflation factor calculated for the current year.

Personal taxes

Individuals pay income and capital gains tax on income derived from all sources, including the income from foreign sources.

Aliens are taxpayers if resident. They pay income related taxes on income originating in Colombia. After five years of continuous or accumulated residence, they also pay taxes on income received abroad.

If an alien is non-resident, tax is levied on Colombian source income.

Rates for income tax are defined annually in a progressive table depending on the amount of the income.

Rates of personal income tax

Resident nationals and aliens pay income tax based on a progressive rate schedule, with 35% being the highest marginal rate. In the 2000 tax year, this rate was applicable to earnings of COP $75,000,000 (approximately US$ 37,500) or more.

Non-resident investors are subject to a 35% tax on income generated in Colombia; the tax is usually withheld at the source of payment. In the case of dividends or profits on which the distributing company has paid the tax, the levy will be only 7%.

Some other important rates of withholdings tax for payments (or credits) to the accounts of foreign companies without domicile in Colombia and non-resident are:

	Income tax	*Remittance tax*
Interest, commissions, fees, royalties, leases know-how	35%	7%
Technical services and technical assistance provided from abroad	10%	–
Use of cinematographer film (base 60%)	35%	7%
Turnkey contracts and other contracts for material work	1%	1%
Computer programs (base 80%)	35%	7%
Machinery leased for construction, maintenance and repair of civil works performed by Colombian contractors under contracts subject to international public tender	2%	1%
Other payments not listed above	14%	1%

Exemptions

For salaried employees not required to file, income and capital gains tax are the sum of all withholdings made according to the table published annually by the authorities, as applied to all payments or credits with the exception of:

- indemnities for occupational accident or sickness;
- indemnities for the protection of maternity;
- the employee's funeral expenses;
- severance pay and interest on severance, if average monthly income for the last 6 months does not exceed Col$ 5,200,000

(2001) (if average monthly income is Col$ 6,000,000 or more, 100% of the amount received is taxable);

- pensions, which are taxed only over the level of 50 legal minimum salaries;
- 30% of labour payments; and
- service and other bonuses received by pilots and seamen.

Other taxes

Import tax

The import of goods is subject to the following taxes, unless otherwise provided for in special regulations:

- goods imported under temporary licences are subject to sales tax based on cost, plus import duties tax on a long term basis;
- foreign goods entering Colombia are subject to customs clearance tax or duties at rates shown in the official rate tables.

The 1.2% levy on the value of imports is levied for the cost of customs services provided by the Colombian authorities. This does not apply to:

- goods imported by participants of the so-called Vallejo Plan (a Colombian exports support policy);
- goods imported from countries where Colombia has free trade agreements; or
- goods imported by the Colombian armed forces for national defence or security uses.

Stamp tax

Stamp tax is charged on documents. This is payable on private instruments expressing obligations, or their extinction or modification, including documents made outside Colombia for which the obligation is to be discharged within Colombia.

The general rate of 1.5% is applied to the total value of a contract. There are special rates that apply to certain types of documents, persons or exemptions.

Financial operations tax (FOT)

FOT is equal to 0.003% of the value of the transaction. This applies to transactions conducted by customers from credit institutions with funds deposited in cheque or savings accounts. However, this does not include transfers between accounts held by the same person with the same institution, payment from credit institutions depositing in regular accounts, or savings accounts and the issuers of cashier's cheques.

Tax treaties

Colombia has signed double-taxation agreements with other countries to avoid dual taxation, with the following being the most important:

- agreements with the United States, Argentina, Germany, Chile, Brazil, Italy, France and Venezuela concerning air and maritime shipping;
- agreements with Venezuela on regulations governing taxation of state investment and international transport companies; and
- agreements with Andean Community countries to avoid dual taxation on Andean companies with multilateral investments – these agreements apply to individuals residing in an Andean Community country and concerns income and net worth tax (there is no tax on net worth in Colombia; the tax is applied only in the country where income is earned.

Withholding tax

Withholding tax currently is applied to all national taxes (income tax, sales tax and stamp tax). It is used locally in industry and trade taxes.

For alien non-residents, the income tax is settled by the withholding taxes.

Exchange control

Exchange is under the control of the National Tax Administration and Central Bank.

Cyprus

Nexia Poyiadjis

Corporate taxes

Taxable entities

Resident companies are liable to income tax on worldwide income. Capital gains are taxed under the capital gains tax law. Under Cyprus law, a company is resident for tax purposes in the place where its central management and control is exercised.

Non-resident companies

Where a non-resident company is trading in Cyprus through a permanent establishment, usually a branch, it must first obtain Central Bank approval and register with the Registrar of Companies. Profits of such branches are taxed at the normal rates, on profits earned during the calendar year.

The tax liability is often reduced under double tax agreements.

Taxes imposed

There is no separate legislation dealing with the taxation of corporations. Companies, local and international business, are taxed under the provisions of the Income Tax law.

Companies are assessed to tax on a current year basis, with special provisions for international business companies and their expatriate employees.

Income tax is normally payable six months after the end of the accounting period and is based on the profits of that accounting period.

Rates of tax

Resident companies are taxed at:

- 20% for profits up to CYP£ 40,000;
- 25% for profits over CYP£ 40,000.

The following exceptions exist:

- public companies registered in Cyprus and incorporated in the Cyprus Stock Exchange are taxed at rates which are one half of the normal rates, for the first four years after their inclusion in the Stock Exchange, and this exemption is subject to a maximum annual reduction in tax liability of CYP£ 100,000;
- companies engaged in the bus transportation industry do not pay any tax on the profits used for the purchase of new buses.

Rates for international business companies

The term 'international business' denotes a company that is wholly owned by non-Cypriots and which derives its income totally outside Cyprus, irrespective of its place of management and control.

Such companies pay tax at the rate of 4.25% on their net profits.

No withholding or additional taxes are paid on the payment of dividends to the shareholders, regardless of the relevant provisions in any double tax agreements between Cyprus and other countries.

Income subject to tax

General rules

Profit chargeable to income tax is computed by adding together the various sources of income (trading profits, rents, investment income, but not capital gains) and then deducting the normal deductions and reliefs.

Capital gains and losses

Capital gains are taxed under a separate law, the capital gains law of 1978, and is levied at the rate of 20% on gains arising from the disposal of immovable property or the disposal of shares of companies, the assets of which consist mainly of immovable property.

The gain is computed by deducting from the sale proceeds the original cost of the property, or its market value at 27 June 1978 (where the property was acquired before that date).

Dividends

Companies are obliged to withhold 20% tax on the payment of dividends to its shareholders. The tax is then assumed to have been paid by the recipient of the dividend, but there is also an option available to include the gross dividend in the tax computation and to receive relief for the tax already paid.

A company can set off tax withheld on dividends it pays, with tax suffered on the receipt of dividend income. A restriction of six years from the receipt of the dividend income applies to this set off.

The paying company is required to provide its shareholders with a certificate showing the amount of dividend, the tax withheld and whether the dividend is paid out of income that has been taxed or not.

No tax is withheld on dividends payable to non-resident companies, and prior approval of the Commissioner of income tax is normally required to obtain this exemption.

Interest

The taxation of interest is identical to that of dividends.

Stock/inventory rules

Stock and work in progress are valued at the lower of cost and net realisable value. FIFO is generally used.

Deductions

General rules

Taxable profits are calculated in accordance with generally accepted accounting principles with certain statutory adjustments.

- Expenses incurred wholly and exclusively for the production of income are deductible and they must be of a revenue nature.
- Capital expenditure can only be deducted by means of tax depreciation relief (capital allowances).
- Political donations are not deductible. Charitable donations up to an amount of CYP£ 20,000, and one half of the excess over CYP£ 20,000, are deductible if made for educational, cultural or other purposes in Cyprus.
- Company formation expenses are not deductible.

- Losses on sales of buildings or investments cannot be deducted from income unless such assets are held as trading stock. Relief may however be available under the capital allowances system.
- Entertainment costs are allowed for both business purposes and staff.
- General provisions and provisions for contingent or future losses are not usually allowable.
- Interest payable on a business loan is allowable. However, where investment companies acquire fixed assets out of business loans, the interest relating to the period up to the date on which the asset commences producing income is considered as a capital expense and is not allowable.

Depreciation

Depreciation is replaced in the tax computations by capital allowances known as 'wear-and-tear' allowances. Such allowances are calculated on a straight-line basis and are based on the cost of all fixed assets except land and private motor vehicles. The present rates of wear-and-tear allowances are:

Commercial buildings	3%
Hotel buildings	4%
Industrial buildings	4%
Plant and machinery	10%
Furniture and fittings	10%
Commercial vehicles	10%
Computer hardware	10%
Computer software	20%

Higher rates may be applicable if it can be established that the assets have a shorter working life.

It is possible under certain circumstances to claim 100% wear-and-tear allowances.

Investment allowances

Additional allowances for fixed assets are given for new or imported second-hand fixed assets in the year they are first used.

No such allowances are allowed to offshore companies for assets held abroad.

Balancing additions and deductions

When business assets previously depreciated are either sold, destroyed or scrapped, the proceeds of the sale price over the written down value of the asset at the date of sale is brought into account in the tax computation as a charge, but this amount cannot exceed the wear-and-tear allowances already granted.

Investment incentives and special benefits

The following special incentives are presently available:

- reduced tax rates for public companies quoted in the Stock Exchange;
- reduced tax rates in private companies when investing in machinery;
- special investment incentives are included for international business entities as outlined below.

International business legal entities

- Reduced tax rate (4.25%). Exemption from capital gains tax on property situated abroad. No stamp duty.
- Reduced tax rate for international business branches (4.25% or nil).
- Exemption from tax for international business partnerships.
- 10 year tax holiday for manufacturing businesses producing new products.
- Reduced tax rates for expatriate employees of international business entities.
- Shipping profits fully exempt from taxation and ship crew salaries fully exempt from taxation.
- Relief on exports repatriated professional fees and repatriated earnings earned abroad.

Non tax incentives

- Duty-free facilities (household goods except furniture, private motor vehicles, televisions etc.) for international business entities and their employees.
- Operation of bonded factories and warehouses.

- No import duties for entry to the EC.

Related party transactions

Provided such transactions are made at arm's length, and then both revenue and capital transactions are treated in the normal way.

Losses

Losses incurred during the year from a trade or business are first set off against profits of that year from other sources. Any unrelieved losses are then carried forward and set off against profits of the next 5 years.

Losses from agriculture cannot be set off against profits from other sources.

In the following cases no losses are allowed to be carried forward:

- if within a period of three years there is both a change in ownership of a company and a major change in the nature of trade carried on by the company;
- if at any time the scale of activities in a trade carried on by a company has become small or negligible.

Corporate groups

Each corporation is taxed separately and no provision exists for loss relief between group companies. Although parliament has passed a law that enables group relief to be available, this is still subject to the official ministry of finance regulations.

Personal taxes

Taxation on income

Income tax is levied under the Income Tax Law 58 of 1961 as amended by subsequent laws, the most important being Law 5 of 1977 which introduced special provisions for international business companies, Law 40 of 1979 which changed the year of assessment from preceding year basis to current year basis and Law 58 of 1991.

Taxable individuals

Residents

Resident individuals are liable to income tax on income accruing in, derived from or received in Cyprus. However, resident individuals are effectively chargeable on worldwide income as income accruing abroad; whether remitted to Cyprus or not, it is deemed to be income derived from Cyprus and subject to income tax if it consists of:

- income of a trade or business controlled or managed in Cyprus;
- income of a person exercising a profession outside Cyprus where that person also carries on a profession within Cyprus;
- investment income.

Non-residents and temporary residents

Individuals who are not resident in Cyprus, or who are in Cyprus temporarily for any purpose and for periods not exceeding six months in any one year to 31 December, are not liable to income tax on any income accruing outside Cyprus (even if remitted to Cyprus).

Source of income

Employment income

Gains or profits from any office or employment, irrespective of whether the person is serving in Cyprus or elsewhere (including the estimated annual value of any accommodation or of any other allowance granted in respect of employment, whether in money or otherwise) are taxed.

Income tax on expatriate individuals

Resident aliens who are employees (including those who are directors of limited companies) are taxed at lower rates depending on where the duties are performed.

- Where duties are performed wholly within Cyprus, foreign individuals are taxed at rates ranging from nil to 20% on any remuneration for services rendered within Cyprus to offshore companies or partnerships.
- Where the duties of employment are rendered partly in Cyprus and partly overseas, income for services rendered in Cyprus is taxed at 50% of the rates and income rendered from services rendered abroad is not taxed at all (if paid through a bank

operating in Cyprus). The actual calculation is established by time apportionment.

- Where the duties of employment are rendered overseas and the employee is not paid through a bank operating in Cyprus, then the employee's salary is taxed at one tenth of the normal tax rates.
- The first CYP£ 2,000 per annum of foreign pensions remitted to Cyprus by any person are tax-free. Any excess is taxed at a flat rate of 5%.

All the expatriate groups, as taxed above, are entitled to full personal allowances and deductions since 1995.

Business income

Gains or profits from any trade, profession or vocation are subject to income tax. However, 100% of the income remitted from abroad by a Cypriot residing in Cyprus is tax free if his interest in the business is at least 15%.

In addition to the usual business deductions, since 1 April 1987, 60% of the profits connected with the provision of professional services abroad are exempt. Where similar services are performed in Cyprus, the ratio of foreign profits to local profits is deemed to arise in the same ratio as foreign turnover to local turnover.

Farming and agriculture

Since 1991, 30% of the income of an individual from farming or agriculture is exempt provided that such income does not exceed CYP£ 10,000.

Pensions

Pensions and annuities are generally taxable, except for certain exceptions (mainly of political appointments e.g. the presidential pension). As mentioned earlier, pensions received in Cyprus from abroad are taxed at 5% on a remittance basis on any amounts in excess of CYP£ 2,000 (the first CYP£ 2,000 being tax free).

Exempt income

The main exemptions from tax are:

- sums received by way of retirement gratuity, commutation of pension, death gratuity or as consolidated compensation for death or injuries;

- income arising from scholarships;
- all interest derived within Cyprus from capital imported from abroad with the consent of the Minister of Finance;
- the emoluments of foreign diplomatic and consular representatives if not Citizens of Cyprus;
- the income of charitable institutions, provident funds, co-operative societies, non-profit organisations;
- 30% of the amount invested to acquire first issue shares in a company listed in the Cyprus Stock Exchange (assuming the shares are held for one full year).

Dividends

Dividends are subject to 20% withholding tax at source, however, as from 1 April 1996, there is an option to the recipient individual to not include the income from the dividends in their computation of taxable income such that 20% tax suffered at source becomes final tax on the dividend.

The above only relates to dividends paid out of profits that have already incurred income tax at the hands of the company.

The treatment of dividends at the hands of the paying company and the receiving company, as well as foreign shareholder issues, are dealt with in the corporate section.

Interest

The taxation of interest is identical to that of dividends.

As well as the fact that income from interest is taxable, close companies (those controlled by less than five people) are taxed on imputed interest of 9% annually on loans or other grants to connected persons.

Rentals and royalties

Rents, royalties, premiums or other profit arising from property are taxable. The value of the benefit derived by the owner of the land from the erection by the tenant of a structure which becomes the owner's property, is also taxable.

Allowable deductions from such income are:

- interest paid on loans in connection with the construction of the building;

- 3% per annum on the cost of the construction of the building, excluding the cost of the land;
- 20% of the annual rental income is allowed as a deduction towards the repairs and renewals of the building.

Losses

Any losses resulting from any of the above activities, except capital losses, may be set off against any other income or other salary of the same year of assessment and any balance may be carried forward and set off against income from any source of the following year of assessment.

Losses from farming activities cannot be set off against other losses but must be set off against future profits from the same source.

If a person delays the submission of accounts from a particular year for more than six years, no losses can be carried forward for that year.

Personal allowances and deductions

The following is a table of the most common personal allowances:

	CYP£
For each child under 16 years old.	500
For each child receiving secondary education in Cyprus.	500
For each child receiving tertiary education in Cyprus.	1,500
For each child in the National Guard.	500
For each person over the age of 65.	1,500
All life premiums are allowed as a deduction provided they are paid to a company that has a base in Cyprus, that the insurance specifies an amount payable at death and the premium is less than 7% of the amount insured. The deduction is subject to a maximum of one-sixth of the taxable income before deduction of the personal allowances.	
Married couples' allowance.	500

Other deductions:

- interest from government bonds is not taxed;
- interest for housing loans up to a maximum of CYP£ 500 is deducted from taxable income.

Special family rules

Husband and wife are treated separately for income tax purposes. Most reliefs are apportioned to husband and wife in accordance with their taxable incomes, with the opportunity to transfer any unused relief to the other party.

Rates of tax

Personal income tax rates are as follows:

Band (CYP£)	*Rate (%)*	*Tax on band (CYP£)*	*Cumulative tax (CYP£)*
0 – 6,000	Nil	Nil	Nil
6,000 – 9,000	20	600	600
9,000 – 12,000	30	900	1,500
12,000+	40	–	–

Payment of taxes

Payroll deductions

Tax in respect of salaries and wages is deducted at source by employers at the prescribed rates and paid over monthly under the Pay-As-You-Earn tax collection system.

Self-employed individuals

A self-employed individual must file a provisional return during January in the year of assessment showing his estimated taxable income for that year. Provisional assessments are paid in three equal instalments, on 30 July, 30 September and 31 December of each year.

Taxable period

The year of assessment is 31 December.

Other taxes

Capital gains

Capital gains tax is imposed at a rate of 20% on all gains arising out of the sale of immovable property. There is a lifetime exemption of the first CYP£ 10,000 of gains.

The following are exempt:

- foreign nationals, whether resident or ordinarily resident, are not taxed on the disposal of immovable property outside Cyprus;
- cypriots are not taxed on the disposal of immovable property outside Cyprus, providing the property was acquired while the individual was resident abroad;
- non-residents, regardless of nationality, are not taxed on the disposal of property in Cyprus, provided it was acquired with funds received from abroad;
- gains up to CYP£ 15,000 from the sale of agricultural land by a farmer;
- subject to certain conditions, the first CYP£ 50,000 of gains arising from the disposal of a house used by the owner for his own habitation.

Value added tax (VAT)

Value added tax is applied on all imports and taxable supplies made in the republic by a taxable entity in the course of its business.

A taxable person for VAT purposes is the person who makes taxable supplies.

The legislation provides for a zero rate and a standard rate of 10%.

Registration for VAT purposes is compulsory for businesses with taxable supplies exceeding CYP£ 12,000 per annum, or CYP£ 3,000 in any one quarter.

International business entities without physical offices in Cyprus are not required to register for VAT. International businesses with physical offices in Cyprus are not required, but may register for VAT.

Special contribution for defence

All business profits, including salaries, dividends, interest and rents are subject to a 2% contribution for defence. Employers are also required to contribute an amount equal to the contribution of their employees. Offshore companies and their employees are not subject to this tax, except that such companies must contribute in respect of their Cypriot personnel.

Immovable property tax

All immovable property in Cyprus, with minor exceptions (such as agricultural land used by its owner for agricultural purposes), is subject to immovable property tax.

This is levied on the market value of the property as at 1 January 1980 at rates of up to 0.35%.

Estate duty

The Estate Duty Law 1962 was suspended for persons who died after 1 January 2000. The following provisions relate to the imposition of estate duty for persons who died prior to 1 January 2000.

The imposition of tax on the estate of a deceased person is governed by the Estate Duty Law of 1962 and its subsequent amendments.

Taxable property includes:

- the property of a deceased person, domiciled in Cyprus, wherever situated in the world;
- the property in Cyprus of a person not domiciled in Cyprus;
- gifts made by the deceased three years prior to his death;
- gifts irrespective of the date of transfer where the donor retains a benefit;
- life insurance and provident fund capital payments.

Value of the estate

The value is based on the market value of the property at the date of death. In the case of a gift, this is the lower of market value at the time of the gift and market value at the time of the death.

Rates

The rates, revised from 28 March 1997, are as follows:

Value of property	*Rate of tax*	*Cumulative tax*
0 – 20,000	Nil	Nil
20,001 – 25,000	10	500
25,001 – 35,000	13	1,800
35,001 – 55,000	15	4,800
55,001 – 80,000	17	9,050
80,001 – 105,000	20	14,050
105,001 – 150,000	23	24,400
Over 150,000	30	–

The most significant deductions are as follows:

Deductions	*CYP£*
For surviving spouse	75,000
For each child under 21 years of age	150,000
For each child over 21 years of age	75,000
Donations to charity	Up to 20,000
Donations to government or local authority	Full amount

Assets of a person not domiciled in Cyprus, such as bank deposits in Cyprus, shares in offshore companies and shares in Cyprus shipping companies, are tax exempt.

Stamp duty

Stamp duty is levied on certain documents at various, generally small, rates. International business companies are exempt from stamp duty on documents relating to their ordinary business activities.

Municipality tax

All town municipalities charge various taxes annually on companies and on individuals, the most important of which is the professional tax.

Withholding taxes

Cyprus law requires taxes to be withheld at source on interest, dividends, royalties and certain other amounts paid to non-residents of Cyprus. The following table illustrates, with minor adjustments, the rates currently in force.

	Paid from Cyprus		
	Dividends	*Interest*	*Royalties*
	%	%	%
Non treaty countries	20	20	10
Treaty countries:			
Austria	10	0	0
Bulgaria	0	0	0
Canada	15	15	10
China	10	10	10
Czech republic	10	10	5
Denmark	15	10	0
France	15	10	0
Germany	10	10	0
Greece	25	10	0

Hungary	0	10	0
Ireland	0	0	0
Italy	0	10	0
Kuwait	10	10	5
Norway	0	20	0
Poland	10	10	0
Romania	10	10	5
Russia	0	0	0
Sweden	5	10	0
United Kingdom	0	10	0
United States	0	10	0
Yugoslavia	10	10	10

Under Cyprus legislation, the withholding tax on dividends paid by a Cyprus local company to a foreign company is fully refundable. International business company dividends are paid without any withholding tax.

In the absence of a treaty, there is withholding tax of 20% on dividend payments made to foreign shareholders. In the presence of a treaty, its provisions prevail.

Exchange controls

Although Cyprus has exchange controls, these are applied very liberally by the Central Bank of Cyprus. In practice, most of the day-to-day transactions are dealt with by the commercial banks.

All investments in Cyprus by non-residents require the prior approval of the Central Bank of Cyprus. The criteria that the Central Bank imposes are generally the benefits accruing to the Cyprus economy. Up to 100% foreign participation in local companies is permitted.

International business entities in Cyprus have no exchange control restrictions and can freely transfer funds anywhere in the world. Permission for foreigners to establish of an offshore entity is usually readily given on the production of satisfactory bank references and on the condition that no business activity is carried out in Cyprus.

Czech Republic

Audit Plus

Corporate taxes

Taxable entities

Resident companies

Resident companies are liable to corporate income tax on their income from worldwide sources.

Non-resident companies

Non-resident companies are liable to corporate income tax only on income arising in the Czech Republic.

Tax year and filing requirements

The tax year is the calendar year, or a fiscal year, that is defined as 12 consecutive calendar months. A tax return must be filed within three months after the end of the tax year or within six months if a chartered tax adviser is acting on behalf of the company, or if a mandatory statutory audit is performed.

Taxes imposed

All taxes on income are imposed at a national level. The Czech tax system holds no special advantages or disadvantages for foreign companies or branches of foreign companies in terms of tax rates. Some exemptions are provided for non-trading branches where attributable profit is taxable. This profit must be negotiated with the local financial office.

Rates of tax

The corporate tax rate for both resident and non-resident companies is 31%.

Income subject to tax

General rules

Income subject to tax is income from all activities. Withholding tax applies to dividends and other capital gains. Taxable profit is based on accounting profit adjusted under the tax law.

Stock/inventory valuation

Stock is valued at historical cost. Various methods for valuing trading stock are acceptable for tax purposes with the exception of LIFO.

Capital gains and losses

Capital gains are included in ordinary taxable income and taxed at the standard corporate tax rate of 31%.

Dividends

Dividends are subject to a withholding tax of 15%; lower rates may be applied where a tax treaty exists.

Deductions

General rules

Most expenses are deductible provided they are incurred in the normal course of business. Certain expenses, such as food, drink and gifts are not deductible and certain deductions, such as travel expenses, are limited.

Depreciation and amortisation

Two methods of depreciation and amortisation are permitted in accordance with tax law. These are:

- straight line; and
- reducing balance.

Approximate rates for the straight line method are:

- buildings 3.4%
- machinery 8.7–18.3%
- vehicles 28.6%

Certain assets, such as land and works of art, are not depreciable.

Royalties

Royalties are deductible provided the amount is justifiable against the services provided.

Interest

All interest payments are considered to be business expenses and are therefore deductible. There are some restrictions regarding interest payable to parties which directly or indirectly control or own the company. The maximum permissible related party debt/equity ratio is 4:1, and interest paid in excess is considered as a dividend and taxed as such.

Dividends

Dividends paid are not deductible. One half of the withholding taxes from dividends is deductible in the year when dividends are paid.

Bad and doubtful debts

Write offs are permitted under special legislation (see act on reserves for purposes of determining the income tax base). Relief is available ranging from 20%, where the debt has been outstanding for more then six months, to 100%, where it has been outstanding for more than three years. There are special provisions as to how these debts would be treated.

Reserves and provisions

Reserves are allowed only in special circumstances under specified legislation. The most common reserves are for fixed asset maintenance where the expected life of the asset is six years or more.

Employees' and directors' remuneration and benefits

Employees' and directors' remuneration and benefits are generally deductible.

Specifically non-deductible expenses

Food, drink and gifts for business partners are non-deductible. The remuneration and benefits of non-executive directors and members of supervisory boards are non-deductible. Penalties and fines, environmental charges and some taxes such as real estate transfer tax are non-deductible.

Foreign source income

Tax paid abroad on the foreign source income can be offset against tax paid in the Czech Republic on worldwide income. However, the maximum amount deductible is limited to the level of local taxation. Where a double taxation treaty is in force, foreign source income is taxed accordingly.

Investment incentives and special benefits

New investment incentives are in function as of 1 May 2000. Their criteria are complex since they cover such parameters as sectors, invested funds, ratio machinery and equipment/total funds, environmental standards, districts and so on and so forth.

Concessions include relief from tax liability for a five or ten year period, exemption on customs and VAT on certain types of machinery, training and jobs grants, and the development of the infrastructure within this project. These investments are generally focused on multi-national and global investors and not for small and medium businesses.

In all companies, a tax deduction is available at a rate of 10% of an investment in qualifying fixed assets purchased in the current tax year.

Losses

Losses may be offset against the profits of the seven subsequent tax periods.

Corporate groups

Corporate groups are not yet treated as a single fiscal entity under Czech law, although they may pay dividends equal to dividends received, without the deduction of withholding tax. A corporate group is recognised where the parent company owns at least 20% of the shares.

Liquidation of a company

An individual shareholder is subject to income tax at a rate of 15% on liquidation distributions, to the extent that these exceed the paid-up share capital of the company.

Capital taxes

Capital duty

There is no capital duty in the Czech Republic.

Net worth tax

There is no net worth tax in the Czech Republic.

Personal taxes

Taxable individuals

Residents

Resident individuals are taxed on their worldwide income irrespective of source. Czech tax law and double taxation treaties grant relief from double taxation. An individual who resides in or visits the Czech Republic for 183 days or more, in any year, will be treated as resident.

Non-residents

Non-residents are normally subject to income tax solely on income arising in the Czech Republic.

Tax year and filing requirements

The taxable period is the calendar year. Residents are not required to file a tax return if they receive income only from an employment.

A return must be filed by the end of March, or the end of June if a chartered tax adviser is used.

Taxes on income

The most significant taxes on income are taxes from employment and other non-independent activities, and income tax on entrepreneurs.

Sources of income

Employees' remuneration and directors' fees

Employment income is taxed as ordinary income. It includes all payments in cash, benefits in kind and personal capital insurance paid by the company. There are a limited number of benefits which are not taxable.

Business income

Individuals must report income from business (usually a sole proprietor or a share of income from a partnership), income from agriculture, forest and water business and income from other undertakings such as the professional activities of solicitors, auditors, lawyers and artists, etc.

Capital gains

Capital gains are treated as income for tax purposes.

Dividends

Dividends are generally taxed at a rate of 15% and the tax is withheld by the paying company.

Interest

Interest from long term bank or savings accounts is subject to withholding taxes at a rate of 15%.

Rentals

Rent receipts are subject to income tax.

Royalties

Royalties paid are not subject to withholding tax. Royalties received are taxed as normal income.

Social security benefits

Social security benefits are not taxable, although contributions are tax deductible.

Pensions and annuities

Pension receipts are not subject to tax. Annuities are taxed with other income.

Exempt income

Tax regulations allow for tax relief for various types of income, usually where unconnected with the business.

Foreign source income

The foreign source income of individuals is generally treated in the same way as the foreign source income of corporations (see above).

Personal allowances and deductions

Resident taxpayers are granted tax-free allowances, as follows:

	Czech crowns per year (CZK)
Each taxpayer	38,040
Each child living with the taxpayer	23,520
Students (additional)	11,400
Disabled and other special cases	50,040

Expenses relating to income are generally deductible.

Non-resident taxpayers are only granted an allowance of CZK 38,040 per year.

Losses

Losses can be offset against income from other sources in the current year with the exception of employment income. Where offset is not possible, the excess losses can be carried forward to the subsequent 7 years.

Special family rules

Income derived from a business can be divided between a married couple in the ratio of 30:70 or 50:50 under special conditions.

Special treatment for expatriates

There is no special treatment for expatriates in the Czech tax system.

Rates of tax

General

The 2001 tax rates for residents are:

Band in Czech crowns (CZK)		*Rate*
0 to 109,200		15 %
109,201 to 218,400	16,380 CZK + 20% in excess of 109,200 CZK	
218,401 to 331,200	38,220 CZK + 25% in excess of 218,400 CZK	
331,201 +	66,420 CZK + 32% in excess of 331,200 CZK	

Provincial and local taxes

There are no provincial or local taxes on income.

Withholding tax

A 15% withholding tax is levied on dividends distributed to individuals and 15% is also withheld from bank and savings account interest.

Payment of tax

Payroll deductions

Tax is deducted from wages and salaries by the employer. Tax deducted can be offset against an individual's final income tax.

Prepayment Tax

Advance payments are based on tax paid in the previous year.

Estate and gift tax

Gifts and inheritances are taxable in the Czech Republic. The rates depend on:

- the amount received; and
- the relationship between the parties.

Wealth tax

There is no wealth tax in the Czech Republic.

Social security contributions

Both employers and employees must contribute to social funds. Percentages are computed at 35% of income (or gross wages in the case of employees).

	Employer	*Employee*	*Total*
Social fund	26.25%	8.75%	35%
Health insurance	9%	4.5%	13.5%

Various exemptions apply.

Other taxes

Treatment of partnerships

Profits made by a partnership are allocated to the partners in accordance with their profit shares and taxed in the partners' hands.

VAT and sales taxes

Most goods are subject to 22% VAT, while most services are taxed at 5%. Certain essential goods are taxed at 5% and qualified services at 22%. A zero rate applies to the export of goods and services.

Other taxes

- excise duty (levied on alcohol, tobacco and fuel);
- road tax;
- real estate tax;
- real estate transfer tax.

Exchange control

There is limited foreign exchange control. All types of investments are allowed for non-residents, although real estate property is limited and a special buying procedure is recommended.

Tax treaties and withholding taxes

Country	*Normal Dividends*	*Participation Dividends*	*%*	*Royalties %*
Albania	15	5	5/nil	10
Australia	15	5	10	10

Austria	10	10	nil	5
Belarus	10	10	5	10
Belgium	15	15	10	5
Brazil	15	15	15/10	25
Bulgaria	10	10	10	10
Canada	15	10	10	10
China	10	10	10	10
Croatia	5	5	0	10
Cyprus	10	10	10	5
Denmark	15	15	nil	5
Egypt	15	5	15	15
Estonia	15	5	10	10
Finland	15	5	nil	5
France	10	10	nil	5
Germany	15	5	nil	5
Greece	local rates	local rates	10	10
Hungary	15	5	0	10
Iceland	n/a	n/a	n/a	n/a
India	10	10	10	10
Indonesia	15	10	12.5	12.5
Ireland	15	5	0	10
Israel	15	5	10	5
Italy	15	15	nil	5
Japan	15	10	10	10
Kazakhstan	10	10	10	10
Korea	10	5	10	10
Latvia	15	5	10	10
Lebanon	5	5	nil	10
Lithuania	15	5	10	10
Luxembourg	15	5	nil	10
Malaysia	10	10	12	12
Malta	5	5	nil	5
Moldova	15	5	5	10
Mongolia	10	10	10	10
Netherlands	10	nil	nil	5
Nigeria	15	12.5	15	10
Norway	15	5	nil	5
Poland	10	5	10	5
Portugal	15	10	10	10
Romania	110	10	7	10
Russia	10	10	nil	10
Singapore	5	5	nil	10
Slovak Republic	15	5	nil	5
Slovenia	15	5	5	10
South Africa	15	5	0	10
Spain	15	5	nil	nil
Sri Lanka	15	15	nil	10
Sweden	10	nil	nil	5

Switzerland	15	5	nil	10
Thailand	10	10	10	15
Tunis	15	10	12	15
Ukraine	15	5	5	10
United Arab Emirates	5	nil	nil	10
United Kingdom	15	5	nil	10
USA	15	5	nil	10
Venezuela	10	5	10	12
Vietnam	10	10	10	10
Yugoslavia	15	5	nil	10

Minimum participation requirements are normally 25%.

The double taxation treaty with Iceland was concluded on 28 December 2000 and the wording of the treaty is not yet available.

Anti-avoidance measures

Transactions of an artificial nature carried out solely for the purpose of avoiding tax may be ignored or replaced by the transaction that was commercially intended.

Denmark

Nexia Preben Larsen
Statsautoriserede revisorer

Introduction

Most Danish taxes are levied at a national level, with the exceptions of *'kommuneskat'*, *'amtskommuneskat'* and real estate tax (local taxes). The tax year is the calendar year, although companies and other businesses may choose alternative year ends.

Corporate taxes

Taxable entities

Resident companies

A company which is resident in Denmark is liable to corporation tax on its worldwide income and capital gains. A company is resident in Denmark if it is incorporated in Denmark or has its central management and control located in Denmark.

The two principal forms of resident, limited liability companies are the joint stock company (aktieselskab – A/S) registered under the Danish Companies Act and the private company (anpartsselskab – ApS) registered under the Danish Private Companies Act. The ApS is similar to the A/S, but is subject to less stringent regulations.

The capital requirements for companies are currently as follows:

	DKK
Limited companies	500,000
Private companies	125,000

For tax legislation, the Danish territories do not include the Faroe Islands and Greenland as these two territories have their own tax legislation.

Non-resident companies

Non-resident companies are generally taxed on the business income from a Danish branch/permanent establishment and on income from real property situated in Denmark. The taxation includes any capital gains derived from the sale of business and assets pertaining to a branch/permanent establishment or from real property in Denmark.

Tax year and filing requirements

Company tax is levied at the national level on all types of income, including capital gains. It is calculated on the basis of the taxable income of an income year.

Companies have the right to choose any income year as long as it runs to the end of a month.

Companies must file the tax return no later than six months after the end of the income year. If the income year ends between 1 January to 31 March, the tax return must be filed by 1 July in the same calendar year.

The tax authorities will make an estimate of the taxable income if no tax return is filed. If the tax return is not filed on time, a tax addition is paid of DKK 200 per day each day the limit has been overdue, however this amount cannot exceed DKK 5,000.

If certain conditions are met, both the tax authorities and the taxpayer are entitled to make changes to the tax return within a period of three years and four months after the end of an income year.

Taxes imposed

The taxes assessed can be paid either in a lump sum or in two advance instalments:

Lump sum payment

The entire tax assessed for an income year is payable on 20 November in the following year. As an example, if the financial year ends 31 December 2000, the tax return should be submitted before 1 July 2001 and tax is payable no later than 20 November 2001.

Advance payment

Companies can pay an advance tax on 20 March and 20 November in an income year but once a company has chosen to make use of the advance tax payment scheme, the decision cannot be rescinded.

The advance tax payment scheme is compulsory if the company's first income year began after 29 January 1992. The scheme also becomes compulsory if the company's taxable income exceeded DKK 10,000,000 two years prior to the actual income year.

Parent companies and their subsidiaries may enjoy joint taxation as long as certain conditions are met and they will have a joint and several liability for the tax payment.

Rates of tax

The corporation tax rate applying to resident and non-resident companies is 30% as from the income year 2001. If the companies do not make use of the advance tax payment scheme, the calculated tax is increased with 10%.

Income subject to tax

General rules

Resident companies are taxed on worldwide income, including business profits, certain capital gains, dividends, interests and royalties. Most usual business expenditure pertaining to operations (but not to capital) are tax deductible.

Non-resident companies are taxed on business income derived from a permanent establishment or real property situated in Denmark. Capital gains from the sale of business assets pertaining to a permanent establishment or from real property in Denmark are also taxable.

Stock/inventory rules

Inventory is valued at the end of the year on the basis of either market value or costs (including freight, duty etc.). For inventory produced by the company, indirect production costs can be added.

Companies can choose either the FIFO method or the weighted average cost method of valuation, but they may not use the LIFO or base stock methods.

Capital gains and losses

Certain types of capital gains realised by companies are included in the ordinary taxable income and taxed at the ordinary income tax rate of 30%.

The most common types of assets subject to capital gains tax are machinery and other disposals of business assets, real property and certain intangible assets (e.g. patent rights, goodwill, trademarks and copyrights).

The gain arising from the sale of real property is calculated in two parts:

(a) the part of the gain relating to depreciation claimed in prior years is recaptured as a capital gain and the full amount is included in the taxable income;

(b) any additional gain is taxed in full if the period of ownership is less than three years; losses are deductible, but only against income derived from the sale of real property.

A minor deduction in the gain is provided if the property is acquired before 1 January 1999 and if it has been owned for more than three years.

After three years' ownership, the calculated income from the property is reduced by 5% in each subsequent year until and including the ninth year of ownership. This reduction is gradually being abolished with a transitional period until the year 2007.

The purchase price will be increased by an amount of DKK 10,000 (a supplement) in the year of purchase and in every other year of ownership. The supplement will not be granted in the year of the sale unless the purchase and sale of the property are effected in the same year.

Gains arising from the sale of shares owned for less than three years are added to the ordinary capital income. A loss on shares owned for less than three years can be carried forward for five years, but can only be offset against a taxable gain deriving from the sale of shares that are also owned for less than three years.

Capital gains and losses on shares owned for more than three years are neither taxable nor deductible provided the company does not trade in shares.

Gains on the sale of goodwill are taxable and losses are deductible from the taxable income.

The purchaser of goodwill may write-down the cash purchase price over a period of seven years and at a rate of a seventh each year. Goodwill purchased before 1 January 1998 can be written down over a period of ten years.

Denmark

If goodwill is transferred between related parties, the buyer can only write-down on an amount corresponding to the seller's taxable gain plus the remaining part of the seller's depreciable goodwill – and not from the purchase price.

Gains on bonds, mortgage deeds, instruments of debt and other money claims are subject to special rules.

For claims repaid or amortised after 27 December 1990 and debt raised after the same date, the following rules apply:

- when assessing the taxable income, gains from claims and debts are to be included; losses are deductible; gains from claims and debts in both Danish Kroner and foreign currencies are taxable;
- losses originating from trade accounts in consolidated but not jointly taxed companies are deductible; if the companies are jointly taxed, there will be no deduction for losses on such accounts.

Regarding other accounts, profit from debt owed to consolidated companies is not subject to any tax if the creditor is not allowed to deduct the loss.

Gains or losses derived from the sale, disposal or renunciation of rights which are limited in time, such as patent rights, trademarks and copyrights, are included in the taxable income.

Dividends

Dividends received by a resident company are subject to income tax. However, a dividend from a Danish subsidiary is tax-exempt provided that the parent company has owned at least 25% of the share capital in the subsidiary for at least one year during which period the dividend is declared.

Dividends received from foreign subsidiaries are exempt, if the above conditions have been met. In addition, the following demands must be met:

- the foreign subsidiary must be a 'company' according to Danish rules, this request will probably be fulfilled if the subsidiary is regarded as a company in the country in which it is domiciled;
- the foreign company must not be a 'financial company', i.e. if more than one-third of the income in the foreign subsidiary is derived from financial business (or more than one-third of the assets are financial assets) the subsidiary is regarded as a financial company;

- if the subsidiary is regarded as a financial company the consequence is that controlled foreign corporation rules will apply, i.e. forced joint taxation will take place; the effect of a forced joint taxation is that the Danish company will be taxed on all the income in the foreign subsidiary.

Dividends declared by a Danish company are subject to 28% withholding tax.

The tax is the final levy for non-resident companies if the above-mentioned conditions of ownership etc. are not met. If the conditions are met, dividends can be distributed without any taxes being withheld.

If the conditions are not met but a double taxation treaty has been concluded, the foreign shareholder may request a refund of the difference between the 28% withheld and the rate specified in the relevant double taxation treaty.

Danish resident companies (fully liable to tax) owning less than 25% of the share capital of a company must include 66% of the taxable dividends in the income of the dividend receiving company.

Deductions

General rules

Expenses related to the business income, e.g. expenses incurred to obtain, secure and maintain the taxable business income, are deductible when computing the taxable income.

Depreciation and amortisation

Plant and machinery

Plant and machinery used exclusively for commercial purposes is pooled and depreciated in accordance with the declining-balance method. The pool basis is the opening, written-down value at the beginning of the tax year, less disposals during the year, plus acquisitions during the year. The rate of depreciation is discretionary, however, subject to a ceiling of 25% (as from the income year 2001) of the base costs. The basis for depreciation of industrial or commercial buildings is the initial cost.

New acquisitions of DKK 9,800 each or less, or with an expected useful lifetime not exceeding three years, may be written-down in full for tax purposes in the year of acquisition. However, the items must not be part of existing equipment. If for example a printer has a price of less than DKK 9,800 it will not be tax deductible as it can only function together with a computer (purchase price, e.g. DKK 5,000) bringing the total cost above DKK 9,800.

The costs of company cars are added to the pool for plant and machinery.

Ships are written down in the same way as plant and machinery.

Specific regulations apply to rental assets. Depreciation is not available in the year of acquisition. The rental assets will be shown in a separate balance basis. In return, the declining balance basis can be depreciated at 50% (as from the income year 2001) in the income year following the year of acquisition. The depreciated balance will then be included in the general balance basis in the third year.

Buildings

Buildings for industrial and commercial use are depreciated according to the straight-line method. The rate of depreciation is discretionary. The maximum rate is 5% per year.

The basis for depreciation of industrial or commercial buildings is the initial cost. If an industrial or a commercial building is improved or rebuilt, the cost may be deducted from the taxable income if it amounts to no more than 5% of the basis of the tax depreciation. The excess cost may be capitalised and depreciated. No depreciation is allowed on separate office buildings or on land.

Special installations

Special installations in industrial and commercial buildings are depreciated with up to 5% per year. The rate of depreciation is discretionary.

Advance depreciations

Operating equipment acquired after 3 October 2000 can no longer be depreciated in advance.

Goodwill and other fixed assets

Intangibles such as trademarks, patent rights, goodwill and copyrights may be written-off on a straight-line basis over their useful lives. Goodwill purchased after 19 May 1993 can be depreciated at a rate of

1/7 over a period of seven years. If goodwill is purchased before 1 January 1998, the period is ten years.

Royalties

Royalties are tax deductible provided that the amount is justifiable.

Interest

Interest expenses related to the business income are tax deductible.

If the debt/equity ratio exceeds 1:4, interest on loans from related parties can be reduced when calculating the taxable income. However, if the Danish company can prove that a loan could have been obtained from an unrelated party on the same terms as the loan from a related party, no reduction is made.

There are no other special restrictions on interest paid to an associated company provided that the interest is at a commercial rate.

Dividends

Dividends paid out are not deductible.

Entertainment expenses

Entertainment expenses may only be deducted up to 25% of the total cost. However, travel and hotel costs (not meals) for foreign business trips promoting the sale of goods or services abroad are fully deductible.

Currency fluctuations

Gains or losses on claims and debts in foreign currency must be included in the taxable income. The gains or losses are taxable/deductible when realised. If approved, a company may use the accrual method, provided that this method is used for all claims and debts.

Investment incentives and special benefits

Financial grants are available to Danish and foreign enterprises establishing business activities in regional development areas. The grants may comprise loans at very low interest rates or cash grants. Grants may also be obtained to finance project planning and research and development projects.

Related party transactions

Transactions between related parties must be based on the principle of arm's length, otherwise the authorities may adjust the transaction.

In January 1998, transfer pricing regulations were introduced and companies must now have documentation showing as a minimum how prices between related parties are determined.

Losses

Net operating tax losses may be carried forward for five years and set off against taxable profits.

Corporate groups

A Danish resident company may obtain permission to be taxed on a combined income basis with a 100% owned subsidiary – domestic as well as foreign.

One aspect of group taxation is that taxable losses in one company can be off set against taxable income in another company, enabling losses to be utilised earlier than if the companies were being taxed separately.

It is not possible to exploit a deficit incurred before the joint taxation, but the loss bearing company may use the deficit against its own future income.

If the foreign subsidiary is a 'financial' company, joint taxation is mandatory in the Danish parent company.

Personal taxes

Taxable individuals

The extent to which the income of an individual is subject to Danish tax depends on where he is resident in Denmark.

Residents

Resident individuals are taxed on their total income, regardless of source, but Danish tax law and double tax treaties provide relief from double taxation.

An individual is considered to be resident once he has lived in

Denmark for six months and he will then be taxed as a resident from the date of his arrival.

Non-residents

Non-residents are taxed on income arising from:

- personal services performed in Denmark;
- a permanent business establishment or from real property situated in Denmark;
- dividends from Danish companies;
- royalties from Denmark.

Tax year and filing requirements

The taxable period is the calendar year. After each taxable period, all taxpayers must in principle prepare a tax return to be filed not later than 1 May in the year following the taxable period. Using the agreed figures of the income tax return, the final tax will be calculated by the tax authorities. If the tax authorities believe that they have all necessary information about the taxpayer they will forward the final tax statement together with the pre-printed tax return in the month of April. The difference between the final tax and the tax paid in advance during the income year will *either* be refunded to the taxpayer in May/June in the year following the income year *or* will be paid by the taxpayer in three instalments in the year following the income year. If the amount due is less than approximately DKK 14,000, it will be paid in the second year following the income year.

If the taxpayer does not file a tax return, the tax authorities will estimate the taxable income and fines will have to be paid.

The tax authorities and the taxpayer may, if certain conditions are met, amend the taxable income within a period of three years and four months after the year end.

Taxes on income

General

Income taxes are levied by national and local authorities. The Danish tax regime operates with two types of income: ordinary and share income.

Employees pay a minor contribution to the Supplementary Pension Scheme.

In addition, employees pay a gross tax, i.e. a labour market contribution (known as 'AM-bidrag') of 9%, on the basis of the employment income (see 'Social security' below).

Ordinary income

Generally speaking, ordinary income includes all types of recurring income and is divided into capital income and personal income.

The different types of ordinary income cannot be off-set against one another because they are subject to different tax rates (see 'Rates of tax').

Capital income has been defined thoroughly in the law, which means that any income that has not been defined as capital income is regarded (and taxed) as personal income. Capital income includes:

- interest, receivable and payable;
- taxable gains and losses on financial assets and debts;
- assessed capital yield in private enterprises according to the special business taxation scheme (see 'Business income');
- capital gains on the disposal of shares (if not taxed as share income).

Dividend income

Dividends are taxed according to special rules (see 'Dividends').

Sources of income

Employment income and directors' fees

Employment income is taxed as personal income and includes all payments in cash, as well as other benefits received from the employer such as meals, housing, car, etc.

An employee may deduct expenses such as travel, unemployment insurance, trade organisation, subscriptions, trade literature, in order to arrive at net employment income. In addition, married employees who temporarily maintain two households may deduct certain expenses thereby incurred.

Pension scheme payments, which are made by an employer on behalf of an employee, are not taxable, provided that the payments are made under an approved superannuation scheme.

Gifts and bonuses, and dismissal payments are regarded as employment income, meaning that the employer has to withhold a certain amount of tax. Dismissal payments and jubilee bonuses are taxable as personal income. Amounts below DKK 8,000 are, however, tax-free.

Business income

Business income before interest (less losses) is taxed as personal income, regardless of the type of business or profession. Expenses are deductible to the extent that they are incurred in order to obtain, secure and maintain the taxable business income. Interest income/expenses relating to the business is taxed as capital income.

Business income may also be taxed according to a special business taxation arrangement which gives a private enterprise the same taxation position as that of companies. An assessed capital yield of the enterprise is taxed as capital income, whereas other net profit withdrawn for private consumption is taxed as personal income. Net profit not withdrawn for private consumption is subject to a preliminary 30% fixed rate of taxation and when the income is eventually withdrawn for private consumption the withdrawal will be taxed as personal income and a credit of the preliminary paid taxes of 30% will be granted.

The business taxation arrangement is optional and when submitting the income tax return, the taxpayer can choose whether to join or withdraw from the arrangement after the relevant year of assessment.

Capital gains

Unless specifically prescribed by law, capital gains are not taxed. Taxable capital gains are generally taxed as capital income. Losses can be offset against gains and net losses can be set off for five years.

The most important assets subject to tax as capital income are shares and real estate.

Shares

Gains realised after less than three years of ownership are taxed as capital income. Losses can be carried forward for five years, but can only be offset against other gains from the disposals of shares which were owned less than three years, and cannot be deducted from taxable income.

Gains made from shares owned for three years or more are subject to tax on the same conditions applying to gains or income from dividend ('aktieindkomst').

Losses can be carried forward for five years, and the taxable value of the loss can be off-set against ordinary income tax payable.

Gains from shares of an amount of less than DKK 38,500 are taxed at 28% and gains above this level are taxed at 43%.

Total basis for spouses is DKK 77,000.

Specific regulations apply to quoted shares.

Real estate

Capital gains from the sale of real estate are taxed as capital income. Losses can be deducted from other profits from the sale of commercial property. Additional losses can be carried forward in the following five fiscal years and can be deducted from profits from the sale of other property.

A minor deduction in the gain is provided if the property is acquired before 1 January 1999 and if it has been owned for more than three years.

The disposal of a private residence is tax exempt provided that the owner does not trade in real estate or a similar business.

Dividends

Dividends up to DKK 38,500 are taxed at a rate of 28%. The tax is withheld by the dividend paying company and is considered a final tax. Dividends of more than DKK 38,500 are taxed at a rate of 43%. In case of non-resident shareholders, the 28% withholding tax is regarded as a final tax. The tax may be reduced in accordance with a double taxation treaty.

Interest

Interest received is taxed as capital income. There is no withholding tax on interest. Interest paid, such as interest on mortgages, may be netted off against interest received.

Foreign currency

Individuals not subject to tax on their trade must include gains and losses on claims and debts in foreign currencies when assessing the taxable income if the annual net gain or net loss exceeds DKK 1,000.

Gains from the disposal or full or partial repayment of debts in Danish Kroner must be included when assessing the taxable income if the debt returns interest at a rate which is lower than the minimum interest rate at the time of the debtor's acceptance of the obligation. The official interest rate is calculated on the basis of the highest suggested repayment amount. There is no deduction for losses.

The minimum interest rate has been 4% from 1 January 2001.

Social security benefits

Contributions based on need and paid by public authorities in accordance with the Act on Social Aid are not included in income.

Pensions and annuities

Pensions paid out from an annuity assurance or pension savings with recurring payments are subject to tax. A duty of 40% is imposed on lump sum payments from a capital insurance, and from savings for pension purposes if paid out according to the original scheme.

Rentals

The owners of real estate are liable to tax of the value of their property ('Ejendomsværdiskat'), unless the housing is fully or partly let out. The tax is calculated from the public assessment.

The tax is calculated as 1% of the part of the property value that does not exceed DKK 2,684,000 and 3% of the value exceeding this amount.

This tax has been introduced in 2000 and some temporary rules will ensure that taxation according to the new rules are not more severe than the rules applied before 2000.

Tax will also have to be paid for properties situated abroad and for Danish properties if the owner lives abroad.

Royalties

Royalties are taxed as personal income and in the case of payments to non-residents a 30% tax is withheld at source. This tax only applies to royalties paid for the use of, or right to use, patents, designs, formula or processes, trademarks, etc. It does not apply to royalties paid for the right to motion pictures, musical or literary works, etc., or payments for the right to use machinery, vessels, buildings, etc., (leasing payment). Double tax treaties may modify the rate of tax.

Personal allowances and deductions

The most important personal deductions are an integral part of the general system described above, i.e. negative income such as interest and business losses may be off set against positive income.

As a general rule, other deductions, e.g. for expenses defrayed in connection with acquiring employment income, may not be deducted directly from the income, rather the tax value of the deductions is off set against the taxes on the income (see 'Rates of tax').

Danish residents over 18 are entitled to a tax free allowance of DKK 33,400 and persons under the age of 18 DKK 24,800.

Each spouse has a personal allowance and if one spouse cannot utilise the allowance, it can be transferred to the other.

Contributions to pension schemes (with recurring re-payments) may be deducted from personal income. For private pension schemes, lump sum contributions are deductible over a ten year period at a rate of 10% per annum. However, a deduction of DKK 36,500 may always be obtained up to the amount of the payments already made.

Contributions to lump sum payment schemes cannot exceed DKK 36,500 per annum and the contributions are only deductible in the capital income.

Losses

Generally speaking, losses can be deducted from other income.

Losses not utilised can be carried forward for five years. No other specific rules apply to professionals.

Special family rules

With few exceptions, all members of a family are taxed individually.

When calculating taxes, a standard personal allowance of DKK 33,400 is given. If one spouse cannot use the allowance, it can be transferred to the other spouse. Similarly, the unused basis deduction of DKK 177,900 in connection with the calculation of the intermediate tax (see below) may be transferred to the other spouse.

Special treatment of expatriates

Subject to certain conditions, foreign nationals employed by a Danish employer may choose to pay tax according to the so-called 'Professor Regulation'.

The employee has to meet the following rules in order to be included by the regulations:

- the employee must be fully liable to tax in Denmark in connection with the beginning of the employment;
- the employee must initialise his employment by being included by the 'Professor Regulation';
- the monthly salary of the employee should be at least DKK 56,500 before deduction of labour market contribution ('AM-bidrag') and supplementary pension scheme;
- the employee is not allowed to take either direct or indirect part of the management of, the control with, or the capital of the company in which he is employed;
- the employee has to perform his job in Denmark;
- the period of taxation of 25% cannot last for any longer than 36 months; and
- the employment must be reported to the Danish Tax Authorities within 8 days.

Consequently, the employer must withhold labour market contribution ('AM-bidrag') at 9% before calculating the national tax (A-skat) at 25% on earned income. No expenses can be deducted from the earned income prior to the payment of the 'AM-bidrag' and income taxes.

Income from research activities in connection with an approved research project is not subject to the minimum earned income requirement of DKK 56,500.

Rates of tax

Local taxes are always calculated at a flat rate. The tax rate may vary a few percent depending on the municipality (average local rate is approximately 31%).

The labour market contribution ('AM-bidrag') of 9% is deducted from the personal income before calculating the taxes (see section on Social Security Contributions).

National taxes are calculated at the following rates (2001):

- 6.25% of the taxable ordinary income (personal income plus positive capital income less deductions);
- an intermediate tax of 6% on personal income plus positive capital income if these two amounts exceed DKK 177,900;
- 15% on personal income, plus positive capital income, plus payments to a lump sum pension scheme with a deduction of DKK 276,900.

Example:

Personal income		350,000
Capital income		-30,000
Deductions		-20,000
Taxable income		300,000
Labour Market Contribution ('AM-bidrag'), 9% of	350,000	31,500
Local taxes:		
Taxable income	300,000	
'AM-bidrag'	-31,500	
31.0% hereof	268,500	83,235
National taxes:		
Personal income	350,000	
Capital income (if positive)	0	
Deductions	-20,000	
'AM-bidrag'	-31,500	
6.25% hereof	298,500	18,656
Personal income	350,000	
Capital income (if positive)	0	
'AM-bidrag'	-31,500	
Basic allowance	-177,900	
6.0% hereof	140,600	8,436
Personal income	350,000	
Capital income (if positive)	0	
'AM-bidrag'	-31,500	
Basic allowance	-276,900	
15.0% hereof	41,600	6,240
Tax value of personal allowance, 37.25%	33,400	-12,441
Total taxes and 'AM-bidrag'		135,626

Reduction for tax ceiling

The sum of tax rates cannot exceed 59%. In the above example, the total rate of taxation amounts to 31.0% + 6.25% + 6% + 15% = 58.25%.

Reductions in the upper tax rates only occur in the municipalities in which the local tax rate exceeds 31.75%. The rate of 31.0% is an average local tax rate. The reduction is given in the basis used when computing the 15% tax.

Withholding taxes

Withholding taxes are withheld on royalties paid to non-residents.

Tax credits

When calculating taxes, credit will always be given for taxes paid in other countries on income also taxed in Denmark. The tax credit can never exceed that part of the Danish taxes, which can be attributed to the foreign income. This of course only applies where a double taxation treaty does not apply another method.

Payment of tax

Before each tax period an advance income assessment is made for all taxpayers. Using the estimated taxable income an advance tax will be calculated. This can be paid in three different ways:

- deductions from employment income;
- prepayments;
- withholding tax on dividends.

Payroll deductions

Deductions from employment income are always calculated based on the expected taxable income, by giving a deduction and applying the relevant percentage to the amount so calculated. Thus, variations in employment income will automatically cause an adjustment to the tax withheld.

Prepayments

Prepayments are made in 10 equal instalments and are only necessary if the employment income is not sufficient to allow the deduction of the total amount of advance tax.

Estate and gift taxes

The transfer of assets by inheritance on death is subject to estate tax if the deceased was a Danish resident. Transfers of assets by lifetime gifts are subject to gift tax if the donor or the beneficiary is a Danish resident. However, tax will always be assessed on the inheritance or gift of real property located in Denmark, regardless of the residence of the deceased or the donor.

Estate tax is a flat-rate 15% of the value of the estate exceeding DKK 210,600.

If one or more of the beneficiaries are not closely related to the deceased, an additional estate tax of 25% must be paid on the part of the estate that is passed on to such beneficiaries. The estate tax of 15% is deducted from the value of the estate before the surtax of 25% is calculated, i.e. the estate tax for beneficiaries other than close relatives is 36.25%.

Gift taxes previously paid are not credited against the estate tax.

Spouses do not pay estate tax.

Lifetime gifts to close relatives are subject to a flat-rate gift tax if the gift within one year exceeds DKK 46,800 per donee.

Gifts to a donor's children, grandchildren, parents, or sons and daughters-in-law are subject to a 15% gift tax. The latter can only receive a yearly gift of DKK 16,400 tax-exempt. Gifts to grandparents will be subject to a 36.25% gift tax.

Transfers between husband and wife are exempt.

Gifts to persons not mentioned above will, as a rule, be liable to income tax.

Wealth tax

Denmark has no wealth tax, effective from 1997.

Social security

Social security is mainly financed through income taxes and sales taxes. Employees contribute an insignificant amount of less than DKK 100 to the Supplementary Pension Scheme every month.

The 'AM-bidrag' is intended to finance education, sickness benefits, unemployment benefit etc., and is levied at a rate of 9% (8%, plus a special pension payment of 1%) on personal income before any deductions. The 'AM-bidrag' can be deducted from income before calculating any income taxes.

Other taxes

Partnerships

Profits generated by a partnership are allocated to the partners according to their profit shares and taxed in the partners' hands. Certain types of limited partnerships may be taxed as companies.

VAT and sales taxes

VAT is levied on all goods and services at 25%, excluding sales of real property, personal transport, education, and cultural activities.

Generally, the tax is calculated quarterly as the difference between the tax charged and the tax paid, but companies dealing in the export of goods and services may receive a reimbursement of VAT on exports on a monthly or weekly basis and export companies may receive the reimbursement in advance. This rapid reimbursement system, which is optional, means that companies must have two VAT registration numbers, the second relating to exports only.

Act on duties on the wage bill

Companies supplying zero-rated services, such as banks, insurance companies, other commercial institutions, doctors, dentists, education, travel agencies, etc., are covered by the Act on Duties on the Wage Bill if they employ paid labour.

This duty is calculated on the basis of the company's wage bill total plus profit, less deficit (profit or deficit originating from foreign activities are disregarded). The wage bill duty is 2.5%.

For commercial companies the duty basis is computed on the wage bill base, plus 90%. The wage bill duty is 4.5%.

Real estate tax

An annual tax is levied on the value of real property at rates from 1.6–3.4%.

Other duties

Customs duties are levied on goods imported from countries outside the EU at varying rates. Excise duties are levied at very high rates on tobacco, wine, beer, motor vehicles, etc.

Exchange control

There are no restrictions with regard to the transfer of money between Denmark and foreign countries and a permit is not needed in relation to the transfer of money into or out of Denmark, no matter which currency is used.

In principal, such transfers must, however, be effected by a currency broker, i.e. a bank, and transfers of more than DKK 60,000 must be reported to the Danish National Bank. Residents must also advise the tax authorities of any account or deposit being opened with foreign banks or financial institutions.

Foreigners taking up residence in Denmark must report such accounts and deposits to the tax authorities within three months of arrival.

Double tax relief

Resident companies may claim a credit for foreign income taxes paid, restricted to the lesser of the foreign tax or the part of the Danish tax on foreign income.

Tax treaties and withholding taxes

Dividends from foreign subsidiaries are tax-exempt as mentioned above, as long as the Danish company owns at least 25% of the share capital during a period of one year.

Withholding taxes

According to the tax treaties the following withholding tax rates apply in respect of dividends paid to foreign residents. As a result of the Danish participation exemption ruling, no withholding tax should be levied on distributions made to a parent company resident in an EU member state, as long as it has owned a considerable interest (i.e. 25% or more) in the subsidiary for at least one year. For further information see above.

Country of residence	*Normal (standard) dividends (%)*	*Participation dividends (%)*	*Minimum participation requirements (%)*
Non-treaty countries	25	25	25
Selected treaty countries:			
Australia	15	15	n/a
Austria	10	0	25
Belgium	15	0	25
Brazil	25	25	n/a
Canada	15	5	50
Cyprus	15	10	25
Finland	15	0	25
France	0	0	n/a
Germany	15	0	25
Hungary	15	5	25
Indonesia	20	10	25
India	25	15	25
Ireland	15	0	n/a
Italy	15	0	25
Japan	15	10	25
Korea	15	15	n/a
Luxembourg	15	0	25
Malta	15	5	25
Netherlands	15	0	25
New Zealand	15	15	n/a
Norway	15	0	25
Pakistan	15	15	n/a
Portugal	15	0	25
Singapore	10	5	25
Spain	15	0	25
Sweden	15	0	25
Switzerland	25	0	25
United Kingdom	15	0	25
United States	15	5	95

Egypt

Abou Saada & Partners

Introduction

The income tax system in Egypt is regulated by the New Tax Law, No. 187 for the year 1993 (enacted from 1 January 1994 under the unified tax on income of natural persons), as well as by corporate income tax, customs duty, sales tax, stamp duties and tax on real estates.

Major developments

A new Investment Guarantees and Incentives Law, No. 8 for 1997:

- consolidates tax incentives; and
- sets out activities supported by the government (see later) – especially outside the Nile Valley.

Corporate taxes

Taxes on income and corporations

Rates

The rate of tax on annual net profits is 42%, except for oil exploration and producing companies for which the rate is 42.55%, and except for industrial and export activities for which the rate is 34%. In all cases, profits less than EGP 18,000 p.a. are subject to a 2% exemption. Several activities are tax exempt.

Capital gains taxes

Capital gains are treated as part of ordinary business income and are taxed accordingly. Asset replacement may, under certain conditions, attract tax exemption.

Branch profit taxes

Branches of foreign corporations and entities operating in Egypt are taxed at 42% on their annual net profits earned in Egypt, except for oil exploration and production companies which are taxed at 42.55%.

Foreign tax relief

Branches of foreign banks and corporations and other entities operating in Egypt are liable for corporate tax only on the profits arising from activities in Egypt. Consequently, relief for foreign taxes is not relevant. However, entities with a permanent establishment are subject to corporate tax at 42% on net profits. Interest earned outside Egypt, net of foreign taxes, are subject to the 34% rate (see 'Tax on Movable Funds').

Companies resident in countries with double taxation agreements with Egypt are treated in accordance with the provisions of those agreements.

Payment of taxes

Corporate tax based on audited financial statements must be paid within one month of the shareholders' annual meeting approving the accounts or within a month of the date in the company's articles (on which the annual meeting must approve the accounts). Branches of foreign companies must submit their tax returns within six months of their financial year end date. The payment of tax must be accompanied by:

- an audited tax declaration;
- a copy of the audited financial statements and several other schedules; and
- an extract of the resolution at the annual meeting, approving the profit distributions.

In addition, any board of directors' resolution relating to profit distribution must be sent to the Tax Authority (ETA) within one month of the board meeting.

Other matters

Workers' participation in profits

10% of the distributed profits of branches or foreign companies operating in Egypt (and of the distributed profits of Egyptian corporations) must be set aside for distribution to labour working for them.

Tax cards

Every entity operating in Egypt must have a tax card issued by the Tax Authority as evidence of having a tax file and must keep proper books of account as specified by law. Entities operating in Egypt may only deal with other entities in possession of a tax card, which states that tax returns have been filed annually, and report to the ETA on a quarterly basis all payments and contracts entered into with individuals and companies.

Tax authority

Any business operating in Egypt must advise the ETA of any payments made to any contractor or supplier of goods or services and of any contracts entered into with any of the above; they must withhold the following percentages from all payments over EGP 10.00 and pay the tax deducted quarterly to the ETA for the account of such a person (these rates are subject to change):

Contracting and supplying	1%
Services	3%
Commissions (with certain exceptions)	10%
Professional fees over EGP 500	15%
Professional fees under EGP 500	10%

Corporate entities, branches of foreign corporations and several other named enterprises that lease property or sell goods for the purpose of trading or manufacturing, must add a percentage ranging from 1%-5% to the amounts collected on account of the payee's tax liability.

Every entity starting or terminating operations in Egypt must advise the ETA accordingly within one month of the start or termination of its activities.

Personal taxes

Rates

Income tax is first levied on the various sources of individual income as follows:

Tax on moveable funds

This tax is usually withheld at source, at the rate of 32%. Otherwise, it is due within 15 days of receipt of income. The tax is levied on:

- interest payments;
- most income received by Egyptians or non-Egyptians normally resident in Egypt, from sources outside Egypt, net of foreign taxes;
- interest payments to non-residents;
- all amounts paid and benefits given to non-executive members of corporate boards;
- remuneration and allowances over EGP 5,000 per annum paid, and benefits given, to executive members of corporate boards for executive duties that are in excess of amounts paid to other non executive members (the first EGP 5,000 is subject to the tax on salaries; see below); and
- representation allowances paid to chairmen and executive members of corporate boards in excess of EGP 3,000 per annum In addition, payments in excess of EGP 18,000 per annum to chairmen (and all members of corporate boards that are subject to tax on moveable funds) will be subject to a 2% levy to support the financial resources of the state.

Tax on salaries

This tax is withheld at source from payments to those working in Egypt for less than six months in any calendar year, and for foreigners working less than six months. Payments include salaries, overtime, bonuses, fringe benefits, and allowances and all other payments and benefits. This tax is also levied on the first EGP 5,000 of amounts paid to executive directors of corporations for executive directors who own more than a nominal share in the equity of the corporation (only four named persons can be subject to this tax for amounts over EGP 5,000, see Tax on Moveable Funds above). The tax rate of 20% is on the first EGP 50,000 earned per annum and 32% on amounts over EGP 50,000, after deducting the allowances.

The following annual allowances are usually granted.

- Family allowances:
  - single person — EGP 2,000
  - married persons without children, or widower with children — EGP 2,500
  - married persons with children — EGP 3,000
- Social security contributions.
- Punitive and unpaid sick leave deductions.

- Life insurance and pension fund premiums not exceeding EGP 1,000 or 15% on income (whichever is less).
- Hardship allowance. EGP 480
- Representation allowance. EGP 2,500
- Productivity allowance. EGP 3,000
- Amounts paid to the representatives of regional offices of foreign companies and establishments in Egypt are taxed only on the portion of their income attributable to their activities in Egypt.
- Accommodation allowances for foreign experts, provided their employment in Egypt is for a period of more than six months.
- 10% of total income (after certain allowances) as an allowance for earning the income.
- Additional allowance. EGP 2,000

Unified annual tax

Tax is assessed annually on the total income from all sources in the tax return (excluding income from moveable funds and salaries, which is taxed separately). The tax rates used for the unified annual tax assessment are as follows:

Taxable income

Over EGP	*Under EGP*	*Tax on lower amount*	*Percentage on excess*
0	2,500	0	20%
2,500	7,000	500	27%
7,000	16,000	1,715	35%
16,000	–	–	40%

The family allowances noted for the tax on salaries are deductible if not claimed elsewhere. Individuals subject to this tax must file a wealth declaration with the EYA at the beginning of the activity and every five years thereafter. In addition, a 2% levy to support the financial resources of the state is levied on income in excess of EGP 18,000 per annum.

Tax on income from non-commercial professions

This tax applies to net revenues from non-commercial professions as practised independently by the taxpayer, whether the profits result from exercising the profession or activity in Egypt or abroad, provided that the Head Office (or permanent centre for the taxpayer's exercise of the profession) is in Egypt.

Allowable expenses include: social insurance payments, 15% of net profit for professional consumption, life insurance premiums to the extent of the lesser of EGP 1,000 or 15% of net profit, and certain donations.

Losses may be carried forward for five years. Certain allowances are deductible if not claimed elsewhere. Tax returns must be filed by 31 March each year when the tax payment is due. Amounts paid to non-resident foreign professionals are subject to a flat rate of tax at 20%. Such amounts are not subject to any other tax.

Tax on commercial and industrial profits

This tax is levied on commissions, the letting of commercial and furnished premises, selling assets, buildings, or dealing in real estate, exploitation of natural resources, poultry farms, animal husbandry and land reclamation. Only 80% of profits in excess of EGP 80,000 arising from industrial activities are taxed; similarly, only 70% of export activities are taxed. The tax is on annual net profits after deducting expenses. The family allowances noted for tax on salaries are deductible if not claimed elsewhere.

Local income taxes

Capital gains taxes

An individual's capital gains are added to income and taxed accordingly, except for the first sale of real estate or building sites within the boundaries of Egyptian cities. These are subject to a tax flat rate of 2.5% of the total value. At present, individuals are taxed only on income and not subjected to a wealth tax on the value of their assets.

Capital gains are exempt on profits of re-evaluation of assets owned by individual or partnerships if given as shares in kind on incorporating joint stock entities.

Foreign tax reliefs

Dividends and interest received from abroad by Egyptian residents, net of foreign taxes paid, are subject to the tax on moveable funds at 32%. Citizens from countries having double tax agreements with Egypt are treated in accordance with the provisions of these agreements. In general, these agreements provide that individuals resident in Egypt for less than six months in any year are taxed in their country of origin and not in Egypt (albeit under certain conditions).

Tax period

The fiscal year for individuals is the calendar year.

Other matters

Sole traders and partnerships are taxed according to the type of income. Each partner is separately taxed.

Income taxed on non-residents

Liability to tax

Non-residents are taxed only on income earned in Egypt.

Rules

The tax rates vary with the type of income and are withheld at source.

- A tax rate of 20% for the first EGP 50,000 earned per annum and 32% on amounts over EGP 50,000 (neither subjected to any relief) are levied on amounts (including rent) paid to foreign experts, provided that their total duration in Egypt does not exceed six months.
- A flat rate of 20% (not subjected to any relief) is withheld at source from amounts paid to foreign non-residents carrying out professional work in Egypt.
- 32% is applied on the gross amount of royalties; however, royalties paid to residents of countries which Egypt has a double taxation treaty usually are subjected to tax at 15%.
- Dividends are not subject to withholding tax because they are paid out of profits that have already been taxed or are exempt.
- Interest payments are subject to 32% tax on moveable funds (see item nine).

Tax treaties

Egypt has double taxation agreements, which include the following countries:

Algeria	Finland	Lebanon	Romania	Tunisia
Austria	France	Libya	Saudi Arabia	United Kingdom
Belgium	Germany	Japan	Slovakia	United States
Canada	Greece	Jordan	Sudan	Yugoslavia
Czech	India	Kuwait	Sweden	
Denmark	Italy	Morocco	Switzerland	
Ethiopia	Iraq	Norway	Syria	

Other taxes

Directors' remuneration

The remuneration of directors is subject to the 32% tax on moveable funds. In addition, payments in excess of EGP 18,000 per annum to chairmen and members of corporate boards, who are subject to the tax on moveable funds, are subject to a 2% levy to support the financial resources of the states.

Other significant taxes

Sales (value added tax) – SVAT

The SVAT applies to all non-exempt domestic and imported goods and services and is due upon the sale of goods or the rendering of services. Imported goods are subject to tax when released from customs. The following are exempt from SVAT:

- goods brought in by diplomatic missionaries (except food, alcohol and tobacco);
- local dairy products;
- bread, pasta and milled products (except imported fine flour);
- meat and fish (except caviar and smoked salmon);
- domestic fruits and vegetables;
- offal and food industry waste used for animal feed;
- papers, books and magazines;
- clothing distributed by the Supply and Home Trade Ministry; and
- natural gas, butane and petrol.

Goods and services exported outside Egypt, as well as goods and services imported/ exported within the free zone area in Egypt, will not be subjected to tax. In addition, goods in transit through Egypt are also exempt from SVAT.

Computation of tax

Tax is computed by reference to the value of the commodity. In the case of domestically produced goods, the value of the product for tax purposes is taken at its selling price in the open market under normal circumstances. In the case of imported goods, the value is calculated as that applicable for customs duty purposes plus customs duty. The tax rate for all goods and services is 10%, however, some listed goods and services have different tax rates such as cars, TV sets, home appliances and some tourist services and food products.

Taxes on payroll (social security)

Monthly combined social insurance contributions up to EGP 1,000 are paid to a central organisation. These contributions cover medical care, old age, industrial accidents and unemployment. The first EGP 500 of the basic wage are subject to a 40% contribution, of which 14% is borne by the employee and 26% by the employer. The second EGP 500 of any other remuneration is subject to 35% contribution of which 11% is borne by the employee and 24% by the employer.

Taxes on natural resources

Net profits from the exploitation of natural resources are taxed at 42%, except oil exploration and production companies, which are taxed at 42.55%. In addition, government concession fees and levies are payable.

Stamp duty

Stamp duty is charges on payments from government agencies at 2.4%, and on contracts, bank loans, documents, receipts, checks, certificates, bank accounts, salaries and advertisements at rates ranging from 0.08% – 35%.

Capital gains

Capital gains are treated as ordinary business profits and are taxed accordingly. In some cases, where assets are replaced, the tax paid on profits realised from the sale of the asset may be recovered within three years.

Depreciation and depletion

Depreciation is computed on the straight-line method, and the rates are negotiated with the ETA. The rates are based on the type of asset and the number of hours worked. The following rates are common:

Buildings	2% – 5%
Furniture and fixtures	6% – 15%
Plant and machinery	10% – 15%
Office and account machines	12.5% – 20%
Motor vehicles	20% – 25%

The above allowances are for tax purposes only and replace the depreciation provided in the accounts.

Treatment of dividends

There is no withholding tax. Dividends are either paid out of corporate profits, which are taxed at 42% or 34%, or out of exempt profits. 90% of local dividends received by corporate entities are deducted from their taxable profits (100% of dividends are deducted if received by a corporation from a corporate entity in which it has participated in its equity on formation). Dividends received abroad are subject to the tax on movable funds at 32%, after allowing for foreign taxes as a deduction from income.

Loss carry-over

Corporate losses may be carried forward for a maximum of five years. Individuals may also carry forward losses for five years, provided they are not offset against profits from other sources.

Transactions between related parties

Revenue transactions are treated as ordinary transactions, except that transactions between spouses, father and mother and underage children, are ignored for tax purposes.

Consolidation of income

Specific taxes are levied on each source of income as far as individuals are concerned. Related corporations may not file consolidated tax returns.

Other matters

In addition to normal expenses, the following may be allowable for tax purposes:

- amounts in lieu of rent on property;
- amortisation of assets subject to depletion;
- taxes paid other than the unified tax and/or corporate tax;
- all donations up to 7% of the annual net profit;
- doubtful debts provision limited to 5% of the annual taxable net profit; and

- amounts set aside for employee pension funds not exceeding 20% of total payroll.

The tax law also provides the following tax exemptions and benefits for corporations:

- workers' participation in profits;
- all amounts paid to members of a corporate board;
- allowance of attendance paid to the shareholders on the occasion of holding the general assemblies; and
- an amount to the central bank's declared interest rate, calculated on the paid-up capital of listed private or public corporations (under certain conditions).

Incentives and grants

Profits arising from the following activities with certain conditions are exempt from tax for five years, if set up in development areas or financed by the Social Fund for ten years, and for twenty years if set up or moved out of the Nile Valley.

- Land reclamation and cultivation.
- Mining and industry (excluding tobacco and alcoholic beverages).
- Animal, poultry and fish production.
- Tourist services.
- Industrial and agricultural land food stores and haulage.
- Air transport.
- Oil and energy exploration.
- Residential housing and leasing.
- Infrastructural activities.
- Medical and clinical centres.
- Financial leasing.
- Underwriting.
- Venture capital.
- Information technology.
- Projects financed by the Social Fund for Development.
- Maritime transport.

The above activities also attract fringe exemptions, including stamp duties and reduced customs on machinery, and (in some cases) land from the government free of charge.

Profits arising from the following are also exempt from tax:

- interest received from local banks;
- 90% of profits and dividends received from investments, agricultural land and real estate;
- profits arising from corporate mergers, reorganisations and divestitures;
- profits or dividends received by a corporation from a corporate entity in which it has participated in its equity formation;
- dividends paid by an investment company that derives income from shares and debentures;
- free zone companies under Law 8 for 1997 are exempt from corporate tax;
- American entities operating in Egypt and financed by the USAID; and
- certain government agencies.

Exchange controls

Any individuals or corporations may freely operate a bank account in foreign currencies. Dealing in foreign bank notes is not allowed.

France

Auditeurs & Conseils Associés

Corporate taxes

Taxable entities

Resident companies

Resident companies are liable for corporate income tax on profits derived from France (including capital gains) and on other profits subject to double taxation treaty provisions. Companies are resident if they are incorporated in France.

Non-resident companies

Non-resident companies, concerning the business carried out in France, namely through their permanent establishment, are liable for corporate income tax in the same way as resident companies.

In addition, net profits earned by the French branches of foreign companies are subject to a 25% withholding tax ('branch tax'), whether or not the profits are repatriated, which can be reduced or eliminated by tax treaties where certain conditions are fulfilled.

Furthermore, this withholding tax is not applied in a case where the head office of the French branch is located in a country of the European Union, which is subject to corporate income tax in that country.

As a consequence, the branch of a foreign company can sometimes be taxed more heavily than a subsidiary.

Taxes imposed

Most French taxes are levied by the State under a single unified system which is codified in the General Tax Code (*'Code General des Impôts'*).

Companies may choose their fiscal year which is not necessarily the calendar year. It is the regular period provided for in the company's articles' by-laws. A tax return must be filed three months after the period ends. However, if the company ends its financial year on 31 December, the time limit in order to file the tax return is, in principle, postponed until 30 April.

The corporate income tax is paid in instalments.

Indeed, four instalments based on the preceding year's profits must be paid during the year, the balance being paid or reimbursed at the time when the tax return is filed.

For instance, if a company ends its financial year on 31 December, the instalments must be paid as follows:

1st instalment:	15 March (with minimum corporate income tax, i.e. IFA);
2nd instalment:	15 June;
3rd instalment:	15 September;
4th instalment:	15 December;
Liquidation balance:	15 April of the following year.

Rates of tax

On operating profits:-

	2000	*2001*	*2002*
Common rate	33 1/3%	33 1/3%	33 1/3%
Additional contributions	10%	6%	3%
Total Rate	36 2/3%	35 2/3%	34 2/3%

On long term capital gains:-

	2000	*2001*	*2002*
Common rate	19%	19%	19%
Additional contributions	10%	6%	3%
Total Rate	20.9%	20.14%	19.6%

An additional social contribution (CSB: *'Contribution Sociale sur les Bénéfices'*) of 3 1/3% computed on the corporate income tax of 33.3% (and on the long term capital gains taxed at 19%) is due when the turnover exceeds MFF 50. However, there is an allowance of MFF 5. Thus, this additional tax is applied only if the taxable result exceeds MFF 15.

Those companies owned by more than 75% of individuals, and with a turnover of less than FF 50 million, will apply a corporate income tax rate of:

- 25% in 2001; and
- 5% in 2002

on the first FF 250,000 of taxable income (instead of the standard $33^1/_3\%$).

Furthermore, the French tax code provides a minimum corporate income tax (IFA) due even if the taxable income of the company is a loss.

The minimum corporate income tax can be offset against the corporate income tax of the two following years. The amount of the minimum corporate income tax from FF 5,000 to FF 250,000 depends on the turnover of the company. There is no minimum corporate income tax if the turnover is less than FF 500,000.

Income subject to tax

General rules

For tax purposes, income is calculated in accordance with French (generally) accepted accounting principles and adjusted according to specific tax rules.

Income in France is determined on the basis of the engagement rules, i.e. income must be taken into account when its subject is realised even if the company has not yet received payment.

There are specific rules concerning some kinds of incomes, namely capital gains and dividends, which can be deducted from the accounting result to be taxed under specific regimes.

Capital gains and losses

A distinction is made between short and long term capital gains and losses. A short term capital gain is subject to corporate income tax at the common rate.

A net long term capital gain, i.e. the gain after offsetting the long term capital losses, is subject to a reduced rate of 19% (plus additional contributions).

Beginning with fiscal years commencing on 1 January 1997, the special regime of long term capital gains and losses concerned only royalties on licences and software and so on (except royalties on trademarks) and on sales of shares under certain conditions. Indeed, the shares must correspond to a shareholding in a company which has been held for at least two years (it is the case when the percentage of shareholding exceeds 5% of the capital shares).

If a company opts for the long term regime, the company must allocate 81% of the capital gains to the special reserve of long term capital gains. In case of distribution of this reserve, a complementary corporate income tax would be due in order to tax the capital gain with the normal rate.

When long term losses exceed long term gains, the excess can be carried forward for ten years and offset against future long term gains.

Ordinary tax losses can also be offset against long term capital gains.

Dividends

In principle, dividends are included in taxable income except if the company opts for the parent-subsidiary tax regime. The special parent-subsidiary tax regime can be applied when the shareholding of the parent company exceeds 5% of the share capital and this company keeps its shareholding over two years or makes a relevant commitment.

In this framework, dividends received by holding companies are exempt from taxation except for 5% of their gross value (including *'avoir fiscal'* for French companies and tax credit for foreign companies according to international conventions).

In addition, in the case of distribution of these amounts by a holding company, the *avoir fiscal* and tax credit can be offset against equalisation tax (*précompte*) if any. The terms *avoir fiscal* and *précompte* are specific to French law and local advice is recommended.

Foreign dividends

As a rule, dividends received from abroad by a French company are taxed in France at the normal rate of corporate income tax, except in the case of a special parent-subsidiary tax regime. No tax credit is granted for taxes paid abroad unless different rules are provided in tax treaties.

Distributions of foreign dividends by a French company or a French holding company to its individual shareholders are subject to French income tax with *avoir fiscal* (for French residents) or to a withholding tax of 25% of the gross amount (for foreign residents). This rate may be reduced or cancelled in tax treaties. In addition, the equalisation tax (*précompte*) may be due.

Equalisation tax

The equalisation tax at the rate of 33⅓% is due in the case of the distribution of:

- untaxed results at the common rate (33⅓% plus special contributions); and
- results taxed more than five years earlier.

The tax credit and *avoir fiscal* can be offset against the equalisation tax.

Inventory rules

Inventories must be valued at the cost of goods sold or at the current market value on the closing date of the tax year, whichever is lower. Costs can be determined using the average cost or FIFO method (LIFO is not generally accepted) and should include buying expenses. For the purpose of valuing the work in progress of finished goods, costs should include both direct and indirect manufacturing costs. Where the selling price is less than the cost, a provision may be recorded.

A special provision for the increase in the value of inventory (*'provision pour hausse des prix'*) may be recorded when, at the end of a fiscal year, the cost of an item of inventory has increased by more than 10% compared with the cost of a similar item at the end of one of the two preceding fiscal years. This provision must be added back to taxable profits within six years.

Deductions

General rules

Expenses are generally deductible provided they are incurred for the benefit and in the normal course of business. They must be adequately supported and their amounts reasonable.

However, some overly luxurious expenses are not deductible for tax purposes.

Depreciation and amortisation

Wasting fixed assets are depreciated over their useful lives as follows:

	Years
Industrial buildings	20
Commercial and residential buildings	20-50
Fixtures and fittings	10
Machinery and equipment	5-10
Vehicles	4-5
Software	1

Depreciation is usually calculated using the straight-line method. The reducing balance depreciation method can only be used where the asset is new and is of a type specified in a list of assets published by the fiscal authorities.

No depreciation is allowed on land, trademarks or goodwill. However, if the realisable value falls below the book value, a deductible reserve may be set up.

Start-up expenses must be written off as soon as possible. This will normally be in the first year in which there are profits sufficient to absorb them and may not be later than five years from the year in which they were incurred.

For depreciation to be deductible in full, the accounts must show a charge at least to normal straight line depreciation. Failure to show such a charge leads to a permanent loss of relief.

Special depreciation allowances are available in certain cases as a matter of economic policy.

Some investment in water purification, pollution and noise control may be depreciated by 100% in the first fiscal year.

Software and energy saving equipment may be depreciated over a period of 12 months.

Royalties

Royalties are normally deductible under the same conditions as any other expense.

Interest

Interest payable is normally deductible unless paid to shareholders, in which case:

- it is not deductible if the capital is not fully paid up;

- it is deductible only up to an amount corresponding to a loan which does not exceed 150% of the company's nominal capital if the shareholders manage the company or own more than 50% of the capital stock; this restriction is not applicable to interest paid to a French parent company but does apply to interest paid to a foreign parent company (though non-discriminatory provisions in double taxation treaties may sometimes avoid this – in this case a tax claim is necessary); and
- the interest is limited to the average yearly rate applied by the bank establishment for loans over two years (6.03% for the fiscal year ended December 2000).

Bad and doubtful debts

Write-offs and provisions are deductible, provided they relate to the normal course of business and are duly documented.

Employees' and directors' remuneration and benefits

Employees' and directors' remuneration and benefits are deductible, provided their amount is reasonable and corresponds to the effective amount of work performed.

Main non-deductible expenses for tax purposes

The following expenses are not deductible for tax purposes:

- corporate income tax and penalties attached to this tax;
- fines;
- excessive depreciation on a private car;
- tax on company cars; and
- extravagant expenses.

In addition, there can be timing differences regarding the following expenses, i.e. they can be deducted only in the following year. Thus, the amount paid or reserved during the year must be added back to the tax result and the amount paid during the previous year is deducted from the tax result.

- Organic tax, a social security tax of 0.13 % of the turnover.
- Construction tax: 0.45 % of the gross salaries. This tax is due only if the company has more than 10 employees.
- Unrealised exchange gains and losses.
- Employee's participation in profits (a profit sharing plan).

Dividends

Dividends paid are not deductible.

Investment incentives and special benefits

Investment incentives are available according to French regional development policy.

They are mainly regional development grants, location grants for certain non-industrialised activities, research and development activities and decentralisation indemnity. Their amounts depend on the investment amount and the number of jobs created. These particular incomes are taxed according to particular rules currently on the same terms as that of the depreciation of the investments financed.

They are regulated by a public agency called DATAR which has offices in Paris, London, New York, Chicago, Tokyo, Madrid, Berne and Stockholm as well as in French Embassies (commercial offices).

Foreign source income

The foreign source income can be taken into account in the accounting and taxable results of the company. However, the foreign incomes are not, in principle, taxable in France. Thus, if there is a tax treaty signed between France and the country concerned, double taxation can be avoided by two methods: by exempting the income or by tax credit as provided by the tax treaty.

A tax credit granted is generally equal to the amount of taxes actually paid abroad.

Related party transactions

Transactions between related parties must be on an arm's length basis. Otherwise, the tax authorities can reassess the taxable result.

In case of a tax audit, French companies must provide all elements regarding the transfer pricing policy of the group within 60 days.

To receive the information in case of difficulty, the French tax authorities may use the international tax administrative assistance, if any, or may themselves compute the French tax result of the company.

Losses

A loss incurred during a given fiscal year may be carried forward for five years. After this period the loss cannot be offset against profits. However, deferred tax depreciation losses can be carried forward indefinitely except in case of a transfer of activity. In this case, deferred tax depreciation losses retroactively become ordinary tax losses.

In addition, any carry-forward of losses (ordinary tax and deferred tax depreciation losses) are lost if a company changes its principal activities. In the case of a merger, the losses of the target company (i.e. the absorbed company) are also lost. However, the Financial Ministry can grant an agreement in order to allow the absorbing company to use the target's losses.

A loss incurred in a fiscal year can be carried back under certain conditions against the undistributed profits of the preceding three fiscal years. However, any tax refund arising can only be reimbursed five years after the loss arose, or treated as a payment of tax due in the intervening five year period. This receivable of carry-back can be used to request a loan as a warranty for French banks.

Corporate tax group

In France, under certain conditions, a group of companies can opt for the consolidated tax regime. In this case, the parent company pays the corporate income tax on the taxable income of the group to the French tax authorities.

All the companies in the group must opt for this regime before the end of the previous financial year for which the tax regime will be applied. The option must be made on the basis of the draft provided by the tax authorities and the following conditions must be fulfilled:

- the parent company must hold directly or indirectly at least 95% of the capital shares of its subsidiary;
- the parent company must not be held over 95%, if there is a further parent company subject to French corporate income tax; and
- each company in the group must have the same dates of the opening and closing tax year of 12 months.

In the case of a consolidated tax group, all the taxable income and losses of companies in the group are added in order to determine the taxable income of the group. In addition, the taxable income of the group must be adjusted, namely in case of intra-group transactions.

The option covers five years and can be renewed.

However, if a company leaves the tax group, its losses created during the tax-consolidated period are lost since they are transferred to the parent company in the year of their creation.

Personal taxes

Taxable individuals

Residents

An individual, whether a French or foreign national, who has his *'tax residence'* in France is subject to tax on the whole of his income from whatever source. However, the tax treaty can consider what kind of income must only be taxed in another country.

An individual is a French tax resident according to the French tax code in the following situation:

- if he has his permanent home or principal place of sejour in France (namely if he stays in France for more than 183 days per calendar year);
- if he carries out an occupation or employment in France, except where this is incidental to a foreign activity; or
- if the centre of his economic interests is in France.

The tax treaty uses in principle the same criteria in order to determine the country in which the tax residence is located, i.e. the country of permanent residence, the country in which the individual has his interest (personal and economic), the country in which he usually lives (principal place of sejour).

Non-residents

An individual who is not resident in France is subject to tax only on his income arising from France, unless excluded by tax treaty.

Taxes on income

In France, individual income tax is levied at the national level. Individuals also pay social security contributions.

Sources of income

Income tax is assessed on total income which is the sum of net income from each source on a worldwide basis for the French resident. Generally, losses can only be offset against income from the same source. When the year's income is insufficient to offset, losses can be carried forward over a period limited to five years.

Employment income and directors' fees

Wages and salaries include remuneration of employees as well as directors of corporations and the non-controlling directors of private limited liability companies.

Assessment is made on the total remuneration, including benefits in kind made available to the recipient during the calendar year, whether actually drawn or not. It does not include damages for breach of employment contract, payments in connection with training, reimbursement of expenses, social security payments or contributions to retirement funds and other social security schemes.

A lump sum salary deduction of 10% is allowed (minimum and maximum limits FF 2,350 and FF 78,950 respectively for 2000). A taxpayer can choose to deduct the true expenses instead of applying the lump sum of 10%.

Remuneration after deduction for expenses is subject to a further relief of 20%, which must not exceed FF 144,400 for 2000. Also, wages are taxed at 72% (with the lump sum of 10 %) of the net received.

A director with either a minority or majority holding benefits from the 10% and 20% relief described above.

Business income

Industrial and commercial profits include profits from industrial and commercial operations when carried out by an individual or a company not subject to corporate income tax.

Taxable income is based on the net profit of the taxpayer's business for the accounting period ended during the calendar year. The period end date can be freely chosen by the individual at the commencement of his business. Profits are computed on an accruals basis.

A special tax system known as the retrieval basis exists for the '*micro-enterprise*' (a very small company).

This system concerns individual companies with an annual turnover not exceeding the following limits:

- FF 175,000 for service suppliers;
- FF 500,000 for other companies.

For these two categories the amount of expenses is evaluated by the tax authorities on a lump sum basis, nevertheless, the common rate of taxation is applicable to the related profits.

A distinction is made between professional and commercial profit and non-professional industrial and commercial profit.

Losses incurred in a professional business may be offset against income from all sources

Losses incurred in the case of the non-professional activity may be offset only against income from the same source. When this income is lower than the losses in a given year, they may be carried forward for a five year maximum time limit.

Taxation of non-commercial profits ('benefices non commerciaux')

Non-commercial profits include income from a profession, from the holding of a non-commercial office and from other non-commercial activities.

Income from the licensing or sale of patents or know-how are taxable under this category, generally at a flat rate of 26% (in the case of a company, the rate is 19%). However, receipts arising from dealings in trademarks are taxable in the normal manner.

In general, non-commercial profits are computed on a cash basis but the taxpayer may elect to compute on an accrual basis.

Non-commercial profits are assessed either on a notional or an actual basis, the actual basis being compulsory where gross receipts exceed FF 175,000 per annum.

Payments in this category to persons not having a professional base in France are subject to a $33\frac{1}{3}$% withholding tax which can be reduced or suppressed by tax treaties.

Agricultural profits

Agricultural profits include all farming profits earned by owner farmers and tenant farmers and profits from forestry. These profits are assessed on an actual basis, or on a notional basis when annual receipts are not higher than FF 500,000. The actual basis determines net income in accordance with generally accepted accounting principles (the accrual basis) for a 12 month period.

Agricultural losses may be offset against other source income where the total of the other income is less than FF 350,000. Where the total of other income exceeds FF 350,000, agricultural losses may only be offset against agricultural profits over the subsequent five years.

Capital gains

Real property

If real property (real estate) is sold less than two years after acquisition, the capital gain is added to the other sources of income after a flat rebate of FF 6,000.

If the property is sold more than two years but less than 22 years after acquisition, the capital gain is computed by deducting the inflated acquisition cost from the selling price. The capital gain is then reduced by 5% per year held after two years.

Gains on property held for more than 22 years are exempt.

Non residents are subject to 33% withholding tax (or 50% for persons who deal in real property) on capital gains. The rate of 33% can be reduced or suppressed by tax treaty.

Movable assets

Capital gains on moveable assets (personal property) in the form of private or listed shares are exempt if the yearly total sale is less than FF 50,000 (for 2000). Capital gains are subject to income tax of 26% where the total sale proceeds of the year exceed the limit. Non-residents are not subject to this tax.

Capital gains taxation can be postponed in case of an exchange of shares, namely due to a merger or acquisition.

Furthermore, losses can only be offset against income from the same source, but may be carried forward over a period limited to five years.

Dividends

Dividends paid by a French company subject to corporate income tax to individuals domiciled in France, or to resident companies being able to benefit from the parent company regime, carry a tax credit (*avoir fiscal*) equal to 50% of the dividends. The rate of the tax credit can be limited to 25% in the other cases. The *avoir fiscal* is available to the shareholder as a tax credit against income tax due. Any excess is payable in cash to individuals.

An example for individuals domiciled in France is as follows:

	FF
Dividends received	100
Avoir fiscal	50
Taxable income	150
Theoretical tax at, say, 50%	75
Avoir fiscal	- 50
Tax effectively due	25

The *avoir fiscal* is also available to non-residents under some tax treaties.

French residents may deduct FF 16,000 for married couples and FF 8,000 for single individuals from the dividends of French companies and interest on bonds issued in France, if their taxable income does not exceed FF 299,200 for a single person and FF 598,400 for married people.

Interest

French residents can elect to be taxed on interest either by way of a final withholding tax of 25 % or by adding it to their other sources of income.

In the latter case, married couples may deduct FF 16,000 (FF 8,000 for individuals) from dividends and bond interest received if their taxable income does not exceed FF 299,200 for a single person and FF 598,400 for married people.

Income from immovable property unfurnished

This category includes rents received by transparent companies (partnerships) not subject to corporate income tax (i.e. non-commercial companies) and by individuals.

The net income is the rent actually received in the year plus the landlord's expenses borne by the tenant less the tenant's expenses borne by the landlord, less various landlord's expenses, such as repairs and maintenance expenses, the wages of a house porter and interest on money borrowed to finance the preservation, acquisition and construction of the property.

To determine the net taxable income, the net rent is reduced by 14%. This deduction covers depreciation and administration expenses.

Personal allowances and deductions

There are a few expenses which can be deducted from total income (including alimony and support payments to parents and children). A few of these expenses may invite a percentage reduction in tax or be subject to specific rules as follows:

- 25% for child care expenses (children under the age of 7) up to a limit of FF 15,000 per child;
- 50% for domestic employee expenses limited to FF 45,000 – thus the reduction is limited to FF 22,500;
- cost of shares in limited cases;
- some expenses on a rental building (directly or by the sale of a share); and
- some expenses on 'DOM-TOM' (overseas departments and territories) under specific conditions.

No special rules or relief is available to the citizens of foreign countries.

Special family rules

The head of a household is taxable on the aggregate of his and his spouse's income and the income of all dependant children. Any child (whether living with the taxpayer or not) constitutes a dependant unless married or over 18. An unmarried child over 18 years old may elect to continue to be treated as a dependant if under 21, or under 25 and a full-time student.

Married people cannot file French income tax returns separately except in particular cases.

The personal tax system is progressive but an individual's liability is adjusted in accordance with his family circumstances by application of the family quotient. The individual's income is split into a number of parts, which is determined as follows:

Single adults	1	part
Married couples	2	parts
Married couple with 1 child	2.5	parts
Married couple with 2 children	3	parts
Each additional child	1	part

The tax savings arising from each child is limited to FF 12,440 (for 2000 income) for each half part.

Rates of tax

Residents

The 2001 rates (assessing the 2000 income) are as follows:

Bands FF	*Rate (%)*	*Tax on Band FF*	*Cumulative*
0 – 26,600	0	0	0
26,600 – 52,320	8.25	2,122	2,122
52,320 – 92,090	21.75	8,650	10,772
92,090 – 149,110	31.75	18,104	28,876
149,110 – 242,620	41.75	39,040	67,916
242,620 – 299,200	47.25	26,734	94,650
Over 299,200	53.25		

Payment of tax

An individual who is subject to income tax must file a return before the end of February of each year in respect of his and his family's income during the preceding year.

Two-thirds of the preceding year's tax has to be paid; the first third before 15 February and the second third before 15 May. The balance is paid in September or October of the year following that in which the income was received. The taxpayer can elect to pay the advance payments in ten monthly instalments.

Social taxes

There are additional 'social' taxes which apply differentials depending on the nature of income, as well as a general contribution of 7.5% (CSG), a Social Debt Reimbursement (RDS) of 0.5% and a social contribution of 2% (*'prélèvement social'*) i.e. a total of 10%. These taxes are, namely, applied on financial income, real property and dividends and are payable in October of the year following that in which the income was received.

Estate and gift taxes

Taxes are the same for both estates and gifts.

Heirs and legatees must declare the property belonging to the deceased within six months of death. Property which must be declared includes all property located in France and where the deceased is a French resident, or where the heir has been a French resident for more than six years, worldwide property must also be declared.

An allowance of FF 300,000 is calculated on each part belonging to the deceased's children, with an allowance of FF 400,000 for the surviving spouse.

Duties on each taxable part of the gift or estate are as follows:

- between husband and wife, and between grandparents, parents and children, the rates vary from 5% to 40% according to the taxable basis (the schedule is progressive);
- between other parties the rates vary from 35 % to 60%; and
- certain estate and gift tax treaties are in force for the avoidance of international double taxation.

Wealth tax

Wealth tax was restored in 1989.

This tax is assessed on worldwide property for residents and on properties located in France or non-residents.

The tax schedule has the following banded rates:

Basis of taxation FF	€	*2001 Rate (%)*
Below 4,700,000	720,000 €	0.00
4,700,001 – 7,640,000	720,000/1,160 000 €	0.55
7,640,001 – 15,160,000	1,160 000/2,300 000 €	0.75
15,160,001 – 23,540,000	2,300 000/3,600 000 €	1.00
23,540,001 – 45,580,000	3,600 000/6,900 000 €	1.30
45,580,001 – 100,000,000	6,900 000/15,000 000 €	1.65
Over 100,000,000	Over 15,000 000 €	1.80

This wealth tax is payable by 15 June of each year on the value of the assets at the 1 January of the year.

Social security contributions

Whatever their nationality, all persons working in France are, in principle, subject to social security payments.

However, nationals of EC states seconded to France for a maximum of 12 months may, in principle, be exempt.

The rates of social security contributions that cover widowhood, sickness, old age pensions, family allowances and unemployment apply to all employees and are as follows:

Assessing basis FF	*Employers %*	*Employees %*	*Total*
Part of the wage up to 179,400	32.96	18.30	51.26
Part of the wage up to 717,600	24.89	12.34	37.23
Part of the wage up to 1,435,200	19.80	8.85	28.65

The rates for retirement benefits depend on employment status, as follows:

'Cadres' FF (top and middle management)	*Employers %*	*Employees %*	*Total %*
Part of the wage up to 179,400	4.50	3.00	7.50
Part of the wage up to 717,600	12.50	7.50	20.00
Part of the wage up to 1,435,200	12.50	7.50	20.00
Total of wage	0.22	0.13	0.35

'Non cadres' (employees)	*Employers %*	*Employees %*	*Total %*
Part of the wage up to 520,920	4.50	3.00	7.50
Part of the wage between 179,400 and 538,200	12.50	5.00	12.50

There is no minimum or maximum contribution. The above schedule includes payroll taxes and therefore reflects the total charges on salaries except for banks, insurance companies and other companies not fully subject to VAT which are subject to an additional payroll tax (*'taxes sur les salaires'*).

Other taxes

VAT and sales taxes

Value added tax (VAT) is a general tax on consumption charged on all goods and services consumed or used in France whether of French or foreign origin. Exports are not taxed and the tax on the cost of production is reimbursable.

The principal rates of VAT are as follows:

- 2.1% on press and medicines (which are reimbursable by the Social Security);
- 5.5% on water, food, agricultural products, passenger fares, hotels, books and other medicines; and
- 19.6% on everything else since 1 April 2000.

Property tax

This local tax is charged on all the buildings of an owner. Tax is assessed on the rental value of the premises.

Habitation tax

This tax must be paid by the persons who occupy a dwelling on 1 January. Tax is assessed on the rental value of the premises.

Registration taxes on the transfer of business and real estate are as follows:

FF	*Rate (%)*
For a business	
Part of the price over FF 150,00	4.8%
For real estate	4.89% of the market value

Additionally, the transfer of a building may be subject to the VAT in the case of first time transfer (except the sale to an estate agent) and where the sale is realised within a time limit of five years after the completion date.

Withholding taxes

France withholds taxes mainly on royalties, dividends and non-commercial profits. Royalties include amounts paid to a non-resident for services rendered or utilised in France by a purchaser established in France. There is generally no withholding tax on interest (whether from negotiable bonds or other loans), even for non-treaty countries.

We must note that within the European Union, the withholding tax on dividends can be avoided if the foreign parent company owns more than 10% of the French company for more than two years. This tax exemption is subject to specific formal conditions.

The following table shows the rates of withholding tax in force for payments of royalties and dividends for selected countries:-

Country of residence	*Royalties (a) (%)*	*Dividends (%)*
Non-treaty country	$33^1/_3$	25
Selected treaty countries:		
Argentina	18	15
Australia	10	15
Austria	0	15
Belgium	nil	15 (d)

Brazil	10/15/25 (b)	0
Cyprus	5 (h)/nil	15/10 (d)
Denmark	nil	nil
Egypt	15/25	25 (d)
Germany	nil	15/nil/(l) (n)
Hungary	nil	15/5 (f)
India	nil	10
Indonesia	10	15/nil (d)
Ireland	nil	0
Italy	5 (c)	15/5 (d)
Luxembourg	$33^1/_3$ (o)/nil	25/15/5 (f) (m) (i)
Malta	10/nil (c)	15/5 (d)
Netherlands	nil	nil
New Zealand	10	15
Nigeria	12.5	15/12.5 (d)
Norway	nil	15/nil (l)
Pakistan	10	15
Poland	10 (c)	15/5 (d)
Portugal	5	15 (j)
Saudi Arabia	nil	nil
Spain	5	15 (f) / nil (l)
Sweden	nil	0/nil (l)
Switzerland	5	15/nil (d)
Thailand	15/5 (e)	20/15 (f)
Turkey	10	20/15 (e)
United Kingdom	nil	0 (d)
United States	5 (c)	15/5 (d)

Notes

a) Certain amounts that are not considered to be royalties according to the tax treaty provision may be tax exempt if they are business profits;
b) 10% for film, television or copyright royalties and 25% for trademarks;
c) Nil for arts, literature or scientific royalties, except for Italy in the case of software;
d) Lower rate applies to companies holding more than 10% of the distributing company's capital;
e) Lower rate may apply as provided in the treaty;
f) Lower rate applies to companies holding more than 25% of the distributing company's capital;
g) Lower rate applies to companies holding more than 50% of the distributing company's capital;
h) 5% for film and television royalties;
i) Lower rate applies to companies holding more than 25% of the distributing company's share capital; a higher rate applies to dividends received by holding companies which are resident in Luxembourg;

j) No withholding tax is payable if the conditions of application of the EC Directive of 23 July 1991 are fulfilled; these conditions are:
   — management headquarters in the EU;
   — holding exceeds 25% for more than two years;
   — no refund of *avoir fiscal* in excess of the withholding tax as provided for by treaty, and
   — not applicable if the ultimate shareholder is a non-EU resident, except where it can be demonstrated that this is not for tax avoidance purposes.

k) Higher rates may apply, as provided in the treaty.

l) No withholding tax applies to companies holding more than 10% of the distributing company's capital.

m) Withholding tax of 25% applies to companies' Luxembourg holdings.

n) Withholding tax of 15% applies where dividends are distributed by a company which is subject to corporate tax.

o) $33^1/_3$% if the royalties are paid to a holding company.

Other treaty countries

Algeria, Bahrain, Bangladesh, Benin, Bulgaria, Burkina Faso, Cameroon, Central Africa, China, Congo, Ghana, Ivory Coast, United Arab Emirates, Ecuador, Finland, Gabon, Iceland, Iran, Israel, Jordan, Kuwait, Madagascar, Malawi, Mali, Mauritania, Monaco, Morocco, Niger, New Caledonia, Oman, Philippines, French Polynesia, Qatar, Quebec, Romania, Saint Pierre et Miquelon, Senegal, Slovak Republic, South Africa, Togo, Trinidad and Tobago, Tunisia, Ex-USSR, Venezuela, Vietnam, Yugoslavia and Zambia.

Germany

BTR Beratung und Treuhand Ring GmbH Wirtschaftsprüfungsgesellschaft

Introduction

In July 2000, the legislative bodies passed an extensive and radical Reform of Business Taxation. The core elements of the reform are the reduction of tax rates and the system change at shareholder level, namely the changeover from the tax credit system to a classic dividend taxation system. Most changes for corporation and personal income tax have been in force since the beginning of 2001. However, some rules will not enter into force until 2002.

Most taxes are levied at national level, with the exception of municipal trade tax and property tax (levied at community level) and certain other relatively minor taxes. The tax year is the calendar year, although companies and other businesses may have other year ends.

From the year 2002 onward, all tax law figures and all income assessments/measurements will be denominated in euros.

Corporate taxes

Taxable entities

Resident companies

All companies domiciled (registered) or managed in Germany are liable to corporate income tax on their worldwide income (subject to existing bilateral tax treaties) from all sources. They are also subject to municipal trade tax ('Gewerbesteuer').

Non-resident companies

Non-resident companies with a permanent establishment in Germany are liable to corporate income tax and municipal trade tax on all German-sourced income effectively connected with that permanent establishment (including capital gains).

Other non-resident companies are subject to a final withholding tax on certain German-based income.

Tax year and filing requirements

The tax year is the calendar year, but the financial year of a company may be any fixed 12 month period provided for in the company's articles of association. A change from the calendar year to any other year end date is possible on application, provided cogent economic reasons are given. In principle, the tax return must be filed by the end of May in the year following the end of the tax year. In certain cases, filing can be postponed for up to 14 months. The German internal revenue office will make a tax assessment and, in the absence of a tax return, will make a tax estimation.

Taxes imposed

A resident company is liable to corporate income tax and municipal trade tax. The taxes are normally payable within one month of receiving a notice of assessment. Quarterly advance payments of the tax are obligatory during the tax year and are normally based on the tax due in the preceding year. Interest is charged on late payments and on an entity's tax liability if taxes are assessed 15 months after the end of the tax year. In the case of repayments, interest is also reimbursed.

Rates of tax

Distributed and retained profits of resident as well as of non-resident companies are subject to corporate income tax at 25%. In addition, the solidarity surcharge ('Solidaritätszuschlag'), amounting to 5.5% of corporate income tax, is also levied.

Municipal trade tax is levied on the profit calculated for corporate income tax purposes, modified by some add-backs (e.g. 50% of interest payments on long term debts) and deductions. The tax rate depends on the levy rate of the respective local community. The levy rate of communities with 50,000 or more inhabitants is normally between 35% and 50%. The effective tax rate is between 15% and 20%, taking into account that the municipal trade tax is a deductible item in terms of its own calculation. It is also a deductible item in calculating corporate income tax.

The overall tax burden for corporations (corporate income tax, the solidarity surcharge, municipal trade tax) is normally between 37.5% and 42.5%.

Income subject to tax

General rules

The method of determining commercial profits is to be consistent from year to year and can only be changed if this is justified by sound business practices and accounting standards, and provided the purpose of the change is not to gain incidental tax benefits.

Stock/inventory valuation

Stock is to be valued in accordance with accounting standards at the lower of cost (FIFO or LIFO) or net realisable value. Other methods may be employed, provided cogent economic reasons are given.

Capital gains and losses

With the exception of capital gains from the sale of shareholdings, there is usually no special treatment of capital gains and losses. They are treated as normal income and tax is levied at the full rate. On disposal of certain fixed assets, such as land and buildings, the resulting capital gain may be transferred to a replacement reserve, provided that it is intended that the sold asset will be replaced by a new one fulfilling the same function, or that replacement has already occurred. The acquisition costs of the new asset must be reduced by the amount of the reserve.

Capital gains from the sale of shareholdings in foreign corporations are exempt from taxation. According to the new law, the same is true for shares in domestic companies. The new rules will apply as of the beginning of 2002 if the fiscal year of the company whose shares have been sold is the calendar year. If the fiscal year is not the calendar year (e.g. 1 July to 30 June), the new law applies later (e.g. from 1 July 2002 onward). The said tax exemption doesn't depend on a minimum holding period, a minimum participation share, or an active operations proviso. However, there are exceptions for gains arising from earlier tax-deductible write-downs and for shares received in exchange for contributions in kind brought into the company on a book-value basis. Capital losses and write-downs will correspondingly no longer be creditable against tax.

Dividends

The underlying corporate income tax is no longer creditable, but the dividend is exempt from corporate income tax and municipal trade tax for the German parent company. The tax exemption does not depend on a minimum holding period, a minimum participation share, or an active operations proviso.

Dividends are normally subject to a withholding tax of 20% plus 5.5% solidarity surcharge or to a lower rate if so provided for by a corresponding tax treaty. The German withholding tax is creditable or refundable for residents against their individual or corporate income tax. Foreign withholding taxes on dividends of a foreign subsidiary of a German corporation cannot be imputed or refunded.

Special provisions apply if German taxpayers own at least 50% of the shares of a foreign company, which is subject to a low level of taxation (tax rate under 25%) and has passive income (controlled foreign corporations, or CFC for short). The shareholder then has to pay a special corporate income tax of 38% on the profits of such a corporation. If the CFC pays dividends to the German corporation, the dividend is tax-free.

Deductions

General Rules

Expenses directly or closely connected with the conduct of a business are generally tax-deductible. Many expenses which are deemed to lie within the scope of personal needs (such as food and drink) are only partly deductible. Certain expenses are subject to a maximum limit.

Operating expenses incurred in connection with tax-free dividends of German subsidiaries are not deductible in as far as they are directly and financially related to these dividends. The same is true for operating expenses incurred in connection with tax-free capital gains. If a German corporation receives foreign dividends, 5% of these dividends are deemed to constitute non-deductible business expenses, which means that only 95% of the foreign dividend is tax-free. Consequently, the actual expenses are completely deductible.

Depreciation and amortisation

Various methods of depreciation and amortisation are permitted; provided that they are in accordance with generally accepted accounting principles (GAAP), sound business practices, and the tax laws. The depreciation and amortization basis of tangible and intangible fixed assets is historical cost. The residual value and the useful life of the assets are taken into account.

Methods normally accepted are:

- straight-line;
- declining balance;
- depreciation on the basis of the utilization of the asset.

Acceptable rates are:

- buildings 2% – 5%;
- plant, machinery, office equipment 6.25% – 20%;
- vehicles 16.66%;
- goodwill 6.66%.

Small and medium sized companies can claim an additional 20% depreciation on the cost of movable assets in the year of acquisition. They may establish a depreciation reserve of up to 40% of the planned acquisition of assets in the prior year.

Certain assets, such as land, are not depreciable.

Royalties

Paid royalties are deductible as business expenses to the extent that they are at arm's length rates. If they are paid to non-residents, they are subject to a withholding tax of 25%.

Interest

In principle, all interest payments are considered to be business expenses and are therefore deductible. There are special rules for interest in connection with tax-free dividends. For municipal trade tax purposes, interest payments are only partly deductible.

There are thin-capitalisation rules applying to loans of foreign shareholders. In general, a foreign shareholder's loan may not exceed 150% of the respective equity (safe haven of 1.5:1). If the German corporation qualifies as a holding company, the safe haven is 3:1. Interest payments on the exceeding amounts are not deductible and are deemed to be dividend distributions.

Bad and doubtful debts

Debts can be valued on a specific basis, on a general basis, or on a combination of the two. Write-offs and provisions are deductible.

Reserves and provisions

In general, reserves and provisions are allowed if they comply with the accounting principles and are in accordance with sound business practices and the tax laws.

Employees' and directors' remuneration and benefits

Employees' and directors' remuneration and benefits are generally deductible.

Special non-deductible expenses

Corporation income tax, the solidarity surcharge, gifts exceeding € 40, and 50% of salaries and bonuses paid to members of a supervisory board are not deductible. Benefits given to shareholders in cash or in kind are treated as income of the corporation and as dividends paid to the shareholders.

Foreign-source income

Resident companies are liable to corporate income tax as well as the solidarity surcharge on their worldwide income. However, foreign-sourced income other than dividends, interest and royalties, is mostly exempt from German tax where so provided for by a corresponding bilateral tax treaty with the other country. As regards interest income and royalties, a credit for withholding tax is generally applicable. There is no credit for withholding tax on foreign tax-free dividends.

German municipal trade tax is not levied on any branch offices domiciled abroad.

Investment incentives and special benefits

Regional grants and grants for certain types of investment may be obtainable. In particular, investment grants may be available in the five new federal German states in the Eastern part of Germany.

Related party transactions

Transactions between companies or other persons under common control may be subject to revision if they are not carried out at arm's length and under the rules set out in the tax laws and anti-avoidance legislation ('Aussensteuergesetz' [German Foreign Tax Relations Act]). All deviations from market value must be adjusted.

Losses

If a loss arises, it may alternatively be offset against the profits of the preceding tax year (carry-back) up to an amount of € 511,500 or carried forward for an indefinite period for an offset against income arising in subsequent years (carry-forward). Losses exceeding € 511,500 may only be deducted from the income of subsequent years. Major changes in shareholder structure and the objects of the business may lead to a lapse or non-deductibility of such losses.

Corporate groups

German resident companies and registered branch offices of foreign companies may form corporate groups, providing they meet certain legal requirements and conditions. In particular a majority interest and a profit and loss absorption agreement must exist between the group companies, effective for a minimum period of five years. Profits and losses within the group are then offset against each other. There are different prerequisites for a group taxation with respect to municipal trade tax.

Tax free mergers and disposals

Mergers may be tax exempt provided certain conditions are met, particularly when assets or shares are exchanged for shares.

Liquidation of the company

An individual shareholder will in principle be subject to income tax on liquidation distributions to the extent that these exceed the paid-up capital; 50% of the difference is taxable (semi-income-system, see below). If the shareholder is a company, then a loss on liquidation is not deductible and a surplus is not taxable.

Capital taxes

Capital duty

Capital duty is no longer levied on any contribution to the capital of a company in exchange for shares.

Net worth tax

This tax was abolished with effect as of 1997.

Treatment of branch offices (branch office profits tax)

The profits of foreign branch offices are treated as foreign-sourced income (see above).

German branch offices of foreign companies will normally be subject to corporate income tax. There is no special branch office profits tax.

Personal taxes

Taxable individuals

The extent to which the income of an individual is subject to German tax depends on whether he is resident in Germany.

Residents

A person is resident if he has accommodation in Germany, which is more than casual or temporary, or if he is physically present in Germany for more than six months. An individual who is resident in Germany is subject to income tax on his worldwide income.

Non-residents

Non-residents are normally subject to income tax on certain defined income arising in Germany. Former residents of Germany have a special status for a certain period.

Tax year and filing requirements

The taxable period is the calendar year. Spouses can choose to file a separate or joint tax return.

Residents are not required to file a tax return if they meet the following conditions:

- they have received income from employment which has been subject to wage tax, and
- they have not received other income in excess of € 410, and
- they have not been granted a reduction in wage tax payable for the year concerned (e.g. special home-depreciation allowance, etc.).

In other cases a return must be filed by 30 May of the year following the year in question (in certain cases postponement is possible).

Residents who are not required to file a return may do so voluntarily if they expect a refund.

Non-residents are required to file a return if they have certain German-sourced income.

The revenue office will make an assessment. In the absence of a tax return, a tax estimation may be made.

Taxes on income

The income of an individual is subject to income tax and the solidarity surcharge. Wage tax on income received as an employee as well as withholding tax on interest income and dividends are imputed. If the individual runs a business, municipal trade tax is also levied.

Social security contributions are payable by both employers and employees and are levied by independent bodies.

Sources of income

Employment income and directors' fees

An employee (including a director) who is resident in Germany is normally taxed on all his earnings arising within the tax year. Most benefits in kind are taxable, partly (e.g. company car) on a lump-sum basis. Deductions are available for parts of the employees' social security contributions. Travelling expenses to and from work (fixed amounts) and other employment-related expenses are also partly deductible. Every employee is entitled to a lump-sum deduction of € 1,044, if he can't prove higher expenses.

Business income and income from self-employment

For income tax purposes, income is determined on the basis of the financial statements of each business. Accounts are normally drawn up in keeping with the calendar year, but other tax years may be permitted for business income. Income from self-employment is determined by cash basis accounting.

Dividends

According to the new semi-income system, half of the dividend is subject to income tax, the other half is tax-free. Operating expenses (especially interest expenses) related to these dividends, are only

50% deductible, irrespective of whether the shareholder has received dividends in the respective year or not.

The semi-income system has been in force for foreign dividends since 1 January 2001. For dividends from German corporations the new system is normally applicable from 2002 onward.

Dividends of German corporations are subject to a withholding tax of 20% plus the 5.5% solidarity tax or to a lower rate if so provided for by a corresponding tax treaty. Although only 50% of the dividend is taxable, for residents domestic and foreign withholding tax is totally creditable against their individual income tax liability.

An exception to the semi-income system exists where German taxpayers own at least 50% of the shares of a foreign company, which is subject to a low level of taxation (tax rate under 25%) and has passive income (controlled foreign corporations, or CFC for short). The shareholder has to pay a special personal income tax of 38% on the profits of such a corporation. If the CFC pays dividends, half of the dividend is taxable.

Interest

Interest revenue is taxable and generally subject to 30% withholding tax plus 5.5% solidarity surcharge if paid by a bank to a resident and not to a non-resident. In some cases a withholding tax of 25% is also imposed on non-residents. Interest revenue of up to € 1,601 (individual tax return) or up to € 3,202 (joint tax return) is exempt in computing taxable income and there is no withholding tax if a corresponding application was made at the bank(s) in question. Tax credit is granted with respect to the withholding tax.

Rentals

Rental payments received from letting real estate are subject to income tax. Deductions are allowable for expenses, including interest expenses and depreciation. Calculation of rental income is effected on a cash basis.

Royalties

Royalties received are taxed as normal income, subject to a deduction for expenses and depreciation of the costs of such rights. Royalties paid are only subject to withholding tax at a rate of 25 % if they are paid to non-residents.

Social security benefits

Certain social security payments are taxable as of a certain limit of the tax rate on normal income.

Pensions and annuities

Pensions received from a former employer are generally taxed as income from former employment. A certain percentage of annuities are taxed according to the age of an individual at the time when such payments commenced.

Exempt income

Certain types of income are exempt from personal income tax, including certain social security payments or parts of them, employees' reimbursed travel expenses, and any foreign income exempt under the provisions of applicable tax treaties.

Alimony is normally exempt, unless the payer claims a deduction. The taxable and deductible amount is limited to € 13,805.

Capital gains

Capital gains made in the course of operating a business are treated as taxable income.

Private investment gains are generally tax exempt, provided the asset was held longer than the statutory period of limitation for speculative transactions (shares and securities 12 months, real estate 10 years). However, a capital gain on the disposal of shares is taxable if the shareholding amounts to 10% or more of the total share capital. This threshold has been reduced to 1% from 1 January 2001 onward for shares in foreign companies. If shares in domestic companies are sold, the new law will apply as of the beginning of 2002 if the fiscal year of the company whose shares have been sold is the calendar year. If the fiscal year is not the calendar year (e.g. 1 July to 30 June), the new law comes into force later (e.g. 1 July 2002).

Shareholders are obliged to pay tax on capital gains from the sale of shareholdings within the scope of the semi-income system. This means that half of the capital gain is subject to income tax at the level of the shareholder, the other half is tax-free. The aforesaid principles apply regardless of whether the shareholdings are held as corporate assets or as private assets and apply both to German as well as to foreign shareholdings, unless, due to the provisions of an existing tax treaty with the respective other country, Germany is not entitled to tax such profit. Losses are also only 50% tax-deductible.

For capital gains stemming from a sale of the business or from a participation in a partnership, a reduced tax rate is possible up to an amount of € 5 million, provided certain requirements are met.

Foreign-source income

Residents are liable to pay personal income tax as well as the solidarity surcharge on their worldwide income. However, foreign-sourced income other than dividends, interest and royalties, is mostly exempt from German tax (although it is included in the calculation of the applicable German tax rate) where so provided for by a corresponding bilateral tax treaty with the other country. For dividends, interest income and royalties, a credit for withholding tax is generally granted.

German municipal trade tax is not levied on any branch offices domiciled abroad.

Personal allowances and deductions

Various standard allowances/deductions are available, the levels of which depend on marital status, children, etc. The following expenses are deductible, or allowances are granted, either in whole or in part:

- interest income allowance of € 1,601 (unmarried) or € 3,202 (married);
- social security payments;
- insurance payments for life and accident cover;
- donations to charitable, scientific or cultural institutions and political parties;
- church taxes and church donations;
- tax consulting fees;
- special depreciation allowance for a person's personal home;
- child allowance;
- alimony payments.

For non-residents, the above allowances and deductions are normally not applicable.

Losses

Where an individual sustains a loss he may alternatively offset it against the positive income made in the preceding tax year up to an amount of € 511,500 or carry it forward for the purpose of offsetting it against income made in subsequent years. Losses exceeding € 511,500 may only be deducted from the income made in subsequent years. Losses carried back and forward must be offset against the same type of income. If a full offset against the same income source is not possible, the remaining loss is only partially deductible in the current tax year and the balance must be carried forward.

Special family rules

Income may be declared separately by both spouses or by filing a joint return. Non-residents may not file a joint return. Children of all ages declare all their income separately from their parents.

Special treatment for expatriates

No special treatment is available for expatriates.

Rates of tax

General – resident and non-resident

Illustrative 2001 and 2002 rates for residents are:

	Separate return		*Joint return*	
€	*Income Tax (€)*	*Solidarity Tax (€)*	*Income Tax (€)*	*Solidarity Tax (€)*
5,000	–	–	–	–
10,000	620	–	–	–
20,000	3,242	178	1,240	–
30,000	6,240	353	3,716	204
50,000	14,448	794	9,514	523
75,000	26,507	1,457	18,344	1,008
100,000	38,633	2,124	28,896	1,589
150,000	62,887	3,458	53,014	2,915
200,000	87,128	4,792	77,266	4,249

The maximum tax rate in 2001 and 2002 is 48.5%. This rate is reduced to 47% for 2003/2004 and to 42% for 2005 and later.

Provincial and local taxes

Municipal trade tax is levied on taxable business income. Depending on the levy rate of the respective local community, the tax rate varies between approximately 15% and 20%. The tax may be deducted from its own basis as well as from the basis for income tax. In addition to this, part of the municipal trade tax is creditable against income tax. Thus, in many cases, the municipal trade tax means no additional tax burden. However, careful tax planning is necessary to avoid losses of imputation credits.

In addition to income tax, a church tax of 8% to 9% of income tax is levied on church members according to the respective number of children and the federal German state in which they have their residence. Paid church tax may be deducted from income for income tax purposes.

Land tax is levied at local level.

Withholding taxes

20% withholding tax plus 5.5% solidarity tax is levied on dividends. Under the majority of double taxation conventions concluded with Germany, the withholding tax rates are reduced (see below). Interest payments rendered by a bank to a resident and not to a non-resident are generally subject to a 30% withholding tax. These taxes may be offset against the final amount of payable income tax (where a corresponding refund can be claimed).

Tax credits

Wage tax, prepayments, and withholding tax on dividends and interest income may be credited against a person's income tax liability.

Payment of tax

Income tax is to be paid within one month of the date of its final assessment.

Interest is charged on late payments and on an entity's tax liability if taxes are assessed 15 months after the end of the tax year. In the case of repayments, interest is also reimbursed.

Payroll deductions

The employer deducts wage tax from wages and salaries. The amount deducted is off-settable against the final amount of payable income tax (where a corresponding refund can be claimed).

Prepayments

Quarterly prepayments are obligatory during the tax year and are normally based on the tax due in the preceding year.

Estate and gift taxes

Gifts and inheritances are taxable in Germany. The rates depend on:

- the amount/value received;
- the relationship of the recipient to the benefactor.

Lifetime transfers are charged at the same rates as those bequeathed mortis causa.

Rates vary from 7% to 30% for transfers made to a spouse and children, from 12% to 40% for other relatives, and from 17% to 50% for unrelated parties. Various exemptions apply, depending on the relationship in question and the type of gift. The transfer of a family home to the spouse is tax exempt and, where certain conditions are met, business property is only partially taxable. Germany has only concluded estate and gift tax treaties with six other countries, and these treaties in most cases applying only to estate tax and not to gift tax.

Wealth taxes

Wealth tax has been abolished from 1997 onward.

Social security contributions

The German social security system consists of:

- state pension, to which everyone is entitled to contribute, whether or not they are employees; employees must pay contributions subject to a maximum limit;
- state unemployment insurance, which only applies to employees;
- state health insurance contributions must be paid by all employees, however, if an employee's income exceeds a certain amount, he or she is free to leave the state health insurance system (by taking out private insurance); other individuals (e.g. the self employed) may contribute on a voluntary basis;
- state nursing-care insurance contributions must be paid by everyone, employees pay such contributions subject to a maximum limit.

The total sum of contributions is generally paid 50/50 by the employer and the employee.

Other taxes

Treatment of partnerships

Partnerships are pass-through entities: they are not subject to taxation as such, but instead the individual partner's share of such earnings is subject to the respective partner's liability to pay income tax or corporate income tax. Consequently, only the respective partner is entitled to protection under the terms of a corresponding tax treaty. However, the partnership itself is subject to municipal trade tax.

VAT and sales tax

Most goods and services supplied within Germany are subject to 16% VAT, but certain essential goods and services are taxed at a rate of 7%. Germany is part of the European Community's (EC) VAT system. A zero rate applies to the export of goods and services outside the EC.

The deduction of VAT paid is in some cases limited to 50%, e.g. on company cars with private use.

Other taxes

Transfer tax – 3.5% on transfers of real estate.

Excise duties – levied on alcohol, tobacco, fuel, etc.

Property tax – a local tax based on the assessed value of the property levied on the owner.

Exchange control

There are no restrictions on the export or import of capital but reporting requirements must be met.

Tax treaties and withholding tax

Under the majority of double taxation conventions concluded with Germany, the withholding tax rates are reduced. German withholding tax rates on dividends, interest income and royalties covered by select tax treaties (and, where applicable, European Directives) currently in force are:

Country of residence	*Dividends*[1]	*Interest*	*Royalties*
Non-treaty countries	20	0/25[2]	25
Select treaty countries:			
Argentina	15/15	15	25
Australia	15/15	10	10
Austria	15/0	0	0
Belgium	15/0	15	0
Brazil	15/15	15	15
Canada	15/15	15	0
Czech Republic	15/5	0	0
Cyprus	15/10	10	0
Denmark	15/0	0	0
Egypt	15/15	15	15
France	15/0	0	0
Greece	25/0	10	0
Hungary	15/5	0	0
India	10/10	10	10
Indonesia	15/10	10	10
Ireland	15/0	0	0
Italy	15/0	10	5
Japan	15/15	10	10
Kenya	15/15	15	15
Korea	15/10	15	15
Luxembourg	15/0	0	0
Malaysia	15/5	15	10
Malta	15/5	10	10
Mauritius	15/5	25	15
Netherlands	15/0	0	0
New Zealand	15/15	10	10
Norway	15/0	0	0
Pakistan	15/10	20	10
Poland	15/5	0	0
Portugal	15/0	15	10
Singapore	15/10	10	0
South Africa	15/7.5	10	0
Spain	15/0	10	5
Sri Lanka	15/15	10	10
Sweden	15/0	0	0
Switzerland	15/5	0	0
Thailand	20/15	25	15
Turkey	20/15	15	10
United Kingdom	15/0	0	0
United States	15/5	0	0

[1] The first rate is applicable for normal dividends and the second rate is applicable for participation dividends or dividends paid under European Directives. The minimum participation requirements

vary from 10% to 25% depending on the applicable tax treaty in question.

[2] In general there is no withholding tax on interest payments made to non-residents (see above).

If the withholding tax limitations provided for by the double taxation treaties are lower than the national German withholding tax rate, there is no solidarity tax on the withholding tax.

Other treaty countries

Bangladesh, Bolivia, Bulgaria, Chile, Costa Rica, China, Columbia, Ecuador, Emirates, Estonia, Finland, GUS States, Iceland, Israel, Iran, Ivory coast, Jamaica, Kazakhstan, Kuwait, Latvia, Liberia, Lithuania, Mexico, Mongolia, Morocco, Namibia, Paraguay, Philippines, Romania, Slovakia, Trinidad and Tobago, Tunisia, Ukraine, Uruguay, Venezuela, Vietnam, Yugoslavia, Zambia, Zimbabwe.

Anti-avoidance measures

Where an investment is held in a company in a low tax area, the authorities may look carefully at the real place of management. Transactions of an artificial nature carried out solely for the purpose of avoiding tax may be ignored or replaced by the transaction that was commercially intended. If, for example, the shares of a German company are held by a mere holding company which has no commercial activities of its own and is only set up in order to benefit from a corresponding tax treaty (treaty shopping) or from a corresponding EU directive (directive shopping), the holding company would be ignored in terms of any taxation issues.

Hong Kong

Charles Mar Fan & Co.

Introduction

On 1 July 1997, Hong Kong became a Special Administrative Region ('SAR') of the People's Republic of China ('PRC'). The Basic Law of Hong Kong SAR states that under the principle of 'one country, two systems' the socialist system and its policies will not be practised in Hong Kong. Hong Kong SAR is authorised to exercise a high degree of autonomy and enjoy executive, legislative and independent judicial power including that of final adjudication.

The laws in force in Hong Kong prior to 1 July 1997, including the common law, the rules of equity, ordinances, subordinate legislation and customary law shall be maintained, except for any that contravene the Basic Law, subject to any amendment by the legislature of the Hong Kong SAR.

The Basic Law specifically states that Hong Kong SAR shall practise an independent taxation system and shall, taking the low tax policy previously pursued in Hong Kong as a reference, enact laws on its own concerning types of taxes, tax rates, tax reduction allowances and exemptions, and other matters of taxation.

Corporate taxes

Taxable entities

Companies and partnerships (of which a company may be a partner) are subject to Hong Kong profits tax on profits arising in or derived from Hong Kong. Foreign income, whether or not remitted to Hong Kong, is not taxed except where it is considered to have arisen in, or derived from operations carried on in Hong Kong. Residence of the company is not relevant for Hong Kong tax purposes.

Tax year and filing requirements

Tax returns are usually issued in April each year and are required to be filed within one month. However, by special concession the following extensions for filing are usually granted:

Accounting year end	*Tax return due date*
1 April to 30 November	30 April of the following year
1 December to 31 December	31 July of the following year
1 January to 31 March	15 November of the same year

Companies are normally required to submit audited accounts in support of profits tax returns. Tax returns and computation of taxable profits are usually prepared by accountants.

Taxes imposed

Profits tax is levied on profits which arise in, or derive from Hong Kong.

There are no payroll, turnover, sales, value added, or capital gains taxes in Hong Kong.

Rates of tax

Profits tax for corporations is levied at 16% on the corporation's assessable profits.

Income subject to tax

General rules

For a liability-to-profits tax to arise it is necessary:

- for a trade, profession or business to be carried on in Hong Kong;
- for the profits to arise in, or derive from, Hong Kong.

Whether or not a business is carried on in Hong Kong and whether or not profits are derived from Hong Kong is largely a matter of fact, but guidance is taken from the following test to determine the source of profits for Hong Kong tax purposes: 'Where do the operations from which the profits in substance arise take place?'

Certain receipts, including royalties for the use of, or right to use, patents, etc., in Hong Kong are deemed to be receipts arising in or derived from a trade or business carried on in Hong Kong.

In the case of receipts from the exhibition of films and artistic works or royalties from patents and other intellectual property (other than from associated companies), the assessable profits are taken as 10% of the receipts.

Interest income derived from deposits placed in Hong Kong with an authorised financial institution is exempt from profits tax with effect from 22 June 1998, except for interest income on deposit which is used to secure or guarantee money borrowed. This exemption is not applicable to interest earned by a financial institution from its Hong Kong business, which is subject to Hong Kong profits tax.

Stock valuation

Stock should be valued in accordance with generally accepted accounting practice and in most cases at the lower of cost and net realisable value. The FIFO and average cost methods are most common. LIFO, base stock and replacement cost methods are not permitted. The method adopted must be consistently applied.

Capital gains and losses

Capital gains are not subject to tax in Hong Kong nor are capital losses deductible for tax purposes.

Dividends

Dividends, whether from a Hong Kong source or otherwise, are not taxable.

Deductions

General rules

Outgoings and expenses are allowable deductions to the extent to which they are incurred in the production of taxable profits.

Depreciation

Industrial buildings qualify for an initial allowance of 20% on cost (excluding the cost of land) occupied for the purpose of a qualifying trade. Qualifying trades include trades carried out in mills, factories or similar premises. In addition, an annual allowance of 4% on the qualifying expenditure is also available.

Commercial buildings (buildings used for the purposes of trade, other than industrial buildings) qualify for an annual commercial building allowance of 4% on the cost of construction (excluding the cost of land).

Machinery and equipment qualifies for an initial allowance of 60% of the cost. In addition, an annual allowance in respect of wear and tear is also given at prescribed rates, ranging from 10% to 30%, on the reducing balance method. Since 1 April 1998, an immediate 100% write-off has been allowed for prescribed plant or machinery used for a manufacturing process, computer hardware, computer software and computer systems.

Refurbishment concession

Capital expenditure on the renovation or refurbishment of a building or structure, other than a domestic building or structure, is deductible at a rate of 20% a year over a five-year period.

Royalties

Royalties paid, which are commercially realistic and are incurred for the production of taxable profits, are deductible.

Interest

There are detailed rules governing the deductibility of interest paid. Basically, it will be deductible if it is incurred for the production of taxable profits and any one of the following conditions is satisfied:

- the lender is a financial institution;
- the lender is a public utility company and the money has been borrowed at a rate of interest not exceeding the prescribed prevailing rate;
- the money has been borrowed from a person other than a financial institution and the sum payable by way of interest is chargeable to Hong Kong tax;
- the money has been borrowed from a financial institution or an overseas financial institution and the repayment of the principal or interest is not secured or guaranteed by a deposit made by the borrower or a related party (unless the interest therefrom is subject to Hong Kong tax);
- the money has been borrowed other than from a related party and used to finance the purchase of trading stock or plant and machinery, or the interest relates to the public issue of debentures or other documents.

Dividends

Dividends paid are not deductible.

Bad and doubtful debts

Specific provisions or write-offs of trade debts are deductible, while general provisions for doubtful debts are not.

Reserves and provisions

General reserves and provisions are not deductible.

Employees' and directors' remuneration and benefits

Employees' and directors' remuneration and benefits are deductible.

Specifically non-deductible expenses

Expenses of a domestic or private nature, including the cost of travelling between residence and place of business, any disbursements or expenses not incurred for the production of assessable profits, any expenditure of a capital nature, and any sum recoverable under an insurance or contract of indemnity are specifically non-deductible.

Foreign source income

Foreign source income is generally exempted from profits tax.

Investment incentives and special benefits

There are no specially enacted investment incentives.

Related party transactions

If inter-company charges made by foreign affiliates are commercially realistic and are incurred in the production of Hong Kong profits, they are normally allowable for Hong Kong tax purposes. If, however, a Hong Kong resident company conducts business with a closely connected non-resident company in such a way that profits, or profits in the Hong Kong company, are suppressed, the non-resident can be deemed to be doing business in Hong Kong and hence liable to Hong Kong profits tax in respect of his profits from such business.

Losses

Trading losses are deductible from other taxable profits arising in the year of assessment and any unutilised losses may be carried forward and deducted from any taxable profits of future years, without time limit. Specific legislation has been enacted to prevent the obtaining of a tax advantage by acquisition of a company with accumulated tax losses.

Corporate groups

There are no provisions for taxing groups of companies as a single entity or for offsetting losses of one company against the profits of another.

Tax free mergers and disposals

Profits or losses arising from the merger or disposal of subsidiaries are capital transactions and are not subject to profits tax.

Liquidation of a company

Distributions to shareholders which exceed the paid-up capital on liquidation of a company are not usually subject to profits tax as this gain is treated as a capital gain.

Taxes on capital

Capital duty

Capital duty at the rate of 0.1% is payable on the authorised capital of a company and is capped at HK$ 30,000.

Net worth tax

There is no net worth tax on companies.

Treatment of branches

Where a branch is an extension of a foreign corporation, the foreign corporation is the entity liable for profits tax on its Hong Kong sourced income.

The basic method of ascertaining the assessable profits of a branch is as follows:

- if branch accounts are kept which show the true profits arising in Hong Kong, these are adopted and adjusted in accordance with all the rules of profits tax;
- in a case of failure to provide accounts for the branch, or where

such accounts do not reflect the true position of the Hong Kong branch, assessable profits may be ascertained by adjusting to worldwide profits in accordance with profits tax principles and an apportionment on the basis of Hong Kong turnover to worldwide turnover.

Personal taxes

Taxable individuals

Individuals who derive income from within Hong Kong are liable to Hong Kong tax.

Residents

Liability to Hong Kong tax is based on the source of income rather than on whether the individual is resident in Hong Kong.

Tax year and filing requirements

The tax year ends on 31 March each year. An assessor may give notice in writing to any individual requiring that individual to furnish a return within a reasonable time (usually within 2 months). Where a return form is not received from the Inland Revenue Department (IRD), an individual is required to notify the IRD in writing within four months after the end of the tax year if he has earned income subject to tax.

Return forms, in respect of profits tax, are issued on 1 April each year and must be submitted within one month although, by concession, filing dates are normally extended to 31 July for those businesses with accounting dates ending from 1 December to 31 December, and to 15 November for those businesses with accounting dates ending between 1 January and 31 March.

The Business Registration Ordinance requires every person who carries on a business in Hong Kong to apply to the IRD for the registration of that business within one month of commencement of business. The application for business registration is the first advice that the IRD receives of the existence of a new business entity.

Taxes on income

The income tax system is schedular. Tax is levied separately on salaries, profits and property but an individual resident in Hong Kong may elect for personal assessment on total income so that all sources are aggregated.

Sources of income

Employment income

For employees whose income is from an employment, liability arises in respect of salaries tax as follows:

- employees who render services in Hong Kong during visits not exceeding a total of 60 days in a basis period are exempt from Hong Kong tax on the income from their employment. Where more than 60 days are spent in Hong Kong, and the employment has a Hong Kong source, the total income is subject to Hong Kong salaries tax;
- a person whose employment is considered to have a non-Hong Kong source will be liable to salaries tax only on remuneration relating to services rendered in Hong Kong. In the case where his visits to Hong Kong have exceeded 60 days in the tax year, time apportionment is permissible.

An employment is considered to have a non-Hong Kong source where the following conditions apply:

- the contract of employment was negotiated and entered into outside Hong Kong;
- the employer is resident outside Hong Kong;
- the remuneration (or the greater part of it) is paid outside Hong Kong.

A director's fees from a company managed and controlled in Hong Kong are taxed irrespective of where the related services are rendered or whether or not the director visits Hong Kong.

Included in income chargeable to salaries tax are:

- base salary, leave pay, fees, commission, bonus, gratuity;
- benefits-in-kind that can be converted into cash, or which represent the assumption by the employer of a personal liability of the employee;
- any gain realised by the exercise of a right to acquire shares obtained as the holder of an office or as an employee.

The rental value of a place of residence which is provided rent-free, or partly rent-free, by the employer or where an employer reimburses whole or part of the rent paid by the employee. The rental value is deemed to be a percentage of total income (excluding the cost of housing) as indicated below:

Type of accommodation	%
Hotel, one room	4
Hotel, not more than two rooms	8
Other	10

The rental value may be abated by any rent paid by the employee which is not reimbursed by the employer.

Pensions derived wholly from Hong Kong

In the case of a pension attributable to services rendered in any official employment, other than employment in the Government, that part of the pension not attributable to services rendered in Hong Kong is excluded from tax.

Business income

An individual carrying on business in Hong Kong is subject to profits tax at 15% on profits arising in or derived from Hong Kong, determined in the same way as for a corporation.

Capital gains

Gains from the realisation of capital assets are not taxed in Hong Kong.

Dividends

Dividends are exempt from income tax.

Interest

Interest is exempt from tax on an individual's income.

Rentals

Property tax is levied on the owner of land or buildings situated in Hong Kong at the standard rate of 15% on the rent receivable, less an allowance of 20% for repairs and outgoings.

Hong Kong

Royalties

Royalties received from the use of or right to use a trademark, copyright, secret process, and other intellectual property rights in Hong Kong, are deemed to arise from a business or trade carried on in Hong Kong and are liable to profits tax.

Pension and annuities

Any sum received by way of commutation of pension under a recognised occupational retirement scheme or the Pensions Ordinance or contributions withdrawn from Mandatory Provident Fund Scheme are exempt from tax.

Any sum received from an annuity is exempt from tax.

Exempt income

Alimony payments by way of maintenance from a husband or former husband are specifically exempt.

The value of any holiday warrant or passage granted by an employer to an employee is specifically exempt.

Foreign source income

Income derived by a person from services rendered outside Hong Kong is excluded from the charge to salaries tax if, in the territory where the services are rendered, the person is chargeable to, and has paid, tax of a substantially similar nature as salaries tax in respect of that income.

Personal allowances and deductions

The following allowances are generally granted to a taxpayer:

	2001/2002 (HK$)
Single taxpayer	108,000
Married taxpayer	216,000
Allowance for 1st and 2nd child (each)	30,000
Allowance for 3rd to 9th child (each)	15,000
Single parent allowance	108,000
Dependent parent/grandparent allowance	
– not residing with taxpayer	30,000
– residing with taxpayer	60,000
Dependent brother/sister allowance	30,000

Disabled dependent allowance	60,000
Home mortgage interest	100,000
Elderly residential care expenses	60,000
Training allowance (up to a maximum of)	40,000

Expenses are deductible insofar as they are wholly, exclusively and necessarily incurred in the production of income that is subject to salaries tax.

Charitable donations made to approved charities are allowable where the aggregate is not less than HK$ 100, but the allowance is restricted to 10% of income in the assessable tax year.

Losses

Where an individual sustains losses from his business, the taxpayer may carry the losses forward indefinitely to offset against future assessable income. Alternatively, the taxpayer may make an election for personal assessment, under which profits and losses from all sources will be aggregated.

Special family rules

Each spouse is separately charged to salaries tax on his or her income from employment. A married couple who do not wish to be separately assessed must make an election to that effect.

Special treatment for expatriates

There is no special treatment for expatriates.

Rates of tax for 2001/2002

Band (HK$)	*Rate (%)*
First 35,000	2
Next 35,000	7
Next 35,000	12
On the remainder	17

Maximum tax is limited to tax at the standard rate of 15% on the total taxable income, less allowable deductions but before personal allowances.

Provincial and local taxes

There are no provincial or local taxes on income.

Withholding taxes

There are no withholding taxes.

Tax credits

There is no tax credit system.

Payment of tax

Final salaries tax plus 75% of the provisional salaries tax is usually paid in January to March of the year following the year of assessment and the balance of the provisional salaries tax is paid approximately three months later. The due dates of payments are fixed by the Commissioner and are stated in the notice of assessment from the Inland Revenue Department.

Prepayment

A provisional assessment of salaries or profits tax is made, based on the salary or profits for the preceding year. The amount so paid is applied against the agreed final liability for the current year and any excess paid is applied against provisional tax payable for the succeeding year.

Estate tax and gift tax

Estate duty is levied on the principal value of all property located in Hong Kong which is inherited on the death of an individual. It is not levied on property located outside Hong Kong. Included in inherited property are any gifts exceeding HK$ 200,000 made within three years prior to the date of death, with the exception of gifts made in consideration of marriage. The Hong Kong assets of a controlled company (i.e. a company controlled by five or less persons) are also liable for estate duty in certain circumstances.

Estates with a value not exceeding HK$ 7,500,000 are exempt. The present estate tax rates range from 5% on estates with a value between HK$ 7,500,000 and HK$ 9,000,000, 10% on estates with a value between HK$ 9,000,000 and HK$ 10,500,000 and 15% on estates with a value exceeding HK$ 10,500,000. These rates are not progressive and marginal relief is available where the aggregate value of the estate just exceeds a point on the scale of estate tax rates.

There is no gift tax in Hong Kong.

Wealth tax

There is no wealth tax in Hong Kong.

Social security contributions

Social security is accepted as a government responsibility and is administered by the Social Welfare Department. There is no deduction from salaries.

Other taxes

Treatment of partnerships

A partnership is included in the definition of a person and is treated as a separate entity for the purposes of the Inland Revenue Ordinance. The assessable profits of a partnership are computed in exactly the same manner as for any other business (except where one or more partners elect for personal assessment, or where a company is a partnership) and are taxed at the standard rate of 15%.

The senior partner is responsible for filing the return on behalf of the partnership. Tax is recoverable out of the assets of the partnership or from any partner or partners.

VAT and sales taxes

There is no VAT or sales tax.

Sales taxes

With the exception of a first registration tax on automobiles, there are no sales or purchase taxes in Hong Kong.

Rates

Rates are assessed on land, houses and premises at 5% of the rateable value (which is generally related to the rent earned).

Excise taxes

Hong Kong is a free port and there are no general tariffs upon imported goods. However, liquor, tobacco and hydrocarbon oils are subject to tax whether they are imported into or manufactured in Hong Kong for local consumption.

Hong Kong

Stamp duty

Stamp duty is charged on the transfer of shares and landed properties in Hong Kong.

Exchange control

There is no exchange control.

Tax treaties and withholding taxes

There are no tax treaties and withholding taxes in force.

Anti-avoidance measures

Transactions of an artificial or fictitious nature carried out solely for the purpose of avoiding tax may be disregarded by the Inland Revenue Department.

Hungary

Metrum Auditing Ltd.

Introduction

Hungary has a classical tax system, which was introduced at the end of the eighties. Hungarian taxes currently in force include corporate tax, personal income tax and value added tax. The tax system accommodates the increasingly sophisticated business environment and further harmonisation steps are expected in support of Hungary's application to join the EU.

Corporate taxes

Taxable entities

Hungarian tax laws distinguish between resident and non-resident corporate taxpayers and the corporate tax obligations of the taxpayers is determined differently for each.

Taxation of dividends receivable is based on a different set of regulations and again differentiates between resident and non-resident corporate entities.

Resident companies

- Business organisations – limited liability companies
- Joint-stock companies
- State enterprises, etc. – including partnerships and co-operatives.

Foundations and non-profit organisations are also corporate taxpayers if certain conditions are satisfied. Resident corporate taxpayers have an unlimited tax liability and they are subject to tax on their worldwide income.

Non-resident companies

- Foreign enterprises performing business activities through a domestic permanent establishment.

- Foreigners receiving Hungarian-source interest, royalties and remuneration for performing and artistic activities.

Non-resident corporate taxable entities have a limited tax liability in Hungary. They pay corporate tax only on the Hungarian-source income originating from the permanent establishment.

Tax year and filing requirements

The tax year corresponds to the calendar year if the taxpayer does not choose a different one. If a non-calendar business year is chosen, the tax year follows.

In the course of the tax year, advance tax payments must be paid by way of self-assessment on a monthly or quarterly basis, depending on how much tax was paid in the previous tax year. Tax advances must be paid on a monthly basis by taxpayers whose corporate tax exceeded HUF 5 million and on a quarterly basis in all other cases.

By 20 December, all resident and non-resident taxable entities must have paid tax advances at 90% of the expected tax liability.

Corporate tax returns must be filed by 31 May of the year succeeding the tax year.

Taxes imposed

There are no other national taxes in Hungary, except for corporate tax, over the income of companies.

The local business tax introduced in Hungary encumbers the income before taxation, its basis being the net sales revenue originating from business activities conducted in the jurisdiction of the local municipality, reduced by material costs, value of recharged services, subcontractor fees, and the acquisition value of goods sold. The rate of local tax is 2%.

The local tax advance is paid twice a year. Beyond local business tax, the local municipalities may introduce in their jurisdiction other so called 'communal' type taxes and property type taxes as well whose rate is not high. A number of municipalities grant tax incentives.

Rates of tax

The corporate tax rate levied at national level is 18% with a reduced rate of 3% for Hungarian off-shore companies (locally incorporated, foreign owned and operating outside Hungary).

Income subject to tax

General rules

Resident companies must pay taxes in respect of both domestic and foreign income. The tax base includes business revenue from ordinary activities.

Inventory valuation

There are no special tax rules pertaining to the valuation of inventories. Inventories must be valued in accordance with the rules of the accounting act which prescribes valuation at an acquisition cost. The valuation of self-produced inventories is on the basis of the lower of either the production cost or market value. Losses in value as per the accounting act may not be set against taxable income.

Capital gains and losses

Capital gains originating from the sale of fixed assets are taxed similarly to other business income.

Two special rules in relation to the accounting of capital gains and loss are drawn to the attention of readers:

- upon the sale or contribution in kind of tangible and intangible assets and inventories, the taxable amount must be increased if the equivalent accounted as revenue differs by 10% from the normal market price (an arm's length rule);
- in relation to the sale and contribution in kind of securities and shares, the corporate tax law contains an additional rule relating to acquisition costs; the taxable amount on sale must be increased if the acquisition value of the securities exceeded the market value by over 10% on the date of acquisition, as well as if revenue from the subsequent sale of securities does not reach 90% of the normal market price.

Dividends

For resident corporate taxpayers, dividends received domestically or from abroad are tax free. Revenues from dividends and shares received from controlled foreign companies are not exempt (normally from companies in lower tax paying jurisdictions which are controlled by a Hungarian parent company).

If private individuals or non-resident taxpayers receive the dividends, dividend tax deducted by the payer must be paid. In accordance with this rule, non-resident taxpayers must pay 20% dividend tax or a rate determined by double taxation agreements for received dividend. If the non-resident spends the dividend on the founding of a new Hungarian company or to subscribe new capital to an existing company, it does not have to pay dividend tax on such an amount in Hungary.

Deductions

General rules

All costs closely related to the activities may be deductible from taxable income. Costs are listed in detail in the legislation which may not be deducted from the tax base.

Depreciation and amortisation

The schedule to the law lists in detail the depreciation rates and rules which may be set against taxable income.

For tax purposes the full acquisition value of the asset may be deducted from the tax base during the foreseeable usage term of the asset, whereas the accounting act only allows the depreciation of the acquisition value as reduced by the anticipated residual value.

Scheduled depreciation may not be accounted for on certain assets. Such assets include land, estates, forests or works of art. However, extraordinary depreciation may be accounted for such assets, as well, if certain conditions are met.

Acceptable rates are:

Buildings	2%
Rented out buildings	5%
Machinery, equipment	14.5%
Computer equipment	33%
Vehicles	20%

Royalties

For resident taxpayers, royalties received are included as taxable income. For foreign organisations it is taxed at source by the resident royalty payer. The corporate tax rate is 18% if there is no double taxation agreement in effect. Royalties are deductible as a business expense.

Interest

Interest paid may be accounted as a business cost, and interest received is included in taxable income for resident corporate taxpayers. It is taxed at source for foreign payee organisations.

In relation to interest, the rule on thin capitalisation should be noted. Interest payable by taxpayers on loans outstanding in the tax year may be deductible from the tax base as cost only up to a certain amount. A three-to-one debt-to-equity ratio is imposed and interest on loans beyond this ratio is not deductible irrespective of the entity receiving the interest. Interest paid to a bank is an exception to this rule.

From 2001, amounts of interest and royalty received by associated enterprises exceeding the normal market interest rate and royalty is deemed to be a dividend.

Reserves and provisions

The tax base must be reduced by a percentage of overdue receivables outstanding on the final date of the tax year. Recognised rates of loss in value:

- 2% of the value of the receivable upon a default of 90-180 days;
- 5% upon a default of 181–360 days;
- 25% upon default beyond 360 days.

The above provision may not be applied by banks and investment companies.

The value of irrecoverable debt also reduces taxable income. Debt is deemed to be irrecoverable if proved to be so, or is such through judicial proceedings.

Non-deductible expenses

In relation to costs which may not be deductible in accordance with tax law or practice, a further rule stipulates that services to a value of HUF 200,000 not including VAT, may be deductible if by the nature of the services it can clearly be determined that the use of the services is justified on the basis of reasonable business conduct.

Tax incentives

Tax incentives for investments and regional incentives

Taxpayers are entitled to such a tax incentive for investments in projects for production purposes in the value of HUF 1 billion. The tax incentive also depends on the satisfaction of a number of conditions and its rate – a 50% or 100% tax incentive – on where the investment is implemented, e.g. in an underdeveloped region or a region where unemployment exceeds 15%.

Tax incentives for small and medium-size businesses

Small and medium-size businesses have enforced tax deductions for interest paid on loans lent by banks for the procurement or production of tangible assets taken out after 31 December 2001. The rate of tax incentives is 40% of paid interest in the tax year but no more than HUF 5 million per tax year.

Investment incentives for micro and small businesses

Micro and small businesses may reduce their tax base by the value of (amongst others) real estate, technical equipment, machinery, vehicles, accounted as 'incomplete' investment in the tax year, but by no more than HUF 10 million.

Off-shore companies

Off-shore companies pay tax at 3%. Limited liability companies and joint-stock companies registered in Hungary and in 100% foreign holding are deemed to be off-shore companies in Hungary. An important rule regarding these companies stipulates that off-shore companies may only conduct commercial activities abroad and may only perform services whose place of performance is deemed to be abroad according to the act on value added tax.

Related party transaction

The legal relationships and contracts between related parties must at all times be judged on the basis of normal market prices. If the parties do not contract at a normal market price, thereby also influencing the profit before taxation, the tax authority has the statutory right to modify the tax base of the contracting parties and accordingly determine the tax obligation. However, by way of issuing a mutual statement, the contracting parties – satisfying specific conditions – may also apply a tax base varying from the one determined according to the price applied by them. The law stipulates several methods for determining the normal market price.

Losses

Taxpayer companies without a previous owner may reduce their tax base by the losses incurred in the year of establishment and the three tax years thereafter for an unlimited period, without further authorisation from the tax authority.

If the tax base is negative in any given tax year, pre-tax profit may be reduced by such amount in the subsequent five tax years, if authorised by the tax authority.

Personal taxes

Taxable individuals

Residents

An individual is deemed to be a resident if his domicile or habitual place of abode is in Hungary. Tax is levied on the income of resident individuals earned in any form.

Non-residents

If the individual has neither a domicile, nor a habitual place of abode in Hungary, residence is determined according to the domicile and habitual place of abode in the other state. Tax is levied on the Hungarian-source income of non-resident private individuals.

Tax year and filing requirements

Individuals must submit tax returns once annually for all income earned in the tax year by 20 March of the year succeeding the tax year. The tax year corresponds to the calendar year. Individuals satisfy the tax obligation by way of self-assessment, but in relation to some private individuals, the employer or the payer may also file the tax return according to the statement issued by the individual.

Some individuals do not have to submit a tax return, including those receiving only a pension, or certain other income such as that originating from the sale of movable properties, if their related income is no more than HUF 200,000 per year, or the cost reimbursement received in relation to expenses of employment. However, there are types of income for which separate tax returns must be submitted in all cases.

Taxes on income

The income of individuals is subject to personal income tax at progressive rates set out later in this chapter and social security contribution and employee contribution. The employer and the payer are obliged to deduct from the income of employment.

Sources of income

Income from dependent services

In Hungary, where employment income allowances are received by members of business organisations for personal participation, or where there is the remuneration of elected officials in companies, e.g. members of the supervisory board, etc., no costs are allowed against this income.

Income from independent services

Income from all other personal activities not belonging to the above category are independent services, such as income to private entrepreneurs.

Private persons may deduct costs from the revenue of the activity in two ways. They may either choose the itemised cost accounting method, that is he settles costs actually incurred and certified in relation to the activity in an amount not exceeding the revenue, or considers 10% of the revenue as cost which may be accounted without certification.

Dividends

Dividends received by individuals are taxed at 20% or 35%. Individuals must pay 20% tax on the amount of dividend within a limit set by reference to the prime rate of the National Bank valid on the first date of the year in which the dividend was declared. The rate is 35% for dividends exceeding the limit.

For dividends received from abroad, tax paid abroad on the dividend may be credited against the 20% dividend tax payable in Hungary. If the dividends originate from a non-treaty state, the rate of dividend tax payable in Hungary cannot fall below 5%, irrespective of the amount of dividend tax paid abroad.

Interest

Interest as defined by law is taxable at a rate of 0% in Hungary (so it increases the rate on which other income is taxed while not itself being taxable). Interest income attracting the 0% rate is interest on savings deposits, publicly offered stocks, loans offered by private individuals, if it exceeds by no more than 5% the prime rate of the National Bank on the date of the transaction, or interest on loans offered by private individuals to a company, but no more than HUF 10,000 annually for private persons. Interest not belonging to a category defined by law, or paid interest exceeding the specified amount is deemed as other income of the individual and is included in consolidated taxable income.

Royalties

There are no special rules on the taxation of royalties. Royalties are included in consolidated taxable income which is taxed according to the progressive rates.

Taxation of pensions and similarly taxed income

Pensions, various social security aids, support and scholarships offered to students of higher education are tax-free. If, however, the private person earns income from other sources, the amounts received for pensions (etc.), must also be considered when determining the tax rates applied to other income.

Capital gains

It may generally be said that all gains earned on any assets, including movables assets, real estate or securities, is taxable income where the taxable amount is determined by deducting costs spent on the acquisition, disposal and certain enforcement expenditure from the sale price. The tax rate on capital gains is 20%.

Income from the leasing of real estate

A private person may choose how to pay taxes on income from the leasing of real estate. He may either satisfy his tax obligation with 20% taxation at source, in which case he may not set costs against the income, or he pays taxes on it as part of his consolidated income and he may also deduct costs on the same basis as for the independent services.

Foreign source income

Where they are available, double taxation agreements exempt many categories at foreign source income from taxation in Hungary, but such income is included to determine the tax rate of other income. In relation to income taxed at source – dividends, interest, royalties – the agreements generally stipulate that taxes already paid abroad may be deducted from taxes payable in Hungary.

Personal allowances and deductions

From 2001, the following tax table is applicable for determining Hungarian personal income tax obligations for both residents and non-residents:

20%	on HUF 0–480,000
30%	on HUF 480,001–1,050,000
	HUF 96,000 tax and 30% on the amount over HUF 480,000
40%	over HUF 1,050,001
	HUF 267,000 and 40% on the amount over HUF 1,050,000

From 2001, the statutory rate of the tax base is exempt from tax under the title of family benefit, depending on the number of supported family members.

Tax benefits set against personal income tax

The taxable amount is reduced by the specified rate under the following titles:

- the employee benefit may be effected for private individuals whose annual income does not exceed HUF 1,050,001. The tax on the annual income may be reduced by 10% of earned wages, but by no more than HUF 3,000 per month;
- 25% of pension contributions paid on a mandatory basis may be deducted from taxes;
- amounts exceeding mandatory amounts paid to private pension funds, and the amount paid to voluntary and mutual insurance funds;
- savings and interest on loans for housing purposes;
- public donations and life insurance premiums;
- tuition fees of university, college students;
- increase in the investment portfolio of private persons as investment tax credit.

Some specific activities, such as the development of intellectual properties, enjoy additional tax benefits.

The taxation of private entrepreneurs is a special category and differs from the above rules. Private entrepreneurs pay taxes on work wages according to the above table and 18% entrepreneurial personal income tax on business income earned through their enterprise. Private entrepreneurs have the right to accrue losses. After-tax income remaining after deduction of entrepreneurial personal income tax: entrepreneurial dividend funds, being profits after income taxes, are levied with a 20% and 35% dividend tax according to the calculations stipulated by law.

There are social security contributions payable on income by both the employee and the employer:

- 3% health insurance contribution paid by the employee – 11% paid by the employer;
- an 8% pension contribution from the employee is allocated to the state pension insurance fund and 6% to the individual's private pension fund (the employer pays pension contributions at a rate of 20%);
- an additional 1.5% employee and 3% employer contribution is payable from wages to the Solidarity Fund.

Other taxes

VAT obligation

Sales of goods and services within Hungary incurs a VAT payment obligation. The general VAT rate is 25%, applicable for most products and services. Some products and services have reduced tax rates of 12% and 0%. The 0% rate is for exported products and product sales deemed to be exported products. Some services enjoy an activity based tax exemption.

Excise duties

Excise duties are payable in Hungary for mineral oil, alcoholic products, beer, champagne and tobacco.

Duties

Inheritance, gifts and capital transfers have a duty payment obligation. The amount of the inheritance and gift duty depends on the object of the gift and inheritance, and the relationship between the recipient and the donor. The general rate of inheritance and gift duty is progressive from 11% to 21% (2.5% – 4/5% for inherited homes, 5% – 10% duty for homes conveyed as gift). The duty on onerous transfers of property is 10% and there is a rate of 2% to 4% for sales of apartments.

Rules on foreign exchange

Exchange controls exist whereby a few transactions require the prior authorisation of the exchange control authority. Several other transactions and activities involve a subsequent reporting obligation.

Double taxation agreements and their application, withholding taxes

Hungary currently has double taxation agreements with 56 countries. The local application of any agreement requires the non-resident to certify his foreign status and in some cases issue a statement of his beneficial owner status.

Country	*Dividend (%)*	*Interest (%)*	*Royalties (%)*
Albania	5/10	0	5
Australia	15	10	10
Austria	10	0	0
Belgium	10	15	0
Brazil	15	10/15	15/25
Bulgaria	10	10	10
Cyprus	5/15	10	0
Czech Rep.	5/15	0	10
Denmark	5/15	0	0
Rep. of South Africa	5/15	0	0
United States	5/15	0	0
United Kingdom	5/15	0	0
Egypt	15/20	15	15
Finland	5/15	0	5
France	5/15	0	0
Philippines	5/20	15	15
Greece	10	10	10
The Netherlands	5/15	0	0
Croatia	5/10	0	0
India	15	15	40(20)
Indonesia	15	15	15
Ireland	5/15	0	0
Israel	5/15	0	0
Japan	10	10	10
Yugoslavia	10	0	10

Canada	5/10/15	10	10
Kazakhstan	5/15	10	10
China	10	10	10
Korea	5/10	0	0
Kuwait	0	0	10
Poland	10	10	10
Luxembourg	5/15	0	0
Malaysia	10	15	15
Morocco	12	10	10
Malta	5/15	10	10
Moldavia	5/15	10	0
Mongolia	5/15	10	5
Germany	5/15 (25)	0	0
Norway	10	0	0
Italy	10	0	0
Russia	10	0	0
Pakistan	15/20	15	15
Portugal	15(10)	10	10
Romania	5/15	15	10
Spain	5/15	0	0
Switzerland	10	10	0
Sweden	5/15	0	0
Singapore	5/10	5	5
Slovak Rep.	5/15	0	10
Slovenia	10	0	10
Thailand	15/20	10/25	15
Turkey	10/15	10	10
Tunisia	10/12	12	12
Ukraine	5/15	10	5
Uruguay	15	15	15 (10)
Vietnam	10	10	10

India

Sharp & Tannan

Introduction

Companies are assessed to tax under the Income Tax Act 1961 at rates prescribed annually by the Finance Act, for the financial year from 1 April to 31 March by reference to their taxable income for the previous financial year. A substantial portion of the tax payable for the year is paid as advance tax on estimated income (taking into account certain adjustments at source).

Corporate taxes

Taxable entities

Resident companies

A company is resident in India if it is incorporated in India or the control and management of its affairs is situated wholly in India throughout the year.

Resident companies are liable to income tax on worldwide income including capital gains.

Non-resident companies

All other companies are non-resident companies and are only liable to tax on the following income:

- income received or deemed to be received in India or accruing or arising or deemed to be accruing or arising in India;
- capital gains on assets in India;
- income, such as royalties and technical service fees for services rendered in India.

Where a non-resident company has a business connection in India, a part of its worldwide income is deemed to accrue even though it may not in practice have accrued or been received in India. The term 'business connection' is not defined but is wide ranging in its application. It includes, for example, a branch office, an agent, a factory or subsidiary to sell a non-resident parent's product, or a financial connection between a resident and non-resident company.

The liabilities are often reduced under tax treaties.

Tax year and filing requirements

The tax return in respect of the financial year must be filed on or before 31 October following the end of that financial year. The law requires that all companies must file a return of income irrespective of whether a loss is made. The assessing officer may accept the income tax return as filed or, alternatively, may initiate assessment proceedings by issuing a notice within 12 months from the end of the month in which the return is filed. The proceedings must be completed within two years of the end of the relevant financial year.

It is obligatory to obtain a Permanent Account Number (PAN) and a Tax Deduction Account Number (TAN).

Taxes imposed

All taxes on income are imposed at a national level. The tax treatment of companies varies according to their residential status. The status depends on whether a company is a domestic company or a foreign company. A domestic company is an Indian company or any other company which has made, in respect of its income liable to tax under the Act, the prescribed arrangements for declaration and payment within India of dividends, including dividends on preference shares. Domestic companies are normally resident companies since, in addition to being Indian companies, the control and management of their affairs is also wholly carried out in India.

'Foreign company' denotes a company which is not a domestic one. Foreign companies are normally non-resident companies.

Rates of tax

Income tax

Domestic companies

The rate of income tax for domestic companies is 35%. The Government has temporarily announced a surcharge of 2% on income tax.

A further corporate tax is levied on distributed profit at the rate of 10% (plus the temporary surcharge of 2% as above) on the amount of dividends declared, paid or distributed.

Foreign companies

Business profits or other income.	48%
Dividends.	Nil
Interest (payable by government or an Indian concern on monies borrowed or debt incurred in foreign currency).	20%
Royalties and fees for technical services (provided these are received in consideration of an agreement made after 31 May 1997).	20%

Where the tax payable on the total income as computed under the Act is less than 7.5% of the book profits, the tax payable shall be deemed to be 7.5% of such book profit plus the temporary surcharge of 2%.

Tax on capital gains

Domestic companies

Gains (proceeds less allowable cost) resulting from the transfer of capital assets are taxed at the rates applicable to business profits.

In the case of long term capital gains, tax is payable at a rate of 20% plus a surcharge of 2% after taking into account any cost indexation benefit. Long-term capital gains include the following:

- the transfer of shares in a company and/or securities listed in a recognized stock exchange in India and the transfer of units of the Unit Trust of India and the units of specified mutual funds which have been held for more than 12 months;
- the transfer of other assets held for more than 36 months.

All companies must pay long-term capital gains tax of 10% (plus surcharge of 2% thereon) on a capital gain from shares and listed securities if they do not claim indexation benefit.

Foreign companies

Gains (i.e. proceeds less allowable cost) resulting from a transfer of short term capital assets are taxed at the rates applicable to business profits. Long term capital gains (as defined above) are taxed at the rate of 20%.

In the case of long term capital gains arising on a transfer of shares or debentures of an Indian company which was originally acquired using foreign currency, foreign currency translation benefit is applicable instead of cost indexation benefit.

Income subject to tax

General rules

Taxable income is calculated by aggregating the different sources such as property, business or professions, capital gains other than long-term capital gains, and income from other sources.

Gains are calculated by deducting from the proceeds of any disposal, purchase costs, improvement costs and incidental costs such as selling and legal costs. Since 1 April 1981, a company has been able to obtain relief against inflation by opting to substitute the 1 April 1981 market value for original cost on assets purchased or acquired prior to that date.

Capital gains

Business re-organisations, i.e. amalgamations or demergers, are tax neutral.

The fair market value of an asset lost or destroyed, which is recovered under an insurance policy on account of a force majeur, is taxed as a capital gain.

In relation to a capital asset (being goodwill of a business, or a trade mark or brand name associated with a business, or a right to manufacture, produce or process any article or thing, tenancy rights, stage carriage permits or loom hours) the cost of acquisition will be taken as 'nil' unless actually paid for acquiring the same.

Capital gains on the transfer of certain capital assets used in a business (such as plant and machinery, land or buildings or rights to these) arising in the course of moving an industrial undertaking from a notified urban area to any other area are eligible for exemption within one year prior or three years subsequent to the date of transfer, provided the taxpayer purchases or constructs new capital assets for the purposes of conducting business in the new area. Either the value of the capital gain or the cost of the new asset is exempt, whichever is lower.

If the new asset is transferred within three years from the date of its acquisition, the capital gains on such transfer are computed by reducing the cost of the asset by the amount of the exemption from capital gains achieved on the earlier transfer of the original asset.

Long term capital gains tax is not payable if the sale proceeds or capital gains are invested in specified bonds for a locked-in period of three years.

In the case of foreign companies where a capital gain arises on the transfer of shares or debentures of an Indian company originally acquired using foreign currency, the capital gain is computed in that foreign currency.

No capital gains tax is payable by a foreign company which, in the process of a demerger, transfers the shares held by it in an Indian company, provided the shareholders continue to hold at least three quarters of the shares of the resulting foreign company and such transfer does not attract capital gains tax in the country in which the demerged foreign company is incorporated.

Stock/inventory rules

Stock and inventory are generally valued at the lower of cost or market value on a FIFO basis. There are no standard rules prescribing the method of valuation of inventories except that the valuation must include all taxes and duties, etc. Any method adopted for valuation must be followed consistently thereafter.

Deductions

General rules

Taxable trading profits are calculated in accordance with generally accepted accounting principles after making certain statutory adjustments. Only expenditure laid out wholly and exclusively for business purposes is allowed. Most expenses incurred in earning income can be deducted, with some exceptions. Additional common adjustments are as follows:

- capital expenditure on fixed assets may be depreciated (see below); up to 31 March 2005, companies engaged in the business of bio-technology or in the business of manufacture or production of any drugs, pharmaceuticals, electronic equipment, computers, telecommunication equipment or chemicals, helicopters, aircrafts or computer software, are entitled to deduction of 150% of revenue and capital expenditure (exclusive of land and buildings) incurred on in-house scientific research and development facilities as approved by the prescribed authority;

- certain expenses, such as payment of bonuses, leave encashment, contributions to gratuity funds, provident funds, superannuation funds, interest on loans from public financial institutions and statutory payments such as excise duty and sales tax, are allowable when paid;
- general provisions and provisions for contingent or future losses are not usually deductible;
- business restructuring expenses and voluntary retirement payments to employees are amortised and are tax deductible over a period of five years.

Depreciation and amortisation

Depreciation is calculated on the written down value of categories of assets at the rates specified in the income tax rules.

Categories of assets include tangible assets such as buildings, plant and machinery or furniture, and intangible assets such as know-how, patents, copyrights, trademarks, licences, franchises and other intellectual property. The same percentage of depreciation is applied to items within the same category.

Where an asset is acquired outside India by a non-resident and imported to India for business or professional use, the value of the asset is calculated as actual cost less depreciation, according to Indian rates in force since the asset's acquisition.

Buildings

Buildings including items such as roads and bridges attract depreciation at a rate of 5% on the declining balance on mainly residential buildings and 10% on other buildings. Temporary buildings are 100% depreciable in the year of addition.

Furniture and fittings

The general rate applicable to this category of asset is 10% of the written down value.

Plant and machinery

The general depreciation rate for this category is 25% although higher rates of 50% and 100% are available on certain energy-saving and pollution-control equipment. No depreciation is allowed on imported motorcars although cars of Indian manufacture are entitled to depreciation at 20%.

Depreciation is allowed at 60% on computers.

On sale or transfer of assets, proceeds are credited against allowances within the relevant category. Where such proceeds exceed the category value, the excess is charged as a short-term capital gain.

Intangible assets

The general rate applicable to this category of assets is 25% of the written down value.

Royalties

Royalties and fees paid for technical know-how are allowed on either cash or on an accruals basis according to the company's accounting method. Payments of royalties and fees related to achieving sales are allowable expenses.

Telecom licence fees

Capital expenditure incurred for acquisition of a licence from the Department of Telecommunications to operate basic and cellular telecommunication services is amortised and tax deductible over the licence period.

Interest

This is normally allowed on a cash or accruals basis depending on the method adopted by the company.

Royalties, fees for technical know-how and interest payable outside India are deductible only if withholding tax has been paid to the government.

Dividends

Dividends paid are not deductible.

Investment incentive and special benefits

There are many investment incentives. The main incentives are listed below, but it should be noted that there are numerous conditions to be satisfied before the exemptions can be claimed.

The following rates on profits and gains are computed for non-residents as a percentage of gross receipts prior to deduction:

Categories	*Incentives*
New industries in free trade zones or electronic hardware technology parks or software technology parks or in any Special Economic Zones engaged in the business of exports.	Income fully exempt for ten consecutive assessment years from the date of manufacture of articles or things or computer software.
Newly established 100% export oriented undertakings.	Income fully exempt from tax for ten consecutive assessment years from the date of manufacture.
Industrial undertaking commencing manufacture or production in the North Eastern region of units or parts on or after 1 April 1998, subject to certain conditions.	Income fully exempt from tax for ten consecutive assessment years from the commencement of production.
An enterprise owned by a company registered in India or by a consortium of such companies by an agreement with any government or statutory body begins developing, maintaining and operating any infrastructure facility on or after 1 April 1995.	Income fully exempt for ten consecutive assessment years fall within an initial 15 years (20 years in case of some specified infrastructure facilities) from the date of commencement of operation and maintenance of such infrastructure.
A company commencing provision of telecommunications services, basic or cellular including radio paging, domestic satellite services or network of trunking and electronic data interchange services, broad band and internet services, at any time on or after 1 April 1995 but before 31 March 2003.	Income fully exempt for first five years and 30% exempt for a subsequent five years, such that the ten consecutive assessment years fall within an initial 15 years.
A company which begins to develop, develops and operates or maintains industrial park/ Special Economic Zones between 1 April 1997 to 31 March 2006, as per the scheme framed by the Central Government.	Income fully exempt for ten consecutive years that fall within an initial 15 years.

An industrial undertaking which is set up in any part of India for the generation or generation and distribution of power at any time between 1 April 1993 and 31 March 2006.	Income fully exempt for any ten consecutive years that fall within the initial 15 years.
An industrial undertaking which starts transmission or distribution of power by laying a network of new transmission or distribution lines at any time during the period beginning from 1 April 1999 to 31 March 2006.	Income fully exempt for ten consecutive assessment years that fall within the initial 15 years.
A small-scale industrial undertaking manufacturing or producing units or parts or operating cold storage plant at any time between 1 April 1995 to 31 March 2002.	30% of income exempt for an initial period of ten consecutive assessment years.
An industrial undertaking in a notified under-developed state, commencing manufacture or production of units or parts or operating cold storage plant at any time between 1 April 1993 to 31 March 2002.	Income fully exempt for initial five years and 30% exempt for a subsequent five years. Where such industry is set up in the North Eastern region it is 100% exempt for an initial ten years.
Industrial undertaking located in an under-developed district (Category 'A') commencing manufacture or production of units or parts or operating cold storage plant at any time between 1 October 1994 to 31 March 2002.	Income fully exempt for initial five years and 30% exempt for a subsequent five years.
An industrial undertaking located in an under-developed (Category 'B') district commencing manufacture or production of units or parts or operating cold storage plant at any time between 1 October 1994 to 31 March 2002.	Income fully exempt for initial five years and 30% exempt for a subsequent five years.
A hotel owned by a company registered in India, and approved by a prescribed authority prior to 1 April 1999, where not located within the municipal jurisdiction	50% of income is exempt for an initial ten assessment years.

of Mumbai, Delhi, Calcutta, Chennai, which commences its operation in a notified hilly area or rural area or a place of pilgrimage between 1 April 1997 and 31 March 2001.	
Hotels in any other type of areas (excluding those within the jurisdictions of Mumbai, Delhi, Calcutta or Chennai).	30% of income is exempt for an initial ten assessment years.
A company registered in India carrying out scientific and industrial research and development, where approved by prescribed authority, before 1 April 1999.	Income fully exempt for the first five years.
An undertaking commencing the commercial production of mineral oil on or after 1 April 1997 in any part of India other than the North Eastern region, or which commences the refining of mineral oil on or after 1 October 1998.	Income fully exempt for an initial seven years.
A company engaged in developing and building for a housing project on or after 1 October 1998 where completion is prior to 31 March 2003.	Income is fully exempt.
An industrial undertaking setting up and operating a cold chain facility for agricultural produce on or after 1 April 1999 but before 31 March 2003.	Income fully exempt for an initial five years and 30% exempt for a subsequent five years.
Income from projects outside India.	Exemption on 50% of income provided it is taxable under the Indian Income Tax Act and the consideration is remitted to India.*
Approved hotels and tours operators	Exemption on 50% of income attributable to earnings in convertible foreign exchange plus balance profit is credited to Reserve, calculated on a proportional basis.*

Housing projects, in certain areas	Exemption on 50% of income provided the equivalent amount is debited to the profit and loss account and credited to a housing project reserve account.*
Income from export of goods, computer software, film software, as also development of computer software outside India.	Exemption on 100% of the income derived from export, calculated on a proportional basis.

*Available only to Indian companies and these deductions are being phased out (i.e. truncating 20% each year) over a period of 5 years, i.e. available only for the year ending on 31 March 2005.

The following rates on profits and gains are computed for non-residents as a percentage of gross receipts prior to deduction:

Shipping business	7.5%
Exploration for mineral oils and providing services in connection therewith/hiring of equipment for such activity	10%
Aircraft operation	5%
Civil construction such as turnkey power projects	10%

Special rates applicable to certain incomes

Tax is levied at special rates on gross income in the following cases:

Overseas financial organisations (offshore funds)

Nature of income	*Tax rate*
Income from units purchased in foreign currency.	11.20%
Long term capital gains from units purchased with foreign currency.	11.20%

N.B. Indexation benefit will not apply to the above capital gains.

Non-residents

Nature of income	*Tax rate*
Interest/dividends other than declared, distributed or paid by domestic company, in accordance with a government notified scheme and purchased in foreign currency.	11.20%

Long term capital gains on the above shares or bonds.	11.20%

N.B. Neither indexation benefit nor foreign currency translation benefit is allowed in computing the above capital gains.

Foreign institutional investors

Nature of income	*Tax rate*
Income on securities (other than dividend and units) listed on a recognised Stock Exchange in India	22.40%
Capital gains on securities:	
—long term	11.20%
—short term	33.60%

Related party transactions

Transactions between companies or other persons under common control are deemed to take place at market value where profits or capital gains would otherwise be understated.

New legislation is being introduced to curb avoidance of abuse of transfer pricing. It aims at providing a statutory framework leading to computation of reasonable, fair and equitable profits and tax in India on account of international transactions between residents and non-resident associated enterprises. The provision stipulates determination of an 'arm's length' price in international transactions on the basis of:

- comparable uncontrolled price method;
- re-sale price method;
- cost plus method;
- profit split method;
- transactional net margin method;
- any other method to be prescribed.

Where more than one price can be determined by the most appropriate method described earlier, the arm's length price shall be the arithmetical mean of two or more prices. The relevant rules are being formulated.

Losses

Capital losses can be offset only against capital gains. Other category losses can be offset against different category income in the same year at the option of the taxpayer, so trading losses can be offset against general income and capital gains. Unused business and capital losses can be carried forward for offset against income over eight years.

In the case of closely held companies, losses cannot be carried forward and offset unless at least 51% of the voting shares remain in the same hands.

Unused depreciation is not treated as a business loss. Unused depreciation can be carried forward indefinitely for offset against business income.

Corporate groups

Neither consolidated tax treatment nor provision for group relief of losses is available. However, depreciation is allowed on the tax written down value of assets transferred between a parent company and its wholly owned subsidiary and there is no tax on any capital gain arising on such a transfer provided certain conditions are fulfilled. The same principle is applicable in the case of mergers or demergers.

Mergers and demergers do not result in any tax liability on the transfer of business or assets provided the prescribed conditions are fulfilled.

Exchange controls

India employs exchange control regulations which have recently been significantly amended. Procedures for obtaining permission from the Reserve Bank of India have also been simplified. Companies in which foreign ownership is up to 51% have been put on a par with domestic companies. Where foreign ownership exceeds 51%, companies are required to obtain the Reserve Bank of India's approval for specific transactions. The government has also introduced the Liberalised Exchange Rate Management System through which the rupee has been made fully convertible on trade account.

Foreign investment standards have been eased and for a range of industries there is a system of automatic approval for prescribed industries where the foreign equity is 50%, 51%, 74% and 100%. Where investment is of higher magnitude permissions must be sought from the Foreign Investment Promotion Board (FIPB).

There are no restrictions on the remittance of profits, dividends, interest or royalties from India to non-residents provided the agreement under which the payments are made has been approved in advance by the central government through the Reserve Bank of India.

Personal taxes

Resident

Resident individuals are taxable on their worldwide assessable income.

An individual is resident under either of the following conditions:

- if present in India for a total period of 182 days or more during a financial year;
- if present in India for a total period of 60 days during the current financial year and at least 365 days in total during the preceding four financial years.

The financial year is the 12 month period ending on 31 March.

Resident but not ordinarily resident

Resident but not ordinarily resident individuals are taxable on their Indian income plus any other income derived from a business controlled, or a profession set up, in India.

A resident but not ordinarily resident individual is one who is resident for the current financial year but either:

- was not a resident for any of the nine out of ten financial years preceding the current year;
- was not present in India for a total period of 730 days or more during the preceding seven years.

Non-residents

Non-resident individuals are taxed on income, which is received, or accrued or has arisen in India (or is *deemed* to be received, accrued or has arisen in India). A non-resident individual is one who does not fulfil the conditions for residency described above.

Tax year and filing requirements

The taxable period is the financial year, that is, 12 months ending 31 March.

Any individual whose total net income exceeds certain limits is required to file a return. Additionally, the assessees fulfilling certain economic criteria are required to submit income tax returns irrespective of whether or not their income exceeds the threshold.

Individuals are also required to obtain and quote a Permanent Account Number relating to specified transactions.

The filing dates for individuals subject to income tax are: on or before 31 July for all assessees, except in the case of assessees, who are required to file a return of income on account of one of the six economic criteria who are required to file the return by 31 October of the assessment year.

Taxes on income

Income tax is levied by the central government. The taxable income of an individual is his gross assessable income (other than exempt income) derived from all sources, including capital gains, during the financial year (irrespective of the accounting year adopted by the taxpayer), less allowable deductions. No tax is levied on the first Rs.50,000 of the income. The marginal rate of tax increases in stages according to different levels of taxable income.

The maximum marginal rate of tax for the year ended 31 March 2001 (for both resident and non-resident individuals) will be 30% for taxable income in excess of Rs 150,000. In addition to the income tax, individuals in the band of income of Rs 60,000 and Rs 150,000 are required to pay a surcharge on income tax at the rate of 12% and those having income exceeding Rs 150,000 are required to pay a surcharge on income tax at the rate of 17%. For the year ending 31 March 2002, the income tax rates have remained the same and the surcharge on income tax as stated before has been reduced to 2%.

In addition to income tax, the state government may levy a profession tax up to Rs 2,500 per annum which is deductible from the taxable income.

Sources of income

Employment income

Income from employment consists of salaries, wages, bonuses, pensions, taxable benefits and any other employment related earnings. Salary income is deemed to accrue or arise in India if it is paid or payable for service rendered in India. Therefore, salary and other allowances paid in the home country are taxable in India where an expatriate renders services in India (subject to tax treaty provisions).

Standard deductions at various stages of salary income are allowed in respect of expenses incidental to employment, irrespective of the actual expenses incurred. However, no standard deduction is allowed for employees drawing salary above Rs 500,000 per annum.

Benefits in kind are normally valued at the standard rates specified in the income tax rules, which may or may not bear any relation to the employer's actual cost. Tax on employment income, after certain allowable deductions have been made, is deducted at source by the employer.

The issue of stock options to employees is taxed as a capital gain on the difference between the option price and the price realised on sale or transfer.

Dividends on capital gains arising from Global Depository Receipts are taxable at a flat rate of 10% plus surcharge in the hands of resident employees.

Business income

In general, business income for tax purposes is determined according to generally accepted principles as adjusted by the specific income tax rules.

Any business having an annual turnover of more than Rs.4,000,000 or any professional organisation with gross receipts of more than Rs 1,000,000 are required to undergo a tax audit.

Losses

Business losses are fully deductible from any other income for the same year, and thereafter only against business income (not necessarily from the same business) within the subsequent eight years. Losses from speculative business can only be offset against profits from other speculation activities in the same year or subsequent eight years. Carry back of losses is not permitted.

Unused depreciation allowance

Unused depreciation is not treated as part of business loss and can be carried forward indefinitely for set-off against business income.

Subject to certain conditions, the conversion of an owner-managed business into a partnership or a partnership into a limited company is permissible without attracting a liability to capital gains tax.

Capital gains

Capital gains arising from transfer of short-term as well as long term capital assets are included in gross taxable income. A long term capital asset is one which is held for a period of at least one year in the case of shares or securities listed on a recognised stock exchange in India or the units of an Indian unit trust or of specified mutual funds, and three years in the case of any other asset. Depreciable assets used for business purposes are not subject to capital gains computation. However, the net proceeds on a sale of such assets are deducted from the business asset categories maintained for depreciation purposes.

While short term gains are taxed at an applicable rate, long term gains are taxed at 20% plus a surcharge of 12% or 17% thereon as the case may be (2% after 1 April 2001). Taxable long term gains are determined after taking cost indexation benefit into account. For non-resident individuals, a long term capital gain arising on transfer of shares or debentures of an Indian company originally acquired with foreign currency will be subject to the application of the foreign currency translation benefit rather than the cost indexation benefit.

Tax on long-term capital gains is limited for all those assessed, to 10% plus surcharge of 12% to 17% thereon as the case may be (2% after 1 April 2001) on the capital gains on sale of shares and listed securities prior to adjustment against the cost inflation index. Where the tax on capital gains exceeds 10% plus applicable surcharge, the cost inflation index benefit is not available on the excess.

Capital losses may be offset against capital gains in the same head for the same year or for a subsequent eight years.

Tax on capital gains accrues to the owner of shares and certain securities when the company buys back the shares or specified securities. In computing the gain, the cost indexation benefit or currency translation benefit is available.

Exempt income

The main categories of exempt income are:

- agricultural income, although such income is taken into account for rate purposes;
- any receipts up to Rs 5,000 which are casual and non-recurring in nature, unless these are related to business or are subject to capital gains tax;

- interest on certain government securities or savings schemes;
- remuneration received by foreign diplomats;
- certain types of redundancy benefits received by an employee, within specified limits;
- income from newly established businesses in a free trade zone, electronic hardware park or software technology park, or from newly established 100% export-oriented undertakings;
- dividends from Indian companies, income from the Unit Trust of India and mutual funds received by investors.

Interest and royalties

Gross interest and royalties are included in the gross taxable income of an individual. A deduction is allowed for bank commission, bank charges or any other expenditure incurred wholly and exclusively for the purposes of making or earning such income.

Rentals

The higher of actual or notional rental income from residential property is chargeable to income tax. Total exemption is allowed in respect of any one residential property which is self-occupied. A standard deduction of 30% of the annual value rent is allowed in respect of property where the computation is based on higher of the actual or notional rent in respect of self-occupied property. The deduction for interest is allowable to the extent of Rs 30,000 in the case of properties acquired or constructed prior to 1 April 1999; in respect of properties which are constructed with borrowed capital after 1 April 1999 and the construction of which is completed before 1 April 2003, the deduction has been enhanced from Rs 100,000 to Rs 150,000.

Personal allowance and deductions

No separate personal allowance is available, but income up to Rs.50,000 is taxed at a nil rate. In computing the net taxable income of an individual, the following are wholly or partially deductible:

- donations for specified purposes, subject to certain conditions;
- profits and gains from certain types of newly established industrial undertakings in specified areas;
- certain specified income of residents which results in inflow of foreign currency to India;
- income from interest on specified government securities up to Rs 9,000.

Rebate from income tax

A taxpayer can claim an income tax rebate at the rate of 20% of the qualifying amount of certain investment or expenditure. The maximum qualifying amount is restricted to Rs.80,000 and covers payment of insurance premium in India for the protection of the taxpayer and his family, investment in certain specified savings schemes, annuity schemes, equity linked mutual funds and mortgage payments and approved investments made in equity shares or debentures for the purposes of providing infrastructure, telecommunications or the generation or distribution of power.

A resident individual who is 65 years of age, or more, can claim rebate from tax liability up to Rs 15,000.

Special family rules

All individuals are taxed only on their own personal income irrespective of marital status. However, in certain cases 'clubbing provisions' are applicable to prevent tax avoidance by diverting income to a spouse or certain other relatives. Minors' income in excess of Rs.1,500 is clubbed with the income of the parent with higher income.

Rates of tax

Income tax: the same rates are applicable to residents and non-residents.

Band (Rs.)	*Rate (%)*	*Tax on band (Rs.)*	*Cumulative tax (Rs.)*
0–50,000	Nil	Nil	Nil
50,001–60,000	10	1,000	1,000
60,001–150,000	20	18,000	9,000
150,001	30 total	19,000	19,000 plus 30% of the amount by which income exceeds 150,000

For the year ended 31 March 2001, surcharge at the rate of 12% on income tax is levied against persons with income of more than Rs.60,000 but less than Rs.150,000 and on income exceeding Rs.150,000 at the rate of 17%. For the year, the said surcharge is reduced to 2% on income tax.

Payment of tax

Advance tax is required to be paid in three instalments (due on 15 September, 15 December and 15 March) based on the estimate of income for subsequent year ending on 31 March. The cumulative instalments paid at the respective due dates should not be less than 30%, 60% and 100% respectively of the total advance tax payable. Total advance tax payable is calculated but after taking due credit for tax deducted at source.

Estate duty

There is no inheritance tax in India since the abolition of the Estate Duty Act in March 1985.

Gift tax

Gift tax was abolished with effect from 1 October 1998.

Wealth tax

Wealth tax is levied on net wealth consisting of specified assets in excess of Rs 1.5 million as at 31 March every year. In the case of residents, the tax is charged on the value of net assets located anywhere in the world. For non-residents only net assets in India attract this tax.

Social security

All social security contributions are required to be paid to the relevant funds maintained by the government or to other recognised funds.

The following social security schemes are statutorily applicable:

- the Provident Fund scheme covers all employees earning not more than Rs 5,000 per month at the time of the scheme becoming applicable to an employer; contributions up to 12% of the salary are required to be made by the employer and the employee;
- out of 12% of an employer's contribution, 8.33% is transferred to the Pension Fund from which the employee will receive a monthly pension after retirement from employment;
- the employee is entitled to gratuity if he has completed a minimum of five years' service; the Payment of Gratuity Act applies to establishments having more than ten employees; an employer can cover the yearly increase in gratuity liability by paying annual contribution based on actuarial valuation of gratuity liability to an approved gratuity fund.

Other taxes

Real estate property tax

Levied at varying rates on the assessed value by the respective local authorities.

Excise duty

Levied by central government at various rates on a wide range of products manufactured in India.

Service tax

Levied by central government at 5% on specified services.

Sales tax

Levied by central as well as state government at various rates on a wide range of products sold in India.

Customs duty

Levied by central government at varying rates on a wide range of products imported into India.

Stamp duties

Certain legal and other documentation, as well as share transfer deeds require stamping with varying rates of stamp duty.

Exchange controls

All foreign exchange transactions are governed by the Foreign Exchange Management Act, with Reserve Bank of India as the monitoring authority. Permission is required for the transfer of money, assets and rights as follows:

- within India by non-residents;
- outside India by residents.

In general, a strict approach is adopted in respect of transactions involving the outflow of cash and capital from India.

Withholding taxes

Income tax is withheld from all payments to a non-resident, except dividend. The rates of deduction in respect of payment in the form of fees for technical services, royalties and interest are prescribed. Any other payment is subject to withholding tax at the rates agreed with the assessing officer.

The following table illustrates the rate currently in force:

Country	*Interest* (%)	*Royalty* (%)	*Fees for technical services* (%)
Non-treaty countries	20	20	20
Treaty countries:			
Australia	15	10/15/20	10/15/20
Austria	20	20	20 (net basis)
Bangladesh	10	10	20
Belgium	10/15	20	20
Brazil	15	15/20	20
(25% for royalty on trademarks and others 15%)			
Belarus	10	15	15
Bulgaria	15	15/20	20
Canada	15	15/20	10/15/20
China	10	10	10
Cyprus	10	15	10
Czech Republic	10	10	10
Denmark	10/15	20	20
Finland	10	20	20
France	10/15	20	20
Germany	10	10	10
Greece	20	20	20
Hungary	15	20	20
Indonesia	10	15	20
Israel	10	10	10
Italy	15	20	20
Japan	10/15	20	20
Jordan	10	20	20
Kazakhstan	10	10	10
Kenya	15	20	20
Korea	10/15	15	15
Libya	20	20	20
Malaysia	20	20	20
Malta	10	15	10
Mauritius	20	15	15
Mongolia	15	15	15

Morocco	10	10	10
Namibia	10	10	10
Nepal	10/15	15	20
Netherlands	10/15	20	20
New Zealand	10/15	30/10	30/10
Norway	15	*not prescribed*	10
Oman	10	15	15
Poland	15	22.5	22.5
Philippines	10/15	15	20
Qatar	10	10	10
Romania	15	22.5	22.5
Russia	10	10	10
Singapore	10/15	15/10	15/10
Spain	15	10/20	20
Sri Lanka	10	10	20
South Africa	10	10	10
Sweden	10	10	10
Swiss	15/10	10/15	10/15
Syria	7.5	10	20
Tanzania	7.5	10	20
Thailand	10/25	15	20
Trinidad & Tobago	10	10	10
Turkey	10/15	15	15
Turkmenistan	10	10	10
United Arab Emirates	5/12.5	10	20
United Kingdom	10/15	*10/15/20	*10/15/20
USA	10/15	*10/15/20	*10/15/20
Uzbekistan	15	15	15
Vietnam	10	10	10
Zambia	10	10	20

*In some states the tax rate applicable to interest paid to banks and financial institutions carrying on bona fide banking business is 10% and interest paid to the government/quasi-government authorities and Central Bank of the state is exempt from tax.

Individuals

Tax is deducted at source on employment income at the applicable rates after allowing certain deductions. Withholding taxes are deducted at source from certain gross payments made to both residents and non-residents. These are later offset against the final liability.

	*Residents** (%)	*Non-resident Indians* (%)	*Other non-residents* (%)
a.(i) Interest other than interest on securities	10	See (k) below	See (k) below
(ii) Interest on debentures or securities other than Central or State Government securities	10	–	–
b. Winnings from lotteries/ crossword puzzles	40	40	40
c. Winnings from horse races	40	40	40
d. Insurance commission	10	See (k) below	See (k) below
e. Interest on moneys borrowed or debt incurred in foreign currency	–	20	20
f.(i) Income by way of long-term capital gain on specified assets referred to in Section 115E	–	10	–
(ii) Investment income and other term capital gains	–	20	20
(iii) Income from bonds or shares (other than dividends referred to in	–	10	10

	Section 115-O) purchased in foreign currency or capital gain arising from their transfer			
g.	Payments to contractors (exceeding Rs 20,000)	2 (other than advertisement contract)	See (k) below	See (k) below
h.	Payments to sub-contractors	1% per advertisement contract	See (k) below	See (k) below
i.	Rent (exceeding Rs 120,000 p.a.)	15	See (k) below	See (k) below
j.	Professional/ technical fees exceeding Rs 20,000	5	See (k) below	See (k) below
k.	All other income	The higher of 20% of the actual rates applicable as if such income has been the total income	The higher of 30% of the actual rates applicable as if such income has been the total income.	The higher of 30% of the actual rates applicable as if such income has been the total income

* The surcharge at the rate of 10% of the tax payable by residents is imposed with effect from 1 April 1999, i.e. Assessment year 2000/01.

Indonesia

Johan, Malonda & Rekan

Introduction

The major taxes in Indonesia are levied at national and provincial levels. Tax subjects also include mass and socio-political organisations.

Corporate taxes

Taxable entities

Resident companies

Resident companies are subject to corporate income tax on their worldwide income. A company is resident if it is incorporated in Indonesia. A branch of a foreign company, which is a permanent establishment, is liable to corporate income tax on their Indonesian source profit and its parent company's income from similar type of business and businesses closely related with that of the permanent establishment.

Non-resident companies

Non-resident companies are liable to corporate income tax (by way of a withholding tax) on their Indonesian source income.

Tax year and filing requirements

The financial year of a company is detailed in the company's articles of association. Companies must file their corporate income tax returns within three months of the close of their financial year. The maximum permitted extension period is six months from the due date of the income tax return. The tax authorities are not required to issue tax assessments except for those companies which have undergone a tax audit.

The tax return for employee income tax follows the calendar year, not the book year of the company.

Tax returns not audited within ten years of the relevant financial year end are final. The expiry date may be extended for cases of criminal offence.

Payment of tax

Companies must pay their current year taxes in monthly instalments based on the preceding year's corporate income tax liability, less tax withheld by third parties divided by 12. Monthly instalments of income tax prior to the filing of annual tax return follows the tax instalment paid in the last month of the preceding book year. Certain income, such as rent, interest, royalties and specific services are subject to withholding tax. Withholding tax may be taken as a tax credit, except if treated as final tax. The balance of the current year tax liability must be settled at the latest by the 25th day of the third month after the accounts year end, prior to filing of the corporate income tax return.

Rates of tax

The corporate income tax rates on taxable profits are as follows:

- 10% on the first Rupiah 50 million;
- 15% on profits above Rupiah 50 million up to Rupiah 100 million;
- 30% on profits above Rupiah 100 million.

Income subject to tax

General rules

Income from all sources worldwide is subject to tax, less allowable expenses. The method used to determine taxable profit must be consistent from year to year. Any change must be approved by the tax authorities.

Inventory valuation

Allowable methods for valuing inventory are the FIFO and average methods.

Capital gains and losses

A company's capital gains or losses are treated as income and is subject to normal tax rates. Sales of land and buildings by a company are subject to a 5% income tax which is treated as tax credit. Land and buildings sold by individuals are subject to a 5% final tax. The buyer is subject to a 5% excise net of allowable deduction. Applicable values are market price or selling price, whichever is higher.

The selling of shares through the Stock Exchange is subject to a 0.1% final tax. Founder's shares are subject to an additional 0.5%.

Bonds sold through the Stock Exchange are subject to a 0.03% final tax on the gross amount of the transaction.

Dividends

Dividends include bonus shares declared from a non-cash capital paid-in source such as 'revaluation increment' or capitalization of capital paid in excess of par value.

Dividends received by a company from another company incorporated in Indonesia are not subject to corporate income tax provided all of the following criteria are met:

- source of dividends is retained earnings;
- a minimum of 25% ownership from paid-in capital;
- conducts active business besides investments.

Deductions

General rules

Expenses incurred in the course of generating, collecting and maintaining the income of a company are wholly tax deductible, with the exception of benefits in kind provided to employees, such as motor cars, housing, medical expenses, donations, provision for bad debt (except for banks and financial institutions) and provision for retirement benefits. Provisions may be deductible when they are realised. Normal entertainment expenses incurred for business purposes may also be deductible. Free meals are tax deductible if provided to all employees

Depreciation and amortisation

Depreciation charges are effective since the month the costs are incurred.

The straight-line method of depreciation is permitted for buildings at the following rates:

Indonesia

Permanent buildings	5%
Temporary buildings	10%

There are four categories of other fixed assets permitted to apply the declining or straight-line method of depreciation with varying rates, as follows:

	Useful life	*Straight-line*	*Declining balance*
Category I			
Motorcycles, wooden furniture and equipment, dies, jigs and moulds	4 years	25%	50%
Category II			
Metal furniture and equipment, air conditioners, computers, printers, cars, buses, trucks, containers and the like. Machinery for agriculture, plantation, forestry, fishery, food & beverage, and light industrial, logging and construction equipment, heavy equipment for transportation, warehousing and communication, telecommunication equipment, equipment for semi conductor industries.	8 years	12.5%	25%
Category III			
Machinery for general mining other than oil and gas. Machinery for textile, timber, chemical and machinery industries. Heavy equipment, docks and vessels for transportation and communication. Telecommunication equipment.	16 years	6.25%	12.5%

Category IV			
Metal furniture and equipment, heavy machinery for construction, railways, wagons and floating docks, transportation and communication equipment.	20 years	5%	10%

Long term prepaid expenses are amortised on the declining balance or straight-line method as follows:

Prepayment period	*Declining balance*	*Straight-line*
Within 4 years	50%	25%
Within 8 years	25%	12.5%
Within 16 years	12.5%	6.25%
Within 20 years	10%	5%

The initial costs to obtain right on land cannot be amortised. But official expenses incurred for the extension of right on land can be amortised over its beneficial period or maximum 20 years.

Buildings under construction and other fixed assets under installation are depreciated, commencing the month these assets are ready for usage.

With the approval of the Director General for Taxes, depreciation may commence when the company starts commercial operations or when the asset starts earning revenue.

Royalties, interest, management and services fees

The above expenses are deductible provided transactions are at arm's length and properly documented.

The Minister of Finance is empowered to issue a regulation on the debt to equity ratio, to determine the amount of interest deductible from income. No decision has been issued to date.

Foreign source income

Dividends, interest and royalties are added to income. Withholding taxes, if any, may be taken as a tax credit.

Related party transactions

The tax authorities are empowered to make adjustments on related party transactions if they deem that the transactions are not made on an arm's length basis.

Losses

Tax losses, which must be confirmed by the tax authorities, may be carried forward for five years to offset against profits. For certain industries or undertakings, the Minister of Finance can extend the carry-forward offset period to a maximum of ten years.

Corporate groups

The tax law does not allow a parent company to file consolidated tax returns. Each entity must file its own tax return. The lower tax rate can also be applied to all subsidiaries.

Tax on property

Land and buildings owned by a company are subject to property tax. The tax is based on the market value of the land and buildings and is payable annually.

International organisations

International organisations as ruled by the Minister of Finance are exempted from tax provided that:

- Indonesia is also a member of that organisation;
- the organisation is not involved in revenue deriving activities in Indonesia;
- the organisation is engaged in providing loans to the government with funds coming from contributions of its members.

Loan forgiveness

Profit from loan forgiveness is in principle taxable. Exemption up to a certain percentage is possible if the loan restructuring is conducted through an institution as determined by the government.

Social organisations

Contributions received by an organisation from its members who are conducting business and professional services are taxable.

Written-off accounts receivable

The above is tax deductible provided the following conditions are met:

- recorded at cost in the commercial profit and loss statement;
- its collection is conducted through the Court of Justice, Government Public Auction Agency or a statement regarding the debt write-off prepared by a notary public;
- published in the mass media or certain publications; and
- a list submitted of an uncollectible Accounts receivables to the Director General of Taxes.

Investment tax facilities

Investments conducted under the foreign or domestic capital investment scheme (PMA and PMDN) may enjoy certain tax facilities if conducted in a certain line of business or in certain areas.

The tax facilities are as follows:

- reduction in net income of up to a maximum of 30% divided over six years, from investments made;
- accelerated depreciation and amortisation;
- carried forward losses of more than five years up to a maximum of 10 years;
- income tax on dividends of 10%, except when the tax treaty states a lower rate.

Bonded zones

Companies operating in bonded zones may enjoy the following facilities:

- postponement of import duties;
- exemption from Value Added Tax and Luxury Sales Tax;
- exemption from import withholding tax (income tax article 22);
- exemption from excise duties.

Integrated economic development zones (KAPET)

Companies operating and domiciled in KAPET zones may enjoy the following facilities:

- reduction in net income of up to a maximum of 30% divided over 6 years from investments made, commencing commercial production;
- accelerated depreciation and amortisation;
- compensation of carried forward losses for up to a maximum of 10 years;
- income tax on dividends of 10%, except when the tax treaty states a lower rate.

Companies operating in bonded zones located in KAPET zones enjoy the facilities of both zones.

Venture capital

Income received by a venture capital company from its venture business partner is exempted from tax provided:

- the venture business partner is a small or medium sized company, or it is engaged in the business sectors determined by a Finance Minister decree;
- its shares are not traded in the Stock Exchange in Indonesia.

Pension fund

Income received by a Finance Minister approved Pension Fund from investments in certain businesses as determined through a Finance Minister decree is exempted from tax.

Mutual fund

Interest income from bonds received by a Mutual Fund Company during the first five years of its operations since establishment or the obtaining of an operating license is exempted from tax.

Language and currency used for accounting purposes

Only English and the US Dollar are allowed to be used in the company's accounts other than Bahasa Indonesia and Rupiah. The company is required to report such intention at the latest three months prior to the related book year. Tax returns must be filed in Bahasa

Indonesia. For newly established companies such intention must be reported within three months after its establishment date.

Liquidation of a company

Upon liquidation, the amount which shareholders receive in excess of the paid-up capital is in principle subject to tax.

Investment tax facilities

Investments conducted under the foreign or domestic capital investment scheme (PMA and PMDN) may enjoy certain tax facilities if conducted in certain line of businesses or in certain areas.

The tax facilities are as follows:

- reduction in net income of up to a maximum of 30% divided over six years, from investments made;
- accelerated depreciation and amortization;
- carried forward losses of more than five years up to a maximum of ten years;
- income tax on dividends of 10%, except when the tax treaty states a lower rate.

Personal taxes

Taxable individuals

Residents

An individual is resident if he lives in Indonesia in excess of 183 days within a 12 month period or arrives in Indonesia during a fiscal year with the intention of remaining. A resident is subject to income tax on his worldwide income.

All 'resident taxpayers' with income above the minimum taxable income are required to have a 'Tax Registration Number'.

Non-residents

A non-resident is subject to income tax on his Indonesian source income at a rate of 20%. The tax rate is reduced for residents of tax treaty countries.

Tax year and filing requirements

The tax year for an individual is the calendar year. Individuals are required to file tax returns if their income is above the minimum tax exempted amount. They must file their tax returns by the following 31 March with a possible six-month extension. Taxes must be paid at the latest on 25 March. Non-residents are not required to file tax returns, as tax on their Indonesian source income is withheld by the payer. It is not mandatory for the tax authorities to issue tax assessments every year, but they may do so within ten years of the end of the relevant tax year. If no assessment is issued within the ten year period, the tax becomes final. The expiry date is extended if tax authorities can prove that a taxpayer has committed a criminal tax offence.

Non-residents' income from services may be exempted from tax if they fulfill the time-test period regulated in the tax treaty.

Payroll taxes and social security contributions

All employers are required by law to calculate, withhold and pay the income tax on their employees' income. Social security contributions are paid by both employers and employees. Companies are responsible for depositing the contributions monthly with a government agency.

Sources of income

Employment income

All emoluments provided by employers, except benefits in kind, are taxable. Benefits in kind provided to employees employed by companies or international organisations, which are not liable for corporate income tax, are subject to final tax or are assessed based on a calculation norm like deemed profit, are taxable. Contributions to government approved pension funds and social security are deductible. Severance pay and retirement pensions paid in full upfront are subject to a final tax, as follows:

- Rupia 25,000,000 or less is exempted from withholding tax;
- Rupia 25,000,000 to Rupia 50,000,000 – 5 % final tax;
- above Rupia 50,000,000 to Rupia 100,000,000 – 10 % final tax;
- above Rupia 100,000,000 to Rupia 200,000,000 – 15 % final tax;
- above Rupia 200,000,000 – 25 % final tax.

Business income

The taxable income of a business is calculated in accordance with generally accepted accounting principles consistently applied from year to year. Accounts must be prepared on a calendar year basis.

Capital gains

Capital gains are treated as normal income. The selling of shares on the Stock Exchange is subject to a 0.1 % final tax on the gross amount of the transaction. The selling of founder shares are subject to an additional 0.5% final tax. Land and buildings sold by an individual are subject to a 5% final tax. Land and buildings sold by a company are subject to a 5% provisional income tax. This tax may be refundable if there is an overpayment of corporate income tax. The transfer of fixed assets to a limited liability company as paid up capital must be at market value. Grants between parents and children, and inherited estates, are tax free.

The purchaser of land and buildings is subject to a 5% excise duty on the purchases of land and building rights after subtraction of a deductible amount.

Dividends, royalties, interest, rent and services

The above categories of income are generally subject to withholding tax at 15% to 20% of the gross income, which represents a tax credit for the recipient, provided that it is not a final tax. The effective rate is lower if charged on net income (1.2% to 7.5%). These types of income are liable to the normal tax rate, except for interest on term deposit, savings accounts and rents from land and buildings on which withholding tax is the final tax.

Final withholding taxes cannot be treated as tax credit.

Social security and pensions

Social security and pension contributions are deductible but the benefits are taxable.

Foreign source income

Foreign source income is subject to income tax. Withholding tax may be taken as a tax credit.

Personal allowance and deductions

Resident taxpayers are granted tax-free allowances as follows:

	Rupia
Single taxpayer	2,880,000
Spouse	1,440,000
For each child, up to a maximum of three children	1,440,000
Separate allowance for wife whose income is not from her husband's business	2,880,000
Employees are entitled to 5% of their income for employment expenses to a yearly maximum of	1,296,000

All expenses for individuals carrying on business are in principle deductible. Exceptions are the same as for corporate income tax.

Special provisions

The income of an individual becoming or ceasing to be a taxpayer during a calendar year is annualised to arrive at his income tax liability.

Losses

Tax losses can be carried forward for five years against future profits. Initial losses in specified industries can, with approval from the Minister of Finance, be carried forward for a maximum of ten years.

Rates of tax

The income tax rates for individuals are as follows:

Up to Rupia 25,000,000	5%
Above Rupia 25,000,000 – Rupia 50,000,000	10%
Above Rupia 50,000,000 – Rupia 100,000,000	15%
Above Rupia 100,000,000 – Rupia 200,000,000	25%
Above Rupia 200,000,000	35%

Provincial and local tax rates

There are no provincial or local taxes on income.

Withholding taxes

Withholding tax at 15% is levied on income from non-bank interests, dividends, royalties, fees and rents received by Indonesian residents. Withholding tax on interest from time deposits and saving accounts is final 20%. Not final withholding tax can be taken as tax credit by the recipient of income from these sources. All income (from whatever source) is subject to income tax. In principle all income tax withheld represents a tax credit, except for final tax. The effective tax rate is lower if levied on net income ranging 1.2% to 7.5%.

Payment of tax

Individuals must pay their income taxes monthly based on the preceding year income tax liability less any taxes withheld from income, divided by 12. Monthly instalments of income tax prior to the filing of annual tax return follows tax instalment paid in the last month of the preceding book year. Individuals owning more than one place for trading and shopping centres are subject to a 1% monthly prepaid income net on their sales.

Estate and gift tax

Generally, there are no estate and gift taxes in Indonesia.

Taxes on property

Land and buildings are liable to tax assessed annually based on the value of the land and buildings. The tax is due at the end of the calendar year. The tax on land and buildings replaces wealth tax.

Other taxes

Joint operations

Profits made by a joint venture or partnership are allocated to the partners in accordance with their profit shares and taxed in the partners' hands.

VAT and sales tax

All manufactured and imported products are liable to VAT at 10%. In addition to VAT, certain luxury goods are subject to sales tax. The rate of sales tax is 10% to 75%. The luxury sales tax is applied to the manufacturer or the sole agent for imported goods. A zero rate of VAT applies to the export of goods.

With the exception of certain services, all services with its benefits utilised in Indonesia are liable to VAT at 10%.

In principle, all second-hand fixed assets owned by a company not for trading are subject to VAT if sold.

Road tax

Road tax applies to all motor vehicles and is payable annually in amounts which depend on vehicle market value.

Transfer tax

Transfer tax applies on the purchase and transfer of ownership of motor vehicles.

Excise duties

Excise duties apply to cigarettes and alcohol.

Exchange control

Indonesia has no exchange controls. Approved investment joint venture companies are required to report on the realisation of investment. Indonesian companies and individuals receiving loans from overseas must report to the Central Bank for statistical purposes.

Transactions reaching US$ 10,000 are subject to reporting requirements.

Foreign investments

Except for certain types of business closed to foreign investment, as stated in the 'negative list', all other businesses can be owned by foreign individuals or companies. Foreign investors may buy shares in existing non-public and non-foreign investment companies, and change the company's status to a foreign investment company.

Tax treaties and withholding taxes

Under the majority of double taxation conventions concluded by Indonesia, the 20% dividend tax rate is reduced. The withholding tax of 20% on interest, royalties and technical fees paid to non-residents is also reduced under the tax treaties as follows:

Country of Residence	*After Tax Profit of Permanent Establishment*	*Interest*	*Royalties*	*Portfolio*	*Dividends Substantial Holdings*
	%	%	%	%	%
Non-treaty countries	20	20	20	20	20
Treaty countries:					
Australia	15	0/10	10/15	15	15
Austria	12	0/10	10	15	10
Belgium	15	0/10/15	10	15	15
Bulgaria	15	0/10	10	15	15
Canada	15	0/10	10	15	10
Czech	12.5	12.5	12.5	15	10
Denmark	15	0/10	15	20	10
Finland	15	0/10	10/15	15	10
France	10	0/10/15	10	15	10
Germany	10	0/10	10/15/7.5	15	10
Hungary	0/20	0/15	15	15	15
India	10	0/10	15	15	10
Italy	12	0/10	10/15	15	10
Japan	10	0/10	10	15	10
Jordan	20	10	0/10	10	10
Kuwait	10	0/5	20	10	10
1Luxembourg	10	0/10	12.5/10	15	10
Malaysia	12.5	0/15	15	15	15
Mauritius	10	0/10	10	10	5
Netherlands	9	0/10	10	15	10
New Zealand	0	0/10	15	15	15
Norway	15	0/10	10/15	15	15
Pakistan	10	0/15	15	15	10
Philippines	20	0/10/15	15	20	15
Poland	10	0/10	15	15	10
Romania	12.5	12.5	12.5	15	12.5
Seychelles	20	10	10	10	–
Singapore	15	0/10	15	15	10
South Africa	–	10	10	15	10
South Korea	10	0/10	15	15	10
Sri Lanka	20	0/15	15	15	15
Sweden	15	0/10	10/15	15	10
Switzerland	10	0/10	12.5	15	10
Syria	10	0/10	15/20	10	10
Taiwan	5	0/10	10	10	10
Thailand	20	0/15	10/15	15	15
Tunisia	12	0/12	15	12	12
Turkey	20	10	10	15	10
Ukraine	10	10	10	15	10
United Kingdom	10	0/10	10/15	15	10

Indonesia

U S A	10	0/10	10	15	10
Uzbekistan	10	10	10	10	10

Ireland

Oliver Freaney & Company

Introduction

Ireland has continued to lower corporate and personal tax rates in recent years. The reduction in rates has been partly offset by restrictions to reliefs, such as capital allowances. The tax year for companies is normally the company's accounting period, provided the latter is not greater than 12 months. Individuals had been assessed on income earned to 5 April each year; in the case of a trade or profession, tax is payable on profits of the accounting year ending in the income tax year. The income tax year will be aligned with the calendar year with effect from 1 January 2002. A transitional tax 'year' will run from 6 April 2001 to 31 December 2001.

Corporate taxes

Taxable entities

Resident companies

Resident companies are liable to corporation tax on their worldwide income, including capital gains. Companies are resident in Ireland if their central management and control is situated in Ireland. Thus, companies incorporated outside Ireland can be resident in Ireland. With effect from 11 February 1999, companies incorporated in Ireland will be regarded as resident in the state even if managed and controlled from abroad. This place of incorporation rule does not apply where the company or a related company carries on a trade in the state and either the company is ultimately controlled by persons resident in an EU or a treaty country, or else the company or a related company are quoted companies. In addition, where a company is regarded as not resident under a tax treaty between Ireland and another state, then the place of incorporation rule will not apply.

Non-resident companies

Non-resident companies are liable to corporation tax on trading profits and other income derived from an Irish branch and also on capital gains realised in respect of assets used or held for the purposes of the branch.

Other income arising in Ireland is subject to income tax and not to corporation tax.

Apart from branch assets referred to above, capital gains tax is chargeable on gains derived from:

- land;
- exploration and exploitation rights in designated areas; and
- unquoted shares which derive the greater part of their value from such land, minerals or exploration and exploitation rights as is mentioned above.

Taxes imposed

All taxes on income are imposed at the national level.

Corporation tax is charged on profits of an accounting period. If an accounting period exceeds 12 months then it is subdivided into shorter periods not exceeding 12 months. The rate of tax is determined by reference to the appropriate rate or rates for that year. If the rate changes, profits of accounting periods straddling the change over date are apportioned on a time basis. Tax is payable six months after the end of the accounting period.

Income tax is levied on individuals and non-resident companies. Income tax is normally applied to non-resident companies by withholding at source from rents, interest and royalties.

Rates of tax

Corporation tax

With effect from 1 January 2001 the rate of corporation tax for trading income, with the exception of certain land dealing activities, is 20%. Companies whose total trading income (other than income taxable at the 10% or 25% rates) for an accounting period is less than £200,000 are taxed on such income at the 12.5% rate. Manufacturing companies, however, are eligible for a 10% rate on their profits – see investment incentives later in the chapter.

Non-trading income, certain land dealing activities, income from working minerals and petroleum activities are taxed at the 25% rate.

Capital gains tax

The rate of capital gains tax is 20%.

Resident companies

Retained profits and distributed profits are (in general) charged at the same rate. Exceptions apply to the undistributed profits of closely held resident companies providing professional services, or services of any description to professional partnerships or persons, and also to the undistributed rental income and investment income of closely held resident companies. In these cases, a 20% corporation tax surcharge is imposed on the relevant after-tax income retained, depending on the activity of the company.

With effect from 6 April 1999, dividends and other distributions made by resident companies are subject to withholding tax at the standard rate of income tax (currently 20%). Distributions to Irish resident companies may be made without deduction of withholding tax. In addition, residents of EU or tax treaty states, companies ultimately controlled by residents of EU or tax treaty states and quoted companies of EU or tax treaty states, are entitled to an exemption from withholding tax, subject to providing a declaration and evidence of residence.

Non-resident companies

Such companies are liable to income tax at 20% on Irish source income not derived from or attributable to a permanent establishment in Ireland.

Income subject to tax

General rules

Income for tax purposes is calculated in accordance with established principles of commercial accounting, as adjusted by reference to the income tax legislation.

Capital gains and losses

Gains are calculated by deducting from the proceeds of sale or disposal the original cost, improvement costs and incidental expenses of sale, such as commissions and fees. The acquisition and improvement costs are indexed upwards to take account of inflation. There are restrictions on the indexation of acquisition and improvement costs of development land. Capital losses cannot be increased by indexation and may only be offset capital gains of the same or subsequent years.

Only capital losses on development land may be set against development land capital gains.

Dividends

Dividends from one Irish resident company to another are not liable to corporation tax. However, if received by closely held resident companies and not distributed onwards, such dividends are liable to the corporation tax surcharge referred to above.

Dividends received from abroad are taxable. Relief is given for foreign tax suffered, either as a deduction or a credit. In general, a credit is given where a Treaty exists, otherwise a deduction is given. 'Credit' means an offset of the foreign tax paid against the Irish tax liability. 'Deduction' means a deduction in computing taxable income for the foreign tax paid.

Deductions

General rules

Expenses are deductible for tax purposes with certain exceptions:

- only expenses which are wholly and exclusively incurred for the purposes of the trade are normally deductible;
- no capital expenditure can be deducted except as depreciation/ capital allowances;
- capital losses, entertainment expenses, general provisions and dividends are not deductible.

Capital allowances

Plant and machinery

With effect from 1 January 2001, plant and machinery and motor vehicles qualify for a straight-line deduction of 20% over 5 years.

Industrial buildings

Factories and similar premises, including warehouses, used in manufacturing trades qualify for an allowance of 4% per annum on a straight-line basis. If the premises are more than 25 years old the allowances may not be available. The allowance is available in respect of buildings only. It is not available in respect of site cost.

Hotels

Qualifying expenditure on hotels is allowed at 15% per annum on a straight-line basis for the first six years and 10% in year seven. If the hotel is more than ten years old, the allowance may not be available.

Other allowances

Special rules provide for relief for the following costs:

- scientific research;
- mining development;
- dredging;
- patent rights.

Royalties

Patent royalties are deductible from the total relevant trading income on a cash payment basis. Other royalties (for example, know-how) are allowed as a normal business expense on an actual basis.

Interest

Interest payable as a trade expense is normally deductible in computing profits of a trade. However, interest payable to a parent company not resident in a treaty country is not, in general, deductible and is treated as a distribution.

Non-trading interest payable to non-residents is normally allowed as a deduction only if income tax is withheld on payment, unless:

- the appropriate double taxation agreement provides for zero withholding tax and an exemption certificate has been obtained;
- the interest is payable out of foreign income.

The paying company must be resident in Ireland. The regulations are complicated and there are many restrictions on this relief.

Investment incentives and special benefits

The standard rate of corporation tax on trading income is to be reduced on a phased basis as follows:

- 20% for the year 2001;
- 16% for the year 2002;
- 12.5% for the year 2003 and subsequent years.

Manufacturing relief

Companies engaged in manufacturing in Ireland are eligible for a 10% rate of corporation tax on all manufacturing profits arising between 1 January 1981 and 31 December 2010. In order to qualify, a reasonable degree of manufacturing must be carried on in Ireland but goods need not be entirely manufactured there. Although profits from retail sales and sales into EU intervention and construction work are excluded, the manufacture and sale of goods for the construction industry (e.g. concrete blocks) can qualify. Software development and data processing can qualify as does engineering and architectural design and planning services for non-EU works and fish production on a fish farm.

Certain non-manufacturing companies which contribute towards the development of the Shannon region may also qualify for the 10% tax rate under a licensing system. This relief expires on 31 December 2005. Activities which qualify must fall within one or more of the following:

- repair or maintenance of aircraft;
- trading operations which contribute to the use or development of Shannon Airport;
- trading operations which are ancillary to the above operations or to any other operations consisting of the manufacture of goods.

Cash grants are available for machinery, buildings and staff training.

Financial services centre

The financial services centre is located in the Custom House Docks area of Dublin. In 1986, the Government recognised the potential of the area for redevelopment.

The Government included in the Finance Act 1987 a provision for the application of a 10% rate of corporation tax to international financial services and other activities associated with such services located on the site. Approved companies engaged in the provision of financial services will qualify for the 10% rate of corporation tax until the year 2005. Such companies would include those engaged in fund management, treasury management, financial advice and dealing and brokerage operations.

Here is a summary of tax incentives available (as underlined by Dublin's International Financial Services Centre):

- rate of corporation tax – the rate may be increased if the company so desires because of home country controlled foreign corporation rules;
- no withholding tax is deductible by a company at the Centre in respect of dividends paid to a parent company located in a country with which Ireland has ratified a Taxation Convention;
- tax treaties in most cases allow for the repatriation of profits with little or no taxation in the home country;
- stamp duty – in general, most financial transactions carried out at the centre will not attract stamp duty (documents prepared in Ireland in respect of foreign transactions and executed abroad are exempt from stamp duty);
- value added tax – International Financial Services are, in general, not liable to VAT;
- capital gains tax – gains from the sale of stocks and shares by Financial Institutions and Insurance Companies will not normally be liable to capital gains tax but will be treated as trading income eligible for the 10% rate of corporation tax.

Related party transactions

Payments to or receipts from companies or other persons under common control may be subject to revision to market value. This is especially the case where one of the entities is eligible for the 10% rate of corporation tax. However, the Revenue Commissioners are highly unlikely to challenge a highly profitable 10% tax rate company trading on favourable terms with overseas associated companies.

Losses

Trading losses can usually be off-set against all income (including capital gains) of the year of loss or the preceding year. Any balance remaining can be carried forward indefinitely, provided the trade is continued, but only against profits from the trade in which the loss was incurred. Anti-avoidance provisions exist to prevent, in certain circumstances, the carrying forward of trading losses where the ownership of a company changes.

In the case of other losses, for example rental losses, relief is more restricted.

Corporate groups

Each company within a group is taxed as a separate entity. However, group relief may be claimed to set-off trading losses and certain other deficits (such as excess interest charges, but not capital losses) incurred in one company against the profits of the same period of another company in the group. Companies wishing to take advantage of these provisions must be EU residents and one must be at least 75% owned by the other or both must be at least 75% owned by a third EU resident company. The loss or deficit can only be set-off against profits earned in the period of loss; thus, a loss could not be surrendered for set-off against future profits of another group company. The relief applies only in respect of activities within the charge to Irish tax.

There is a similar relief available for certain consortium companies.

Restrictions exist on the offsetting of losses, excess capital allowances or excess charges on income (where those losses or excesses arise in a trade which is otherwise taxable at 10%). Losses of such companies can only be claimed under group and consortium relief against profits of another group company, which itself is liable to the 10% rate of taxation.

Personal taxes

Taxable individuals

Residents

Liability to income tax is determined by residence rather than citizenship. An Irish resident is liable to income tax on all of his income wherever arising. An individual is treated as resident in Ireland for a tax year if he or she:

- spends 183 days or more in Ireland in that tax year;
- spends 280 days in Ireland, combining the number of days spent in the country in that tax year and in the preceding tax year.

Presence in a tax year by an individual of not more than 30 days in Ireland will not be recognised for the purpose of applying the two-year test. Presence in the country for a day means the personal presence of an individual at the end of the day (midnight).

An individual coming to Ireland who is not a resident and who can show that he or she intends to remain in the country and be resident in the following year, may elect to be treated as resident for the year of arrival. It is not possible to elect to be non-resident.

An individual who has been resident in Ireland for three consecutive tax years becomes ordinarily resident from the beginning of the fourth tax year. An individual who has been ordinarily resident in Ireland ceases to be ordinarily resident at the end of the third consecutive year in which he or she is not resident.

An individual who is resident but not domiciled will not be liable to income tax on income arising abroad (i.e. outside Ireland and the UK). Such income is only taxed if remitted to Ireland. Irish and UK incomes are fully liable in the hands of a resident, irrespective of domicile.

Broadly speaking, an individual is domiciled in the country or state which he regards as his permanent home. He acquires a domicile of origin at birth, normally that of his father, and retains it until he acquires a new domicile by choice. To acquire a domicile of choice, a person must sever his ties with his domicile of origin and settle in another country with the clear intention of making his permanent home there. Long residence in a country will not necessarily prove that a person has acquired a domicile of choice there unless he indicates an intention to settle permanently.

Non-residents

A non-resident is liable to tax only on income arising in Ireland.

Double Taxation Agreements frequently provide exemption for certain types of Irish income such as interest.

Tax year and filing requirements

Individuals had been assessed on income earned to 5 April each year, in the case of a trade or profession tax is payable on profits of the accounting year ending in the income tax year. The income tax year will be aligned with the calendar year with effect from 1 January 2002. A transitional tax 'year' will run from 6 April 2001 to 31 December 2001. The filing requirements for the two different tax year ends are as follows:

Taxable period

The tax year ends on 5 April.

Individuals must make a return of income on or before a specified date, i.e. not later than 31 January in the year after the year of assessment to which the return relates.

For example:

Year of assessment	*Specified date*
2000/01	31 January 2002

The tax year ends on 31 December.

Individuals must make a return of income on or before a specified date, i.e. not later than 31 October in the year after the year of assessment to which the return relates.

For example:

Year of assessment	*Specified date*
2001	31 October 2002

Returns must be made whether requested by the Revenue or not and persons who fail to meet this requirement will be subject to a 5% surcharge on their income tax liability for the year if the return is submitted before the expiry of two months after the specified date and a surcharge of 10% thereafter.

In the absence of tax returns, personal allowances may be withheld. Where a person defaults in making a return or the Inspector is dissatisfied with the return, the Inspector may make an assessment.

Taxes on income

Individuals are subject to PAYE (income tax by deduction at source) on all employment income paid in the state. Most other types of income are subject to tax by self-assessment. In addition to ordinary income tax, Pay Related Social Insurance (PRSI) is payable on earnings. Certain earnings of writers, artists and composers are exempt from tax; also exempt is income from certain patent royalties, forestry operations and stallion services.

Sources of income

Employment income

In general, all income is taxable including all payments from the employer. Deductions are allowed for expenses, wholly, exclusively and necessarily incurred in the course of an employment and for payments to approved superannuation schemes and for qualifying interest payments.

An employee allowance of IR£ 2,000 is also allowable in general at the standard rate of tax (20%).

Any benefits arising from an employment will be treated as remuneration of the employment. If personal allowances are sufficient, they will normally be restricted under the payroll deduction system (PAYE) by the amount of the benefit in order to simplify collection of the tax arising on the benefits.

Business income

Income from trades or professions is assessable on a current year basis i.e. on the profits arising in the accounts period ended in the tax year (1 January – 31 December). Capital allowances, based on capital expenditure during the basis period for the assessment are granted at the following rates:

- plant and equipment, 20% straight-line for five years;
- industrial buildings, 4% per annum straight-line;
- motor vehicles, 20% straight-line for five years.

Allowances for non-commercial vehicles are subject of a ceiling of IR£ 17,000.

Trading losses, either monetary or resulting from capital allowances, can be set against income of any description arising in the year and may be carried forward against future trading income.

Social security benefits

Most social security benefits are now liable to income tax.

Capital gains

The rate of Capital Gains Tax is 20%. Gains are calculated by deducting from the proceeds of sale or disposal the original cost as well as improvement costs and incidental expenses of sale, such as commissions and fees. The acquisition and improvement costs are indexed upwards to take account of inflation; indexation cannot be used to increase a loss. In the case of land with development value, indexation relief is restricted.

Resident individuals are chargeable to capital gains tax on gains wherever arising. Non-resident individuals are only chargeable to capital gains tax on gains derived from:

- land or minerals situated in the state;
- exploration and exploitation rights in designated areas;
- unquoted shares deriving the greater part of their value from the above assets;
- assets used for the purpose of a trade carried on in Ireland through a branch or agency.

Individuals who are resident but not domiciled in Ireland are only taxable in respect of gains arising outside Ireland and the UK if they are remitted to Ireland. The gain is taxable to the extent of the remittance only.

Capital gains had been assessable in the year ended 5 April. They will be assessed on a calendar year basis with effect from 1 January 2001. A transitional tax 'year' will run from 6 April 2001 to 31 December 2001. Tax is payable on or before 1 November following the end of the tax year. From 2002 it will be payable on 31 October. Capital losses may be set against capital gains, but may not be set against income. Unused losses may be brought forward and set against future gains. Losses on the disposal of land with development value can be set against any gains, however development land gains may only be reduced by development land losses.

An individual is granted an exemption from tax for the first IR£ 1,000 of a gain made in each tax year. No transfer between spouses is allowed.

Dividends

Dividends paid by an Irish resident company will now be subject to withholding tax of 20%. An individual shareholder will be taxable on the gross dividend (i.e. before withholding tax) but will be entitled to a credit for the tax withheld by the company paying the dividend. Provided a declaration is completed, an exemption from withholding tax can be obtained by an individual resident in an EU state or a country with which Ireland has a double tax agreement.

Interest receivable

Interest from which Irish tax is withheld at source is no longer liable to any further Irish income tax. Interest not taxed at source is normally assessable on the amount of interest received during the year of assessment. Generally speaking, this includes interest received from banks and building societies and some other institutions. Such interest is subject to 20% Deposit Interest Retention Tax (DIRT). Deposit accounts held by non-residents are exempt from Retention Tax.

Rentals from property

Deductions in computing profit from rentals include management expenses, maintenance costs, rent payable, rates and insurance as well as the cost of any services or goods a landlord is legally bound to provide under the terms of a lease. Since 23 April 1998 no relief is available for interest on money borrowed for the purchase, repair or upkeep of residential premises. Interest on funds borrowed before that date (and on borrowings for non-residential lettings) continues to be deductible. Capital allowances can be claimed on certain fittings and fixtures. Expenditure incurred on the building of certain houses or apartments in designated areas for letting as residential dwellings is allowable as a deduction against the rental income from the property or other properties in the state. Such a deduction is subject to certain conditions being fulfilled. Allowances are also granted where industrial buildings or hotels are let.

Royalties

Royalties received for imparting industrial and technical know-how will normally be treated as trading receipts and the usual trading deductions will apply. Patent royalties received by the inventor may be exempt from tax but successive amendments to legislation have introduced extensive anti-avoidance in this area.

Foreign source income

All foreign source income is taxable where an individual is resident and domiciled in the State. Where the income is received from a country with which Ireland has a tax treaty, a credit is given for withholding taxes and sometimes, in the case of dividends, a credit is also given for some of the corporate taxes paid by the foreign company paying the dividends.

In the absence of a tax treaty, Irish unilateral provisions apply. This generally takes the form of a deduction from the foreign taxable income of the foreign tax directly paid.

Personal allowances and deductions 2001

Exemption thresholds

Income tax is levied on income subject to exemption limits of IR£ 8,200 (married couple) and IR£ 4,100 (single and widowed persons). For married couples aged 65 years and over the exemption limit is IR£ 15,000. For single persons in the same age bracket the limit is IR£ 7,500. Non-exempt individuals are granted the following personal allowances: single person IR£ 5,500, married couple IR£ 11,500 and widowed IR£ 6,500. These allowances are granted at the standard rate of tax. For the short tax 'year' in 2001, allowances will be reduced to 74% of the normal annual amounts.

Interest payable

Deductions are allowed for qualifying interest payments. Interest on money borrowed for the purchase, repair or improvement of an individual's sole or main residence is allowed at the standard rate up to a maximum of IR£ 4,000 (married & widowed) and IR£ 2,000 (single). A higher allowance is available for the first 5 years of an individual or couple's first mortgage. With effect from 1 January 2002 relief for interest payable will be allowed at source.

Medical expenses

The amount claimable is the excess of the cost over IR£ 100 for each individual, or over IR£ 200 for a family.

Other deductions

Deductions are also allowed as follows:

- an allowance for medical insurance premiums (standard rated), with effect from 6 April 2001 relief will be allowed at source;
- other less common allowances such as a limited rent allowance, are also available.

Non-residents are in general not entitled to personal allowances and reliefs unless so entitled under the terms of a Double Taxable Convention or if the person is an Irish citizen, or non-resident for health reasons, in which case they are entitled only to the same proportion of personal allowances as their Irish source income bears to their worldwide income.

Special family rules

Joint assessment of husband and wife is automatic unless they opt for separate or single assessment. In the case of joint assessment, the income of the husband and wife is aggregated, as are the allowances, reliefs and tax bands. If a couple elect for separate assessment then each spouse is taxed as a single person but any unutilised allowances, reliefs or tax bands of one may be passed to the other. Under single assessments a couple are taxed as if unmarried. In general, the income of a minor child arising out of a capital gift by a parent is treated as the income of the parent.

Rates of tax

Single and widowed persons (excluding lone parents with qualifying children)

Band (*IR£*)	*Rate* (*%*)
0 – 20,000	20
Balance	42

Lone parents (single or widowed) with qualifying children

Band (IR£)	*Rate* (*%*)
0 – 23,150	20
Balance	42

Married persons assessed jointly

Band (IR£)	*Rate* (*%*)
0 – 29,000*	20
Balance	42

* Can be increased by as much as £11,000 if each spouse has income.

For the short tax 'year' in 2001, the bands will be reduced to 74% of the normal annual amounts.

Payment of tax

Payroll deductions

Remuneration from employment is taxable at source if the paying point is in Ireland. Tax is based on the actual income, after personal allowances, of the tax year. Deductions are also made by the employer for social insurance and remitted to the Collector General simultaneously, with deductions for income tax.

Resident individuals who are paid from points outside Ireland are directly assessed to income tax by their local Inspector of Taxes.

Preliminary tax

Other income tax is payable in one instalment on 1 November each year. This tax will become payable on 31 October from 2002 onwards. It is known as 'Preliminary Tax' which means the amount of tax which, in the opinion of the chargeable person, is likely to be payable by him for the year of assessment. This tax is payable even though the Inspector of Taxes has not given a notice in respect of same. The amount of the Preliminary Tax paid must be at least 90% of the final liability or 100% of the previous year's liability to avoid interest charges. Capital gains tax is payable on or before 1 November following the year of the gain. This will be payable on 31 October from 2002 onwards.

Estate and gift taxes

The rate of tax for both gifts and inheritances taken on or after 1 December 1999 is 20%. Gifts and legacies (except for those received prior to 2 December 1988) to which the same group threshold (see below) applies are aggregated in order to determine the rate of tax.

The entire property in the gift or inheritance is taxable where, at the time of the gift or inheritance, the disponer is resident or ordinarily resident in the state, or the donee or successor is resident or ordinarily resident in the state, or the property is situated in the state.

Where the disponer or the donee/successor is non-domiciled, he/she will not be considered to be resident or ordinarily resident in the state until 1 December 2004 and then only if he/she has been resident in the state for the five consecutive tax years preceding the relevant date.

The tax is payable by the donee/beneficiary and not by the donor although, in the event of default by the donee, the donor may be held accountable.

To avoid international double taxation there is an estate and gift tax treaty in force with the UK and an estate tax treaty in force with the USA.

Group thresholds

Inheritances and gifts from a spouse are exempt. There is no maximum limit.

The following are the relevant group thresholds:

- where the donee is the child, or minor child, of a deceased child of the disponer the first IR£ 316,800 is exempt. This applies to both gifts and inheritances; in the case of inheritances taken by a parent from a child, the limit is also IR£ 316,800;
- where the donee is a lineal ancestor, a lineal descendent (other than a child or minor child of a deceased child), a brother, sister or a child of a brother or sister of the disponer, the exemption limit is IR£ 31,680.

In any other case, the exemption limit is IR£ 15,840.

Wealth tax

There is no wealth tax in Ireland.

Social security

Pay Related Social Insurance (PRSI) is payable as follows:

	Employee
PRSI*	4.0% (income ceiling IR£ 28,250)
Health[ø]	2.0% (no income ceiling)
	6.0%

* First IR£ 100 earnings per week is ignored.
* Exempt if earnings per week do not exceed IR£ 226.
[ø] Not payable on income less than IR£ 280 per week.

Contributions are payable on gross earnings less allowable superannuation contributions up to the ceiling shown.

Other taxes

Value added tax

Value added tax is payable on goods and services at rates between zero and 20%. Exported goods qualify for the zero rate. Developed property is liable at 12.5%. Most fuels and restaurant meals are taxable at 12.5%.

Property taxes

Property taxes on residential properties was abolished from 5 April 1997.

Stamp duty

The maximum rate is 6% on commercial property and it applies to transfers of certain property, including all land and buildings, valued at over IR£ 60,000.

Residential property is subject to the following rates:

	First-Time	*Other Owner Occupiers*	*Investors New Properties*
Up to IR£ 100,000	Nil	Nil	3.00%
IR£ 100,001 – IR£ 150,000	Nil	3.00%	3.00%
IR£ 150,001 – IR£ 200,000	3.00%	4.00%	4.00%
IR£ 200,001 – IR£ 250,000	3.75%	5.00%	5.00%
IR£ 250,001 – IR£ 300,000	4.50%	6.00%	6.00%
IR£ 300,001 – IR£ 500,000	7.50%	7.50%	7.50%
Over IR£ 500,000	9.00%	9.00%	9.00%

The investor rate for second hand properties is 9%.

Share transfers are liable at 1%.

Exchange control

With effect from 1 January 1993 all exchange controls have been removed.

Withholding taxes

Tax at 20% is withheld at source from dividends, patent royalties, rents and certain interest paid to non-residents. This is subject to tax treaties which may provide for a lower or nil rate of withholding tax. There is no withholding tax on copyright royalties paid to non-residents. Subsidiary or branch profits may be repatriated from Ireland free of Irish tax other than tax on profits.

The following table illustrates the rates currently in force for patent royalties and interest:

Country of Residence	*Royalties (%)*	*Interest (%)*
Non-treaty countries	20	20
Selected treaty countries:		
Australia	10	10
Austria	nil	nil
Belgium	nil	15
Canada	nil	15
Cyprus	nil	nil
Denmark	nil	nil
Finland	nil	nil
France	nil	nil
Germany	nil	nil
Italy	nil	10
Japan	10	10
Luxembourg	nil	nil
Netherlands	nil	nil
Norway	nil	nil
Pakistan	nil	30*
Sweden	nil	nil
Switzerland	nil	nil
United Kingdom	nil	nil
United States	nil	nil
Zambia	nil	nil

*A tax treaty cannot impose a withholding tax greater than that provided for in domestic legislation, i.e. 20%.

Anti-avoidance measures

Income arising to offshore entities where Irish resident individuals have the power to enjoy it may be assessable on the individual.

Transactions entered into solely for tax avoidance purposes may be ineffective.

Isle of Man

Crossleys

Introduction

As one of the world's leading offshore centres, the Isle of Man operates a sympathetic tax regime with the only form of direct taxation being income tax. There are no capital gains taxes, death or inheritance taxes, stamp duties, estate duties, turnover or wealth taxes.

The tax year for both companies and individuals runs from the 6 April to 5 April, although companies and other trading entities may have other year ends. Exempt, international and Non-resident Company Duty (NCD) status companies enjoy a favourable tax regime and companies engaged in banking, insurance fund management, the film industry and ship management, can qualify for exemption or a reduced rate. There are no disclosure requirements concerning the beneficial ownership of Manx companies, nor filing requirements with the Registrar of Companies, other than for public limited companies and, therefore, confidentiality is assured.

Corporate taxes and duty

Resident companies

Companies resident in the Isle of Man, except those classified as either an exempt or international company, are subject to Manx income tax on their worldwide income. A company is considered resident for Manx income tax purposes if it is incorporated in the Island or its central management and control is exercised in and from the Island. That is, the majority of its Board of Directors are themselves resident on the Isle of Man and the board meetings are held on the Island.

Exempt companies

An exempt company, which cannot be beneficially owned by an Isle of Man resident, is a Manx incorporated company or one incorporated elsewhere and registered in the Isle of Man under Part XI of the Companies Act 1931. It must have a resident Director and Secretary (who are suitably qualified) and be able to undertake any trade or business, at or from, any premises in the Isle of Man (including Manx territorial waters) other than those which are prescribed. Exempt companies are typically used for private business and Collective Investment Schemes.

Exemption from the payment of income tax is authorised by the Assessor of Income Tax on submission and approval of the relevant application. The exemption fee payable varies from £430 for applications made between 6 April to 30 June, or within 30 days of commencement of trade, to £1,200 for those made between 1 July and 30 September.

By concession the Assessor of Income Tax will allow applications made after 30 September on the basis that the company pays the fee applicable as if it were an international company of £3,600.

Exempt insurance companies

Exempt insurance companies are generally used by Public Limited Companies or other businesses of substance and are more commonly known as captive insurance companies. A captive insurance company may also be an international company (see below). The fees payable, whether the captive insurance company is an exempt or international company are as follows:

- in respect of authorisation – £1,500;
- in the case of an insurer which is authorised to carry on insurance business within classes 1 and 2 – £10,000; or
- in the case of any other insurer – £3,000.

International companies

An international company (as with an exempt company) can be a company incorporated in the Isle of Man or one incorporated elsewhere and registered in the Isle of Man under part XI of the Companies Act 1931 and, unless quoted on a recognised International Stock Exchange, no Manx resident can have any interest. It must have a resident Director and Secretary (who is suitably qualified) and is able to carry on or transact any trade or business, at or from any premises in the Isle of Man (including Manx territorial waters) other than those which are currently prescribed for an exempt company. Unlike an exempt company, an international company can be a public company, but it must ensure that its income and receipts are derived from outside the Isle of Man or from dealings with other international companies or international limited partnerships, unless it arises from approved interest sources.

The legislation provides for a flexible rate of taxation which is chargeable according to the specific requirements of the international company. This can range from a minimum rate of 1% to a sliding scale maximum of 35% of assessable profits, subject to a minimum income tax charge of £430 per annum. Applications have to be made to the Assessor of Income Tax who will have regard to the nature and circumstances of a company's application in determining the appropriate rate.

Non-resident companies

Companies incorporated outside the Isle of Man

Companies incorporated and managed outside of the Isle of Man, which are engaged in business within the Island through a branch, are liable to Manx non-resident income tax at the rate of 18%. The liability to taxation is based on any profit arising from the business activity, except where the income is derived from approved interest sources.

A non-resident company deriving the whole of its trading profits from a trade carried on in the Isle of Man is eligible for the 12% rate of tax on £500,000 of its taxable profits (see below – 'Taxes imposed').

Companies incorporated inside the Isle of Man

An NCD company is a Manx incorporated company, control and management of which is exercised outside the Isle of Man and which has delivered a declaration to that effect to the Registrar of Companies. Such a company is not liable to taxation, but a duty of £830 is charged on the initial filing of its non-resident declaration to the Registrar of Companies and on each subsequent filing of an annual return. Until such time as a declaration is delivered, the company is liable to income tax at a rate of 18% of its profits.

A company may apply to be classified as an NCD on incorporation, or at any time during the year, on the submission of a non-resident declaration. Until the company files a declaration stating it has resumed its residence within the Island, the company's profits will be outside the scope of Manx income tax.

An Order has been made by the Isle of Man Treasury giving effect to a moratorium on the formation of companies of this type with a view to it being a preliminary step to the ultimate winding up of companies currently in existence. In addition, no companies formed after 6 April 1999 may seek NCD status and likewise for existing companies.

Tax year and filing requirements

The tax year, or year of assessment (the fiscal year), for income tax purposes runs from 6 April to the following 5 April. By extra-statutory concession, companies are permitted to have an accounting period end other than 5 April, providing the accounting period is for a period of 12 months. Profits from a trade are normally assessed on a preceding year basis, i.e. the income assessed for 2001/02 on a preceding basis would be income that arose during the period 6 April 2000 to 5 April 2001. Again, by extra-statutory concession, a continuing trade making up accounts for a 12 month period ending in the period 6 April 2000 to 5 April 2001 would form the basis of the assessment for 2001/02. Special rules apply to the commencement and cessation of a trade.

In principle, a tax return should be completed and submitted by 30 June following the end of the previous year of assessment.

Taxes imposed

Income tax is charged at the rate of 18% and is due and payable on 1 January in the relevant year of assessment. If an assessment is not issued until after 1 January for a relevant year of assessment, the income tax assessed is due and payable within 21 days.

For the year of assessment 2001/2002, income tax at the rate of 12% will apply to the income of a company which derives the whole of its trading profits from a trade carried on in the Isle of Man. The 12% rate will apply to the first £500,000 of taxable income being the amount after capital allowances, distributions and loss relief. The 12% rate will not apply to branch operations.

Income subject to tax

General rules

Income tax is charged on a company's income, less allowable reliefs and losses.

Capital gains

Capital gains are not subject to tax.

Dividends

Dividends paid can be treated as capital distributions or as a deduction against a company's taxable profits. Distributions are paid gross and therefore no tax is payable to the island's Treasury at the time a dividend is paid. However, Manx non-resident income tax at the rate of 18% is deductible from dividends paid to non-residents and this has to be paid over to the Treasury within 14 days.

Exempt and International companies generally pay dividends gross.

Deductions

General rules

Any expenditure of a revenue nature incurred wholly and exclusively for the purposes of a trade is eligible for tax relief. Capital items, such as depreciation, are not eligible for deduction but relief is given in the form of capital allowances. The management expenses of an investment company are allowable, but on a restricted basis. Certain expenses incurred in the generation of rental income – namely rates, insurance, repairs and management fees – are allowable in computing taxable income.

Capital allowances (depreciation and amortisation)

Capital allowances are available on a variety of expenditure. Expenditure incurred in respect of plant, machinery, ships, aircraft, industrial and agricultural buildings, hotel and tourist premises can obtain an initial allowance of up to 100%. Non-commercial motor vehicles are eligible for a writing-down allowance of 25% but there are restrictions for 'expensive cars'.

If an asset which has received the benefit of capital allowances is disposed of, a 'balancing adjustment' may arise. The adjustment is equivalent to the sale proceeds on disposal less the tax written down value of the disposed asset. For these purposes, the sales value cannot exceed the original cost. Providing the sale proceeds are reinvested in a similar asset, a balancing charge on a ship or aircraft may be deferred.

Losses

Trading losses of a company may be offset against any other income in the fiscal year of the loss or the subsequent year, or carried forward and offset against future income of the same trade. If a loss is sustained in the final period of trade, terminal loss relief is available and losses are set-off against taxable profits of the previous three fiscal years.

Group relief is available and losses may be transferred, i.e. surrendered and claimed, by one group company to another.

A claim for a particular loss relief must be made within two years of the year of assessment in which the loss was made.

Personal taxes

Taxable individuals

Resident

The worldwide income of any individual who is resident or ordinarily resident in the Isle of Man is liable to Manx income tax. Such income includes earned income, e.g. income from an employment or pension and investment income, e.g. dividends and loan interest. Both husband and wife are taxed as one.

Non-resident

Any individual not deemed resident or ordinarily resident in the Isle of Man is subject to Manx non-resident income tax on any income arising or accruing from the annual profits or gains of any property, profession, trade, employment or vocation situated on or carried out in the Island. By concession, income which originates from approved income sources, such as bank deposit interest, is not taxable, i.e. it is paid gross.

Residence

Residence can be established by choice or determination from the very first day an individual arrives on the Island, or by a person's actions. An individual will always be regarded as a Manx resident for a year of assessment if that person is present in the Isle of Man for six months or more in that year. For this purpose, six months is taken as 183 days. In addition, an individual who undertakes regular visits to the Island which extend on average to three months (90 days) or more each year over a period of four consecutive years will be considered as a resident for tax purposes. An individual who visits the Island and has accommodation available for his use will be considered resident for any year in which he has visited the Island. There is an extra-statutory concession for short term residence.

Tax year and filing requirements

The tax year or year of assessment (the fiscal year) of an individual for income tax purposes runs from 6 April to the following 5 April. Remuneration, such as salaries and Manx sourced pensions, is assessed on an actual basis, so the income assessed for 2001/2002 on an actual basis would be income that arose during the period 6 April 2001 to 5 April 2002. Other income, such as investment income and non-Manx sourced pensions, is assessed on a preceding year basis (see the company section). Special rules apply to the commencement and cessation of residence. There are also provisions to cover short term residence.

A tax return should be completed and submitted by 30 June following the year of assessment.

Taxes imposed

Income, less allowable deductions, is subject to Manx income tax at the standard rate of 12% on the first £10,000 (or £20,000 for a married couples, being fully transferable between spouses) of taxable income and thereafter at the higher rate of 18%. Subject to certain exceptions, income paid to a non-resident is subject to Manx non-resident income tax at the rate of 18%.

Taxes on income

Wages and salaries paid to employees are subject to tax deduction at source under the Income Tax Instalment Payments scheme. Social security contributions are payable by both employers and employees and are payable to the Government, with any income tax deductions made by the 19th day following the end of the previous month.

Sources of income

Employment income

An employee who is resident in the Isle of Man is taxed on all his emoluments for a tax year, which include 'benefits in kind'. A benefit in kind may be regarded as the financial benefit obtained by employees by reason of their employment. The benefit is the value in 'money or money's worth'. Benefits usually take the form of expenses met by the employer or the provision/use of particular assets, e.g. a motor car. Deductions are available for various personal and other allowances.

Business income

Profits from trades, professions and vocations are computed in the same manner as for companies and are normally assessed on a preceding year basis. Accounts may end on a date other than 5 April providing the accounting period is for a period of 12 months and ends in the preceding fiscal year ended 5 April. Special rules apply to the commencement and cessation of trade.

Partnerships

Whilst a partnership is regarded as a separate entity for income tax reporting purposes, each partner is responsible for the income tax payable on his proportion of the partnership's income with any ultimate tax liability being determined after consideration of any personal allowances and reliefs. A partnership is considered resident for taxation purposes where the central management and control is conducted. A non-resident partner of a Manx partnership will be subject to Manx non-resident income tax in respect of his share of the partnership income arising or accruing from within the Isle of Man.

Social security benefits

Payments of social security benefits are generally taxable with some exceptions such as sickness benefit and maternity allowance.

Pensions

Pensions, other than invalidity and war pensions, are taxable as earned income.

Capital gains

Capital gains are not subject to tax.

Dividends

Dividends are normally assessed on a preceding year basis with special rules applying to commencement and cessation. Dividends from Manx sources are received gross, unless paid to a non-resident.

Interest

Bank interest from sources within the Island is paid gross to residents and non-residents alike. Other interest paid to a non-resident is subject to Manx non-resident income tax at the rate of 18%.

Rentals

Income received from property rental, or under the terms of a lease, are taxable. Certain expenses relating to property are allowable (see the company section).

Royalties

Royalties are taxed as normal income.

Personal allowances and deductions

Personal allowances

Resident taxpayers are entitled to tax-free allowances against any income. The level at which these are received depends upon an individual's circumstances.

Allowances for 2001/02 are as follows:

	£
Single person	7,700
Married couple	15,400
Single parent	5,270
Blind person	2,120

Deductions

In addition to personal allowances, a resident taxpayer is able to claim relief for the following annual expenditure.

Life Assurance Relief

50% of the premiums paid, subject to restrictions.

Retirement annuity premiums

If an individual is employed or self-employed and the income received is from a non-pensionable employment (net relevant income), tax relief can be claimed on the premiums paid. This is restricted to 17.5% of the net relevant income for individuals up to the age of 50 and rises to 27.5% for those who are over the age of 61. The ability to enter into new policies ceased on 1 July 1988 when they were superseded by Personal Pension Schemes. Contributions to existing policies are still permitted and qualify for relief.

Personal pension schemes

Individuals contributing to Personal Pension Schemes are able to obtain income tax relief on the premiums paid of 17.5% up to the age of 35, rising to 40% for those who are over the age of 61.

Interest paid

Interest paid to any financial institution whose profits are subject to Manx income tax is eligible for relief, without restriction.

Deed of covenant

An individual may obtain tax relief for covenanted payments to a charity or for children or grandchildren in full time education (ages 18 to 25 only). The maximum amount which can be covenanted to children or grandchildren in respect of each donee is £5,000. Charitable donations, which are not under a deed of covenant, are limited to a maximum of £5,000 in total.

Losses

Loss relief for an individual follows that available for a company, but in addition, losses sustained by a married person may be restricted to the spouse who has incurred the loss only and set off against the claimant's own earned income and then his investment income. If necessary, losses may then be set off against his spouse's earned and investment income.

Where a loss is sustained in a trade within the first four years of assessment, losses may be carried back and offset against any other income of the previous three years.

Other taxes

Estate, gift tax and wealth taxes

There is no estate, gift or wealth tax in the Isle of Man.

Indirect taxes

There are a number of indirect taxes within the Isle of Man. The principal indirect tax is Value Added Tax (VAT), which is charged on the purchase and sale of goods and services. VAT sales are either exempt, zero-rated or standard rated (which is currently levied at

17.5%). Tax on supplies of fuel and certain accommodation is levied at 5%.

Tax treaties

The Isle of Man has currently only one formal double taxation arrangement and that is with the United Kingdom. An information agreement exists with the United States of America with regard to the international operation or chartering of ships.

Other taxes

Exchange control

There are no exchange controls in the Isle of Man.

Trusts

Trusts controlled and managed in the Isle of Man are subject to taxation on their worldwide income. Where a trust deed precludes an Isle of Man resident settlor or beneficiary from benefiting under the settlement, no Manx income tax will be levied providing the income of the trust only arises or accrues from outside the Isle of Man. Trusts that trade in the Isle of Man are subject to Manx income tax at 18%. A Manx resident trust which trades in another jurisdiction is also subject to Manx income tax at 18%, subject to the availability of double taxation relief.

International limited partnerships

An International Limited Partnership comprises a General Partner and one or more Limited Partners. The General Partner must be a company (other than one prescribed) which is resident, has a place of business in the Isle of Man and complies with any other requirements as may be prescribed. At least one director and the secretary (who are suitably qualified) must also be resident in the Isle of Man.

All Limited Partners, other than those which are International Companies, must be resident outside the Isle of Man and not conduct any trade or business other than those which are currently prescribed for an Exempt Company. No Island resident may have an interest in an International Limited Partnership.

The income and receipts of an International Limited Partnership should be derived from outside the Isle of Man or dealings with other

International Companies or International Limited Partnerships, unless it arises from approved interest or dividend sources.

The legislation removes the restriction on the number of members of a limited partnership (previously 20) and is particularly useful for collective investment schemes, ship management and ownership of other investment vehicles.

A limited partnership can be classified as an International Limited Partnership for any year of assessment on submission and approval of the relevant application to the Assessor of Income Tax. An application for a certificate of status should be sent to the Assessor of Income Tax no later than 30 June or within 30 days of commencement of trade. The application should be accompanied by a fee of £430 or such other sum as may be prescribed and once approved an International Limited Partnership will not be subject to Manx income tax in respect of the income it receives.

Israel

Haft & Ziv
Strauss Lazer & Co.

Introduction

The British Mandate Government enacted Israel's original income tax laws in 1941 prior to the establishment of the State of Israel. Since then, the legislation has been amended or extended more than 200 times.

Six basic laws cover taxation on income and capital gains, as follows:

- Income Tax Ordinance;
- Income Tax Law (Inflationary Adjustments) 1985;
- Encouragement of Capital Investments Law 1959;
- Industry Encouragement Law (Taxes) 1969;
- Land Taxation Law (Appreciation, Sale & Acquisition) 1963 (formerly Land Appreciation Tax Law 1963);
- Value Added Tax Law 1975 (a profit tax on the income of banks, insurers and various other financial institutions).

Other laws make tax provisions relating to specific fiscal activity, such as that concerning mutual funds.

In May 2000, a public committee for income tax reform ('Ben-Bassat Committee') has published recommendations to change the tax policy in many fields e.g. taxation on regular income, capital markets, capital gains, land betterment, estates, gifts, international taxation etc. Also, the government intends to enact significant changes in the prevailing encouragement legislations.

One of the Ben-Bassat Committee recommendations is to change the tax system from a territorial system to a personal system, so that, if implemented, an Israeli resident's income (from any source world-wide) will be subject to tax in Israel.

As a result of current economical and political events, the probability of the proposals of the public committee being accepted as legislation is quite unclear.

Corporate taxes

Taxable entities

Resident companies

Israeli companies are taxed on business income and capital gains worldwide.

Passive income (i.e. interest, dividends, royalties) is taxed in Israel if initially received in Israel.

Non-resident companies

Foreign companies (not incorporated in Israel) are liable for income tax on all income that is generated in the conduct of trade or business in Israel and income effectively connected with it.

Tax year and filing requirements

The tax year of a company is the calendar year.

Corporate income tax returns are due within five months following the close of the taxable year (31 December). An extension may be requested for periods of up to eight months. For public companies, the entire tax liability must be paid with the extension request. All tax returns must include financial statements and a statement of adjustment and must be audited by an Israeli Certified Public Accountant (CPA).

Taxes imposed – advance payments

Estimated taxes on income for the current year must be paid either in ten fixed instalments or in twelve instalments based on a percentage of the company's turnover.

Rates of tax

Companies are subject to tax at the rate of 36% imposed on the taxable income.

The 2000 tax rates for companies are as follows:

	When all income is distributed		*When all income is not distributed*	
	Income	*Tax*	*Income*	*Tax*
	(New Israel Shekels)			
Taxable income	100	–	100	–
36% company tax	36	36	36	36
	64		64	
Dividend distributed*:				
25% withheld at source	16	16	–	–
Net retained income	48		64	
Total tax		52		36

* Generally, there is no withholding between two Israeli companies.

Investors in approved enterprises enjoy various benefits such as tax holidays, reduced tax rates, grants, and government aid for approved research and development programs.

Income subject to tax

General rules

Corporate tax is levied on gross income, less allowable deductions. Most companies are required to use the accrual basis method of accounting to determine taxable income. Service companies, which do not own inventory or stock, may use the cash basis method.

Adjustment for inflation

High inflation rates in the early 1980s caused the enactment of Income Tax Law (Inflationary Adjustments) 1985. This law caused taxes to be calculated on real income rather than on profit resulting from inflation, as measured by the Israeli Consumer Price Index (CPI), thus protecting equity from inflationary erosion.

The main adjustments created by this law are:

- the excess of equity over depreciated fixed assets, all adjusted to the changes of the CPI during the year, and deductible from the taxable income (up to 70% of the current taxable income); if the outcome of equity, less depreciated fixed assets, is negative then the results are to be added to the taxable income.

- Tax losses which have been carried forward are linked to changes in the CPI.
- Depreciation is linked to changes in the CPI.
- Capital gains on sales of traded stocks are taxable under this law; certain companies' gains from the sale of stocks are exempt from taxation – owing to the zero change of the CPI in year 2000, it is expected that the implementation of this adjustment will be frozen in the near future.

US Dollar adjusted reports

Certain qualifying entities are allowed to present their financial reports and to manage their books of accounts in US Dollars or to link their Israeli currency figures to the exchange rate of the US Dollar rather than the CPI.

Capital gains

For tax purposes, capital gains include two components:

- *Inflationary gain* – the part of the gain derived from linkage to the CPI;
- *Real gain* – the difference between the total capital gain and the inflationary gain.

The inflationary gain has been exempt from tax since 1 January 1994 and is subject to 10% tax on the accrued portion before that date.

The real gain is subject to the company income tax rates, generally 36%.

Capital losses

Capital losses may be set off against real capital gains and land appreciation gains and may be carried forward for up to seven years. The same rule applies to land appreciation tax.

Losses from foreign securities may be set off only against gains from foreign securities.

The payment of capital gains tax may be deferred under the following circumstances:

- *Transfer of assets against shares* – If assets are transferred to a company in exchange for shares, payment of capital gains tax may be deferred until the assets or the shares are sold, provided that immediately after the transfer the transferor holds shares representing at least 90% of all the rights in that company;

- *Rollover* – Capital gains tax on the sale of depreciable assets may be deferred until the assets are sold where the consideration is used to purchase replacement assets within twelve months after, or four months before, the date of the sale; the capital gain is then deducted from the cost of assets acquired and depreciation is calculated on the reduced amount.

Dividends

Dividends paid to Israeli individuals or foreign residents (both individuals and companies) are subject to withholding taxes of 25%. However the 25% tax rate may be reduced according to the relevant tax treaty.

Dividends paid to an Israeli company from another Israeli company are exempt from tax.

Deductions

General Rules

Companies may deduct from gross income the ordinary and necessary expenses of carrying on a trade or business that are paid or incurred during the tax year. Where the cost benefits more than one year, it must be capitalised and either depreciated or amortised.

Depreciation and amortisation

Tangible property is depreciated using the straight-line method, which recovers cost in equal amounts over the life of the asset. Industrial companies may elect to apply an accelerated depreciation method.

Royalties

Royalty expenses are deductible in accordance with the arm's length principle.

Interest

Interest paid or accrued on indebtedness, which is neither directly nor indirectly incurred to produce non-taxable income, is deductible.

Bad and doubtful accounts

Generally, taxpayers must identify bad debts. Specific write-offs are based on the collectibility of the receivable.

Losses

Business losses are offset against all income of the same year and may be carried forward without limit. However, carried forward losses from business may be offset only against business income. Business losses may not be carried back.

Losses from property rental can be offset only against income from the same building in future years. Losses may not be carried back.

Employees and directors remuneration and benefits

Generally, employees, and directors remuneration and benefits are deductible, without limit.

Specifically non-deductible expenses

Expenses that may not be deducted from current taxable income include:

- expenditure not related to the generation of such income;
- capital expenses;
- cost of improvements to fixed or rented assets, which were not paid or accrued for the purpose of income generation;
- interest and linkage differentials on debts to the income tax authorities;
- fines;
- personal expenses;
- charitable contributions, although a 35% tax credit is available for contributions to approved institutions (the 35% tax credit is limited to 30% of the taxable income, or NIS 2,000,000 whichever is lower; any surplus, on 30% of income or on NIS 2 million, is carried forward up to three years); and
- entertainment, travel abroad, and car maintenance are deductible to certain limits.

Foreign source income

The foreign source income of domestic companies is generally taxable and foreign tax credits are available. Foreign companies are taxed only on Israeli source income, which is effectively connected with a trade or business.

Investment incentives and special benefits

Encouragement of capital investments law

In an effort to encourage capital investment in industry, tourism and real estate development by both foreign nationals and Israelis, and to increase export and generate jobs, Israel provides tax benefits to investors under The law for Encouragement of Capital Investment, whereby status as 'approved enterprise' is granted to investments made by companies incorporated in Israel, to foreign companies registered in Israel, and to Israeli-registered partnerships which meet specific criteria. The investment may be made in either a new facility or an existing expansion, which must be located in a designated development zone ('A', 'B' or 'Other' zones).

Two authorities in the Ministry of Industry and Trade deal with approved enterprises. The Investment Centre evaluates applications and grants approvals, while the Investment Authority encourages foreign investment in Israel through worldwide representation. The tax relief provisions of this legislation are included in many double taxation treaties with other countries such that, if an investor pays reduced tax on Israeli income, the allowable deduction in the home country is equivalent to what would have been taxed in Israel, less tax relief. These benefits are granted to the investor rather than the fiscal authority's home country.

Tax relief

Income from an approved enterprise owned by a foreign resident company is subject to reduced company tax, plus 15% tax on dividends. Payment may be deferred if it can be demonstrated that profits were reinvested in the business and not repatriated.

The benefit period in this regard is the first year in which the company has taxable income, net of losses, to 12 years from the start of operations or 14 years from the grant of approval, whichever is earlier. The Investment can extend the benefit period under special circumstances.

Investment grants

Grants in the form of subsidies may be given to manufacturing, industrial equipment and building leasing, tourism and agriculture. Amounts vary according to project location, and are a set percentage of the investment in fixed assets. The grants are tax exempt and must be deducted from the cost of fixed assets when computing depreciation.

Alternative benefits

A company owning an enterprise approved after 1 April 1986 may waive the investment grant and receive in lieu a full exemption from company tax for periods varying in accordance with location of plant and the percentage held by foreign residents, as follows:

	Development zone		
	A	*B*	*Other*
	years	*years*	*years*
More than 25% foreign held:			
Tax exemption period	10	6	2
Reduced tax rate thereafter	–	4	8
Total benefit period	10	10	10
Less than 25% foreign held:			
Tax exemption period	10	6	2
Reduced tax rate thereafter	–	1	5
Total benefit period	10	7	7

Approved property

The construction of an industrial building and acquisition of machinery and equipment for lease to a manufacturing enterprise, are entitled to the same benefits as an approved enterprise.

The law for encouragement of capital investments provides exemption from Land Appreciation Tax (a capital gains tax on land) where a shareholder, owning at least 50 residential units, sells his shares in a company owned by foreign residents and engaged in the construction, leasing or selling of residential apartments. All shareholders must be foreign resident individuals and none may hold more than 5% of the company's capital. The company must be approved by the Income Tax Commissioner as owned by foreign residents holding real property.

The following benefits are granted to the owner of an approved property first leased between 1 September 1991 and 31 December 2001, where at least 50% is leased for residential purposes for a period of at least five out of seven years following completion of construction, and more than 50% of the building space is retained within five years.

- Exemption from property tax on the land used for the approved property.
- Reduced tax for an unlimited period on the sale of the property.
- Reduced company tax proportionate to the percentage of foreign residents' control.
- The taxable inflation surplus component of the capital gain is subject to 10% tax.
- Accelerated depreciation at 20%.

Acquiring apartments and land

Support is available for the purchase of residential apartments for new immigrants.

Foreign experts

An Investment Centre approved, non-resident foreign expert employed on a specific project in Israel pays a maximum tax of 25% for three working years. This period may be extended for another five years.

Approved foreign experts can deduct their housing costs and part of their living expenses from their taxable income during the initial 12 months of their stay in Israel.

International trade companies

The law for encouragement of capital investment allows international trade companies incorporated abroad to establish offices in Israel without paying Israeli taxes, as follows:

- the company's income and capital gains from selling assets abroad are exempt for ten years from the first year the company has taxable income, subject to recommendation by the Investment Centre;
- for a 20 year period from the first year the company has taxable income, the sale of shares by foreign resident shareholders are exempt from capital gains tax;
- dividends, paid out of tax exempt income within 20 years from the first year the company has taxable income, are exempt from withholding tax when paid to foreign residents;

- the multi-national company must be engaged in international trade outside Israel.

Interest on foreign currency loans from abroad

A 25% tax withholding is imposed at source on interest paid on foreign currency loans received from abroad, unless reduced by a double taxation treaty. The Income Tax Commissioner is authorised under certain circumstances to reduce this tax rate.

The Industry Encouragement (Taxes) Law 1969

A special law was enacted in 1969 to encourage industrial activity. A summary of its main clauses is as follows:

An industrial company is one in which the income each year is 90% derived from manufacturing. Interest, capital gains and dividends are not treated as income from an industrial enterprise, but a company is treated as an industrial company where 90% of its income is derived from hotels.

The costs of registering an industrial company, issuing shares and their becoming listed on the stock exchange are deductible over a three-year period.

12.5% of patent and know-how costs can be amortised annually.

A group of industrial companies may file consolidated returns if certain conditions are met.

Tax benefits for research and development

Israeli tax law permits, under certain conditions, a tax deduction for expenditure (including capital expenditure) in scientific research and development projects, where approved by the relevant Israeli government ministry. Expenditure not so approved is deductible over a three-year period.

Free trade zones

A free trade zone was established in Eilat pursuant to a law enacted in 1985 aimed at promoting business activity (mainly tourism), attracting industrial activity and international trade and encouraging residence in Eilat. This legislation provides several tax incentives, as follows:

- exemption from indirect taxation on imported goods purchased in foreign currency by tourists, and exemption from employers tax;

- exemption from VAT of goods imported for use in Eilat and of services provided in the Eilat area;
- tax credit of up to 10% of the taxable income from employment, business or occupation of resident individuals;
- employers also receive tax credit at the rate of 20% of the net salary and wages paid to their employees, up to a limit equivalent to the tax withheld at source from these employees.

Free export processing zone

In June 1994, the Knesset passed new legislation which called for the designation of certain areas as free export processing zones (FEPZ) in which specified business and commercial activities are free to operate in a non-regulated and tax preferential environment. The major features of an FEPZ are:

- full exemption from corporate and income tax for 20 years, 15% tax on distributed income;
- full exemption from import and export licence requirements;
- full exemption from quota requirements and import regulation;
- possibility to repatriate profit in full;
- elimination of all bureaucratic procedures (permits, registration and approvals);
- freedom to independently negotiate labour contracts; and
- utilities and telecommunications provided by free tender and negotiation.

The first FEPZ, geared to high tech and light industry, is to be established near the city of Be'er-Sheva so as to provide sufficient land space with close access to its ample available human resources and to the technological manpower and facilities of Ben-Gurion University (while still being situated near to the commercial and transport infrastructure of Israel's central areas).

Plans for similar concessions to be granted also to the banking and financial services sectors are currently being discussed by government agencies and committees.

Personal taxes

Taxation of individuals

General

Calculation of the taxable income of individuals is similar in principle to that of corporations, however, most individuals are exempt from tax on income from the sale of quoted securities, personal household income (not part of a business or occupation), interest and linkage differences, life insurance, mutual funds and other savings. Married couples are, generally, separately assessed.

Self-employed individuals are entitled to make limited deductions for pension payments, certain savings plans, income loss insurance and social security. All resident individuals are entitled to tax credits as follows:

- personal allowance;
- married allowance;
- single parent family allowance;
- donations restricted to a 35% credit (also applies to foreign residents who are liable to tax in Israel);
- life insurance premiums and deposits with pension and provident funds.

Individual income tax rates for 2000

		Annual Income		
Rate of Tax	*Income*	*Accumulated Income*	*Accumulated Tax*	*Monthly Income from 1 Jan 2000*
%	*NIS*	*NIS*	*NIS*	*NIS*
10	Up to NIS 23,280	23,280	2,328	Up to 1,940
20	Next NIS 23,400	46,680	7,008	Next 1,950
30	Next NIS 76,200	122,880	29,868	Next 6,350
45	Next NIS 99,840	222,720	74,796	Next 8,320
50	In excess of NIS 222,720	–	–	In excess of NIS 18,560

These tax brackets are adjusted in accordance with the changes in the CPI.

Income from dividends, interest, rental of residential dwellings, etc., is taxed differently. Allowances or credits are granted for savings in pension funds, life insurance, etc.

Israel

The lowest tax rate applies to earnings from personal exertion. Income from passive sources is taxed at 30% and higher. Income of senior citizens (60 and over) – even if such income is not from personal exertion – is taxed at a rate of 10% or higher.

Individual's income from business is subject to the Adjustment for Inflation Law, and losses may be carried forward.

Capital gains

For tax purposes, capital gains include two components:

- inflationary gain – the part of the gain derived from linkage to the CPI;
- real gain – the difference between the total capital gain and the inflationary gain. The inflationary gain has been exempt from tax since 1 January 1994, and is subject to 10% tax on the accrued portion before that date. The real gain is subject to regular individual and company income tax rates.

Sales of stocks

Capital gains on the sale of securities traded on the Tel Aviv Stock Exchange (TASE) are exempt from capital gains tax.

Israeli individuals are subject to tax at a rate of 35% on the real gain in foreign currency terms of foreign securities, i.e. they are exempt from taxes on exchange rate differences. Gains from the sale of stocks of industrial or industrial holding companies traded on an approved stock exchange abroad are subject to tax regulations as if they are traded on TASE.

The first stock registration on a stock exchange is considered to be a tax event. However, one can postpone the tax event to the day of disposition.

According to the Ben-Basat Committee recommendations, income of Israeli residents from capital gains on securities traded on a stock exchange, including securities of an Israeli company traded abroad (e.g. an industrial company), and capital gains from interests received from outside of Israel, will be subject to a 25% tax rate.

Benefits to foreign residents

Foreign residents are subject to the same tax rates as Israeli residents. However, if they invested foreign currency, they may choose to calculate the gains in the original currency rather than in Israeli currency.

The inflationary gain on the sale of shares of an Israeli company, purchased originally with foreign currency, is exempt from tax if the calculation is based on the changes in the specific exchange rates of the Israeli currency.

Exemptions

For individuals, the main exemptions (under the Income Tax Ordinance) are as follows:

- Employment severance, with limits.
- Gains from the sale of securities traded on the TASE, provided the individual is not taxed according to the Income Tax Law (Inflationary Adjustments), and does not engage in the business of trading in securities.
- Interest received on a foreign currency deposit in an Israeli bank by a new immigrant for 20 years from the date of his immigration. According to Ben-Basat committee recommendations, this exemption applies for only ten years.
- Foreign sources income received by a new immigrant in Israel, for seven years from his immigration date. According to the Ben-Basat Committee recommendations, this exemption shall apply for up to ten years from the date of immigration but shall exclude, however, any new immigrants who have been former residents.
- Income from renting residential real estate is exempt from income tax up to a ceiling of NIS 6,970 per month. This exemption is valid till 31 December 2000.

  According to Ben-Basat committee recommendations, that ceiling of NIS 6,970 will be reduced to about NIS 3,000. The income tax liability from residential rental fees will be calculated in accordance with one of the following alternatives:

  a) rental income will be calculated less deduction of expenses according to the regular tax rate of the assessee; or

  b) tax will be paid at the rate of 10% of the rental income, without deduction of expenses. Interest and linkage differential income on taxes are due.

- Linkage differences on 'preferred loans' which are not deemed business income of a business in the hands of the recipient.

Linkage differential income is financing income arising from the linking of monetary assets to the Consumer Price Index. An amount equal to the difference created by such linkage is included in the interest on items whether the terms of the finance allow for linkage or not.

Tax paying

Employees

Income tax is withheld at source from salaried employees and wage earners (PAYE). The amount withheld takes into account the personal allowances and other deductions to which the employee is entitled (most are not applicable to foreign residents, and some apply only to new immigrants). If an individual's total annual income falls below an annually adjusted limit, he is not required to file an annual tax return.

Foreign residents

Tax at 25% must be deducted from payments paid to foreign residents. The rate of deduction is less than the standard rate of deduction in order to reduce the administrative burden. Other rates of tax (see table above) apply according to double taxation treaties.

A foreign resident may pay lower tax rates based on the table above. No tax is imposed in Israel on an income yielded to a foreign resident from non-Israeli sources.

Deductions at source from non-employment income

Type of payment	*Rate of deduction*
Authors	50%
Artists, supervisors, lecturers, office services, directors (according to type of remuneration)	50%
Athletes (not salary)	30%
Withdrawals from supplementary education funds	50%
Payments to employer from provident fund	40%
Unauthorised payments from provident fund	35%
Insurance commission	40%
Land rental fees	35%
Clothing, metal, electricity and electronics, and transportation labour	30%
Diamond polishing and diamond trade	30%
Building and transportation labour	30%
Agricultural labour	30%
Agricultural produce	15%

Interest and linkage	45%
Interest on debentures	35%
Loan fees (shares)	40%
Income on an agreement of forward exchange rates	35%
Dividends	25%
Interest or dividends on foreign securities	35%
Proceeds upon sale of foreign securities	5%
Services or assets	20%, 30%

Reduction of the rates of deduction requires approval by the income tax assessing officer.

National and Health Insurance (social security)

Both employers and employees pay for National Insurance. The employees' share includes compulsory health insurance.

The rates are percentage of income and refer to the monthly income:

	Monthly Salary (NIS)		
	0 – 3,174	3,175 – 25,388	25,389 – 31,735
Employee's share	5.76%	9.70%	9.70%
Employer's share	4.93%	4.93%	–

These rates refer to Israeli residents. The tax brackets are usually updated on a quarterly basis and are valid for December 2000.

Other rates apply to the self-employed and to residents who have only (or mostly) a passive income.

Other taxes

Estate and gift tax

Neither estate tax nor gift tax are imposed in Israel.

According to Ben-Basat Committee recommendations, estate tax may be levied at the rate of 10% on the net estate of Israeli resident individuals (assets less liabilities, other taxes, expenses related to death and estate management fees) in excess of NIS 2 million.

Furthermore, gift tax will be levied at the rate of 10% on the difference between the accrued value (against the individuals reporting to the tax authorities) of the gifts and NIS 2 million.

Value added tax (VAT)

General

A uniform rate or 17% (17/117 of gross turnover) is imposed on the sale of goods and services, rental income and interest (not applicable to banks and insurance companies). Input VAT is deducted from output VAT.

Unprocessed fruits and vegetables, exports, services provided to tourists and certain other income from foreign sources are zero-rated.

Diamonds, jewels, residential rental income, securities and a limited number of transactions and dealers are exempt from VAT.

Profit tax and wages tax

According to the VAT Law banks, insurance companies, stock exchange members, underwriters and certain financial institutions pay a wages tax of 17% on wages paid by them in addition to a profit tax of 17/117 of their profits, net of wages tax, instead of VAT.

Income computation is identical to the computation for corporate income tax, except that tax is not imposed on dividends from a company which is liable for profits tax. Prior year losses are not deductible from profit tax.

The profit and wages tax is deducted from taxable corporate income.

These institutions are not considered VAT dealers, thus they cannot recover VAT paid out of their consumption.

Wages tax on not for profit institutions

Non-profit institutions pay an 8.5% wages tax instead of VAT. These institutions are not considered VAT dealers, thus they cannot recover VAT paid out of their consumption. These institutions are subject also to Employees Tax of 4% of wages paid.

Treaty withholdings

The following table summarises withholding tax rates on dividends, interest and royalties in accordance with various tax treaties. It should be noted that the data listed below is subject to specific provisions of each treaty.

	dividends %	*interest* %	*royalties* %
Non-treaty countries	25	25	25
Treaty countries			
Austria	25	15	0/10[1]
Belgium	15	15	0/10[2]
Canada	15	15	0/15[3]
China, People's Republic of	10	7/10[4]	10
Czech Republic	5/15[5]	0/10[6]	5
Denmark	25	25	10
Finland	5/10/15[7]	0/10[8]	10
France	5/10/15[9]	5/10	0/10[10]
Germany	25	0/15	0/5[11]
Greece	25	10	10
Hungary	5/15[12]	0	0
India	10	0/10	10
Ireland	10	5/10[13]	10
Italy	10/15[14]	10	0/10[15]
Jamaica	15/22.5[16]	0/15[17]	10
Japan	5/15[18]	0/10[19]	10
Netherlands	5/10/15[20]	10/15[21]	5/10[22]
Norway	25	25	10
Philippines	10/15[23]	0/10[24]	15
Poland	10/15[25]	5	5/10[26]
Romania	15	0/5/10[27]	10
Singapore	0	15	0
South Africa	25	25	0/15[28]
South Korea	5/10/15[29]	7.5/10[30]	2/5[31]
Spain	10	5/10[32]	5
Sweden	0	25	0
Thailand	10/15[33]	10/15[34]	5/15[35]
Turkey	10	0/10[36]	10
United Kingdom	15	15	0/15[37]
United States of America	12.5/15/25[38]	10/17.5[39]	10/15[40]
Uzbekhistan	10	10	5/10[41]

Notes

1 10% for films.

2 0% for certain copyrights.

3 0% for certain copyrights.

4 7% applies to interest on loans from financial institutions.

5 5% applies to substantial holding (15% holding).

6 0% applies to governmental loans.

[7] 5% applies to substantial holding (25%); 10% applies to dividends from 'approved enterprise'; 15% all others.

[8] 0% applies to certain governmental loans.

[9] 5% applies to substantial holding (10%).

[10] 0% applies to certain kinds of copyrights of literary, artistic, or scientific works.

[11] 0% applies to certain kinds of copyrights of literary, artistic, or scientific works.

[12] 5% applies to substantial holding (10%).

[13] 5% applies to certain loans.

[14] 0% applies to substantial holding (25%).

[15] 0% applies to certain kinds of copyrights of literary, artistic, or scientific works.

[16] 15% applies to substantial holding (10%).

[17] 0% applies to certain governmental loans.

[18] 5% applies to substantial holding (25%).

[19] 0% applies to certain governmental loans.

[20] 5% applies to substantial holding (25%); 10% applies to dividends from 'approved enterprise'; 15% all others.

[21] 10% applies to certain governmental loans.

[22] 10% applies to films.

[23] 10% applies to substantial holding (10%).

[24] 0% applies to certain governmental loans.

[25] 10% applies to substansial holding (15%).

[26] 5% applies to industrial interest.

[27] 0% applies to certain governmental loans; 5% applies to certain loans.

[28] 15% applies to films.

[29] 5% applies to substantial holding (10%); 10% applies to dividends from 'approved enterprise'; 15% all others.

[30] 7.5% applies to certain governmental loans.

[31] 5% applies to industrial royalties.

[32] 5% applies to certain certain loans.

[33] 10% applies to substantial holding (25%).

[34] 10% applies to certain governmental loans.

[35] 5% applies to certain kinds of copyrights of literary, artistic, or scientific works.

[36] 0% applies to certain governmental loans.

[37] 15% applies to films.

[38] 12.5% applies to substantial holding (10%); 15% applies to dividends from 'approved enterprise'; 25% all others.

[39] 10% applies to loans from financial institutes.

[40] 15% applies to industrial royalties.

[41] 5% applies to certain kinds of copyrights of literary, artistic, or scientific works.

Italy

Consulaudit, Spa – Arietti & Associati Srl

Introduction

Since 1 January 1998, many changes have been introduced in the Italian tax legislation that substantially re-designed and rationalised the entire tax system.

The first aim of the Tax Reform was to reduce the large number of different taxes that were collected at a national level and to introduce new taxes (like ICI and IRAP) that are paid directly to the local or regional public bodies to enable them to finance their budgets.

The second aim of the Reform was to reduce the overall tax pressure to favour a general development of the economy and a new impetus towards business investment. Special permanent tax incentives were introduced, such as the Dual Income Tax system, which in the long run should allow substantial tax savings for those businesses that continue to re-invest their profits.

In the approach to the political elections of May 2001, many new tax proposals were put forward to the attention of the electors. As a consequence, the next couple of months may reveal a new Reform based upon the principles sponsored by the winner of the elections.

Corporate taxes

Taxable entities

Resident companies

Companies resident in Italy are taxed on their worldwide income, including capital gains. A company is resident if it is registered in Italy or if its administrative headquarters or principal business purposes are located in Italy during the greater part of the tax year.

Resident companies liable to corporate income tax include:

- stock corporations (SpA), limited liability companies (Srl), the permanent establishments of foreign companies and other entities; and

- other public or private bodies, such as various types of informal associations whose main purpose is the carrying on of a business activity.

Non-resident companies

Non-resident companies are taxed only on income and capital gains deemed to be earned within the Italian territory, subject to tax treaty provisions.

Tax year and filing requirements

The tax year corresponds to the company's financial year, which may be any fixed 12 month period as stated in the company's articles of association.

A tax return for corporate tax (IRPEG), local tax (IRAP) and real estate tax (ICI), must be filed within one month from the shareholders' approval of the annual accounts.

Tax inspections may occur within five years from the submission of the relevant tax return. If the tax return is not appropriately filed, an estimated assessment may be raised up to six years from the relevant year.

Taxes imposed

IRPEG (*'Imposta sul reddito delle persone giuridiche'*) is a national tax levied on the income of corporate bodies. This is known as a dual income tax because a portion of the net income may be taxed at a lower rate to encourage capitalisation of companies.

IRAP (*'Imposta regionale sulle attività produttive'*) is a local tax levied on the net production value realised within a region according to categories of business activity. IRAP is applicable for tax periods commencing after 30 September 1997. From the same date, the former local tax (ILOR) has been abolished.

IRPEG and IRAP payments, based on the previous year's return, must be made in two advance instalments before the company's financial year end (usually in the fifth and eleventh months of the tax year). The balance must be computed and paid when filing the annual tax return.

ICI is paid in two instalments in June and December of each calendar year.

Rates of tax

IRPEG 36% (ordinary rate); it will be reduced to 35% from January 1 2003.

19% (ordinary reduced rate).

7% (reduced rate for corporations listed on the Stock Exchange).

IRAP 4.25% (ordinary rate).

2.5% – 4.25% (agriculture).

4.25% – 5.4% (banks, financial institutions and insurance companies).

ICI 0.4% – 0.7% (rates are fixed within this range by each local municipality).

Income subject to tax

General rules

The taxable income of corporate bodies for IRPEG includes:

- business profits;
- income from land and buildings;
- non-operating profits;
- capital income;
- capital gains from the disposal of assets, including real estate; and
- income earned abroad.

The Dual Income Tax system taxes, at the lower rate of 19%, a portion of the annual net profits corresponding to the 'deemed interest remuneration' of any capital increase (such as increase of common stock and increase in the retained earnings) achieved by the company after 30 September 1996. The actual amount of the 'capital increase' is then further increased by 40% to favour a quicker start-up of the mechanism. The Ministry of Finance annually determines the 'deemed interest remuneration rate' applicable to capital increases (currently 7%).

For corporations admitted to the Stock Exchange, the reduced corporation tax applicable is 7% for the three initial tax periods (instead of 19%).

Non-operating companies' minimum tax

The minimum tax system for 'non-operating'; companies and partnerships has been fully revised with effect from 31 December 1996. A company is deemed to be 'non-operating' if its annual turnover, and the increase of its inventory at year end, does not exceed the sum of the following calculation:

- 1% of the acquisition cost of financial investments (shares, participations, long term financial receivables etc.);
- 4% of the acquisition cost of real estate, ships and aircraft; and
- 15% of the acquisition cost of all other fixed assets.

The above items, assumed gross of any allowable depreciation and apportioned for the actual period of ownership, are averaged over the last three tax periods.

Where, based upon the above calculation, a company qualifies as 'non-operating', its taxable income will be determined by applying the following percentages to the acquisition cost of its fixed assets (as shown in the current year annual accounts):

- 0.75% of the acquisition cost of financial investments;
- 3% of the acquisition cost of real estate, ships and aircraft; and
- 12% of the acquisition cost of all other fixed assets.

Under this rule, fixed assets acquired under lease contracts are treated as freehold assets.

Several exceptions apply to this taxation system, particularly with regard to newly formed companies.

The IRAP local tax is imposed on all professional and business activities involved in the production of goods or services. Although IRAP has been substituted for other income taxes, it cannot itself be considered as an income tax because it is levied on the 'net value of production', even where net income is negative.

The 'net value of production' is determined as follows:

- plus profit (or loss) before taxes;
- plus cost of labour including directors' fees;
- plus write-off provisions on fixed assets and receivables;

- plus provisions for risks and contingencies;
- plus interests and other financial costs;
- plus extraordinary costs, expenditures and capital gains;
- less financial income (including interest, dividends); and
- less extraordinary incomes and capital gains.

Interest and premiums from public securities issued before 20 September 1986 are tax exempt. Interest on public securities issued after September 1986 are fully taxable. The withholding tax (12.5%) previously applicable is no longer applicable if the interest is earned by business entities. Non-residents may be entitled to receive interest on public securities free of withholding tax if the relevant double taxation treaty applies.

Stock/inventory rules

Stock must be valued at lower of cost or selling price. Cost can be determined using any accepted evaluation method (LIFO, FIFO or weighted mean). In any case, the stock cannot be valued lower than the LIFO value.

Capital gains and losses

Capital gains are subject to corporate income tax (IRPEG) as normal taxable income. Capital losses are fully deductible from taxable income.

Gains realised on the sale of fixed assets owned for longer than three years may be taxed in equal instalments over five tax periods, including the year in which the gain is realised.

Capital gains realised on business reorganisation procedures may be, by option, separately taxed at the rate of 19%. Such capital gains are those arising in the case of a merger, division, or sale of business, and the sale of shares owned for longer than three years. The option must be exercised in the tax return for the year the gain is realised.

Gains on the transfer of sale of immovable property are, in addition, subject to INVIM (*'Imposta comunale sull'incremento di valore degli immobili'*). The tax rate ranges from 5% to 30% and is applied on the difference between market value, as at 31 December 1992, and the original cost. Sales of real estate that occur after 31 December 2002 will not generate any capital gain liable to INVIM.

Non-resident companies are chargeable to income tax on capital gains in the same way as a resident company, but only on assets located in Italy (unless treaty provisions apply).

Dividends

Dividends received from other Italian companies are subject to IRPEG. As the profits of the paying company may have already been subject to corporation tax, a relief is granted to the recipient shareholder in the form of a tax credit. The tax credit must be added to taxable income and then deducted from total tax due.

As the tax credit is linked to the corporate tax paid or deemed payable by the distributing company, there may be no tax credit available to the shareholders.

Full tax credit on dividends (currently 58.73%) is available to shareholders to the extent that the distributing company has actually paid an equivalent amount of IRPEG (tax credit from what is known as Basket A) or has enjoyed specific tax exemptions or tax reductions in relation to listed revenue items (tax credit from Basket B). While the tax credit from basket A may be offset against all other income and may be claimed back, the tax credit from basket B, as it does not arise from actual corporate tax paid by the distributing company, may be used only to offset the tax liability related to the dividend received.

Equalisation tax has been abolished from 1 January 1998.

Foreign dividends

Only 5% of dividends paid by an EU resident subsidiary are assessed as taxable income of the parent company in Italy provided the following conditions (EU directive 90/435) are met:

- participation by the Italian company in the EU resident subsidiary has to exceed 25% and have been owned for longer than one year;
- the foreign subsidiary is subject to corporate tax in its country of residence.

If the EU directive cannot be applied, only 40% of the dividends received from other foreign subsidiaries (10% owned or more) are taxable in the hands of the parent company. Dividends received from subsidiaries located in a 'low tax jurisdiction' are usually fully taxable for the recipient.

As foreign dividends are partially exempt from Italian corporate tax, no tax credit for the underlying tax is usually granted. Special rules are applicable to dividends received from a treaty country.

Deduction

General rules

The basic principle is that taxable income is ascertained from the accounts and no cost can be deductible if it is not charged to the profit and loss account. However, adjustments may be required for exempt items, non-deductible expenses and special reliefs. The most important items subject to adjustment are:

- *leasing* – for leased fixed assets the lessee is entitled to deduct the rent paid if the contract period is longer than 50% of the useful life of the asset as determined for tax purposes (for real estate the lease period cannot be lower than 8 years);
- *maintenance and repairs* – expenditure is deductible up to a maximum of 5% of the acquisition cost of depreciable fixed assets at the beginning of the year (any excess is deductible in equal instalments over the following five years);
- *company cars* – only 50% of depreciation and running costs are tax deductible;
- *social welfare and charitable contributions* – they are deductible up to stated limits, if made for specifically qualifying purposes;
- *general and administrative overheads* – they are non-deductible up to the amount of tax exempt income;
- *provisions for risks and contingency* – such provisions are restricted to specific cases determined by law; and
- specific rules apply to writing off patents, trademarks, goodwill, training expenses, research and development expenses and advertising expenses.

Depreciation and amortisation

Depreciation of all fixed assets, except land, is allowable for tax purposes but, to be deductible, it must be included in the accounts and in the register of depreciable assets.

Depreciation cannot be claimed for tax purposes in excess of the amount shown in the accounts. Only the straight line method of depreciation is permitted.

Depreciation may not be calculated, for tax purposes, at rates in excess of those approved by the Minister of Finance for any specific business sector.

The following rates (minimum and maximum) are currently in force:

- buildings 3%–7%
- plant and machinery 6%–30%
- furniture and office equipment 12%
- vehicles 20%–30%

In the year in which the assets are purchased, the depreciation rate is reduced by 50%. In addition to ordinary depreciation, accelerated depreciation may be claimed on fixed assets. This allowance is granted for the initial three years from the date of purchase of new assets, and for one year only in the case of secondhand assets. In each relevant year the accelerated depreciation claimed for any given asset cannot exceed the ordinary depreciation allowed, so the total depreciation cannot exceed twice the ordinary rate.

Restrictions have been introduced for company cars whose depreciable acquisition cost cannot exceed Lire 35 million.

Royalties

Royalties are deductible if paid with reference to an intangible asset used to produce taxable revenues. They can be paid abroad upon payment of a withholding tax of 30%, unless treaty protection applies.

Interest

In principle, all interest payments on loan stock (and other debts of a company) are considered to be business expenses and are therefore deductible.

Interest expenses on the purchase of fixed assets are added to the cost of the asset until the tax period in which it is brought into use. They are, therefore, tax relieved by depreciation at the relevant rates.

Interest expenses incurred are deemed to be non-deductible up to the amount of tax-exempt interest and premiums earned. Anti-avoidance measures disallow tax deductions claimed for interests paid on bond loans if the interest rate is three points higher than the Official Discount Rate (currently 4.75%).

There are no special rules for payments of interest to associated companies. There is no debt/equity legislation in respect of the deductibility of interest. Furthermore, interest on acquisition loans is fully deductible.

Dividends

Dividends paid are not deductible.

Bad and doubtful debts and other provisions

In general, provisions which are not specifically allowed by law cannot be deducted.

- A provision for bad and doubtful debts, not exceeding 5% of the total amount of commercial receivables, is deductible until the accumulated reserve is equal to 5% of the total receivables. Specific rules are given for banks and financial institutions.
- An annual deductible provision aimed at covering foreign exchange losses may be calculated based upon the difference between receivables and payables denominated in foreign currency.
- An annual provision for the recurring maintenance of ships and aircrafts is allowed up to 5% of the acquisition cost of each ship or aircraft.
- Specific rules are prescribed with reference to other deductible provisions concerning premium deals.

Employees' and directors' remuneration and benefits

Employees' and directors' remuneration are fully deductible. Most of the benefits in kind are tax deductible to the extent that a corresponding amount is assessed as income of the recipient.

The taxable value of a fringe benefit is usually calculated by reference to its actual market value, determined on an arm's length basis.

The taxable values of common benefits provided to employees, and hence the amount deductible for corporate taxes, are as follows:

Cars	30% of a notional mileage cost corresponding to 15,000 Km per year.
Loans	50% of the difference between the actual interest paid by the employee and the interest computed using the Official Discount Rate in force.

Housing	30% of the difference between the current market rent and the rent actually paid by the employee.

Specifically non-deductible expenses

Gifts and entertainment expenses above Lire 50,000 are deductible, based on ⅓ of their total amount, in five equal instalments over five financial years, including the year in which the expenses were incurred.

Other specifically non-deductible expenses include:

- fines;
- income taxes, IRAP and ICI;
- expenses not connected with business activity;
- other expenses specifically listed by law; and
- costs related to transactions carried out with a counterpart resident or domiciled in a low tax jurisdiction (unless they are proved to be genuine and supported by business reasons); a tax ruling may however be obtained before the transaction is actually carried out.

Foreign source income

Italian companies are fully taxable (at corporate tax level) on foreign income from all sources. A resident company is taxed on foreign branch income and may set off branch losses against trading income from other sources.

Taxes paid abroad on foreign source income are deductible as a credit against IRPEG (tax against tax) in order to avoid double taxation.

Foreign source income is generally subject to IRPEG. A tax credit is usually available only if the foreign tax has been actually paid or assessed. If the foreign income was not disclosed in the tax return, the taxpayer may not subsequently claim the tax credit when such income is ultimately assessed by the Revenue. The tax credit is generally equal to the actual tax paid abroad, but it cannot exceed the amount of the Italian tax corresponding to the foreign income declared. For countries where a double taxation treaty exists, different rules may be applicable.

Controlled foreign corporations (CFCs)

Starting from January 2001, a CFC legislation has been introduced in the Italian tax system. Tax is imposed on Italian shareholders (corporate or individuals) in respect of profits made by controlled corporations (+50% voting rights) established in low tax territories as detailed in a special 'black list'. The legislation will not apply to a CFC carrying on a genuine commercial operation with unconnected parties in its territory of residence.

Investment incentives and special benefits

General rules

For a number of years the government has been using incentives to encourage industrial investment and to direct investments to particular areas, principally through tax incentives, subsidised loans and grants to companies operating in under-developed areas. The amount of grant is usually based upon the investments made and the number of jobs created, but it cannot exceed limits stated by the EU directive.

Tax incentives

These laws provide for a ten year tax holiday period for new business activities set up in the territories of Southern Italy or exemptions from local taxes for new activities based in specified depressed areas of the Central Northern region of the country. However, during the last few years, most of these permanent tax incentives have been abolished.

Selected tax incentives currently in force are listed below:

- companies that previously enjoyed exemption from local taxes (namely ILOR) are now entitled to a corresponding partial exemption from IRAP;
- tax credits of up to Lire 60 million per year are available to medium to small businesses based in Southern Italy which increase their number of employees;
- tax credits of up to 60% of the value of new industrial assets, grants and subsidies, are available to companies investing within certain territories defined by directives of the European Community;
- tax credits for investment made in research and development, including the hiring of newly qualified employees;
- corporation tax reduction for new investments in fixed assets: a portion of the annual taxable income, corresponding to the 'net increase' of specified fixed assets, qualifies for a lower taxation at the rate of 19%; it is a temporary tax incentive enforced only for the tax periods 1999, 2000 and 2001.

Related party transactions

There are no special rules. Actual prices may be replaced by market values where there is evidence of transactions not at market rates. The 'transfer pricing' rules usually apply only where one of the parties is non-resident, but in certain cases these provisions also apply to domestic transactions.

Losses

For corporation tax purposes, tax losses may be carried forward for five years against future income, which need not be from the same source, but they may not be carried back. Special rules apply when tax losses occur alongside tax-exempt proceeds and where 'non-operating companies' are involved.

Tax losses suffered in the first three tax periods after a company's incorporation may be carried forward without any limitation. Special rules apply in cases of change of ownership or change of business to limit the use of previous years' tax losses.

Corporate groups

There are no provisions for group relief. Corporate tax paid in excess by one company may, under certain conditions, be transferred to another group company to offset its current or future tax liability.

Tax free mergers and disposals

Mergers and divisions are generally deemed to be neutral for tax purposes. Since November 1997, it is possible to increase the value of the assets of the merged company (or of the beneficiary company resulting from the division) by paying a substitute tax of 19% of the step-up. However, substitute tax is not due on the extent to which the step-up corresponds to an equivalent amount of capital gains already subjected to tax in the hands of previous vendors of the shares.

A company may transfer a portion of its business to a subsidiary in exchange for shares issued by the subsidiary without incurring any capital gain tax liability, provided that the shares received are recorded in the accounts of the contributing company at the same value as the hived-down business. For tax purposes, the hived-down assets and liabilities maintain their original historical value in the accounts of the recipient subsidiary.

Liquidation of the company

An individual shareholder is subject to personal income tax on liquidation distributions, to the extent to which they exceed the original share capital contribution. If the shareholder is a company, the loss on liquidation is deductible and any surplus is taxed.

Capital taxes

Capital duty

A flat capital duty of € 130 is levied on any shareholder's cash contribution to the capital of a company. In case of contributions in kind, the tax rate may range between 1% and 15% of the market value of the asset.

Net worth tax

Abolished from 1 January 1998.

Treatment of branches (branch profit tax)

Profits arising from foreign branches are treated as foreign source income and are therefore subject to corporate tax (IRPEG).

For local tax (IRAP) purposes, a share of the total 'net value of production' of the company, proportionally corresponding to cost of labour incurred in the foreign country, is exempt from taxation in Italy. If the branch has operated in the foreign country for a period not exceeding three months, then all its profits are liable to IRAP.

Italian branches of foreign companies are required to file a tax return and pay IRPEG on profits originated in Italy. IRAP is due if the branch has been operative for more than three months.

International tax treaties provide special rules to avoid double taxation. Negotiations are in progress to review the wording of those treaties which have been concluded with other countries in order to adjust current provisions, which still refer to the old local tax (ILOR), to accord with the new IRAP tax.

Personal taxes

Taxable individuals

Individuals who are either resident or non-resident in Italy, and earning income in Italy, are subject to personal income tax.

Residents

In addition to those registered among the national resident population for the greater part of the tax year (183 days), those who maintain their domicile or abode in Italy – according to the Civil Code rules – are also deemed to be resident.

Residents are subject to personal tax on worldwide income, unless otherwise provided for by tax treaties.

Non-residents

Non-residents are subject to personal income tax only on the income earned in Italy, unless otherwise provided by tax treaties.

Withholding tax is levied on the following sources of income:

- royalties;
- dividends;
- interest on bonds and similar securities;
- interest on current accounts; and
- professional fees.

Tax year and filing requirements

The tax year is the calendar year. Individuals are not required to file a tax return where they:

- do not receive any income;
- receive only exempt income, or income subject to definitive withholding tax; or
- receive income solely from employment or pensions.

Business entities are always required to file a tax return, even where no taxable income is earned.

Tax returns must be filed by 30 June, following the end of the tax year.

Assessments may be raised up to the end of the fifth year (or sixth year where no tax return has been filed), subsequent to the submission of the return.

Taxes on income

There are two levels of taxation:

- a national taxation known as IRPEF (*'Imposta sul reddito delle persone fisiche'*) and;
- a local taxation known as IRAP (*'Imposta regionale sulle attività produttive'*), applicable only to business and professional activities.

Both employees and employers pay social security contributions.

Sources of income

Employment income and directors' fees

An employee, including a company's director, is taxed on all salaries, compensation and benefits in kind received during the tax period by virtue of an employment contract. However, termination payments and, in particular cases, payments of previous years' salaries, are separately subject to income tax to avoid an undue increase in the annual tax bracket. No expense deductions are allowed against employment income

Business income

This includes income generated by an industrial or trading enterprise owned by an individual or by a partnership, rather than by a corporate entity.

The same regulations apply as for corporate tax in determining the taxable income and payment of tax due. However, tax is charged at progressive rates rather than at the corporate rate. Starting from year 2001, by option it is now possible to separately tax business profits at the corporate rate instead of at the progressive personal tax rate; special rules are applicable to the case.

If the annual turnover is lower than Lire 600 million, only VAT records are required to be kept. Such records should be integrated with all other non-VAT records concerning income and expenditure. If the annual turnover is higher than Lire 600 million, a full set of accounts is required.

For certain businesses, the 600 million Lire threshold is increased to Lire 1 billion.

Capital gains

Capital gains, excluding those arising on the sale of an individual's business concerns, are included in the income of a taxpayer in the year in which they are realised and are taxed at the rate corresponding to the tax bracket of the taxpayer. Certain capital gains may, by option, be taxed over a five year period.

Capital gains on disposals of real estate owned for longer than five years are exempt from tax. Capital gains realised on the sale of a residential house are also exempt.

Capital gains arising on disposals of shares and similar securities are liable to a substitute tax. The taxation system applies a 27% rate to the amount of the net capital gain realised. Capital losses can be carried forward to set off future capital gains.

A reduced rate of 12.5% is applied to capital gains realised on the disposals of shares and similar securities if the number of shares disposed does not exceed the following percentages (non-qualified shareholding):

- 20% or 25% of the share capital (for companies *not* listed on the Stock Exchange); or
- 2% or 5% of the share capital (for companies listed on the Stock Exchange).

Dividends

Dividends received from Italian companies are subject to IRPEF.

As profits of the paying company may have already been subjected to corporation tax, an ordinary tax credit equal to 58.73% of the dividend may be granted to the shareholder (56.25% from year 2002 and 53.85% from year 2004). The 'ordinary' tax credit (Basket A) must be added to taxable income and deducted from total tax due. The 'limited' tax credit (Basket B) is added to the gross dividend received and then deducted from the net income tax related to the dividend itself.

From 1 July 1998, individuals owning non-qualified shareholdings may opt for a definitive taxation by means of a withholding tax of 12.5% of the dividend received; if the option is exercised, the dividend must not be reported in the annual tax return and no tax credit is granted.

Italy

Dividends received from non-residents are fully taxable except where treaty provisions apply.

Interest

Interest on securities, bank deposits, current accounts and bond loans are subject to a withholding tax ranging from 12.5% to 27%. Once the withholding tax is levied, individuals are no longer required to include the income received in their taxable income. All other interest income is fully taxable and must be disclosed in the personal tax return.

Interest and profit derived from an Italian mutual fund is tax-free because the mutual fund has already suffered a definitive substitute tax of 12.5% on its annual increase in value.

From 1 July 1998, profits realised on financial investments, if such investments are managed or administered by an authorised financial operator (a bank, financial agent, stockbroker, etc.), may be taxed according to one of two methods, as follows:

- substitute tax of 12.5% levied immediately on each single capital gain actually realised on non-qualified shareholdings, options and futures; capital losses previously incurred are deducted from the capital gain (*'Risparmio amministrato'*); or
- substitute tax of 12.5% levied on the annual increase of the value of financial assets administered by an authorised financial operator; the taxable base includes all dividends, interests, capital gains and losses earned in a relevant tax period, computed on an accrual basis (*'Risparmio Gestito'*).

These two methods allow anonymity to the taxpayer, as all taxes are levied and paid to the Revenue by an authorised financial operator.

Rentals and real estate income

Income from buildings and land is subject to IRPEF, whether or not rent is paid. The public registry determines and annually reviews a notional taxable income. Where rent paid is higher than the notional income, the actual rent is used to determine taxable income.

Royalties

Royalties received are fully subject to income tax, but a standard 25% deduction is allowed (regardless of the actual expenses incurred).

Professional income

Professional income is assessed on a cash basis. All expenses incurred are generally tax deductible (even though some limitations apply to travel and entertainment expenses, car expenses, training expenses, real estate depreciation and lease instalments on fixed assets).

Social security benefits

Social security contributions are deductible and benefits received are taxable.

Pensions and annuities

Pensions are subject to income tax in the same way as employment income. Life annuities are taxed based on 60% of the amount received.

Foreign source income

Italian residents in receipt of foreign source income, other than from employment, are subject to IRPEF unless otherwise provided for by a tax treaty. A tax credit is generally granted when the income has been taxed in the other country.

Personal allowances and deductions

National income tax

Taxable income is reduced by the following main allowable deductions:

- total amount of compulsory social and health contributions paid;
- donations to charitable entities (within limits); and
- a share of the expenses (25% – 41%) incurred for energy savings and building restructuring.

The total tax payable is also reduced by an amount equal to 19% of the following expenses incurred:

- interest paid to EU lenders on mortgages related to the purchase of a residential house with an annual roof limit of Lire 7 million;
- specialist medical fees and general medical fees exceeding a fixed amount of Lire 250,000; expenses for the purchase of transportation means for disabled persons;

- life insurance premiums and non-compulsory social contributions up to maximum amount of Lire 2.5 million;
- expenses incurred in connection with the funeral arrangements of close relatives (up to Lire 3 million for each person);
- expenses incurred to enrol and attend secondary school and university (within limits); and
- certain gratuities (within limits).

Losses

Business losses may be used to offset business profits of the following five years. Tax losses suffered in the three tax periods after commencement of the business may be carried forward without time limits.

Losses from professional activities may be offset against other income derived in the year concerned.

Losses cannot be carried forward for local tax (IRAP) purposes.

Special family rules

A husband and wife are taxed separately, but the income of minor children is added to the income of their parents.

Special treatment for expatriates

No specific facilities are granted to expatriates.

Rates of tax

General

Current law has fixed the following tax rates:

IRPEF Tax Rates

Tax Bracket	Up to 20 million	From 20 to 30 million	From 30 to 60 million	From 60 to 135 million	Over 135 million
Year 2000	18.5%	25.5%	33.5%	39.5%	45.5%
Year 2001	18%	24%	32%	39%	45%
Year 2002	18%	23%	32%	38.5%	44.5%
Year 2003	18%	22%	32%	38%	44%

Residents and non-residents

The above rates apply to both resident and non-resident taxpayers.

Withholding taxes

Withholding taxes are levied on professional fees, royalties, interest and dividends.

Professional fees are subject to a withholding tax of 20% if payment is made to a resident, and 30% if payment is made to a non-resident.

Royalties from patents paid to residents are subject to 20% withholding tax. If payment is made to a non-resident and a non-treaty reduction applies, the withholding tax rate is 30%.

Interest on securities is subject to a withholding tax ranging between 12.5% and 27% for both residents and non-residents. Interest on bank accounts is subject to withholding tax at 27%; such interests are not subject to further taxation or disclosure.

Tax credits

On foreign source income, a tax credit equal to the taxes paid abroad is usually given. However, the tax credit allowed cannot be higher than the Italian tax corresponding to the foreign source income concerned.

For the calendar year 2001, the following personal tax credits are granted to individuals:

Non income earning spouse	*ranging from:* Lire 817,552 to Lire 1,057,552
Each child and other dependant relatives (amount to be divided between the parents)	Lire 516,000
Employment and pension income	*ranging from:* Lire 100,000 to Lire 2,200,000
Pension income only	*ranging from:* Lire 90,000 to Lire. 430,000

Payment of taxes

Payroll deductions

Tax is withheld by the employer from the employee's salary with reference to individual tax brackets, taking into account the personal tax credits available.

Prepayments

Income taxes due for the fiscal year must be paid in two advance instalments equal to 95% of the total taxes paid for the previous year. The first instalment (38%) must be paid before 31 May, the second (57%) is payable before 30 November. The balance due for the fiscal year is payable before 31 May of the following year.

Estate and gift tax

Transfers of estates, goods and rights by inheritance or gift are subject to a cumulative tax, with certain exemptions and reliefs, computed by reference to the value received by the beneficiary and taking into account his relationship with the deceased or donor. The tax is charged on the net value of the existing assets at the date of succession and is payable by the recipients. If the deceased or the donor was resident abroad, tax is applicable only to the assets existing on the Italian territory.

The value of the estate is increased by a notional 10% for cash, jewellery and furniture, even if such items have been declared at a lower value.

Deductions may be made in respect of certain liabilities, medical and funeral expenses, if supported by relevant documentation. Inheritance taxes paid abroad may be deducted from the inheritance tax due.

Tax rates may range from 4% for closer relatives (spouse and children) to 8% for non-related beneficiaries. Inheritance tax must be paid within 60 days from the date of the assessment issued by the Revenue. By option, an amount equal to 80% of the total tax due may be paid over a five year period – in this case interests are due and the beneficiary must provide a valid guarantee.

The beneficiary's tax return must be filed within six months of the date of death.

Inheritance tax paid abroad may be deducted from the inheritance tax due in Italy on the same asset; to avoid international double taxation there are certain estate and gift tax treaties in force.

Wealth tax

There is no wealth tax in Italy.

Social security contributions

Contributions must be paid by both the employer and employee at rates according to the type of employment. The employer bears the major part of the cost, generally contributing about 40% of gross salary. The employee pays between 8% and 10%, which is deducted from his salary. All foreign individuals are liable to social security if they possess a work permit (subject to social security conventions and the EU Directives).

The self-employed pay social contributions at rates between 10% and 18%.

Other taxes

Treatment of partnerships

Income from partnerships flows through to the individual partners and is included in their individual returns. Local tax, however, is assessed on the partnership as an entity. Business incomes earned by partnerships may, by option, be taxed at the corporate rate (currently 36%).

VAT and sales tax

VAT is levied on the sale of goods and services at rates of 4%, 10% and 20%.

Several exceptions apply.

Stamp duty

Stamp duty is imposed on certain deeds, documents and registers.

Real estate tax (ICI)

Real estate tax (ICI) is imposed on the notional value of property. The tax rates are annually fixed by each municipality council and may range between 0.4% and 0.7%. Payments are due twice a year in June

(50%) and December (the remaining 50%). Tax returns must be submitted only where real estate assets have been acquired or disposed during the relevant tax year. Special reductions apply to the taxpayer's first residential property.

Exchange control

Foreign transactions and foreign investments exceeding Lire 20 million must be disclosed to the Exchange Control Authorities. Special rules apply with reference to their disclosure in the income tax return in the case of residents owning, at the end of the tax period, foreign assets worth more than Lire 20 million. For statistical purposes, resident taxpayers must disclose in the tax return all financial transactions within the tax period which are higher than Lire 20 million and are related to foreign financial investment.

Tax treaties and withholding taxes

Under the majority of double taxation treaties concluded by Italy, withholding tax rates are reduced or waived completely. The following table shows the maximum rates currently in force:

Country of residence	*Royalties (%)*	*Interest (%)*	*Dividends (%)*
Non-treaty countries	22.5	12.5/27	27
Selected treaty countries:			
Argentina	10/18	15-20	15
Australia	10	10	15
Austria	0/10	10	Nil (a)
Belgium	5	15	Nil (a)
Brazil	21/15	15	15
Canada	0-10	15	15
Czech Republic	0-5	Nil	15
Cyprus	Nil	10	15
Denmark	5	15	Nil (a)
Egypt	15	25	32.4
France	5	10	5/Nil (a)
Germany	0-5	10	10/Nil (a)
Greece	5	10	Nil (a)
Hungary	Nil	Nil	10
India	21	15	32.4
Ireland	Nil	10	Nil (a)
Japan	10	10	15/10 (b)
Kenya	15	15	20/15
Korea	10	10	15/10 (b)
Luxembourg	10	10	Nil (a)
Malaysia	15	15	10

Malta	0-10	10	15
Netherlands	5	10	Nil (a)
New Zealand	10	10	15
Norway	5	15	15
Pakistan	30	30	25/15
Poland	10	10	10
Portugal	12	15	Nil (a)
Singapore	15/20	12.5	10
Spain	4/8	12	Nil (a)
Sri Lanka	10/15	0-10	15
Sweden	5	15	Nil (a)
Switzerland	5	12.5	15
Thailand	5/15	10/15	20/15
Turkey	10	15	15
UK	8	10/Nil (e)	Nil (a)
USA	5/8/10	15	15/10 (d) /5 (c)

Notes

'Nil' no withholding tax is levied.

(a) No withholding tax is levied on dividends paid to a parent company, provided that an interest of 25% or more has been held for at least one year.

(b) If the recipient owns at least 25%.

(c) If the recipient owns at least 51%.

(d) If the recipient owns at least 10%.

(e) No withholding tax is levied on sales, on credit, of equipment or goods.

Other treaty countries

Albania, Algeria, Bangladesh, Bulgaria, China, Colombia, Ivory Coast, Ecuador, Estonia, Ethiopia, Ghana, Indonesia, Finland, Iraq, Israel, Kazakhstan, Kuwait, Lithuania, Macedonia, Malaysia, Morocco, Mauritius, Mexico, Philippines, Russia, Romania, Senegal, Saudi Arabia, South Africa, Tanzania, Thailand, Trinidad and Tobago, Tunisia, United Arabic Emirates, former USSR countries, Venezuela, Vietnam, former countries of Yugoslavia, Zambia.

New treaties with Argentina, Kenya and Senegal have been already approved and ratified but they are not yet in force.

New Treaties with Cuba, Denmark, Ethiopia, Gabon, Georgia, Lettonia, Lebanon, Mozambique, Oman, Senegal, United States of America, Ukraine and Uzbekistan have been signed but not yet ratified.

Negotiations are in progress with the following countries: Byelorussia, Canada, Croatia, Jamaica, Ireland, Syria, Slovenia, Trinidad and Tobago, and Uganda.

Anti-avoidance measures

A general anti-avoidance provision exists and is applicable to all taxpayers.

Transactions carried out without proper and valid business reasons, with the aim of avoiding obligations or charges imposed by tax legislation, may be adjusted by the authorities to reflect the proper application of the rules avoided.

The anti-avoidance provision applies if one of the following transactions is carried out by the taxpayer:

- merger, division, reorganisation, liquidation or payment to the shareholders of company reserves other than those based on ordinary profits;
- contribution of assets made to other companies and other contracts that may cause a transfer of the ownership or possession of a business;
- sale or disposal of company receivables;
- sale or disposal of tax credits;
- merger, division, contribution of assets, exchange of shares made in accordance with the EU directive 90/434; or
- transactions involving shares, options and foreign currencies.

Before carrying out one of the above transactions, the taxpayer may submit a request for a ruling based on a detailed description of the planned transaction.

Japan

Sawamura & Co.

Introduction

Tax rates on corporate and individual income have been reduced. There were no significant changes in the tax system in 2000. As a result of the long recession, the government intends to allow companies to reorganise easily without tax penalties. To facilitate this, capital gains arising on the exchange of stocks and transfer of stocks are deferred if certain conditions are met. Fiscal unity or consolidated returns within groups may be introduced in 2002.

The government financial year ends on 31 March. The tax year for individuals is the calendar year, and companies can select their own fiscal year. An advance tax ruling system is not available although unofficial guidance or advice may be available from the tax authorities. A tax examination, generally including a physical audit of the accounting records of taxpayers, is carried out at least once in the course of three to five years.

Corporate taxes

Taxable entities

Resident companies

Resident companies (those corporations which have their registered offices in Japan) are taxable on worldwide income and capital gains.

Non-resident companies

Non-resident companies are taxable on income derived from sources within Japan. These corporations may be divided into the following categories, which are treated differently for tax purposes:

- non-resident companies with a branch or a fixed place of business in Japan, which are subject to corporation tax only on their entire income from sources within Japan;
- non-resident companies which:

- undertake construction, installation or assembly activities or provide services for the supervision of such activities for more than one year;
- carry on business in Japan through agents.

Non-resident companies are subject to corporation tax on the aggregate of income derived from the utilisation, sale or disposal of assets located in Japan, rental income arising in Japan, and that part of income from interest, dividends and royalties which is attributable to their business in Japan. Other gross income is subject to a flat 20% withholding tax or such rate as is laid down in the relevant tax treaty.

Any other non-resident companies are normally only taxable on the aggregate of income from the utilisation, sale or disposal of an asset in Japan, professional fees, occasional income and rent. Income such as interest, dividends and royalties is subject to a flat 20% withholding tax, unless the rate is reduced by tax treaty provisions.

The taxable income of non-resident companies is, in principle, subject to the same rules and tax rates as those applied to resident companies.

Tax year and filing requirements

The financial year of a company may be any fixed twelve-month period provided in the company's articles of incorporation. Tax returns must be filed and taxes must be paid within two months after the financial year end. Companies with fiscal periods exceeding six months are generally required to file interim tax returns for the first half year and to make provisional tax payments within two months after that period end. A one-month extension for tax filing and payment may be granted.

A company which maintains the appropriate standard of accounting records may apply to the tax authorities to use a blue tax return (as opposed to a white tax return). Certain privileges are then available, including the carry forward of losses and other general tax deductible provisions. In order to benefit from these privileges, the majority of corporations file blue tax returns.

Tax imposed

Taxes imposed on a corporation are national tax, local taxes and enterprise (or business) tax. Local taxes consist of a prefectural inhabitant tax and municipal inhabitant tax. Tax rates are normally set from 1 April each year. Corporation taxes are chargeable according to the tax year in which their accounting period ends.

Because Japan has a declaration system, companies are responsible for filing tax returns and paying taxes within time limits. In the case of failure to file and pay by the due dates, penalties are imposed by the tax authorities. In addition, if any under declaration of income is discovered during a tax examination, additional tax and penalties are levied.

Rates of tax

National tax

Corporation tax rates applicable to the fiscal year commencing on 1 April and thereafter are as follows:

	Budget 1999	*Budget 2000*
Corporations with stated capital of more than Yen 100 million	30%	30%
Corporations with stated capital of Yen 100 million or less		
– income over Yen 8 million	30%	30%
– income up to Yen 8 million	22%	22%

Local taxes

Tax authorities may determine the precise rate (applied as a percentage of the national corporation tax payable) within the following bands:

Prefectural inhabitants tax	5%–6%
Municipal inhabitants tax	12.3%–14.7%

In addition, per capita tax is payable, depending on the amount of issued share capital and capital surplus and the number of employees.

Enterprise tax is charged on taxable income at rates, which vary according to the level of such income.

Taxable income	*1999 rate*	*2000 rate*
Up to Yen 4 million	5.0%	5.0%
4 to Yen 8 million	7.3%	7.3%
Over Yen 8 million	9.6%	9.6%

This a deductible expense for corporation tax purposes in the period of actual payment.

Effective tax rate

The normal effective corporation tax rate combining the national and local taxes, except for per capita tax, is approximately 41.8% in Tokyo for a corporation with more than Yen 100 million of stated capital.

Extra taxes

For a family company, additional income taxes are levied on undistributed income less allowance (the minimum Yen 15 million). Aggregate tax rates are:

For taxable income less than Yen 30 million	11.7%–12.10%
For taxable income Yen 30 to 100 million	17.6%–18.11%
For taxable income more than Yen 100 million	23.5%–24.10%

Income subject to tax

General rules

Corporation tax is levied on the net income of each accounting period (measured under generally accepted accounting principles), adjusted in accordance with the requirements of general tax laws.

Within specified limits, foreign taxation suffered by a domestic Japanese corporation is deductible from Japanese national and local tax liabilities.

In order to take full advantage of certain tax concessions (particularly concerning the deductibility of special reserves, the carry-forward and carry-back of tax losses, and special depreciation), corporations must register under the blue tax return scheme. Once registration is obtained (within given time limits), subsequent renewal is not required.

Stock/inventory valuation

Inventories are valued at cost, or the lower of cost or market value. Inventory cost is the total of the purchase price of materials, labour costs and all related expenses, including those directly incurred in making inventory available for sale or consumption. Cost may be determined on a FIFO, LIFO or any other consistent basis used in the financial statements.

Capital gains and losses

The capital gains and losses of a corporation are subject to normal corporation tax. However, a special additional tax is imposed on capital gains from the sale or transfer of land or the right to use land owned by a corporation. The capital gain is calculated by deducting acquisition costs and direct and indirect expenses of sale from the proceeds. The resulting gain is taxed at 5% in addition to the ordinary corporation tax payable. A capital loss on such land can be deducted from income for tax purposes. This additional tax rate rises to 10% on gains from the sale of land owned for periods of less than five years. Local inhabitant tax is due on such national tax at the normal rates. The additional tax rates do not apply to land sold to government bodies. The gains and losses on the revaluation of securities at the financial end are taxed if the securities are held for the purpose of sales.

The additional tax on capital gains on the sale of land was suspended for a period from 1 January 1998 to 31 December 2000.

Dividends

Dividends received from domestic Japanese corporations in which the investing company owns more than 25% of the shares are exempt from tax. Only 80% of the dividends received from domestic Japanese corporations, other than the above, are exempt from tax.

Ordinary dividends received from a foreign company in which a Japanese corporation holds at least 25% of the issued share capital, normally attract a tax credit in respect of the underlying foreign tax according to the percentage of after tax earnings distributed.

Deductions

General rules

Costs and expenses incurred by corporations in the conduct of business are generally deductible for tax purposes. Some business related expenses not wholly or necessarily incurred for the purpose of the trade are partly or entirely disallowed. For estimated losses or expense provisions there are specified calculation methods for tax purposes.

Depreciation and amortisation

The value of the deductible depreciation of tangible assets is computed by applying consistently either the straight-line method or the reducing balance method over the useful lives of the assets as laid down by the tax authorities. Amortisation of intangible assets is computed by the straight-line method over the useful life of the assets.

Japan

Software is categorised as an intangible asset and depreciated over three years by the straight line method if it is for R&D or sales by coping. In all other circumstances it is depreciated over five years.

Royalties

Royalties payable are allowed as a normal business expense.

Interest

In principle, all interest incurred in earning income is deductible.

Thin capitalisation rules are designed to counter the substitution of debt for equity finance. In very broad outline, if corporate debt to a parent or its related companies (50% or more shareholding) is greater than three times the related party's equity, the amount of the interest payment relating to the excess debt will be disallowed for deduction, provided that the total debt of the company exceeds total equity by more than three times. The most important consideration is that total debt must exceed total equity by three times, if not, then the thin capitalisation regulations will not apply, even if related party debt is greater than three times related party equity.

Dividends

Dividends should be approved at the annual shareholders' meeting, although interim dividends are declared by the Board of Directors. Both dividends are accounted for as appropriation of earnings and are accordingly not deductible for tax purposes.

Bad and doubtful debts

The general provision for doubtful accounts is set at either the rate specified by the tax law or at the rate of actual bad debts within the past three years of each company. Specified rates effective from 1997 and future reductions are as follows:

Type of business	*1997*	*1998*	*1999*	*2000*	*2001*	*2002*
			(× 1/1,000)			
Bank and finance	3.0	2.5	2.0	1.5	1.0	0.5
Consumer credits	13.0	10.5	8.5	6.5	4.0	2.0
Wholesalers/retailers	10.0	8.0	6.5	5.0	3.0	1.5
Manufacturers	8.0	6.5	5.0	4.0	2.5	1.0
Others	6.0	5.0	4.0	3.0	2.0	1.0

As from 2003, only the actual bad debts loss rate will be accepted for income tax purposes. For smaller corporations, whose capital is Yen

100 million or less, the application of provision rate for 1997 is still allowed. A 50% provision for bad debts due from companies in insolvency is generally allowed.

Provisions and reserves

Japanese tax law is very strict in allowing deductions for provisions for estimated losses and expenses, such as employees' bonuses, employees' retirement benefits, sales returns, product warranty and regular repairs. These provisions will be reduced or abolished over five years.

Reserves are deductible for tax purposes although they are not necessarily required for financial purposes. Among others, special depreciation of specified assets, overseas investment losses and program development qualify for specific industrial incentives.

Employees' and directors' remuneration and benefits

Salaries, wages, bonuses, social insurance contributions and other benefits are deductible expenses. Directors' salary must be approved by the shareholders meeting and it is deductible insofar as it is not excessive. Bonuses to directors as approved by the shareholders are accounted for as an appropriation of earnings and are accordingly non-deductible.

Specifically non-deductible expenses

Taxes and fines

National corporation tax, prefectural inhabitants tax, municipal inhabitants tax, penalties and fines are non-deductible.

Contributions and donations

There are various kinds of expenditure under this heading. It is stipulated that a corporation may deduct a part of such expenses up to the amount equal to the sum of 1.25% of its taxable income and 0.125% of stated capital. Contributions to governments and charitable organisations, or for other government approved purposes, are fully deductible.

Entertainment expenses

No entertainment expenses incurred by a corporation with capital over 50 million yen may be deducted. However, 80% of such expenses are allowed for small corporations, within limits these are 3.2 million yen per annum for corporations with capital of 10 million yen or less and Yen 2.4 million per annum for corporations with capital over Yen 10 million and up to Yen 50 million.

Undisclosed payments

Any payments disbursed in the period from 1 April 1994 to 31 March 2002, where the recipient and purpose of payment are non-disclosed, are additionally taxed at a rate of 40%. Local tax is levied on national tax.

Write down of assets

A write down to market value is an allowable expense in the event of damage due to disaster or obsolescence in the case of inventory or fixed assets, and substantial decline in the price of listed shares.

Foreign source income

There is no tax exemption for foreign source income, except for overseas technical service income (see investment incentives and special benefits). A foreign tax credit is generally given, if any foreign tax is levied at source on income.

Investment incentives and special benefits

Special depreciation

Special initial depreciation is allowed in addition to ordinary depreciation in the first year of use, principally for machinery and equipment used for pollution control, energy saving and in high technology industries at varying rates up to 30% of the acquisition cost. Such special depreciation is also available for other specified types of assets and in designated development areas.

Accelerated depreciation

Special accelerated depreciation is allowed in addition to ordinary depreciation on machinery used by small and medium sized enterprises (capitalised at 100 million yen or less) for fishing and textile industries, newly built rental housing, buildings used as warehouses and grain silos at rates ranging up to 55% of ordinary depreciation for the first five years.

In place of the special initial depreciation of 30% of the acquisition cost for certain equipment, a corporation may opt for a tax credit of 7% of the total acquisition cost.

Free access zone in Okinawa

With the approval of the Free Access Zone in Okinawa, various tax incentives will be implemented in addition to exemption of custom duties.

Included are the following:

- a 35% income deduction on the operating income of a manufacturing company in the zone for the first ten years;
- exemption from enterprise tax and property taxes for the first five years;
- investment tax credits of 8% for factory buildings and 15% for machinery and equipment.

Special reserves

A number of special reserves are permitted under the tax laws and are eligible as corporate tax deductions. They must, however, be calculated according to specified formulae and be recorded in the accounting records and financial statements.

Specific tax laws are implemented by the government from time to time to encourage investment and industrial activity. The more interesting provisions are outlined below.

Communication equipment

In order to promote investment, specific communication equipment of less than Yen 1 million is fully deductible as an expense where a corporation acquires the equipment in the periods from 1 April 1999 to 31 March 2001.

Overseas technical service income

If a corporation incurs overseas income directly or indirectly from licensing industrial rights and providing technical services, a special deduction is allowed at the following rates:

Royalty on license of patents and know-how	6%
Fee on provision of engineering and technical assistance services	12%

Such deductions shall not exceed 25% of the taxable income.

Related party transactions

Transactions (both domestic and overseas) between related parties must be conducted at market value. Under social tax legislation, the authorities have the power to substitute for tax purposes the value of similar transactions calculated under arm's length pricing criteria for the actual value.

Losses

In principle, a corporation which files a blue tax return may carry back losses to the previous year or carry losses forward for up to five years.

The entitlement of a corporation to carry-back operating losses incurred in the periods ended between 1 April 1992 and 31 March 2002 was suspended except for a corporation meeting with certain specified conditions. Losses incurred in these periods may only be carried forward.

Corporate groups

There are no special tax rules relating to groups of companies. All companies are taxed individually and there is no group relief.

Under tax haven measures, where a domestic corporation owns 5% or more shares of a foreign subsidiary in a lower tax country and 50% or more of the shares are owned by Japanese investors, that portion of undistributed earnings of the foreign company is included in the taxable income of the domestic corporation. If a foreign company is either taxed at rates of more than 25% or is engaged in substantial business of which it has management control, that company shall be excluded.

Tax free mergers and disposals

If a merger transaction is structured properly, no tax liability need arise. Any appreciation of asset values is subject to tax at the rate of 27.1% and additional tax is applied to the appreciation of land value (although exemption has been granted since 1998).

Any gains on the disposal of subsidiary or affiliated companies are taxed in a similar manner to general trading income. In certain cases where a company disposes of shares of subsidiary or affiliated companies of which land is over 70% of its total assets, gains from such disposal shall be deemed gains on land sales and subject accordingly to additional taxes at 5% or 10% based on the length of investment. However, an exemption of such tax was given for the disposals incurred between 1 January 1998 and 31 December 2000.

Liquidation of a company

Upon liquidation of a company, taxes are levied on any profits from disposition of the company's assets and extra taxes are also applicable to capital gains on land. Distribution of net earnings (in excess of the paid-in capital by shareholders) is subject to 20% withholding tax, which is deductible from the recipient's tax liabilities.

In the recipient corporation, the distribution income is treated in the same way as dividend income. Any loss on the investment is an allowable deduction for tax purposes.

Capital taxes

Capital duty

Registration tax is due at 0.7% on an increased amount in the stated capital.

Net worth tax

There is no net worth tax levied on companies. However, various taxes are levied for holding properties and equipment.

Treatment of branches (branch profit tax)

The profits of branches of foreign companies in Japan will normally be subject to corporate income tax. There is no extra tax for such branches.

Personal taxes

Taxable individuals

Residents

An individual is a resident if he has a Japanese domicile or has resided continuously in Japan for one year or more. There are two categories of residents, as follows:

Japan

Permanent resident

A permanent resident is one who is domiciled in Japan either as a citizen of Japan or as someone who has his permanent home in Japan. This definition includes non-Japanese citizens who have lived in Japan for more than five years. A permanent resident is liable to income tax on his/her worldwide income.

Non-permanent resident

A resident who has no intention of living permanently in Japan is classified as a non-permanent resident, unless he has had his domicile or residence in Japan for more than five years, in which case he is deemed to be a permanent resident. Most expatriates working in Japan are therefore non-permanent residents and are normally treated as such from their date of arrival in Japan, provided they intend to stay in Japan for at least one year.

A non-permanent resident is assessed on Japanese source income and on any income from outside sources which is paid in or remitted to Japan.

Income remitted to Japan will usually include cash in any currency brought into Japan, funds borrowed in Japan to be repaid outside Japan, drawings from an employer and transfers to Japan of securities or other valuable assets in lieu of a transfer of earnings.

Non-residents

An individual who does not fall into either of the above categories is deemed to be non-resident and is liable to income tax on Japanese source income only, regardless of where paid. However, many tax treaties will exempt from Japanese tax the employment income of a non-resident who works in Japan for less than 183 days during a calendar year.

Domicile

A domicile is defined as the territory where an individual has 'the base and centre of his living'. A Japanese citizen will normally be considered as domiciled in Japan (and therefore resident) unless he has lived outside Japan for more than one year.

An expatriate living continuously in Japan for one year or more is deemed to have a domicile in Japan, although until he has spent five years there, he will continue to be classified as a non-permanent resident.

Tax year and filing requirements

The taxable period is the calendar year.

With some exceptions, residents are required to file national income tax returns by 15 March of the following year and taxes are due on the same date. Non-residents are also required to file tax returns if they have certain Japanese source income, such as business and property income. Residents leaving Japan permanently must file tax returns and pay taxes before departure.

Residents having only employment or director's remuneration of less than Yen 20 million a year are exempt from filing tax returns because employers are required to adjust their annual national income taxes due in December salary payments. However, if a resident has income over Yen 200,000 in total from another source (excluding the main employment and retirement income), or specific tax deductions apply, they must file tax returns.

In cases of failure to file by the due date or the under declaration of any income, additional taxes and penalties are levied. Extension of the due date of tax filing is not normally permitted. Inhabitant tax returns are exempt where national tax returns are filed or there is only employment income.

Taxes on income

Taxes on income consist of national income tax, prefectural and municipal inhabitant taxes and enterprise tax. National income tax is assessed on taxable income arising in each calendar year. Tax rates are applied separately to each of the three categories of taxable income, i.e. gross income, retirement income and forestry income.

Local inhabitants tax is assessed in full by both prefectures and municipalities on an individual who is resident in Japan on 1 January in any year, and is based on the individual's income reported for national income tax purposes in the previous year. In view of this, careful consideration should be given by taxpayers as to timing of their permanent departure from Japan. For practical purposes both prefectural and municipal taxes can be treated as components of one system of local inhabitants tax.

Employment income and directors' salary

This includes salaries, wages, bonuses and allowances. The full value of allowances is normally treated as a taxable benefit in kind and includes family allowance, housing allowance and company houses. If an employee pays to his employer an amount calculated as the economic rent for the accommodation, which is determined based on a property taxation value, no taxable benefit will arise. Otherwise, the taxable benefit is the value of the economic rent, except in the case of directors in which case it is normally 50% of the market rent. For some other allowances, a deduction is available in respect of the attributable business element. Employer's social insurance contributions and contributions to approved pension funds are tax-exempt. Some other benefits, such as office to home commuting allowance, meal subsidy up to 50% of costs, subsidy to employees' recreational party or trips comprising not more than four nights (including overseas trips), are in general tax free.

Taxable employment income is gross assessable income as explained above, less an employment deduction. Employment income deduction is calculated as below:

Gross receipt (thousand Yen)	*Income deduction (thousand Yen)*
Under 1,625	650
1,625 to 1,800	Receipt × 40%
1,800 to 3,600	Receipt × 30% + 180
3,600 to 6,600	Receipt × 20% + 540
6,600 to 10,000	Receipt × 10% + 1,200
Over 10,000	Receipt × 5% + 1,700

Business income

Income from a self-employed business or professional activity is classified as business income. Necessary expenses directly incurred and expended during a tax year for carrying on a business are allowed in computing the net income arising in that year.

If a taxpayer maintains proper accounting records, he may be permitted to submit a blue tax return rather than a normal white tax return. The blue tax return confers significant tax advantages in computing net business income and also net rental and forestry income. These include the charging of specific tax allowable general provisions and depreciation allowances, together with greater flexibility in utilising tax losses.

Under the Blue Tax Return System, a business income deduction in the amount of Yen 550,000 is allowed in 2000.

Losses arising can normally be offset against other income in a prescribed order, firstly against recurring income (such as income from interest, dividends, rentals and employment), secondly against income of a temporary nature (such as capital gains and occasional income), thirdly against forestry income and finally against retirement income.

Any net losses remaining may be carried forward for three years or back for one year, provided that a blue tax return is filed in the year the losses are incurred. Otherwise very limited relief is available.

Capital gains

Gains are treated differently, depending on whether they arise from the sale of land and buildings, the sale of securities or of other assets. Gifts or donations are also normally regarded as taxable disposals.

For gains from the sale of assets other than land and buildings and securities, an allowance of up to Yen 500,000 is available each year against short term gains (on assets held for less than five years), with any excess being available to reduce long term gains. The net taxable capital gain which is included in the income tax computation comprises the net short term gain and 50% of the net long term gain.

For gains from the sale of equity securities with effect from 1 April 1989, gains from sale of the stocks of corporations or convertible bonds, less any losses, are taxed separately at a flat rate of 26% (national and local taxes) without aggregation with other taxable income. If such securities are listed on the recognised stock exchanges, the taxpayer may elect to suffer a 1% withholding tax on the gross proceeds from the sale of securities. On the gains realised within one year after the initial public offerings of newly listed stocks, 13% tax is levied where those securities had been held by the taxpayer for more than three years. Capital gains on the transfer of securities which are acquired between 1 April 2000 and 31 March 2005, held for more than three years and transferred within one year after the initial public offerings, are taxed at 6.5% if those securities are issued by certain small or medium-sized companies.

Gains from sale of land and buildings

With repsect to long term gains, where the property sold was held for more than five years, the aggregate tax for 2000 is as follows:

Taxable gains (million Yen)	*Rate*
Up to 60	26.0%
Over 60	32.5%

If land is sold for a housing development project which meets required qualifications, or to a public corporation, the aggregate tax rate is 20% for gains under 40 million yen and 26% for gains over Yen 40 million.

Taxable gains are computed on gross proceeds less acquisition costs and expenses (less depreciation), sales commissions and the applicable deduction. The deductions are:

Case of disposition	*Deduction (Yen)*
Normal disposition (minimum)	1 million
Expropriation by government or agencies	50 million
Approved land development programme	20 million
Approved residential land programme	15 million
Farm land development programme	8 million

Capital gains on the disposal of residential property, which has been held for ten years or more, are taxed at 14% on the gains up to Yen 60 million after Yen 30 million of the residential property deduction, and 20% on the gains over Yen 60 million.

The aggregate deduction is limited to Yen 50 million per taxpayer per year.

With respect to short term gains, capital gains arising from the sale of land and buildings held for less than five years are taxed at the greater of 52% (of such gains) or 110% of the amount that is the national tax on total short-term capital gains and other income (less the national tax on the short term capital gains) calculated by applying general income tax rates.

Capital losses are normally offset against other source income in the tax year.

Dividends

Dividend income includes all distributions of profits, distributions of gains by investment trusts and fixed interest amounts paid to shareholders during the first two years of a company's trade. Dividends are subject to a 20% withholding tax.

Normally, dividend income is added to other sources of income for the purposes of higher rate tax, with credit being given for the withholding tax suffered. However, a taxpayer may elect to keep his dividend income separate and suffer instead a flat rate of withholding tax of 35%. This election can only be made where dividend income from a single company does not exceed Yen 500,000 and provided no more than 5% of that company's equity is owned by the taxpayer.

Interest

Most interest on bank deposits and bonds is subject to 20% withholding tax. Interest and dividends on securities issued outside Japan and paid to Japanese residents through a Japanese paying agent are also subject to 20% withholding tax. Interest receivable on loans made by an individual for business purposes is normally classified as business income.

Rental

Rental income includes income arising from the lease of land, buildings, ships and aircraft. All reasonable and necessary expenses incurred, including depreciation and interest, are deductible in calculating the net income subject to tax.

Rental business losses can generally be offset against other sources of taxable income, subject to certain limits.

Royalties

Royalties are subject to 10% withholding tax up to Yen 1 million and 20% over Yen 1 million. Royalties received are taxed normally, subject to deduction for related expenses and depreciation of the cost of the rights.

Social security benefits

Social insurance contributions made by taxpayers are fully deductible. Benefits received for unemployment, casualty damages and medical care are tax-exempt, although pension annuities or lump sum payments at retirement are subject to tax.

Pensions and annuities

At retirement or severance, employees may be entitled to receive from employers or pension funds either or both a lump sum payment and pension annuities. Only 50% of retirement income, that is the lump sum payment less a special deduction which is calculated based on length of service and/or disability, is separately taxed.

Forestry source income

Special deductions are allowed from income derived from the sale or transfer of timber which has been owned for over five years.

Exempt income

Exempt sources of income include:

- interest from approved employee savings schemes, established for house purchase or retirement purposes;

- interest received, up to specified limits, by elderly or disabled people and widows with dependant children;
- academic prizes;
- insurance payments for damages;
- maintenance payments.

Foreign source income

The foreign source income from dividends, interest, royalties and business are normally taxed and foreign taxes suffered at source are normally credited against Japanese tax liabilities.

Personal allowances and deductions

Allowances

An annual personal allowance of Yen 380,000 is available for each taxpayer. An additional allowance of Yen 380,000 is available for each dependant (including a dependant spouse) providing the dependant's taxable income does not exceed certain limits. Further allowances are available for elderly, handicapped and widowed persons and, in certain circumstances, an additional spouse allowance of Yen 380,000 may be claimed.

Deductions

Deductions are also allowed for accidental losses, housing loan interest, medical expenses, social security contributions, life and non-life insurance premiums and donations although there are some limitations.

Losses

Any loss from a source of income, except for losses in sources of dividends, miscellaneous income, security stock transactions and temporary income, are offset against any categories of income in the same year, subject to certain conditions. A net loss can be carried forward for three years, if the taxpayer files a blue tax return.

Special family rules

Tax is imposed on the individual who earns the income and capital gains. A joint tax return system is not applied in Japan.

Special treatment for expatriates

For expatriates working in Japan, salary income in respect of services performed in Japan is treated as Japanese source income regardless of where, by whom, or in which currency the payment is made. Overseas living allowance, children's education allowance, provision of company house (approximately 50% of monthly rent for a leased house for directors, depending upon size) and other benefits are included in taxable income. Relocation allowance and once a year home leave allowance are generally tax-free. Social security, mortgage subsidies and share options are not normally taxed in Japan, provided such costs are borne by the parent company outside Japan.

If the expatriate is not a permanent resident under Japanese tax rules, a pro rata deduction from the gross salary income is available for any days spent working outside Japan, as far as such a portion of income or more is received outside Japan and not remitted to Japan.

Rates of tax

National tax

National tax rates for 2000 are as follows:

Band Yen	*Rate (%)*	*Tax on Band Yen*	*Cumulative Tax Yen*
Up to 3,300,000	10	330,000	330,000
3,300,000 – 9,000,000	20	1,140,000	1,470,000
9,000 000 – 18,000,000	30	2,700,000	4,170,000
Over 18,000,000	37	–	–

The above rates are applied separately to each of the three categories of taxable income.

Local inhabitants tax

For all practical purposes, municipal and prefectural local taxes can be considered as a single component. Using Tokyo as an example, the combined local tax rates for 2000 are as follows:

Band Yen	*Rate (%)*	*Tax on Band Yen*	*Cumulative Tax Yen*
Up to 2,000,000	5	100,000	100,000
2,000,000 – 7,000,000	10	500,000	600,000
Over 7,000,000	13	–	–

Withholding tax

The standard rate of withholding tax is 20% for dividends and interest. Withholding tax tables for salary and wages and for bonuses are set showing the marginal rate of 35% of the amount which exceeds Yen 1,760,000. Royalties, fees to writers, entertainers, sports players, designers, lawyers, accountants, and other professionals are normally subject to tax at 10% up to Yen 1 million and to tax at 20% over Yen 1 million.

The withholding tax rate for overseas payments of dividends, interest and royalties is 20%, unless the tax treaty in existence between Japan and the recipient country provides for lower rates. Salary to a non-resident director is subject to tax at 20%.

Tax credits

The following annual credits are available to reduce an individual's tax liability (although no tax refund is permitted if total credits exceed the year's tax liability, the excess credits may normally be carried forward):

- foreign tax paid or withheld on income arising abroad;
- *dividends:* the annual credit allowed is 10% of total taxable dividend income provided aggregate taxable income is less than Yen 10 million; for amounts more than Yen 10 million, a credit of 5% of dividend income is given; this is in addition to the credit available for withholding tax suffered on dividend income;
- *research and development expenditure:* the tax credit given depends on the value and nature of the expenditure and is only available against business income;
- *acquisition of a residential property:* subject to restrictions on size, use and the taxpayer's income level, a tax credit of 1% of the principal amount of housing loans up to Yen 10 million, 1% of the additional Yen 10 million and 0.5% of the additional loan less than Yen 10 million is available for the first six years of ownership; a special tax credit is available for an initial 15 years when the taxpayer acquires a residential property from 1999 through 2001.

Payment of tax

Payroll deductions

Withholding tax (national) and inhabitant taxes are deducted from salaries and wages by an employer. The withholding tax is adjusted at the year end to settle the ultimate national tax liability of each employee.

Prepayments

All taxpayers with an estimated national tax liability of more than Yen 150,000 (after allowance for tax deducted at source) will be assessed on one third of that amount, to be paid in two instalments in July and November. The balance of tax due is payable on submission of the tax return, at the latest by 15 March of the following year. One half of the final tax payment may be deferred until 31 May. A refund of excess tax might take a couple of months after the tax filing.

Where there is no prepayment for inhabitant taxes, the taxes are paid either by 12 monthly deductions from the taxpayer's salary or by four equal payments per annum.

Estate and gift taxes

Inheritance tax

Inheritance tax is levied on an individual who is in receipt of assets under an inheritance or bequest. The administrator or executor of the deceased's estate has no liability to tax or obligation to file any tax returns.

Taxpayers domiciled in Japan at the time of their inheritance will be taxed on all assets acquired through inheritance or bequest, irrespective of the location of the assets or the domicile of the deceased. Taxpayers not domiciled in Japan are only liable to tax on assets which are located in Japan. The method of computation of the tax involves aggregating all properties inherited plus any gifts to heirs or legatees within three years of the date of death. A basic exemption of Yen 50 million is given plus Yen 10 million for each statutory heir. Each heir is taxed on his or her share under the bequest. The tax payable by an heir other than a spouse, child or parent of the deceased is increased by 20%. The rates of inheritance tax increase in bands, from 10% on the first Yen 8 million of the taxable inheritance to 70% on the excess above Yen 2,000 million.

Tax credits are available for the surviving spouse, minors under 20 and handicapped heirs. Credit for gift tax previously suffered is also available.

Relief is available for successive inheritances and the inheritors of agricultural property.

Gift tax

Gift tax is levied annually on the recipients of gifts. Similar domicile rules apply as for inheritance tax. An annual exemption of Yen 600,000 is available. An individual who has been married for twenty or more years may claim a 'once in a lifetime' exemption of 20 million yen in respect of a gift from his or her spouse of residential property, or of money for acquiring such a property. The rates rise in bands, from 10% on the first Yen 1.5 million to 70% on the excess over Yen 100 million.

Wealth tax

There is no wealth tax in Japan.

Social security contributions

Pension insurance

Insurance is compulsory for all employees and for the self-employed.

Different levels of contribution are made for different schemes but the employer matches the premiums paid by the employee to reach a total premium level of around 17.3% of remuneration.

Employee insurance

Contributions paid by the employee (through a deduction from remuneration) for employment insurance are normally 0.4% of gross salary, with the employer contributing a further 0.75%.

Health insurance

Health insurance is compulsory for all employees and the self-employed. Where private insurance societies have not been established by the employer, a National Health Insurance scheme is available. Target premiums of around 7% are split between the employee and the employer.

A liability for social security contributions, in respect of non-permanent residents, usually only arises if their salaries are paid direct by an employer from within Japan. Salary costs recharged to Japanese companies or branches from abroad would not normally fall into this category and hence would not trigger a liability.

Nursing care insurance

Nursing care insurance has been introduced in 2000 and is compulsory for employees aged over 40. The rate is 0.75%.

Other taxes

Treatment of partnerships

Profits made by a partnership are allocated to each partner in accordance with his profit share and are taxed as partners' income. Certain types of partnership may be taxed as a corporation.

Consumption tax

Consumption tax is charged at 5% of sales value on a wide variety of goods and services consumed in Japan. This tax is similar to the European Value Added Tax System.

Some separate excise taxes remain, including those on petroleum products, alcohol and tobacco.

Securities transactions tax was abolished with effect from 31 March 1999.

Other taxes

Fixed asset tax

The municipal tax authorities assess an annual property tax on individuals registered on 1 January as owners of land, buildings and depreciable, tangible business assets. Whilst in principle the market value of the property is used to compute the tax payable, in practice a special lower valuation is used as the tax base for land and buildings and is decreased even further for residential use. The standard rate of tax is 1.4% but may, in some municipalities, rise to 2.1%. The tax is payable in four instalments.

Real property acquisition tax

A prefectural tax of 4% of the appraised market value of land or buildings is assessed on an individual acquiring real property. Exemptions from tax are available if the property is below a certain value or if residential housing is constructed within a specified period on the purchased land.

Special landholding taxes

The municipal authorities also impose a special tax on the acquisition and annual ownership of land above a prescribed size, at 3% and 1.4% respectively of the acquisition cost. Real property acquisition and fixed asset taxes are credited against this tax.

Business office tax

Certain municipalities (primarily the large cities) impose taxes on office buildings. For new buildings the tax is set at 6,000 yen per square metre of floor space and is payable within two months of construction. Buildings with floor space of less than 2,000 square metres are exempt. In addition, an annual tax on existing buildings is levied at the rate of 600 yen per square metre of total office space, plus 0.25% of total remuneration paid to employees. Small businesses with less than 100 employees or a floor area of less than 1,000 square metres are exempt.

Stamp duty

Persons preparing taxable documents such as contracts transferring assets or rights, promissory notes, share certificates and receipts are liable to stamp duty, which is paid by means of stamps which are attached to the document. The tax rates vary for the different categories of documents and the value of the consideration involved.

Exchange control

Under exchange control legislation, prior notification of capital transactions to the Ministry of Finance is in principle not required but ex post facto notification will suffice for investments. Capital transactions require prior notification for certain industries such as agriculture, petroleum and those which threaten national security, disturb public order or hamper public safety, or may have significant impact on the economy or fundamental industries.

Generally, remittances from Japan are free from controls. Certain banks or securities companies are required to submit ex post facto notification where foreign exchange business is taking place. Netting, multi-netting, offsetting or pooling of accounts have no limitations.

Tax treaties and withholding taxes

Japan requires income tax to be withheld at source on interest, dividend, royalties, professional fees and certain other amounts paid to residents and non-residents. The following table illustrates the usual rates currently in force:

Country of resident	*Royalties (%)*	*Interest (%)*	*Dividends (%)*
Non-treaty countries	20	20	20
Selected treaty countries:			
Australia	10	10	15
Austria	10	10	10/20 (c)
Belgium	10	10	10/15 (b)
Brazil	12.5/15/25 (a)	12.5	12.5
Canada	10	220	10/15 (b)
China	10	10	10
Denmark	10	10	10/15 (b)
France	10	10	5/15 (d)
Germany	10	10	5/15 (d)
India	20	10/15 (e)	15
Indonesia	10	10	10/15 (b)
Ireland	10	10	101/5 (b)
Italy	10	10	10/15 (b)
Korea (South) (i)	12	12	12
Luxembourg	10	10	5/15 (b)
Malaysia (i)	10	10	10/15 (b)
Netherlands	10	10	10/20 (c)
New Zealand	20	20	15
Norway	10	10	5/15 (b)
Pakistan	Nil	0/20 (h)	15/20
Philippines	15/25 (g)	10/15 (f)	10/20 (b)
Russia	10	10	15
Singapore	10	10	5/15 (b)
Spain	10	10	10/15 (b)
Sweden (i)	10	10	10/15 (b)
Switzerland	10	10	10/15 (b)
Thailand	15	10/20 (e)	15/20 (b)
United Kingdom	10	10	10/15 (b)
United States	10	10	10/15 (b)

(a) 25% for patent and 15% for film royalties.

(b) Lower rate for 25% or more shareholdings.

(c) Lower rate for 50% or more shareholdings.

(d) Lower rate for 15% or more shareholdings.

(e) Lower rate of 10% applies generally to banks.

(f) Lower rate for interest on debentures.

(g) Lower rate for film royalties.

(h) Interest on debentures or loans is exempt.

(i) Tax treaties have been amended in 2000.

Anti-avoidance measures

In general, all transactions should be carried out on an arm's length basis. Transactions with affiliated parties are normally reviewed carefully by tax authorities and the authorities have powers to assess further income or adjust such transactions where they result in tax avoidance.

Under the tax haven countermeasures in Japan, undistributed profits of a foreign company in tax haven countries shall be included in the taxable income of a Japanese domestic corporation, where such a corporation owns 5% or more of shares of the foreign company. The foreign company is defined as a company which is located in a tax haven country, which does not levy tax on income or whose income tax burden is under 25% of the income, and of which more than 50% of the shares in the aggregate are owned directly or indirectly by Japanese companies.

Transfer-pricing countermeasures also apply for a foreign subsidiary where 50% or more of shares are owned by the Japanese corporation directly or indirectly. If transactions between corporations are not concluded following the arm's length principle, the prices of such transactions are adjusted so that the taxable income of the Japanese corporation may increase.

Jersey

Langtry International

Introduction

Jersey, Britain's premier offshore financial centre, operates a well-regulated, low tax regime with various investment vehicles available for use internationally such as exempt companies, international business companies, non-resident companies, limited partnerships and trusts.

Taxation of companies

Taxable entities

Resident companies

Companies, which are resident in Jersey, are liable to Income Tax on their worldwide income. Companies are resident in Jersey if they are incorporated there (except exempt companies – see below) or if their business is managed and controlled there.

Exempt companies

Companies registered in Jersey or overseas can be exempt from Income Tax if they are Collective Investment Funds or are companies in which no Jersey resident has a beneficial interest. Details of the beneficial owner(s) have to be supplied to the Jersey Financial Services Commission. Such exempt companies are treated as non-resident for tax purposes and:

- pay no income tax on income arising outside the Island;
- are not required to deduct Jersey income tax from interest or dividend payments;
- pay no income tax on interest arising from Jersey bank deposits;
- make no income return (other than for Jersey income excepting bank deposit interest) and are not required to file accounts (except in respect of a Jersey trade);

- can appoint local directors and have board meetings in Jersey.

The present exempt company fee is £600 per annum.

International business companies

An International Business Company (IBC) can be a company incorporated in Jersey or an overseas company, which is controlled and therefore resident in the Island or indeed the Jersey branch of a non-resident company. As for an exempt company, Jersey residents are denied access to the IBC.

IBC's are fully resident in Jersey for tax purposes and pay tax on profits from international activities at the following rates:

Profit	*Rate of Tax*
First £3 million	2.0%
Next £1.5 million	1.5%
Next £5.5 million	1.0%
Remainder	0.5%

Subject to a minimum tax liability of £1,200 annually, income sourced within the Island (such as bank deposit interest) will continue to be taxed at the rate of 20%.

Non-resident companies

Exemption from income tax is granted to companies incorporated in other (typically low or nil tax) jurisdictions that are controlled in Jersey. This concession is available on the basis that the company does not undertake a trade and is not beneficially owned by a resident of Jersey.

Taxes imposed

The year of assessment for income tax is the calendar year.

Profits from trade are normally assessed on a preceding year basis (e.g. accounts for the accounting year ended 30 June 1997 equal 1998 assessment). Special rules apply to the commencement and cessation of trade. All other income is assessed on an actual basis.

Taxpayers are issued with assessments in the year following the year of assessment and tax is payable the day following the issue of an assessment.

Rates of tax

Income tax is charged at a rate of 20%

Income subject to tax

General rules

Income tax is charged on the taxpayers income less allowable reliefs and losses.

Capital gains and losses

Capital gains are not subject to tax.

Dividends

Dividends paid are not deductible in arriving at the taxable profit of a company.

Dividends from Jersey resident companies are paid out of taxed profits and the payment of a dividend does not advance any liability by the company with respect to the income tax due on its taxable profits. Dividends are effectively paid net and no payment of tax has to be made to the Revenue authority at that time. No further Jersey tax is payable by the shareholders and repayment may be claimed if the tax deducted at source exceeds the shareholders tax liability.

Exempt companies generally pay dividends gross.

Deductions

General rules

The expenses allowable in computing trading profits are those incurred wholly and exclusively for the purposes of the trade. Where a company's business consists mainly in the making of investments, relief is allowed for expenses of management (e.g. directors' fees).

Certain expenses relating to let property are allowable in computing the taxable amount of rental income.

Depreciation

Depreciation charged in the accounts is not deductible in computing profit chargeable to tax. Instead, capital allowances are given for expenditure incurred on plant and machinery (including glasshouses). In general, a pool of expenditure is maintained which is adjusted annually to include the cost of new acquisitions and deduct the sale proceeds of assets sold. A capital allowance of 25% of the reducing balance of the pool is allowed. If sale proceeds exceed the value of the pool, a 'balancing charge' will arise which will be taxed as income of the trade. On cessation of trade, a 'balancing allowance' may arise. All items of plant and machinery are pooled, except for 'expensive cars' and assets used only partly for the purposes of the trade.

Losses

Companies (and individuals) may offset trading losses against any other income generated in that year of assessment. Unrealised losses may be carried forward and deducted from the profits of the same trade indefinitely, but relief must be taken in the first available year.

Special rules exist regarding opening or closing losses.

Corporate group

There is no legislation dealing with group relief for losses, although by concession the authorities do permit arrangements which have the same effect.

Personal taxes

Taxation of individuals

Resident

An individual who is resident and ordinarily resident in Jersey is subject to income tax on his worldwide income on an arising basis. A wife's income is aggregated with her husband's for tax purposes.

An individual who is resident but not ordinarily resident in Jersey is subject to income tax on his income generated in Jersey and on his worldwide income on a remittance basis.

Non-resident

An individual who is not resident or ordinarily resident in Jersey is liable to income tax only on Jersey sourced income other than, by concession, bank deposit interest.

Non-residents who are British subjects are entitled to make a claim for proportional reliefs whereby a proportion of the Jersey personal allowances available to residents are allowable. This relief is available in the same proportion as the individual's Jersey income bears to his worldwide income.

Taxes on income

The year of assessment is the calendar year.

Income tax is charged at a rate of 20%, and is assessed about nine months following the year of assessment and is payable the day following the issue of an assessment.

Sources of income

Employment income

An employee who is resident in Jersey is taxed on all his emoluments for a tax year. Deductions are available for various personal and other allowances and relief for life assurance premiums, medical insurance premiums and bank interest paid.

Business income

Profits from trades, professions and vocation are computed in the same way as for companies and are normally assessed on a preceding year basis. Special rules apply to the commencement and cessation of trade.

Trading losses can be offset against other income for that year of assessment or carried forward against future profits from the same trade.

Partnerships

Partnerships are taxable as separate entities, however an individual's share of partnership profit forms part of his taxable income for the purposes of obtaining deductions for personal allowances and reliefs.

Limited partnerships

The passing of the recent Limited Partnership (Jersey) Law has introduced the concept of Limited Partnerships (LP's) the essential characteristics of which are that they have limited and general partners.

Jersey

The Limited Partners have limited liability but have no authority to act for the Partnership (the management being conferred exclusively on the general partner(s)).

The partners themselves may be individuals, companies, other LP's or any legal person. The LP is tax transparent and as long as the partners are not residents of the Island they will be exempt from taxation in Jersey.

Social security benefits

Payments of social security benefit are taxable other than for maternity, sickness, accident or a death grant.

Pensions

Pensions other than invalidity pensions and war pensions are taxable.

Capital gains

Capital gains are not subject to tax.

Dividends

See Business Income above.

Interest

Bank interest is paid gross and is taxable in the hands of the recipient. Other interest paid by a resident is subject to the standard rate of 20% income tax whether paid to a resident or to a non-resident.

Rentals

Rentals and other receipts arising from leases or ownership of land are subject to income tax. Certain expenses relating to let property are allowable.

Royalties

Royalties are taxed as normal income.

Personal allowances

Resident taxpayers are granted tax-free allowances, the level of which depends on the domestic circumstances of the taxpayer.

Allowances for 2000 income are as follows:

Single person	£2,600
Married man	£5,200
Earned income relief	£3,400 (maximum)
Wife's earned income relief	£4,500 (maximum)
Child allowance	£2,500 (per child)
Child allowance	£5,000 (per child in further education)
Allowance for single parent family	£4,500
Dependent relative relief	£1,500
Housekeeper relief	£1,500

Deductions

For disbursements or expenses to be deductible in computing profits chargeable to tax, they must be incurred wholly and exclusively for the purpose of the trade, profession, employment or vocation.

Estate and gift tax

There is no estate or gift tax in Jersey. Probate duty is levied for the first £50,000 at £50 per £10,000, and thereafter at £75 per £10,000.

Social security

An employee contributes 5.7% of his employment income, with an earnings limit of £2,446 per month. His employer contributes an additional 6.3% of the employee's income to the same limit. Self-employed individuals pay a flat rate of £293.52 per month. In certain circumstances this may be reduced according to an individual's earnings.

Other taxes

Income tax on trustees

Trustees resident in Jersey are strictly liable to income tax on all sources of income but where there are no beneficiaries resident in Jersey, by concession, it is only Jersey source income other than Jersey bank deposit interest which is taxed.

Exchange control

There are no exchange controls.

Double tax relief

Double tax relief treaties exist with the United Kingdom and Guernsey and between Jersey and France with regard to air transport and shipping profits.

Anti-avoidance measures

Additional assessments can be levied by the Comptroller of Income Tax to counter transactions, the main purpose of which is to avoid or reduce income tax.

Kenya

Carr Stanyer Gitau & Co.

Introduction

The economy

Kenya has a free enterprise economy. State intervention is limited to a few agencies designed to promote services and infrastructure. The main areas of economic activity are agriculture, however, tourism and light industries are increasingly gaining importance. The government has a vision of turning the nation into an industrial one by the year 2020. To this end, a number of Export Processing Zone Enterprises have been established centred mainly in Nairobi, Mombasa and their surrounding areas. Significant tax concessions have been legislated as incentives. The formation of a regional trade body known as Common Market for Eastern, Central and Southern Africa (COMESA), bringing together countries of this region, is also geared towards expanding the market.

The principal export commodities are coffee, tea, pyrethrum, horticultural crops and (lately) flowers. A number of industries in motor vehicle assembly, oil refinery, cement, canning factories and food processing have been established. With its many game parks, attractive beaches and good standard of accommodation, Kenya has a very attractive tourist industry.

Kenya is the seat of the region's United Nations offices, UNEP and HABITAT Headquarters, and a large network of international companies, and it is also a liaison centre for organisations with relief efforts in Somalia and Southern Sudan.

Many commercial banks (locally and foreign incorporated) operate in Kenya. There is now a vibrant stock exchange market open to foreign investors. However, there has been minimal real economic growth and the level of unemployment has been high in the last five years. The commercial climate, nevertheless, can change overnight.

Government policy on foreign investments

The Government is actively promoting and encouraging foreign investment. All exchange control requirements regarding the repatriation of profits have been abolished.

There is a Foreign Investment Protection Act under which a certificate of Approved Enterprise is given if a proposed investment is likely to benefit the Kenyan Economy. Holding this certificate entitles an enterprise to the repatriation of both capital and profits. The Investments Promotion Centre (IPC) operates as a 'one-stop' service office for the investor's requirements regarding immigration and work permits, approvals by the office of the President and various government ministries. The IPC also provides information on investment opportunities in Kenya.

A major development in Kenya's tax system is the establishment of a Quasi-Government Board – the Kenya Revenue Authority (KRA) – which came into force on 1 July 1995.

The KRA brought under one administration the collection of the major taxes, namely Income Tax, Customs and Excise, and VAT. Higher revenue yields are expected through greater administrative efficiency and employment of high-powered staff to minimise tax evasion.

Other key tax changes have been the introduction of a self-assessment tax system, an instalment tax system and the Personal Identification Number (PIN).

These features have led to reduced tax rates for both corporations and individuals, resulting from increased controls and efficiency in the total taxation machinery and widening of the tax base.

Corporate taxes

Resident companies

Resident companies are taxable on their worldwide income. A company is resident if it is incorporated under Kenyan law, or management and control are exercised in/from Kenya or the Minister has gazetted the company to be resident.

Non-resident companies

Non-resident companies are taxable on all income that is derived from within Kenya such as business, interest, dividends and rental incomes.

Tax year

The tax year, commonly called the year of income, runs from January to December. Where the financial year of an organisation is different, then its income is taken to be income of the tax year in which the financial year ends. Self-assessment tax returns are due for filing by 30 June for 31 December year end taxpayers. For all other taxpayers, the due date is six months after the end of accounting year.

Taxes imposed

Corporation tax, which is of national character, favours resident companies which pay tax at lower rates.

Tax payers are required to pay their taxes within the accounting year through an instalment tax system if:

- their tax payable is over Kshs. 40,000 per annum; and
- their income (other than emoluments) is over 50% of their total income.

The basis of determining the instalment tax payable is either an estimate of the current year's profit or the preceding year assessment multiplied by 110%. Instalment tax is payable quarterly as follows:

	Proportion	*Due Date*
1st instalment	27.5%	end of 4th month
2nd instalment	27.5%	20th of 6th month
3rd instalment	27.5%	20th of 9th month
4th instalment	27.5%	20th of 12th month

Rates of tax

Processing	*Resident company*	*Non-resident company*	*Export zone enterprises*
since 1992 to 1997	35%	42.5%	first 10 years nil
1998 – 1999	32.5%	40%	next 10 years 25%
with effect from 2000	30%	37.5%	–

Income subject to tax

General rules

Taxable income is the business profit adjusted to allow for capital deductions, to disallow non-business expenses and exclude non-chargeable income.

Stock/inventory rules

Stocks are valued at the lower of cost and net realisable value. No particular method of valuing stock is approved for tax purposes. All methods such as LIFO, FIFO, base stock method and average cost methods are acceptable.

Capital gains and losses

Capital gains tax was suspended in 1985.

Dividends

Dividends are subject to withholding tax of 5% if they amount to more than Kshs. 150. Dividend income is taxable in the year of payment and not when declared. Distribution of accumulated company profits in a voluntary winding up concern is deemed as payment of dividends. Dividends received by a company controlling more than 12.5% of the voting power of the paying company are not taxable. Dividends earned from outside Kenya are not chargeable. Companies are expected to distribute at least 40% of their tax profits as dividends and 100% of their investment income. Withholding tax, deducted on dividends other than from designated co-operative societies, is final tax.

The non-resident rate of withholding tax is 10%.

Deductions

General rules

Allowable expenses are those which are wholly and exclusively incurred in the production of income.

Depreciation and amortisation

Depreciation and amortisation are added back in tax computation, while wear and tear allowances are allowed. Fixed assets are classified into four groups:

Assets	*Class*	*Rates of Wear and tear*
Tractors, combine harvesters, heavy earth-moving equipment and other heavy self-propelling machines.	I	37.5%
Computers, copiers, calculators and duplicating machines.	I	30%
Other self-propelling vehicle, including aircraft.	III	25%
All other machinery including ships.	IV	12.5%

The qualifying capital expenditure is the actual cost of the asset, but for class III the qualifying capital expenditure is limited to Kshs. 500,000 on a non-commercial motor vehicle in 1997 and Kshs. 1,000,000 with effect from January 1998.

Deduction on interest, dividends and royalties

Royalties and interest wholly and exclusively incurred in the production of chargeable income, or determining tax losses, are deductible. A dividend payment is a distribution and is therefore not deductible.

Bad and doubtful debts

Only specified bad debts are allowable.

Reserves and provisions

They are not deductible.

Capital allowances

	Year of first use of plant and machinery	*Rate*
Investment deduction allowance (calculated on cost of building and machinery used for manufacturing purposes) – all eligible assets, single allowance.	2000/01 2001/02 2002/03 2003/04	100% 85% 70% 60%
Industrial building allowance (on cost net of any investment deduction) on straight-line basis:		
– industrial buildings;		2.5%
– hotels.		4%
Farmworks allowance allowed on structures (excluding machinery) necessary for proper operation of a farm (straight-line method)		33%
Mining allowance on capital expenditure incurred in mining specified minerals:		
– year 1;		40%
– year 2-7.		10%

Employees and directors' remuneration and benefits

Contributions to a registered pension scheme or provident fund are deductible. Contributions to the provision of benefits-in-kind or housing by the employers are also deductible in ascertaining the taxable value. A director's remuneration is deductible, yet it is taxed on his or her personal income.

Specifically non-deductible expenses

- Expenditure or loss which is not wholly and exclusively incurred in the production of the income.
- Capital expenditure or any loss, diminution or exhaustion of capital.
- Expenditure incurred by a person in the maintenance of himself, his family or establishment, or for any other personal or domestic purpose.
- Expenditure or loss which is covered by an insurance contract.
- Income tax or tax of a similar nature paid on income.
- Expenditure incurred in Kenya by a non-resident person not having a permanent establishment in Kenya in the production of income from management or professional fees, royalties, interest and rents.
- Loss incurred in a hobby business.

Personal taxes

Taxable individuals

The taxation of individuals depends on status of residence.

Residents

An individual is considered resident if he has a permanent home in Kenya and was in Kenya for any period of time in a year of income, or was present in Kenya for a period or periods of at least 183 days in the year of income, or was present in Kenya in the year under consideration and each of the two preceding years of income for periods averaging 122 days in each year of income. Residents are better treated tax-wise. They are allowed personal reliefs and lower tax rates. A person leaving or arriving in Kenya is considered resident to/from the date of departure or arrival respectively.

Non-residents

Tax is charged on income derived from Kenya only.

Tax year and filing requirements

The tax year is the calendar year. Individuals and unincorporated persons are now required to adopt 31 December as their accounting year end. A tax file may be opened by the tax department on request or on receipt of some information. The department is empowered to have power to access information from several authorities.

Every legal person (individual or corporate) is required to register with the Income Tax Department and obtain a Personal Identification Number (PIN) certificate. A PIN certificate is required before one can transact or obtain services from several public institutions.

There is a yearly issue of returns to all registered taxpayers which must be completed, signed and submitted within six months after their respective financial year end.

Taxes on income

Tax on salary, Pay-As-You-Earn (PAYE), is deducted and paid on a monthly basis and offset against final income tax at the end of the year.

Sources of income

Employment income

Resident and Non-Resident employees and directors are taxed on salary and benefits in kind for each year of income. Contributions to an approved pension/provident fund scheme and also Registered Home Ownership Savings Scheme are tax deductible from employment income subject to a maximum of Kshs. 150,000 per annum and Kshs. 48,000 per annum respectively. Few other expenses, for example protective clothes, qualify for allowance but the Income Tax Department has to authorise.

Business income

Trading profits are calculated from accounts prepared on sound accounting principles and later adjusted to meet the requirement of the tax law. A business loss is carried forward and offset against future profits. Graduated tax rates are used in assessing an individual's tax liability. A partnership is not a taxable person and any profit or losses are allocated amongst the partners who are taxed on them.

Social security benefit

Employer's contributions to National Social Security Fund is allowable as an expense. National Social Security Fund is a compulsory savings scheme.

Pensions and annuities

The first Kshs. 150,000 of pensions payment per annum is exempt from tax. Annuities are taxable depending on their nature and calculation.

Capital gains

Taxation of capital gains was suspended in 1985.

Dividends

Dividend income is subject to withholding tax at 5% and 10% for non-residents. Any interest on loans borrowed to purchase shares is allowable against the dividend earned. Dividend income is taxable in the year it is paid. Withholding tax is final tax on qualifying dividend income.

Interest

All interest, irrespective of the amount, is subject to withholding tax of 15% and taxable on the receiver. Withholding tax is final tax for qualifying interest income, i.e. interest up to Kshs. 300,000 from Housing Development Bonds and an interest received by an individual from Banks and Financial Institutions; housing bonds are subject to 10% withholding tax.

Rent

A rent account is required for each financial year which shows gross rent and expenses which should be wholly and exclusively incurred in the production of income. This is a specified source of income.

Royalties

Expenses incurred to earn the royalty are allowable against this income. Withholding tax is applicable on the gross income on payment, but offset against the final tax liability.

Consultancy, agency or contractual fees

Any person paying consultancy, agency or contractual fees to an individual is required to withhold a tax of 2% of the gross amount payable if the aggregate amount is 24,000 Shillings, or more, in a month.

Tax on tax

If an employer pays a salary and then decides to pay the tax thereon, the tax the employer pays is a taxable benefit on the employee. To arrive at the tax eventually paid, a series of sub-assessments have to be done until the reassessable benefit is negligible/minimal.

Foreign source income

Where an individual is resident for tax (whether expatriate or citizen), all employment income earned in Kenya and outside Kenya is charged to tax at the graduated resident rates of tax. The individual will also be entitled to a personal relief.

Exempt income

Exempt income includes:

- the first Kshs. 360,000 lump sum paid from a pension fund and Kshs.240,000 paid from a registered provident fund;
- income from most agricultural boards and all agricultural shows;
- interest on tax reserve certificates;
- the first Kshs. 150,000 paid as pension per annum;
- management or professional fees and royalty or interest payable under an agreement where the government is a party to, or guarantor; and
- dividend income received by a resident company with the following characteristics:
  - dividend received by a company which controls more than 12.5% of the voting powers of the company-paying dividend;
  - dividends from investment income of a life insurance fund of a resident; and

– a bonus issued on debentures and redeemable preference shares.

Personal taxes

The personal tax allowances are as follows:

	2000 *Kshs p.a.*	*2001* *Kshs p.a.*
Personal relief applicable to all resident individuals	9,600	11,520
Mortgage relief on owner occupied properties	up to Kshs 100,000 on interest paid on approved borrowings.	

A married woman's business income is taxed on the husband if the two spouses are living together.

A married woman may opt to file a separate return from that of her husband in respect of income consisting of her employment, professional or self-employment.

Rates of tax

Individual, wife's employment and wife's professional income rates of tax from 1998:

	2000 (K£)	*2001* *(K£)*	*Rate* (%)
The first	5,220	5,472	10
The next	5,220	5,472	15
The next	5,220	5,472	20
The next	5,220	5,472	25
All income over	20,880	21,888	30

Note: Kshs. 20 = 1 K£

Instalment tax should be paid to cover 100% of the total tax liability as shown below:

Instalment	*1st*	*2nd*	*3rd*	*4th*
1 January 1993	–	–	60	20
1 January 1994	–	15	60	25
1 January 1995	–	30	45	25
1 January 1996 et seq	25	25	25	25

For those taxpayers who derive at least two-thirds of their income from agricultural, pastoral, horticultural or similar activities, their payment should be as below:

	%	%
1 January 1993	60	20
1 January 1994	75	25
1 January 1995 et seq	75	25

Withholding tax

It should be paid within 30 days of deduction.

Description of Income	*Rates* %
Non-resident:	
Management of professional fees	20
Royalties	20
Rent	30
Dividends	10
Interest	15
Pension retirement annuity	5
Entertainment (Public or private)	20
Contractual, Agency Consultancy fee	20
Resident:	
Dividends	5
Interest	15
Insurance Commission	10
Interest on Housing Development Bonds	10
Contractual, Agency or Consultancy fees	2

Payments of tax

Payroll deductions

PAYE deductions should be paid by the employer on or before the ninth day of the month following the month to which the deductions relate.

Prepayments

Prepayments are made in the form of an instalment tax, which is a self-assessment, before the total liability is finally determined.

Tax credits

Tax credits are carried forward for offset against future tax liabilities. The same may be repaid to the taxpayer if claimed.

Estate taxes

An individual is taxable on his income including accrued income up to the date of death. Return of income up to the date of death should be submitted by the personal representative. During the administration period, any taxable income is assessable on the trustee, executor or administrator of the estate of the deceased at the rate of 30%. During the trust period, the trustee is still liable to deduct tax at the appropriate rate. Where any income is distributed to the beneficiaries, they are assessed on the grossed-up income with credit for tax paid at 30%.

Other taxes

Other taxes include Value Added Tax (VAT) and Customs and Excise duty. VAT, which replaced sales tax as from 1990, is levied on the supply of goods and services in the course of furtherance of a business. The standard rate of VAT is 18%. Other rates are 'O', 10% and 25%.

Exchange control

The Exchange Control Act was repealed in 1995.

Double taxation relief

There are double taxation agreements between Kenya and Zambia, USA, UK, Canada, Denmark, Norway, Sweden, Germany, Tanzania and Uganda.

Anti-avoidance measures

- An authorised tax agent is responsible for any failure, omission, claim, statement or deduction, whether or not due to negligence or to the disregard of law.
- After-tax profits should be distributed as dividends, which should be taxed on the recipients. In case of non-distribution, the Tax Department is supposed to be paid an amount by the company equal to the tax avoided.
- Suspicious transactions may be reversed, as directed by the department, to counter avoidance of tax or the reduction of liability.
- Omission of income is punishable by double the tax evaded in addition to the tax actually chargeable, as well as a fine not

exceeding Shillings 200,000 or imprisonment for a term of two years, or both such a fine and imprisonment.

- Where additional tax is charged to a taxpayer due to wilful or gross neglect or fraud on the part of an authorised tax agent, the agent is guilty of an offence and liable to a fine not exceeding Kshs. 50,000 for each return, statement or other documents.
- Penalty for late submission or non-submission of return of income is 5% of liability subject to a minimum of Kshs. 1,000 and Kshs. 5,000 for individual and corporate taxpayers respectively.
- Any shortfall in the amount of instalment tax paid is penalised by 15% of the shortfall multiplied by a factor of 1.1, while unpaid tax attracts a penalty of 20% and late payment interest at the rate of 2% per month from the due date.

Korea

Samduk Accounting Corporation

Introduction

In recent years Korea has seen a lowering of the corporate and personal income tax rates and a broadening of the tax base.

Most taxes are levied at a national level, with the significant exception of real estate tax (levied at local level) as well as certain other relatively minor taxes.

The tax fiscal year is the calendar year, although some corporations may have other year ends.

Corporate taxes

Taxable entities

Resident companies

Resident companies are liable to corporate income tax on their worldwide income, including capital gains. A company is resident if it is incorporated under Korean law.

Non-Resident companies

Foreign corporations (corporations with their head offices in a foreign country) are taxable only on income derived from sources within Korea.

Tax is not levied on the liquidation income of a foreign corporation.

A foreign corporation with a business location in Korea is required to file a tax return in accordance with corporation tax law as applied to domestic corporations. If it has no business location in Korea, tax is withheld on Korean source income in accordance with Korean corporation tax laws and any tax treaty in effect.

Tax year and filing requirements

A corporation tax return, together with supplementary financial information, must be filed no later than three months from the date of finalisation of financial accounts.

A corporation with a business period exceeding six months must designate a six-month period from the beginning of the business period as an interim tax prepayment period. Prepayments of tax must be made within two months of the end of the interim period.

Taxes imposed

There are two types of taxes imposed on the income of domestic corporations:

- national tax (or corporation tax); and
- local government tax (or resident tax).

Rates of corporation tax

The amount of corporation tax due is calculated by applying the following tax rates to taxable income.

Domestic corporations including those whose stocks are listed on the Korean Stock Exchange:

Taxable income not exceeding Won 100 million	16% of taxable income
Taxable income exceeding Won 100 million	Won 16 million plus 28% of the amount in excess of Won 100 million

Income subject to tax

General rules

Corporation tax is charged on the income for each business year and includes the following items:

- income accruing in each business year;
- liquidation income (excluding the liquidation income of a non-profit making domestic corporation or foreign corporation); and
- capital gains.

Stock/inventory rules

Stock is valued in accordance with sound business practice, in most cases at the lower of cost or market value. The FIFO and average cost methods are most common. The LIFO and retail inventory methods are also permitted.

Capital gains

Capital gains from the disposal of land and buildings are subject to a special surtax, in addition to the normal corporate tax charged on the gains. The special surtax is 15% of the gain or 30% where the property was transferred without registration.

Dividends

Dividends paid are not deductible in arriving at taxable income. Dividends are subject to a withholding tax of 15%, or a lower rate where this is prescribed by a tax treaty.

Withholding tax on dividends is a credit or refund for resident companies against their corporate income tax.

Dividends received both from Korea and from foreign sources are taxed at the full corporate income tax rate, while 90% of the amount of dividends received by institutional investors from listed corporations and 'over-the-counter' registered corporations is not included in taxable income.

Deductions

General rules

Expenses directly or closely connected with the conduct of the business are generally wholly or partly tax deductible. Any expenses considered to contain a personal element (such as food and drink) are only partly deductible.

Certain expenses are subject to a maximum amount that can be deducted.

Depreciation

Different methods of depreciation are permitted, provided that they are in accordance with generally accepted accounting principles and sound business practice.

The depreciation base of an asset is its historic cost. The residual value and useful life of the asset are taken into account. Certain assets, such as land, are not depreciable.

Accepted methods are as follows:

- straight-line method for buildings and intangible fixed assets; and
- straight-line method or declining balance method for other tangible fixed assets.

The useful lives of assets are as follows:

• buildings	20-40 years
• plant, machinery, office equipment and vehicles.	4-16 years

Interest on debts incurred in order to purchase or construct property, plant, and equipment must be capitalised.

Assets with an acquisition cost of under Won 1,000,000 may be expensed directly against income.

Amortisation

Expenses corresponding with future revenue must be capitalised and subsequently amortised. These include organisation expenses, premiums on debentures and research and development costs.

Amortisation periods are set out in the tax legislation.

Royalties

Royalties payable are allowed as a normal business expense.

Interest

In principle, all interest payments on loan and other debts of a company are considered to be business expenses and therefore deductible.

Dividends

Dividends paid are not deductible.

Goodwill and other fixed assets

Goodwill that is purchased is treated as a capital asset and written-off over a period of five years.

Goodwill created by the company cannot be capitalised and depreciation of the goodwill is not allowed.

Patents purchased for a lump sum are valued in the same manner as other depreciable capital assets.

Reserves and provisions

Redundancy reserves

The amount of severance pay which can be expensed during a year is the lower of:

- an amount equivalent to 10% of total wages paid to employees who have been in service for one year or more; or
- 40% of the total liability for severance pay at the year end, less the balance of the reserve recognised for tax purposes in the prior year.

In addition, actual severance payments in excess of the reserve for severance allowances can be expensed.

Bad debt reserves

Reserves for bad debts up to a maximum of 1% (2% for financial institutions) or last year's experienced ratio of accounts receivable, including VAT, as of the closing date of the respective business year. The residue after deducting actual bad debts is included in income of the following year.

Security transaction reserves

Security transaction reserves of companies engaged in security businesses are deductible up to an amount equivalent to 30% of the net profits from securities transactions during the business year. The remained amounts, after offsetting actual losses, are included in the gains of the third year from the year in which the reserves were appropriated to the loss.

Tax credits

The following tax credits are available:

Credits for foreign tax

Where a domestic company has paid or is liable to pay foreign corporation tax, the tax paid or payable abroad is deductible from Korean corporation tax, up to the tax amount of tax equal to the ratio of income from foreign sources to total taxable income.

Credit for loss caused by disaster

Where a domestic company is deemed to have difficulties in paying tax because it has lost 30% or more of the total value of its assets due to a disaster, a tax amount equal to the ratio of the value of the lost assets to the value of total assets is deducted from the company's corporation tax liability.

Related party transactions

Transactions between companies or other persons under common control may be subject to revision if they are not carried out in accordance with arm's length principles.

Furthermore, if a transaction is not at arm's length, it may be treated as a deemed dividend distribution.

Losses

A company may carry forward losses for up to five years.

Corporate groups

There are no special tax rules relating to groups of companies. All companies are taxed individually and there is no group relief.

Personal taxes

Taxable entities

Residents

An individual is resident if he plans to make his domicile in Korea permanently or has resided continuously in Korea for more than one year. The tax authorities treat a person as resident if his occupation would normally require a continuous presence in Korea for one year or more. Residents are subject to income tax on their worldwide income and are permitted to take all deductions allowable under Korean tax laws.

Non-residents

An individual is non-resident if he is not domiciled in Korea and has resided in Korea for less than one year. Non-residents are only subject to tax on income from sources in Korea.

Non-residents are allowed the same deductions, personal allowances (except spouse allowance, dependant allowance and other similar allowances) and tax credits as resident taxpayers.

Taxes on income

Taxes on income consist of national income tax and local resident tax. The taxable income of individuals is determined on a calendar year basis. Taxable income consists of the various categories of income, namely worldwide income, retirement income, capital gains and forestry income.

Local resident tax is assessed by local government on Korean domiciliaries, as well as individuals liable for Korean income tax.

Sources of income

Individual income tax is grouped into four types:

- worldwide income tax;
- retirement income tax;
- capital gains tax; and
- forestry income tax.

Taxable worldwide income is made up of interest, dividend income, real estate income less necessary expenses, business income less necessary expenses, salaries and wages and other income net of necessary expenses. Worldwide income tax is computed on taxable worldwide income by applying progressive income tax rates. The most important sources of income are described in further detail below.

Employment income

This includes salaries, wages, remuneration, pensions, bonuses and any other amounts receivable in return for services.

The total value of salaries and wages in each taxation period, after deduction of necessary expenses, is subject to withholding tax according to a withholding tax computation table prepared by the government.

Business income

Business income is defined by the tax laws of Korea as revenues for the accounting period, less necessary expenses incurred in that period. Accounting practice with respect to allowances and reserves is defined in the laws and regulations of Korea. Expenses that are limited or not permitted for tax purposes include depreciation, provision for bad debts, provision for severance indemnities, entertainment expenses and charitable contributions exceeding specified limits.

Taxable business income generally does not include amounts received as tax refunds, interest received on tax refunds or revaluation of assets.

A balance of net losses may be carried forward for five years.

Interest income

Interest income received by residents is normally taxable and includes interest on bank deposits, public bonds and debentures, and distributions by bond investment trusts. Where such income is fully taxed at source, individuals are not required to report it on their tax returns. In the same way, minor amounts of interest that are received by individuals on bank current accounts and specified issues of Korean government bonds are generally excluded from the annual tax return; the tax, if any, on such interest is withheld at source.

Interest from regular bank deposits, bonds and securities issued by the government or local authority and securities investment trusts is subject to a 20% withholding tax, whilst interest from private loans is subject to a 25% withholding tax.

Dividends

For tax purposes, dividends include distributions of profits to stockholders by ordinary business corporations, distributions of gains by securities investment trusts (other than bond investment trusts), excess distributions to stockholders in connection with a liquidation (or merger), certain undistributed profits (imputed dividends) as prescribed by income tax law, and the par value of stock dividends received, except those declared from capital surplus and asset revaluation surplus. To mitigate the burden of double taxation, income tax law provides for a tax credit on dividends received for individuals. Dividend income from a company is subject to 20% withholding tax.

Real estate income

Real estate income includes all income from the lease of land, fixtures, and the rights on real estate, mining and factory buildings. Taxable income is the net income in each taxation period after deduction of necessary expenses and losses carried forward within five years.

Other income

Other income includes prize money, fees on copyrights receivable by an individual other than a writer, royalties for the use of films and tapes for radio and television broadcasting and other similar items. Taxable income is the total amount of income less necessary expenses. Remuneration for giving a specific lecture and similar income is subject to a deduction of 75% as a necessary expense.

Other income is subject to 20% withholding tax.

Retirement income

The tax on retirement income, including severance pay, is computed on the basis of the following formula:

- (retirement income x 50% – retirement income deduction) x number of years of continuous employment = taxable annual retirement income;
- annual retirement income tax is calculated by applying income tax rates to the taxable annual retirement income; and
- annual retirement income tax is multiplied by the number of years of the continuously employed to then give the retirement income tax.

Capital gains

Capital gains arising from transfers of land, buildings, and rights to real estate are taxed at a rate of 20% to 40%, depending on whether the property is held for more or less than two years and registered with the appropriate government office. Capital gains arising from transfer of land or building that is held for less than two years are taxed at a rate of 40%, but gains arising from transfer of assets transferred without registration are taxed at a rate of 65%. And capital gains arising from transfer of shares in a non-listed company are taxed at a rate of 20%, but in case of small or mid-sized companies' shares, the rate is 10%.

In determining the taxable income from capital gains, individuals are allowed a standard deduction of Won 2,500,000. The standard deduction for capital gains is not allowed in the case of the transfer of land, building or rights held without registration.

The special deduction for long term possession of land or real estate is as follows: 10% of the capital gain if the possession period exceeds three years but does not exceed five years, 15% of the capital gain if the possession period exceeds five years but does not exceed ten years and 30% of the capital gain if the possession period exceeds ten years.

Forestry income

Forestry income is derived from the sale or other transfer of forestry held for five years or more. The costs of acquisition, forestation, cutting, transportation and selling are deductible. In addition, a deduction of Won 6,000,000 is allowed.

The formula for computing forestry income tax payable is as follows:

- gross income – (acquisition cost + capital expenditure + related direct sales expense + special deduction of Won 6,000,000) = taxable forestry income; and
- income tax rates are applied on the taxable forestry income.

Foreign source income

See 'tax credits' below.

Personal allowances and deductions

Allowances

For the purposes of national income tax, certain personal allowances or exemptions are deductible. Resident taxpayers are permitted a basic allowance, an allowance for a spouse living with the taxpayer, an allowance for each dependant maintained by the taxpayer in one household, and a special allowance for donations and contributions.

No deduction is allowed, however, for a spouse or dependant with an independent income. There are additional allowances for taxpayers, spouses, or dependants who are physically handicapped.

Deductions

Gross income in each category is subject to itemised deductions appropriate to the category. On employment income, for example, employment income deduction, insurance deduction, medical expenses and education expenses are allowable. The net income of each category is then aggregated. The total of certain supplementary deductions must be offset against worldwide income. An excess deduction is applied against retirement income, capital gains, and forestry income in that order.

Special family rules

Where a spouse of the main income earner receives dividend, interest or real estate income (excluding dividend and interest income subject to separate taxation), such income is aggregated with the taxable income of the main income earner of the household for the taxation of worldwide income.

The term 'main income earner' means the member of the household who earns the highest income.

Rates of tax

National tax

Income tax on worldwide income is the aggregate of amounts calculated by applying each tax rate successively to income in the relevant tax band:

Income Band Won	*Tax Rate (%)*	*Tax on Band Won*	*Cumulative Tax Won*
10–10,000,000	10	1,000,000	1,000,000
10,000,001–40,000,000	20	6,000,000	7,000,000
40,000,001–80,000,000	30	12,000,000	19,000,000
80,000,001+	40		

The tax on severance pay is calculated by dividing taxable income by the number of years in service, then applying the tax rates and multiplying this amount again by the number of years in service.

Tax rates on capital gains are as follows:

- land, buildings or other assets held for more than two years – 20-40%;

- land, buildings or other assets held for less than two years – 40%; and
- assets transferred without registration – 65%.

Local resident tax

Korean domiciled individuals and individuals liable to Korean income tax are subject to a resident tax as follows:

- per capital tax at a nominal rate; and
- per income rate at 10% of the amount of individual income tax.

Tax credits

Where the dividend income from domestic companies of a Korean resident is included in worldwide income, an amount (calculated as follows) is deducted from the worldwide income tax liability:

- 19% of the dividend income is added to the amount of dividend actually received by the shareholder;
- this figure is then used to calculate the shareholder's individual income tax;
- thereafter, 19% of the dividend income (as calculated above) is credited against the calculated individual income tax amount or refunded to the shareholder.

Where a resident has paid or is to pay income tax abroad, the tax amount paid or payable is deducted from the amount of Korean income tax owed (within the limit of an amount equivalent to: the amount of the income tax owed without application of this credit and the ratio of income from foreign sources to total taxable income). If the foreign tax amount paid, or payable, exceeds this limit, the excess portion may be carried over for five years.

When a resident loses 30% or more of the total value of his business assets due to one or more disasters, an amount equal to the tax due (without application of this credit), times the ratio of the value of the lost assets over the total value of assets owned prior to the disasters, is subtracted from the amount of tax due in the year of the disaster(s).

For a wage and salary income earner, 30% (or 45% if the total tax amount is less than Won 500,000) of the calculated tax amount may be subtracted from the amount of tax due up to Won 600,000 per year.

Payment of tax

Taxable period

Taxes are assessed for the calendar year.

Interim prepayment for worldwide income tax

A resident with worldwide income is required to make interim prepayments of worldwide income tax. The prepayments (each equivalent to half of the worldwide income tax paid or payable in the preceding year) are due at the end of November.

Pre-returns and estimated payment

Real estate dealer

An individual who operates a real estate business must file a return showing the profit on sales of land and buildings by the end of the month, following the month in which the sale takes place. An amount equivalent to 20-65% of the profit must be paid as income tax on real estate dealing business. A 10% special tax credit for pre-returns and estimated payment is allowed.

Capital gains

A resident who transfers assets subject to capital gains tax must file a return on the capital gains within two months after the month in which the transfer takes place and pay tax thereon.

A special tax credit for pre-returns and estimated payments is allowed. The pre-return tax payable is calculated by applying the capital gains tax rates to the profit earned and deducting 10% of the calculated tax.

Final return and payment

Return on tax base

A resident who receives worldwide income, retirement income, capital gains or forestry income in a tax year is required to file a return for each category of income by the end of May of the following year.

Payment of tax

A Korean resident must pay any balance due after the deduction of credits and estimated payments with the return.

A Korean resident with a tax liability exceeding Won 10 million may pay a part of the tax in instalments within 45 days of the end of the payment period.

Tax withholding

A person paying interest, dividend or business income arising from a free occupation prescribed by Presidential Decree, Class A wages and salaries, and from retirement income or other income is required to withhold income tax thereon at the relevant rates at the time of the payment and pay it to the government by the tenth day of the following month.

Estate and gift tax

Inheritors and legatees who acquire assets located in Korea by inheritance or bequest are subject to inheritance tax even if they are not domiciled in Korea. Inheritance tax is imposed after deducting the following amounts from the total value of the assets acquired on death and assets gifted to an inheritor within the preceding ten years.

Public taxes on death

- Public imposts;
- funeral expenses between Won 5 million and Won 10 million;
- debts.

Itemised deductions

- Basic deductions:
  - general – Won 200 million;
  - inherited family businesses – Won 300 million;
  - inherited farms, fisheries, and forestry – Won 400 million;
- deduction for dependants:
  - Won 30 million per person;
- deductions for minors:

if the inheritor or legatee, or a member of the inheritor's or legatee's family is a minor, an annual deduction of Won 5 million is granted to the minor until the individual reaches 20 years of age;

- deductions for the elderly:

  if the inheritor or the legatee, or a member of the inheritor's or legatee's family is over 60 years old, a deduction of Won 30 million is granted to that person;

- deductions for the disabled:

  in the case where the inheritor or the legatee, the inheritor's spouse or the legatee's spouse, or a member of the inheritor's or legatee's family is disabled, an annual deduction of Won 5 million is granted to that person until the individual reaches 75 years of age.

Lump sum deductions

- General – Won 500 million;
- Inherited family businesses – Won 600 million;
- Inherited farms, fisheries, and forestry – Won 700 million.

The taxpayer may choose either itemised deductions or lump-sum deductions, as follows.

Deductions for spouse

Where the bequeathed is a known resident, the actual amount inherited by the individual's spouse is deducted if it falls within the range of Won 500 million to Won 3 billion.

Deductions for financial assets

If financial assets are a part of the inheritance, the following amounts are allowed as deductions:

- for amounts between Won 20 million, the total amount of the inherited financial assets is deducted;
- for amounts that fall within the range of Won 20 million and Won 100 million, Won 20 million can be deducted;
- for amounts that exceed Won 100 million, 20% of the total inherited financial assets can be deducted, however, only deduction up to Won 200 million is allowed.

Deductions for losses

- Losses incurred as a result of natural disasters and other unforeseeable circumstances are allowable.
- An amount equivalent to the value on a loss which is the result of fire, collapse of buildings, explosions, environmental pollution, natural disasters, etc., which have affected the inherited property, is allowed.

Rates of inheritance tax increase in bands from 10% on the first Won 100 million of the statutory inheritance to 50% on the excess above Won 3,000 million.

A person who acquires assets by inheritance is liable to file a tax return within six months of the inheritance, together with detailed statements concerning the deducted amounts. The taxable value is determined by the government, based on the filed tax return.

Gift tax

A Korean domiciled individual who is gifted an asset is subject to gift tax. A non-Korean domiciled individual who acquires assets located in Korea by gift is also subject to gift tax. Donors are also liable to pay gift tax on the basis of joint responsibility.

Gift tax is imposed on the balance after deduction of the following amounts from the value of the assets donated, subject to certain limitations.

Deductions for family gifts

In cases where a Korean resident individual receives family gifts from the following individuals, he is granted a deduction:

- spouse – up to Won 500 million;
- lineal family members – up to Won 30 million for all individuals, except minors for whom up to Won 15 million is allowed; and
- other family members – up to Won 5 million.

Deductions for losses

- Losses incurred as a result of natural disasters and other unforeseeable circumstances are allowable; and
- an amount equivalent to the value on a loss, which is the result of fire, collapse of buildings, explosions, environmental pollution,

natural disasters, etc., and which have affected the gifted property, is allowable.

The tax rates are in bands from 10% on the first Won 100 million to 50% on the excess over Won 3,000 million. Similar return and payment rules apply, as for inheritance tax.

Wealth tax

There is no wealth tax in Korea.

Social security

The gross earnings of employees, including pensions and medical insurance, are subject to social security. The total contribution is equally shared between the employer and the employee.

Other taxes

National taxes

- Value added tax (VAT) is imposed on the additional value which accrues at each stage of transfer of goods or services from one party to another. The rate is currently 10%.
- Tax on sales (output tax) of a company during a six-month period (where an interim return should be filed and paid after the first three months) less tax already assessed at a previous stage (input tax) on purchased goods or services during the same period. These taxes must be fixed and settled in every six-month period.
- A zero rate applies to the supply of goods for export, services furnished from outside the Republic of Korea, international navigation services for ships or aircraft and foreign currency earnings derived from goods or services supplied to a non-resident or foreign corporation with no permanent establishment in Korea. A non-resident who has not resided in Korea for more than one year is entitled to a zero tax rate benefit on the condition that the country in which the individual is resident allows the same tax benefit to Korean residents.

Special excise tax

A special excise tax is assessed on sales of special items and on entrance fees earned by certain entertainment and gambling establishments.

Special items are grouped into classes for the purpose of tax assessment, as follows:

	Tax rate
Class 1: including luxury items such as slot machines, golf requisites, motorboats, snow and water skiing apparatus and scooters, air-conditioners and movie projectors.	30%
Class 2: Coffee and cocoa; following items levied 10.5% – refrigerator, electric washing machine, color TV, grand pianos, crystal glassware.	15%
Class 3: including such items as soft drinks, nutrition preparations, sugar, certain cosmetic products.	10%
Class 4: including items such as jewellery, pearl, tortoise-shell, coral, amber, ivory, precious metal products, luxury cameras and accessories, watches, carpets, fur skin and furniture.	30%
Class 5: Group 1 including automobiles with an engine displacement in excess of 1,500 cc.	7%–14%
Class 5: Group 2 Gasoline	Won 691 per litre

Entertainment and gambling establishments such as horse race tracks, special steam bath houses, gaming rooms, golf courses, bicycle tracks and casinos are subject to a special excise tax of 20% or Won 200 – Won 50,000 per person.

Asset revaluation tax

An individual may revalue his assets on 1 January, 1 April, 1 July or 1 December of each business year. A company may also revalue its business assets from the beginning date of the business year and every three months thereafter (i.e. 3, 6, 9, or 12 months after the start date) until 31 December 2000. The revaluation is usually determined by the Korea Appraisal Board and is computed from the start of the taxpayer's chosen date. The revaluation is subject to an asset revaluation tax of 3% (1% for land revaluation), payable upon submission of the revaluation return or in instalments made over the course of one year, where the tax exceeds Won 10 million. A gain on revaluation is not subject to individual income tax or corporate income tax.

Depreciation is calculated on revaluation and extended estimated life and is a fully deductible expense for income tax purposes. Any revaluation gain remaining after adjustment can be capitalised.

Education tax

Education tax is revenue raised for the purpose of education through payers of a special excise tax, payers of liquor tax and taxpayers engaged in the banking and insurance business.

Education tax rates are as follows:

Tax base	*Tax rate*
Special excise tax	30%
Liquor tax	10-30%
Gross revenue or individual or enterprise performing banking or insurance business	0.5%
Per capita inhabitant tax	10-25%
Registration tax	20%
Horse race tax	20%
Property tax, aggregate land tax	20%
Automobile tax	30%
Transportation tax	15%
Tobacco consumption tax	40%

Securities transaction tax

A securities transaction tax is imposed on stock market transactions. A dealer in securities or a seller of securities must withhold and pay to the tax authority 0.5% of the value of each security transaction on or before the tenth day of the month following the date of the transaction.

Telephone tax

A 10% telephone tax is imposed on telephone bills.

Local taxes

Acquisition tax

Persons who acquire real estate, motor vehicles, heavy equipment, trees, boats, aircraft, golf memberships, condominium memberships and health club memberships through purchase or inheritance, are liable to acquisition tax.

The base cost for acquisition tax is the declared price at the time of acquisition of the property or assets.

Tax rates:

- 2% of the value of the acquired property or the amount of an annual instalment;

- in the case of acquiring a villa, golf course, high class dwelling house, luxury amusement place, land for the non-business purposes of a corporation or a luxury boat – 500% of the above tax (corresponding to 10% of the value of the article); and
- in the case where taxable articles for business purposes are acquired in specially designated areas of restricted population growth, for example the Seoul Metropolitan area (except when foreign investors build new plants or expand existing ones by using assets acquired by the end of 2001) – 300% of the above tax rate (2%), which corresponds to 6% of the value of the property.

Registration tax

Persons who register the acquisition or transfer of real estate, rights to property or other titles in the official register, are liable to registration tax.

The base cost for registration tax is the value at the time of registration of the property or assets registered.

Property	*Tax rate (%)*
Real estate acquired by purchase	3.0*
Reservation of rights to real estate	0.8
Rights to property other than ownership	0.2
Vehicle	5.0
Company incorporation	0.4

* Threefold registration tax applies up to 31 December 2001 in Seoul, Pusan and Taegu, except on foreign investment.

Automobile tax

Individuals who own registered cars. Buses or trucks are subject to an automobile tax also. Cars, buses and trucks are classified as business or non-business use. Automobile taxes vary according to engine capacity, type and weight of vehicles.

Property tax

Owners listed in the buildings, vessels or aircraft taxation register at the beginning of the payment period, must pay property tax annually.

For a residential house or lot, the rates for a house range from a minimum of 0.3% for amounts less than 12 million to a maximum of 7% for amounts exceeding Won 40 million. For non-residential buildings, the rates range from a minimum of 0.3% to a maximum of 7%.

Workshop tax

Employers with 50 or more employees, or whose combined office and plant space is 100 Pyong (330 m^2) or more, are liable to workshop tax. Space used for employees' welfare is excluded from the taxable space.

Workshop tax rates are 0.5% of salaries and wages (payable monthly) and Won 250 per square metre of office and plant space, payable in July of each year.

Exchange control

For the past few decades Korea has maintained strict capital controls under the Foreign Exchange Control Act. Although the Act may have been effective in curbing the excessive flight of capital, especially in the early stage of economic development when foreign capital was very necessary for economic growth, it has increasingly become a bottleneck for foreign investment.

From 1 July 1998, all foreign exchange transactions relating to foreign investment in Korea, such as equity market investment, bond market investment and mergers and acquisitions of Korean companies, have been liberalised, with the exception of investment in onshore and offshore Won-denominated deposits. Moreover, the designated foreign exchange bank system is no longer in effect so that foreign investors wishing to invest in the capital markets need not handle all of their foreign exchange transactions through a single foreign exchange bank based in Seoul. Almost all transactions relating to residents' foreign borrowings have also been liberalised.

From 1 April 1999, the current positive list system of capital account transactions changed to the negative list system. This implies that all capital account transactions, except those on the negative list, were liberalised. This has resulted in 72 of the 91 kinds of capital account transactions listed in the OECD Code of Liberalisation of Capital Movements becoming liberalised.

Withholding taxes

Korea requires income tax to be withheld at source on interest, royalties, professional fees and certain other amounts paid to residents and non-residents. The following table illustrates the standard rates currently in force:

Country of residence	*Dividends %*	*Interest %*	*Royalties %*
Non-treaty countries	25	25	25
Treaty countries:			
Australia	15	15	15
Austria	10 (o)	10	10
Bangladesh	10	10	10
Belgium	15	10	10
Brazil	15	10 (e)	25 (aa)
Bulgaria	5 (v)	10	5
Canada	15	15	15
China	5 (t)	10	10
Czech	5 (t)	10	10
Denmark	15	15	10 (n)
Egypt	10 (p)	10 (s)	15
Finland	10 (p)	10	10
France	10 (c)	10	10
Fiji	10 (p)	10	10
Germany	10 (c)	10 (e)	15 (b)
Greece	5 (p)	8	10
Hungary	10 (p)	–	–
India	10 (p)	10 (r)	15
Indonesia	10 (p)	10	15
Israel	5 (u)	7.5 (x)	2 (y)
Italy	10 (p)	10	10
Ireland	10 (o)	–	–
Japan	5 (t)	10	10
Kazakhstan	5 (u)	10	10
Kuwait	10	10	15
Luxembourg	10 (p)	10	15 (b)
Malaysia	10 (p)	15	15 (b)
Mexico	– (u)	5	10
Mongolia	5	5	10
Morocco	5 (t)	10	5 (ab)
Netherlands	10 (p)	10 (e)	15 (b)
New Zealand	15	10	10
Norway	15	15	15 (b)
Northern Ireland	15 (h)	10 (e)	–
Pakistan	10 (f)	12.5	10
Poland	10 (o)	10	10
Portugal	10 (z)	15	10
Philippines	10 (p)	15 (g)	15 (g)
Romania	10 (p)	10	10 (d)
Russia	5 (w)	–	5
Singapore	10	10	15
South Africa	5 (p)	10	10
Spain	10 (p)	10	10
Sri Lanka	10 (p)	10	10

Sweden	10 (p)	10 (e)	15 (b)
Switzerland	10 (p)	10	10
Thailand	20 (h)	10	15
Tunisia	15	12	15
Turkey	15 (q)	15 (i)	10
United Kingdom	5 (a)	10	2 (m)
United states	10 (j)	12	10 (k)
Uzbekistan	5 (p)	5	2 (y)
Vietnam	10	10	10

Notes:

(a) rate applicable where equity holding is at least 25%, otherwise the rate is 10%;
(b) a 10% rate applies to industrial royalties;
(c) rate applicable where equity holding is at least 25%, otherwise the rate is 15%;
(d) a 5% rate applies to patent royalties;
(e) rate applicable where loan is from a financial institution and over a period of seven years, otherwise the rate is 15%;
(f) rate applicable where equity holding is at least 20%, otherwise the rate is 12.5%;
(g) a 10% rate applies to certain loans or royalties specified in Philippine law;
(h) rate applicable where equity holding is at least 25%, otherwise the rate is 15%;
(i) a 10% rate applies to loans over two years;
(j) rate applicable where equity holding is at least 10%, otherwise rate is 15%;
(k) rate applicable on copyrights of literature, music, film, television or radio broadcast, otherwise the rate is 15%;
(l) rate applicable where equity holding is at least 30% and over US$100,000, otherwise the rate is 10%;
(m) rate applicable on use of equipment, otherwise the rate is 15%;
(n) rate applicable on commercial investments, otherwise the rate is 15%;
(o) rate applicable where equity holding is at least 10%, otherwise the rate is 15%;
(p) rate applicable where equity holding is at least 25%, otherwise the rate is 15%;
(q) rate applicable where equity holding is at least 25%, otherwise the rate is 20%;
(r) rate applicable when interest earnings belong to financial institutions' revenue, otherwise the rate is 15%;
(s) rate applicable where loan's period is over three years, otherwise the rate is 15%;
(t) rate applicable where equity holding is at least 25%, otherwise the rate is 10%;
(u) rate applicable where equity holding is at least 10%, otherwise the rate is 15%;

(v) rate applicable where equity holding is at least 15%, otherwise the rate is 10%;
(w) rate applicable where equity holding is at least 30% and US$ 100,000, otherwise the rate is 10%;
(x) rate applicable when interest earnings belong to financial institutions' revenue; otherwise the rate is 10% and interest of debentures are none;
(y) rate applicable on use of equipment, otherwise the rate is 5%;
(z) rate applicable where equity holding is at least 25% over 2 years;
(aa) rate applicable on a trade mark right, otherwise the rate is 15%;
(ab) rate applicable on a copyright, otherwise the rate is 10%.

Lebanon

Usamah Tabbarah & Co.

Introduction

Taxpayers are required to maintain accounting records in the Arabic language. All taxpayers must adopt the accounting period 1 January to 31 December.

Corporate taxes

Taxable entities

Resident companies

All companies, irrespective of their nature and objectives, are subject to tax based on profits and income derived from all activities, including industrial, commercial, non-commercial trades and revenue derived from movable capital assets.

Non-resident companies

All profits, receipts and proceeds are taxable, including amounts paid to companies that have no business offices in Lebanon.

Tax filing requirements

Companies are required to file their tax returns by 31 May following the tax year. Partnerships and individuals must file their returns by 31 March following the 31 December year end.

Corporate tax rate

The profit of shareholding companies, such as joint stock companies, limited liability companies and limited partnerships in respect of sleeping partners, are subject to a tax at a rate of 15% on their proportion of the income.

Tax on dividends

The dividends or distributed profits of Lebanese shareholding companies are subject to a tax of 10%.

Tax on foreign company undistributed profits

The undistributed profits of foreign companies operating in Lebanon are treated as fully distributed and are subject to tax after deducting 15% from taxable profit and 10% from reserves.

Income subject to tax

General rules

The profit liable to tax is calculated by totalling income from various sources, such as operating profit from commercial or industrial trades, real estate transactions, hire of services, development of underground resources, brokering, commission agents, receipts from any remunerative operations and dividends.

Inventory valuation

Inventory valuation at cost is acceptable.

Deductions

General rules

Taxable profits are calculated in accordance with generally accepted accounting principles with certain statutory adjustments as follows:

- expenditure incurred wholly and exclusively for business purposes relevant to the period is allowed; partners' remuneration and work performed outside Lebanon are separately taxed;
- depreciation on capital expenditure can be deducted; and
- all reserves and provisions, whether specific, general or contingent, are disallowed except those which arise from legal action against a company.

Depreciation

Generally, a depreciation charge is allowed on qualifying fixed assets in use.

Royalties

Royalties are generally allowed as a deductible expense. Tax at 50% is charged on 15% of the royalty payable.

Interest

Interest charges are fully deductible.

Dividends

Dividends and other distributions paid to partners by companies are not deductible.

Capital gains

Capital gains are taxed separately at 10%.

Losses

Unabsorbed losses can be carried forward for a maximum period of three years.

Remuneration paid to foreign individuals, companies and institutions

Amounts paid in Lebanon as remuneration for the activities of individuals, companies or institutions that have no business offices in Lebanon, as well as any profits, receipts or proceeds realised in Lebanon by these individuals, companies or institutions, are taxable as follows:

- the net taxable amount is fixed at a lump sum of 15% of the basic income and at 50% if the income represents an indemnity for services rendered; and
- profit resulting from a total or partial assignment is subject to income tax at a rate of 6%.

Tax on payments from public and private funds

Tax is levied on all income from salaries, wages, allowances' benefits and retirement benefits, public and private, as well as life annuities paid in Lebanon by a public fund to any individual resident in Lebanon or abroad, or by a private fund to any individual living abroad in return for services rendered in Lebanese territory.

Rates of tax

Band (Lebanese Pounds)	*Rate (%)*
0 – 6,000,000	2
6,000,001 – 5,000,000	4
15,000,001 – 30,000,000	7
30,000,001 – 60,000,000	11
60,000,001 – 120,000,000	15
Above 120,000,000	20

Partnerships

In partnership or limited partnership companies, each partner is personally taxed on his share of profit.

Personal taxes

Taxable individuals

All individuals are taxed based on profits from industrial, commercial and non-commercial trade, skilled trades, professions, salaries, wages and retirement benefits, revenue from movable capital assets, real estate transactions, leasing or hiring of commercial or industrial service, income from the development of underground resources, brokering and commission income as well as incidental income or profit from a remunerative operation not otherwise liable to income tax. No income is exempt from tax except by explicit provision in legislation.

Tax assessment and tax-free allowances

Tax liability is assessed on actual profits after deduction of the tax-free allowance of Lebanese £7.5 million for an unmarried taxpayer. For married taxpayers, this allowance increases by a further Lebanese £2.5 million and for each child an extra allowance of Lebanese £500,000 is given up to a maximum of five children.

Rates of tax

Band (Lebanese £)	*Rate (%)*
0 – 9,000,000	4
9,000,001 – 24,000,000	7
2,400,001 – 54,000,000	12
54,000,001 – 104,000,000	16
Above 104,000,000	21

Withholding taxes

Withholding tax is deducted from third party services on deemed profits computed on 15% of the sub-contracted amount at a rate of 50%.

Luxembourg

Fiduciaire Resource SA
Resource Révision Sàrl (Chartered Accountants)

Corporate taxes

Taxable entities

Resident companies

A company is resident in Luxembourg if it has been incorporated in Luxembourg or if it is effectively managed in Luxembourg. A resident company is liable to corporate tax on its worldwide income whether or not that income is received in Luxembourg.

Non-resident companies

Non-resident companies operating through a permanent establishment in Luxembourg will be charged corporate tax and trade tax on profits arising in, or derived from, that permanent establishment.

Tax year and filing requirements

The tax year is the calendar year. Companies may have different accounting periods in which case the tax year is the year ending in the calendar year in question. Tax returns must be filed by 31 May after the end of the tax year. Postponement is possible.

Taxes imposed

Corporate income tax must be paid each year and is calculated on net profits realised by the company.

A net worth tax is payable and is based on the net worth of the company.

Municipal business tax must be paid each year and is calculated on income. This tax is deductible for the purposes of computation of corporate income tax.

Rates of tax

The maximum corporate income tax rate is 30% on taxable profits. The rate is lower if the annual taxable profit does not exceed F.Lux 600,000. The tax is exclusive of unemployment contributions which represent 4% of the corporate income tax payable.

The municipal business tax rate based on income is approximately 9%.

Income subject to tax

General rules

Total profits for corporate tax purposes are obtained by totalling all sources of income and profits (including trading profits and capital gains). The basis of total profits for corporate taxation is determined by the increase of net assets between the beginning and the end of the accounting period, increased by distributions of profit and reduced by contributions of the shareholders to the capital of the company.

Capital gains and losses

Capital gains are treated as income for tax purposes. Under certain circumstances, capital gains realised on the sale of assets belonging to a company for more than five years may be reduced by the cost of the replacement upon revaluation of the original acquisition cost (real estate). Capital gains are tax free in 1929 holding companies, which are special types of holding companies that attract various tax privileges. Capital gains meeting the Luxembourg affiliation privilege conditions are exempt.

Dividends

Dividends paid by taxable companies suffer a withholding tax of 25%. There is no withholding tax applied on dividends distributed by a 1929 holding company.

Dividends received from a corporate company in which the Luxembourg company has an investment of more than 10% (participation privilege or acquisition privilege of at least F.Lux 50 million) are exempt from corporate taxes. Luxembourg withholding tax paid is refundable, but foreign withholding tax is often only partly creditable.

Where there is a double taxation treaty in place, the withholding tax rates may be reduced.

Stock inventory rules

Stock is normally valued at the lower of cost or market value.

Foreign income

In general, foreign source profits and income are aggregated with Luxembourg profits, and income. However, in order to avoid double taxation, Luxembourg has entered into a number of tax treaties. Beside the double taxation treaties, Luxembourg grants unilateral relief by way of tax credits for foreign taxes paid. Dividends received from a company in which the receiving company owns more than 10% of the share capital are tax-free.

Deductions

General rules

Expenses related to the normal business of the company are fully deductible for the computation of corporate taxes in general. Income upon which the computation of the municipal business tax is based is adjusted according to specific factors. There is a tax-free allowance of F.Lux 700,000 on income.

Depreciation

In general, the straight-line basis is used for computation of depreciation. Depreciation rates are fixed on the basis of the expected useful economic life of the assets. Under certain circumstances, an accelerated depreciation may be used (e.g. for sophisticated high-tech equipment). Normal rates for depreciation are:

Real estate	1.5–4%
Machinery and equipment	10–15%
Vehicles	20–25%

Excessive depreciation is not deductible.

Royalties

Royalties paid according to arm's length principles are fully deductible.

Interest

Interest paid in relation to the business of the company is fully deductible. However, the company must take into account the arm's length principle for interest paid to shareholders or related parties. Excessive rates will be considered to be a hidden distribution of profits.

Investment incentives and special benefits

Investment incentives

Those Luxembourg authorities which are willing to participate in national economic development offer a wide number of incentives. Examples of such incentives are the free disposal of land for industrial sites, capital allowances up to 25% for the acquisition of land and equipment and loans given by the state-owned investment bank at advantageous rates of interest.

Tax incentives

Luxembourg offers many tax incentives for new investments and for newly incorporated companies. These incentives are available in various forms, as follows:

Tax reduction tax relief is granted for the first eight years of business and consists of a reduction of 25% of the taxable income for companies which are likely to improve the general and regional balance of the economy.

Investment allowance of 12% is given on all new supplementary investment except for investment in real estate. A further 6% is granted on investments up to F.Lux 6m and a supplementary 2% on the surplus over F.Lux 6m.

Both the tax reduction and investment allowance are granted by law and may be reported over the subsequent ten years.

Upon special request, the government may allow tax relief for a maximum period of ten years on the taxable income of directors and managers living in Luxembourg.

A number of other allowances can be negotiated with the institutions of the European Commission.

Holding companies

A holding company is one which exists with the sole objective of the holding of investments. Luxembourg 1929 holding companies are exempt from all municipal and corporate income taxes, and pay only an annual subscription tax of 0.2% on the effective value of the shares they issue. Large holding companies, with assets in excess of

F.Lux 1,000,000,000, can apply for holding milliardaire status. They are then exempt from subscription tax. However, dividends, bonuses to directors and any interest paid are subject to tax as follows:

- interest on securities 3%;
- dividends and bonuses to directors 0.1% to 3%.

The minimum tax payable by a milliadaire company is F.Lux 2,000,000 per annum.

Collective investment undertakings, such as investment funds or investment companies, are exempt from all corporate income tax and are liable only to an annual subscription tax ranging from 0% to 0.06% on the net asset value.

Related party transactions

All transactions between related parties must be on an arm's length basis for tax purposes.

Losses

Losses arising during the year can be deducted from operating profits. Any unused balance of losses can be carried forward indefinitely.

Corporate groups

Under certain circumstances a controlled company's results may be added to those of a controlling parent company and taxed as a single company. This is only possible for tax purposes if a resident company is no longer under its own control, such as the financial, organisational and economical control is in the hands of the controlling parent. Financial control is exercised when the controlling company owns more than 99% of the voting shares of the subsidiary.

If the parent company owns 75% of the capital and if at least 75% of the other shareholders agree, the benefit of fiscal integration may be granted.

Capital taxes

Incorporation tax must be paid from the date of incorporation and on subsequent capital increases. This tax is deductible for income tax purposes. The rate is normally 1% on the subscribed capital.

Net worth tax must be paid each year and is calculated on the net assets. This tax is not deductible for income tax purposes. The rate is 0.5%.

Personal taxes

Taxable individuals

Residents

Individuals resident in Luxembourg are taxable on their worldwide income. An individual is treated as resident for income tax purposes if he is domiciled (i.e. has accommodation available for his use on a long term basis) or 'habitually resident', defined as present in Luxembourg other than for a temporary purpose for more than 183 days in any year. The tax year is the calendar year.

Non-residents

Non-resident individuals are taxable only on income arising in Luxembourg. Losses can be carried forward or offset against income from other categories. Income tax payable is on at least 15% of Luxembourg income, other than in the case of salaries and pensions.

Tax year and filing requirements

The tax year is the calendar year. Returns should be filed within three months of the end of the year. Postponement of filing is possible.

Taxes on income

Individuals are subject to income tax, capital gains tax and estate tax.

Taxable income is calculated by reference to specified categories, according to different rules, though losses made in one category may be offset against the income from another.

Sources of income

Employment income

In general, all income is taxable including all payments from an employer. Certain overtime payments are, however, exempt. A flat amount of F.Lux 21,000 plus a minimum of F.Lux 15,600 for travel expenses are deducted for expenses incurred in the course of employment. Benefits in kind are added to taxable income.

Business income

Business income comprises income from trade, commercial and industrial activity, except income from agricultural and certain professions. Profits on the disposal of assets are included in business income. Profits realised at the time of liquidation of part, or all, of the business are taxed at a reduced rate after deduction of an amount varying between F.Lux 400,000 and F.Lux 1,000,000.

Income from professions

Income from professions includes the earnings of medical doctors, architects, lawyers, auditors and directors of limited liability companies.

In principle, gains realised by those engaged in the 'liberal' professions on the disposal of the immovable property of their business are taxed at normal income tax rates, but such gains may be reinvested tax free within two years.

Capital gains

Capital gains are treated as income for tax purposes. Profits realised on the disposal of moveable property up to six months after its acquisition date, or profits realised on immovable property up to two years after its acquisition date, are treated as speculative profits and taxed at the normal income tax rates. Non-speculative gains on immovable property are usually taxed at half the normal rate.

Acquisition costs of assets are adjusted to take account of inflation.

This principle does not apply to profits realised on the disposal of the taxpayer's main residence and these gains are tax free, subject to conditions.

Gains from the disposal of investments amounting to 25% or more of a company's equity are taxable.

A special deduction of F.Lux 2,000,000 for the above (F.Lux 4,000,000 for married couples) is given once every ten years.

Gains realised on the disposal of other shares are treated as follows:

- taxed at normal tax rate if sold up to six months after their acquisition;
- tax-free if sold six months after their acquisition.

Luxembourg

Personal allowances and deduction

A number of allowances are available, but the most important is the standard deduction which amounts to F.Lux 18,000. The tax tables are adjusted to take family circumstances into account.

Rates of tax

The Luxembourg tax system for personal taxes is based on a high progression of tax rates. The tax rates applied depend on the family situation of the taxpayer (e.g. where married and a parent). The maximum rate payable is :

- 42% on taxable income + 2.5% unemployment contributions (year 2001);
- 38% on taxable income + 2.5% unemployment contributions (year 2002).

The following are examples of Luxembourg taxation for 2001 (including a 2.5% contribution to the unemployment fund):

Income (F.Lux)	*Tax class 1 (F.Lux)*	*Tax class 2 (F.Lux)*	*Tax class 2.2 (F.Lux)*
1,000,000	136,653	33,251	0
3,000,000	975,082	658,665	584,865
6,000,000	2,266,582	1,950,165	1,876,365

Notes

Tax Class 1: single;
Tax Class 2: married without children;
Tax Class 2.2: married with two children.

Withholding tax

There is currently no withholding tax on interest of any kind paid in Luxembourg. An allowance of F.Lux 60,000 (or F.Lux 120,000 under collective taxation) is granted on all investment income.

Dividends paid by resident companies are subject to a withholding tax of 25%.

Losses

Losses from a business or profession can be carried forward without limit. The offset of other losses is restricted.

Special family rules

The family is treated as a unit for tax rate purposes (see under 'Rates of Tax').

Estate and gift taxes

The worldwide property of an individual domiciled in Luxembourg at the time of his death is subject to estate duty. Rates vary according to the nature of the relationship with the beneficiary and the value of the estate. The heirs of non-resident individuals pay tax only on property located in Luxembourg.

Individuals (Heirs)	*Resident (%)*	*Non-resident (%)*
Direct descendants	nil	10–12
Spouse with children	nil	10–15
Spouse without children	5	10–15
Brothers and sisters	6	10–16
Others	10–15	10–15

Lifetime gifts made by domiciled individuals are taxable at rates varying from 1.8% to 14.4% and tax is payable by the notary who deals with registration of the gift.

Wealth tax

Individuals resident in Luxembourg are subject to wealth tax on their net worldwide assets at 0.5% per annum subject to an allowance of F.Lux 100,000 for the taxpayer, his spouse and each child.

Social security

Social security contributions are payable by employer and employee at approximately 13% and 10% respectively of gross remuneration up to a maximum of approximately F.Lux 234,390.

Other taxes

VAT

A value added tax (VAT) is levied on most sales of goods and services at a standard rate of 15%. An intermediate rate of 12% applies to some goods and services including fuel, tobacco and professional services. A reduced rate of 3% applies to certain food, books and transportation and of 6% to gas and electricity.

Exchange controls

Luxembourg has no exchange controls.

Foreign income

In order to avoid the double taxation of income, Luxembourg applies both exemption and credit systems. The exemption system applies to agricultural and commercial revenues, professional income salaries and rent. Under this system Luxembourg uses a progression clause and taxes payable on income in Luxembourg are calculated on the worldwide income of the resident taxpayer. The credit system is applied to all dividends, interest and royalties received from abroad.

Withholding taxes

Luxembourg withholds a 25% tax on dividends distributed to shareholders, except for 1929 holding companies where no tax is withheld at source. No withholding tax is applied to interest. In order to avoid double taxation and in certain cases to reduce the withholding tax rate, Luxembourg has entered into double taxation treaties. The following table shows the rates of withholding tax currently in force:

Country of residence	*Royalties* (%)	*Dividends* (%)
Non-treaty countries	12	25
Treaty countries:		
Austria	nil/10	0(c)
Belgium	nil	0(c)
Brazil	25/15	0
Bulgaria	5	5
Canada	10/0	10
China	10/6	5
Czech Republic	10/0	5
Denmark	nil	0(c)
Finland	nil/5	0(c)
France	nil	0(c)
Germany	5	0(c)
Greece	7/5	0(c)
Hungary	0	5
Indonesia	12.5/10	10
Ireland	nil	0(c)
Italy	10	0(c)
Japan	10	5
Malta	10	0

Morocco	10	10(a)
Netherlands	nil	0(c)
Norway	nil	5(a)
Romania	10	5
Singapore	10/6	5
Slovakia	10/0	5
South Korea	10/12	10(a)
Spain	10	0(c)
Sweden	nil	0(c)
Switzerland	nil	0/5
Thailand	15	5/15
Tunisia	12	10
Vietnam	10	5/10
United Kingdom	5	0(c)
United States	nil	0/5(d)

Notes

(a) Recipient company owns at least 25%.

(b) Recipient company owns alone or with other subsidiary companies 10%.

(c) As a result of the implementation of the EC Parent-Subsidiary Directive there should be no withholding tax levied on distributions made to a parent company resident in an EC member state provided a substantial interest (i.e. 25% or more) has been held for at least two years.

(d) The 5% applies if the recipient company has either sole ownership, or ownership with other subsidiary companies of 10%. The 0% applies if the US recipient has held more than 25% of the voting rights for an uninterrupted period of two years.

Malawi

Graham Carr

Corporate taxes

Income of companies

Basis

Taxable income of a company is accounting profit excluding capital items, adjusted for non-allowable and tax free items and capital allowances. These adjustments are calculated in the same manner as for a non-incorporated business run by a sole trader or partnership. The year in which assessable income is charged to tax is on the same basis as for unincorporated businesses.

Income tax rates

	2000/01	*99/2000 & 97/99*	*96/97 & 95/96*
Locally incorporated companies	35%	38%	38%
Locally incorporated companies (export processing zones)	0%	0%	0%
Locally incorporated companies (priority industries)	0% to 15%	0% or 15%	–
Branches of companies not locally incorporated	40%	43%	43%
Life assurance business	21%	24%	24%

The 1996/97 and 1995/96 rates include a temporary drought levy of 3%. The word temporary has now been removed since 1 April 1997. The 0% income tax rate for priority industries shall apply for a period not exceeding 10 years (or as the Minister may designate).

Minimum (turnover) tax

The following represent minimum amounts of tax payable by companies in business from the year 2000/01:

Income banding		*Tax payable*
Income exceeding	*but not exceeding*	
MK 200,000	MK 200,000	MK 5,000
	MK 500,000	MK 25,000
MK 500,000	MK 500,000	MK 50,000
MK 2,000,000	MK 5,000,000	MK 100,000

Dividends and management fees

A dividend received by one Malawi company from another is treated as taxed income in the receiving company and is not included when computing taxable profits of that company. The effect of this is that if a dividend is paid to a loss making company, there can be an overall tax disadvantage to the group as the dividend cannot be used to reduce the loss, and this has had an effect on the tax planning of groups of companies in Malawi.

Groups of companies favour charging management fees around the group to reflect services carried out by one company for another. Management fees are currently treated as allowable expenses if the companies involved can demonstrate that they are bona fide charges and are not merely tax saving devices.

Dividend tax account

All companies incorporated in Malawi are to maintain a dividend tax account from 1 April 1992. The account, which is carried forward from year to year, is operated as follows:

- it is opened with seven thirteenths (7/13) of the retained profits at 1 April 1992;
- it is increased by the amount of all income taxes paid on the taxable income of the company; and
- it is reduced by the amount of income tax which relates to dividends distributed by the company, using the rate of tax applicable to companies at the date of distribution (currently 35%).

If the distribution of a dividend would result in the dividend tax account of a company being reduced to below zero, the company must pay additional income tax for the year of assessment within which the dividend is distributed, sufficient to bring the resulting negative balance to at least zero.

Export processing zones and priority industries

To encourage exports, certain areas have been designated Export Processing Zones. In addition from 1997/98, certain industries have been designated as Priority industries. Exporters within these zones and companies within these industries enjoyed the following income tax benefits:

- the corporate tax rate is reduced to 0% indefinitely for companies in export processing zones and for a period up to ten years (or as the Minister may direct) for priority industries; certain priority industries will continue to pay tax at a reduced rate of 15%;
- no duty on capital equipment and raw materials;
- no excise taxes on purchases of raw materials and packaging materials; and
- no surtaxes (value added tax).

Capital allowances

The following capital allowances are currently granted by the Commissioner General in respect of capital expenditure on assets used for the purpose of the taxpayer's trade.

Investment allowances

These are given on new and used industrial buildings, industrial plant and machinery, and farm fencing. A rate of 40% is given on new items and 20% on used items. Investment allowances can only be claimed if the assets are brought into use during the year of assessment and used in the process of manufacture (including farming). They are deducted from the tax value.

If investment allowance is claimed, the taxpayer may not also claim an initial allowance in that year.

Initial allowances

These are granted in the year the assets are brought into use in respect of the following items of capital expenditure at the following rates:

• plant and machinery	20%
• office equipment, fixtures and fittings	20%
• motor vehicles (excluding private passenger vehicles)	20%
• farm implements	20%
• computers	20%
• industrial buildings	10%

Initial allowances and annual allowances may both be claimed together and are both based on the tax value.

Annual allowances

These are granted each year as long as the asset remains in use in the taxpayers trade. They are calculated by the reducing balance method (except where indicated) at the following annual rates:

• industrial buildings	5%
• plant and machinery	10-25%
• office equipment, fixtures and fittings	10%
• motor vehicles, saloon cars etc.	20%
• vans, lorries, pick-ups, buses, trucks, etc.	25-33%
• farm implements/fencing	10%
• farm improvements	5%
• computers (straight-line basis on original cost)	20%

These rates may be increased for, say, multi-shift usage of plant and machinery. In certain circumstances, tractors and motor vehicles used extensively may attract capital allowances up to 33%.

Industrial buildings

Industrial buildings include buildings used for the following purposes:

- making an article, subjecting goods or materials to a manufacturing process;
- hotels;
- processing or distributing fish;
- transport, dock, electricity or bridge undertaking; or
- any other activity declared by the Minister of Finance to be making an important contribution to the national development.

Specifically excluded as industrial buildings are retail shops, warehouses, offices and dwelling houses. Where an industrial building includes office accommodation, as long as expenditure on offices does not exceed 20% of the total expenditure on the building, the entire building is treated as an industrial building.

Manufacturers or farmers may also include staff housing used by the full time employees as industrial buildings and claim capital allowances accordingly. In the case of staff housing, used by people who can control 5% or more of the voting equity, only one third of normal capital allowances is granted.

A manufacturer is defined as the owner of a business carried on in an industrial building as defined below and the owner of a plantation producing tobacco, tea, sugar, coffee or any crop approved by the Minister of Finance.

Export allowances

For all exporters, including manufacturing in bond, the following income, and other, tax benefits are available:

- an amount of 12% of export revenues for non-traditional exports (ie. other than tobacco, tea, coffee, and sugar) is allowable as a deduction when calculating taxable profits to taxpayers who should register with the Malawi Export Promotion Council;
- an amount of 25% of international transport costs is allowable as a deduction when calculating taxable profits;
- no duties on the imports of capital equipment used mainly in the manufacture of exports;
- no surtaxes (valued added tax);
- no excise taxes on the purchase of raw materials and packaging materials made in Malawi; and
- no duties on capital items and raw materials.

Training allowance

An amount of 50% of the costs incurred by a taxpayer during the year of assessment in training an employee is allowable as a deduction in the calculation of taxable profits. To qualify, the employee being trained must be a Malawian and the training must be to enable the employee to attain a qualification at degree, diploma or certificate level.

Designated areas

A taxpayer who is eligible for an investment allowance shall, in addition, be given an allowance of 15% for the investment in an area designated for the purpose of such an allowance by the Minister of Finance.

Fringe benefits tax

Description

'Fringe benefit' means any asset, service or other benefit in kind provided by, or on behalf of, an employer to an employee, if such benefit includes an element of personal benefit to the employee.

Benefits in kind are taxable on the employer paying the benefit at the rate of company income tax. The recipient of the benefit is not liable to tax on the benefit and the tax is not an allowable expense for the determination of taxable income of the employer.

Employers should, within the month they begin to provide benefits to employees, register with the Commissioner General by completing a fringe benefits tax form, and the tax is payable on a calendar quarterly basis.

The employer should keep records showing the nature of the benefits provided, the names of those receiving the benefits, and the taxable value of the benefits. Employers do not have to calculate and pay fringe benefits tax where the beneficiary of the fringe benefits is an employee whose annual taxable income does not exceed MK 5,000.

An employer who fails to register, or to pay fringe benefits tax due, shall be liable to a penalty of 20% of the fringe benefits tax due.

The following is a summary of the tax treatment of common benefits in kind:

- free housing is taxed according to scales set by the Commissioner General; the taxable value is calculated as the higher of the following:
  - for property rented by the employer, the rent actually paid, or for a property owned by the employer, the open market rental value;
  - for furnished housing 12% of employee's gross salary;
  - for unfurnished housing, 10% of employee's gross salary; or
  - the taxable value may be reduced by the amount of any contribution made by the employee; the taxable value may be further reduced by 50% where the accommodation is owned by the employer;
- personal use of company vehicle is taxed according to scales by the Commissioner General; the taxable value is 15% of cost effective from 1 July 1998;
- the taxable value may be reduced by the amount of any contribution made by the employee;
- school fees are taxed at 50% of the cost of fees and related expenses paid directly to the Institution;

- travel fares from the country of recruitment to Malawi at the beginning and end of a contract are not taxable as long as the contract has been approved by the Commissioner General; other travel for holidays paid by the employer is taxable on the employer at cost, even if the employee's contract states that he is entitled to such benefit;
- in the case where cash is given to enable employees to meet excess expenses, as opposed to that which is normally applicable as per the employer's stipulated benefits, such cash excess is a taxable benefit; and
- for other fringe benefits, including electricity, water, security guards, household items, watchmen, gardeners and any other provisions, the taxable value is the cost to the employer less any contribution from the employee. However, where the property is owned by the employer, the cost of a gardener, security guard and watchman shall not be classed as taxable benefits.

Companies and self-employed persons

The tax is payable by quarterly provisional payments within 14 days of the calendar quarter. Seasonal income earners can apply to the Commissioner for special payment dates. Any additional tax arising at the year end (ie. after computation) is payable on filing of the tax return.

At the beginning of every year of assessment, each taxpayer must estimate the total amount of income tax that is likely to be payable by him in that year of assessment.

The total provisional tax estimated should not be less than 90% of the actual tax liability for the year of assessment.

There are penalties for failure to operate provisional tax and for underpayments.

Provisional tax need not be paid by individuals whose taxable income for the year is estimated not to exceed MK 30,000 or whose income exceeds MK 30,000, but is derived from employment or pension from which PAYE tax is being deducted, or a combination of these two situations – which includes non-employment income and exceeds MK 30,000 or non-pension income of not more than MK 30,000.

Withholding tax

When making certain payments, as listed below, the payer must deduct the percentage specified from the amount being paid and remit the amount so deducted to the Department of Taxes. When making the deduction, a triple copy Withholding Tax Certificate must be completed and the original copy (A) sent to the Inspector of Taxes, the second copy (B), sent along with the balance of payment to the person being paid, and the third copy (C), retained.

Contained in the Taxation Amendment Act, with effect from 1 April 1997, the issuing of a withholding tax exemption certificate was abolished, rendering all payments listed below subject to withholding tax. However, in a subsequent press release the government has changed this provision and companies and individuals operating a business are now free to apply for a Withholding Tax Exemption Certificate.

If the recipient of a payment holds a valid Withholding Tax Exemption Certificate or is a non-taxable person, withholding tax should not be deducted. This applies to all payments other than rent, bank interest, royalties, fees, commissions and payment of casual labour.

Rates applicable

The following rates apply from 1 April 1997:

Royalties	20%
Rents	20%
Payment of over MK 1,000 for any supplies to traders and institutions under tender or similar arrangement:	
– foodstuff (effective from 1 April 1998 as per Taxation (Amendment) Act 1998)	7%
– other	10%
Fees and commissions	20%
Carriage and haulage	10%
Payment of over MK 1,000 for tobacco and other farm products (effective 1 April 1998)	7%
Payment to contractors and sub-contractors	10%
Payment for public entertainment	20%
Payment for casual labour or services of over MK 500	20%
Bank interest in excess of MK 500	20%
Interest of treasury bills, stock, bonds, or promissory notes raised by, or for, the Government	15%

Withholding tax suffered may be offset against tax charged on the taxpayer's income tax assessment.

Failure to deduct any withholding tax renders the holder personally liable to pay the amount and remit a 20% penalty.

Malawi branches of non-resident companies

Branches of non-resident companies operating in Malawi are taxed on their profits at the rate of tax for companies plus 5%, giving a current rate of 40%. In respect of all other taxation matters, they are treated in a similar manner to Malawi incorporated companies.

Personal taxes

Liability of non-resident to Malawi tax

Non-resident individuals who have income arising in Malawi are liable to tax in Malawi at the rate of 15% on that income. It will normally be necessary for tax to be paid on such income before the exchange control authorities will grant permission for remittance of such income.

Companies incorporated in Malawi in which there are non-resident shareholders are taxed at the same rate of tax as Malawi-owned companies. However dividends remitted to non-resident shareholders were subject to a surcharge of 15% until 31 March 1995. This provision was removed from 1 April 1995.

Position of individuals and companies carrying out short term contracts in Malawi

As a general rule, a non-resident of Malawi employed by a non-resident employer to work in Malawi for periods of less than six months (for example a consultant) is not liable to pay tax in Malawi on that income where a Double Taxation Agreement applies. Non-resident companies which operate in Malawi on a one-off basis (for example a short building contract) are liable to tax in Malawi on the basis of profits arising in Malawi on that contract.

Income of individuals

Taxable income is defined as assessable income less allowable expenses. In the case of employees, the principal source of assessable income is salaries. Employers do not have to operate PAYE on salaries which are not more than MK 24,000 per annum, inclusive of overtime and taxable allowances.

Income tax rates

The following bandings apply to individuals:

	2000/2001	
	Band	*Rate*
First	24,000	0%
Next	18,000	15%
Next	18,000	25%
Excess over	60,000	35%

Income of individuals from unincorporated businesses

Taxable income of such individuals is based on their profit and loss accounts adjusted for any non-allowable items and capital allowances, losses and gains and the tax is at the rates set out above.

Minimum (turnover) tax

The following represent minimum amounts of tax payable by individual taxpayers in business from 1 July 1999.

Income banding				*Tax payable*
Income		not exceeding	MK 100,000	nil
Exceeding	MK 100,000	but not exceeding	MK 500,000	MK 5,000
Exceeding	MK 500,000	but not exceeding	MK 1,00,000	MK 7,500
Exceeding	MK 1,000,000			MK 10,000

Filing of income tax returns

Individuals

It is mandatory for employees who earn more than MK 30,000 per annum to prepare and deliver a tax return. Tax returns are made up to 30 June, the last day of the tax year (31 March up until 1996/97 tax year) and are required to be submitted by 31 December. A penalty of MK 1,000 is charged for late submission of an income tax return.

Businesses

Business income tax returns are to be filed within a period of 180 days after the end of the accounting year.

Payments

Individuals in employment

Employees who receive weekly or monthly salaries have tax deducted under the Pay-As-You-Earn (PAYE) scheme. Employers must pay the tax to the Collector of Taxes by the 14th of the month following the deduction. Any shortfall in the PAYE deducted during the year is payable by the employer and recoverable from the employees.

Every employer shall, within 45 days after the end of each year of assessment, furnish the Commissioner with duly completed Tax Deducted (PAYE) Certificates.

Interest on overdue tax is charged at 15% plus a penalty at the rate of 5% of the overdue amount for every month the tax remains unpaid.

Other taxes

Surtax

Surtax is payable by all manufacturers of taxable goods and suppliers of taxable services. The general rate is 20%, although there are some exceptions. Surtax is administered by the Department of Customs and Excise of the Malawi Revenue Authority.

Stamp duties and fees

The following are the current rates of the more common stamp duties and fees in Malawi:

Incorporation of a company

Registration of authorised capital

An amount of MK 50 for the first MK 1,000 authorised capital, plus MK 15 for each subsequent MK 2,000 authorised share capital or part thereof is payable.

Memorandum of Association and Articles of Association of a company

An amount of MK 100 is payable.

Increase in authorised capital of a company

An amount of MK 20 per MK 2,000 authorised nominal share capital or part thereof is payable.

Transfer of shares

No stamp duty has been payable since 2 April 1992.

Estate duty

The value of the estate comprises all assets of the deceased at the date of his death less funeral expenses and debts due at the date of death. In addition, any gifts or transfers of property for less than full value made within three years of death must be included in the value of the estate.

Duty is payable by the executors of estates of deceased individuals based on the value of the estate subject to detailed rules as to succession.

Airport tax

A charge of US$ 20 is made for each non-resident passenger and MK 150 for each Malawian passport holder or foreign passport holder with a Permanent Residence Permit leaving the country on an outward trip by plane. It is collected at the airport at the time of departure.

Property tax (rates)

This is levied by local authorities on the value of all properties, whether commercial or private, owned by a taxpayer in that district. They are payable half yearly, generally in June and December.

Hotel and food tax

This is charged at the rate of 10% on the cost of hotel accommodation and meals.

Double taxation agreements

Malawi currently has double taxation agreements with the following countries:

Denmark

France

Kenya

Netherlands

Malawi

Norway

Republic of South Africa

Sweden

Switzerland

United Kingdom

United States of America

As a general rule, income which would be taxed both in Malawi and another country is only taxed once under these agreements.

Malaysia

Robert Teo, Kuan & Co.

(Readers: please note, that the information here was correct at January 1999)

Corporate taxes

Basis of taxation

Resident companies

A company is resident in Malaysia for tax purposes if its management and control are exercised in Malaysia. Generally, a company is considered resident in Malaysia if the meetings of its Board of Directors are held in Malaysia, even if the companies are not incorporated in Malaysia.

Resident companies are liable to income tax on income accruing in or derived from Malaysia. Foreign income received in Malaysia by a resident company is not subject to Malaysian income tax. However, resident companies carrying on the business of banking, insurance and air and sea transport operations are taxed on worldwide income whether or not the income is received in Malaysia.

Non-resident companies

Non-resident companies are liable to income tax on income accruing in or derived from Malaysia. Foreign income received in Malaysia is not subject to Malaysian income tax.

Tax year and filing requirements

The tax year is the calendar year, but a company may adopt any accounting period as its financial year. Tax returns are normally issued to taxpayers in late February or March of each calendar year.

Companies must complete and submit their returns within 30 days of issue or within an extended date approved by the Malaysian Inland Revenue. Companies with a financial year ending prior to 30 September are normally allowed up to 31 May of the following year to submit their tax returns. In the absence of a return, the Inland Revenue may raise an estimated assessment.

Taxes imposed

All taxes on income are imposed at national level.

Payment of tax

Income tax is normally payable within 30 days after the service of a notice of assessment notwithstanding any appeals or objections. However, companies with an annual tax liability exceeding RM 1,000 are required to pay tax in five bi-monthly instalments for each year of assessment based on their estimated tax liability.

Rates of tax

The rate of income taxes for companies whether resident or not is 28%. However, for certain companies that are not resident in Malaysia, interest income is taxed at the rate of 15% under the double taxation agreements between Malaysia and the countries concerned. For companies carrying on petroleum operations the tax rate is 38%.

Income subject to tax

General rules

Income subject to tax is based on generally approved accounting standards as adjusted by specific rules provided in the Income Tax Act and is assessed in Malaysian Ringgit (RM).

Only expenses which are incurred wholly and exclusively in the production of income are deductible. Taxable income is determined after deducting allowable expenses, capital allowances and any other reliefs allowed under the Income Tax Act. The method of determining commercial profits should be consistent from year to year but can be changed if justified by sound business practice, provided the purpose of the change is not one of tax avoidance.

Stock/inventory valuation

Stock must be valued at the lower of cost or market value. Base stock and LIFO methods are not acceptable.

Capital gains and losses

Any gain on the disposal of chargeable assets is subject to real property gains tax. Chargeable assets include the following:

- real properties situated in Malaysia;
- shares held in a Real Property Company (RPC).

An RPC is a 'controlled company' which owns real property, shares, or both in another RPC, the market value of which is more than 75% of the value of its total tangible assets. A 'controlled company' is a company with not more than 50 members controlled by not more than five persons.

Apart from the above, there is no capital gains tax in Malaysia.

Dividends

No withholding tax is imposed on dividends paid by a Malaysian company. Malaysia adopts an imputation system of taxing corporate income. The income tax paid by a company on its profits is utilised to frank dividends paid to shareholders.

A Malaysian company paying a dividend to its shareholders is required to deduct the underlying tax at a rate of 28% on the gross dividend. This underlying tax is available as a credit for resident shareholders against their individual or corporate income tax liability.

Dividends received from Malaysian sources are taxed at the full corporate tax rate. The tax deducted at source from the Malaysian dividends is available to offset against the tax on the dividends.

Capital gains made upon the disposal of long term investments are not taxable except where they relate to investments made in an RPC (as defined above).

Deductions

General rules

Expenses incurred wholly and exclusively in the production of gross income from a business are deductible against the gross income. Certain expenses are specifically disallowed under the Malaysian Income Tax Act.

Depreciation and amortisation

Various methods of depreciation and amortisation are permitted provided that they are in accordance with generally accepted accounting principles and sound business practice. The depreciation and amortisation of tangible fixed assets is based on historical or re-valued cost.

Methods normally accepted are:

- straight-line;
- reducing balance;
- depreciation on the basis of the utilisation of the asset.

Acceptable rates are:

- office equipment, furniture and fittings – 10%-20%;
- motor vehicles – 10%-20%;
- buildings – 2%.

Certain assets, such as freehold land, are not depreciated.

Royalties

Royalties are deductible as business expenses if they are incurred in the production of income.

Interest

In general, interest expense incurred wholly and exclusively in the production of gross income is allowable as a deduction for tax purposes. The deductibility of interest on borrowed money which is also used for non-business purposes is restricted to the extent of the borrowings used to finance non-business assets.

Bad and doubtful debts

Bad debts and provision for specific trade debts are deductible against business income.

Reserves and provisions

In general, reserves and general provisions are not allowed. They can only be allowed when actually incurred wholly and exclusively in the production of gross income.

Employees' and directors' remuneration and benefits

Employees' and directors' remuneration and benefits are generally deductible. However, leave passages and entertainment allowance given to employees or directors are not deductible.

Specifically non-deductible expenses

Specifically non-deductible expenses include the following:

- domestic or private expenses;
- lease rentals exceeding RM 50,000 for a motor vehicle which is not licensed for commercial use;
- employer's contributions to an unapproved pension, provident or savings schemes;
- employer's contributions to approved pension schemes in excess of 19% of the employee's gross remuneration;
- entertainment expenses and entertainment allowances;
- cost of leave passages for employees;
- non-approved donations;
- interest or royalty or contract payment derived from Malaysia from which withholding tax has not been deducted and remitted to the Malaysian Inland Revenue;
- certain other expenses specifically not allowed under the Malaysian Income Tax Act.

Foreign source income

Foreign source income is not taxable if received in Malaysia by a resident company. Foreign source income received by a company not resident in Malaysia is not taxable.

Investment incentives and special benefits

Incentives are provided under the Promotion of Investments Act 1986 and the Income Tax Act 1967. The main incentives are as follows:

- pioneer status;
- investment tax allowance;
- reinvestment allowance;
- industrial adjustment allowance;

- double deduction of certain expenses;
- incentives for:
  - approved agricultural projects;
  - tour operators;
  - approved investments;
  - overseas construction sectors;
  - research and development.

Related party transactions

Transactions between companies or other parties under common control may be ignored if they are not carried out on an arm's length basis.

Losses

Current business loss may be offset against income from any source for the same year. Unabsorbed business losses brought forward can be utilised only against the statutory income from all business sources of subsequent years.

Losses can be carried forward indefinitely until permanent cessation of the business.

Unused capital allowance can be carried forward for use against the adjusted same source income of subsequent years. Unabsorbed capital allowances can be carried forward indefinitely. In the event that a business source ceases, the unabsorbed capital allowance remains permanently lost.

Corporate groups

There is no group relief for losses in Malaysia other than group relief for companies involved in approved livestock farming and the cultivation of approved crops that have been identified for group relief. Group relief is only available for application to an approved project submitted to the Ministry of Agriculture before 31 December 1999.

Tax free mergers and disposals

Mergers are not taxable except where the properties or investments in an RPC are involved (as defined above). However, exemption can be obtained if certain conditions are satisfied, particularly when the merger meets the government's policy on capital participation and the 'Malaysianisation' of companies.

Liquidation of company

Distribution on liquidation is not subject to tax in the hands of the shareholders.

Taxes on capital

Capital duty

Capital duty is levied on the authorised issued capital of a company.

Net worth tax

There is no annual net worth tax levied on companies.

Treatment of branches (branch profits tax)

Branches of foreign companies in Malaysia are subject to income tax at 28% on their income derived from Malaysia. Interest is taxed at a rate of 15% except where a different rate is provided under a double taxation treaty with the country concerned.

Personal taxes

Taxable individuals

The extent to which the income of an individual is subject to Malaysian income tax depends on the resident status of the individual.

Residents

The resident status of an individual is determined by his physical presence in Malaysia. An individual is regarded as resident for tax purposes if he satisfies one of the following conditions:

- he is present in Malaysia within the relevant calendar year for a period or periods amounting to 182 days or more;
- he is present in Malaysia within the relevant calendar year for a period of less than 182 days, but was present for 182 or more consecutive days as follows:

- in the calendar year immediately preceding the relevant calendar year;
- in the calendar year immediately following the relevant calendar year;

a temporary absence from Malaysia shall be included in the 182 days where the temporary absence is for the following purposes:

- in connection with his service in Malaysia and owing to service matters or attending conferences or seminars or study abroad,
- owing to ill health involving himself or a member of his immediate family,
- in respect of social visits not exceeding 14 days in aggregate;

- he is in Malaysia in the relevant calendar year for a period or periods amounting in all to 90 days or more, having been with respect to each of any three of the calendar years for the four years of assessment immediately preceding that particular year of assessment, either:
  - resident in Malaysia,
  - present in Malaysia for a period or periods amounting in all to 90 days or more in the calendar year in question;
- he is resident in Malaysia for the calendar year subsequent to the relevant year, having been so resident for each of the three calendar years immediately preceding the relevant year.

Non-residents

Non-residents are subject to income tax on income accruing in or derived from Malaysia. Foreign income received by non-residents in Malaysia is not liable to income tax.

Tax year and filing requirements

Income tax is levied on income accruing in the calendar year which is the basis year for a year of assessment. A business carried out by an individual may adopt an accounting period other than the calendar year.

Tax returns are normally issued to taxpayers in late February or March of each calendar year. Taxpayers must complete and submit the returns within 30 days of issue or within an extension period approved by the Malaysian Inland Revenue. In the absence of a return, the Inland Revenue may raise an estimated assessment.

Taxes on income

Income tax is levied at national level. Individuals with an annual tax liability exceeding RM 1,000 must pay their tax liability in five bi-monthly instalments as specified by the Inland Revenue. For employed individuals with an annual liability exceeding RM 500, payments are by monthly salary deductions.

In any other case, income tax is normally payable within 30 days after the service of a notice of assessment notwithstanding any appeals or objections.

Payment of tax

Individuals with an annual tax liability exceeding RM 1,000 must pay their tax liabilities in five bi-monthly instalments as specified by the Inland Revenue.

In any other case, tax raised must be settled within 30 days of the service of an assessment notwithstanding any appeals.

Payroll deductions

For employed individuals with an annual tax liability exceeding RM 500, payments are by monthly salary deduction.

Prepayments

It is the Malaysian Inland Revenue's policy to collect tax in advance in respect of expatriate employees (pay-as-you-earn scheme).

Payments are by salary deduction. The amount deducted is offset against the final tax payable.

The Director General of the Inland Revenue is empowered to issue a provisional assessment in the absence of a tax return.

Sources of income

Employment income and directors' fees

An employee (including a director) employed in Malaysia is taxable on his full remuneration for such employment, notwithstanding that part of his income may be paid to him outside Malaysia. Most benefits-in-kind are taxable.

Deductions are available in respect of subscriptions to professional bodies and employees' contributions to an approved provident or pension fund.

Business income and losses

Taxable income is calculated in accordance with generally accepted accounting standards as adjusted by specific rules provided in the Income Tax Act. A business may adopt any accounting period as its financial year.

Losses

An individual's current business loss (adjusted) can be utilised against any other sources of income in the same basis year. Unutilised business loss can be offset against income from all business sources in subsequent years.

Losses can be carried forward indefinitely until permanent cessation of the business.

Unutilised capital allowance can be carried forward to be utilised against the adjusted income of subsequent years from the same business source. Unabsorbed capital allowance can be carried forward indefinitely. In the event that a business source ceases, the unabsorbed capital allowance remains permanently lost.

Dividends

Malaysia adopts the imputation system of taxation whereby tax paid by a company on its profits is utilised to frank dividends paid to shareholders.

Dividends received are net of tax (i.e. tax is deducted at source at 28%). However, individuals are required to declare the gross dividend received in their tax returns. The tax deducted at source from the dividend is offset against the tax payable. In cases where the tax deducted is in excess of the tax payable, the difference is refunded to the individual.

Interest

Withholding tax at the rate of 5% is required to be withheld and remitted to the Inland Revenue in respect of interest paid to a resident individual by an approved bank, finance company or institution. However, their certain interest is specifically exempted from withholding tax or income tax. Most interest income is taxable when it is paid or credited.

Rentals

Rental received from the letting of properties is subject to income tax. Deductions are allowed for expenses incurred such as quit rent, assessment, insurance, interest on loans obtained to finance the property, maintenance of the property, etc.

Royalties

Royalties paid to a non-resident individual attract a 10% withholding tax. Income received by an individual resident in Malaysia from royalties or payments in respect of the following is exempt from tax:

- publication of, or the use of or the right to use, any literary work or any original painting (amount exempted RM 20,000);
- publication of, or the use of or the right to use, any artistic work and recording discs or tapes (amount exempted RM 6,000).

Social security benefits

Social security contributions are payable by both the employer and employee. No tax relief is given to the employees on their contributions.

Pensions and annuities

Pensions received by an individual who is a resident in Malaysia are exempt from income tax, in the following circumstances:

- on reaching the age of 55;
- on reaching the compulsory age of retirement from employment specified under any written law.

Where a person receives more than one pension, the exemption is only applicable to the larger pension.

Payments received by way of an annuity are generally subject to income tax.

Exempt income

Incomes which are exempt from tax are provided for specifically under the Income Tax Act and the Promotion of Investments Act. They include the following:

- death gratuities;
- compensation for loss of employment and payments for restrictive covenants;
- interest on government securities or bonds and corporate bonds;
- income from employment exercised in Malaysia for a period not exceeding 60 days;
- income up to RM 12,000 per annum from translation of any musical composition, books or literary work;
- other income exempted from income tax as specifically provided in the Income Tax Act and the Promotion of Investments Act.

Capital gains and losses

The provisions for capital gains and losses for corporations also apply to individuals. Capital gains on the disposal of long term investments are not taxable except where they relate to investments made in an RPC (as defined above).

Foreign source income

Foreign income received in Malaysia by an individual resident in Malaysia is taxable. Bilateral or unilateral relief is given if the foreign income has suffered tax in the foreign country.

Foreign income received in Malaysia by an individual not resident in Malaysia is not taxable.

Personal allowances and deductions

The reliefs available to an individual resident in Malaysia are summarised as follows:

	RM
Personal and dependant relief	5,000
Wife relief	3,000
Child relief:	
— per child	800
— per handicapped child	5,000

Enhanced child relief for children above 18 years old who are studying at universities, colleges or similar establishments in Malaysia (four times normal relief)	3,200
Insurance premiums/approved fund contributions (maximum)	5,000
Insurance premiums for education and medical benefits (maximum)	2,000
Medical expenses incurred in respect of parents (maximum)	5,000
Cost of support equipment for a disabled person (maximum)	5,000

No reliefs are available to a non-resident person.

Income tax rebates for individuals

Individual

A rebate of RM 110 is given to an individual against his tax payable if his chargeable income does not exceed RM 10,000. The same rebate applies to a wife who is assessed separately.

Wife

A further rebate of RM 60 is given if a wife has no income or where the wife elects for combined assessment and combined chargeable income does not exceed RM 10,000.

Income tax rebate for islamic religious dues

Full rebate is given against the tax payable in respect of Islamic religious dues paid.

Purchase of computers

A tax rebate of RM 400 is granted to an individual who has purchased a personal computer. The tax rebate can only be enjoyed once in every five years and is limited to one computer per family.

Levy

Any individual who has paid a fee (levy) for the issue of an Employment Pass, Visit Pass (Temporary Employment) or Work Pass is entitled to claim that fee as a rebate against the income tax payable by the individual employee.

Special family rules

A wife's income from all sources is separately assessed from that of her husband unless she elects for her income to be combined with that of her husband. A wife assessed separately from her husband is entitled to the same personal reliefs as that of her husband except for the children's relief which is given to the person maintaining the children. Where a wife is assessed separately, her husband is not entitled to any wife relief.

Special treatment for expatriates

There is no special treatment for expatriates. The extent to which an expatriate individual is taxed depends on his resident status.

Rates of tax

General – resident and non-resident

For residents, the rate of tax is on a graduated scale on the chargeable income after deduction of reliefs. Rates of tax are as follows:

Chargeable income	*RM*	*Rate (%)*	*Tax RM*
On the first	2,500	0	0
On the next	2.500	2	50
On the first	5,000		50
On the next	5,000	4	200
On the first	10,000		250
On the next	10,000	6	600
On the first	20,000		850
On the next	15,000	10	1,500
On the first	35,000		2,350
On the next	15,000	16	2,400
On the first	50,000		4,750
On the next	20,000	21	4,200
On the first	70,000		8,950
On the next	30,000	26	7,800
On the first	100,000		16,750
On the next	50,000	29	14,500
On the first	150,000		31,250
In excess of	150,000	30	

For non-residents, the rates of tax are as follows:

	Rate (%)
Business, employment and other income	30
Royalties	10*
Rental of moveable properties	10*
Technical or management fee	10*
Interest	15*

* The rates of tax may vary in accordance with the double tax treaties which Malaysia has signed with the countries concerned.

Provincial and local taxes

The federal government levies income tax in Malaysia. There are no provincial and local taxes on income. However, the state governments impose assessment and quit rent on properties and licence fees for various businesses carried out within their municipalities.

Withholding taxes

Withholding tax must be withheld and remitted to the Inland Revenue within 30 days of payment or crediting in respect of the following payments made to non-residents:

	Rate (%)
Interest	15
Royalties	10
Remuneration of public entertainer	15
Special classes of income under Section 4A of the Malaysian Income Tax Act, 1967	10
(the above tax is a final tax and the rate of tax may be varied in accordance with the double tax treaties which Malaysia has signed with the countries concerned).	
Non-resident contractor, consultant or professional in respect of the service portion on contract payments	20
The above tax will be treated as payment on account of the following taxes:	
Tax liability of non-resident contractor, consultant or professional	15
Tax liability of employees of the non-resident contractor, consultant or professional	5
	20

Estate and gift taxes

Estate duty has been abolished in Malaysia. There is no gift tax in Malaysia.

Wealth tax

There is no wealth tax in Malaysia.

Social security contributions

The Social Security Organisation (SOCSO) comprises a compulsory insurance scheme managed by the Malaysian Government whereby employees are covered in the event of disablement or death due to employment injury.

All employers (registered with the SOCSO Board) and qualifying employees are required to contribute to the SOCSO, at specified rates.

Other taxes

Treatment of partnerships

The profits and losses made by a partnership are apportioned to the partners in accordance with the partnership agreement. The partners are required to include in their personal tax return their share of the profit or loss. A partnership is also required to file a separate tax return.

VAT and sales taxes

There is no VAT in Malaysia. Currently, sales tax is imposed on all goods (unless exempted) manufactured in, or imported into Malaysia. Service tax is levied on certain services at the rate of 5%.

Other

Stamp duty	– levied on documents as provided under the Stamp Act 1949.
Custom duties	– levied on import and export of goods.
Sales and service tax	– levied on goods and services.
Local taxes	– assessment and quit rent on properties. – licence fees for various businesses.

Exchange control

Malaysia has a very liberal exchange control system which enables business to deal freely in foreign exchange with very little or no restriction except with Israel, Serbia and Montenegro where special restrictions apply.

New measures were imposed with effect from 1 September 1998 with the intention of curbing speculation of the Malaysian Ringgit (RM), the regaining of monetary independence and the insulation of the Malaysian economy from the prospects of further deterioration.

These new measures include the following:

- payments within Malaysia must be made in RM; generally, residents are freely allowed to make payments to non-residents for any purpose up to RM 10,000 in RM or its equivalent in foreign currency;

residents are freely allowed to make payments to non-residents, in foreign currency only, for amounts exceeding RM 10,000 equivalent;

- non-residents are free to make direct and portfolio investments in Malaysia; they are allowed to repatriate dividends, interest, rental, commissions and profits freely, subject to the completion of a simple statistical form for remittances of more than RM 10,000 equivalent in foreign currency in each case and the presentation of the necessary documentary evidence to the banks concerned;
- a levy in the form of exit tax is imposed on foreign funds on investments in shares, bonds and other financial instruments as follows:

Funds brought into Malaysia before 15 February 1999:

- the principal amount repatriated after one year from 1 September 1998 or one year from the actual date the amount came into Malaysia (where this is after 1 September 1998) will not be subject to any levy;
- if the principal amount is repatriated within one year, it will be subject to levy at a decreasing rate, depending on the duration the principal amount is held as follows:

Period held	*Rate of levy (%)*
Up to 7 months	30
Exceeding 7 months – up to 9 months	20
Exceeding 9 months – up to 12 months	10
Exceeding 12 months	0

- any profit realised during the one-year period will not attract levy, even when it is repatriated after the one year period;
- any profit realised on investments made during the one-year period, even if realised after the one-year period, is exempted from the levy;
- profits realised and repatriated on investments made after the one-year period, are subject to a levy of 10%.

Funds brought into Malaysia on or after 15 February 1999:

- the principal amount is not subject to levy upon repatriation;
- profits realised and repatriated within 12 months of the date when the investment is made are subject to a levy of 30% of the profit;
- profits realised and repatriated within 12 months of the date of investment are subject to a levy of 10% of the profits;
- profits realised during the 12 month period of the investment, but repatriated after 12 months of the date of investment, are subject to a levy of 10%.

The following funds are not subject to levy on repatriation:

- Foreign Direct Investments (FDI);
- investment in properties;
- repatriation of funds by non-residents arising from transactions on the shares of companies listed on the Malaysian Exchange of Securities Dealing & Automated Quotation Bhd (MESDAQ);
- capital gains from Islamic financial instruments;
- income received from holdings in Malaysian Government Bills, Treasury Bills and Private Debt Securities.

An FDI is an investment made by a non-resident in:

- a company where the non-resident is entitled to exercise or control the exercise of not less than 10% of the votes attached to the voting shares of the company;
- a company where the directors are accustomed, or are under an obligation, whether formal or informal, to act in accordance with the directions, instructions or wishes of the non-resident;
- a body, whether corporate or non-corporate, where the management is accustomed, or is under an obligation, whether formal or informal, to act in accordance with the directions or wishes of the non-resident.

- restrictions are imposed on the usage of funds held in External Accounts;
- import and export of currency notes;
- a non-resident traveller visiting Malaysia is permitted to carry with him the following currency notes:

Import of currency notes (upon arrival)

- any amount of foreign currency notes and traveller's cheques denominated in foreign currencies;
- RM currency notes up to RM 1,000.

Export of currency notes (upon departure)

- foreign currency notes and traveller's cheques up to the amount brought into Malaysia;
- RM currency notes up to RM 1,000 only.

- a non-resident is required to declare to the Immigration Officer upon arrival the amount of foreign currencies and traveller's cheques carried by him into Malaysia.

Tax treaties and withholding taxes

Malaysia has signed tax treaties with 52 countries. In most of the double taxation agreements into which Malaysia has entered, the countries of residence are accorded tax-sparing credit.

In respect of dividends paid by companies exempt from tax under the Promotion of Investments Act 1986, the recipients are also exempt from Malaysian income tax on such dividends. If the recipients are also taxed on the dividends in another country of residence, the country of residence will usually give credits as if Malaysian tax has been paid.

Withholding tax rates currently in force are:

Country of residence	*Royalties* (%)	*Interest* (%)	*Technical/ management fees* (%)	*Dividends* (%)
Non-treaty countries	10	15	10	Nil
Treaty countries:				
Arab Republic of Egypt	10	15	10	Nil
Argentine Republic (a)	10	15	10	Nil
Australia	10	15	10	Nil
Austria	10	10/15	10	Nil
Bangladesh	10	15	10	Nil
Belgium	10	15	10	Nil
Canada	10	15	10	Nil
Czech Republic	10	12	10	Nil
Denmark	10	15	10	Nil
Finland	10	15	10	Nil
France	10	15	10	Nil
Germany	10	15	10	Nil
Hungary	10	15	10	Nil
India	10	15	10	Nil
Indonesia	10	15	10	Nil
Ireland	8	10	10	Nil
Italy	10	15	10	Nil
Japan	10	10/15	10	Nil
Malta	10	15	10	Nil
Mauritius	10	15	10	Nil
Mongolia	10	10	10	Nil
Netherlands	10	15	10	Nil
New Zealand	10	15	10	Nil
Norway	10	15	10	Nil
Pakistan	10	15	10	Nil
Papua New Guinea	10	15	10	Nil
People's Republic of China	10	10	10	Nil
Philippines	10	15	10	Nil
Poland	10	15	10	Nil
Republic of Albania	10	10	10	Nil
Republic of Fiji	10	15	10	Nil
Republic of Korea	10	15	10	Nil
Republic of Turkey	10	15	10	Nil
Republic of Uzbekistan	10	10	10	Nil
Romania	10	15	10	Nil
Russia	10	15	10	Nil
Saudi Arabia (b)	10	15	10	Nil
Singapore	10	15	10	Nil

Sri Lanka	10	10	10	Nil
Sweden	10	15	10	Nil
Sudan	10	10	10	Nil
Switzerland	10	10	10	Nil
Thailand	10	15	10	Nil
United Arab Emirates	10	5	10	Nil
United Kingdom	8	10	8	Nil
United States of America (a)	10	15	10	Nil
Vietnam	10	10	10	Nil
Zimbabwe	10	10	10	Nil

(a) Double taxation agreements with the Argentine Republic and the United States of America only cover shipping and airline profits.

(b) The double tax agreement with Saudi Arabia only covers airline profits.

(c) Malaysia has also signed double taxation agreements with the following countries:

- Islamic Republic of Iran;
- Jordan;
- Kuwait;
- Myanmar;
- Namibia.

(d) Malaysia is in the process of concluding double taxation agreements with Libya and Spain.

(e) Where the rate of tax on the above payments is not specifically mentioned in the respective double taxation agreement, the tax rate in the Income Tax Act 1967 will apply.

Anti-avoidance measures

The Inland Revenue may disregard or vary transactions and make such adjustments as it thinks fit in respect of transactions considered to be of an artificial nature.

Mauritius

Hajee Abdoula & Ramtoola

Introduction

Within the present decade, the Mauritian taxation system has undergone reformation with the introduction in the early 1990's of the Pay-As-You-Earn (PAYE) system together with the Current Payment System (CPS). In 1995, a new Income Tax Act was introduced to replace Income Tax Act 1974. In 1998, the Minister of Finance replaced the existing Sales Tax with Value Added Tax (VAT). All these changes have been introduced with the intention of modernising the taxation system in Mauritius.

The Republic of Mauritius runs a self-assessment system based on the global system of taxation and income tax is assessed on a preceding year basis from 1 July to 30 June.

Most taxes are levied by the central government, with the exception of certain minor taxes which are levied by the municipalities.

Corporate taxes

Taxable entities

Resident companies

Resident companies are liable to corporate income tax on their worldwide income.

A company is resident if it is incorporated in Mauritius or has its central management and control in Mauritius.

Non-resident companies

Non-resident companies are liable to corporate income tax on income derived from Mauritius.

Companies in the freeport zone

A company licensed under the Freeport Act 1992 is not liable for income tax, however, freeport zone companies are liable to tax on income from any activities outside the zone.

Unit trust schemes

Each trustee of a unit trust scheme is liable to income tax on the chargeable income, which is the difference between the net income derived by the trust and the aggregate amount distributed to the beneficiaries under the terms of the trust deed.

Any amount distributed to the beneficiaries under the terms of the trust deed is liable to income tax in the hands of the beneficiaries.

Sociétés/partnerships

Resident *sociétés* and partnerships are not liable to income tax, but every associate of a resident *société* or partnership is liable to income tax on his/her share of income.

A non-resident partnership or *société* is treated as a company and is liable to income tax on income derived in Mauritius.

Non-resident offshore trusts remain tax-exempt.

Resident offshore trusts are required to file tax returns and are governed by the same tax regime as offshore companies.

Resident companies, companies in the freeport zone, offshore companies, etc.

Further to the Finance Act 2000, some major changes have taken place for taxation levied on companies.

The tax payable by local companies (assuming they are not exempted in any way) will drop from 35% to 25% as from assessment year 2001/02. For offshore companies, the distinction between companies incorporated pre- and post-July 1998 is maintained.

Offshore companies incorporated before July 1998 will still have the right to choose whether to be governed by the Income Tax 1974 (and may elect to be taxed at 0%) or be governed by the Income Tax Act 1995 (and be taxed at 15%). However, this right has to be exercised on or before 30 June 2002, otherwise conversion will be automatic.

For offshore companies incorporated after 1 July 1998, the rate of income tax will remain at 15% (with the option to elect a higher rate).

The result is that by 30 June 2002, all offshore companies (irrespective of their dates of incorporation) will be taxed at 15% and may claim a deemed tax credit of 90%. However, as from the year of assessment commencing 1 July 2003, all offshore companies will be governed by the same tax regime – taxable, that is, at 15% with the deemed tax credit reduced to 80%.

Most offshore companies will actually pay tax in the jurisdiction in which they operate. They will still be able to claim credit for the actual tax paid. In effect, most of them will see their effective rate fall to 0%. However, documentary evidence must be produced before actual tax credit may be claimed.

Offshore companies can be 100% foreign owned, but (generally) cannot conduct transactions with residents of Mauritius. There has been some relaxation of this general rule. An offshore company can hold debentures in any company incorporated under the Companies Act 1984. Prior to the Act, an offshore company could only hold debentures in a foreign company, in another offshore company or in a offshore trust.

International companies

The International Companies Act 1994 provides that an international company is not resident in Mauritius for tax purposes.

Offshore Trusts – the chargeable income of a trust (net income less trust expenses and distributions to beneficiaries) is taxed under the Income Tax Act 1974 at between 0% to 35% for trusts registered prior to 1 July 1998. The trustees can, by irrevocable notice to the Offshore Authority and the Commissioner of Income Tax, elect for the chargeable income of the trust and the income of the non-resident beneficiaries to be taxed under the Income Tax Act 1995. In cases where the election is not made for the non-resident beneficiaries to be governed by the Income Tax Act 1995, they shall be exempt from income tax on the income derived from the trust.

The chargeable income of a trust registered after 1 July 1998 is governed by the Income Tax Act 1995 and, therefore, taxed at 15%. The income of non-resident beneficiaries will also be taxed at 15%. The trustees of an offshore trust may at any time deposit with the Offshore Authority a declaration of non-residence with respect to that trust. A declaration of non-residence must be in writing and signed by one or more of the trustees of the trust. Where a declaration of non-residence has been deposited for an offshore trust, the trust is regarded as not resident in Mauritius for the purposes of the Income Tax Act 1995 and where none of the income of the trust is subject to income tax in Mauritius, the trustees shall be exempt from any requirement under the Income Tax Act 1995 to file a return or to supply any information (with respect to the income or distributions to beneficiaries of that trust).

A declaration of non-residence shall have effect for the year of assessment in which it is deposited and all subsequent years of assessment. A declaration of non-residence may at any time be revoked by notice in writing to the Offshore Authority and the Commissioner of Income Tax (and such revocation shall have effect for the year of assessment in which it is given).

The Finance Act 2000 has brought two changes for international companies. The first change is that bearer shares have now been cancelled and will have to be converted to registered shares.

The second change requires the registration of shareholders, directors and secretaries of international companies.

Tax year and filing requirements

The tax year is the fiscal year to 30 June and taxes are paid on a previous year basis, though companies and other businesses may have other year ends.

Rates of tax

All taxes on income are imposed at national level. The rates of corporate income tax are:

For Tax Incentive Companies	15%
For companies listed on the Mauritian Stock Exchange	25%
For other companies	35% (25% as from assessment year 2001/02)

Tax incentive companies

The Income Tax Act 1995 made provision for a new category of companies termed, 'Tax Incentive Companies'. These include companies:

- holding an export enterprise certificate;
- holding a strategic local enterprise certificate;

- holding a modernisation and expansion enterprise certificate (other than a company engaged in the manufacture of goods excisable under the Excise Act 1994);
- holding an industrial building enterprise certificate;
- holding a pioneer status certificate;
- registered with the Small and Medium Industries Development Organisation;
- holding an export service certificate under the Export Service Zones Act 1981;
- holding a development certificate under the Development Incentives Act; and companies
- holding a hotel management service certificate under the Hotel Management (Incentives) Act 1982.

Also included are:

- investment trust companies listed on the Mauritian Stock Exchange or designated as an approved investment institution under section 50A of the Stock Exchange Act 1988;
- mutual funds authorised under the Companies Act 1984;
- trusts or trustees of a unit trust scheme;
- companies holding a housing development certificate;
- polyclinics holding a health development certificate under the Health Development Certificate Act 1992;
- manufacturing companies;
- corporations certified to be engaged in international business activity by the Mauritius Offshore Business Activities Authority as established under the Mauritius Offshore Business Activity Act 1992;
- companies holding an Offshore Banking Licence under the Banking Act 1988;
- companies engaged wholly in the management of venture capitals funds and companies holding a strategic local enterprise certificate under the Industrial Expansion Act 1993;
- venture capital funds;
- bus companies;
- companies engaged in the agro-based industry;

- companies deriving at least 75% of their income from agriculture, fishery and livestock (other than sugar cane cultivation);
- companies whose main activity is to provide lease financing;
- a companies deriving at least 75% of their income from the construction of buildings, roads and bridges;
- companies holding a pioneer financial services certificate;
- companies holding a fishing development certificate;
- companies holding a leisure development certificate;
- companies holding a regional development certificate issued under the Development Incentives Act;
- companies engaged in the provision of secondary or tertiary education;
- companies operating a duty-free shop;
- offshore management companies;
- companies engaged in software development;
- companies engaged in the Freeport zone; and
- companies running restaurants.

Listed companies and the subsidiaries of listed companies

Companies listed on the Mauritian Stock Exchange together with the subsidiaries of a listed company, other than Tax Incentive Companies, are liable to tax at a rate of 25%.

Other companies

The rate applicable to companies other than Tax Incentive Companies and listed companies is 35%. However, as from assessment year 2001/02, this rate of tax will fall to 25%.

Income subject to tax

General rules

The chargeable income of a company is the net income of the company for that income year.

Capital gains and losses

There is presently no capital gains tax in Mauritius, except for capital gains on land parcelling, and no capital loss is allowable as a deduction from other income. However, companies whose principal activity is trading in shares are exempt to tax on the profit made as a result of trading in those shares listed on the official Stock Exchange.

Dividends

Dividends paid by a company are not deductible in arriving at taxable income and are not subject to any withholding tax.

Dividends received by a company from another resident company are not taxable in the hands of the recipient.

Stock/inventory rules

Stock should be valued in accordance with sound business practice, in most cases at the lower of cost or market value. The FIFO and average cost methods are most commonly used, whereas LIFO and the base stock method are not permitted.

Deductions

General Rules

Expenses incurred exclusively to generate gross income in the business are generally allowable.

Depreciation and capital allowances

In arriving at the profit chargeable to taxation, depreciation is disallowed and is, therefore, added back to trading profit. Instead, capital allowances are given for investment in certain assets. The allowance is on a straight-line basis and tends to be as follows:

Industrial premises excluding hotels	5%
Hotels	20%
Plant or machinery costing 10,000 rupees or less	100%
Plant or machinery costing more than 10,000 rupees:	10%
– ships or aircraft;	
– aircraft leased by a company engaged in aircraft leasing;	100%
– furniture and fittings;	10%
– motor vehicles;	20%

– electronic and high precision machinery or equipment, computer hardware and software;	25%
– other.	20%
Agricultural improvement on agricultural land	20%
Capital expenditure on scientific research	20%
Any other item of a capital nature other than non-industrial premises	5%

Royalties

Royalties are deductible on business expenses to the extent that they are at arm's length rates. The withholding tax on royalties is 35%.

Interest

In principle, all interest payments on loan stock and other debts of a company are considered to be business expenses and are therefore deductible, except for interest payment on debentures issued by reference to shares, in which case such interest is treated as distribution.

Interest earned by offshore companies on deposits in Mauritius are tax-exempt

Dividends

Dividends paid are not deductible in arriving at taxable income and are not subject to withholding tax.

Doubtful debts

Only trade debts written off are deductible in arriving at the profit chargeable to corporate income tax. A provision for bad debts (specific or general) is disallowed.

Goodwill and other intangible assets

No allowances are made in respect of the amortisation of goodwill and other intangible assets.

Investment allowances

In addition to the capital allowances deductible in computing chargeable income, an investment allowance can be claimed at the rate of 25% of:

- the capital expenditure incurred on the construction of industrial premises (including hotels) used for the production of gross income;
- the cost of the acquisition of new machinery or plant (except road vehicles) used for the production of gross income in the income year in which the expenditure was incurred; or
- the cost of computer software or a new bus of a seating capacity of not less than 30.

In the event of any of the above being sold or scrapped within five years of acquisition, the allowance is clawed back.

Losses

Where a company has incurred a loss in any year, it is entitled under certain conditions to carry forward the loss for offset against future profits. Losses carried forward are lost should there be a change in ownership of more than 50% in any particular income year.

Corporate group losses

For corporate taxation purposes, companies (other than Tax Incentive companies) are treated as separate entities (whether or not they form part of a group of companies) and no group relief is available. Wholly owned subsidiaries incorporated after 1 July 1993 and operating as tax incentive companies are allowed to offset losses against the profit of the parent company.

Contributions to superannuation funds

Payments made under an approved superannuation fund by a company to provide a pension allowance to its employees are an allowable expense. In addition, payments made under an approved scheme for the medical expenses of its employees and their dependants are also an allowable expense.

Contribution to road funds

Contributions to any approved road fund are an allowable expense for tax purposes.

Contributions to sports clubs and sports training centres

Any expenditure not exceeding Rs 1,000,000 incurred by a company on contributions to any sports club or sports training centre set up by the Mauritian Government is allowed as a deduction from gross income.

Donations to charitable institutions

Donations of up to Rs 200,000 made to charitable institutions are allowable.

Marketing and promotional expenses

Companies engaged in tourism or export activities are allowed to deduct twice the amount of any expenditure incurred in an income year on overseas marketing, export promotion (including participation in international trade fairs), overseas advertising and the preparation of tenders for the export of goods or services.

Pre-operational expenses

Pre-operational expenses for tax incentive companies incorporated after 30 June 1993 are tax deductible.

Tax credits

Over and above the deductions stated above, companies can take advantage of the following tax credits which are deductible against tax payable.

Investment tax credit

Companies subscribing to share capital in a tax incentive company or listed company can deduct 10% of the amount actually paid in cash over a period of three income years. The deduction cannot exceed Rs 300,000 in any income year.

Tax credit to modernisation and expansion enterprises

A company, which is the holder of a modernisation and expansion certificate under the Industrial Expansion Act of 1993 and which incurs capital expenditure of Rs 10 million within two years from the date of the issue of the certificate, can (on the acquisition of new plant and equipment or technology for modernisation and expansion) deduct over a period of three years a maximum of 10% of the capital expenditure so incurred (3.33% per annum). This is in addition to deductions available for normal capital allowance purposes.

Tax credit for exports

In order to encourage the export of goods manufactured or produced locally (other than tea, sugar or their by-products) or the provision of services outside Mauritius, companies other than tax incentive companies can take advantage of reduced income tax rates as follows:

Qualifying export sales	*Tax credit*
10% or over but not exceeding 30%	30%
Over 30% but not exceeding 50%	45%
Over 50%	60%

Related party transaction

Transactions between companies, or other persons under common control, may be subject to revision if they are not carried out on an arm's length basis.

Personal taxes

Taxable individuals

The extent to which the income of an individual is subject to Mauritian tax depends on whether he is resident in Mauritius and the 'situs' (source) of the income.

Residents

A resident individual is one who has been present in Mauritius for a period (or periods amounting to) more than 183 days within the income year, or for an aggregated period of 270 days or more within that income year and the two preceding years.

An individual who is resident in Mauritius is subject to income tax on his worldwide unearned income. Earned income is taxable to the extent that it is received in Mauritius. Relief is available for any income tax paid abroad.

Non-residents

Non-residents are normally subject to income tax on income arising in Mauritius. The liabilities of non-residents may be reduced by the relevant double taxation agreement.

Tax year and filing requirements

The taxable period is the fiscal year to 30 June.

Each taxpayer must, for the purposes of assessment of income tax, furnish a return in the form approved by the Commissioner. All returns must be submitted by the end of September.

Tax on income

The main tax on income is income tax. Social security contributions are payable by both employers and employees. Employers are required to pay a levy along with the tax to the Industrial and Vocational Training Board.

Source of income

Income from employment

An employee (including a director) who is resident in Mauritius is normally taxed on all his emoluments for a tax year under the PAYE system. Income from an employment, profession or vocation earned by a married woman living with her husband is tax assessed separately. All benefits in kind are taxable.

Business income

For income tax purposes, trading profits are calculated in accordance with generally accepted accounting principles. Accounts must normally be prepared for a 12 month period up to the end of the tax year, which is 30 June. Where an individual sustains a loss in his business, he may offset that loss against future business income.

Social security benefits

Most social security benefits are exempt from tax.

Pensions and annuities

Pensions received from a former employer are taxed as emoluments for the year. Annuities are also taxable.

Capital gains

Gains made in the course of a business are treated as taxable income, except for a profit on the sale of investments quoted on the Official Stock Exchange. Speculative and investment gains are generally tax-exempt, provided they are not made in the course of a business.

Mauritius

The transfer of a business to a company or to the children of an individual is tax free, subject to certain conditions being met.

Dividends and interest

Dividends received from any Mauritian resident company are tax-free.

Interest received on monies deposited with a bank for a continuous period of three years is also tax-free. However, bank deposits for less than three years are subject to tax, but interest received up to Rs 75,000 is exempted. For a couple, the limit is Rs 150,000.

Interest payable on bonds issued by certain statutory and corporate bodies are also tax-free.

Rental income

Rents received from real estate are subject to income tax. Deductions are allowed for expenses.

Royalties

Royalties and similar payments (including patents, copyrights, trademarks, goodwill, franchises and know how) are exempt.

Personal allowances and deductions

Resident taxpayers are granted tax-free allowances, the level of which depends on marital status and whether they have any children.

The allowances are as follows:

	Y/E 30 June 2001
Single person	Rs 65,000
Dependant non-working wife	Rs 50,000
Child under the age of 18 (limited to 3 children)	Rs 20,000
Child over the age of 18 and receiving full time instruction	Rs 20,000
Child attending the University of Mauritius or a polytechnic in Mauritius	Rs 50,000
Child attending a university or a polytechnic abroad	Rs 100,000

Child attending a technical school	Rs 30,000
Dependant handicapped child	Rs 50,000
Handicapped person maintained by the taxpayer	Rs 50,000

Deductions

Deduction from employment and agricultural income

Taxpayers who receive income from employment or agriculture are allowed a deduction of 15% of gross emoluments from employment and net income from agriculture. The maximum limit is Rs 100,000 for each type of income.

Taxpayers who receive a pension are allowed to deduct an amount equal to their pension or Rs 65,000, whichever is the lower.

Expenses

Expenses relating to income are generally deductible, although some types of expenses may be subject to flat rate or percentage limits.

The following expenses are also deductible:

- interest up to a limit of Rs 200,000 on secured loans for the purpose of construction, acquisition or improvement of a house (the same limit is also applicable to a loan that has been jointly contracted by a couple); interest relief here may be shared in any proportions;
- premiums payable on life assurance, personal pension schemes and contributions to medical schemes (the total deduction available in respect of these three items is limited to Rs 80,000, or 20% of net income, if the latter exceeds Rs 400,000 in an income year);
- medical expenses up to a maximum of Rs 20,000 if treatment is undergone locally or Rs 30,000 if treatment is abroad;
- donations of Rs 20,000 made to approved charitable institutions and other specific donations;
- most alimony payments;
- fees or expenses up to a limit of Rs 25,000 payable to a recognised institution for self education or training, whether by distance learning or otherwise;
- expenses of Rs 25,000 incurred by the members of professional bodies for continuing professional education;

- expenses of Rs 8,000 incurred by a taxpayer in relation to tuition fees or school fees for his dependant child;
- 40% of qualifying investments up to a limit of Rs 50,000 (any excess is deductible in the two subsequent income years, subject to a maximum of Rs 50,000 in any income year);
- to qualify for this relief the taxpayer should subscribe in the share capital of a company which is either a Tax Incentive Company or listed on the Stock Exchange or which invests in units or newly issued securities of investment trust companies or contributes to an approved medical savings scheme or investment club formed in accordance with the Stock Exchange Act 1988; and
- amounts invested in Retirement Saving Plan (RSP) approved by the Commissioner of Income Tax also qualify for investment relief – the maximum amount allowable is Rs 50,000.

Non-residents

With certain exceptions, non-residents are not entitled to any allowances.

Special treatment for expatriates

Expatriate staff of an offshore bank, offshore company or company operating in the Freeport Zone are entitled to a reduction of 50% of the amount of income tax payable on emoluments derived from these entities.

Expatriate employees of a pioneer status enterprise, an export enterprise or any company engaged in electronics and technological activities are allowed relief by way of deduction from income tax otherwise payable by him of an amount equal to 50% of the income tax payable on emoluments derived by him from the company, provided that the number of employees entitled to the deduction shall not exceed two per company.

Rates of tax

The rates of tax for the year to 30 June 2001 are:

Band	*Rate (%)*
Rs1 – Rs 1,923	15
Above Rs 1,923	25

Special rates of tax apply to small income earners and to income derived from agriculture (excluding sugar cane).

Payment of tax

Annual returns

Payment of tax is made under the PAYE System for employees and the Current Payment System (CPS) for individuals receiving business, professional or rental income.

Under the CPS System, a self-employed taxpayer is required to submit one CPS return by 31 March in the fiscal year for the preceding period 1 July to 31 December, and one annual return by 30 September following the end of the fiscal year.

Estate and gift tax

Gifts and estates are not taxable in Mauritius.

Wealth tax

There is no wealth tax in Mauritius.

Social security

Payment for social security is made by means of contributions to the National Pension Funds. Both employees and employers contribute at a rate of 3% and 6% of basic salary, respectively.

Other taxes

Registration fees

A one-off fee is payable on all authorised share capital and increases in authorised share capital.

Transfer tax

A transfer tax of 13% is payable on transfers of real estate. There are no taxes on the transfer of securities, with the exception of unquoted companies holding real estate where a transfer tax of 13%, based on the value of the real estate, is payable.

Value added tax (VAT)

This new tax was introduced in September 1998 to replace the existing sales tax. Most goods and services are taxed at 10%, but certain essential goods and services are not taxable. It is mandatory for entities which have an annual turnover of Rs 3 million per year or more to register for VAT. Exports are taxable at 0%.

Customs and excise duties

This is levied on almost all imports into Mauritius with certain exceptions. The rate of duty varies according to the category of goods and various treaties.

Customs levy

A levy is applied to all goods entering Mauritius. The current rate is 17%.

Tenants' tax

This is a local tax based on the value of property and is levied on the tenant.

Property tax

This is a local tax based on the value of property and levied on the owner.

Exchange control

There is no exchange control in Mauritius.

Foreign tax credit

Where a Mauritian resident derives income from a foreign country and pays foreign tax in that country in respect of the income, a credit is allowed for foreign tax against the Mauritian tax computed, with reference to the same income. Foreign tax credit is only available for the amount of income actually received in Mauritius and is given only for foreign tax paid of a similar nature to Mauritian income tax.

Where a credit for foreign tax is allowable in respect of any income, the amount of the credit shall not exceed the amount of income tax payable on that income.

Withholding taxes

There are no withholding taxes in Mauritius.

Anti-avoidance measures

Any arrangement shall be void for income tax purposes if, and to the extent that, its purpose (or one of its purposes) is tax avoidance.

Tax treaties

Mauritius, being a tax-planning jurisdiction, has focused the development of its offshore sector on the use of a growing network of double taxation agreements. Currently, Mauritius has agreed 25 tax treaties with the following countries:

Belgium, Botswana, China, France, Germany, India, Indonesia, Italy, Kuwait, Luxembourg, Madagascar, Malaysia, Mozambique, Namibia, Oman, Pakistan, Singapore, Sri Lanka, South Africa, Swaziland, Sweden, Thailand, United Kingdom, Zimbabwe and Nepal.

Double taxation avoidance treaties summary table

Country		*Dividends (max rate)*			*Interests (max rate)*		*Perm Est*	*Capital Gains*
	Tax sparing Clause	*Portfolio*	*Other*	*Banks*	*Other*	*Royalties (max rate)*	*Min duration Activity (months)*	
Belgium	Yes	5% (b)	10%	10%	10%	(e)	6	(d)
Botswana	Yes	5% (a)	10%	12%	12%	12.5%	6	(d) (h)
China	Yes	5%	5%	Exempt	10%	10%	12	(d) (g)
France	No	5% (b)	15%	(e)	(c)	15%	6	(d)
Germany	No	5% (a)	15%	Exempt	(c)	15%	6	(d) (g)
India	Yes	5% (b)	15%	Exempt	(c)	15%	9	(d)
Indonesia	Yes	5% (a)1	10%	Exempt	10%	10%	6	(d)
Italy	No	5% (a) (k)	15% (k)	(c)	(c)	15%		(d)
Kuwait	Yes	(e)	(e)	(e)(m)	(e) (m)	10%	9	(d)
Luxembourg	Yes	5% (b) (i)	10% (b) (i)	(e)	(e)	(e)	6	(d)
Madagascar	No	5%	10%	10%	10%	5%	6	(d)
Malaysia	Yes	5% (b) (j)	15% (j)	15%	15%	15%	6	(d)
Mozambique	Yes	8% (a), 10% (b) 1	15%	Exempt	8%	5%	6	(d)
Namibia	Yes	5% (a)	10%	Exempt	10%	5%	6	(d)
Nepal	Yes	5% (a)2, 10%(b)	15%	10%	15%	15% (l)	6	(d)
Oman	Yes	(e)	(e)	(e)	(e)	(e)	6	(d)
Pakistan	Yes	10%	10%	10%	10%	12.5%	6	(d)
Singapore	Yes	(e)	(e)	(e)	(e)	(e)	9	(d)
South Africa	Yes	5% (b)	15%	(e)	(e)	(e)	9	(d)
Sri Lanka	Yes	10% (b)	15%	10%	10%	10%	6	(d) (g)
Swaziland	Yes	7.5%	7.5%	5%	5%	7.5%	6	(d)

Sweden (f)	Yes	5% (b)	15%	Exempt	15%	15%	6	(d) (h)
Thailand	Yes	10%	10%	10%	15%	5% (l), 15%	6	(d)
U.K.	Yes	10% (b)	15%	Exempt	(c)	15%	6	(d)
Zimbabwe	Yes	10% (a)	20%	Exempt	10%	15%	6	(d) (g)

Notes (general)

- Dividends, interests and royalties derived from Mauritius by offshore entities are tax-exempt; no capital gains.
- Double taxation is eliminated by the credit method, i.e the taxpayer's country of residence will grant a credit for taxes paid in the source country.
- When a resident of Mauritius is recipient of dividends from a company which is resident of the treaty country, the recipient is entitled to a tax credit which shall take into account the tax paid in the treaty country by the company paying the dividend in respect of the profits out of which the dividend is paid.
- The recipient is the beneficial owner of the dividends/interests/royalties. Such income is taxed in the recipient's country of residence, but may also be taxed in the source country according to the laws of that state.
- A resident of Mauritius receiving will be allowed a tax credit corresponding to the amount of tax levied in the treaty country.
- Services and activities, including building site or a construction, installation or assembly project, may constitute a taxable presence.

Notes (specific)

(a) Shareholding at least 25%, subject to detailed rules on the member of such investments held.

(b) Shareholding at least 10%, subject to detailed rules on the member of such investments held.

(c) Interest taxed in recipient's country of residence, but may also be taxed in source country according to the laws of that state.

(d) Gains from alienation of any property (movable & immovable) forming part of the business property of a permanent establishment may be taxed in the country where the permanent establishment is situated; gains from alienation of ships or aircraft are taxable in the state in which the alienator is resident.

(e) Dividends/interests/royalties are taxable only in the recipient's country of residence according to the laws of the state.

(f) Treaty applicable only for offshore companies.

(g) Gains from the alienation of shares of a company may be taxed in the company's country of residence.

(h) Gains from alienation of any property including derived by an individual holding 'dual' residence, are subject to taxation at any time during the next 10 years following the date on which the individual has ceased to be a resident of the first state of which he was a resident.

(i) Dividends derived by a company resident in Luxembourg from Mauritian sources are exempt from tax in Luxembourg, provided that the Luxembourg company holds at least 10% of the shareholding of the Mauritian company and that the latter is subjected to tax of at least 15% in Mauritius.

(j) Dividends paid by a company which is resident of Malaysia to a resident of Mauritius who is the beneficial owner, are exempt from any tax in Malaysia which is chargeable on dividends.

(k) Such tax shall be deemed to have been paid at an amount not exceeding 15% of the gross amount of the dividends.

(l) In the case of copyright of literary, artistic or scientific work (excluding cinematographic films, tapes or discs for radio or television broadcasting).

(m) In the case of interest paid being effectively connected with a permanent establishment, the beneficial owner of the interest is taxed at a maximum of 5%.

Treaties awaiting ratification are: Cyprus, Lesotho and Russia.

Treaties awaiting signature are: Bangladesh, Croatia and Malawi.

Treaties being negotiated are: Canada, the Czech Republic, Greece, Portugal, Tunisia, Uganda, Vietnam and Zamia.

Mexico

Gossler, S.C.

Introduction

Mexico has reformed its tax system with the aim of increasing the amount of tax collected and improving taxpayer compliance with the tax regulations.

Corporate taxes

Companies liable to taxation

Resident companies

Resident companies are assessed on their worldwide income.

A company is considered resident if its head office or controlling director is located within Mexico. A company incorporated under Mexican law will be considered resident.

Non-resident companies

Foreign companies and individuals who are permanently established in Mexico for the purpose of carrying out business activities, or who have a Mexican fixed base for carrying out professional activities, will satisfy the tax requirements which apply to resident companies, subject to the applicable international double taxation treaties.

Taxes imposed

Mexico has a single income tax levied on a federal basis.

The tax year is the calendar year and tax is paid when the annual tax return is submitted (returns must be submitted within three months of the end of the tax year).

Payment of the annual tax is by monthly or quarterly advance payments, depending on the level of income involved. An adjustment is made in the seventh month of the financial year. If the payments made are in excess of the tax due, either a credit or reimbursement will be made upon request.

There is no requirement to make advance payments of tax during the first business year.

There is an additional tax on assets of 1.8% of the asset value, regardless of losses or gains on those assets. This tax is not paid during the first four years of business.

Rates of tax

Income tax is charged at a rate of 35%, or 30% (32% for 1999) where profits are reinvested. The balance of 5% (3% for 1999) is payable on dividend distributions.

Income subject to tax

General rules

The whole of a company's income, including income from foreign sources is subject to taxation and it is mandatory to account for a gain resulting from the decrease in real value of a debt due to inflation.

Non-taxable income includes assets and capital revaluations, capital increases and payments made by shareholders to cover losses.

The tax authorities are empowered to calculate estimated levels of income. Since 1997, transfer-pricing regulations apply to transactions and particular attention is paid to transactions with non-resident related parties.

Capital gains and losses

These arise from the holding of assets, from investment with fixed or variable income, or from their disposal.

A return generated by bank deposits and other fixed rate investments is taxable in so far as it exceeds inflation. In the event that inflation is in excess of a generated return, a loss is recognised and is tax deductible in the financial year.

For fixed assets sale, the historical acquisition cost (adjusted to current value) is deducted from the income arising from the disposal, and the gain thus calculated is treated as taxable income. Where there is a loss, the amount is deducted from taxable income.

On a disposal of company shares, the purchase cost (adjusted to current value) may be deducted from income.

Dividends

When distributing dividends, a company must calculate corporation tax of 35% on the amount of the dividend multiplied by a factor of 1.5385. The tax is treated as a charge on the company.

Dividends arising from the net fiscal profits account (CUFIN), or from the net fiscal profits reinvested account (CUFINRE), are not subject to tax as the balance of these accounts represents amounts on which the company has already paid tax. The balance of these accounts is adjusted in line with inflation.

If it is decided to pay tax at 35% then dividend distributions will be deemed to be distributed out of CUFIN, a net profit account. But if it is decided to pay tax at 30%, then any dividend distributed will be deemed to be paid out of the CUFINRE account, net profit after taxes. Dividends will be free from taxes as the CUFIN account is in balance.

Since 1999, dividends paid to resident or non-resident individuals are subject to a 5% withholding tax on the value, resulting from multiplying the dividend value by the 1.5385 factor.

An individual shareholder can elect to combine his dividend with his other income to obtain a rate lower than 40% via a reimbursement for excess tax paid.

Repayments of capital by reductions (or through a company liquidation) are treated in the same way as dividend distributions.

Stock/inventory valuation

The cost of raw materials and finished goods acquired is deducted from profit in the financial year, whether the stock is sold or not.

Tax on assets is assessed on replacement value or on the most recent purchase value.

Deductions

General rules

Legislated deductions include those for the acquisition of raw materials and goods for processing and sale, depreciation, overheads and interest.

Both general and specific conditions must be met with respect to certain types of expense. The principal condition is that an expense must be strictly necessary for business purposes.

Certain deductions are subject to limits, for example cars and related costs, travel expenses and aircraft charges.

Certain categories of expense are non-deductible.

Depreciation and amortisation

Depreciation is determined by applying a statutory percentage (straight-line method) and these are:

Buildings	5%
Vehicles	25%
Office equipment	10%
Industrial plant	variable
Computer equipment	30%

The value resulting from these calculations is adjusted to take into account inflation between the acquisition date and the year end when the deduction is applied.

Real property is not depreciable.

Intangible assets reducing operating costs or enhancing product acceptance for a period within the life of the company are known as deferred costs and are written down by 10% per annum. Those whose effect is for an unlimited period are known as deferred charges and are written down by 5% per annum.

Payments made prior to the commencement of business operations, and those made with respect to patents, trademarks, commercial names and transfer technology royalties, are written down at the rate of 10% per annum.

Royalties

Royalty expenses are deductible as an ordinary and necessary expense, including such payments to residents abroad.

Interest

Interest paid or accrued related to a company's business activity is tax deductible. It is necessary to calculate the inflationary component of any debts on which interest accrues, as well as those which do not generate interest, in order to determine which are deductible and which exceed inflation.

Where the inflationary component is higher than the interest accrued, an inflationary gain results, thereby representing taxable income. An inflationary gain is the profit obtained when the real value of a debt decreases as a result of inflation over a period of time.

Dividends

Dividends paid are not tax deductible.

Bad and doubtful debts

These may be deductible upon production of the relevant legal documentation, or of documentation which demonstrates the practical impossibility of recovery, or when the statutory time limit for collecting debts has been reached. The statutory time limits for collection are dependent upon the nature of the business.

Certain conditions as set out in the tax regulations must be met in order to demonstrate the impossibility of recovery and must demonstrate through documentation that all possible means of debt recovery have been exhausted.

Trade credit

Trade credit is not deductible.

Special rules

Companies involved in activities relating to agriculture, livestock, fishing or forestry, as well as the surface transport of cargo or passengers must observe a special tax system known as 'simplified rules'. This system follows the principle that no tax is due, provided that no resources are withdrawn from the business with the aim of increasing the capitalisation of these sectors of the economy.

Under the simplified rules the taxable base is the amount by which receipts exceed outgoings. This is also known as the 'cash flow system'.

Activities relating to the livestock industry benefit from a 50% reduction in taxes, bringing the rate down to 17.5%.

Investment incentives and special benefits

Several fiscal benefits apply to the following:

- agriculture, livestock and forestry sectors;
- air and/or marine transportation;
- investments in research and development.

In addition, import duty reductions are available on fixed assets acquired for the production of export items.

Transfer pricing

Since 1997, in accordance with OECD international rules, transfer pricing regulations have been adopted.

Included in these rules is a requirement for taxpayers to keep up to date documentation with respect to international related party transactions such as sales, royalties, services, interest and so forth, in order to avoid an estimated adjustment from the tax authorities.

Article 65 of the Income Tax Law provides various methods as described in the OECD guidelines for companies to meet the transfer pricing regulations.

Losses

These may he deducted from taxable profit within a period of 10 years from the date they were incurred.

The deductible amount is adjusted to account for inflation in the second period of the accounting year in which it is incurred. A balance in excess after initial and subsequent write-downs is adjusted with reference to the National Index of Consumer Prices (published by Banco de Mexico) in line with inflation for the period ending in the last month of the accounting year in which it is written down and that of the period immediately preceding it.

Corporate groups

Groups formed by a holding company with at least one or more subsidiaries can opt to calculate their tax liability based on consolidated results – thereby potentially benefiting from a compensation of 60% of the losses of one or more of their companies against profits earned during the financial year by other companies in the group. Prior approval to exercise such an option must be obtained from the Ministry of Finance and Public Credit and an opinion must be obtained from an authorised public accountant regarding the financial status for taxation purposes of all companies in the group.

Personal taxes

Residents

Any individual who has established his residence in Mexico is resident, unless he remains in another country for more than 183 days (not necessarily consecutive) in any calendar year and can certify tax residence in the other country.

An individual who is resident in Mexico is subject to income tax on his worldwide income as it arises.

Non-residents

Non-residents are subject to tax on income arising in Mexico, including interests, royalties, fees and salaries.

Non-residents are taxable if they are domiciled in Mexico in order to carry out a business activity or maintain a fixed base from which to offer professional services. Income is subject to tax not because it is derived from these establishments but because the source of income is located in Mexico.

Taxes on income

Any income of an individual resident in Mexico is liable for income tax, except in expressly exempted cases.

Sources of income

Services

This type of income arises from the provision of services either as an employee or self-employed individual.

An employer must deduct at source from income received by an employee appropriate amounts of tax and make an annual return, except where the employee informs the employer in writing of his intention to complete his own return.

Certain employee benefits are not included in income tax, for example, overtime payments, gratuities and social security payments.

An employee is not allowed to make deductions when preparing an annual tax return, however, subsidies and credits to his salary are allowed, representing a tax reduction.

A self-employed individual can deduct expenses related to his activities. During the course of the financial year he must make quarterly advance payments in settlement of his tax liability.

Companies making payments to a self-employed individual must withhold 10% tax at source, which the individual may use as credit towards his provisional quarterly payment.

Business income

Individuals carrying out business activities must calculate their taxable earnings by deducting permitted items from their taxable income and applying tax at a rate of 35%.

Individuals must keep a net taxable earnings account detailing tax payments. They can make withdrawals from this without incurring additional tax liabilities.

Individuals have the option not to distribute profits of the fiscal year and to transfer these to other income. Notification takes place via an annual return. The additional tax of 5% (from 30% to 35%) is payable upon distribution of dividends – CUFIN and CUFINRE accounting methods apply (see above under Corporate taxes, dividends).

Where business income is lower than US$ 2,200 the previous year, a business may elect to calculate their tax liability according to the 'simplified rules' method. The main principle of this method is that no tax is due, provided that no resources are withdrawn from the business.

Individuals who carry out business activities solely in the livestock, agriculture and transport industry, must calculate liability according to the simplified rules.

Social security benefits

Social security payments and receipts are not deducible but benefits are exempt from income tax, provided that they do not exceed established limits.

Pensions and retirement benefit

Income derived from these sources is tax-free to the extent that they do not exceed nine times the minimum salary. Tax is due on amounts in excess of this limit.

Capital gains

Any profit derived from the transfer of rights is treated as a capital gain. The profit is generally taxable on the difference between disposal value and original acquisition cost.

With respect to sales of assets not resulting from business activity (for example real estate, buildings and movable assets), the tax liability is calculated by deducting historical cost adjusted to current value to account for inflation between the date of acquisition and the date of disposal.

Profits or losses from the sale of shares are added to or deducted from the adjusted historical cost, as are dividends received and paid by the company, to determine the amount to be deducted from the proceeds received.

Dividends

When dividends are distributed among shareholders, tax is paid by the company. Individuals may elect to include the dividends with their other income and apply for a progressive rate of tax to achieve a reimbursement of taxes, as the cumulative rate of tax will be lower than the 40% rate. At no time will a higher rate of tax result.

Interest

Taxable interest payments may arise from sources in the finance industry, from investments in the public sector in general, and from other kinds of financial operations.

Tax is due at a rate of 2% on investments in the finance industry and is deducted at source by the institution paying the interest. Public sector investments are, in many cases, treated in the same manner although there are cases where no tax is payable.

Where interest is generated by means other than those mentioned above, the annual tax is payable according to a progressive rate up to a maximum of 40% of the total gross income. Where a company pays the interest to an individual it must withhold 20% at source.

Rentals

Costs incurred during the year may be deducted from tax on rents from letting real estate or a deduction is allowed for repairs and insurance of 50% for residential houses and 35% for other buildings.

Royalties

Individuals receiving royalty income are subject to tax at a progressive rate and must complete an annual return.

Other income

Income from competition prizes and raffles is subject to tax at a rate of 15%. No deductions are allowed. Payment is due from those awarding the prize.

Individuals receiving other forms of income, such as debt cancellation, gains on currency exchange, dividends from abroad, working of underground resources, operating concessions and gifts in excess of the tax free allowance, are subject to tax and must make an annual return.

Personal allowances and deductions

Personal allowances

There are no personal allowances for taxpayers or their family members. A tax liability can only be reduced via a general credit, which varies according to the amount of income received.

Deductions

In addition to deductions relating to each type of income received, an individual may deduct the medical fees and hospital charges which he pays for himself, his wife, parents, grandparents, children and grandchildren, provided those receiving treatment do not earn more than one minimum salary between them in a calendar year. The funeral costs of such family members may also be deducted up to an equivalent of one minimum salary, as well as donations made during the year. Obligatory school transportation can be deducted.

Special family rules

There are no special rules, as each member of the family pays tax on his or her own income, although certain income may be split between married couples depending on the marriage contract.

Tax rates

General

The tax rate is 40% for individuals and 35% for companies. It is sometimes lower where progressive rates apply.

Provincial rates

There are no provincial rates.

Rate of deduction at source

This varies according to the corresponding tax.

Tax credits

A credit against taxable amounts included in the annual return is allowed for income taxes paid to foreign countries. The credit should not be higher than the tax that would have been paid in Mexico.

Wealth taxes

Mexico has no wealth tax.

Social security

Company and individual employers must make social security contributions on behalf of their employees ranging from 17.37% to 25.46% of the employee's basic income. The employee also contributes (at a lower rate).

In addition, employers must contribute an amount equal to 5% of employee salary to the National Institute for the Promotion of House Building to give the employee the possibility of acquiring his own home and 2% in addition to salary to enable him to have funds to draw upon.

Other taxes

Employees' profit sharing schemes

Company and individual employers must distribute 10% of specially assigned profit to their employees. In some cases, this payment is limited to an equivalent of one times the employee's salary.

Since 1992, workers' profit sharing has been deductible in amounts exceeding the social security payments made to employees.

Value added tax

This tax is charged at a rate of 15% throughout the country (except along the border) where the rate is 10%. It is not paid on exports or food products which are zero-rated, thereby enabling tax to be repaid.

Other taxes

Tax on assets

Since 1989, in addition to income tax, a minimum tax of 1.8% of the adjusted value of the taxpayer's assets has been payable, thereby reducing certain liabilities.

State and municipal taxes

Tax on property purchase

The acquisition of land and buildings is subject to a tax rate of 2% over building value.

Payroll taxes

In the majority of states, tax at the rate of 2% is due on the payment of wages.

Real estate taxes

Owners of land and buildings must pay tax to the local council estimated on the value of assets according to the specific rules applied by each city.

Mexico

Special tax on products and services

This indirect tax is due principally on the consumption of taxable goods and services (such as telephone services, alcoholic drinks and cigars) and is applied at different rates.

Exchange control

Since 1992, there has been no exchange control.

Tax treaties and withholding taxes

Mexico has signed tax treaties with the following countries: Australia, Austria, Argentina, Belgium, Brazil, Canada, Chile, China, Colombia, Czech Republic, Denmark, Ecuador, Finland, France, Germany, Greece, Hungary, India, Indonesia, Ireland, Israel, Italy, Japan, Korea, Luxembourg, Malaysia, Netherlands, Nicaragua, Norway, Panama, Poland, Portugal, Romania, Singapore, Spain, Sweden, Switzerland, United Kingdom, USA and Venezuela.

Withholding tax deducted on payments to non-residents is based on the following rates:

Salaries in pesos	*Income*
0–125,896	Exempt
125,897–1,014,160	15%
1,014,161	30%
Financial leasehold	15%
Professional fees & rentals	21%
Interests	varying (from 4.9% to 40%)
Technical assistance & royalties	15 to 40%
Shares sale on total income	20%
If decided to pay on profits tax (always with auditor's opinion)	40%

Country	*Dividend %*	*Interest %*	*Royalties %*
Belgium	5/15(a)	10/15 (j)	10
Canada	10/15 (b)	15 (u)	15
Chile5/10 (c)	15 (z)	15 (z)	
Denmark	0/15 (d)	5/15 (k)	10
Ecuador	5	10/15 (l)	10
Finland	0	10/15 (m)	10
France	0/5/15 (i) (s)	14.9/10/15 (w) (x)	
Germany	5/15 (e)	10/15 (n)	10
Ireland	5/10 (f)	5/10 (k)	10
Israel	5/15 (a)	10/15 (n)	10
Italy	15	15 (n)	15
Japan	5/15 (a) (s)	10/15 (m)	10

Korea	0.15 (g)	5/10/15 (o)	10
Netherlands	5/15 (e)	5/10/15 (m) (q)	10
Norway	0/15 (d)	10/15 (l)	10
Portugal	10	10	10
Romania	10	15	15
Singapore	0	5/15 (k)	10
Spain	5/15 (a)	5/15 (k)	10
Sweden	0/5/15 (f) (t)	10/15 (l)	10
Switzerland	5/15 (a)	10/15 (l)	10
UK	0	5/10/15 (p) (r) (v)	10
United States	5/15 (h)	4.9/10/15 (w) (x)	10
Venezuela	5	4.95/10/15 (m) (y)	10

Notes

(a) 5% rate applicable for companies holding 25% or more of share capital.

(b) 10% rate applicable for companies holding 25% or more of voting rights.

(c) 5% rate applicable for companies holding 20% or more of share capital.

(d) 0% rate applicable for companies holding 25% or more of share capital.

(e) 5% rate applicable for companies holding directly or indirectly 10% or more of share capital.

(f) 5% rate applicable for companies holding directly or indirectly 10% or more of voting rights.

(g) 0% rate applicable for companies holding 10% or more of share capital.

(h) 5% rate applicable for companies holding 10% or more of voting rights. Further, the general 15% withholding tax is reduced to 10% after five years.

(i) The rate of 0% for individuals or corporations applies where the recipient of the dividend directly or indirectly owns at least 50% of its share capital and is a resident of a third state. It must also own at least 10% of the voting rights of the company.

(j) 15% withholding tax is reduced to 10% from the fifth year of the agreement under which the interest arises.

(k) 5% rate applies to payments to banks.

(l) 10% rate applies to payments to banks after five years.

(m) 10% rate applies to payments to banks in respect of interest from bonds and securities that are regularly traded on a recognised securities market.

(n) 10% rate applies to payments to banks, insurance companies and pension funds after five years.

(o) 5% rate applies to payments made to banks after five years; 10% rate applies to payments to banks during the first five years.

(p) 10% rate applies to banks, insurance companies and interest derived from a security trading on a recognised securities market during the first three years.

(q) 5% rate applies to insurance companies and interest derived from a security trading on a recognised securities market.

(r) 5% rate applies to banks, insurance companies and interest derived from a security traded on a recognised securities market after three years.

(s) The 5% rate applies when the share capital has been owned for at least six months before the conclusion of the fiscal period. However, a rate of 0% applies in some cases.

(t) 0% rate applies where the recipient company holds directly at least 25% of the voting rights and at least 50% of the voting rights of the recipient company are owned by Swedish residents.

(u) 10% rate applies for interest paid to banks and insurance companies from bonds and securities that are regularly traded on a recognised securities market.

(v) 10% rate applies to payments by banks, where the recipient is not an insurance company or bank, after three years.

(w) 4.9% rate applies to payments to banks and insurance companies in respect of interest from bonds and securities that are regularly traded on a recognised securities market, after five years. A rate of 10% applies, in respect of the above, during the first five years.

(x) 10% rate applies for interest paid to banks and insurance companies from bonds and securities that are regularly traded on a recognised securities market, after five years.

(y) 4.95% rate applies in respect of interest paid to banks and insurance companies.

(z) The rate agreed by Chile and Mexico for interest and royalties may be reduced if Chile enters into a treaty agreement with another country at a lower rate than the current agreed rate of 15%.

Morocco

Fiducia

Corporate taxes

Taxable entities

Resident companies

Corporation tax is charged on profits on business activities carried out by Moroccan resident companies. This includes income and capital gains derived from activities in Morocco and on profits which are attributed to Morocco under double tax treaty provisions.

A company is deemed resident if it is incorporated in Morocco.

Non-resident companies

Companies not resident in Morocco are subject to corporation tax on all income or profits related to the assets they own in Morocco and to their operations and activities carried out in Morocco (including on a casual basis).

Tax year and filing requirements

The fiscal year runs from 1 January to 31 December but a company may choose its accounting period end date. Where the profits of an accounting period straddle two fiscal years (and where tax rates have changed), they are apportioned and charged at the appropriate rates.

A tax return must be filed three months after the accounting period end. Penalties and interest charges are imposed if this deadline is not met.

Corporation tax is payable quarterly during the accounting period based on the preceding year's profits. The balance is payable on the tax return filing date or may be deducted from the next year's instalments if a surplus has been paid.

Taxes imposed

Companies are liable to corporation tax on their profits, which is imposed at a national level. Certain activities, such as non-profit organisations, co-operative companies, agricultural companies and similar, are exempt.

Rates of tax

- From January 1996, the rate of 35% is applicable to all profits.
- A 10% withholding tax on payments made to non-resident companies provides a full discharge from any direct tax.
- Non-resident companies may opt for the notional assessment scheme at 8% of the contract amount. This rate discharges any liability to the return on shares (or on participations), tax from equivalent withholding and from the 10% withholding tax;
- A minimum tax must be paid by all companies other than non-resident companies opting for notional assessment, whatever the level of profits of the company. The minimum tax is calculated on sales income plus incidental and financial income. The rate of taxation is 0.5% (or 0.25% for certain companies).
- Companies which are listed on the stock exchange for the first time between 1 January 2001 and 31 December 2003 are eligible for a tax relief on 25% to 50% of profits achieved during the following three years.

Income subject to tax

General rules

All income is subject to corporation tax, including trading profits, incidental and financial income, extraordinary income and capital gains.

Stock/inventory valuation

Stock must be valued at the lower of cost or selling price. Cost can be based on average cost or the FIFO method (LIFO is not generally accepted) and should include purchasing expenses. For valuing work in progress or finished goods, cost should include both direct and indirect manufacturing expenses. Where selling price is less than cost, a provision may be made to reduce stock value to cost.

Capital gains and losses

- *Immovable property:* capital gains are set against capital losses. Where capital gains exceed capital losses in a fiscal year, the excess is subject to corporation tax at the normal rate, but a deduction (25% to 100%) is allowed in accordance with special rules. If losses exceed gains, the excess is deductible from other income.
- *Movable property:* capital gains on shares are subject to the same rules as above. However, where shares are held as fixed assets companies may elect for a final 15% tax.

Dividends

Dividends received from Morocco resident companies and paid out of income subject to corporation tax are exempt income.

Deductions

General rules

Expenses are generally deductible provided they are incurred for the benefit of the enterprise and in the normal course of business. They must be adequately supported and reasonable in amount.

Depreciation and amortisation

Wasting fixed assets are depreciated over their useful lives as follows:

	Years
Industrial buildings	20
Commercial and residential buildings	25
Fixtures and fittings	10
Machinery and equipment	10–15
Vehicles	4–5

Depreciation is usually calculated using the straight-line method. The reducing-balance method can only be used where the asset is new and is of a type specified in law.

Motorcars qualify for writing down allowance – restricted where the cost is more than MAD 200,000.

No depreciation is allowed on land, trademarks, securities or goodwill. However, if the realisable value of these assets falls below book value, a tax deductible reserve may be set up.

Company formation expenses must be written off as soon as practicable. This will normally be in the first year in which there are profits sufficient to absorb them and cannot be later than five years from the year in which they were incurred.

For depreciation to be deductible in full, the accounts must be charged with at least the equivalent to a normal straight-line depreciation charge. Failure to charge depreciation leads to a permanent loss of relief.

Royalties

Royalties are normally deductible under the same conditions as any other expense.

Interest

Interest payable is normally deductible, unless paid to shareholders, in which case:

- it is not deductible if the capital is not fully paid up;
- it is deductible only up to an amount corresponding to a loan which does not exceed the company's nominal capital; and
- the interest is limited to the yearly average rate on treasury bonds.

Bad and doubtful debts

Write-offs and provisions are deductible provided they arise in the normal course of business and are properly documented.

Reserves and provisions

Reserves and provisions for contingent or future losses can only be allowed:

- where incurred wholly and exclusively for operating purposes; or
- where the current value of the contingency can be accurately estimated.

Reserves and provisions made by companies to cover investment expenses, construction or the acquisition costs of housing for personnel or exhausting mines, are allowed in accordance with specific tax rules.

Employees' and directors' remuneration and benefits.

Employees' and directors' remuneration and benefits are deductible provided the amount is reasonable and can be justified by the services performed.

Specifically non-deductible expenses

- Delinquency charges and penalties for breaking fiscal law are not allowable.
- 50% of expenses exceeding MAD 10,000 are not deductible when they are paid in cash.

Foreign source income

Foreign business income is exempt from tax in Morocco.

Investment incentives and special benefits

- Exporting companies enjoy a full exemption for an initial five year period and a 50% reduction in tax thereafter.
- Manufacturing companies and companies that operate in under-developed geographical zones enjoy a 50% reduction for an initial five years.

In addition, equipment can be depreciated on a reducing balance basis.

Related party transactions

Transactions between related parties must be on an arm's length basis.

Losses

Losses incurred during an accounting period can be carried forward and deducted from the profits of the next accounting period. Unrelieved losses may be carried forward and relieved up to the fourth year after the initial loss. The four year limit applies to the loss before depreciation as the loss arising from depreciation can be carried forward indefinitely.

Corporate groups

Each company within a group of companies is taxed separately and losses cannot be transferred between companies.

Tax-free mergers and disposals

Provisions allow for capital gains taxation to be deferred in the course of mergers between companies.

Liquidation of a company

Cash distributions or property received at the end of company liquidation are taxed in accordance with stamp duty rules. In addition, the excess of proceeds received by shareholders over the original subscription cost of the shares is taxable as a dividend.

Capital taxes

There is no tax on net worth.

Treatment of branches (branch profit tax)

Branches of foreign companies are charged to corporation tax in the same way and at the same rate as Moroccan resident companies.

Personal taxes

Basis of taxation of individuals

Residents

Individuals ordinarily resident in Morocco are subject to tax on their worldwide income.

An individual is ordinarily resident in Morocco if any of the following applies:

- if he or she has their permanent home or is present in Morocco for 183 days (not necessarily consecutive) in any one year;
- if he or she carries on an occupation or employment in Morocco, except where this is incidental to overseas activity; or
- if he or she has the centre of his/her economic interests in Morocco.

Non-residents

Individuals not ordinarily resident in Morocco are subject to tax only on their income arising in Morocco, unless excluded under a double tax treaty.

Tax year and filing requirements

Income tax is assessed annually on the total income earned by the taxpayer during the previous year. However, wages and similar income have tax debited during the year, subject to adjustments for total income where necessary.

Taxes on income

Individual income tax is imposed at a national level. Individuals also pay social security contributions.

Sources of income

Total taxable income is the aggregate of various descriptive categories. The net income of each of these categories is separately assessed according to its own rules.

Income categories include:

- professional income;
- farming income;
- wages and similar income;
- real estate income and capital gains; and
- income and profits derived from securities.

Losses can only be offset against income from the same source. Where there is insufficient income to allow for a total or partial deduction, the loss can be carried forward for a maximum of four years.

Employment income and directors' fees

Employment income includes remuneration paid to employees, directors of corporations and the non-controlling directors of private limited liability companies.

Assessment is on the total remuneration, including benefits in kind, made available to the recipient during the calendar year, whether actually drawn or not. It does not, however, include allowances granted to cover expenses incurred in the course of the work-related activity, social security payments or contributions to retirement funds, disability pensions, family allowances and other social security allowances.

The net taxable income is calculated by then deducting from gross taxable income the following:

- work related expenses, which are set at the rate of 17% on the salary, provided this does not exceed MAD 24,000; and
- contributions related to retirement pay and pensions.

Tax collection method

- *The pay-as-you-earn-method (PAYE):* PAYE is administered by the employer or agent responsible for payment where the employer is resident or settled in Morocco. An amount is withheld on behalf of the Treasury from each payment.
- Taxpayers resident in Morocco and receiving wages, allowances or salaries from public or private employers or payers resident, settled or having their head office outside Morocco, are taxed through a register.

Business profits and losses

Professional income:

- professional income includes income from commercial, industrial and handicraft activity, real estate development, housing development or asset trading and professional services, when carried out by an individual or a company not subject to corporation tax;
- taxable income is based on the net profit of the taxpayer's business for the accounting period ending during the calendar year;
- net income is calculated using the net actual profit scheme provided by law, however, taxpayers working as sole traders or in partnership may opt for one of two schemes provided for by law, namely the standard profit scheme and the simplified net income scheme;
- these optional schemes are applicable to those with turnovers below certain limits according to specific rules.

Agricultural profits:

- agricultural profits include all farming profits earned by farmers and tenant farmers;
- agricultural profits are computed on an accruals or notional basis when annual turnover is not higher than MAD 2,000,000.

Dividends

Individuals resident in Morocco are subject to a final withholding tax on dividends received from resident companies which are liable to corporation tax at a rate of 10%, 15%, 20% or 30%, in accordance with special rules.

This tax also applies to dividends paid to non-residents, except where relief is given under a double tax treaty.

Interest

Moroccan residents can elect to be taxed on interest, either by way of a final withholding tax or by aggregating it with their other sources of income.

In the latter case, the taxpayer is taxable on the whole of his income (including the gross dividend) with credit for the withholding tax deducted.

Rentals income

The net income earned from immovable property is the rent actually received in the year, plus landlord's expenses borne by the tenant, less tenant's expenses borne by the landlord.

The net rent determined as above is then reduced by 40%. This deduction covers depreciation, various landlord's expenses and administration expenses.

Royalties

Income from licensing, sale of patents, dealing in trademarks and in know-how are normally taxed under the category of professional income.

However, copyright royalties paid to Moroccan residents are exempt. Copyright royalties are subject to a 10% withholding tax when paid to non-residents, unless relief is given under a double tax treaty.

Social security benefits

Certain benefits are exempt from income taxes. These include: family allowances, disability pensions, life annuities and temporary allowances granted to victims of work-related accidents and allowances covering sick leave, accident and maternity leave.

Pensions and annuities

Pensions received by Moroccan residents from pension funds are taxed as income. A deduction of 35% of the pension is allowed. A relief of up to 80% is allowed on pensions received by foreign citizens who are resident in Morocco.

Exempt income

Tax is not charged on voluntary payments made as compensation for breach of an employment contract, or on stock options.

Capital gains

Immovable property

Capital gains are treated as a professional income and will benefit from deductions depending on their acquisition date, except on property which is not utilised by the taxpayer in his trade or profession. In this case, capital gains are subject to a special final tax at the rate of 15% when realised.

Movable property

Capital gains on shares are treated as professional income and as benefit from deductions, depending on their acquisition date (provided they are business assets). Otherwise, they are subject to a final tax of 10%, 15%, 20% or 30% in accordance with special rules.

Foreign sources of income

Residents of Morocco are fully taxable on foreign income as it arises. Relief is allowed against a tax liability for any foreign taxes payable directly on the income.

Personal allowances and deductions

Taxpayers benefit from a tax deduction corresponding to 10% of the amount of the following:

- premiums or contributions relating to life insurance contracts of a ten-year period subscribed to mutual or insurance companies established in Morocco (the calculation basis of the deduction cannot exceed MAD 9,000 annually);
- dividends from shares listed in the Moroccan stock exchange provided that the calculation basis for the deduction does not exceed MAD 5,000; or
- the purchase cost of shares listed in the Moroccan stock exchange, provided that the calculation basis for deduction does not exceed MAD 16,500.

Special family rules

A deduction of MAD 180 for each dependant, not exceeding a total of MAD 1,080, is deductible from taxable income each year.

The taxpayer's dependants are his wife and his own children, his legally adopted children (where they are under 21 years of age or under 25 and a full-time student), provided that their own income does not exceed MAD 12,000.

Rates of tax

Residents

Income is taxed as follows for the fiscal year 15 January 2001 to 31 December 2001:

Band (MAD)	*Rate %*	*Tax on band (MAD)*	*Cumulative tax (MAD)*
0 – 20,000	0	0	0
20,001 – 24,000	13	520	520
24,001 – 36,000	21	2,520	3,040
36,001 – 60,000	35	8,400	11,440

Income above MAD 60,000 is taxed at the rate of 44%.

Income tax is levied at the national level only (there are no local taxes on income).

Remuneration is taxed at the rate of:

- 30%, if paid to individuals who do not belong to an employer's permanent staff (other than those described below); or

- 17% in the case of remuneration paid by public or private educational or vocational training establishments to teachers other than those employed on a permanent basis.

Non-residents

Income such as interest, royalties, rents, etc., paid to non-residents is subject to a 10% withholding tax.

Withholding taxes

Taxes are withheld on:

- wages and salaries;
- remuneration paid to non-residents;
- dividends; and
- interest.

Payment of tax

Payroll deductions

Income tax is deducted from wages and salaries by payroll deduction.

Returns and assessment

An individual who has income chargeable to tax is required to file a return before the end of March of each year in respect of his income during the preceding year.

The fiscal authorities will raise assessments based on this return form.

Estate and gift taxes

Taxes are the same for estates and gifts.

An individual's heirs and legatees must declare the property belonging to the deceased at the time of death. The property to be declared includes all property located in Morocco.

Duties on each taxable part of the gift or estate are as follows:

- a rate of 1% between husband and wife; grandparents, parents and children; and between brothers and sisters; and

- a variable rate of 2.5% to 5% between other parties.

Wealth tax

There is no wealth tax in Morocco.

Social security contributions

Whatever their nationality, all individuals employed in Morocco are (in principle) subject to social security payments.

These payments cover sickness, old age pensions and family and retirement benefits.

The rates are as follows:

	Employers (%)	*Employees (%)*	*Total (%)*
Illness, maternity, disability	0.44	0.22	0.66
Retirement contributions	6.08	3.04	9.12
Family allowances	8.87		8.87

Other taxes

VAT and sales taxes

Value added tax (VAT) is a general tax on consumption and is charged on most goods and services consumed or used in Morocco, whether of Moroccan or foreign origin.

There are five rates as follows: 7%, 10%, 14% and 20%, as well as a zero rate applying to certain goods and services (in particular to exports).

Exchange control

The Ministry of Finance exercises control over all foreign currency transactions, but delegates certain powers to authorised banks.

Direct investments enjoy automatic freedom to transfer invested capital and income. This transfer is not subject to any special authorisation and is done directly through the banks.

Tax treaties and withholding tax

Income tax at 10% is withheld from interest, rents, copyright and design royalties, dividends, non-commercial profits and all amounts paid for services rendered or used in Morocco, to a non-resident by an employer or agent established in Morocco, unless eliminated by tax treaty.

The following table shows a selection of tax treaties in force between Morocco and other countries:

Country of residence	*Effective date*
Algeria	28 May 1993 (approved)
Belgium	18 February 1975
Canada	9 November 1975
Denmark	1 January 1992
Egypt	28 May 1993 (approved)
Finland	9 November 1979
France	14 September 1971
Germany	1 November 1974
Italy	10 August 1983
Libya	28 May 1993 (approved)
Luxembourg	16 February 1984
Netherlands	10 June 1987
Norway	18 December 1975
Romania	31 August 1987
Spain	16 April 1985
Sweden	1 January 1961
Switzerland	21 July 1995 (approved)
Tunisia	26 June 1979
United Arab Maghreb (UMA)	14 July 1993
United Kingdom	29 November 1990
United States	1 January 1981

Selected treaty countries

	Royalties (%)	*Interest (%)*	*Dividends (%)*
Belgium	5–10	15	15
Denmark	10	10	10–25
France	5–10	10–15	15
Netherlands	10	10–25	10–25
USA	10	15	10–15

The Netherlands

Horlings, Brouwer & Horlings

Introduction

Most taxes are levied at a national level, with the significant exception of real estate tax (levied at local level) and certain other relatively minor taxes. The tax year is the calendar year although companies and other businesses may adopt different year end dates for their accounts.

Corporate taxes

Taxable entities

Resident companies

Resident companies are liable to corporate income tax on their worldwide income including capital gains. A company is resident if it is incorporated under Dutch law. A foreign incorporated company which has its central management located within the Netherlands will also be subject to Dutch taxation as a resident company.

Non-resident companies

Non-resident companies are liable to corporate income tax on certain Dutch source income.

The major income components are the profits of a business carried out in the Netherlands through a permanent establishment or a permanent representative and income from immovable property in the Netherlands.

Tax year and filing requirements

The tax year is the calendar year but the financial year of a company may be any fixed 12 month period provided for in the company's articles of association. In principle, the tax return must be filed within five months after the end of the tax year. In certain cases the filing can be postponed for up to 14 months.

The inspector must raise an assessment within three years of the end of the tax year concerned. In the absence of a return, an estimated assessment may be raised.

Taxpayers, including Dutch companies and the Dutch permanent establishments of foreign companies, may adopt a currency other than the Dutch guilder and report their annual taxable result in this foreign currency. It is anticipated that this measure will reduce the administrative burden of international operating companies.

Taxes imposed

All taxes on income are imposed at a national level. The Dutch tax system grants no special advantages or disadvantages to foreign companies or the branches of foreign companies with regard to rates of tax. Tax is normally payable within two months of the receipt of an assessment. A provisional assessment may be issued during the taxable period in which the income is earned. For certain provisional assessments, payment may be made in instalments.

Rates of tax

The corporate income tax rate for 2001 is 30% for the first NLG 50,000 taxable profit and 35% for the taxable profit that exceeds the first NLG 50,000.

Income subject to tax

General rules

Profits subject to tax are based in principle on commercial profits less losses and certain gifts. Commercial profits are defined as the total sum of all profits, including capital gains, realised through the conduct of a business enterprise and are measured in guilders or functional currency. The method of determining the commercial profits should be consistent from year to year and can be changed only if justified by sound business practice (provided the purpose of the change is not to gain an incidental tax benefit).

Stock/inventory valuation

Stock should be valued in accordance with sound business practice, in most cases at the lower of cost or market value. The FIFO and average cost methods are most common. LIFO and the base stock method are also permitted.

Capital gains and losses

There is no special treatment for capital gains or losses (except those falling under the participation exemption, see below). They are treated as normal income and taxed or relieved at the full rate. On disposal of a fixed asset, any capital gain may be transferred tax free to a replacement reserve. Assets which are depreciated over a period longer than 10 years have to be replaced by a new one fulfilling the same function. Taxation of capital gains on intangible assets may also be deferred, provided the asset is not held as a portfolio investment. The book value of the new asset must be reduced by the amount of the reserve, however, it cannot be lower than the book value of the asset disposed of. Reinvestment must in principle take place within three years, following the year in which the disposal of the asset took place.

Dividends

Dividends paid are not deductible in arriving at taxable income. Dividends are normally subject to a withholding tax of 25% or to a lower rate where prescribed by a tax treaty. This tax is creditable or refundable for residents against corporate income tax. Dividends received both from Dutch and foreign sources are taxed at the full corporate income tax rate, subject to any credits available. An exemption is available if the participation exemption applies.

Dividends and capital gains arising from investments in other companies, both Dutch and foreign, are exempt from corporate income tax in the hands of the recipient, provided the shareholding is at least 5% of the nominal paid-up share capital and is not held as stock-in-trade (participation exemption).

Shareholdings under 5% may also be deemed to qualify in certain cases.

For holdings in foreign companies there are two further requirements:

- the foreign company must be subject to a national profits tax in its own country;
- the holding must not be of a portfolio-type investment.

For EU shareholdings the portfolio investment provision does not apply provided at least 25% of the shares are held and the company in which the shares are held is subject to normal taxation. Expenses incurred in connection with a foreign qualifying participation (including interest expenses) are not deductible for Dutch corporate income tax purposes. Currently our High Court has asked the European Court of Justice whether this is discriminatory for EU shareholdings. If the answer is yes, then the expenses should be deductible.

Capital gains made upon the disposal of a qualifying participation (as defined above) are tax-free. Capital losses are not deductible in such cases. However, losses sustained upon the winding-up and liquidation of a company in which a qualifying participation is held, may be deductible in the year in which the liquidation is completed if the Dutch holding company has held at least 25% of the shares in the foreign subsidiary during the five years prior to liquidation. A liquidation loss is not deductible if the activities of the liquidated subsidiary are continued within the group or if the loss can be compensated by the liquidated company or a group company.

A parent company which owns at least 25% of the shares in a subsidiary is allowed to write down its investment during the first five years after the date of acquisition or incorporation of the subsidiary. The facility only gives temporary relief because if after five years the value has not increased, the amount of the write down must be released to the profits in equal parts of 20% per annum.

Deductions

General rules

Expenses directly or closely connected with the conduct of the business are in general wholly or partly tax-deductible. Expenses considered to contain a personal element (such as food and drink) are only partly deductible, when a substantial shareholder works for the company. Certain expenses are subject to a maximum limit.

Depreciation and amortisation

Various methods of depreciation and amortisation are permitted, provided that they are in accordance with generally accepted accounting principles and sound business practice.

The depreciation and amortisation basis of tangible and intangible fixed assets is historical cost. The residual value and the useful life of the asset are taken into account.

Usually accepted methods are:

- straight-line;
- reducing balance (provided the asset's value to the business decreases more in early years);
- depreciation on the basis of the utilisation of the asset;

- a decreasing yearly percentage.

Acceptable rates are:

Buildings	1-3%
Plant, machinery, office equipment	10-20%
Vehicles	20-30%
Goodwill	20%

Certain assets, such as land, are not depreciable.

Royalties

Royalties are deductible as business expenses to the extent that they are at arm's length rates.

Interest

In principle, all interest payments on loan stock and the other debts of a company are considered to be business expenses and are therefore deductible, unless the interest is paid on a loan to acquire a foreign qualifying participation.

Furthermore, in the following transactions the interest may be disallowed unless there is a bona fide commercial reason for the transaction:

- declaration of dividend or repayment of capital;
- contribution of capital in an entity which is loaned back;
- loan from a related entity or a related individual which is used to fund the above transactions;
- loan from a related entity or a related individual in order to acquire a Dutch resident related company.

In the last two examples the interest expense is deductible if the recipient is effectively taxed at a rate which is 'reasonable'. It has not yet been determined which rate should be considered reasonable but the interest deduction is denied if, and to the extent that, the recipient has unutilised losses or credits for any unpaid taxes.

Dividends

Dividends paid are not deductible.

Bad and doubtful debts

Debts can be valued on a specific or a general basis or a combination of the two. Write off's and provisions are deductible.

Reserves and provisions

In general, reserves and provisions are allowed if they are in accordance with sound business practice. There are also some special fiscal reserves which, under certain conditions, can be formed even though they are not in accordance with sound business practice.

Employees' and directors' remuneration and benefits

Employees' and directors' remuneration and benefits are generally deductible. However, some allowances given to employees or directors which contain a private element (such as food and clothing) are 90% deductible.

Foreign source income

Foreign source income, other than dividends, interest and royalties, is generally exempt from Dutch tax (subject to progression, which is not material for corporate income tax) provided a treaty applies or else the income has been taxed in the other country. For dividends, interest and royalties from treaty countries and from listed developing countries, a credit for withholding tax is generally given. Where participation exemption applies, no credit is given as the income is exempt.

Investment incentives and special benefits

A tax deduction of between 3% and 28% is available for investments in qualifying fixed assets up to a maximum figure of NLG 575,168 per annum. Regional reliefs are available for investment in under-developed areas. Other reliefs can be obtained for certain types of investment, e.g. for investments which improve the environment.

Related party transactions

Transactions between companies or other persons under common control may be subject to adjustment if they are not carried out on an arm's length basis. Furthermore, non-arm's length transactions may be treated as informal capital (resulting in 0.55% capital duty) or as a deemed dividend distribution (subject to dividend tax of up to 25%).

Losses

Unrelieved losses can be carried back three tax years and can be carried forward indefinitely. Losses should be offset in the order in which they arise. Losses may lapse on a major change of shareholders and business.

Corporate groups

A Dutch parent company and its resident subsidiaries may be considered as one entity (the fiscal unit) for tax purposes where a number of requirements are fulfilled. This means that the assets and liabilities of the subsidiaries are considered, for tax purposes, to belong to the parent company. The principal advantage of opting for fiscal unity is that the taxable profits and losses of all companies within the fiscal unit are pooled.

Furthermore, certain reorganisations are possible on a tax-free basis. The major conditions are as follows:

- the parent company holds at least 99% of the subsidiary;
- the financial years of the parent and subsidiary are the same;
- the shares are held throughout the financial year concerned;
- the companies must be Dutch (provided a number of conditions are fulfilled);
- foreign incorporated companies, which are resident in the Netherlands, can become part of a fiscal unity (both as the parent and the subsidiary company).

In the past, foreign companies which intended to acquire a Dutch resident company often first incorporated a Dutch subholding company which subsequently acquired the target company financing the acquisition with debt. Interest expenses could be offset against the profits of the target due to fiscal unity. Recent legislation may limit the deductibility of such interest expenses to the profits of the subholding company only. Where the acquisition of a target is financed by way of an inter company loan, the interest expenses may only be offset against the profits of the subholding. An acquisition funded by external debt, however, will in principle remain unaffected.

Group finance companies

Dutch companies may form a risk reserve for a number of finance activities under the group finance companies regime. The Dutch company should be part of an international group, although the finance function need not be its sole activity. However, its activities should be conducted solely from the Netherlands. In order to qualify, the entity must meet both the 'country test' and the 'activity test'.

Country test

The entity should perform finance activities for group companies, which are established in at least four countries or two continents. In principle, the entity should receive, of its gross income, at least 5% per country or 10% per continent but a limited pooling (either per country or continent) is possible. The entity's activities may also include the financing of Dutch group companies subject to certain ratios.

Activity test

The company must finance assets or business activities of the group, including the financing of participations irrespective of whether participation exemption is applicable. This includes financial and operational leasing but excludes the financing of third parties and passive investments.

Addition to the reserve

The entity may add 80% of its annual profits from the qualifying finance activities to the reserve, including the income from short-term investments which are held to fund acquisitions and which are in line with the activities of the group. A maximum addition to the reserve should not exceed 80% of the taxable income of the Dutch company, otherwise there is no ceiling to the reserve.

Release of the reserve

There is a taxable and tax-free release of the reserve. A taxable reserve is released to annual profit. This applies to previous write-downs of loans and liquidation losses for which a provision was made in the past. A tax-free release can apply in the following circumstances:

- the entity may write down 50% of the acquisition cost of participation but should at the same time reduce the cost price of the participation by the same percentage;
- the entity may take a fully tax-free release for capital contributions to a group company which relate to the assumption of a liability by the group for a risk, which cannot be borne by the entity itself;
- the same applies to the acquisition cost of a participation, which in the opinion of the Ministry of Finance entails extraordinary risks.

Voluntary release

The facility provides for a voluntary release whereby the reserve is released during five years in equal parts and is taxed at a special rate of 10%. A mandatory release applies if the company ceases to be a Dutch resident, is being liquidated or no longer meets the conditions. In this case the release is taxed at 35%.

Tax-free mergers and disposals

Mergers can be tax exempt if certain conditions are met, particularly where assets or shares are exchanged for shares.

If the participation exemption is applicable, the disposal of subsidiaries is tax-free. This is generally preferable to a disposal of assets since any gain is not realised for tax purposes.

Liquidation of the company

An individual, substantial interest shareholder will in principle be subject to income tax (25%) on liquidation distributions to the extent that these exceed the paid-up capital.

If the shareholder is a company, the loss on liquidation is deductible and any surplus is taxed. However, if the participation exemption is applicable, a surplus is tax exempt while a loss may be deductible (depending on the circumstances).

Other taxes

Capital duty

Capital duty is levied at 0.55% of any contribution to the capital of a company in exchange for shares, including share premium and informal capital. Exemptions apply in the case of certain mergers and reorganisations.

Net worth tax

There is no annual net worth tax levied on companies.

Real estate transfer tax

The acquisition of Dutch immovable property and certain rights in immovable properties is subject to a 6% real estate transfer tax. A number of exceptions are available, for example, in cases of intra-group restructuring.

Incentives for foreign investors

In 1993, the Dutch Ministry of Finance published a resolution on 'Greenfield Investments' which provides for a potentially very attractive framework to foreign investors who intend to invest in the Netherlands. If the investment is at least NLG 10 million, and if a certain number of permanent jobs are created in the Netherlands, the effective corporate tax rates can be reduced substantially in a number of ways. Examples of this are taxation on a cost plus basis, amortisation of know-how and/or goodwill and accelerated depreciation.

The investment must be within a number of specific categories including distribution centres, head office activities and research and development.

Treatment of branches (branch profits tax)

The profits of foreign branches are treated as foreign source income (see above).

Branches in the Netherlands of foreign companies will normally be subject to corporate income tax. There is no separate branch profits tax.

Personal taxes

In order to stimulate the economy and employment opportunity, the basic rates of taxation are lowered. The reduction in taxation on labour has been financed by reductions in total collective expenditure and by increases in indirect taxes, such as VAT and environmental levies.

By lowering the taxation on income from employment, together with a shift from direct to indirect taxation, the Netherlands economic structure and its international competitive edge will be strengthened. Greater emphasis on environmental levies (such as those on energy consumption) will make a significant contribution towards achieving sustainable economic development.

In designing the new taxation system, the basic requirement was seen to be a more simple system which can be incorporated into the existing fiscal structure. The new arrangements must improve the operational efficiency and cost effectiveness of the collection system.

Main points of the Income Tax Act 2001

The Income Tax Act 2001 contains many changes to the existing taxation laws. The most important of these are:

- introduction of the 'box' system;
- introduction of the Investment Yield Tax;
- reduction of the rates in the existing taxation brackets;
- alterations to a number of deductions;
- personal allowances to be replaced by the 'Levy Rebate';
- individual taxation.

The 'box' system

The former income tax system was based on just one taxable income. This taxable income was made up of all the income that you received in a year such as your salary or social security payments, interest, the notional rental value of your own home, etc. Various deductions could then be made to arrive at your taxable income. These include mortgage interest relief and certain exceptional expenses. Under the new system you will not have one, but three taxable incomes, each of which falls into a 'box'. Each box has its own tax rate:

- box 1: taxable income from work and home ownership (progressive rate);
- box 2: taxable income from a substantial (business) interest (fixed rate of 25%);
- box 3: taxable income from savings and investments (fixed rate of 30%).

Each form of income is taxed in one box only: there can never be double taxation.

If the income in a box is negative, this cannot be set off against a positive income in one of the other boxes. However, it is possible to set the negative amount off against a positive income in the same box in past or future years.

The table below shows the box in which the various types of income are taxed.

A short explanation of each box follows:

Box 1 type of income	*Rate*
Taxable income from employment and home ownership	Sliding scale rising to 52%

Taxable income from employment and home ownership comprises:

- business income;
- wages, salary, social security payments, pension, etc.;
- the property you use as your principal residence (fixed rental value minus mortgage interest);
- gains from other activities;
- gains from self-employment;
- periodic receipts and payments (such as alimony);
- negative expenses relating to income provisions (e.g. refunds of life assurance or annuity premiums).

The taxable income is subject to deduction for:

- expenses relating to income provisions (e.g. life assurance premiums);
- childcare expenses;
- individual allowances.

Box 2 type of income	*Rate*
Taxable income from a substantial shareholding	25%

Box 3 type of income	*Rate*
Taxable income from savings and investments	30%

The fixed assumed yield has been established at 4% per annum. This amount is taxed at the rate of 30%.

The assumed yield is calculated according to the average market value of capital and assets*, minus outstanding debts in any one year (to arrive at the 'yield assessment base').

*Capital and assets include:

- shares and savings deposits;
- (rights to) real estate (other than the principal residence);
- other (moveable) property not in personal use.

The current 'wealth tax' *(vermogensbelasting)* has been abolished.

Taxable individuals

The extent to which the income of an individual is subject to Dutch tax depends on whether he is resident in the Netherlands.

Residents

Residence is 'determined according to circumstances'. Major factors are physical presence, having a home at one's disposal, location of family and centre of economic and social activities.

A person who leaves the Netherlands and returns within one year without having been resident elsewhere will be treated as resident in the Netherlands for the intervening period. A person who arrives in the Netherlands in the course of a year will be considered a resident from the date of arrival if it is his intention to stay. An individual who is resident in the Netherlands is subject to income tax on his worldwide income.

Non-residents

Non-residents are normally subject to income tax on:

Box 1

- business income;
- wages, salary, social security payments, pension, etc;
- the property you use as your principal residence (fixed rental value minus mortgage interest);
- gains from other activities;
- gains from self-employment;
- governmental benefits;
- negative expenses relating to income provisions (e.g. refunds of life assurance or annuity premiums);

less:

- expenses relating to income provisions (e.g. life assurance premiums);
- childcare expenses;

Box 2

- substantial shareholdings in companies residing in the Netherlands;

Box 3

- (rights to) real estate located in the Netherlands.

A wide network of double taxation agreements reduces liabilities of non-residents.

Box 1

Besides the income from employment and home ownership, this box also includes income which derives from past employment, such as (state and private) pensions and unemployment insurance benefits (*'werkloosleidswet'*).

Business income

For income tax purposes, trading profits are calculated in accordance with generally accepted accounting principles. Accounts must normally be prepared for the calendar year (other tax years are not normally permitted).

Gains made in the course of business are treated as taxable income. The transfer of a business to a company or to an employee is tax-free, subject to certain conditions. Rollover relief is available for capital assets in certain cases.

Wages and directors' remuneration and fees

An employee (including a director) who is resident in the Netherlands is normally taxed on all his emoluments for a tax year. Most benefits in kind are taxable. Deductions are available for employees' contributions to an approved pension fund and some social security contributions. For expenses incurred for commuting by bike or public transport, fixed amounts can be deducted. All other expenses incurred are not deductible anymore.

Gains from other activities

This is any income which is not directly derived from paid employment (in the form of wages or salary), or from self-employment. For example, this could be income derived from giving lectures, consultancy work or any form of freelance activity.

Individual allowance

The individual allowance is the sum of the following deductions:

- expenses in relation to personal (maintenance) obligations (e.g. alimony);
- losses from financial loans to starting businesses (the so-called 'Auntie Agatha' scheme);
- expenses relating to the maintenance of children under 27 years of age, where such maintenance is your direct responsibility;
- exceptional expenses incurred by yourself, your partner, or any children under 27 years of age (e.g. as the result of chronic illness, invalidity or death);
- weekend expenses for disabled children over the age of 27;
- school and study costs;
- expenses for the maintenance of listed buildings;
- deductible gifts and donations.

It is possible that the income in box 1 will be less than the sum of all deductions making up the individual allowance. If this is the case, you can deduct the remainder of the allowance from the income in box 3. If a proportion of the personal allowance still remains, this can then be deducted from the income in box 2.

Rate

The tax rate on income in box 1 is progressive, i.e. there is a sliding scale whereby the tax burden becomes greater in proportion to your income. The rates for box 1 are:

Taxable income from employment social and home ownership		*Percentage including security premiums*	
More than	*Less than*	*Under 65*	*Over 65*
0	NLG 32,769	32.35%	14.45%
NLG 32,769	NLG 59,520	37.60%	19.70%
NLG 59,520	NLG 102,052	42.00%	42.00%
NLG 102,052		52.00%	52.00%

Box 2

All income deriving from a substantial shareholding is taxed. In general, a substantial shareholding exists if you either directly or indirectly own at least 5% of the issued share capital in a corporation. It does not only include shares, but also options, profit shares and receivables on the company. There are additional attribution rules in respect of spouse, partners and certain other family members.

Gains from a substantial shareholding include: liquidation gains and gains from a redemption of the company's shares, the transfer of shares in the course of a legal merger and the emigration of the substantial shareholder, which is treated as a deemed disposition of the shares. In the latter case, an assessment will be raised which must be paid if the shares are sold within a period of ten years.

Gains from a substantial shareholding, including dividends, are taxable at a fixed rate of 25%. Losses are likewise deductible. A negative taxable income can be offset against taxable income from box 2 in the three preceding and all the next years. If you do not have a substantial shareholding anymore and a loss is still not offset, you get a tax credit of 25% of that loss which can be offset against the taxes due on other boxes.

In addition, there are a number of deeming provisions which the substantial shareholder is required to report for tax purposes. These include a minimum income from employment (generally speaking he is deemed to earn an income of not less than NLG 84,000 per year), income from loans made by him to the corporation (interest equals normal market rate) and income from leasing property to the corporation (rent equals normal market rate and capital gain is taxable).

Box 3

Box 3 taxes the income derived from savings and investments. A significant change when compared to the existing situation is that the income from savings and investments will no longer comprise separate interest, dividend and rental revenues. The new system is based on a fixed yield (or return) on your assets and it is this yield which becomes taxable by means of the Investment Yield Tax. Interest paid and other costs cease to be deductible.

The taxable income in box 3 is calculated at 4% of the economic value of your property, minus the amount of your outstanding debts, based on the average balance over the course of the year. The new Investment Yield Tax will apply to such assets as real estate, stocks and shares, saving deposits and non-exempt endowment insurance. The house which you use as your principal residence does not fall under the Investment Yield Tax.

A number of assets are exempt from the Investment Yield Tax. They include: works of art (unless purchased primarily for investment purposes) and moveable property for personal use. Exemptions apply to 'social' investments such as green or ethical investments (maximum NLG 103,539, double for married couples), 'incubator' investments (maximum NLG 103,539, double for married couples) and exempted endowment insurance.

Everyone benefits from a basic tax-free allowance of NLG 39,785. This allowance will replace the interest and dividend allowance. If you are over 65 you are entitled to an extra allowance if certain conditions are met.

Deduction of interest payments on consumer credit (for televisions, cars etc.) has been restricted since 1997. Debts (including consumer credit loans) reduce the assessment base for saving and investments in box 3, as debts can be subtracted from the assessment base on which the 4% yield is calculated. Debts in excess of the threshold amount of NLG 5,509 are tax deductible.

The levy rebate

The former basic personal allowance (that part of your income which was not taxable) has disappeared and been replaced by the '*heffingskorting*' or Levy Rebate. This is in effect a discount on the amount of tax you have to pay.

The Levy Rebate comprises a general rebate together with a number of supplementary rebates. While everyone is entitled to the general levy rebate, the amount will depend on personal circumstances.

General levy rebate

The general levy rebate for taxpayers under 65 will be up to NLG 3,473 per year. The general levy rebate for taxpayers over 65 will be up to NLG 1,552. If you have a partner who does not have an independent income, he or she is nevertheless entitled to the general levy rebate. This amount will be credited directly to your partner.

Your general levy rebate may be increased by one or more of the following rebates provided you meet the corresponding requirements:

	Amount Under 65 (NLG)	*Amount Over 65 (NLG)*
Employment rebate	(Max) 2,027	906
Child rebate	84	38
Supplementary child rebate	423	189
Combination rebate	304	136
Single parent rebate	2,779	1,242
Supplementary single parent rebate	(Max) 2,779	(Max) 1,242

Senior citizens rebate	(Max) 520
Supplementary senior citizens rebate	(Max) 547

Individual taxation

Each partner is taxed on his or her own income. A partner is defined as a spouse or a legally registered partner. Under certain conditions, couples living together that are not married or registered may also be regarded as partners, in the same way as they are now.

For so-called joint income items and joint deduction items, couples have a choice as to which partner is to be taxed on which part of the income. Any system of dividing the income and allowances between the partners is permissible, provided all income is declared, i.e. the partners shares add up to 100%.

Deductions must never exceed 100% either, of course. This division will be possible for:

- income from home ownership;
- gains from savings and investments;
- childcare expenses;
- gifts, donations and exceptional expenses.

Each partner will be entitled to exactly the same rebate, even where he or she has little or no personal income. In that case, a proportion of the general levy rebate will be paid to the partner with the low income in the form of a provisional tax refund. The amount to be paid will be no more than the partner with the higher income is liable to pay in tax. The levy rebate will therefore never exceed the amount of the couple's joint tax liability.

Home ownership

This section contains information on home ownership and mortgages, endowment insurances and home ownership as well as second homes.

Home ownership and mortgages

There are no changes to the way in which private home ownership of your first home affects your tax liability. The notional income you derive from your own home is established by means of the 'fixed rental value' of your house, i.e. the sum you would have to pay in rent if you were not the owner. The deduction options for mortgage interest relief and interest charges on loans for purchase, maintenance or improvement of the home are maximised for a period of 30 years.

However, the 'fixed rental value' will apply only to the principal residence.

Each household can have only one principal residence. All other real estate, such as a second home, will fall under the 'Investment Yield Tax' in box 3.

When you buy a new house it could be that at the time of purchase you have not yet sold your old house and are therefore a temporary owner of two residences. The old house is no longer your principal residence and would therefore normally fall under box 3. In order to facilitate the process of house purchase, a temporary relaxation of this rule is to be allowed. In such cases, you may continue to regard the old house as a 'principal residence' for a limited period, provided it is actively being offered for sale. In this way, the mortgage interest on the old house will remain deductible.

The reverse situation is also possible: your new house remains temporarily unoccupied after purchase. Here too, a relaxation of the rules is allowed. You may deduct the mortgage interest on this new house even though it is not (yet) your principal residence, under the condition that it is indeed to become your principal residence in the near future.

The exemptions and allowances for room rental and for the purchase and maintenance of listed buildings will be maintained.

Endowment insurance and home ownership

The purchase of a house is often financed by means of mortgage loans. In many cases, this will involve an (life) endowment policy which will effectively repay the amount borrowed upon maturity, or upon the death of the policyholder. The lump sum payment made to the insured upon maturity contains an element of interest which is currently not taxable. If the insured has paid premiums, the maturity payment is subject to certain tax exemptions, regardless of the purpose to which it is to be put.

The exemption will relate directly to home ownership only. There must be a direct link between the life endowment policy and the outstanding mortgage debt on your property. The policy must clearly show that you intend to use the payment upon maturity to repay the mortgage.

Other forms of endowment insurance schemes which are not intended for paying off the mortgage will be subject to the Investment Yield Tax, although certain types of policy will enjoy exemption, such as those which only provide a payment in the case of invalidity, illness, accident or death (e.g. funeral expenses policies).

A second home

If you are the owner of a second home or other real estate, you will be affected by the Investment Yield Tax of box 3. Here, it is not the notional rent (or 'Fixed Rental Value') that is taxed, but the notional yield on the investment that property represents. Mortgage interest and the costs of maintenance will no longer be deductible. However, the tax payable within box 3 will of course be reduced by the mortgage payments you make on the second home, since outstanding debts of this nature will reduce the assessment base on which the tax is calculated.

Annuities and pension provision

Not all life assurance premiums are deductible. Life assurance premiums on policies related to lifetime annuities for disabled children and grandchildren (over the age of majority) and on periodical payments and benefits relating to disability, illness or accident will continue to be deductible.

Deduction of premiums for a terminable retirement annuity, a surviving dependant's annuity and a bridging annuity is restricted to a basic deduction of no more than NLG 2,283 and only in the event of a demonstrable pension provision shortfall. The maximum amount applies to individuals only and is not transferable.

Alongside your AOW and any other pension provisions made, the new tax system allows you to build up a pension provision of 70% of your final salary at 65. Within these limits, there is scope for deducting premiums for a terminable retirement annuity, surviving dependant's annuity and a bridging annuity.

The extra scope for tax-deductible premiums on individual pension provisions is made up of an annual margin and a reserve regulation. The annual margin gives you the opportunity to compensate the pension shortfall in the actual year in question, while the reserve regulation compensates the pension shortfalls which have arisen if you have failed to take full advantage of the annual margin in previous years.

The amount of your annual margin and reserve regulation is worked out on the basis of your premium calculation base, up to a maximum of NLG 292,589. This premium calculation is made up of the sum of the following income elements:

- profit from business activities;
- taxable income;
- taxable gains from other employment;
- taxable periodical payments and benefits;

less the AOW (state pension) threshold of NLG 21,808. This threshold is applied because the amount of your state pension has to be taken into account when your pension is calculated.

Premiums for life assurance policies to make up a pension shortfall in the year in question are deductible up to the annual margin. To qualify for the annual margin, you must be under 65 on 1 January on the year in question. The annual margin is 17% of your premium calculation base less the amount that you have already built up in that year in respect of your professional pension and fiscal old-age reserve (a fiscal arrangement for the self-employed).

In order to make up previous pension shortfalls there is the option to make up the annual margin that has not been used (reserve regulation). The maximum reserve regulation available is 17% of your premium calculation base up to a maximum of NLG 12,579. The maximum amount for taxpayers aged over 55 at the start of the calendar year is NLG 24,849.

The reserve regulation means that if you have deducted less premiums in one year than the annual margin amount allowed for that year, you can still use the non-deducted amount at a later stage. The non-deducted annual margin can be reserved for a maximum of seven years.

Personal obligations and exceptional expenses

The costs incurred for the maintenance of children over the age of 27 and of immediate relatives will cease to be deductible. However, the current deductions for expenses relating to children younger than 27 will continue to apply.

Exceptional expenses in connection with chronic illness, invalidity, childbirth and death will continue to be deductible, provided they relate to yourself, your partner or children under 27. Expenses incurred on behalf of aunts, uncles, etc., will no longer be deductible. A new deduction is that for the weekend expenses of disabled children over the age of 27.

Deductions for the costs of study and professional training are to be replaced by a higher general education allowance up to a maximum of

NLG 33,056. A threshold of NLG 1,102 applies to this allowance. Expenses for childcare will remain deductible in part, as will gifts and donations.

Employee savings schemes and premium savings schemes

The existing rules applying to employee savings schemes and premium savings schemes will be maintained under the new system at NLG 1,736 for employee savings schemes and NLG 1,158 for premium savings schemes.

The possibility of withdrawing employee savings scheme deposits tax-free within four years is to be extended. This will allow you to withdraw employee savings schemes deposits tax-free for the purposes of starting your own business, to finance a sabbatical or a course of study.

Tax year and filing requirements

The taxable period is the calendar year. In exceptional circumstances a different fiscal year may be permitted.

Returns must be filed by 1 April following the year concerned (in certain cases postponement is possible). Residents who are not required to file a return may do so voluntarily if they expect a refund of a minimum of NLG 26, provided the return is filed within three years.

Non-residents are required to file a return if they have certain Dutch source income.

The inspector must raise an assessment within three years of the end of the year concerned. In the absence of a return, an estimated assessment may be raised.

Special treatment for expatriates

A special facility called the 30% ruling is available to individuals seconded to the Netherlands within an international group or employed by a Dutch employer because they have special knowledge and experience which is not available or scarce in the Netherlands. The employer may pay the employee a tax-free allowance to a maximum of 30% of employment income. The 30% ruling normally applies for ten years (reviewed after a maximum period of five years).

An expatriate is treated as resident or non-resident according to the normal rules, but if he is a resident taxpayer he can opt for non-residence status so that foreign investment income is not taxed.

Payment of tax

Income tax must be paid within two months after the date of the final assessment.

Payroll deductions

An employer deducts wage tax from wages and salaries. The amount deducted may be offset against the final income tax payable (and where applicable a refund can be claimed).

Prepayments

Provisional assessments may be raised during the tax year or subsequently. Payments on provisional assessments may be spread over the tax year concerned with a minimum period of two months.

Estate and gift tax

Gifts and inheritances are taxable in the Netherlands. The rates applied depend on:

- the amount received;
- the relationship of the recipient to the deceased or donor.

Rates vary from 5% to 27% for transfers to spouse and children to 41% to 68% for transfers to unrelated parties. Various exemptions apply, depending on the relationship and type of gift. Non-residents can be subject to tax on certain transfers of Dutch property. The Netherlands has a number of estate and gift tax treaties.

Wealth tax

Wealth tax is abolished as of 2001.

Social security contributions

The Dutch social security system consists of:

- general funds, to which everyone is entitled, whether or not they are employees (e.g. state pension);
- specific industry related funds for different types of benefit (e.g. unemployment benefit, sickness benefit and invalidity

benefit). Rates vary according to the industry and are subject to a maximum limit. Employers' contributions can amount to 25% of salary. State health insurance is not available to higher paid (NLG 64.300) individuals who must therefore insure privately.

Other taxes

Treatment of partnerships

Profits made by a partnership are allocated to the partners in accordance with their profit shares and taxed in the partners' hands. Certain types of limited partnership may be taxed as companies.

VAT and sales taxes

Most goods and services within the Netherlands are subject to 19% VAT, but certain essential goods and services are taxed at 6%. A zero rate applies to the export of goods and services.

Other taxes

Transfer tax of 6% is levied on the transfer of real estate and certain securities relating to real estate:

- excise duties are levied on alcohol, tobacco, fuel, sugar and certain soft drinks;
- property tax is a local tax based on the value of the property and levied on both the owner and the user.

Exchange control

Exchange controls basically consist of a reporting requirement in respect of movements in excess of NLG 20,000 into and out of the country.

Tax treaties and withholding taxes

Under most double taxation conventions concluded by the Netherlands, the dividend tax rate of 25% is reduced or waived completely. There is no withholding tax on interest and royalties paid to non-residents. Withholding tax rates on dividends under selected tax treaties (and, where applicable, European Directives) in force as from 1 January are as follows:

	Normal rate	*Minimum participation required in foreign companies*	*Special rates*
Non-treaty countries	25	–	–
Selected treaty countries:			
Argentina	15	25	10
Australia (a)	15	–	–
Austria (a)	15	25	0 & 5 (b)
Bangladesh	15	10	10
Belarus (c)	15	25 & 50	5 & 0
Belgium (a)	15	25	0 & 5 (b)
Bosnia-Herzegovina	15	25	5
Brazil	15	–	–
Bulgaria	15	25	5
Canada	15	10 (voting stock)	5
China	10	–	–
Croatia (a)	15	10	0
Czech Republic (a)	10	25	0
Denmark	15	25	0 & 0 (b)
Egypt	15	25	0
Estonia	15	25	5
Finland (e)	15	25	0 & 0 (b)
France (a)	15	25	0 & 5 (b)
Germany (a)	15	25(voting stock)	0 &10 (b)
Greece	15	25	0 & 5 (b)
Hungary	15	25	5
Iceland	15	10	0
India (a)	15	–	–
Indonesia	15	25	10 (d)
Ireland (a)	15	25 (voting stock)	0 & 0 (b)
Israel	15	25	5
Italy	15	50 & 10	0, 5 & 10 (b)
Japan	15	25 (voting stock)	5/10 (d)
Kazakhstan	15	50 & 10	0 & 5
Korea (South)	15	25	10
Latvia	15	25	5
Lithuania (c)	15	25	5
Luxembourg (f)	15	25	0 & 2.5 (b)
Macedonia	15	10	0
Malawi	25	–	–
Malaysia (a)	15	25	0
Malta	15	25	0/5 (d)
Mexico	15	10	5
Morocco	25	25	10
Netherlands Antilles (a)	15	25	5 & 7.5
New Zealand (a)	15	–	–

Nigeria	15	10	12.5
Norway	15	25	0
Pakistan	20	25	10
Philippines	15	10	10
Poland	15	25	0
Portugal (c)	10	25	0
Romania (d)	15	25 & 10	5 & 0
Russian Federation (d)	15	25	5
Singapore	15	25	0
Slovakia	10	25	0
Slovenia (a)	15	25	5
South Africa	15	25 (voting stock)	5
Spain (a)	15	50 (25 + 25)	0 & 5 (b)
Sri Lanka	15	25	10
Surinam (a)	20	25	7.5 & 15
Sweden	15	25	0 (b) (d)
Switzerland (a)	15	25	0 (d)
Thailand	25	25	5 (d)
Tunisia	20	10	0
Turkey	20	25	5 & 15 (d)
Ukraine	15	20	0/5
United Kingdom (a)	15	25 (voting stock)	0 & 5 (b)
United States	15	10 (voting stock)	5 (d)
USSR (g)	15	–	–
Venezuela	10	25	0 (d)
Vietnam	15	25 & 50	5 & 7 (d)
Yugoslavia (h)	15	25	5
Zambia	15	25	5
Zimbabwe	20	25	10

Notes

(a) Tax treaties, which are either being renegotiated, or which will be renegotiated soon.

(b) These represent EU countries with which the Netherlands has concluded a treaty. According to the EU parent-subsidiary directive, dividends paid by a Dutch company to its qualifying EU parent company can be paid gross. The treaty rates are the second and the third rates.

(c) These represent new treaties which have been renegotiated and signed but have yet to come into force.

(d) Reduced rates apply only under certain conditions.

(e) Treaties have been renegotiated but are not yet in force. The table shows the old treaty rates.

(f) Treaty benefits do not apply to exempt Luxembourg holding companies.

(g) This treaty can be applied to all the new republics of the former USSR until a new tax treaty comes into force. The new treaties with Belarus, Kazakhstan, Latvia, Lithuania and the Russian Federation are listed above.

(h) This treaty can be applied to Bosnia-Herzegovina, Croatia (see list and a), Slovenia and the Federal Republic of Yugoslavia (Montenegro and Serbia).

New Zealand

Spicer & Oppenheim

(Readers: please note, that the information here was correct at January 1999)

Introduction

Tax reform in New Zealand has slowed down since its peak in the mid-80s with one or two amendment acts now being passed each year and a Government that consults widely, enabling taxpayers and interested parties to have their say about proposed legislation. The Income Tax Act is currently being rewritten and the reforms, which are substantial, are likely to have an effect upon tax outcomes. Valuation of trading stock was recently reformed (and is discussed below) and self-assessment, GST, tax simplification and the tax system are all currently under review. An inquiry into the powers and operation of the Inland Revenue is planned, while a government appointed committee of experts recently produced a report listing possible improvements to the system of tax administration in the country.

Corporate taxes

Taxable entities

Resident companies

Resident companies are taxable on their worldwide income from all sources, with the exception of dividends received from NZ subsidiaries. A company is deemed to be resident in New Zealand (NZ) if it is incorporated in NZ or has its head office or centre of management in NZ, or control by directors is exercised in NZ.

Non-resident companies

Non-resident companies are taxable on income derived from NZ.

Tax year and filing requirements

The tax year is the year ending 31 March, although companies and businesses may (with approval) have other year ends. Tax returns must be filed on or before 7 July in each year (or for companies with a late balance date, on or before the seventh day of the fourth month immediately following the end of the taxpayer's annual balance date). The Commissioner may grant an extension of time where the returns are prepared by a registered tax agent. In the absence of a return, a default assessment may be raised. The Commissioner has no time limits under which to issue an assessment, but cannot amend an assessment later than four years from the end of the income year in which the taxpayer filed the return (assuming the return was not fraudulent or wilfully misleading).

Taxes imposed

All taxes on income are imposed at a national level on a preceding year basis. Companies must pay provisional tax in three instalments in the year of income. When provisional tax paid falls short of the tax assessed, the shortfall, called residual income tax (RIT), is payable during the following year. For a company with a standard balance date (31 March), RIT will be payable on 7 February of the following year.

Rates of tax

A single flat rate of tax is levied on all companies deriving income in NZ at a rate of 33%.

Income subject to tax

General rules

Income for tax purposes is determined in accordance with general accounting principles, but adjusted by taxing statutes to arrive at assessable income.

Stock/inventory valuation

Stock must be valued using a cost valuation method or market selling price (MSP) if MSP is less than cost.

Approved cost valuation methods are cost, discounted selling price or replacement.

Taxpayers are required to comply with generally accepted accounting principles in valuing their trading stock for taxation purposes.

Capital gains and losses

There is no capital gains tax in NZ. However, certain gains from land transactions may be subject to income tax if:

- the taxpayer's intention on acquisition was to sell the land;
- the taxpayer was dealing in land or operating as a builder;
- development is commenced within ten years of acquisition, or at any time if development involves significant expenditure or where the gain resulted through land zoning changes.

Exemptions from income tax are available where the land was occupied as a dwelling, used for business premises, or, if both prior to and subsequent to sale, the land is used in a farming business. Gains on investments in foreign investment funds and from financial arrangements may also be taxable.

Dividends

Dividends received by a company, whether from a NZ or overseas source, are assessable for income tax purposes. An exemption from tax is available for dividends received from wholly-owned subsidiaries. There is relief for tax withheld at source overseas.

Dividends received from an overseas company are subject to foreign dividend withholding payment tax (FDWP) at the rate of 33%, reduced by any foreign taxes paid. FDWP is an advance tax against a shareholder's ultimate tax liability.

A full imputation system operates in NZ.

Deductions

General rules

Expenses are deductible to the extent to which they are incurred in gaining gross income. Expenses of a capital nature are not deductible. There are certain exceptions, as set out below.

Depreciation and amortisation

Straight line and diminishing value depreciation methods are permitted. From 1 April 1995, all companies must use approved economic rates with a loading of 20% for new assets (excluding buildings). Companies may apply to the Commissioner for higher rates should they consider the economic rates to be inadequate. The straight-line and diminishing value rates have been calculated to yield an identical result over the economic life of the asset. An example of the diminishing value rates applicable to certain assets is set out below. The rate will depend on the industry use of the asset.

Buildings	1-4%
Plant and machinery, office equipment	10-33.3%
Dies, moulds	50%
Motor vehicles (business)	20-26%

Land and goodwill are not depreciable.

Fixed life intangible property (e.g. rights to use property) is depreciable.

Royalties

Royalties are subject to the general deduction rule (assuming they are at arm's length rates).

Interest

Interest, to the extent it is payable in gaining or producing gross income, is deductible. Interest on borrowings to finance group company acquisitions is deductible. Excessive interest may be deemed to be a dividend.

NZ has thin capitalisation rules. Generally, the rules will deny a deduction for interest paid on debt to related offshore entities if the debt-to-equity ratio of the payer exceeds 3:1 and 110% of the worldwide debt-to-equity ratio of the taxpayer's group.

Dividends

Dividends are not deductible. Dividends paid to non-resident shareholders are subject to non-resident withholding tax. Dividends paid to residents are subject to withholding tax.

However, a NZ company, subject to certain criteria being met, may pay dividends to non-resident shareholders without the effective impost of further tax in NZ through the Foreign Investor Tax Credit (FITC) regime.

Bad and doubtful debts

Specific bad debts written off are deductible in the year of write-off. Provisions for doubtful debts are not deductible.

Reserves and provisions

In general, reserves and provisions are not deductible.

Employees' and directors' remuneration and benefits

Employees' and directors' remuneration and benefits are generally deductible. Fringe benefit tax (FBT) is payable at the rate of 49% on the value of the benefit provided to employees and directors. FBT is deductible equating to an effective tax rate of 33%. Allowances to employees or directors which contain an entertainment element are 50% deductible.

Specifically non-deductible expenses

Entertainment expenditure is only 50% deductible (subject to certain exemptions and exclusions). Excessive remuneration paid by proprietary companies is not deductible and may be treated as a dividend. Capital expenditure is not deductible (subject to the depreciation rules outlined above) nor are gifts and certain donations.

Foreign source income

Foreign source income is subject to NZ tax and a NZ company is taxed on its worldwide income. A credit for withholding tax is usually given for dividends, interest and royalties from treaty countries. A controlled foreign corporation (CFC) regime operates to tax NZ residents on branch equivalent profits in CFCs. A foreign investment fund (FIF) regime also operates to claw back gains in FIFs into the NZ tax net.

Investment incentives and special benefits

Investment incentives and benefits are rare, reflecting the Government's 'free market' philosophy.

Related party transactions

Transactions between companies or other persons under common control may be subject to investigation by the Revenue authorities if they are not carried out on an arm's length basis. Application of a company's assets for the benefit of shareholders (or entities associated with shareholders) for inadequate consideration may give rise to dividends assessable to the shareholder (or associate). Depreciation claims on assets sold between related parties will be restricted.

Losses

Business losses are fully deductible against business income arising in the same year. Any unutilised loss may be carried forward indefinitely and set off where there is a common 49% ownership continuously throughout the period between loss and set-off. Special rules allow automatic loss set-off in a wholly owned group of companies or the 'transfer' of a loss by means of subvention payment in the case of companies with a minimum 66% common shareholding.

Corporate groups

A parent company and its resident subsidiaries may be considered as one entity for tax purposes under the consolidation regime. A number of requirements have to be fulfilled and the assets and liabilities of all group members are considered, for tax purposes, to belong to the appointed agent of the group. Certain reorganisations are possible on a tax-free basis. All members of the consolidated group must guarantee the tax liability of the group. Not all members of the corporate group need to join the consolidated group for tax purposes.

Tax-free mergers and disposals

As there is no capital gains tax in NZ, mergers do not often give rise to taxation implications (although care must be taken in regard to losses carried forward and imputation credits).

Liquidation of the company

An individual shareholder will, in principle, be subject to income tax (depending on his/her marginal tax rate) on 'excess return amounts' distributed on the liquidation of a company. Broadly, the excess return amount represents assets distributed, less capital gains and paid-up capital. Capital gains may only be distributed tax free upon wind-up.

Capital taxes

No capital taxes exist in NZ.

Treatment of branches (branch profits tax)

Profits of foreign branches of NZ resident companies are taxable in NZ.

Branches of foreign companies in NZ will be subject to corporate income tax at the non-resident rate of 33%. There is no separate branch profits tax.

Personal taxes

Taxable individuals

The extent to which the income of an individual is subject to NZ tax depends on whether he is resident in NZ.

Residents

An individual is deemed to be an NZ resident if that person:

- has a permanent place of abode in NZ (even if he or she also has a permanent place of abode outside NZ);
- is personally present in NZ for longer than a total of 183 days in any 12 month period;
- is absent from NZ on government service.

An individual ceases to be an NZ resident if he:

- is absent from NZ for more than 325 days in any 12 month period;
- does not maintain a permanent place of abode in NZ during that time.

Non-residents

All income derived by non-residents which is sourced in NZ is taxable in NZ. Certain exceptions exist under double taxation agreements.

Tax year and filing requirements

The taxable period is the year ended 31 March, although a different fiscal year may be granted for agricultural and horticultural activities, due to seasonal activities.

Subject to limited exceptions, all residents are required to file a taxation return. Salary and wage earners are generally not required to file income tax returns.

A return must be filed by 7 July in the year of balance date. Time extensions are available where the return is completed by a registered tax agent.

Non-residents are required to file a return if they have NZ sourced income.

The Commissioner is under no obligation to issue an assessment within a certain time period and can issue a default assessment in the absence of a return. However, he cannot amend an assessment later than four years from the end of the income year in which the taxpayer filed the return (assuming the return was not fraudulent or wilfully misleading).

Taxes on income

Individuals are subject only to central government income tax which is levied on a graduated scale depending on the level of taxable income.

Accident Compensation contributions are payable by both employers and employees. Employers must hold cover with a private provider while employees pay a levy to a government agency.

Sources of income

Employment income and directors' fees

An employee (including a director) who is resident in NZ is normally taxed on all his emoluments for a tax year. Benefits in kind are subject to fringe benefit tax (FBT) which is payable by the employer (i.e. non-taxable to the employee). The only expenses claimable against employment are fees paid for the preparation of tax returns.

Income derived by a non-resident performing personal services (other than public entertainers and professional sportsmen) during a visit to NZ is exempt from tax in NZ if:

- he is resident in another country and is present in NZ for not more than 183 days in any income year ended 31 March;
- he is employed by an individual company resident in the other country (in the case of the USA, Singapore, Canada, Sweden, Japan and Malaysia) or resident simply outside NZ (in the case of UK, Australia and Fiji);
- the income is subject to tax in the visitor's normal country of

residence (this is a requirement of the double tax agreements with Australia, Sweden, Japan and Canada only).

If the visit extends beyond 183 days, NZ tax is imposed on the income earned in NZ.

Where the income is derived by a non-resident of a country with which NZ does not have a double tax agreement, the provisions are similar, except that the duration of the visit must not exceed 92 days.

Business income

For income tax purposes, trading profits are calculated in accordance with generally accepted accounting principles. Accounts have to be prepared for the year ending on the taxpayer's balance date. Non-standard balance dates (i.e. other than 31 March) are allowed for certain farming, agricultural and horticultural activities.

Business losses are fully deductible against business income arising in the same income year and unutilised losses may be carried forward indefinitely.

Capital gains

There is no capital gains tax in New Zealand. Certain land transactions may be subject to income tax if:

- the taxpayer's intention on acquisition was to sell the land;
- the taxpayer was dealing in land, developing land or operating as a builder;
- development was commenced within ten years of acquisition, or at any time if development involved significant expenditure;
- the profit resulted from land zoning changes.

Exemptions from tax are available where the land was occupied as a dwelling, used for business, or, if both prior to and subsequent to sale, the land is used in a farming business.

Gains on investments in foreign investment funds and from financial arrangements may also be taxable.

Speculative and investment gains (e.g. sale of shares) are generally tax exempt provided the investment was not acquired with the intention of re-sale. The transfer of a business to a company is tax-free, subject to certain conditions.

Dividends

Dividends are subject to tax at the taxpayer's marginal tax rate (unless the dividend was derived from a capital source on the wind-up of the company). A credit is available for withholding tax deducted from the dividend or imputation tax credits attached to the dividend. An individual who holds shares in a controlled foreign company (CFC) may be taxed on his/her share of the branch equivalent profit of the CFC. Dividends are subject to resident withholding tax of 33%.

A full imputation system operates in NZ.

Interest

Interest is subject to resident withholding tax (RWT) at a rate of 19.5% (or 33% by election). It is taxable in the hands of the recipient at the recipient's marginal tax rate.

Rentals

Rents received from letting real estate are subject to income tax. Deductions are allowable for expenses, including depreciation and interest. Deductibility of expenses is in accordance with the general deductibility rules.

Royalties

Royalties received are taxed as normal income, subject to a deduction for expenses and depreciation of the cost of the rights.

Social welfare benefits

Income-tested benefits are taxable in the hands of the recipient.

Pensions and annuities

Pensions paid on or after 1 April 1990 from a superannuation fund are not assessable for income tax. Annuities paid on or after 1 April 1990 by a life insurer who is subject to the NZ Life Insurance Regime are exempt for taxation purposes.

Exempt income

The following income is exempt:

- alimony, maintenance or child support;

- payments to non-resident entertainers sponsored by any government as part of a cultural programme or sponsored by a non-NZ resident, non-profit making organisation existing for the promotion of cultural activities;
- prize money in respect of any form of racing where the prize is paid out by a club licensed to use the totalisator;
- social welfare benefits which are not guaranteed retirement income or income-tested benefits;
- scholarships or bursaries paid in respect of attendance at an educational institution other than basic grants or independent circumstances grants made pursuant to education regulations;
- income derived from personal services in NZ by non-residents providing professional or expert advice pursuant to any arrangement entered into the by the NZ government;
- benefits paid pursuant to a claim under a sickness or accident insurance policy;
- premiums received on redemption of any inflation-adjusted savings bond;
- compensation for criminal injuries.

Foreign source income

NZ residents are taxable on their worldwide income. Generally, for dividends, interest and royalties from treaty countries and from listed developing countries, a credit for withholding tax is given. A controlled foreign company (CFC) regime operates in NZ to claw back branch equivalent profits of CFCs into the NZ tax net. A foreign investment fund regime operates similarly.

Personal allowances and deductions

Relief is generally given by way of rebates from tax payable rather than by allowances against taxable income. A family support tax credit is available for low income families and low income rebates apply to all taxpayers with annual taxable income not exceeding NZ$ 38,000.

Losses

Where an individual sustains a loss, he may offset it against the positive income in future tax years. Losses not utilised can be carried forward indefinitely.

Special family rules

NZ taxation legislation does not treat the family as a distinct taxable entity. The income from married taxpayers is taxable in the hands of the spouse who earns the income. Family income is only relevant in the case of a family support tax credit applying to low income families. Income earned by dependant children is taxed in the hands of those children. In certain circumstances a child is entitled to a rebate against assessable income.

Special treatment for expatriates

No special rules apply to foreign expatriates employed in NZ. Income derived from personal services in NZ by non-residents providing professional or expert advice, teaching or lecturing, or making investigations pursuant to any arrangement entered into by the NZ government may be exempt for tax purposes.

Rates of tax

The following graduated scale of income tax rates applies to individual taxpayers in NZ.

Band NZ$	*Rate*	*Tax on Band NZ$*	*Cumulative Tax NZ$*
0 – 38,000	19.5%	7410.00	7410.00
38,001 and above	33%	varies	varies

There is no specific tax rate for non-residents and general rates apply.

Provincial and local taxes

There are no provincial and local taxes on income.

Withholding taxes

Withholding tax at 33% is levied on dividends distributed to individuals; 19.5% withholding tax is levied on interest paid to individuals. Withholding tax can be offset against the final personal income tax payable (and where applicable, a refund can be claimed).

Withholding payment regulations define a number of personal service activities (not representing an employee/employer relationship) that are subject to withholding tax. These include commission agents, casual agricultural workers, entertainers, sportspersons and non-resident contractors.

In the case of payments to non-residents, NZ withholds taxes on:

- royalties and interest at 15% and on dividends at 30%, or at lower treaty rates (there is a 2% NZ levy option for interest on non-related party transactions);
- payments in the nature of fees, prize or appearance money at 20% to a non-resident entertainer or professional sportsperson. This is a final liability on such income and the non-resident is not required to furnish a return;
- payments made to non-residents in respect of any 'contract activity' at 15% on gross payments; a 'contract activity' is either work carried on in NZ relating to construction, installation, assembly and similar projects, or consultancy, advisory and other professional or technical services given in respect of such projects for the hire of personnel or equipment to be used in NZ.

Tax credits

The Family Support and Independent Family Tax Credit schemes are designed to assist low and middle income earning families. There are three parts to the scheme:

- Family Support Tax Credit (FSTC) based on both income earned and the number of dependant children in the family;
- Guaranteed Minimum Family Income Tax Credit (GMFI) designed to ensure that families with dependant children receive a statutory set minimum income guaranteed by the State;
- Independent Family Tax Credit (IFTC), also based on both income earned and the number of dependant children in the family.

Eligibility to benefit under these schemes is based on a combination of household income and the number of dependant children in the household. Consequently, eligibility varies from year to year.

A transitional tax allowance is also payable to taxpayers working full time who do not qualify for any family tax credits. The rebate is NZ$ 728 per annum on income up to NZ$ 6,240 and is reduced by 20% for income between NZ$ 6,240 and NZ$ 9,880 per annum, phasing out completely at NZ$ 9,880.

Other rebates include:

- low income (available up to NZ$ 38,000 of income);
- housekeeper (33 cents for each dollar paid, to a maximum of NZ$ 310);
- donations (which, if to approved organisations, may qualify for a

rebate of 33 cents for every qualifying gift or donation to a maximum rebate of $500).

A non-resident who has income from personal services in NZ may claim a proportion of some rebates according to the period spent in NZ.

A credit is also available for overseas tax actually paid, limited to the lesser of the foreign tax or the NZ tax payable on the foreign income.

Payment of tax

Provisional tax is payable in three equal instalments on the seventh day of the fourth, eighth and twelfth months of the taxpayer's income year. Any shortfall between provisional tax and the final tax liability is defined as residual income tax (RIT). RIT is payable on 7 February of the year following balance date for those taxpayers with a standard balance date of 31 March, or on other dates for taxpayers with non-standard balance dates. Provisional tax is based on the previous year's taxable income with an uplift of 105%. Taxpayers may estimate provisional income, but penalties will apply where reasonable care was not taken in making the estimate.

Payroll deductions

All salaries, wages, superannuation and other emoluments (source deduction payments) are required to have tax deducted at source at prescribed table rates. The tax deducted is available as a credit on the annual assessment.

Prepayments

In general, income other than source deduction payments and excluding non-resident withholding income is provisional income. Provisional taxpayers must pay provisional tax in three equal instalments due on the seventh day of the fourth, eighth and twelfth months of the taxpayer's income year. Provisional tax is credited against actual tax when determined.

Estate and gift tax

Estate duty was abolished in New Zealand in 1993.

A person of NZ domicile pays gift duty annually on gifts of any property in NZ and overseas. No gift duty is payable in respect of gifts not exceeding an aggregate NZ$ 27,000 per annum in value. The rates of gift duty are graduated depending on the total value of gifts per annum, with a minimum rate of 5% (for gifts exceeding NZ$ 27,000 per annum but less than NZ$ 36,000) and a maximum of 25% for gifts exceeding NZ$ 72,000 per annum.

Wealth tax

There is no wealth tax in NZ.

Social security

The social welfare system is financed from general taxation and is designed to provide mainly for benefits and pensions to safeguard against the loss of income through age, incapacity, widowhood, unemployment, etc.

Other taxes

Treatment of partnerships

Profits made by a partnership are allocated to the partners in accordance with their profit shares and taxed in the partners' hands.

GST

Goods and services within NZ are subject to 12.5% GST (goods and services tax). There are very few exemptions, and these include financial services, residential rents and donated goods and services. Exports are zero-rated and GST does not apply to sales of goods between private individuals.

Other taxes

Fringe benefit tax (FBT) is levied to the employer on all tax-free benefits provided to employees at a rate of 49% (tax deductible). Benefits include company cars, loans at reduced rates, and goods and services supplied at less than cost.

Customs duties are levied at various rates on a variety of commodities but are gradually being reduced under the Government's free market policies.

Excise duty is applied on beer, tobacco and alcohol.

The imposition of sales tax was largely eliminated with the

introduction of GST but does apply to tobacco, alcoholic drinks, motor spirits and motor vehicles.

Stamp duty is levied on the transfer of commercial property.

Petroleum tax and road taxation is derived from levies on motor spirits.

Exchange controls

There are no exchange controls in New Zealand. Residents are free to send funds overseas without limitation.

Consent is required for an overseas company to carry on business in New Zealand, or to acquire shares in an NZ incorporated company giving 25% or more control (subject to a de minimis amount), or to purchase assets in a 'specified sensitive sector' (broadcasting, media, commercial fishing or rural land).

Tax treaties and withholding taxes

New Zealand has concluded tax treaties with the following countries:

Australia, Belgium, Canada, China, Denmark, Fiji, Finland, France, Germany, India, Indonesia, Ireland, Italy, Japan, Korea, Malaysia, The Netherlands, Norway, Philippines, Singapore, Sweden, Switzerland, Taiwan, Thailand, United Kingdom and the United States of America.

Withholding taxes

Country of residence	*Royalties* (%)	*Interest* (%)	*Dividends* (%)
Non-treaty countries	15 (b)	15 (a)	30
Selected treaty countries:			
Australia	10	10 (a)	15
Belgium	10	10	15
Canada	15	15	15
Denmark	10	10	15
France	10	10	15
Germany	10	10	15
India	30	15	20
Italy	10	10	15
Japan	–	–	15
Korea	10	10	15

Malaysia	15	15 (a)	15
Netherlands	10	10	15
Singapore	15	15 (a)	15
Sweden	10	10	15
Switzerland	10	10	15
Taiwan	10	10	15
Thailand	10 (c)	10 (d)	15
United Kingdom	10	10	15
United States	10	10	15

Notes:

Withholding tax is not imposed where the recipient of the interest has a fixed establishment in New Zealand, but the net interest will generally be subject to assessment at branch tax rate.

(a) Net interest income is subject to reassessment at branch tax rate where the payer and the recipient are associated persons, but withholding tax is the minimum liability. Withholding tax is not imposed where the recipient of the interest has a fixed establishment in New Zealand.

(b) Net income from industrial royalties is subject to reassessment at branch tax rate, but withholding tax is minimum liability.

(c) Some royalties are 15%.

(d) Only applies to interest derived from financial institutions or the sale of certain goods, otherwise 15%.

Anti-avoidance measures

Transactions of an artificial nature carried out solely for the purpose of avoiding tax may be ignored or replaced by the transaction that was commercially intended.

Nigeria

Sulaimon & Co.

Introduction

In accordance with the constitution of the Federal Republic of Nigeria, the federal government levies income tax on all corporate entities wherever they are resident in Nigeria, while the state governments levy income tax on all individuals and non-corporate entities residing within their states. However, certain individuals are subjects to the federal government taxation. These are members of the armed forces, police and the staff of the External Affairs Ministry as well as residents of the Federal Territory of Abuja.

The federal government is also responsible for levying and collecting the value added tax (VAT), which was introduced into the Nigerian taxation system with effect from 1 January 1994, although the proceeds are shared among the three tiers of government (namely the federal government and the state and local governments).

Corporate taxes

Taxable entities

Resident companies

Nigerian companies are taxable on their worldwide profits from all sources, including chargeable capital gains, whether or not such profits are brought into or received in Nigeria. A Nigerian company is a company incorporated under Nigerian law.

Non-resident companies

Foreign companies are taxable on their operations in Nigeria. Capital gains tax is chargeable on that part of their gains which are brought into or received in Nigeria. However, non-resident companies engaged in shipping, airline and telecommunications businesses are taxed on that proportion of their profits which their turnover in Nigeria bears to their worldwide turnover, subject to a minimum tax payable of not less than 2% of the turnover attributable to trade in Nigeria.

Tax year and filing requirements

The tax year is the calendar year commencing on 1 January and ending on 31 December. The financial year of a company may, however, be any 12 month period chosen by the company.

Income tax returns must be filed within 6 months from the end of the company's financial year. Self-assessment filing is now mandatory for all companies regardless of the amount of their annual turnover. A company must file its tax returns whether or not it is liable to tax.

Taxes imposed

The federal government levies company income tax. The only local taxes affecting companies are rates on property used by them. Such taxes may be allowable as deductions in computing the business profits of the companies for tax purposes.

Income is assessed on a preceding year basis and companies are required to submit their annual audited accounts and returns within six months of the end of the accounting year.

Provisional tax equal to tax paid in the immediately preceding assessment year is payable within three months of the commencement of the year of assessment. These provisional payments are offset against the tax liability as finally determined for the assessment year in question. Payment by instalment is allowed in appropriate cases. A 10% penalty and 20% interest are charged on the amount outstanding for late payment of tax. Companies filing self-assessment returns are exempted from provisional tax.

Tax Clearance Certificates (TCCs) covering a period of three years are demanded as a prerequisite to virtually all business dealings with governments, agencies and banks. Special TCCs are required for foreign exchange transactions.

Rates of tax

Normal tax

The standard rate of company income tax is currently 30%.

Special rates of tax

Companies that satisfy both the following conditions are taxed at the special rate of 20% in the first five years of commencement of business:

- the annual turnover of the company is equal to NGN 500,000 or less; and
- the company must be engaged either in manufacturing, agricultural production or mining of solid minerals.

Companies which are yet to commence business after six months of incorporation are required to pay a levy of NGN 500 for the first year, and NGN 400 for each subsequent year of assessment for which they remain dormant.

Capital gains tax

The rate of capital gains tax is 10%.

Income subject to tax

General rules

Profit for tax purposes is calculated in accordance with generally accepted accounting principles, as outlined by the special rules of the Tax Acts. Profits from each source (e.g. trading profit, rent, dividends, interest, fees, etc.) arising in a given accounting period are usually aggregated. Deductions and reliefs against the profits are then taken to arrive at profits chargeable to tax.

Stock/inventory rules

Special stock/inventory valuation methods may be used. Provided these methods are consistently applied, they are acceptable to the Federal Board of the Inland Revenue, although LIFO and base stock methods are not common.

Capital gains and losses

Capital gains are calculated by deducting from the proceeds of disposal the sum of the original cost, improvement costs and incidental expenses such as commissions and fees. A capital loss is similarly determined, although capital losses are not normally relievable.

Nigeria

Dividends

Dividends are subject to a withholding tax of 10%. Dividends received from Nigerian sources are as franked investment income and not liable to any further income tax. Such dividends received by a non-resident company, not otherwise engaged in trade or business in Nigeria, are similarly free from Nigerian tax other than the withholding tax of 10% suffered at source. The withholding tax rate on dividends applicable to residents of treaty countries is 7.5%.

Participation exemption

An exemption was available if the participation exemption applied.

A three-year, tax-free dividend was available to a shareholder, corporate or individual, whose equity shares in the company paying the dividend were paid for in foreign currency between 1 January 1987 and 31 December 1992, provided the shares were not less than 10% of the company's equity capital. If, in addition to these conditions, the company was also engaged in certain priority areas such as agricultural, petro-chemical or liquified natural gas production, the tax-free dividend period was five years.

Although of historical interest in this context, parallel provisions still exist for businesses in Nigerian Export Processing Zones.

Interest payable

Interest payable on foreign loans is exempted from withholding tax on a sliding scale basis depending on the repayment and moratorium period. Where the repayment period, including moratorium, exceeds seven years, there is 100% exemption.

Similar tax relief is available on interest payments on any loans granted by banks to aid investment in agriculture and, with effect from 1 April 1980, on interest payable on bank loans granted to companies manufacturing goods for export.

Deductions

General rules

Expenses are deductible to the extent that they have been incurred wholly, exclusively, necessarily and reasonably in earning profits. In the case of profits from trade or business expenses incurred for the purposes of such trade or business, they are also deductible.

Certain specified expenses are not deductible, as follows:

- capital expenditure and depreciation (capital allowances can, however, be claimed);
- general provisions or provisions for contingent or future losses;
- expenses for the purpose of earning management fees;
- donations to specified bodies and institutions up to maximum allowances of 10% of the company's total profits in the assessment year; and
- rents on residential accommodation for employees in excess of the lower of 100% of the employee's basis salary and the actual rent paid.

Depreciation and amortisation

Capital allowances, comprising investment and, where applicable, initial and annual allowances, are deductible in respect of capital assets in lieu of accounting depreciation. The investment allowances are calculated on cost in the first year, but may not be written down and therefore they are not taken into account in computing other allowances, nor in computing balancing allowances or charges. The initial allowance is calculated on the cost in the first year only. Annual allowances are calculated on a straight-line basis after deducting the initial allowance.

The current rates of capital allowances are as follows:

	Initial (%)	*Annual (%)*	*Investment (%)*
Industrial and non-industrial buildings	15	10	Nil
Plant and machinery:			
Agricultural production	15	Nil	Nil
Other plant and machinery	50	25	Nil
Replacement plant and machinery bought	50	20	Nil
Furniture and fittings	25	20	Nil
Motor vehicles:			
Public transport	95	Nil	Nil
Other	25	20	Nil
Plantation equipment	95	Nil	Nil
Housing estate	50	25	Nil
Ranching and plantation	30	50	Nil

Nigeria

Specific Investment Allowances:

Qualifying expenditure for Companies or organisations engaging in commercial R&D.	Nil	Nil	20
Qualifying expenditure for companies engaging wholly in the fabrication of tools, spare parts and machinery	Nil	Nil	25
To any enterprises on the purchases of locally made plant and machinery	Nil	Nil	15

Notes

A ceiling is placed on annual claims for capital allowances.

For manufacturing and agricultural production companies there is no ceiling on capital allowances. For other companies the ceiling is 66.675% of assessable profits.

Non-depreciable assets

Capital allowances are not available on certain assets which are non-depreciable, e.g. land.

Royalties

Royalties are non-deductible as business expenses, but are subject to withholding tax.

Interest

Interest payments are allowable deductions, but are subject to withholding tax.

Dividends

Dividends paid are non-deductible.

Bad and doubtful debts

Specific debts identified as doubtful are allowable deductions.

Patents and similar assets

Expenditures incurred on patents, licences, secret formulae or processes, or data concerning industrial, commercial or scientific processes and similar assets qualify as research and development expenditure and attract the following capital allowances:

- initial – 95%;
- annual – Nil.

Management fees

These are normally allowed as deductible expenses, but tax must be withheld at the rate of 10%.

Investment incentives and special benefits

Business incentives include:

- a tax holiday period of up to five years for public companies engaged in specified pioneering industrial enterprise;
- exemption from tax on dividends paid by a pioneer company from the profits of such an enterprise;
- graduated incentives granted to businesses established in rural areas on the basis of the infrastructure available, e.g. electricity, water, tarred roads and telephones; and
- full tax holidays for their years for all new industries operating in any Export Processing Zones in Nigeria.

Related party transations

Transactions between related parties considered not being at arm's length and which have the effect of avoiding or postponing tax may be adjusted for tax purposes. The Revenue has very wide powers to counter such avoidance.

Losses

Trading losses can be carried forward and offset against profits of the same trade in a subsequent assessment year. This is limited to four years, after which any amounts still unrelieved will lapse. The only exception to this is to companies engaged in agricultural production where losses can be carried forward indefinitely until fully relieved.

Corporate groups

No special rules apply to groups of companies. All companies are taxed individually and tax losses may not be transferred between the companies in a group.

Capital taxes

Capital duty is payable on nominal share capital at the rate of NGN 2.50 per NGN 200 of share capital.

Net worth tax

There is no net worth tax on companies in Nigeria.

Minimum tax provisions

Any company which has commenced business and has a total profit producing a tax liability of less than the minimum tax will be taxed as described below.

Companies which have been operating for more than four years with a turnover of NGN 500,000 and below, shall be taxed at a minimum of:

- 0.5% of gross profits;
- 0.5% of net assets;
- 0.25% of paid-up capital; or
- 0.25% of turnover or the company for the year,

whichever is the highest.

If turnover is in excess of NGN 500,000, minimum tax will be whatever is payable under the above condition plus 125% of turnover in excess of NGN 500,000. However:

- the minimum tax is not applicable to a company during the first four years after the commencement of its business;
- the minimum tax is not applicable to agricultural trades or businesses as defined in section 9(8) of the Companies Income Tax Act, nor to any company with at least 25% imported equity capital; and
- the minimum tax will apply to partnerships and self-employed individuals at a rate of 0.5% of total income.

Treatment of branches (branch profits tax)

The profits of foreign subsidiaries of Nigerian companies are treated as foreign source income and taxed when relieved, but profits of foreign branches are treated as profits of the headquarter companies.

The branches of foreign companies in Nigeria will be subject to Nigerian tax.

Personal taxes

Taxable individuals

Residents

Individuals are assessed by the state authorities for tax on their income from all sources, including capital gains, when they are resident or deemed to be resident on the first day of an assessment year (1 January) or the date on which they first take up residence in the Nigerian state. The definition of resident includes being present in Nigeria for a period amounting to 183 days or more in any 12 month period commencing in a calendar year and ending either within that same year or the following year.

Rules determining residence in accordance with the nature of primary sources of income are as follows:

- individuals whose duties are performed wholly outside Nigeria (with temporary visits to Nigeria) are not resident in Nigeria but are in foreign employment;
- individuals in Nigerian employment, i.e. whose duties are performed wholly or partly in Nigeria, are resident in Nigeria; and
- individuals whose primary sources of income derive from trade, business or professions undertaken in Nigeria are deemed to be resident in Nigeria, even when not physically present in the country.

Residents are taxed on income accruing in, derived from, received in or remitted to Nigeria.

Rules also exist for the determination of the principal place of residence in cases where an individual has more than one source of income and/or has more than one place of residence in Nigeria. These rules are applied simply in order to determine which tax authority (federal or state) shall be responsible for the assessment and collection of the tax.

Rules for the determination of residence of individuals for tax purposes also apply (with slight modifications) to other taxable individuals, e.g. partnerships, trustees, executors and incorporated entities.

Non-residents

Non-residents are taxed only on income arising in Nigeria. The federal tax authorities assess all liable non-residents.

Tax year and filing requirements

Except in the year in which the income first arises or the year in which it ceases, the taxable period is 1 January to 31 December. Tax on employment income, pension, etc., is an actual basis, whereas tax on business income is on a preceding year basis and subject broadly to the same rates as for companies.

For each year of assessment, every taxable person shall, without notice or demand, complete and submit an income tax return to the appropriate tax authority. The return should indicate the taxpayer's income from all sources for the previous year ended 31 December and include any allowances and reliefs which the taxpayer may wish to claim for the same period. The authorities then assess the tax payable. There is no specific requirement for non-corporate bodies to file their audited accounts with the tax authorities, but this may be required in individual cases. Residents are not usually required to file a return where:

- their only source of income is from employment and where yearly income does not exceed NGN 30,000; or where
- they receive no income chargeable to tax.

Residents who are not normally required to file a return may do so voluntarily, usually if they expect a tax rebate.

Where resident taxpayers fail to make obligatory tax returns, an estimated or bet judgment assessment may be raised within the second half of the year.

Taxes on income

Tax on individuals is imposed by the law enacted by the federal authorities who also regulate taxation throughout the country as a whole, so that the same income is not taxed in the same year by more than one state tax authority. There are no differences in the manner in which taxable income is computed under the states' personal income tax laws. Income tax rates, personal allowances and reliefs are uniform throughout the country.

The administration of tax and collection of the tax are carried out by each state government which also imposes local taxes and rates, and levies and regulates their collection.

Nigerian social insurance scheme

Employees make compulsory contributions of 3.5% of their insurance earnings each month to the Nigerian social insurance trust fund while employers make similar payments of 6.5% per employee per month towards their employees' retirement benefits.

Dividends

Dividends are subject to a withholding tax deduction at source of 10% (7.5% for recipients residing in treaty countries) by the company paying the dividend. Withholding tax is the final due on the dividends.

Interest

Interest is subject to withholding tax at 10% (7.5% for recipients residing in treaty countries) and the withheld tax is the final tax due on the interest.

Rentals

Rents received from the letting of real estate are subject to withholding tax at 10% (7.5% for treaty countries), but the withholding tax is not the final tax due from the local recipients of the rental income.

Royalties

Royalties are treated in the same way as rental income, although the withholding tax rate is 15% for local recipients and residents of non-treaty countries. The withholding tax for treaty countries is 7.5%.

Exempt income

The main exempt items are as follows:

- interest accruing to non-residents on money borrowed abroad by federal or state governments on terms which include the exemption of such interest from tax;
- gratuities paid by federal or state governments as well as gratuities paid to employees in the private sector under a

contract of service (if not exceeding a given period of years, exemption is limited to NGN 1,000 per annum);

- compensation or gratuities payable upon death or injury; and
- benefits received from pension or retirement benefit schemes approved by the Joint Tax Board under the National Provident Fund Scheme, and investment income derived from those fund schemes.

Foreign source income

A foreign tax credit is available to a resident against tax payable by him in Nigeria, limited to the proportion of his total year's tax which his foreign income bears to his total chargeable income.

Income derived from foreign employment is generally exempt from Nigerian income tax. Dividends, interests, rental and royalties are subject to Nigerian tax if they are brought into Nigeria, whether or not a tax treaty exists.

In the absence of a double taxation agreement, Nigerian provisions apply unilaterally.

Personal allowances and deductions

Personal allowances

The following allowances are generally made against incomes from any source:

- a personal allowance of NGN 5,000 is granted to any individual with taxable income of any kind, with an additional allowance of 20% on earned income without maximum limit (earned income includes salary, bonus, fees, pension and business profits);
- child allowance of NGN 2,500 is granted to the parents of unmarried children under 16, or over 16 if the child is receiving full-time education or indentured in a trade or profession (child allowance is granted for a maximum of four children);
- a dependant relative allowance to a maximum of NGN 2,000 is granted to a taxpayer in respect of those dependants whom he maintains;
- a life assurance relief is granted in respect of premiums paid on a life insurance policy taken on the taxpayer's life or that of a spouse; and
- pension or provident fund contributions to an approved pension

or provident fund scheme, including the Nigerian Social Insurance Trust Fund Scheme.

Other reliefs and deductions

These are available on the following:

- subscriptions to professional bodies, where membership is a condition for practising a relevant profession in Nigeria;
- interest paid on loans to build an owner occupied residential house; and on
- rent payable in respect of an employee's residential accommodation.

Non-residents and part-year residents

Non-residents are entitled only to a basic personal allowance of NGN 5,000 plus 20% of earned income while part-year residents are treated in the same way as full residents and are therefore entitled to full personal allowance.

Special family rules

Except for purpose of apportionment of child and dependant relative allowances and the determination of maximum life assurance and similar reliefs, a husband and wife are treated separately. There are no special rules relating to the taxation of husband, wife and children.

Income including investment income earned by dependant children is taxed in the hands of those children, except where the income is considered to have arisen from a fictitious arrangement, in which case it is taxed in the hands of the parents.

Rates of tax

General – resident and non-resident

Band NGN	*Rate (%)*	*Tax on Band*	*Cumulative NGN*
0 to 30,000	5	1,500	1,500
30,001 to 60,000	10	3,000	4,500
60,001 to 110,000	15	7,500	12,000
110,001 to 160,000	20	10,000	22,000
160,001 and above	26		

Minimum tax rate

The minimum tax provision applies even where a taxpayer's allowances and reliefs exceed his income. There is a mandatory minimum tax of 0.5% of total assessable income.

Withholding tax

In principle, withholding tax exists for a wide range of payments made to individual beneficiaries, such as dividends, interest, rentals and royalties. The rate is 15% of royalties and 10% for most other sources for local residents and for residents of non-treaty countries. For residents of treaty countries, the rate of 7.5% tax is deducted at the time when payment is made or credited to any individual, whichever occurs first.

For local residents, the tax withheld is an advance payment to be offset against the ultimate tax liability. For non-residents, it is the final Nigerian tax due on the income. In summary, withholding tax applies at various rates to income, which include the following:

- rent – 10% of the gross rent;
- interest – 1% of the gross interest;
- dividends – 10% of the dividend (the underlying company tax is ignored);
- royalties – 15%;
- management/consultancy fees – 10%; and
- payment for contracts, supplies and services – 5%.

Payment of tax

Payroll deduction

Tax payments on employment income, pensions and directors fees (usually in respect of executive directors) are made by deduction at source under the Pay-As-You-Earn (PAYE) system. Amounts deducted at source may be offset against the final income tax payable for the year and, where there is overpayment, a refund may be claimed.

Prepayment

There are no provisions for the prepayment of personal income tax, except for withholding tax (where applicable).

Wealth tax

There is no wealth tax in Nigeria.

Social security contributions

The Nigerian Social Insurance Trust Fund Scheme, referred to in previous sections, provides the only social security scheme operating nationally. Both employees and employers contribute at the respective rates of 3.5% and 6.5% of the employee's salary. Non-Nigerian employees ordinary by resident in Nigeria, are required to contribute to the scheme.

Other taxes

Treatment of partnerships

Partnership profit is assessable on individual partners in the firm.

Petroleum profits tax

Companies engaged in petroleum operations are taxed under the Petroleum Profits Tax Act. Such companies are exempt from the provisions of the Companies Income Tax Act. The current rate of tax is 85% less certain deductions. The Act contains its own rules on deductions, losses, capital allowances, accounting periods, returns and payment of tax, although the provisions are similar in most areas.

Property tax

This varies from state to state but the most common tax are rates which are calculated on the rateable value of the property (real property).

VAT and sales tax

With the commencement of VAT legislation of 1 January 1994, sales tax was abolished. VAT is levied on a wide variety of goods and services, including the services of financial institutions. There is a flat rate of 5%, with a zero rate on exports.

Stamp duties

Duties in respect of instruments executed individuals are charged by state governments, while duties upon instruments executed between a company and a company or an individual, group or body of individuals, are charged by the federal government.

Customs duties

Custom duties at varying rates are levied on imports.

Excise duties

These are levied at various rates on a wide range of goods manufactured in Nigeria.

Nigerian social insurance trust fund

Contributions are made at 2.5% and 5% per employee, by employees and employers respectively towards old age, sickness and survivor benefits.

Contributions are also made at 1% of annual payroll to the Industrial Training Fund.

Exchange controls

Foreign currency transactions are subject to very strict control by the Federal Ministry of Finance and the Central Bank of Nigeria.

The principal regulations are as follows:

- approval is required for the establishment of businesses involving non-residents and the granting of 'approved investment status' to such investments for the purposes of eventual repatriation of capital and remittance of dividends and other distributions;
- remittable dividends reinvested in new companies will qualify for approved investment status;
- exchange control approval is required of a Nigerian company controlled by non-residents seeking to borrow money in Nigeria;
- payments for imports, which will usually require pre-shipment inspection and certification if the value exceeds NGN 1,000; and
- exchange control regulations which have a bearing on the taxation of individuals are the personal home remittances of non-Nigerian employees resident in Nigeria, formerly at 75%, now deregulated.

Dividends

Dividends used to be allowed as a certain percentage of profit after tax, but they are now completely deregulated.

Technical fees

Technical fees ranging from 1% to 5% of net sales are allowed, subject to a satisfactory report on the implementation of the technical agreement.

Consultancy fees

The maximum allowed as offshore costs is 20% of the cost of the project.

Royalties

Allowable royalties range from 1% to 5% of sales value.

Withholding taxes

Rates of withholding tax are as follows:

	Non-treaty (%)	*Treaty* (%)
Dividends, rents, interest	10	7.5
Royalties	15	7.5
Management services	10	10
Consultancy services	10	10
Technical services	10	10

Withholding tax is payable by a company at the time dividends, interest, etc., are paid or credited, whichever is earlier. For dividends and interests, tax withheld is the final tax due thereon.

Withholding tax rates currently in force may be summarised as follows:

Country of residence	*Normal Dividend* (%)	*Participation Dividend* (%)	*Minimum Participation Requirement* (%)
Non-treaty countries	10	Nil	Nil
Selected treaty countries:			
Australia	7.5		
Denmark	7.5		
France	7.5		
Greece	7.5		
India	7.5		
Italy	7.5		
Portugal	7.5		
South Africa	7.5		
Sweden	7.5		
Switzerland	7.5		
United Kingdom	7.5		
Royalties			
Non-treaty countries	15		
Treaty countries	7.5		
Interest			
Non-treaty countries	10		
Treaty countries	7.5		
Other treaty countries			
Cameroon	7.5		
Ethiopia	7.5		
Gabon	7.5		
Ivory Coast	7.5		
Morocco	7.5		
Republic of Benin	7.5		
Togo	7.5		
Zaire	7.5		

Anti-avoidance measures

There are no specific statutory provisions for dealing with tax avoidance, although section 18 of the Companies Income Tax Act 1979 and section 17 of the Personal Income Tax Decree 1993, both provide measures for dealing with 'any disposition' or 'any transaction' which, in the opinion of the Revenue, has a tendency to reduce the amount of tax payable. Such disposition is defined as including any trust, grant, covenant, agreement or arrangement, and transaction is defined as including transactions between parties, either where one has control over the other or, in the case of individuals, where they are related to one other, or between parties, both of which are controlled by some other party.

The Revenue will normally regard a disposition or a transaction which tends to affect adversely a liability to tax as artificial or fictitious.

Norway

Revisjonsfirmaet Kjelstrup og Wiggen ANS

Introduction

The principal feature of Norway's 'new' tax system (compared with the system prior to 1993) is the introduction of the 'realisation principle' under which only realised costs are tax-deductible. The disallowance of unrealised costs increases the tax base. This is compensated by reduced tax rates.

Corporate taxes

Taxable entities

Resident companies

The most common kinds of resident company are:

- *Limited liability companies (limited by shares) (A/S)* –

  The joint stock company is a separate taxable entity and liable for all taxes.

  The share capital requirement for joint stock companies (A/S) is a minimum of NOK 100,000, and for public joint stock companies the minimum share capital is NOK 1,000,000.

- *Limited partnerships (K/S)* –

  In a limited partnership at least one of the partners has an unlimited liability for the debt of the company (general partner) and at least one partner has a limited liability (limited partner), according to the company rules.

  A limited partnership is not a separate taxable entity and each partner is liable for taxes on his part of the income and capital.

  The limited partner can only deduct losses within the scope of his liability, according to company rules.

- *Unlimited partnerships (ANS) –*

  The partners are personally liable for all debt acquired by the company, without any limitations.

  The partnership is not a separate taxable entity and each partner is liable for taxes on his part of income and capital.

- *Partnership with shared liabilities (DA) –*

  Each partner is liable for his share of any debt incurred by the company.

  The partnership is not a separate taxable entity, each partner is liable for taxes on his part of income and capital.

Non-resident companies

Non-resident companies are taxed on income derived from a permanent establishment and real property in Norway. Similarly, income from offshore activities in Norwegian waters are taxable in Norway.

Tax year and filing requirements

The tax year is by law required to follow the calendar year, although exceptions may be permitted under special conditions (such as for subsidiaries or branches of multinational companies with a different fiscal year). The annual tax return must be submitted by the end of February, however, a general extension of one month followed by a further month may be given by the local tax authorities. If the accounting period ends after 31 December (for example, 30 April) then the return must still be submitted by the end of the following February.

Taxes imposed

Taxes are levied at national level on all types of income, including capital gains. The taxes are calculated on the taxable income of the financial year.

67% of the estimated tax for the year is payable in advance prior to assessment on 15 February and 15 April.

The final assessment is normally issued in September in the year following the financial year, and assessed taxes less advance payments are due in two instalments on 15 September and 15 November. If advance payments are less than 67% of the assessed taxes, interest will be charged.

Rates of taxes

Corporation tax is levied at a rate of 28% of taxable income, including capital gains. This applies to all corporations.

The tax system is based on the principle that taxes should be the same, regardless of whether a trade is operated as a private enterprise or as a corporation. This principle is achieved through a 'person tax' on active owners. If an enterprise has owners who are active in the business, and such owners own 67% or more of the enterprise, a person tax is levied as if the enterprise was liable to personal taxes. Ownership by a spouse, parents and children younger than 18 years is treated cumulatively with that of the active owner. The basis for personal tax is the operating profit of the enterprise reduced by a theoretical interest on the capital employed in the company. Person tax is payable by the company, but is charged at the rates applying to personal taxpayers.

Income subject to tax

General rules

Corporation tax is levied on the corporation's total income, including business profits, capital gains, dividends, interest and royalties.

Stock/inventory valuation

Inventory is defined as:

- objects purchased and intended for sale;
- raw materials;
- work in progress; and
- finished products.

An inventory must be valued at cost on a FIFO basis. Manufacturers must value their products on a direct cost method consisting of raw materials, semi-finished goods, production wages and consumables.

Unsaleable goods must, according to the tax regulations, be carried at their full cost until they are realised. The tax law does not allow a write-down of inventory for obsolescence or for price reduction.

Capital gains and losses

Capital gains realised by a corporation are taxed in the year the gains are realised at the normal corporate tax rate of 28%. The gain is calculated on the difference between sales proceeds and original cost less tax depreciation (tax value).

Corporations may opt to rollover gains against other assets. Assets are for this purpose grouped into categories with the same allowable rate of depreciation (groups of assets are further defined under the heading, 'Depreciation and amortisation' below.) For asset groups (a) to (d), total sale proceeds may be offset against the remaining tax value for the respective group, with the effect that the basis for future depreciation is reduced accordingly.

Gains from the sale of assets in groups (e) to (h) may be transferred to a specific profit and loss account, rather than immediately taxed; 20% of the remaining balance on the profit and loss account must be taken as profit each year. Losses derived from the sale of fixed assets are treated as described for gains above, but with a reverse effect.

Dividends

Dividends from a Norwegian company are paid out of taxed profit. Dividends received by resident companies or personal taxpayers are tax-free for the recipient (see, 'Personal taxes – dividends' for new rules on dividends received by personal taxpayers).

Dividends paid to foreign shareholders are subject to withholding tax (see table below). Dividends from foreign sources paid to a Norwegian shareholder are taxable in Norway. Taxes withheld at source may be offset against local taxes on the same income.

Deductions

General rule

Expenses related to business income, which are incurred to obtain, secure and maintain the taxable business income, are deductible. There are some exceptions to this general rule as follows:

- provisions to cover future losses and claims are not deductible (tax allowance for accrued costs can only be obtained if the taxpayer has a contractual obligation to pay the expenses at the end of the financial year and the liability can be accurately estimated); and

- entertainment and gifts to business connections are not tax deductible.

Depreciation and amortisation

Capital assets with a useful life of less than three years, or with a purchase price less than NOK 15,000, may be expensed. Other fixed assets must be capitalised and depreciated by employing the declining balance method at maximum rates and in groups as outlined below:

(a)	Office machines etc.	25%
(b)	Acquired goodwill	20%
(c)	Trailers, trucks, buses, taxis and vehicles for the transportation of disabled persons	20%
(d)	Cars, tractors, other movable machines, other machines, equipment, instruments, furniture and fixtures	15%
(e)	Ships, vessels and drilling rigs	14%
(f)	Aircraft, helicopters	12%
(g)	Industrial buildings, hotels, rooming houses and restaurants	2% (6%)
(h)	Office buildings	0% (1%)

An option to depreciate at higher rates in groups (g) and (h) is covered in special regulations. The highest rates are applied to business properties in the countryside and to buildings with a short lifetime.

For assets in groups (a) to (d), which will normally consist of a number of assets, depreciation is calculated on the balance of the group. If the balance is negative because of sales, the negative balance shall be taken to income every year at the rate equal to the group's depreciation rate. This means that the gain (loss) is taxed (deducted) over time at the same rates as the depreciation rates for the assets.

Assets in groups (e) to (h) are depreciated on the basis of the individual asset's balance. Gains and losses are to be treated as described above under, 'Capital gains and losses'.

If any balance of the groups (a) to (d) or an individual asset's balance in groups (e) to (h) result in an amount of less than NOK 15,000, positive balances may be expensed and negative balances may be taken to income.

Land and dwelling houses are not subject to depreciation.

Royalties

Royalties are tax deductible, provided the amount is justifiable against the services rendered.

Interest

Interest expenses related to business income are tax deductible. There is no special restriction on interest paid to an associated company abroad provided the interest is at a commercial rate.

Dividends

Dividends declared are not tax deductible.

Bad and doubtful debts

Outstanding receivables will normally be nominally valued and possible losses are deductible only when they are realised. This means that a provision for doubtful debtors cannot be deducted. A loss is deemed realised when a debtor is declared bankrupt, his/her business is liquidated or it can be finally proven that the debt cannot be collected. In addition, a debt is deemed lost if it is not settled six months after the debt is due for payment (provided normal procedures for debt collection are followed). In addition to the actual losses suffered as explained above, a minor general provision may be made to cover unrealised losses. This deduction is calculated by use of a special formula based on the taxpayer's loss history over the previous two years, as follows:

$$\frac{\text{Realised losses last 2 years}}{\text{Credit sales last 2 years}} \times 4 \times \text{accounts receivable at year end}$$

For new companies in the year of formation and the two subsequent years, a general provision of 2% of outstanding receivables may be claimed.

Provisions

Provisions to cover future expenses, calculated in accordance with general accounting principles, are not tax deductible.

Wages, use of company owned car and other fringe benefits

All payment of wages from an employer to an employee is subject to taxation in the hands of the employee.

When the employer covers private expenses for an employee, such as car expenses, telephone, newspapers and individual insurances (life/accident/pension), these are treated as taxable benefits in the hands of the employee. An employer must pay social security tax at the same rate applied to wages.

Non-deductible expenses

As a basic principle, expenses related to entertainment and gifts are not deductible. There are, however, some exceptions.

Entertainment expenses are deductible if they do not exceed NOK 200 per person and no wine or liquor is served. If this amount is exceeded, or wine or liquor is served, no part of the bill is deductible.

Presents to employees are deductible under certain conditions and limits when the employees or the company celebrates certain events.

A company is entitled to give presents to employees (on an equal basis covering all employees) up to a limit of NOK 500 per employee, without any taxation of the employees. However, the employer cannot deduct these expenses in his tax return.

Small tokens of gratitude given to business connections are considered to be deductible, such as flowers at anniversaries and trivial mass-produced gift items with a company logo.

Membership subscriptions of most kinds are not deductible.

Foreign source income

Income from foreign sources is taxed in accordance with provisions set out in the tax treaty with the country concerned. In cases where there is no tax treaty, foreign source income is taxed in Norway at normal rates. Reductions may be claimed in the taxes assessed on such income for taxes paid abroad on the same income. The reduction may not exceed the tax assessed on the foreign source income in Norway.

Investment incentives and special benefits

Certain incentives in the form of grants and low interest loans are available to corporations established in Norway. Such incentives were introduced to promote investment in defined development areas and to promote export industry and the creation of new jobs. Incentives are granted on application and are considered on a case-by-case basis.

Related party transactions

Transactions between related parties are deductible, but must be based on the arm's length principle, and the related expenses must be normal to the company's business.

Losses

Net tax losses may be carried forward for ten years to offset against taxable profits.

Corporate groups

Group contribution can be granted between resident companies where more than 90% of the shares are owned by the same group. Group contribution is also available to resident companies if the ultimate shareholder is a non-resident company. Group contribution is deductible for the giver and is taxable or will reduce the taxable loss for the recipient.

A resident shareholder may claim a tax deduction for a shareholder's contribution to cover a loss in a Norwegian limited liability company which is engaged in new activities. New activity covers the year of establishment and the four subsequent years. The tax deduction is limited to that proportion of the loss which corresponds to the shareholder's proportion of the total share capital.

Currency fluctuation

Realised exchange gains and losses derived from the normal course of business must be included in the taxable income.

Current receivables and payables

An unrealised exchange loss is allowable for tax purposes, but there is no obligation to record unrealised exchange gains.

Long term receivables and payables

For unrealised gains and losses on long term items, the portfolio principle is applied. This means that all long term receivables and payables in foreign currency are treated collectively. Net currency losses can be charged as an expense. Net currency gains are taken as income to the extent that corresponding losses have been claimed in previous years. Differences between long term receivables and payables at the historical rate and at the current rate are recorded on a separate balance sheet account (a revaluation account). Owing to the introduction of the reversal principle, the balance of this account can never be positive.

In recent years there has been a trend towards a reduction in the taxation of net income (gross income reduced by deductible expenses) and an increase in the taxation of gross income.

Tax-free mergers and disposals

Mergers

To implement a tax-free merger, the following conditions must be met:

- it must be carried out in accordance with the Joint Stock Company Act;
- the tax position must be preserved in the merged company; and
- the main motivation for the merger cannot be tax avoidance.

If these conditions are met, the merger will be effective (from a formal and tax point-of-view) 3 months from initial registration in the company registry, during which period any creditors may raise objections.

Demergers

The conditions for a tax-free demerger are:

- only shareholders of the former company can be shareholders of the demerged companies at the conclusion of the demerging process;
- continuity is maintained with regard to tax circumstances; and
- the principal motivation for demerger is not one of tax avoidance.

Where these conditions are met, the demerger will be effective (from a formal and tax point-of-view) according to the same rules for merger.

Liquidation of company

In the year of its liquidation, a company is taxed in accordance with ordinary principles. However, any difference arising between the tax account (i.e. tax written down value and the market value of each asset) will be taxed or deducted in the year of liquidation.

A company in liquidation must request a pre-assessment by the tax-authorities by sending in a tax return declaration up to the day of liquidation.

From the time of registration of liquidation in the company registry, a six month period must elapse in which creditors may make their objections before a final liquidation announcement can be sent and registered and the liquidation becomes effective.

For shareholders, any equity balance after all creditors have been satisfied is to be treated as their compensation for shares, and taxable profit or loss is calculated by deducting cost price adjusted in accordance with the RISK amount (taxable income less taxes and less dividends for the period after the acquisition of the shares) – see capital gains.

Personal taxes

Taxable individuals

The extent to which the income of an individual is subject to Norwegian taxes depends on whether he is resident in Norway.

Residents

Resident individuals are taxed on their worldwide income irrespective of its source, as well as on worldwide property. Norwegian tax law and double tax treaties grant relief from double taxation.

An individual is considered to be resident from the day of his immigration. A temporary stay in Norway will give the individual resident status from the first day if he remains for at least six months.

Upon leaving Norway, an individual will no longer be considered resident from the day he leaves, i.e. the individual has actually emigrated (sold his house, left his job, etc.). Temporary stays abroad will also interrupt his Norwegian tax liability from the day of departure if the stay exceeds one year and the individual is taxed as a resident in the foreign country. If a double taxation treaty gives Norway a substantial right to tax an individual's income, he will be regarded as resident. Temporary stays abroad lasting more than four years also interrupt an individual's tax liability as a Norwegian resident (once such a period of time has elapsed), thus removing the requirement, providing the individual is taxed as a resident in a foreign country.

Wealth taxation applies to all those resident in Norway at the end of the calendar year.

Non-residents

Non-resident individuals are taxed on income arising from employment in Norway or personal services performed in Norway (including fees to the board of directors). Income from a permanent business establishment or from real property in Norway, as well as dividends from Norwegian companies, are also included. If a foreign shareholder is an active participant in the company, he may be liable to pay the highest rate of tax on a deemed personal income from the company.

Non-residents are liable to wealth taxation on their Norwegian property.

Tax year and filing requirements

The tax year reflects the calendar year. The annual tax return must be submitted to the local authorities by the end of January for employees and the end of February for the self-employed. Extensions may be granted.

Taxes on income

Income taxes are levied at both a national and local rate, but all taxes are assessed locally. There are two bases of income taxation: personal gross income and net income. The gross income basis includes remuneration from work, such as salaries, wages, the value of fringe benefits, etc., as well as the calculated work income of self-employed persons and active shareholders whose taxes on personal income can be reimbursed by the company. Capital gains and other non-work income are not included in the personal income basis. The net income basis is the total of all taxable income, whatever the source, reduced by deductible expenses.

Personal income is subject to two taxes: a social security contribution (at differentiated rates, depending on the kind of income) and a top tax (differentiated rates on income over certain limits).

Ordinary income tax (at differentiated rates according to where the individual lives) is levied on net income.

Sources of income

Employment income and directors' fees

Employment income of all kinds is liable to tax. Benefits in kind must generally be valued by the employer and treated in the same way as cash payment.

Business income

Business income (excluding losses) is taxed as ordinary income, irrespective of the type of business and profession. Expenses are deductible to the extent that they are incurred in order to obtain, secure and maintain the taxable business income under the same rules as outlined for companies. After certain adjustments the net result is also included in the gross income assessment.

Dividends

Dividends were, until 5 September 2000, taxed under the imputation system. The shareholder's tax was reduced by the company taxes and the result was a tax-free net dividend for the Norwegian recipient. Dividends received after 5 September 2000 are liable to tax at a rate of 11%. The taxable basis is reduced by NOK 10,000 for personal taxpayers. Active owners who are liable to 'person tax', (as described earlier under 'Rates of taxes'), will only have to pay tax on that part of the dividend received that exceeds the basis for the 'person tax'.

The imputation system does not apply to foreign shareholders for whom a withholding tax will reduce the dividend. Nor does it apply to dividends from foreign companies.

Interest

Interest received is liable to net income tax. There is no withholding tax on interest. Interest paid is deductible without limitations. Only interest on a tax refund or delayed payment of taxes is not taxable or deductible.

Rentals

Rents received from letting real estate are subject to ordinary net income tax. Deductions are allowable for expenses, including depreciation in the case of business premises (not dwellings). If the rent is business income then the net result is in the calculation of personal gross taxes.

Private owners of houses, cottages and freehold flats are taxed on their own use on an estimated income of 2.5% of the taxable value of the house. The taxable basis is reduced by NOK 51,250 per single personal house.

Royalties

Royalties (received and paid) are included in taxable net income.

Social security benefits

Some benefits are tax-exempt, but pensions, sickness and unemployment pay are liable to tax.

Pensions and annuities

Pensions are always taxed as income and so are annuities generally, with some exceptions. The rules concerning annuities are very detailed.

Capital gains

Capital gains are normally included in taxable net income. The gain from selling one's house is tax free, provided the individual has lived there for at least one year in the last two. The same exemption from taxation applies on the sale of private cottages if used privately for five out of eight years proceeding.

All capital gains are taxed at a rate of 28% and gains or losses are calculated in the following way:

Sales value

Less purchase price
Less RISK amount
Less purchase/sales expenses

= Profit or loss

RISK, through the period of ownership, is calculated according to a very detailed set of rules, but (put simply) it represents net (taxable) income after tax and dividend through the period of ownership. The RISK element has been introduced to avoid double taxation, firstly in the hands of the company and secondly in the hands of the shareholder. Thus net profit after tax and dividends are added to the shareholder's cost price of the shares.

Any loss from the sale of shares is deductible in the sales year from ordinary income.

Foreign source income

Income from foreign sources is taxed in Norway as ordinary income, however, tax treaties may provide relief from double taxation.

Personal allowances and deductions

All employees can deduct up to NOK 36,600 from their gross income as a personal allowance to cover unspecified deductible expenses. Part of the costs of commuting (costs over NOK 8,500) are also deductible as well as specified costs of travel to work (where not covered by the employer). If both parents work, they can also deduct nursery costs (up to NOK 30,000 for at least two children up to 11 years of age). The same applies to a single parent.

Elderly people receive an old age allowance of NOK 1,470 per month after the age of 70. There are also other minor allowances, e.g. tax reductions for some (minor) savings, etc. Premiums paid towards private pension insurance are deductible up to a maximum of NOK 40,000.

Persons living temporarily in Norway can generally deduct 15% of their wages to cover some of the costs a resident can deduct according to their actual costs (e.g. private pensions premiums, interest, nursery costs, certain allowances, commuting costs.) This permission is limited to four years.

Special family rules

In the case of married taxpayers, their total income and capital are taxed in the hands of the spouse with the higher income. Each spouse's income can be taxed separately at their request, but wealth taxes are always assessed on a family basis.

Children are generally taxed as part of the family up to an age of 17 years. Personal income from work can be assessed separately from the age of 13.

Losses

A loss is deductible against net income to the same extent as the income or gain is liable to tax. A loss is offset against other income in the same year. A resulting net loss is carried forward for up to ten years.

Special treatment for expatriates

Individuals who have been resident in Norway remain liable to Norwegian tax on gains from selling shares or interests in Norwegian companies up to five years after the year of their departure, irrespective of their citizenship or when the shares were purchased.

Rates of tax

On income taxes for residents and net income tax (provincial/local tax) the net amount, reduced by NOK 27,700 for single persons and NOK 55,400 for families, is taxed at:

- 28% (generally); or
- 24.5% (in the northern part of Norway).

Personal/gross income taxes

Social security contributions are:

- 3% (pensions); or
- 7.8% (salaries, wages and calculated personal income over NOK 504,000); or
- 10.7% (calculated personal income up to the limit above).

Top tax (national tax) is:

- 13.5% (from NOK 277,800 for single person or from NOK 329,000 for families).

The maximum tax rates will consequently be 49.3 % for employees and 52.2 % for self-employed persons.

The same rates apply to non-residents, but their allowances are reduced and the top rates apply on a lower income (based on how many months they have stayed in Norway).

Tax limitation

If the taxpayer's total taxes exceed 80% of net income, wealth taxes (see rates below) can be reduced. The wealth tax on amounts exceeding NOK 1,000,000 cannot be reduced to less than 0.6% of the excess amount.

Withholding taxes

The general rate of withholding tax for dividends is 25%, but tax treaties often modify this.

Tax credits

A treaty will normally regulate a double taxation situation. Norway has often chosen the exemption method, but the credit method is also used. Internal law also contains rules against double taxation, i.e. credit rules for work income, a right to apply for a credit for other income or the right to treat certain paid taxes as an income reduction.

Payment of tax

Payroll deductions

Income tax is deducted from wages and salaries by the employer according to the PAYE system, and is based on an estimated pre-assessment. Total deductions for the year are offset against the appropriate amount calculated from the tax return. A refund may be paid to the individual after the final assessment in the autumn. A tax demand must be paid by the individual himself (not through the PAYE system) and normally in two instalments at 3 and 12 weeks after the final assessment.

Prepayment

Prepayments are used for self-employed persons and in cases where salary is not high enough to cover the taxable liability. These payments are made in four instalments during the income year (on 15 March, May, September and November), based on an estimated tax liability.

Prepayments are offset against the final tax amount assessed in the autumn of the subsequent year. The net difference is refunded or must be paid in the same way as described above.

Estate and gift taxes

Inheritance tax is charged on the value of a resident individual's or Norwegian citizen's estate on death at the following rates:

Value	*To children/parents*	*To others*
NOK 0 – 200,000	0%	0%
NOK 200,000 – 500,000	8%	10%
Over NOK 500,000	20%	30%

Transfers between spouses are exempt.

Norwegian real estate and the assets of a permanent establishment are always taxable in Norway.

The same rates apply to lifetime gifts to children, to persons who will inherit from the deceased according to his will and to gifts given less than 6 months before the donor's death.

Wealth tax

Taxpayers have to declare the value of their assets and liabilities in their income tax return. Wealth tax is assessed on residents at the year end.

Non-residents are subject to wealth tax on real estate and assets belonging to a permanent business establishment in Norway.

Wealth tax rates

Local tax	*Single persons*	*Families*
NOK 0 – 120,000	0%	0%
Over NOK 120,000	0.7%	0.7%
State tax		
NOK 0 – 120,000	0%	–
NOK 120,001 – 540,000	0.2%	–
Over NOK 540,000	0.4%	–
State tax		
NOK 0 – 150,000	–	0%
NOK 150,001 – 580,000	–	0.2%
Over NOK 580,000	–	0.4%

Social security contributions

These are covered under tax rates above.

Other taxes

VAT and sales tax

Value added tax (VAT) is levied on domestic sales of goods and *certain* defined services at a rate of 23% (24% from 1 January 2001). From 1 July 2001, the general rule is that value added tax is levied on domestic sales of goods *and* services. Registered business enterprises are entitled to claim a refund for input VAT suffered on purchases. Input VAT on certain types of goods and services cannot be refunded.

Investment tax

Investment tax, which is included in the VAT system, is calculated according to the business enterprise on goods and certain services consumed in the business at a rate of 7%. Fixed assets directly employed in industrial production are exempt from investment tax. Investment tax is only calculated when a refund for input VAT is claimed.

Employers' contribution to social security

Employers pay a contribution to the national health and pension scheme based on earnings paid to employees. The basis for social security is salaries and wages and are generally all fringe benefits which are not a refund of direct expenses the employee has suffered in the course of performing his job.

The rate of social security contribution differs throughout the country. The country is divided into five zones with rates varying from 14.1% in the central parts of the country to zero in the northernmost areas. For exceptionally high income (i.e. more than NOK 774,000 in 2000), an additional contribution of 12.5% of the excess amount is payable.

Special taxes

Special taxes are charged to the final consumer on spirits, alcoholic beverages, tobacco, cars and fuel for cars.

Tax treaties and withholding taxes

The following withholding tax rates apply with respect to dividends paid to foreign residents. No other payments to foreign residents are subject to withholding tax.

The following rates are in force from 1998. Please note that tax treaties are frequently re-negotiated and rates may alter.

Norway

Country of residence	*Normal dividends*	*Dividend to parent company (see next column)*	*Minimum participation*
Australia	15 %	15 %	
Austria	15 %	5 %	25 % of equity
Belgium	15 %	5 %	25 % of equity
Brazil	15 %	15 %	
Canada	15 %	15 %	
Denmark	15 %	0 %	10 % of equity
Egypt	15 %	15 %	
France	15 %	5 %	10 % of equity
Germany	15 %	5 %	25 % of equity
Greece	20 %	20 %	
India	25 %	15 %	25 % of equity
Ireland	10 %	0 %	25 % of equity with voting rights
Italy	15 %	15 %	
Japan	15 %	5 %	25 % of voting rights
Kenya	25 %	15 %	25 % of voting rights
Luxembourg	15 %	5 %	25 % of equity
Malaysia	0 %	0 %	
Malta	15 %	15 %	
Netherlands	15 %	0 %	25 % of equity
New Zealand	15 %	15 %	
Pakistan	15 %	15 %	
Portugal	15 %	10 %	25 % of equity
Singapore	15 %	15 %	
South Korea	15 %	15 %	
Spain	15 %	10 %	50 % of voting rights
Sri Lanka	15 %	15 %	
Sweden	15 %	0 %	10 % of equity
Switzerland	15 %	5 %	25 % of equity
United Kingdom	15 %	5 %	10 % of equity
United States of America	15 %	15 %	
No tax treaty in power	25 %	25 %	

The above list is not exhaustive and detailed rules apply.

Pakistan

S M Masood & Co.

Introduction

Direct taxes such as taxes on income and wealth are levied at the federal level.

Over recent years, corporate and personal tax rates have been gradually reduced. Withholding and presumptive taxes have been systematically increased and the tax base has been broadened.

Tax holidays are available for computer software exporters, and for hi-tech and agro-based industries.

A new investment policy has been announced giving broad incentives to all sectors of the economy. These include accelerated depreciation allowances and various tax incentives for the formation of holding companies.

Corporate taxes

Taxable entities

Resident companies

A resident company is taxed on its worldwide income. It is taxed on its foreign income when this is earned. Double taxation of foreign income is avoided by means of foreign tax credits. This relief is available to a Pakistan company on the taxed foreign income at the lower of the Pakistan or foreign rate of tax. The undistributed income of a non-resident subsidiary is not subject to tax.

Non-resident companies

A non-resident company is taxable in respect of its profits earned in Pakistan. A non-resident company is liable for tax at the same rate as a resident company.

Tax year and filing requirements

The financial year for tax runs from 1 July to 30 June. However, special income years have been specified for different classes of income. The corporate tax return is due on or before 31 December in the case of an income year closing between 1 January and 30 June, and on or before 30 September in the case of an income year closing between 1 July and 31 December. The Deputy Commissioner of Income Tax must raise an assessment within three years of the end of the relevant assessment year. In the absence of a return, an estimated assessment may be raised.

Taxes imposed

All taxes on income, other than agricultural income, are imposed at the federal level. Foreign companies and their branches are treated on a par with local companies. Tax is usually payable within one month after the receipt of assessment. Provisional assessment is also allowed for recovery of tax.

Rates of tax

The rates applicable to various types of companies are as follows:

Public company	33%
Private company	43%
Banking company	58%

Companies, other than banking companies, are also liable to surcharge at the rate of 5% of the income tax payable. Furthermore, the companies tax liability in all circumstances is restricted to a minimum tax of 0.5% of turnover.

Tax withheld on supplies, contracts and export proceeds is considered as full and final discharge of tax on that income. However, manufacturing companies and non-residents are allowed to opt for assessment of their income on the normal profit and loss account basis.

Income subject to tax

General rules

Income which is subject to tax is based on commercial profits generated, less losses and after certain adjustments. Commercial profits are defined as the total sum of all profits, including gains, realised through the conduct of a business enterprise and are measured in rupees. The method of determining commercial profits should be consistent from year to year and can be changed only if justified by sound business practice and provided that the purpose of a change is not to gain an incidental tax benefit.

Stock/inventory valuation

Stock must be valued in accordance with sound business practice.

Capital gains and losses

All profits or gains arising from the transfer of capital assets are chargeable to tax as deemed income. Capital gains are not chargeable in respect of immovable property or assets which are subject to depreciation. Moreover, profits on the sale of shares in public companies are exempt from tax up to 30 June 2002. All surplus capital losses for the year can be carried forward and adjusted against future capital gains for a maximum of six years.

Dividends

Dividend income received by a company is liable to tax at an inter-corporate tax rate which varies between 5% to 20%, depending upon the type of company receiving it.

Deductions

General rules

All expenses laid out or expended wholly and exclusively for the purposes of earning income are generally deductible. However, expenditure of a personal nature and capital expenditure are not allowable. Certain indirect expenditure, as specifically provided for, is also allowed as a deduction.

Depreciation and amortisation

Normal depreciation is allowable at prescribed rates under the reducing balance method except on ocean-going ships where the allowance is on a straight-line basis.

An extra allowance is provided at 50% of normal depreciation for double shift working and at 100% for triple shift working on machinery and equipment, proportionate to the number of days worked in a year of 300 days. This is available only in the case of machinery and equipment.

Pakistan

Liberal incentives have been allowed for any investment in new industrial undertakings. The rate of accelerated depreciation allowance in the first year on capital expenditure ranges from 40% to 80% depending upon the type of industry. Other industries are entitled to a reinvestment allowance for expansion and BMR at the rate of 50%.

Unabsorbed tax allowable depreciation not offset against the year's income is carried forward and added to the depreciation of the assets of the same business in the following year. Tax allowable depreciation can be carried forward without limit until fully absorbed.

Prescribed depreciation rates are as follows:

	Normal	*Initial*	*Under New Investment Policy*
Buildings	5%	10%	–
Plant, machinery, office equipment	10%	25%	90% to 50%
Vehicles	20%	–	–
Furniture	10%	–	–

No depreciation is allowed on leased assets. However, rentals paid are deductible.

Royalties

Royalties are deductible as business expenses to the extent that they are at arm's length.

Interest

All interest paid in respect of capital borrowed for the purposes of business is considered to be business expenditure and is therefore deductible.

Dividends

Dividends paid are not deductible.

Bad and doubtful debts

Bad debts are allowed to the extent that they are actually written off by the taxpayer and determined to be irrecoverable by the assessing officer.

Reserves and provision

In general, reserves and provisions are allowed if they are in accordance with sound business practice.

Employees' and directors' remuneration and benefits

Employees' and directors' remuneration and benefits are generally deductible. However, allowances and benefits in excess of 50% of salary, excluding benefits, are added towards income.

Specific non-deductible expenses

- Any expenditure where the payment exceeds Rs. 50,000 and is made other than through a crossed cheque or crossed bank draft: this restriction applies to operating expenses only.
- Any payments of expenses on which a company incorrectly fails to deduct tax at source.
- Any expenditure incurred for payment on account of any fine or penalty for violation of any law or rule or regulations for the time being in force.
- Any tax, rate or excess paid on the profit or gains of the business or otherwise levied on the basis of such gains.

Foreign source income

Foreign source income is taxable in the hands of a resident except where the tax treaty specifically assigns taxing rights to another company.

Investment incentive and special benefits

Tax exemptions have been granted to promote industrial investment in the country.

The following income tax holidays are presently available:

Profit & gains received by	*To be set up between*	*Period of exemption*
Computer training (any computer training institute or computer training scheme approved by Central Board of Revenue)	01/01/97 to 30/06/2005	5 years

Pakistan

Venture Capital Companies and Funds	01/07/2000 to 30/06/2007	–
Private power projects (set-up anywhere in Pakistan)	01/07/88 onwards	No limit
Export of computer software (engage in export of computer software and its related services)	No limit prescribed	No limit

Related party transactions

Transactions between related parties may be subject to scrutiny if not carried out on an arm's length basis. Any advance by a private company to its shareholders, which could normally be distributable out of accumulated profit, will be treated as a dividend in the hands of shareholders.

Losses

Operating losses can be carried forward and set against profits in the six years following the year in which the losses were incurred. Surplus tax allowable depreciation can be carried forward indefinitely. No carry-back of losses is permitted.

Corporate groups

Presently there is no facility to offset tax allowable losses within groups.

Tax free mergers and disposals

No specific exemption is available for mergers and disposals.

Liquidation of the company

An individual shareholder will in principle be subject to income tax at the normal rates on liquidation distributions to the extent that this could be distributed out of accumulated profits.

Capital taxes

Capital duty

There is no capital duty.

Net worth tax

There is no annual net worth tax levied on companies.

Treatment of branches (branch profits tax)

Branch profits are liable to income tax at the normal rates, subject to those exceptions provided for in tax treaties with specific countries.

Personal taxes

Taxable individuals

The tax liability of individuals is determined on the basis of residential status.

Residents

An individual will be resident if:

- he is present in Pakistan for a period of, or for cumulative periods amounting to, 182 days or more in any income year;
- he is present in Pakistan for a period, or for cumulative periods amounting to, 90 days in that income year and he has, within the four years preceding that year, been present in Pakistan for an aggregate total of 365 days or more.

Non-residents

A non-resident is an individual who is not resident as outlined above.

Tax year and filing requirements

The taxable period is the financial year. The due date of returns for individuals is 30 September.

Individuals deriving income from dividends, interest or profits, lotteries and supplies on which tax has been deducted at source, are required to file a statement of income which is considered as the final discharge of tax. The assessing officer must raise an assessment within two years of the end of the relevant year of assessment.

Taxes on income

Residents pay income tax on their worldwide income.

Pakistan

Non-residents must pay tax only on their income earned or received in Pakistan.

Sources of income

Employment income and directors' fees

Income received as salaries, wages and allowances is subject to tax. Tax on this income is deducted at source at an average rate of tax by the employer.

Business income

Business income includes the profits and gains of any business or profession which is carried on, or deemed to be carried on, income derived from any trade, professional or similar association, and the value of any benefit (whether convertible into money or not) which arises from business or the exercise of a profession.

In general, any expenditure incurred wholly and exclusively for the purpose of such business or profession is allowable as a deduction against income.

Capital gains

Any profits arising from the transfer of a capital asset, excluding depreciable assets and immovable properties, is liable to tax. An exception is made in the case of income arising from the sale of shares of a public company, which is exempt up to 30 June 2000.

Dividends

Dividends are liable to withholding tax at 10%; this is a full and final discharge of tax on distribution.

Interest

Interest received in an income year on any securities of the federal or provincial government and on debentures or securities issued by a local authority or a Pakistani company is liable to tax. Deductions allowable against this income include interest paid on amounts borrowed for the purpose of investment in these securities and commission paid for realising interest on such securities.

All interest and profits, other than those included above, are subject to withholding tax or tax deducted at source. This is treated as a full and final discharge of tax on that income.

Rentals

Rental income, which cannot be less than the rent payable by the tenant, is chargeable to tax. Allowable deductions against rental income include insurance premiums, interest, land revenue taxes, collection charges, legal expenses, repairs, bad debts and vacancy allowances which have actually been paid/not paid against rental income, with the exception of repairs.

Royalties

Royalty income is taxed in the same way as other income. Non-residents are liable to tax on those royalties which are payable by a person in respect of rights, property or information used or services utilised for business or profits carried on outside Pakistan. The above law is subject to provisions which are included within the tax treaties with various countries.

Social security benefits

Employees are not obliged to pay social security contributions.

Pensions and annuities

Income from a pension received by a citizen of Pakistan is exempt from tax. This exemption is available to pension payments received from one employer only. Specific annuities are also exempt from tax.

Exempt income

The significant classes of exempt income are:

- agricultural income, although such income is taken into account in arriving at an average rate to determine tax on other income;
- the salary income of the employees of a foreign government, where it is paid as remuneration for services to that government;
- salary paid by a foreign government to foreign teachers;
- yield on government saving schemes;
- interest on private foreign currency bank accounts.

Foreign source income

Foreign source income is taxable in the hands of a resident, except when the tax treaty specifically assigns taxing rights to another country.

Personal allowances and deductions

Allowances for house rental are exempt up to 45% of basic salary. Utility allowances are also exempt, up to 10% of basic salary. Medical allowances actually reimbursed are also exempt from tax. Tax rebates are allowed in the case of certain approved donations, legal and medical expenditure. A tax rebate can be claimed at 5% of any children's education expense, subject to maximum expense of Rs 30,000 per child.

Losses

Losses sustained under any heading (except speculation and capital losses) can be offset against income under any other heading in the same year. Surplus business losses can be carried forward and deducted from business income only in the subsequent six years.

Losses from a speculation business can only be offset against profits from another speculation business. Surplus losses can be carried forward and offset against income of the speculation business in the subsequent six years.

Where capital losses are sustained, these can be carried forward and offset against capital gains in the subsequent six years.

Special family rules

A husband and wife are assessed separately as individuals on their own personal income. However, in certain cases clubbing provisions exist.

Rates of tax

General – resident

Income Group	*Income Tax Rate*
Up to Rs 100,000	5%
Rs 100,000 to Rs 200,000	Rs 5,000 + 10%
Rs 200,000 to Rs 300,000	Rs 15,000 + 15%
Rs 300,000 to Rs 500,000	Rs 30,000 + 20%
Rs 500,000 to Rs 700,000	Rs 70,000 + 25%
Rs 700,000 to Rs 1,000,000	Rs 120,000 + 30%
Rs 1,000,000 & above	Rs 210,000 + 35%

A tax rebate of Rs 2,500 and Rs 2,000 is available in the case of salary and non-salary respectively.

Rates of surcharge

The rate of surcharge is 10% of tax payable.

Non-resident

Tax payable by a non-resident is the greater of 20% of total taxable income or the tax that would be payable if the total taxable income were that of an individual resident in Pakistan. The taxpayer can opt to pay tax based upon a proportion of his total worldwide income.

Provincial and local taxes

There are no provincial and local taxes on income.

Withholding tax

	Rate of Tax
Salary	Average rate
Dividends: received by individuals	10%
Profits/interest: received from banks	10%
Rent of house property: annual rental exceeding Rs. 100,000	7.5%
Interest on securities (excluding debentures)	30%
Certain payments to non-residents excluding the above income	20%–30%

Tax credits

Withholding taxes are normally credited against the tax liability. An exception to this is where taxes are deducted at source against dividends, interest or profit and prize bonds. The tax deducted is considered as a final discharge of tax and are, therefore, not available to be credited against the tax liability on normal income.

Payment of tax

Normally, income tax must be paid within one month of the date of assessment.

Payroll deductions

Taxes are deducted at the 'average rate' from salary and wages and may be credited against the final tax liability.

Prepayments

Advance tax must be paid in four equal quarterly instalments in an income year. This will be based upon the tax liability of the latest assessment year where an individual has been assessed at income exceeding Rs 150,000 in the past. A provisional assessment can be raised by the assessing officer for early recovery of tax.

Estate and gift tax

There are no estate or gift taxes.

Wealth tax

Wealth tax is levied at rates ranging between 0.5% and 2.5%.

A basic exemption from wealth tax is available at Rs 1,000,000 or on one residential house of any value. Other exemptions include household effects, government securities and other assets, which are subject to Zakat.

Social security contributions

Employers are required to contribute towards social security at rates prescribed from time to time by the government for each employee earning less than Rs. 3,000 per month. The benefits available include sickness, death grant, medical care, injury, disablement and survivors benefit.

For employees earning less than Rs 3,000 per month, employers pay an additional 5% of those earnings towards the 'Employees Old Age Benefit Scheme'.

In addition to the above, employers are also required to provide group insurance for all permanent workers, together with payments towards gratuity or provident fund schemes for all their employees.

Other taxes

Treatment of partnerships

Partnerships are treated either as registered firms if they are registered with the tax department or as unregistered firms. A registered firm's profits are liable to super tax – this is after the deduction of tax payable by the firm is distributed among partners in their respective shares. However, taxation which takes place in the partners' hands is subject to certain maximum limits. In the case of an unregistered firm, income tax is levied on firm's profits and the partners' share in the firm's income is exempt from tax and only taken into account if he has any other income liable to tax.

VAT and sales taxes

Most supplies and imports are subject to sales tax at 15%. A zero rate is applied to exports.

Capital value tax

Tax is levied at various rates on the purchase of certain assets, the details are as follows:

Motor vehicles:

(Imported)

Cars, jeeps, double cabin pick-ups and station wagons	*Rate*
Not exceeding 800 cc and three wheeler	Nil
Exceeding 800 cc and up to 1000 cc	3.75%
Exceeding 1000 cc and up to 1300 cc	5%
Exceeding 1300 cc and up to 1600 cc	6.25%
Exceeding 1600 cc	7.5%

Air tickets:

	Rate
Air tickets for foreign travel (except in the case of diplomats & aircraft crew on duty)	1.5% of the value of the ticket

Note
Adjustments of Capital Value Tax are available against wealth tax payable to all individuals recorded on the National Tax register (NTN holders).

Zakat

Zakat is deductible in the case of every Muslim at source at 2.5% on the capital element of saving accounts, fixed deposits, government securities, shares and the securities of other organisations, life insurance policies, annuities and the provident fund.

The Zakat year starts on the first day of the Islamic month Ramzan.

Zakat paid is a deductible expense for arriving at income subject to income tax.

Property tax

A local tax is levied by the Provincial Government on urban property at 10% of the annual value of the property.

Exchange control

Exchange controls on the movement of foreign currency has been greatly liberalised and now there is no restriction on such movements.

Tax treaties and withholding taxes

The rate of withholding tax on dividend and interest income is 10%. The rates of withholding tax in force on dividends under selected tax treaties are as follows:

Country of residence	*Normal dividends*	*Participation dividends*	*Minimum participation requirements*
Non-treaty countries	10	10	–
Selected treaty countries:			
Austria	–	10*/20	25(i)
Belgium	–	10/15*	20(i)
Canada	–	15*/20	25(i)
Denmark	–	9.375*	33.34(i)
France	–	10/20*	50
Germany	20	10*	–
Greece	–	–	–
India	–	–	–
Ireland	–	10	50(i)
Italy	25	15	25(i)
Japan	–	9.375*	33.34(i)
Korea	12.5	20	20(i)
Malta	–	15	20(i)

Netherlands Antilles	20	10	25(i)
Norway	–	15	–
Sweden	10	15	25(i)
Switzerland	–	10*/20	50(i)
Thailand	–	25/15	25
Turkey	15	10	25(i)
United Kingdom	20/15(i)	10	25*/50(i)
United States	–	9.37	50

* Engaged in industrial undertaking.

(i) Inter-corporate.

Other treaty countries

Sri Lanka, Libya, Lebanon, Romania, Philippines, Bangladesh, Jordan, Malaysia, Saudi Arabia, Kenya, United Arab Emirates, Mauritius, U'zbikstan, China, Nigeria, Poland, Singapore, Indonesia, Iran.

Paraguay

CYCE – Consultores y Contadores de Empresas

Introduction

In 1991, Law No. 125/91 was passed, enacted by the Executive Power in 1992 and put immediately in effect.

Starting from that year, a new taxation system also came into effect, with previous provisions being derogated. Fiscal reform had a greater positive impact on those with less capability for contribution reducing their taxation.

The Paraguayan tax system is structured on legal provisions based on Law No. 125/91 ('New Taxation System'), the Constitution, and the Civil Code.

The new tax system

Taxes are based on Paraguayan source income.

Paraguayan source

Subject to special provisions, income originating from activities carried out in Paraguay from assets situated or rights used economically in the Republic (independent of nationality, domicile or residence of those intervening in the operations and of the place where contracts are entered into) shall be regarded as being of a Paraguayan source.

The interest of bearer securities shall be regarded as being entirely of Paraguayan source, where the issuing entity is organised or residing in the Republic.

Technical assistance shall be regarded as rendered in the national territory where the same is made use of in the country.

The assignment of use of assets and rights shall be of Paraguayan source where used in the Republic, even on a partial basis within the period agreed upon.

International freights shall be 50% of Paraguayan source where they are used between Paraguay and Argentina, Bolivia, Brazil and Uruguay, and 30% where they are carried out between Paraguay and any other country.

The established percentages refer only to that portion of the journey that is chargeable to transportation carried out in Paraguayan territory and which is to be exclusively observed by those taxpayers domiciled in the country paying the tax (based on accounting according to general tax principles). The present provision is to be applied to transportation of people and goods.

Taxes

Taxes applied in Paraguay are the following:

- income tax;
- single tax;
- agricultural activities tax;
- value added tax;
- selective consumption tax; and
- acts and documents tax.

As for collection, the base generally rests on two main taxes: income tax and value added tax.

Tax rate applied

General

30% applied to net income.

Special

- 35% – the main office must pay the income tax of a Paraguayan source (obtained and credited by the branch) under any section (except for dividends).
- 35% – individuals domiciled or entities residing abroad without a branch, agency, or location in the country.
- 5% of income originating from dividends and profits obtained by individuals domiciled abroad in their capacity as shareholders or partners. The same rate applies for the remittance of dividends or profits made by a Paraguay branch to its main office.

General provisions – tax balance

Taxpayers must annually submit to the Tax Administration their tax balance, which constitutes the basis for determining the income tax for the profit generated by the end of the fiscal year.

Terms for presentation

Annual presentation

The presentation of the tax balance to the Treasury shall include a sworn statement, between the sixteenth and the nineteenth working day of the fourth month following the end of the fiscal year.

Quarterly advances

Between the tenth and sixteenth working day of the first, third, fifth, and seventh months following expiration of the annual sworn statement.

Where the taxpayer had a profit in the previous fiscal year, he must submit four advance payments based on 25% of the Income tax paid the previous year for each instalment.

Origin of the tax burden

Taxes are paid annually, by the end of the fiscal year that covers the period from 1 January to 31 December of each year.

Annual gross income

Determined in an imputed basis, 12% of the total of fiscal values of hectares of rural property that the taxpayer may own (except for exempted hectares and those used in the operations) independent of the fact that an effective use is being made.

The annual lease rate shall be established in cash and by the hectare, and in no case shall exceed 12% of the fiscal value assigned to the leased lot.

Net income – deductible expenses

- Expenses necessary to obtain and keep the income:
  - when an owner shall apply 40% of the gross income;
  - when not, an owner shall apply 45% of the gross income.

- VAT – 30% of the gross income. The surplus may be used in the following fiscal years.

Extraordinary losses – where originated due to natural causes and not covered by insurance, relief is according to the percentage established by the Executive Power from time to time.

Applied tax rate

25% of the net income determined.

Exemption

- Those operating an area not exceeding 20 hectares.
- For properties of up to 100 hectares, 20 hectares are excluded.
- Natural forests or permanent small lakes.

Special systems

Occasionally the Treasury overrides the prevailing rules for simplicity. In this case, the Treasury defines the rules for determining incomes subject to taxation.

- *Alienation in the customs area* – if goods are alienated in customs areas or supervised private warehouses, advance payments shall be made on account of income tax, which shall be applied for the purposes of the relevant payment, according to the bi-monthly expirations of the current fiscal period. The taxable base for the advance payment shall be the CIF value of the transfer, increased by 30%. A 4.5% is to be applied to this amount.
- *Tourism system or special system (imported goods)* – taxpayers importing goods covered under the tourism system shall make a single and final income tax payment of 30% of the estimated profitability of 10% of the cost of imported goods. Such cost will be the taxable customs value, to which customs taxes for import operations (the selective consumption tax, if applicable, and the VAT are to be added).
- *Ticket sales* – net income for the sale of tickets shall be determined by applying a factor of 1.7 to such income, taxing the result at 30%.

Capital tax

The annual tax called 'real estate tax' taxes the 'holding of real estate located in the territory of the Republic'. This tax is collected by the

Mayor's Office. A range of tax rates and exemptions apply depending on the size, location and nature of the land.

Taxable base

The taxable base for determining this tax is the fiscal valuation of properties, established by the National Cadaster Service.

The annual adjustment applied varies according to the consumer price index published by the Central Bank of Paraguay.

Corporate taxes

Value added tax

This tax is applied to the sale of goods and services and the importation of goods.

Paying taxes

Taxes are paid on a monthly basis, being determined by the difference between the fiscal debit and the fiscal credit.

Tax rate

Generally 10% of the taxable base.

How VAT is imposed

When sales are on a retail basis, the VAT must be included in the sale price and should not be separate. In this case, the VAT is not separated in the invoice.

When sales are wholesale, the VAT must be shown separately, distinguishing the 10% on the invoice.

Selective consumption tax

This tax is imposed on the importation of certain goods, generally luxury items.

Taxable base

Taxable base is the following:

- the factory sale price, not including the tax itself and the VAT;
- on imports, the customs value (to which customs duties are to be added) as well as other taxes that have an impact in the operation before the withdrawal of goods, but not including the VAT;
- petroleum-based fuels are taxed on the price for sale to the public as established by the Executive Power.

Differentiated rates are observed, and range from 5% to 50%, depending on the type of product specified by law.

Calculation and payment

The tax is paid on a monthly basis, except for that on fuels, which is paid in weekly periods from Sunday to Saturday.

Tax on acts and documents

The tax is on those executing documents.

Taxable Base

- 1.74% annual on loans, estimating in proportion to time.
- 1.00% transfers within the country.
- 1.50% transfers abroad.

The amounts are payable according to a schedule of instalments laid down by law.

Commercial, industrial and trade licence

It taxes individuals and entities that carry on industrial, commercial, and professional activities within the Republic's capital.

The payment of licences for commercial and industrial companies and financial entities is annual and is made based on the assets of the corporation and accounting statements certified by the Tax Administration (for commercial and industrial companies) and by the Bank Superintendence for companies operating in the banking, financial and insurance system.

The licence tax is calculated based on the amount of the assets, after deducting the values shown in the following accounts:

- memoranda accounts;

- loss;
- nominal accounts; and
- depreciation of assets located in the Asunción district.

The tax is imposed at varying rates depending on net asset values.

The licence tax is paid after deducting the value of goods existing in other districts and, for the deduction, a sworn statement is sufficient evidence of location.

Any industrial, radio and television broadcasting, printing and daily or periodical publication activities operated for profit shall pay the licence tax according to a 25% reduction to the normal scale.

Other licences

Taxpayers	*Licence Tax*
Night clubs, pubs and similar activities	Annual with surcharge of 100% of the scale established earlier
Street vendors and travelling merchants domiciled in Asunción	Annual, the amount ranges between G 2,000 and G 20,000
Individuals and entities operating movie and theatre halls	Special Class G 40,000 Second Class G 20,000 Third Class G 12,000
Individuals or entities operating automobile parking lots for profit	First Class G 18,000 Second Class G 15,000
The basic amounts established correspond to parking lots whose capacity is up to 25 vehicles. If they exceed this quantity, they shall pay an additional amount per each 10 vehicles or fraction in the following category:	
Professionals	First Class G 3,500 Second Class G 2,500
These in practice in the following professions shall pay the annual professional patent according to the following scale:	

• individuals practising college-level professions	G 6,000
• individuals practising non-college level professions	G 3,000
• individuals practising trades such as construction foremen, electricians, plumbers, and others	G 1,500
• car, bus and tractor drivers	G 600
• public transportation inspectors and ticket collectors	G 500
• motorized bicycle and tricycle drivers.	G 300

Vehicle licence tax

The tax is paid annually, based on the Customs Appraisal Value with a basic charge ranging from G7,500 to G34,000, and a further variable charge ranging from zero to 1%.

The tax is reduced by 10% to 50%, according to the characteristics of the vehicle.

Construction tax

Works performed within the capital district pay a tax ranging from 0.2% to 4% of the value of the construction, depending on the nature of the property.

In the case of industrial buildings, a basic tax is applied to the cost of the construction, ranging from G1,000 to G118,000, and a percentage on the excess of the lower limit ranging from 0.00% to 1%.

Tax on loan operations

Moneylenders and pawnshops pay a tax of G4,000 on the amount of each transaction and pawnshops pay on monthly basis according to the level of pledged items.

Notary Publics are not permitted to formalise any loan instruments without evidence of payment of the tax.

Social security contributions

Social security is mandatory and it is part of the tax system.

There are a number of constituents in charge, with variations for certain employment groups as follows:

- Public Employees Retirement and Pension Fund, which goes into the National Treasury with the purpose of paying retirement pensions to public employees (the contribution is 14% of wages);
- Employees Retirement and Pension Fund;
- bank employees have an employer's contribution of 17% and 10% by the employee;
- national electricity administration personnel have a contribution of 5% by the authority and 5% by employees;
- municipal personnel have a contribution of 10% by the employer and 10% by employees;
- the Social Security Institution is the true social security since it is structured on the law on retirement and pension; medical and disability insurance is mandatory for companies that do not adopt other characteristics of social security; contributions are made on wages earned by workers with an employer's contribution of 16.5% and a worker's contribution of 9%.

Improvement contributions

It is established that those individuals whose assets increase in value due to an improvement made by the state, must pay a compensation to finance the costs of the improvement made for public use.

Improvement contributions are:

- stone and asphalt pavement on streets whose cost is distributed among neighbours of the street improved;
- construction of the sewer system;
- construction of the drainage system for Asunción; and
- highway contribution.

Fiscal exemptions

The most common exemption is on investments, which has the object of encouraging inward investments of capital to (for example) create jobs, increase the production of goods and services or to promote exports.

It exempts such activities 100% from customs duties and 59% from income tax law.

In addition to these laws, there are other fiscal exemptions for VAT and income tax.

The taxpayer is granted fiscal benefits with the purpose of stimulating the economic development of the country, which allows certain industrial companies to purchase machinery on beneficial terms as well as obtain fiscal benefits. In addition, one of the essential requirements for the approval of the investment project is the creation of jobs and an application must be submitted by the taxpayer to the Ministry of Industry and Commerce to apply for the exemption.

Special rates apply for sales resulting from reinvestment, forestation and reforestation.

Further benefits apply for corporations until the year 2008, which cover:

a) large companies issuing shares – $\frac{1}{3}$ of the current income tax rate for large companies, if they issue shares exceeding 50% of the percentage they are obliged to issue in law;

b) large companies paying dividends – $\frac{1}{3}$ of the current Income tax rate for large companies distributing dividends in cash, provided not less than 25% of the net profit in the fiscal year is distributed;

c) large companies converting securities into shares – one-third of the current income tax rate for equivalent large companies where such conversion constitutes not less than 15% of the corporation's paid-up capital; and

d) small and medium size companies – 50% of the income tax of large companies, provided they meet the requirements in a), b) and c) above.

In addition, outsourcing operations have special tax laws.

Other national, state, and municipal tax exemptions

Except where stated elsewhere, the outsourcing contract and the activities carried on in fulfilment of the contract are exempted of any other national, state or municipal tax.

This exemption extends to:

- the importing of authorised goods referred to in the outsourcing contract;
- the re-exportation of imported goods under the contract;
- the exportation of goods transformed, manufactured, repaired or assembled under the contract.

Temporary importing

A company having an outsourcing program approved or extended and having its contract formally registered may temporarily import, under the terms of the contract and according to this law and its regulations, a range of authorised goods used in the business process such as:

- raw materials and input for production and exportation;
- machinery, laboratory, measuring equipment for testing their products and those required by quality control; or
- tools, equipment and accessories for industrial security and products necessary for the prevention and control of contamination of the production plant, work manuals and industrial plans, as well as telecommunications and computing equipment for exclusive use by the outsourcing company.

When dealing with raw materials and input, once they have been imported, they must leave Paraguay within a period of six months from the date they are imported. This period may be extended upon request and with sufficient reason and ministerial approval.

Income tax and free zone tax

Users carrying on commercial activities and who, besides exporting to third-party countries, make sales within the territory, shall pay income tax on the proportion of income arising in the customs territory on commercial activities and shall deduct their expenses in the same proportion, as well as paying the free zone tax on gross income originated from their exports to third countries.

Taxpayer's option

In all cases, commercial, industrial, or service companies may choose to pay the free zone tax or the income tax for commercial, industrial and service activities. Having opted one way, the company may not change to the other tax until four fiscal years have passed.

Personal taxes

In Paraguay, there is a proposal on personal income tax that has not yet been approved. Therefore, there are no personal income taxes imposed on the income of individuals at the time of writing.

Portugal

Consulteam, S.A.

Corporate taxes

Taxable entities

Corporate entities (trading companies, civil companies with a commercial structure, cooperative societies and other corporate entities) and unincorporated entities with their head office or effective management in the Portuguese territory, which are deemed to be resident, are subject to corporate income tax (IRC).

Resident companies

Resident entities are liable to IRC on worldwide income from both Portuguese and foreign sources.

Non-resident companies

Non-resident entities are liable to tax only on income from Portuguese sources.

Tax year and filing requirements

IRC is payable for each taxation period which usually corresponds to the calendar year.

A non-resident entity with a permanent establishment in Portugal may adopt any tax period of 12 months, but the adopted tax period must be retained for at least the subsequent five fiscal years.

An income tax return must be filed each year by 31 May or by the end of the fifth month following the end of the adopted tax period.

Taxes imposed

All taxes on income and capital gains are imposed at the national level under a single unified system (IRC).

Value Added Tax (IVA)

IVA is a turnover tax imposed at rates of 5%, 12% and 17%, depending on the products or services concerned, with relief for IVA suffered on purchases.

Real estate transfer tax (Sisa)

Real estate tax (Sisa) is levied on the transfer for consideration of ownership or partial ownership of real estate (immovable property) and is payable by the purchaser. The general rate is 10% on urban property or building land and 8% in all other cases. Acquisition of urban property or of a discrete share intended exclusively for housing purposes is exempt, provided that the amount on which the tax would be levied does not exceed PTE 11,710,000.

Local tax on real estate (CA)

A municipal tax is levied on the net value of property situated in the territory of each municipality. It is divided into rural (0.8%) and urban (0.7 up to 1.3%) property.

Stamp tax ('Imposto de selo')

Stamp duty is levied on deeds and some documents, books, papers, acts and products.

Income tax rates

The general rate of IRC is 32% payable by resident entities liable to tax on the basis of profits and by non-resident entities with a permanent establishment in Portugal.

For resident entities whose main activity is not commercial, industrial or agricultural, the rate is 20%.

Non-resident entities without a permanent establishment are normally subject to IRC at a rate of 25%.

A local surcharge tax ('derrama') may be levied on IRC, at a maximum rate of 10%. Thus if derrama applies, the general rate of taxation on profits is 35.2% (32% + 3.2%).

For non-resident companies without a permanent establishment there are special rates for income derived from a Portuguese source, as follows:

Dividends	25%
Rights of authors and royalties	15%
Capital or investment income	20%(a)
Fees related to the use, or concession of use, of equipment	15%

(a) Not applied on share capital

Income subject to tax

General rules

As a general rule, taxable income is determined on the basis of the return made by the taxpayer, without prejudice to its audit by the tax administration. Thus, an enterprise is taxed on its effective real profit determined on the basis of its accounting.

Stock/inventory valuation

The following criteria for valuing stock are to be adopted and used consistently in subsequent financial periods:

- effective acquisition or production costs;
- standard costs estimated in accordance with the appropriate technical and accounting principles;
- selling prices after deduction of the normal profit margin (only where the calculation is too burdensome or cannot be estimated with reasonable accuracy, and where the deduction does not exceed 20% of the sales price);
- special valuation methods for basic or normal inventory;
- FIFO or LIFO methods are acceptable.

Capital gains and losses

Capital gains and losses actually realised are usually taxable as normal income. However, the tax arising on capital gains resulting from the disposal of fixed assets may be excluded if the realisation value is reinvested in the acquisition, production or construction of elements of tangible assets, provided that the reinvestment is made by the end of the following third fiscal period.

Dividends

Dividends distributed within Portugal by a subsidiary to its direct parent company are subject to withholding tax on each distribution, regardless of whether the receiving company, in turn, constitutes an intermediary holding company.

In calculating income subject to corporate tax, dividend income will be reduced by 95% provided the shares held represent at least 25% of the subsidiary's share capital and have been owned for at least two consecutive years or since incorporation. If the parent company is a SGPS (holding company without any business activity) the requisite shareholding is reduced to 10% and the fixed rate is not applicable. Otherwise, the corporate tax payable will be reduced by the withholding tax previously suffered.

If a company holds less than 25% of another company, it has the right to deduct from corporate tax payable 60% of the tax paid by the second company corresponding to any dividend.

Dividends received from abroad are always subject to corporate income tax at the normal rate.

Deductions

General rules

Expenses are generally deductible provided they are incurred for the purpose of realising income liable to corporate tax and are properly documented. Social expenses (pension funds, health and life insurance which benefits employees, libraries, nurseries, canteens, etc.) are also deductible within certain limits.

Depreciation and amortisation

Depreciation of all fixed assets, except land, is allowable for tax purposes. Normally the straight line method should be used, but the law provides alternatives. Examples of generally applied rates are:

Equipment and machinery	12.5/20%
Buildings:	
Industrial	5%
Others	2%
Office furniture	12.5%
Electronic equipment	20%
EDP equipment	25%
Motor vehicles	20/25%

Accelerated depreciation schemes are available for certain operational fixed assets and there are special rates for certain activities.

Royalties and service fees

Royalties and service fees covering patents, trademarks, trading agreements, manufacturing licenses, know-how and other intellectual property, are deductible as business expenses. Certain transfer pricing measures are in operation to prevent tax avoidance, as outlined below.

Interest

Interest is deductible in the year it is incurred.

Bad and doubtful debts

These are deductible in full where a debt has proven irrecoverable. In addition, a general provision can be carried in the accounts of between 25% and 100% for bad and doubtful debts between six months and two years old.

Reserves and provisions

Provisions are allowed to cover stock/inventory depreciation or costs resulting from judicial processes.

Employees' and directors' remuneration and benefits

Remuneration, extra allowances pensions and retirement payments are generally deductible. However, some allowances given to employees or directors (including food, housing or rent) are deductible only within limits.

Specifically non-deductible expenses

Depreciation of cars is not allowed to the extent that the depreciation relates to the excess value above PTE 6,000,000. One fifth of all costs related to cars, including maintenance, gasoline, insurance and rents are not deductible. Undocumented expenses are not deductible and they incur a further tax of 50% up to 70%.

Foreign source income

Income from a foreign source, other than dividends, interest and royalties, is generally exempt from corporate tax, provided a treaty applies or the income has been taxed in the other country.

For dividends, interest and royalties from treaty countries, a credit for withholding tax is generally given.

Investment incentives and special benefits

Both tax and non-tax incentives are available to encourage investment and to further regional and national interests and increase employment.

Each case requires a specific approach as there are many incentives including tax holiday periods, reduced interest rates, research and development subsidies and accelerated depreciation. Various EC financial incentives are also available, including export credits, regional grants, etc.

Related party transactions

The tax authorities may adjust taxable income to account for differences between the fair market value and the book value of transactions involving related parties.

Losses

Losses can be deducted from the taxable profits of subsequent fiscal years. No carry back is allowed.

Corporate groups

A corporate group consisting of Portuguese resident companies may be treated as a single taxable entity where the holding company has control over all subsidiaries.

Tax-free mergers and disposals

Mergers can be tax exempt where certain conditions are met, particularly where assets or shares are exchanged for shares.

Liquidation of company

Companies in liquidation are taxed according to the profit arising during the liquidation period. If the shareholder is a company then any loss on liquidation is deductible and any surplus is taxed.

Taxes on capital

Capital duty

A contribution to the capital of a company in exchange for shares, including share premium or informal capital is exempt from capital duty.

Net worth tax

There is no annual net worth tax levied on companies.

Treatment of branches (branch profit tax)

Profits of foreign branches are subject to corporate income tax.

Dividends from the Portuguese branch of an EC company are taxed at a rate of 10%.

Personal taxes

Taxable individuals

Individuals, resident or non-resident in Portugal, earning an income in the country are subject to income tax (IRS – *'Imposto sobre o rendimento de pessoas singulares').*

Residents

Resident individuals are subject to tax on their worldwide income from all sources.

An individual is considered to be resident if he:

- is present in Portugal for more than 183 days in the calendar year;
- occupies a house in Portugal on such terms that it may be presumed it is his intention to occupy it on a permanent basis; or
- he belongs to the crew of a ship or aircraft having its home port in Portugal.

Non-residents

Non-resident individuals are taxable on earned income arising within

Portuguese territory, subject to the application of relevant double taxable treaties.

Tax year and filing requirements

The taxable period is the calendar year.

Residents are not required to file a tax return if:

- they have received pension income only, not exceeding PTE 1,825,000 for married couples, or PTE 1,645,000 otherwise;
- they have not received income other than from a sole employment where this does not exceed PTE 63,800 per month.

In all other cases, a return must be filed by 15 March following the relevant period for dependent employment and pensions or by 30 April for other categories.

Residents who are not required to file a return may do so voluntarily where they expect a refund.

Taxes on income

All income is subject to income tax (IRS). This is computed on the aggregate family income.

Sources of income

Employment income and directors' fees

All employment income, comprising salary and wages as well as all benefits in kind as defined in the IRS Code, is taxable.

A withholding tax is levied on income at the time of payment as prepayment of the ultimate tax liability. Rates are based on expected income for the year and take family structure into consideration. Deductions are available for employees' contributions to social security and to an approved pension fund. Professional fees received in each calendar year are taxable after the deduction of related expenses, incurred up to an overall limit.

Business profits and losses

This includes income from all kinds of non-incorporated industries and trades. The income from commercial, industrial or agricultural activity is determined by the consolidated financial statements of the businesses, applying rules laid down by the IRC Code (Corporate Tax).

Dividends

Dividends are taxed at a rate of 25 % for non-residents, unless a tax treaty applies. For residents, dividends are included in annual income.

Interest

Interest is generally subject to withholding tax at 20%.

Rentals

Rents from real estate are fully taxable. All expenses related to rental income are deductible. A withholding tax rate of 15% is levied on rents paid by corporate entities.

Royalties

Royalties paid to non-residents are subject to a 15% rate. For residents, royalties are included in annual income.

Social security benefits

Social security benefits payable upon illness, marriage, death, etc., are exempt.

Pension and annuities

Pensions paid to non-residents are taxed at a rate of 25%. Residents with pensions over PTE 1,523,000 received from a former employer or social security are taxed as for earned income.

Annuities are treated as investment income, but the capital element in a purchased life annuity is exempt from tax.

Exempt income

A termination payment not exceeding 1.5% of monthly fixed salary per year of labour contract is exempt.

Capital gains

Capital gains are profits derived from the transfer of rights or assets. Gains are generally taxable on the difference between disposal proceeds and original acquisition cost, after accounting for inflation based on annual official tables.

Gains on family residences are not taxable to the extent that they are reinvested within two years for the same purpose.

Capital gains arising from securities acquired before 1 January 1989 are not taxed. A special rate of 20% is applicable to net gains earned by non-resident.

Gains arising on properties and rights are reduced by 50% before inclusion as part of taxable income.

Capital gains arising from bonds, investment funds and shares benefit from special rates (from 30% up to 75%).

Foreign source income

Foreign source income is included in annual income, with a deduction for tax paid in the other country.

Personal allowances and deductions

Personal allowances are granted equivalent to 70% of family income up to a maximum of PTE 550,000 to PTE 603,000 or the social security tax paid during the year if higher than that amount.

Up to 30% of medical expenses not reimbursed and interest paid in respect of medical expenses and hospital treatment is allowed.

Payments to a third party by individuals under court order (e.g. alimony) are deductible.

30% of the education expenses of the taxpayer and his dependants are deductible up to PTE 107,200.

25% of the costs incurred in connection with nursing homes or other institutions for care of the elderly are deductible up to PTE 59,200.

A deduction is allowable of up to 30% of the amount expended in the acquisition of new equipment for the use of renewable energies, up to a limit of PTE 100,000 or, in certain conditions, of PTE 120,000.

Allowances relating to debt interest and redemption incurred in the acquisition, construction or improvement of a permanent owner-occupied dwelling house may not exceed PTE 101,000.

Donations are deductible as follows:

- donations to the Portuguese State;
- donations to churches, charitable, scientific or cultural institutions of up to 15% of net income (after considering all other deductions).

Losses

In general, losses are deductible only against the income of the subsequent six years.

Special family rules

The family is regarded as a tax unit, and the income of all members (including dependant children) is aggregated for tax purposes. Any child constitutes a dependant, unless married or over 18. An unmarried child over 18 years old may be considered a dependant if under 25 and engaged in full time study.

The personal tax system is progressive but an individual's liability is adjusted to his family circumstances by application of the family quotient (apportioning system).

Married couples cannot file separately unless they are separated.

Special treatment for expatriates

Expatriates are treated as residents.

Rates of tax

General

The 2001 rates are:

Taxable income (PTE)	*Tax rate* Normal (A) (%)	Average (B) (%)
Up to 800,000	12	12
Over 800,000 – 1,210,000	14	12.6777
Over 1,210,000 – 3,000,000	24	19.4333
Over 3,000,000 – 6,900,000	34	27.6667
Over 6,900,000 – 10,000,000	38	30.8700
Over 10,000,000	40	

The amount of taxable income (if higher than PTE 800,000) is divided into two parts: one equal to the limit of the highest bracket comprised therein, to which the column B rate applies; the other equal to the excess, to which the column A rate corresponding to the next highest bracket applies.

Residents and non-residents

Certain special rates of tax apply, as follows:

Category	*Tax rate*
Winnings from lotteries, raffles, betting, lotto, bingo, winning contests	25%/35%
Income from registered or unregistered shares (exempt if held for more than 12 months)	25%
Pensions received by non-residents	25%
Income from independent professional services if received by a non-resident	25%
Profits payable by an entity subject to corporate tax if derived by a non-resident	25%
Interest on demand and fixed term deposits	20%
Income from securities, as well as income from carry over transactions, disposal or credits or other similar operations	20%
Any income from capital not expressly taxed at a different rate derived by a non-resident	20%
Royalties and income in connection with the disposal or the temporary use of rights on intellectual or industrial property if derived by a non-resident	15%

Provincial and local taxes

Local tax on real estate (CA)

CA is a municipal tax levied on the value of real estate owned by the taxpayer at the end of the previous year. Real estate used for permanent residence may be temporarily exempt, depending on its taxable value. Landowners are required to pay municipal tax at 0.8% on rural land and 0.7% to 1.3% on rural land, on the value of the property. These taxes are applicable at a national level.

Withholding taxes

Category	%
Interest on current and deposit accounts	20
Dividends and bond interest:	
– government bonds	20

– others (a)	25
Gains from lotteries, betting, etc.	25/ 35
Employment income, commissions, pensions and annuities earned by non-residents	25
Fees related to the use of movable assets or the transfer or use of rights, copyrights, patents and know-how earned by non-residents	15
Other capital or investment, income earned by non-residents	20
Employment income	variable
Professional fees, commissions	20
Rents	15

Notes

Except for the last three items, the tax withheld is a final tax unless the taxpayer wishes to file a return.

(a) As a result of the implementation of the EC Parent-Subsidiary Directive withholding tax of 10% is levied on distributions made to a parent company resident in an EC member state, provided a substantial interest (i.e. 25 % or more) has been held for at least two years.

Tax credits

An individual can receive a tax credit or opt to transfer credit to the subsequent year. Refunds, if in excess of PTE 2,000, are made by the end of August.

Payment of tax

Income tax must be paid within five or eight months from the date of final assessment.

Payroll deductions

Social security is deducted from wages and salaries by the employer at rates fixed in accordance with expected income and family situation.

Prepayments

Withholding tax normally serves as prepayment.

A quarterly prepayment system is in force for self-employment, commercial and industrial income and is based on the taxed income of the previous year. Taxes suffered will be offset against the estimated amount due.

Estate and gift taxes

Gift and inheritance tax is levied on the transfer, free of charge, of movable and immovable property, as follows:

On transfers	*Amount of transfers (PTE 000's)* Up to 730	730-2860	2860-7280	7280-14300	14300-35880	35880-71240	Over 71240
In favour of:							
Spouses and descendants	–	3	6	9	13	17	24
Ascendants or brothers and sisters	7	10	13	16	21	26	32
3rd degree collaterals (i.e. uncles, aunts, nephews, nieces)	13	17	21	25	31	38	45
Other persons	16	20	25	30	36	43	50

For the purpose of applying tax rates, the transfer value is divided into two parts. The first part is equal to the upper limit of the next lowest bracket to that in which the full transfer value falls, which is taxed at the corresponding rate for that lower bracket, and the second part is the excess, which is taxed at the rate for the bracket in which the full transfer value actually falls.

This tax may be paid in up to 16 instalments (six monthly).

Wealth tax

There is no wealth tax.

Social security contributions

The social security system provides old age, disability, sickness and unemployment benefits, family allowances, and health and medical care.

Contributions are paid by the employer and the employee at the following general rates:

Employee	11%
Employer	23.75%

The employee's contribution is deducted from his wages and salary by the employer.

Other taxes

Treatment of partnerships

Profits made by a partnership are allocated to the partners in accordance with their profit shares, and taxed in the partners' hands.

VAT and sales taxes

Most goods and services within Portugal are subject to 17% VAT but certain essential goods and services are taxed at 5% or 12%.

Azores and Madeira rates are 4%, 8% and 12%.

The export of goods and some services are exempt.

Real estate transfer tax

Tax of 8% (rural properties) to 10% (urban properties or building land) is levied on transfer of real estate.

Real estate exclusively intended for dwelling purposes is exempt up to PTE 11,710,000 and subject to special reduced rates thereafter.

Excise duties

Excise duties are levied on alcohol, tobacco and fuel.

Local tax on real estate

A municipal tax based on the assessed value of property is levied by the landowners. Rates are 0.8% (rural properties) and 0.7 % to 1.3 % (urban properties).

Stamp tax

Stamp duty is levied on deeds and some documents, books, papers, acts and products.

Exchange control

Foreign exchange transactions are dealt with by authorised banks. All transactions involving foreign investment must be communicated to the official body concerned, largely for statistical purposes.

Tax treaties and withholding taxes

The following table shows the rates in force as reduced by tax treaties:

Country of residence	*Dividends*	*Interest*	*Royalties*
Non-treaty countries	25/10	20	15
Selected treaty countries:			
Austria	15	10	10/5
Belgium	15	15	5
Brazil	15	15	10/15
Finland	15/10	15	10
France	15	12/10	5
Germany	15	15/10	10
Italy	15	15	12
Spain	15/10	15	5
United Kingdom	15/10	10	5
USA	15/10	10	10

Other treaty countries:

Norway, Switzerland, Ireland, Bulgaria, Mozambique, Venezuela, Poland, Czech Republic and Republic of Korea.

Anti-avoidance legislation

The tax administration can make adjustments to profits in order to prevent either the transfer of business between related companies or the internal transfer of results between different sectors of the same entity subject to different tax regimes. These adjustments are based on special relations between the taxpayer and other parties whether or not subject to IRC (corporate tax), the establishment of conditions different than those usually agreed between independent persons carrying out transactions of the same nature, or a determination on the basis of accounting records of profits different from those that would be determined in the absence of such relations.

Payments to entities resident in countries with a privileged taxation system, allocation of profits of companies resident in such countries, as well as thin capitalisation are subject to special measures aimed at the prevention of tax avoidance.

Incentives Granted to Micro, Small and Medium Enterprises (Dec. see Law no.42/98, of 3rd March and article 45^{0} of Law no.87 B/98, of 31 December)

Micro, small and medium enterprises exercising as their main business a commercial, industrial or agricultural activity as well as non-residents with a permanent establishment in Portugal may, in the 1998, 1999 and 2000 fiscal periods, obtain tax relief for an amount corresponding to 10% of the relevant additional investment, as defined within the purpose of the investment tax credit (Decree-Law no.42/98).

Micro enterprises may also benefit, under certain conditions, from an IRC tax rate of 20% in 1999, 2000, 2001 (namely where their annual turnover does not exceed the amount of PTE 30,000,000, where the company is not a joint stock company, provided at least 75% of the company's shares are owned by individuals – Law no.87B/98).

Puerto Rico

Cardona Irizarry Group

Corporate taxes

Taxable entities

Resident companies – domestic corporations

Domestic corporations (corporations organised under the laws of the commonwealth of Puerto Rico) are liable for income tax on their worldwide income.

Non-resident companies – foreign corporations

Foreign corporations (corporations not organised under the laws of the commonwealth of Puerto Rico) are liable for income tax on all income that is generated on the conduct of a trade or business in Puerto Rico and the income 'effectively connected' with that income. In addition, any income from a Puerto Rican source which is not effectively connected income is subject to a flat 29% tax withholding, except dividends from Puerto Rican corporations and partnerships, which are subject to a flat 10% tax withholding.

Tax year and filing requirements

The tax year of a corporation can be any fixed 12 month period or a 52–53 week year. In order to change its tax year, a corporation must obtain permission from the Puerto Rican Secretary of the Treasury.

Puerto Rican corporate income tax returns are due on the fifteenth day of the fourth month following the end of the taxable year (for the calendar year, corporations must file by 15 April). An automatic extension may be requested for an additional 90 days, but the entire tax liability must be paid with the extension request. In addition, corporations earning over US$ 1,000,000 in gross income must include financial statements audited by a CPA licensed in Puerto Rico, together with the tax returns.

Taxes imposed

Estimated taxes must be paid in four equal instalments made in the fourth, sixth, ninth and twelfth months of the corporation's taxable year. The estimate should be equal to 90% of current earnings or 100% of the previous year's tax liability.

In addition to the regular income tax, an alternative minimum tax is computed to ensure that profitable corporations do not escape income taxation. Alternative tax is compared to regular tax and the higher tax is paid.

Rates of tax

The regular tax of corporations comprises a 20% tax on the company's entire net income plus a surtax computed on net income (after a US$ 25,000 surtax exemption) at the following rates:

Taxable income	*Surtax liability (US$)*
0-75,000	5%
75,001-125,000	3,750 plus 15% on excess over 75,000
125,001-175,000	11,250 plus 16% on excess over 125,000
175,001-225,000	19,250 plus 17% on excess over 175,000
225,001-275,000	27,750 plus 18% on excess over 225,000
275,001 and above	36,750 plus 19% on excess over 275,000

Profits subject to tax

General rules

Corporations are taxed on gross income, less allowable deductions. Generally, corporations use the accrual method of accounting to determine taxable income. However, corporations with no inventory and an average gross income of less than US$ 1,000,000.00 can use the cash basis method.

Stock/inventory valuation

Inventory valuation must conform to the accounting practice of the corporation's industry and it must clearly reflect income. The FIFO method is also permitted, but it may only be used with the cost basis.

Capital gains and losses

Capital gains earned by corporations are taxed at the lower of the regular rate or a fixed 25%. Capital losses, on the other hand, can only be offset against capital gains and are not, therefore, deductible against ordinary income. Capital assets include almost all property except depreciable business property, real property used in a business or other assets held for sale in the ordinary course of a trade or business, such as inventory and trade accounts receivable. Any excess of the sales price over the adjusted basis of the capital asset sold is treated as a capital gain. Any excess of the adjusted basis over the sales price is treated as a capital loss.

Although depreciable property used in a business is not a capital asset, any gain generated in the sale of such property is treated as a capital gain (i.e. eligible for the fixed alternative rate of 25%). However, when the sale of disposal generates a loss, it is treated as an ordinary loss deductible against ordinary income.

Dividends

Dividends paid by a controlled domestic corporation to a domestic corporation are 100% excluded from income. Dividends paid by a domestic corporation to any other corporation are 85% excluded from income, to a limit of 85% of taxable income. Dividends received from foreign sources are 100% taxable, subject to foreign tax credits.

Deductions

General rules

Corporations may deduct from gross income the ordinary and necessary expenses of carrying on a trade or business that are paid or incurred during the tax year. Generally, if the cost benefits more than one year, it must be capitalised and either depreciated or amortised.

Depreciation and amortisation

Tangible property is generally depreciated using the straight-line method, which recovers cost in equal amounts over the life of the asset. Corporations may, alternatively, elect to depreciate property through the Accelerated Cost Recovery system which applies an accelerated depreciation method to 5, 10, 15 and 20 year periods. In addition, residential rental property is depreciated over a 30 year period and non-residential rental property over a 35 year period.

Under the accelerated Cost Recovery System, five and ten year property is depreciated on a declining balance basis at 200% of the existing depreciation rate, whilst 15 and 20 year property, non-residential rental real property and residential real property are depreciated on a declining balance basis at 150% of the existing depreciation rate. Notwithstanding the above, the taxpayer may switch to straight-line depreciation where the use of this method yields a larger allowance.

The capitalised cost of intangibles used in a trade or business, or for the production of income, are amortised over the life of the intangible and over a 15 year period in the case of goodwill.

Royalties

Royalty expenses are deductible as an ordinary and necessary expense, provided they accrue from an arm's length transaction.

Interest

Interest paid or accrued on indebtedness, which is not directly or indirectly incurred to produce non-taxable income, is deductible.

Bad and doubtful accounts

Generally, taxpayers must use a specific write-off method to deduct business bad debts. The specific write-off method is based on the actual value of the receivable.

Reserves and provisions

Generally, no deduction is allowed for reserves or provisions.

Employees' and directors' remuneration and benefits

Generally employees' and directors' remuneration and benefits are deductible if they are considered reasonable. Reasonability is especially requested in closely held corporations and is determined based on compensation paid to employees' and directors' in similar corporations.

Specifically non-deductible expenses

Including those non-deductible expenses mentioned above, are: life insurance premiums (where the corporation is the beneficiary), 50% of meals and entertainment, amounts paid for conventions held outside of Puerto Rico and US territories, penalties, premiums paid to an insurer not authorised to contract insurance in Puerto Rico and any sums paid for the title, use and maintenance of ships (except for ships used for fishing, tourism and transportation).

Foreign source income

Foreign source income is generally taxable for a domestic corporation, however, a foreign tax credit related to such income is available. Foreign corporations are only taxed on Puerto Rican source income and income effectively connected to a trade or business.

Investment incentives and special benefits

Capital investment fund credit

The fund was created to induce private enterprise to invest in high risk government designated projects geared to improving the economic development of Puerto Rico. Investors receive an income tax credit of 25% of the amount invested. In addition, losses generated in the investment, if any, can be credited against income taxes within the subsequent three years. Therefore, in the worst case scenario, investment is recouped in four years through tax credits against income tax.

Incentives for manufacturers and service industries

A reduction in income tax rates (ranging from a 4% to 7% flat rate and a 90% tax exemption on personal property tax and volume of business) is granted to eligible manufacturers and service industries for a period of 10 to 25 years depending on the location of the business. These exemptions are granted in order to promote manufacturing and service industry in Puerto Rico. In addition, incentives in the form of cash grants are available for establishing manufacturing facilities in areas of high unemployment in Puerto Rico. These cash grants can be applied against training for personnel, rent payments during the initial start-up period and freight costs on machinery.

Credits and incentives for tourism

In order to encourage the growth and development of tourism in Puerto Rico, a 50% credit against income tax is available for cash invested in eligible tourism activities. This credit is available in the first two years (25% each year) and any unused portion may be carried forward. In addition, a 90% exemption is provided on income, volume of business and property tax.

Credits and incentives for agricultural businesses

The Agricultural Tax Incentives Act was passed to encourage the permanency and development of agricultural business in Puerto Rico. A 50% credit, similar to the one provided for tourism, is available for investors in agricultural business. Furthermore, a 90% exemption is available on income taxes and a 100% exemption is available on property and volume of business tax.

Related party transactions

Related party deductions and credits are allowed if transactions are made on an arm's length basis. A deduction for accrued expense is allowed only when paid within 90 days.

Losses

Net operating losses can be offset against the profits of the following seven taxable years of the corporation. No carry-back is allowed on operating losses.

Corporate groups

Each company within a group of companies is taxed separately and there is no taxation at group level. However, some credits must be allocated between members of a controlled group.

Tax-free mergers and disposals

There are several methods by which corporations can be merged or acquired in Puerto Rico. In order to obtain a tax-free transaction there must be a valid business reason, such as continuation of control or a continuation of business (the avoidance of tax is not a valid business reason for such transactions). Tax-free reorganisations are not allowed to foreign corporations unless it is established within a period of 183 days after making the exchange (to the satisfaction of the Secretary) that the transaction does not have the objective of avoiding taxes as imposed by the Commonwealth of Puerto Rico.

Liquidation of company

Liquidating distributions in Puerto Rico are treated as payment in exchange for stock. Therefore, such distributions are taxed on the excess of the fair market value of the assets distributed over the basis in the stock, at the lower of the regular rates or the alternative capital gain rates.

Taxes on capital

The government of the Commonwealth of Puerto Rico does not impose any capital or net worth tax.

Treatment of branches

Puerto Rico imposes a 10% branch profit tax on a foreign corporation's dividend equivalent amount. This is in addition to the regular corporate tax on the foreign corporation's 'effectively connected' income. The dividend equivalent amount is the after tax earnings that would have been distributed by the branch if it were a Puerto Rican subsidiary.

Personal taxes

Basis of taxation of individuals

Residents

An individual is usually treated as resident if he resides in Puerto Rico for more than 180 days in the year. Military personnel are treated as resident if they maintain Puerto Rico as their legal residence when they are not stationed in Puerto Rico. Resident individuals are taxed on all income from all sources and may take a credit on taxes paid to other countries on foreign income.

Non-residents

Non-resident individuals are taxable on gross income arising from sources within Puerto Rico, and gross income effectively connected with the conduct of a trade or business within Puerto Rico. Puerto Rican source income, which is not effectively connected with a trade or business in Puerto Rico, is subject to a 20% withholding tax for non-resident US citizens and a 29% withholding tax for non resident aliens, except on distributions from Puerto Rican corporations or partnership profits, which are subject to a 10% income tax withholding.

Tax year and filing requirements

The income tax return for a citizen, resident alien, or non-resident alien with income subject to withholding, is due on the fifteenth day of the fourth month following the end of the taxable year. All other non-resident aliens must file a return on the fifteenth day of the sixth month following the close of the taxable year.

The taxable year for individuals is usually the calendar year, unless a fiscal year is established. There are special rules for non-residents during the first and last years of residency. Taxpayers calculate their own tax liability and file tax returns subject to severe penalties for failure to do so. The government randomly audits returns and may assess additional tax as well as interest and penalties.

Taxes on income

Puerto Rican income tax is calculated on taxable income, which is defined as gross income less allowable deductions and personal exemptions for the taxable year. The municipalities do not impose income tax, however they do levy sales tax and property tax and the rates vary depending on the municipality in which the sales are conveyed and the property is located. Income from services performed in Puerto Rico may also be subject to social security tax.

Sources of income

Employment income and directors' fees

In general, all income for personal services is taxable to the individual who performed the services. Income includes payments in cash as well as the fair market value of property or services received. Certain employee benefits are not included in income if incurred for the employer's benefit under a written plan which is nondiscriminatory, such as accident and health premiums and pension and profit sharing plan contributions. Also, certain non-employee compensation for personal services, such as directors' fees, is taxable for the individual who performs the services.

Business profits and losses

Business income from sole proprietorships is included in the individual's income tax return. In addition, eligible corporations and partnerships which elect for special partnership and 'sub-chapter N' corporation status, must include income earned by those corporations and partnerships in the shareholders' and partners' returns, whether or not distributed by these entities. However, no tax is paid on the profit distributions of these entities. Specific requirements must be met in order to qualify for sub-chapter N and special partnership status.

Deductions of special partnership losses are limited to the smaller loss of the partner with the least share in the partnership, or 50% of any partner's net taxable income. Sub-chapter N corporations' losses are limited to future income or income from other Sub-chapter N corporations.

Dividends

Dividends are any distributions made by a corporation or partnership to its shareholders or partners, whether in money or in other property. Distributions are included in gross income in an amount equal to cash value, plus the fair market value of the property received.

Interest

Holders of loans to the Puerto Rican government and other official bodies (whether federal, state or territory) or their official departments (including administrative departments) pay no tax on the interest therefrom. Most other interest is included in gross income.

Rent and royalties

Rents and royalties are included in gross income for the year received. A property owner is allowed deductions for depreciation, mortgage interest, taxes and other ordinary and necessary expenses incurred in maintaining the property.

Social security benefits

Benefits received under the US social security program are excluded from gross income.

Pensions and annuities

The amount to be included in gross income is the greater of the pension or annuity payments received during the year or 3% of the excess of payments received over the unrecovered cost. Unrecovered cost is that portion paid by the employee (after tax deduction) which has not been recovered in previous years. In addition, taxpayers under 60 years of age may exclude up to US$ 8,000 and taxpayers over 60 may exclude US$ 11,000.

Exempt income

Generally, income from the following sources are excluded from gross income:

- life insurance proceeds gifts and inheritances;

- interest receivable on federal, state, local and Puerto Rican obligations and loans;
- public assistance payments, social security and unemployment benefits;
- a portion of income received from businesses dedicated to specific manufacturing, exporting, tourism, agriculture and film production activities; and
- legislators' travel subsistence payments.

Capital gains and losses

Gains and losses from capital asset transactions are subject to special rules and limitations. Capital assets include: any property held by a taxpayer, except stock in trade or other property included in the inventory; property held primarily for sale to customers in the ordinary course of the taxpayer's trade or business; any trade accounts receivable, depreciable property used in a trade or business, and real property used in a trade or business.

Gain is measured by the excess of property or cash received above the adjusted basis of the property surrendered. The basis is usually the cost of the property, adjusted in accordance with the provisions of legislation, for example, the basis is increased by the cost of capital improvements and decreased by depreciation.

The tax on long-term capital gain (gain from the sale or exchange of a capital asset held for more than six months) is subject to a maximum income tax rate of 20%. However, the taxpayer may opt to include the gain as part of his gross income on the income tax return for the year in which the gain is realised and pay tax at the normal tax rate.

Up to US$ 1,000 of net capital losses are deductible from a taxpayer's other income. The balance is not deductible in the year the loss is sustained, but may be carried over for the next five taxable years. The carry-over is treated as a short term capital loss, even though all or part of it was actually long term.

Foreign source income

Every resident individual is subject to Puerto Rican income tax, even where his income is wholly from foreign sources and a credit is available against foreign taxes paid. However, non-residents do not include foreign source income in return.

Personal allowances and deductions

Standard deduction

Individuals are allowed a standard deduction based on filing status, or they may elect to reduce adjusted gross income by specific itemised deductions. The standard deductions are as follows:

	1999
Joint return of married taxpayer	3,000
Head of household	2,600
Single	2,000
Married individuals filing separate returns	1,500

Specific itemised deductions are allowed as follows:

- mortgage interest on a principal residence and second home located in Puerto Rico;
- real property taxes paid on the principal residence;
- dependant and child care expenses limited to US$ 600 for each dependant, but no more than US$ 1,200;
- 10% of total rent expenses paid up to a maximum of US$ 500;
- 50% of unreimbursed medical expenses in excess of 3% of adjusted gross income;
- charitable contributions exceeding 3% of adjusted gross income, but not over 15% of adjusted gross income;
- dependants' educational expenses, subject to certain limitations; and
- interest paid on debts incurred by the taxpayer for studies at University level.

The following deductions are allowed in addition to the standard or itemised deductions:

- veterans of the US armed forces — US$ 500;
- a maximum of US$ 1,200 (US$ 600 if married, filing separately) for interest paid on car loans;
- pension plan contributions made to plans established by the Federal or Puerto Rican Government;
- married taxpayers filing joint returns where both are employed — US$ 300;
- a maximum of US$ 3,000 (US$ 6,000 if married, filing jointly) for contributions to an Individual Retirement Account (IRA); IRAs

are accounts qualified by the Treasury Department set up to provide for the tax payer's retirement; and

- students in employment who are 25 years of age or younger – US$ 1,000.

Special family rules

Married taxpayers may elect to file personal income tax returns jointly or separately, whichever is more beneficial. However, other considerations may lead taxpayers to file separate returns even though it is not advantageous for tax purposes.

Special treatment for expatriates

There are no special rules for expatriates. However, foreign taxes paid on foreign source income may be credited against Puerto Rico income tax.

Rates of tax

Single	—	applies to unmarried individuals.
Head of household	—	applies to unmarried individuals who have a qualifying dependant residing in the taxpayer's residence.
Joint	—	applies to married taxpayers who file one return, combining income and deductions of both spouses. A joint return is not permitted if either spouse was a non-resident alien during the taxable year.
Married filing separate	—	applies to married taxpayers filing separate returns.

The following rates apply to a married individual living with spouse and filing a joint return, a married individual not living with spouse, an unmarried individual, and the head of a household, estate or trust for taxable years beginning after 31 December 2000.

Taxable income (US$)	*Tax rate*
$0-$2,000	7%
$2,001-$17,000	$140 plus 10% of excess over $2,000
$17,001-$30,000	$1,640 plus 15% of excess over $17,000
$30,001-$50,000	$3,590 plus 28% of excess over $30,000
$50,001 and above	$9,190 plus 33% of excess over $50,000

The following rates apply to a married individual living with a spouse and filing a separate return:

Taxable (US$)	*Income Tax (US$)*
$0-$1,000	7%
$1,001-$8,500	$70 plus 10% of excess over $1,000
$8,501-$15,000	$820 plus 15% of excess over $ 8,500
$15,001-$25,000	$1,795 plus 28% of excess over $15,000
$25,001 and above	$4,595 plus 33% of excess over $25,000

Note:

The above rates do not take into consideration alternative minimum tax and credits against the tax liability.

An alternative minimum tax (AMT) is imposed if it exceeds the regular tax. The AMT is applied to individuals with adjusted gross income over US$ 75,000 (US$ 37,500 if married filing separately). Ordinary and necessary expenses and long term capital gains (if the 20% alternative tax was elected) are subtracted from the adjusted gross income in order to determine alternative minimum taxable income. If the alternative minimum taxable income is between US$ 75,000 and US$ 125,000 (US$ 37,500 and US$ 62,500 if married filing separately) the rate is 10%. If in excess of US$ 125,000 but less than US$ 175,000 (US$ 62,500 and US$ 87,500 if married filing separately), the rate is 15%. If in excess of US$ 175,000 (US$ 87,500 if married filing separately), then the rate is 20%.

Resident and non-resident

Residents, US non-residents and non-resident aliens engaged in trade or business in Puerto Rico are taxed at normal rates. However, non-resident aliens not engaged in trade or business in Puerto Rico are taxed at a 29% flat rate without a right to deductions and personal exemptions.

Provincial and local taxes

There are no local income taxes assessed by the municipalities in Puerto Rico.

Withholding taxes

A 10% withholding tax is applied on the dividends and partnership profit distribution of domestic corporations and partnerships. All other income paid to non-resident individuals is subject to a 20% withholding if the taxpayer is a US citizen; 29% if the taxpayer is a non-resident alien. In addition, income tax is withheld on salaries based on the regular income tax rates and, with certain exceptions, a

7% income tax withholding is required on professional services rendered by a Puerto Rican resident.

Tax credits

A credit is allowed for income taxes paid to foreign countries. Also, there are credits for eligible investments made in high risk business, tourism and agriculture and for contributions made to the educational foundation.

Payment of tax

Payroll deductions

Income taxes are withheld from employees' wages and paid on the fifteenth day of the following month for monthly depositors and on the third day after the payroll payment date for bi-weekly depositors. Bi-weekly depositors are these who have incurred a liability of US$ 500,000 or more in the prior year proceeding; all others are monthly depositors. Local unemployment and disability are payable with quarterly returns.

Prepayments

Tax prepayments are required in the form of estimated taxes. These estimated payments are required on the fifteenth day of April, June, September and the following January for calendar year taxpayers.

Estate and gift taxes

Property transferred by gift or inheritance is subject to estate and gift tax. The progressive gift tax rates are from 2.4% up to a maximum of 52.5% on taxable property in excess of US$ 6,000,000. The graduated estate tax rates are from 3% to a maximum of 70% on taxable estates of over US$ 6,000,000. Puerto Rican residents can deduct from their estate and gift tax returns any property located in Puerto Rico. In addition, gifts made during a calendar year to any person for US$ 10,000 or less may be excluded from the return. Gift taxes previously paid by donor or descendant are credited against the estate tax.

Wealth tax

There is no wealth tax in the Commonwealth of Puerto Rico.

Social security contributions

The federal government requires that all workers and their companies contribute to the Social Security retirement plan. The contribution is presently 6.2% of compensation up to US$ 76,200, for 2000, and US$ 80,400 for 2001, for both employers and employees. Self-employed persons must pay 12.4% on self-employed income up to US$ 76,200 for 2000 and US$ 80,400 for 2001. In addition, employers and employees must each contribute 1.45%, and self-employed persons 2.9%, of compensation to Medicaid.

Other taxes

Treatment of partnerships

Partnerships, like corporations, are taxed at the partnership level. In addition, partnership profits distributed to the partners are taxed at a flat maximum rate of 10% when tax is withheld. If tax is not withheld, dividends are subject to the normal rates.

VAT and sales taxes

Puerto Rico does not have a VAT tax. However, sales tax is computed on hotel lodging, jewellery and public shows.

Other

Excise tax on a range of goods and services exists at a rate of 6.6%.

Property tax is imposed on real property and is prepaid in January and July; personal property tax is levied on personal property used for business; and personal property tax is self-assessed and due in May.

Volume of business tax is a municipal tax computed on gross revenues.

Exchange Control

There is no exchange control in the Commonwealth of Puerto Rico.

Double taxation treaties and withholdings

Dividends and partnership distributions received by foreign corporations are subject to a 10% tax withholding. Also, all other Puerto Rico source income received by foreign corporations not engaged in trade or business is subject to a 29% income tax withholding. There are no double taxation treaties with Puerto Rico, but some treaties of the United States are extended to Puerto Rico.

Anti-avoidance legislation

Although there is no direct anti-avoidance legislation in Puerto Rico, there are many transactions which are disallowed by law when there is no legitimate business reason and the intent is to avoid Puerto Rican taxes.

Russia

Pacioli Audit Company

Introduction

The ground for the present Russian tax system was laid down at the beginning of 1990. The corporate tax law adopted at the end of 1991 provided a single framework for taxing of all legal entities. Since 1991, the law had acquired a number of significant amendments and had been extended by many regulations and instructions related to the interpretation of the law issued by the Presidential Administration, the Ministry of Finance and the State Tax Service. The tax system was cumbersome, offering too many tax exemptions and breaks.

The tax reform in Russia, which had been taking place during the last two years, affected different spheres of its fiscal system, such as the structure and principals of taxation, tax rates and so on.

In 1998, the first part of the Russian Tax Code was adopted where the general principles of taxation and tax control were introduced. The approval of the Tax Code's second part in the middle of 2000, which is in power in 2001, became a continuation of Russian tax reform. The second part of the Russian Tax Code is devoted to certain tax procedures and mechanisms. The passing of the Tax Code is designed to help stabilise the Russian tax system. The total number of taxes is already decreasing and there are prospects of the tax burden decreasing for legal entities and individuals.

Taxes imposed

In accordance with the federal structure of Russia, tax legislation is divided into three levels: federal, territorial and local legislation. The tax list is set up by the Tax Code and tax changes might be introduced by the Tax Code amendments only. Federal taxes are established by the Tax Code, regional and local taxes are regulated by regional and local authorities under the Tax Code control. The taxes imposed include:

- VAT (value added tax);
- excise tax on some types of goods (services) and mineral resources;

- corporate income tax;
- capital tax;
- personal income tax;
- common social tax;
- state duties;
- custom duties and collections;
- taxes on mineral resources usage;
- taxes on mineral and raw material reproduction;
- taxes on carbonic hydrogen production;
- taxes on collection for animal and hydro-biological resources exploitation;
- forest tax;
- water tax;
- ecological tax; and
- federal licence duties.

Corporate taxes

Taxable entities

Resident companies

A company is treated as resident if it is incorporated under Russian legislation. Resident companies are liable to corporate tax on their worldwide income; including capital gains and profits. Tax levied and paid under the laws of other countries on profit earned from overseas businesses is taken into account when assessing taxable profit in Russia. The adjustments must be calculated in line with Russian tax legislation.

An income of non-resident companies derived from Russia is subject to income tax withholding by reference to the source of that income. A non-resident company is liable to income tax at the same rate as a resident company if its business operation in Russia meets the criteria of 'permanent representation'.

Tax year and filing requirements

The income tax year and accounting year is the calendar year. Different fiscal year ends are not allowed. However, a company incorporated after 1 October can delay the filing of its financial statements and tax return in the period to 31 December to the following accounting period.

Companies including foreign entities must file their self-assessed return on a monthly basis. Banks and insurers have different annual filing schedules. Foreign entities, which do not have a taxable permanent establishment, should file an annual tax declaration and report on activity in Russia no later than 15 April of the following year.

Rates of tax

The minimum rate of corporate income tax is 35%, irrespective of the amount of taxable profit. In terms of the budget structure, it comprises three elements: the federal budget rate of 11%, the region rate of 19% (maximum) and the local rate of 5%.

Intermediary services, brokerage and dealing operations, banks and insurers are levied at a maximum rate of 38%.

Income derived from casinos, other gambling and from the recording and distribution of audio-video goods is taxable at 70%.

Income subject to tax

General rules

Gross profit subject to income tax is summarised as commercial profit excluding major indirect taxes less materials and other costs of production deductible under Russian legislation. Exchange gains and capital gains are also taxable. Income received in non-monetary form is calculated under the market price for equivalent goods or services.

Stock/inventory valuation

Inventories are generally valued at production cost and stock applying the average cost, FIFO and LIFO methods. No special reserves are permitted for obsolescence.

Capital gains and losses

In general, capital gains are treated as normal income and taxed at full rate. Profit from sales of fixed assets and other property is calculated on the difference between sales price and historical cost (or net book value for fixed assets or intangible assets).

Dividends

Dividends and interest are generally taxed at 15% at source and are, therefore, not included in income subject to profit tax.

Deductions

General rules

Under Russian statutory regulations, business expenses are deductible for tax purposes if they are wholly incurred for trade or production purposes. This also includes certain start-up costs, payments for research and development, information services charges, consultancy costs, audit costs, external translations costs and so on. A detailed list of deductible expenses is specified by the Government Decree. Certain industries, for example the oil industry, may deduct an additional number of expenses.

Some expenses are deductible only within certain limits (for example, expenses for business entertainment, business travel expenses, advertising, training and property insurance expenses).

Donations to charity and non-commercial institutions are deductible up to 5% of taxable profit.

Depreciation and amortisation

Almost all types of fixed assets may be depreciated except land and natural resources (water, subsoil and mineral resources). In terms of taxation, depreciation is deductible on business assets.

Accelerated rates of depreciation, up to twice the standards rates, may be used only in certain cases. Practically, accelerated rates can be applied to machinery used for increasing production of new product lines. The list of their categories is specified by the Ministry of Industry.

Small-sized companies are eligible for a 50% rate of depreciation on the acquisition cost of the fixed assets in their initial two years.

Intangibles are depreciated by the straight-line method on the basis of their useful life. If the useful life period is undetermined, it is treated as ten years for statutory purposes.

Tangible assets costing less than 100 times the official minimum monthly wage, or those useful lives less than one year, are subject to special regulation. They can be wholly depreciated immediately at 100%, once put into operation.

Royalties

Generally, royalties are deductible for profit tax purposes if the payment is made under a duly registered licensing agreement. Royalties may be calculated as a percentage of sales, otherwise they are treated as intangible assets and their acquisition costs deducted through depreciation.

Interest

Interest incurred on bank loans (including foreign banks) is deductible within established limits. The allowable interest rate depends on the currency of the loan. For double loans it is the interest rate charged by the Central Bank of Russia for loans provided to banks plus 3%. The rate for foreign currency loans is equal to LIBOR plus 3%. To be allowable the loan has to be used for business operations only. Thus, interest paid out on loans used to settle overdue liabilities or borrowed from institutions other than banks (including loans from a parent company), are not tax deductible.

Interest on loans paid to subsidise the acquisition of fixed or intangible assets prior to using the assets, may be capitalised along with the book value of the assets. Interest paid subsequently is charged to the profit and loss account.

Interests on loans used to finance the purchase of assets to be leased under financial leasing are allowable.

Dividends

Dividends paid are not deductible.

Bad and doubtful debts

According to Russian legislation, bad debts and provisions are not tax deductible.

Employees' and directors' remuneration and benefits

Salaries, wages and bonuses are deductible. Hardship allowances granted for work in severe climate conditions are deductible, as far as they are in line with local rates. Redundancy, maternity, sick leave and other payments to employees included in total labour costs are also deductible.

Some remuneration (for example, in the form of the use of the personal automobile) is deductible up to a very low limit.

Non-deductible expenses

The following expenses are not tax deductible:

- training expenses exceeding 4% of an accumulated salary;
- medical costs (other than medical insurance);
- housing benefits, school allowances, club memberships and special entertainment;
- employee bonuses (except those provided for special occasions);
- travel business expenses (exceeding per diem) and accommodation rates specified by state regulation (different for domestic trips and for each country);
- payments to non-state pension funds;
- certain research and development expenditure; and
- advertising expenses exceeding 5% of the sales value.

In general, property insurance expense is tax deductible within the limit of 3% of annual sales. Where fire or other types of insurance coverage are mandatory by law, an insurance premium paid is tax deductible in full.

Foreign source income

Foreign source dividends and interest are taxable in a universal basis as other income. Tax credit is given for foreign tax settled in treaty countries, but the amount of credit cannot exceed the Russian profit tax payable on the foreign source income.

Investment incentives and special benefits

Taxable profit can be reduced by the amount of capital investments for production and housing construction. Generally, the deduction is available for manufacturing enterprises engaged in the development of their own production base if the full amount of depreciation charged on their assets is used before the last reporting date. This deduction is limited to 50% of taxable income in the year of expenditure. However, if fixed assets or incomplete construction are sold out or gratuitously transferred within two years from receipt of this deduction, the taxable profit should be increased by the residual value of the fixed assets.

Related party transactions

There are no special rules.

Losses

Losses are determined in the same way as profits (that is according to Russian statutory accounting rules). Reported losses may be carried forward and used to reduce taxable profits of the subsequent five years, subject to certain conditions. Utilisation of the losses is restricted to 50% of the taxable profit. There is no mechanism for transferring losses to other subsidiaries and other taxpayers. Branches and representative offices may not carry forward tax losses.

There is no loss carry-back provision.

Personal taxes

Taxable individuals

Residents

Residents are natural persons (including resident aliens and stateless persons) who are domiciled in Russia for more than 183 days during a calendar year (not necessarily consecutive). The term 'calendar year' means that a person resides in Russia strictly within one calendar year, and it cannot be used for longer periods; the residence status in Russia is determined annually. Residents are liable for tax on any income in natural and monetary forms arising both in Russia and abroad.

Non-residents

Income earned in Russia by a person who is in the country less than 183 days during a calendar year is liable to tax. Tax liabilities of non-residents who are not domiciled in Russia are reduced by double taxation treaties where applicable. The accounting period for the income tax is a calendar year.

Resident aliens domiciled in Russia are subject to taxes according to common rules. They file a tax return and pay taxes on the flat (basic) rate of 13%. Individuals without a domicile in Russia are liable for taxes on Russian source income. Income of non-residents is payable at a rate of 30%.

Tax year and filling requirements

The taxable period is the calendar year. There is a list of individuals determined in the Tax Code who are liable to file a tax declaration. They include:

- entrepreneurs;
- individuals on income from civil contracts who are not tax agents or dealing with real estate;
- tax residents of the Russian Federation on their income from abroad; and
- individuals on other income which is not taxed by Russian tax agents.

The tax declaration is due on 30 April of the year following the year of account.

Source of income

Employment income and directors' fees

The most important income tax element is tax on wages (withheld at source). Taxable income includes all remuneration received from the employing company as well as other income, in particular benefits in kind supplied by the company. Benefits in kind include payment of public utilities, apartment costs, season tickets, and subscription to books, newspapers and journals, subsistence and several other cases where not covered by legislation.

Business income

Individuals acting as non-incorporated businessmen are subject to taxes on income earned from private business (i.e. self-employed) activity, civil legal contracts, letting and leasing of real estate, sale of property and other activities of a business nature.

Rentals

Rents from letting real estate are taxed after deducting expenses.

Royalties

Patent royalties are subject to tax at the same rate as other income. The taxable income is reduced by the sum of documentary confirmed expenses which were spent on earning the income. If it is not possible to confirm the expenses with documents then the state applies established expense standards for royalties (for example, the expense standard for scientific research expenditure is 20% of income).

Social security benefits

Benefits from a company to an employee are taxed if they exceed state standards or if they are support (relief) expenses or reimbursed expenses (travel expenses and lodgings in business trips) and if they are due to certain employees.

Furthermore, such benefits as pensions, state support, unemployment compensation, survivors' benefit and disablement benefit are not taxed.

Foreign source income

Incomes from foreign sources are taxed at the basic rate. If an income is earned in a foreign currency it will be converted for tax purposes at the official rate effective on the date of receipt. When calculating taxes from foreign sources, the sum paid from the received income abroad will be deducted, subject to certification by the foreign state.

Personal allowance

Residents are granted a tax-free allowance irrespective of marital status. Every taxpayer has a right to certain deductions in their tax computation. There are several types of tax deduction:

- *standard* – the sum of deduction makes up from 300 to 3000 roubles according to the status of the taxpayer;
- *social* – expenses on charity, hospitality and, education (in determined limits);
- *property rights* – property selling, purchasing and construction of houses (in determined limits); and
- *professional* – expenses on profit gaining.

Losses

According to present regulations, losses are not offset against taxable income.

Special family rules

There are no special family rules applicable in Russian taxation terms.

Rate of tax

Rate of tax is established at 13%, except for the following sort of revenues; a tax rate of 35% applies to:

- income derived from all gambling and risk games, including gaming machines;
- prizes (or revenue) from participation in advertised events and projects above 2000 roubles in value;
- free insurance contracts (the sum of the difference between them and the client's insurance instalments multiplied on the refinancing rate of the Russian Central Bank on the date the contract was signed);
- an individual's percentage income on bank deposit (the sum of difference between it and the computed percentage income using 75% of the Russian Central Bank's refinancing rate for rouble *deposits* and its rate of 9% for foreign currency *deposits* for the *deposit* period); and
- an individual's percentage income on bank loans (the sum of the difference between the computed percentage income using 75% of the Russian Central Bank's refinancing rate for rouble *loans* and its rate of 9% for foreign currency *loans* and its rate for the *loan's* period).

Tax rate of 30% applies to:

- dividends; and
- the income tax of non-residents from Russia.

Payment of tax

Entrepreneurs who are not legal entities, private notaries and others involved in business must pay tax advances according to tax notifications in the following order: a half of annual advance payment on 15 April of the year of account, a quarter on 15 October of the same year and a quarter on 15 January of the year following the year of account. The tax authorities calculate the tax amount in accordance with estimated income declared by the taxpayer in tax filing or based on the taxpayer's income of the previous year. Other individuals, including non-residents, are liable to pay tax on 15 July of the year following the year of account.

Wealth tax

There is no wealth tax in Russia.

Other taxes

Personal property tax

The following property is subject to individual property tax:

- *real estate* – dwelling houses, flats, country cottages, garages and other buildings and premises; and
- *personal estate* – motor boats, helicopters, airplanes and other transportation facilities (with the exception of motorcars, motorcycles, self-propelled machines and certain others).

Tax on buildings and premises is paid in accordance with the rate established by the state, but not in excess of 0.1% of their inventory value.

The tax rate on transportation facilities depends on engine power of the transportation mode and is paid in percentages based on the minimum amount of labour remuneration.

Tax partnership

In accordance with the Tax Code, companies and individuals can institute a partnership which does not have a legal entity status. Profits earned by partnership are attributed to the partners according to their share and are taxed in their partners' hands.

Value added tax (VAT)

Value added tax was introduced in 1992 to replace turnover and sales taxes. VAT applied to value added to each element in the chain from producer to customer. Principles underlying the European Union VAT system are also included in the tax regime. Changes to the VAT law in recent years have moved the Russian system even closer to the EU model. The payment of VAT (and other taxes) is governed by the method of accounting chosen by the taxpayer (either the accrual or cash basis).

VAT is levied on sales carried out by legal entities only. The standard of VAT is 20%, although there is a limited list of basic food products, ingredients and goods for children instituted by the government for which a lower rate of 10% is accepted.

For VAT incurred to be recoverable, it must be stated on a separate line on the invoice and payment order. A number of items are not deductible in Russia, including VAT incurred on construction and installation services, VAT on light vans and cars and VAT on items of a non-business nature. In addition, the deductibility of a number of items is significantly restricted, such as VAT on advertising and on hotel accommodation. There is also a special system for restaurants, caterers and retailers. They are required to calculate VAT at 16.67% on the margin between the tax-inclusive final selling price and tax-inclusive purchase price.

Where input VAT exceeds output, the Tax Code law declares that the difference is to be refunded to the taxpayer. In practice, however, actual refunds of VAT are rarely, if ever, made to the taxpayer.

Russian companies which arrange payments for work performed on the Russian territory by foreign legal entities not registered with the Russian tax authority should withhold VAT from any payment and pay the tax on behalf of those foreign entities.

Excise tax

Excise tax is levied at variable rates on a range of luxury goods (e.g. tobacco, beverages, light vehicles, gasoline and certain mineral resources). Tax applies to goods produced or processed and imported into Russia.

For most excisable goods the duty rate is set at a fixed rouble amount per unit. Tax paid on excisable raw materials by domestic producers is allowable for deduction against the tax liabilities payable on the finished goods.

Road taxes

Road tax (tax on the use of roads) is payable at a rate of 1% of whole sales or of the difference between selling and buying prices of goods.

Land tax

Land tax is payable on the use of agricultural pasture and urban allotments. The rate depends on where the land is located.

Exchange control

In compliance with the Federal Laws, the Central Bank of Russia (CB) monitors currency transactions. A list of currency transactions, requiring the receipt of CB licences on their execution, is established by legislation.

The CB issues licences to commercial banks on the execution of currency transactions. Legal entities and individuals have the right to carry out currency transactions only through banks authorised by the CB.

Control measures

There is a civil, administrative and criminal responsibility for violation of the tax legislation in compliance with the Federal laws, which is overseen by the Government Tax Service.

Tax treaties and withholding taxes

Under the statement of the Ministry of Foreign Affairs on January 1992, Russia agreed to honour the tax treaties signed by the former Soviet Union until new tax treaties are drawn up. Unless otherwise provided under the tax treaty, a non-resident foreign legal entity is subject to a 15% withholding tax on its Russian source interest and dividend income and a 20% withholding tax on its income from copyrights, licences or services provided by it in Russia. Income from foreign freight is taxed at 6%.

The elimination of double taxation generally takes the form of a credit for taxes paid to other countries.

	Dividends (%)	*Interests* (%)	*Royalties* (%)
Albania	15	15	15
Austria	0	0	0
Belgium	15	15 (1)	0
Bulgaria	15	15	15
Canada	15	15 (1)	10
Croatia	–	–	–
Cyprus	0	0	0
Czech Republic	–	–	–

Denmark	15	0	0
Finland	0	0	0
France	15	10 (1)	0
Germany	15	5 (1)	0
India	15	15 (1)	15 (2)
Italy	15	0 (4)	0
Japan	15/10	0 (1)	10
Korea (South)	5/10	0	5
Luxembourg	15	5	0
Malaysia	15	15 (1)	10
Mongolia	0	0	0
Netherlands	15	0	0
Norway	20 (4)	0	0
Philippines	–	–	–
Poland	10	10	10
Romania	15	15	10
Slovakia	–	–	–
Spain	18 (4)	0	5
Sweden	5/15	0	0
Switzerland	(5)	(1)	0
United Kingdom	0	0	0
USA	5/10	0	0
Uzbekistan	10	10	0
Vietnam	(5)	–	–
Yugoslavia	–	–	–

Notes

(1) Nil on interest on government guaranteed and Central Bank loans.

(2) The rate of 15% for royalties relating to copyright of literary, artistic and scientific works, other than films, and 20% in all other cases of royalties or fees for technical services.

(3) Applies to interest on banking and commercial credits and loans, interest on current accounts and deposits in credit institutions.

(4) The treaty provides for a tax rate not exceeding 18%. The most favourable norms under Russian legislation prevail.

(5) There is no treaty regulating the taxation of dividends and, therefore, the norm provided for under Russian legislation is applied.

Kingdom of Saudi Arabia

Usamah Ali Tabbarah & Co.

Introduction

The official language of the Kingdom of Saudi Arabia is Arabic. Companies are required to maintain their books and records of account in the Arabic language within the country.

Generally, companies have the option to determine their tax year based on either the Hegira or the Gregorian calendar year.

Corporate taxes

Taxable entities

Resident companies

Companies registered in Saudi Arabia are treated as resident companies. Tax liability is determined based on the nationality of shareholders. Profits on operations, trading, capital gains and other income of companies and establishments fully owned by Saudi nationals and nationals of member countries of the Gulf Co-operation Council (GCC) are not liable to corporation tax. Only profits accruing to foreign individuals (or entities on the shares held by them) are liable to corporation tax.

Non-resident companies

Non-resident companies operating in the Kingdom are liable to corporate income tax on profits earned from their operations in the Kingdom, including capital gains. Foreign individuals or companies are not allowed to carry on a trading business (i.e. sale of goods, import/export activities) in the Kingdom of Saudi Arabia.

Tax year and filing requirements

There is no specific fiscal year in the Kingdom. Companies may settle taxes in accordance with the financial year they have chosen to follow.

A non-resident company, or a joint venture with Saudi nationals owning the entity, should file a final tax return along with its audited financial statements within two and a half months from the end of its financial year and should pay the tax due in full. If audited financial statements are not available within the two and a half month period, the taxpayer should apply for an extension by filing a temporary tax return for a period not exceeding six months from the end of the two and a half month period. However, there is a penalty levied on the unpaid taxes due in the first two and a half month period at the rate of 25%.

A local Saudi company or establishment is not required to file any tax return but should file a Zakat return. Furthermore, it has the option to pay a local tax called Zakat annually, at any time without any delay penalty.

Income tax is payable on the services rendered in the Kingdom by third parties who do not possess a tax file in Saudi Arabia. Tax is deducted at source on deemed profit. Deemed profit is generally calculated at a minimum of 15% of the turnover shown in the taxpayers' accounts and the tax liability is calculated by applying corporation tax rates. However, depending on the services provided, the tax authorities may apply higher percentages to arrive at deemed profits. Certain technical services rendered outside the Kingdom by third parties (because those services are not available within the Kingdom) are exempted from deemed profit where such services are properly supported and certified by external auditors and duly authorised by the proper authorities.

Charges on insurance services rendered in Saudi Arabia by foreign insurance companies who do not have tax files in Saudi Arabia are taxable on the deemed profit basis.

In the case of royalty and commission (agent's commission or any other commission), the full amount charged in the accounts is deemed as profit.

Rates of tax

Corporation tax rates

Band (Saudi Riyals)	*Rate (%)*
0–100,000	25%
100,001–500,000	20%
500,001–1,000,000	25%
1,000,001 and above	30%

Local establishments and companies

A tax called Zakat is paid at 2.5% on the higher of net worth of the business or profit of the local establishments and companies, such as establishments or companies to be fully owned by nationals of Saudi Arabia and of member countries of the Gulf Co-operation Council. There is no penalty for any delay in settling Zakat dues.

Income subject to tax

General rules

Profit subject to corporation tax is calculated by aggregating income from operating profit, investment income, interest income, capital gains and any other sources.

Stock/inventory valuation

Stocks and inventories are valued at the lower of weighted average cost and net realisable value for individual items.

Capital gains

The operational results of the last three accounting periods are taken into consideration in arriving at the amount liable for capital gains tax. The rates of tax applicable depend on the legal status of the seller.

Gains and losses on disposal of fixed assets

Gains and losses are calculated by deducting the net book value of the assets disposed from the sales proceeds at the date of disposal.

Dividends

Dividends or distribution of profits arising out of investments are added to other income to arrive at aggregated taxable profit.

Deductions

General rules

Taxable profits are calculated in accordance with generally accepted accounting principles with certain statutory adjustments, as follows:

- expenditure incurred wholly and exclusively for business purposes relevant to the period is allowed;

- capital expenditure can be deducted by way of depreciation charges for the period of use, computed by applying the straight-line method based on rates approved by the tax authorities; and
- all reserves and provisions (either specific, general or contingent) are disallowed.

The following expenditures are not normally deductible in arriving at taxable profit:

- directors' remuneration;
- partners' remuneration and other benefits;
- agent's commission for foreign companies if the agent's name is not declared on or before bidding for Government contracts;
- social insurance paid outside Saudi Arabia;
- employees' contribution to local social insurance;
- school fees paid outside Saudi Arabia; and
- head office administration expenses.

Depreciation

Generally, a depreciation charge is allowed on qualifying fixed assets from the date the assets are first used. A depreciation charge is computed by applying the straight-line method based on annual rates approved by the tax authorities. If a taxpayer employs lower rates than those approved, he will not be allowed to increase them in future.

Goodwill is not an asset qualifying for depreciation as long as a taxpayer continues his activities, unless goodwill has been purchased for a price. The annual rates of depreciation applied for the most common fixed assets are listed below:

Description of Assets	*Rate (%)*
Furniture and fittings	10
Office equipment	15
Electrical equipment	10
Air conditioners	25
Computers	12.5
Motor vehicles	25
Permanent buildings	3
Temporary buildings in remote areas	15
Construction equipment	12.5
Machinery fixed to ground	7.5
Machinery not fixed to ground	10

Royalties

Royalties are generally allowed as a deductible expense. If payments are made to a foreign party, the full amount paid is treated as profit and taxed on a deemed profit basis.

Interest

Generally, bank interest payments are allowed on an accruals basis. Interest payments made to any foreign bank are not subject to tax on the deemed profit basis, provided such banks have no branches, offices or resident representatives in the Kingdom.

Dividends

Dividends and other distributions paid to shareholders by companies are not deductible.

Investment incentives and special benefits

Investments in other companies (Saudi or non-Saudi), capital expenditure (net book value at balance sheet date) and deferred revenue expenditure are deductible in arriving at the Zakat payable by Saudi companies or Saudi shareholders in mixed companies.

There are no more tax incentives to foreign investors.

New investment could be licensed with 100% foreign investment.

Losses

Trading and operating losses can be offset against other income and capital gains of the same year. Excess losses cannot be carried forward or backward.

Corporate groups

Each company within a group of companies is taxed separately. In consortiums, losses and profits of individual members can be set off against one another to arrive at the net total results of the group.

Dividends or profits can be paid within the group without deduction of taxes at source.

Personal taxes

Taxable individuals

In Saudi Arabia, all personal income taxes have been abolished with the exception of the following.

Non-Saudi individuals

- non-Saudi professionals and self-employed persons rendering services in the Kingdom of Saudi Arabia;
- services rendered by a foreign individual in the Kingdom of Saudi Arabia, other than as an employee.

In both cases, the profit of the professional or the payments made to a foreign individual by a company shall be taxable.

Rates of tax

The following rates of tax are applied:

Band (Saudi Riyals)	*Rate (%)*
0–6,000	0
6,001–16,000	5
16,001–36,000	10
36,001 –66,000	20
66,001 and above	30

Social security

The rate of contributions payable in respect of Saudi workers for annuities schemes is 18%, of which 9% should be paid in full by the employer from the date on which the new law is put into effect on 1 April 2001; 9% should be paid by the contributor on a gradual basis as follows:

6% – paid for one year from the date on which the new law becomes effective;

7.5% – paid for one year with effect from 01/01/1423 A.H. (i.e. from 1 April 2002); and up to

9% – for any further years, with effect from 01/01/1424 A.H. (i.e. from 1 April 2003), and payable thereafter.

The foregoing mode of payment of contributions will apply to those covered by the scheme before or after the new law is put in to effect.

However, the contributions payable in respect of all workers under the occupational hazards will be 2% of the contributory wage and is solely payable by the employer.

Withholding tax on dividends

Dividends are payable out of taxed company profits. No withholding tax is levied on dividends.

Other taxes

A 2% contribution for social insurance is required to be paid by employers on behalf of all employees in certain categories of activities classified as hazardous. Saudi Nationals and their employers must contribute 5% and 8% respectively on the employees' earnings where the total number of employees exceeds 20.

Exchange controls

The Kingdom does not have any exchange control restrictions at present.

Withholding taxes

Income tax is withheld from payments made to non-residents or residents who do not have valid tax clearance certificates for services (such as contracts, sub-contracts, hire of equipment, transport, etc.) if such services are performed within the Kingdom. Payments for services such as consultancy work and patent work (involving royalty payments) are subject to withholding tax, even if such services are performed outside Saudi Arabia.

The method of calculating profit subject to tax on such payments is as follows:

- royalties/commission B total payment made is deemed as profit; and
- all other services B profit is deemed at 15% of the payment made.

Corporate tax rates will be applied in order to calculate the tax due on the profits ascertained on the above basis.

Singapore

Tan & Sitoh Associates

Corporate taxes

Taxable entities

Singapore adopts a territorial basis for taxing income derived from a trade, profession or business carried on in Singapore. Income tax is only charged on income that arises in or is derived from Singapore and any offshore income where it is remitted into Singapore.

Resident companies

Resident companies are subject to tax on profits derived from or accrued in Singapore, or received in Singapore from foreign sources. A company is resident if the control and management of the business is exercised in Singapore.

Non-resident companies

Unless specifically exempt, non-resident companies with no permanent establishment or without a taxable presence in Singapore are only taxable on Singapore sourced income. Foreign sourced income is not taxable.

Tax year and filing requirements

The tax year of assessment is the calendar year. For each tax year, a company is assessed on its income of the preceding accounting year.

Taxes imposed and rates of tax

All companies, whether resident or non-resident, are subject to income tax at the rate of 24.5% on taxable income. Partial exemption applies to a company's chargeable income (other than Singapore dividends) up to S$ 100,000 that is subject to tax at 24.5% as follows:

- up to the first S$ 10,000 of such income, 75% of the income shall be exempt from tax;

- up to the next S$ 90,000 of such income, 50% of the income shall be exempt from tax.

This effectively puts the tax rate at 11.5% for the first S$ 100,000 of chargeable income, making it very attractive for companies to be set up in Singapore, as compared to tax haven countries, to enjoy its extensive Double Tax Treaties. A concessionary rate of tax is applicable to certain offshore income of approved companies or financial institutions for specified activities.

Income subject to tax

General rules

Income for tax purposes is calculated in accordance with generally accepted accounting principles, as adjusted by the specific rules of the Income Tax Act. Allowable expenses, capital allowances and other reliefs are deducted from statutory income (income from each source, such as trading income, rent and interest) to arrive at income chargeable to tax.

Stock/inventory valuation

The Income Tax Act is silent concerning acceptable basis for the valuation of trading stock and work in progress. In practice, the tax authorities accept the FIFO, weighted average and standard costing methods of valuation. Base stock and LIFO bases are not acceptable.

Capital gains and losses

Gains arising from the sale of immovable property, which has been held for less than three years, is treated as income chargeable to tax at the prevailing individual or company tax rate. Tax is charged on:

- 100% of gains made on the disposal of immovable property within the first year of purchase;
- two thirds of gains made on the disposal of immovable property within the second year after purchase; and
- one third of gains made on the disposal of immovable property within the third year after purchase.

Loss arising from the disposal of immovable property within three years of its acquisition is deductible, subject to specified conditions.

In addition, under certain circumstances, the gains arising from the sale of shares in a property based company will be taxed.

Other than the above, there is no capital gains tax in Singapore. Gains on sale of equity shares are not taxed.

Dividends

Dividends received from other companies are taxed as income. However, when a resident company pays a dividend, the dividend is treated as having been paid net of a deemed deduction of income tax at the rate of 24.5%. No additional tax is charged to the company if the dividend is paid out of profits that have been subject to income tax at 24.5%. However, any distribution of untaxed profits by the company, unless exempt under tax incentives, is subject to a 'Section 44' charge of 24.5% of the grossed-up amount. With effect from assessment year 2000, a Singapore resident company can distribute, as an exempt dividend, an amount equal to the tax rebate grossed up at 24.5%.

A Section 44 charge is treated as tax paid in advance to the tax authorities. It is available for offset against any tax subsequently assessed on the company. It is now possible for a resident company to declare and pay dividends to its shareholders, even though it does not have sufficient franking credits, by paying corporate taxes in advance.

Foreign dividends are taxable when remitted to Singapore. They are taxed gross at 24.5%. A tax credit is given according to the amount of tax suffered by the company in the country of source. It is restricted to the Singaporean tax payable before the credit.

If the remitting country does not have a double taxation agreement with Singapore, the foreign dividend is taxed at 24.5% on the net dividends remitted and no credit is given.

There is no withholding tax as such on dividends.

Deductions

General rules

Generally, all expenses and outgoings which are wholly and exclusively incurred in the production of income are deductible, unless specifically prohibited. Expenses of a capital or personal nature and any taxes paid on income (whether Singaporean or foreign) are not deductible.

Subject to certain conditions and restrictions, there are deductions of 200% of the actual expenditure incurred on certain approved projects such as the overseas promotion of the export of Singaporean manufactured goods, maintenance of overseas trade offices, export market development and research and development of new products, processes and qualifying services.

Head office expenses

Head office charges are generally deductible if the basis for the charges is consistent and the expenses are attributable to Singaporean operations. The tax authorities may require an external auditor's certificate and will disallow any capital or disallowable expenses.

A ruling by the Ministry of Finance states that technical assistance fees and management fees for services performed outside Singapore are not deemed to be derived in Singapore, hence not subject to withholding tax, provided that the relevant transactions are at arm's length and not entered into with the intent of siphoning-off Singapore income. Royalty payments are not covered by this ruling. For management fees, an additional requirement is that these should be mere reimbursement or allocation of expenses by head office.

In addition, any profit element included in the charges may be subject to withholding tax at 24.5%. This rate will be reduced with tax treaty countries.

Depreciation and amortisation

Book depreciation of fixed assets is not deductible. Capital allowances may be claimed on plant and equipment and on industrial buildings or structures.

Industrial Building Allowances (IBA)	28% (25% plus 3%) in the first year and 3% per annum for each subsequent year.
Plant and machinery initial allowances	20% of capital expenditure incurred.
Annual allowance	5% to 16% of capital expenditure (depending on type of asset) calculated on the straight-line method).

Accelerated depreciation

A company may claim accelerated allowances of $33^1/_3$% in place of the initial and annual allowances for three consecutive years on capital expenditure incurred for all categories of plant and machinery (excluding motor cars, motor cycles and light goods vehicles).

A 100% annual allowance is available in the first year in respect of capital expenditure incurred on computers, specified office and factory automation equipment, pollution control equipment, certified energy efficient equipment and approved energy saving equipment.

A 20% annual allowance is available on capital expenditure incurred on the acquisition of approved know how and patent rights.

Any unabsorbed capital allowances may be carried forward indefinitely and offset against future income (see 'Losses' below).

Royalties

Royalties paid for the use of patents and the supply of know how are deductible if incurred in the production of income. Royalties paid to non-residents are subject to withholding tax.

Royalty payments made for the following software are exempt from tax:

- downloadable software for end-user;
- site licence; and
- software bundled with computer hardware.

Interest

All interest incurred in the production of income is deductible. However, interest paid to a non-resident is subject to withholding tax. There are no special rules relating to payments to offshore associate companies as long as the payments are made on a commercial basis.

Fees and other payments

A withholding tax of 24.5% (subject to double taxation treaties) applies to management fees, technical assistance fees and director's fees paid to non-residents where such payments are claimed against income chargeable to Singaporean tax, whilst a reduced withholding tax of 15% applies to interest, royalties and rents or other income from movable property.

From income year 2000, withholding tax is exempt on payments made under financial guarantee insurance policies and granted extension of withholding tax exemption on interest rate and bona fide currency swap payments. The exemption does not apply to payments made to non-residents who are permanent establishments in Singapore.

Bad and doubtful debts

A specific or general provision may be made in respect of bad and doubtful debts. A general provision is not tax deductible, while a specific provision is normally allowed as a deduction if it can be established that all efforts to collect has been exhausted.

Reserves and provisions

A reserve is a sum set aside for non-specific purposes and is not tax deductible. A provision is a sum set aside for specific requirements such as holiday pay and travel, retirement benefits, stock obsolescence and future losses.

Generally, provisions are not tax deductible. However, when the expense crystallises it can be written off against the provision and become tax deductible.

Employees' and directors' remuneration and benefits

Generally, employees' and directors' remuneration and benefits are tax deductible.

Specifically non-deductible expenses

The following expenses are not tax-deductible:

- private/domestic expenses;
- expenses incurred on private cars;
- donations made to non-approved institutions; or
- income tax paid.

Investment incentives and special benefits

Investment incentives play a key role in shaping the pace and direction of industrial development. In Singapore, incentives are used for the promotion of new investments in industries and services, including encouraging existing companies to upgrade through mechanisation and automation through the introduction of new products and services and to promote the external economy.

The Economic Development Board (EDB), a statutory board responsible for the planning and promotion of industrial and commercial developments, administers the following tax incentives under the Economic Expansion Incentives (Relief from Income Tax) Act:

- pioneer status;
- development and expansion incentive;
- investment allowance incentive;
- international consultancy services;
- pioneer services incentive;
- approved foreign loan scheme;
- approved royalties and fees;
- post pioneer incentive;
- export enterprise;
- warehousing and servicing incentives;
- investments in new technology scheme; and
- approved art and antiques dealers.

Other incentives administered by EDB and the Singapore Trade Development Board (TDB) include:

- counter trade service;
- business headquarters incentive;
- venture capital incentive;
- operational headquarters incentive;
- export of service incentive;
- treasury and finance centre incentive;
- approved international trade incentive;
- approved oil trader scheme;
- overseas enterprises incentive;
- approved international shipping enterprise;
- approved aircraft leasing;
- counter trade service;
- satellite operations;
- double deduction for R & D Expenses; and on
- expansion incentive.

To further develop Singapore as a leading international financial centre and to promote offshore fund management and a futures market, various tax incentives are provided to the financial, insurance and futures sectors. These include a concessionary tax rate of 10% on income derived from:

- certain approved transactions of the Asian Currency Unit of financial institutions;
- Asian Currency Unit (ACU) income from transactions in all other financial derivatives;
- income derived from trading in interest rate and currency swaps;
- transactions in gold bullion or in any approved commodity or financial futures on any approved exchange/market;
- reinsurance and offshore insurance business; and
- the specified income of approved securities companies, approved trustee companies and approved fund managers.

In addition, the income of the following are tax-exempt:

- that of an approved fund manager; and
- that derived from managing initial public offerings of foreign currency shares.

Dividends paid out of income exempted or subject to the concessionary 10% tax rate are exempt from tax in the hands of the shareholders.

Special tax holidays are available for income derived by financial institutions in Singapore from approved transactions in syndicated offshore loans, credit and underwriting facilities and offshore fund management.

Related party transactions

Transfer pricing may be scrutinised by the tax authorities. Transactions between related parties must be at arm's length and at prices that would apply had the transactions been with an independent party.

Losses

Unabsorbed trading losses and capital allowances may be carried forward to offset future taxable income, provided the company's shareholders and shareholdings remain substantially the same (at least 50%) at the relevant dates.

If the shareholders include a corporation, the tax authorities will review the shareholders/shareholding composition of the corporation before allowing the company to utilise unabsorbed losses and capital allowances.

Corporate groups

There are no provisions in the Income Tax Act for losses in one company to be offset against the profits of another company in the same group.

Treatment of branches

Branches are taxed on income accruing in and derived from Singapore. The branch will not be treated as tax resident in Singapore. Income is subject to tax at the same rate as for resident companies, currently 24.5%.

Personal taxes

Taxable individuals

An individual, whether resident or non-resident, is subject to tax on income derived from or accrued in Singapore. However, a resident individual is also liable to tax on income derived from outside and received in Singapore.

An individual is deemed resident if he satisfies either the qualitative or the quantitative test which respectively investigate whether he has settled or intends to settle in Singapore, or whether Singapore is his usual abode, and whether he is physically present for a total of 183 days or more in a calendar year.

Tax year and filing requirements

Taxes are levied on a calendar year basis. An individual is taxed on his income of the preceding year. For example, tax for the year of assessment 2001 is based on income earned in 2000. Each individual must file an annual return. The due date for filing the return is 14 April each year, unless an extension is granted.

Taxes on income

Singapore income tax is levied at the territorial level only and is on a calendar year basis.

Sources of income

Employees' and directors' remuneration and fees

All income derived from an individual's employment exercised in Singapore is deemed to be Singapore sourced, regardless of whether he enters into his contract of employment or receives his remuneration outside Singapore. Director's fees are deemed to be Singapore sourced income if the company is tax resident in Singapore.

However, the employee will be exempt from Singapore's personal income tax if he or she exercises his or her employment in Singapore for not more than 60 days in the calendar year. The 60 days exemption rule does not extend to public entertainers. The directors of companies are also specifically excluded from the exemption.

An employee in Singapore can exercise two employments, one in Singapore and one outside Singapore. Compensation relating to his offshore duties maybe excluded from a Singapore tax charge. He is not liable to tax on the part of his remuneration paid to him by his offshore employer. Three conditions must apply: no part of the services relating to the offshore employment contract must be performed in Singapore, the remuneration relating to the offshore employment contract must not be remitted into Singapore and the salary cost must not be recharged to the Singapore entity. The apportionment of this remuneration should be on a reasonable and factual basis with reference from the time spent in and out of Singapore.

Apart from payments in cash, benefits in kind which are received in respect of employment are treated as taxable compensation.

Hotel accommodation

The taxable benefit assessable on each adult is S$ 250 per month. Children are assessed at lower rates ranging from S$ 25 to S$ 100 per month, per child, depending on age group. A further 2% of basic salary is added to the above figure to arrive at the total assessable value.

Company-provided housing in lieu of allowance

The assessable value to an employee, excluding a company director, is the lower of the annual value of accommodation or 10% of total employment income reduced by any rent paid by the employee.

The assessable value to a company director is the full annual value of the accommodation if the rented premises are within the Control of

Rent Act and the remuneration received by the director is less than the annual value of the accommodation. Where the conditions do not apply, the assessable value to the director is determined on the same basis as that of an employee.

Home leave passage

Home leave travel costs are taxed at a concessionary rate of 20% of the full passage cost. The concession is limited to one passage for the employee and his wife and two passages for each child per year.

Provision of car

The assessable benefit of a the provision of a car, where petrol cost is borne by the employee, is as follows:

Value of benefit: $^{3}/_{7}$ x [(car cost – residual value) / 10] + (S$ 0.45 per km x private mileage)

Where the car is provided by an employer who also bears the cost of petrol, the benefit is assessed as follows:

Value of benefit: $^{3}/_{7}$ x [(car cost – residual value) / 10] + (S$ 0.55 per km x private mileage)

Business income

Income is determined in accordance with generally accepted accounting principles adjusted by the specific rules of the Income Tax Act. A partnership is not a separate legal entity, therefore each partner is individually assessed on his share of partnership income.

Capital gains

There is no capital gains tax in Singapore. However, with effect from 15 May 1996, gains arising from the sale of immovable property and shares in real property companies which have been held for less than three years will be treated as income. Tax will be charged on:

- total gains made on the disposal of immovable property within one year of purchase;
- two thirds of gains made on the disposal of immovable property within the second year after purchase; or
- one third of gains made on the disposal of immovable property within the third year after purchase.

Exempt income

Income specifically exempted by the Income Tax Act includes interest on deposits in the Post Office Savings Bank (POSB), death gratuities, income of approved pension funds and the first S$ 150,000 of the net annual value of owner occupied residential property.

Dividends

When a company pays a dividend, the dividend carries a tax credit of 24.5%. Any excess tax credit over tax payable will be refunded to the individual if he is tax resident in Singapore.

Interest

Interest income is taxable when it is paid or credited, unless it is tax exempt. Non-resident individuals are exempt from income tax on interest income arising from deposits with approved banks in Singapore.

Rentals

Income from the rental of premises is determined after deducting allowable expenses incurred such as property tax, repairs and maintenance and interest on loans for the purchase of the property.

Royalties

Income from the use of patents and/or supply of know how is taxable. Tax on royalties derived by authors and composers who publish their works in Singapore and derived by inventors and product innovators is based on the lower of 10% of the gross amount of royalties or the net amount of royalties received after deduction of allowable expenses.

Personal allowances and deductions

Reliefs are only available to resident individuals and are as follows:

Personal Reliefs	*S$*
Self	3,000
Earned income:	
Below 55 years	1,000 or 2,000 if physically/mentally disabled

Between 55 and 60 years	3,000 or 5,000 if physically/mentally disabled
Above 60 years	4,000 or 6,000 if physically/mentally disabled
Wife	2,000
Children (1)	
First	2,000
Second	2,000
Third	2,000
Fourth (born after 1987)	2,000
Handicapped dependants (spouse, siblings or children of taxpayer)	3,500
Parents/grandparents (maximum 2)	
— living with taxpayer	5,000
— not living with taxpayer	3,500
Life insurance premiums & Central Provident Fund contributions (max.)	5,000 (2)
Course fees (maximum)	2,500
Foreign maid levy (for married women)	twice the amount of levy paid, maximum up to $8,280)
National Servicemen	2,000, or 1,000 for those who are inactive

Notes

Enhanced child relief to a maximum of S$ 10,000 each for the first four children is available to a married woman with the requisite educational qualifications who elects for separate assessment. A maximum of S$ 15,000 is available for each child below 12 years old.

The amount of relief deducted for each child is:

Child	*below 12 years old on 1 Jan 2000*	*12 years old or above on 1 Jan 2000*
1st	5% of married women earned income	5% of married women earned income
2nd	15% of married women earned income	10% of married women earned income
3rd	20% of married women earned income	15% of married women earned income
4th	(born in 1987 and not adopted) S$ 1,500 + 25% of married women earned income	S$ 1,500 + 15% of married women earned income

	(born on or after 1 Jan 1988 and not adopted)	
	25% of your earned income	15% of married women earned income

Deduction for insurance premiums paid is up to a maximum of S$ 5,000 including the CPF contribution. However, where Central Provident Fund (CPF) contributions are made by the employer and the employee subject to contribution on ordinary wage of up to S$ 72,000 p.a., the full statutory contribution is deductible. There is a limitation to the deduction of CPF contribution from additional wages.

Central Provident Fund contributions (social security)

An employee aged below 55 years who earns wages exceeding S$ 363 a month makes statutory contributions to the Central Provident Fund (CPF) at a rate of 20% of ordinary wages, subject to a maximum of S$ 1,200 per month.

Employees who earn wages of less than S$ 363 a month, or who are above 55 years of age, make contributions at varying rates.

CPF contributions are not required of employees who have been issued Employment/Professional Visit Passes or three-year work permits.

Foreign employees who have made CPF contributions prior to 1 August 1995 are required to continue to do so until their passes or permits expire. They will not need to contribute to CPF upon renewal of their passes or permits.

All CPF contributions in respect of foreign employees made voluntarily or mandatorily under contracts of employment will no longer be tax deductible for either the employer or employee and the employer's contributions will be taxable in the hands of the employee.

Special family rules

Married women are entitled to elect for separate assessment on all of their income.

Income from assets transferred to an unmarried relative under 21 years of age is deemed to be the income of the transferor.

Rates of tax

Rates applicable to resident individuals from year of assessment 2001 (income year 2000) are as follows:

Taxable Cumulative Marginal	Existing Rate	New Marginal Rates (with effect from YA 2001)	Tax on Band	Cumulative Tax
(S$)	(%)		(S$)	(S$)
1 – 7,500	2	0	0	0
7,501 – 20,000	5	3	375	375
20,001 – 35,000	8	6	900	1,275
35,001 – 50,000	12	9	1,350	2,625
50,001 – 75,000	16	12	3,000	5,625
75,001 – 100,000	20	15	3,750	9,375
100,001 – 150,000	22	18	9,000	18,375
150,001 – 200,000	23	21	10,500	28,875
200,001 – 400,000	26	24	48,000	76,875
400,001+	28	26		

Resident individuals are entitled to the 10% tax rebate from 2000 onwards.

Non-resident individuals are liable to tax on employment income at the higher of a flat rate of 15% or the amount of tax payable on such income by a resident individual in the same circumstances.

Non-resident individuals are liable to tax at a flat rate of 24.5% on all income other than employment income. Non-resident directors are taxable at a flat rate of 24.5%.

Payment of tax

Once an assessment is finalised by the Comptroller of Income Tax, a Notice of Assessment is issued. The tax assessed must then be paid within one month of the date of issue of the Notice, notwithstanding any objections that may be raised.

Payroll deductions

There is no requirement to deduct tax at source from employees' monthly remuneration, except in the following cases:

- the employee fails to settle his tax assessment;
- the employee is about to cease employment or depart from Singapore (the monies due to the employee can only be released after the Comptroller grants permission or after 30 days from notification of cessation or departure); and
- non-resident director's remuneration (where the withholding tax is 24.5%).

Estate and gift taxes

There is no gift tax in Singapore.

Estate duty is levied on all movable and immovable property situated in Singapore which passes on death.

An individual who is domiciled in Singapore at the time of death is chargeable with duty on movable property situated outside Singapore.

Duty is charged on the principal value of the estate at the following rates:

Chargeable value of estate	*Rate (%)*
First S$ 12 million	5
Above S$ 12 million	10

Exemption for duty

The following is exempt from estate duty for each individual:

- residential properties with a value of up to S$ 9 million;
- all CPF balances; and
- the balance of S$ 600,000 in value of movable assets which is not covered by the CPF balance.

Other taxes

Property tax

This is levied on immovable properties. It is computed at a uniform rate of 10% of the annual value, which is the gross amount for which the property is expected to be let from year to year. It is payable by the owner half-yearly in advance.

Central provident fund (CPF)

An employer is required to make monthly contributions to the CPF in respect of each employee. Currently the contribution is equal to 36% (maximum S$ 2,160) of each employee's monthly wages. The employer can recover 20% (maximum S$ 1,200) from each employee as the employee's own contribution. A limit on CPF contributions in respect of bonuses and additional wages of up to 4.8 months' pay applies to employees whose annual ordinary wages exceed S$ 72,000. Other details are set out earlier in the chapter.

Foreign worker's levy (FWL)

All non-permanent resident work permit holders are placed on the Levy scheme. The rates of levy payable are as follows:

Category of workers

- Construction workers:

  skilled – S$ 30 per worker, S$ 1 per day, up to S$ 30 per month;

  unskilled – S$ 470 per worker, S$ 16 per day, up to S$ 470 per month;

- Marine workers:

  skilled– S$ 30 per worker, S$ 1 per day, up to S$ 30 per month;

  unskilled – S$ 295 per worker, S$ 10 per day, up to S$ 295 per month;

- Manufacturing workers:

  skilled – S$ 30 per worker, S$ 1 per day, up to S$ 30 per month;

  unskilled – up to 40% of the total workforce, S$ 240 per month, S$ 8 per day, up to S$ 240 per month;

  between 40% to 50% of the total workforce, S$ 310 per worker, S$ 11 per day, up to S$ 310 per month;

- Foreign domestic workers:

  S$ 345 per worker, S$ 12 per day, up to S$ 345 per month.

Skills development fund levy

An employer must pay a levy of 1% of monthly wages or S$ 2, whichever is greater for each employee earning not more than S$ 1,000 per month.

Stamp duties

Stamp duties are imposed at fixed or ad valorem rates on a wide variety of legal documents, according to their nature and value. From financial year 2000, stamp duty on contract notes is abolished and there is further stamp duty relief for corporate restructuring and mergers.

Excise duties

Excise duties are imposed on certain commodities produced in Singapore. Imported goods are subject to custom duties at varying rates.

Goods and services tax (GST)

A GST of 3% is levied on the supply of goods and services made in Singapore by a taxable person in the course of any business carried on by him, including the importation of goods into Singapore with effect from 1 April 1994.

Exemptions

Sale and lease of residential properties and certain financial services are exempt from GST.

Registration

GST registration is compulsory where annual taxable turnover exceeds or is expected to exceed S$ 1,000,000.

GST returns and accounting periods

A GST return must be completed and submitted every quarter by a taxable person.

The period covered by the return is an accounting period which will normally coincide with the company's financial year. A normal GST accounting period is three months.

Exchange controls

There are no exchange controls in Singapore. No prior approval is required from the authorities for any payment, remittance or capital transfer of any currency to any country.

Withholding taxes imposed in a selection of treaties are as follows:

Country of residence	*Royalties* %	*Interest* %
Non-treaty countries	15	15
Selected treaty countries:		
Australia	10	10
Bangladesh	10	10
Belgium	0	15
Bulgaria	5	5 (g)
Canada	15	15 (h)
Czech Republic	10	0
Denmark	15	15 (g)
Finland	10	10 (g)
France	0	10 (b) & (g)
Germany	0	10 (g)
Hungary	5	5 (g)
India	15 / 10 (l)	15 (e)
Indonesia	15	10 (g)
Israel	15	15
Italy	15 / 20 (k)	12.5 (g)
Japan	10	10 (b) & (g)
Luxembourg	10	10 (g)
Malaysia	15	15
Mauritius	0	0
Mexico	10	5 (m) / 15
Netherlands	0	10 (g)
New Zealand	15	15
Norway	7	7 (g)
Pakistan	10	12.5
Papua New Guinea	10	10
People's Republic of China	10	10 (j) & (g)
Philippines	15 (c)	15 (i)
Poland	10	10 (g)
South Africa	5	0
South Korea	15	10 (g)
Sri Lanka	15	10 (f) & (g)
Sweden	0	15 (a) & (g)
Switzerland	5 (c)	10 (d)
Taiwan	15	15
Thailand	15	15 (e) & (g)
United Arab Emirates	5	7 (g)
United Kingdom	10 (n) / 15 (c)	10 (n) / 15 (d) & (g)
Vietnam	5 / 15 (k)	10

Notes

(a) 10% if paid by an industrial undertaking, as defined, to a financial institution;

(b) exempt if paid by an approved industrial undertaking, as defined;
(c) exempt for approved royalties;
(d) exempt if paid on approved foreign loans;
(e) 10% if received by a financial institution (including an insurance company);
(f) exempt if received by a financial institution;
(g) exempt if received by the Government or its local authorities;
(h) exempt if paid to the Export Development Corporation of Canada;
(i) exempt if paid on loan made, guaranteed or insured by specified institutions;
(j) 7% if received by a financial institution;
(k) higher rate applies to literary/artistic royalties;
(l) lower rate applies to royalties in relation to industrial, commercial or scientific equipment;
(m) 5% if received by bank;
(n) for amounts arising or accruing after 1 January 2000.

South Africa

Nexia Levitt Kirson

Residence-based system of taxation

A residence-based system of taxation has been introduced with effect from 1 January 2001. Any person who is considered to be a South African resident will be taxed on their worldwide income although certain categories of income and activities undertaken outside South Africa will be exempt from South African tax. Foreign taxes paid by these residents will however be allowed as a credit against the South African tax liability. Non-residents will still be taxed on their South African sourced income.

Definition of a resident

As far as individuals are concerned, two rules will apply to define what a resident is.

The first rule is based on ordinary residence and means that a person is a resident of South Africa if his or her permanent home, to which he or she will normally return, is in South Africa.

The second rule is time based and a more objective rule. A person will be regarded to be a resident if he has spent during the current tax year as well as during each of the previous three years more than 91 days per tax year in South Africa and he has spent during the previous three tax years in aggregate more than 549 days in South Africa (a portion of a day is regarded as a day).

Immigrants into South Africa will be South African residents from their first day in South Africa. Emigrants will be South African residents until the last day that they leave the country.

As far as persons other than natural persons are concerned, the following will apply:

- a company or trust formed, incorporated or established in South Africa will always be a South African resident;
- companies of which the place of effective management is in South Africa will be a South African resident.

Foreign tax credits

Tax credits in respect of foreign tax paid

To avoid the impact of double taxation where the foreign income of a resident was taxed by a foreign country, the foreign tax paid will be allowed as a credit against the residents South African tax liability. However, it must be noted that foreign tax credits can never exceed South African tax payable on the total amount of foreign income earned by a resident during a year of assessment. Excess foreign tax credits must be carried forward to the following tax year.

The ability to offset excess foreign credits against STC (secondary tax on companies) will no longer apply for years of assessment commencing on or after 1 January 2001.

Foreign tax paid has to be converted to the Rand monetary unit.

Proving of foreign tax credits

An assessment or the equivalent thereof, receipt or an official letter will be accepted as proof of foreign tax paid or payable.

In cases where passive foreign income has been received, for example rental, interest or dividends, and foreign tax was paid thereon, and a person is married in community of property, such foreign tax paid must be allocated between the spouses on a pro rata basis.

Carry-forward period of foreign tax credits

Excess foreign tax credits that have built up since 23 February 2000 may only be carried forward for a period of three years, however for foreign tax credits for years of assessment commencing on or after 1 January 2001, the carry forward period is seven years.

The FIFO (first in first out) principle will apply in utilising excess foreign tax credits of previous years of assessment against the tax liability of the current year.

Prescription period in respect of foreign tax credits

As is currently the case, an assessment is subject to the three-year prescription rule. However, in respect of foreign tax credits, a six-year prescription period will apply. The prescription period commences from the date of assessment. The normal exclusions will still apply in the case of fraud, misrepresentation and non-disclosure.

Conversion rules of foreign income to South African currency

The rules that should be applied to convert foreign income to the South African Rand are as follows:

Foreign dividend	The date that the foreign dividend accrued is the conversion date. Net income of a controlled foreign entity (CFE) is converted at the end of the financial year of the CFE.
Other income	The date that such income is paid or accrued, whichever occurs first.
Foreign tax credits	The date on which the tax is paid. If the tax was not actually paid by the last day of the year of assessment, the ruling exchange rate on such last day must be applied. Foreign tax credits attributable to a foreign dividend are converted on the date of accrual of the foreign dividend.

Main exclusions from residence basis of taxation

International headquarter company

A company is an international headquarter company if 90% of the value of assets represent shares in, and loans to, non-resident subsidiaries (this must be determined at the end of the tax year).

The entire equity share capital must be held directly by non-residents which are not SA residents or trusts. SA residents and trusts may not hold an indirect interest in aggregate of more than 5% in the Headquarter Company. These conditions apply for the entire year of assessment.

If the above requirements are met, the company will not be regarded as a resident.

Residents who are natural persons performing offshore services

The current exemption in terms of shipping crews still applies where the crew is outside the Republic for an aggregate of more than 183 days in a year of assessment.

An additional exemption has been introduced which applies to the foreign employment income of a person, earned while the person is outside South Africa for:

- an aggregate of more than 183 full days in a 12 month period commencing on or ending during a year of assessment;
- 60 full continuous days during the 12 month period.

This exemption does not apply to employees in the service of government or a public entity funded 80% or more from funds voted by Parliament.

Social security

Foreign social security system payouts are permanently exempted.

Foreign retirement funds

Foreign retirement/pension income (e.g. monthly annuity and retirement lump sums) are not taxable. This exemption will be reconsidered in the next three years.

No contributions to foreign retirement funds will be allowed as deductions.

Controlled foreign entity (CFE)

- A CFE means any foreign entity in which a resident or residents hold more than 50% of the participation rights or votes or control of the entity.
- All income, active or passive, will as a general rule be included in the income of resident shareholders in the following instances:
  - (i) when a resident who together with any connected person, holds at least 10% of the participation rights in the CFE; the amount to be included will be an amount equal to the proportional amount of net income of the CFE, determined on the same ratio as such resident's participation rights in relation to the total participation rights in the CFE; the net income of the CFE means an amount equivalent to what the taxable income of the CFE would have been if such CFE had been a resident. The deductions and allowances of the CFE are, however, limited to the income and net losses are therefore not taken into account in determining the taxable income of the resident but are carried forward to future years of assessment; CFE's losses are therefore ring fenced;
  - (ii) when the income of the CFE, which is a company, is not taxed at a statutory rate of at least 27%, the income of the CFE will be taxed in the hands of the resident as it arises and any subsequent dividend thereafter by the company to the resident will be exempt for purposes of the calculation of normal tax (the subsequent dividend will have STC implications).

Instances where income of a CFE is not included in the income of resident shareholders

- Where the income of the CFE, which is a company, has been or will be subject to tax in a designated country at a statutory rate of at least 27%; this income will not be included in the income of resident shareholders.
- Any foreign dividend declared by the CFE from profits, which were previously included in the income of the resident, will also be exempt.
- The income of a CFE will not be included if the income of the CFE is subject to South African tax in the hands of the CFE. This would, for example, be the case where the income was derived from a source in the Republic or deemed to be from a source in the Republic.
- Where the income of the CFE is derived by way of any dividend declared or interest, royalty or rental income paid or payable to such CFE by any other CFE (in relation to the resident), such income will also not be included.
- Where the income is attributable to the business establishment of the CFE and it is not derived from a diversionary transaction in relation to connected persons who are South African residents, the tax on the income will be deferred until a dividend is distributed.

Passive income

Passive income in the form of dividends, interest, royalties, rental income, annuities, insurance income or income of a similar nature will be included on a current basis.

This will not be the case where:

- it does not exceed 5% of the total receipts and accruals of the CFE;
- it arises from the principal trading activities of any banking or financial services, insurance or rental business, except where the income is received from any connected person who is a resident, or from a resident as part of a scheme for the avoidance of taxes, duties or levies.

Foreign income of resident companies

The foreign income of a resident company, for example, income attributable to a foreign branch, will generally be subject to tax.

However, branch income will be exempt if such income was subject to tax in a designated country at a statutory rate of at least 27%. Any other income which was not taxed at that rate in a designated country will be taxed in the Republic and a credit will be granted in respect of any foreign taxes which are proved to be payable in respect of such income.

A loss from activities in a foreign country may be set off against income from sources in foreign countries but a foreign loss may not be set off against South African income. A South African loss may however be set off against foreign income.

Tax on retirement funds (RFT)

The tax on retirement funds will be imposed on foreign income in the form of interest and rental income.

List of designated countries

Algeria, Australia, Austria, Belgium, Canada, Croatia, Czech Republic, Denmark, Egypt, Finland, France, Germany, Israel, Italy, Japan, Republic of Korea, Lesotho, Malawi, Namibia, Netherlands, Norway, Poland, Romania, Slovakia, Swaziland, Sweden, Thailand, Tunisia, United Kingdom, United States of America, Zambia and Zimbabwe.

Please note the above guidelines are only basic guidelines.

Corporate taxes

Tax year and filing requirements

The tax year is the 12 month period ending on the last day in February or any financial year of the company ending during the calendar year in question. Companies are required to submit annual income tax returns within 60 days of their financial year end. Requests for reasonable time extensions are normally granted.

Taxes imposed

Normal tax

Normal tax is charged on taxable income as defined. The taxable income of a company includes all business profits, rent, interest, royalties and other income derived.

Provisional tax payments based on the estimated taxable income for each year are made half yearly. A final 'topping up' payment is made every six months (in the case of February financial year ends, seven months) after the end of the financial year to avoid the payment of interest that might otherwise be payable in the case of companies whose taxable income exceeds R 20,000 and whose original estimates have not met the full tax liability for a particular year.

Levy on financial institutions

A levy is imposed on financial services which are not deductible from taxable income. In the case of deposit-taking institutions and mutual building societies the levy is calculated at a rate of 0.20% of the leviable amount as defined. By virtue of the imposition of VAT on financial services, the levy is not imposed on insurance companies, pension funds and friendly societies.

Marketable securities tax (MST)

MST is payable at a rate of 0.25% on the transfer of shares listed on the JSE Securities Exchange South Africa. No stamp duty is payable on transactions subject to MST.

Secondary tax on companies (STC)

STC is calculated at a rate of 12.5% of the net amount of any dividends declared during a dividend cycle by any company. Because STC is payable on the net amount, only the excess of dividends declared over dividends receivable is subject to the tax. Capitalisation shares do not attract STC.

Donations tax

Subject to certain exemptions, donations tax is payable by resident private companies at a flat rate of 25% on the value of all property disposed of by way of donation or for an inadequate consideration or a consideration less than its fair market value. With effect from 1 October 2001 this rate will decrease to 20%.

Rates of normal tax

Year of assessment ending on or after 1 April 2000.

Normal tax

Corporate entities (other than those mentioned below)	30%
Small business corporations	–

– on first R 100,000	15%
– on excess over R 100,000	30%
Employment companies	35%
Branches of companies having their effective place of management outside the Republic	35%
Gold mining companies	Determined by formula.
Long term insurance companies	Four-Fund approach; 0%–35% dependant on type of fund.
Retirement funds	25% of certain income.

Small business corporation

A small business corporation is a company where:

- the shareholders are natural persons;
- gross income does not exceed R 1,000,000 per annum;
- none of the shareholders own shares in any other company (other than listed companies and unit trusts);
- not more than 20% of the company's gross income collectively consists of investment income (interest, rents, annuities, dividends) and income from personal services (professional services).

Employment company

An employment company is a company:

- which is a labour broker, as defined, and has not been issued with a certificate of exemption;
- where any service rendered on behalf of the company to its client is rendered personally by any person who is a connected person in relation to such company (known as a personal service company).

An employment company is to be taxed as follows:

- the remuneration payable to such a company will be subject to employee's tax with effect from 1 August 2000;
- allowable deductions will be limited to the amount of the remuneration paid to the shareholders, members or other employees;
- net income will be taxed at a rate of 35% and secondary tax on companies will apply to any dividends paid.

A company will not be regarded as a personal service company where it employs more than three full time employees (other than a shareholder or member), none of whom is a connected person in relation to such shareholder or member.

Income subject to tax

General rules

Gross income less exempt income and deductions determine a company's taxable income which is subject to normal tax.

Stock/inventory valuation

Stock is valued at the lower of cost and net realisable value determined on the FIFO basis.

Interest payable and receivable

Legislation is enacted to apply to the treatment of interest earned and interest paid on 'instruments' issued.

'Instruments' include any interest bearing agreement, the terms of which exceed one year, and are issued or acquired at a discount, premium or bears deferred interest. Included in the above arrangements are bills, promissory notes, debentures, deposits with a bank or money lending institution and loans (including shareholder's loans). It does not apply to agreements which qualify for allowances on debtors.

The purpose of the legislation is to ensure that all interest earned by creditors and the interest paid by debtors is spread over the entire period of the transaction.

Companies who conduct their businesses as dealers in instruments can, subject to certain conditions, elect not to be bound by these rules. Where the rules do not apply, the stock of instruments at year end must be valued at market value.

Deductions

General rules

Any expenditure and losses, other than of a capital nature, actually incurred in or outside the RSA (during the tax year) in the production of income, are deductible in the determination of taxable income derived from carrying on any trade within the RSA.

Depreciation and amortisation

The taxpayer is entitled to an allowance of such sum which represents the amount by which the value of any plant, machinery, implements, utensils and articles used for the purposes of trade has been diminished by means of wear and tear during the tax year. Such allowances must accord with the rates determined by the South African Revenue Services as being acceptable in relation to the asset concerned. This allowance does not apply to industrial, hotel or farming machinery, plant, etc., which is provided for below. Wear and tear is not allowed on buildings or other structures of a permanent nature. Annual wear and tear allowances are calculated on the straight-line basis and interest or finance incentive charges in terms of instalment sale agreements are excluded from the cost of the assets when calculating depreciation and the following allowances.

Capital allowances

Initial allowances

Residential buildings

Cost of buildings in 'housing projects' consisting of at least five residential units intended for letting or to be occupied by a bona fide full time employee, and erection commenced on or after 1 April 1982 – 10%.

Annual allowances

Industrial buildings used in manufacture or similar process

Cost of erection of buildings or improvements commenced on or after 1 January 1989 – 5%.

New buildings or improvements to buildings used in a process of manufacture or similar process where the erection of the building or the improvements commenced during the period 1 July 1996 to 30 September 1999 and such building or improvements were brought into use on or before 31 March 2000 – 10%.

The annual allowances may be claimed in full in the year in which the building or improvements were brought into use.

Residential buildings

Cost of buildings in 'housing projects' consisting of at least five residential units intended for letting or to be occupied by a bona fide full time employee, and erection commenced on or after 1 April 1982 – 2%.

Accelerated allowances

New or unused plant or machinery used in a process of manufacture or similar process where:

- acquired and brought into use during the period 1 July 1996 to 30 September 1999 – 33⅓%;
- acquired under an agreement finally signed by every party to the agreement during the period 1 July 1996 to 30 September 1999 and brought into use during the period 1 October 1999 to 31 March 2000 – 33⅓%.

Manufacturing assets brought into use by small business corporations for the first time on or after 1 April 2001 – 100%.

Plant or machinery

Where contractual arrangements for plant or machinery were concluded after 15 December 1989 and brought into use after that date – 20%.

Farming equipment

Any machinery, implements, utensils or articles (other than livestock):

1st year	50%
2nd year	30%
3rd year	20%

Hotels

New buildings	5%
New equipment	20%
Refurbishment	20%
Ships	20%
Aircraft	20%

With regard to the above assets, the allowance may be claimed in full in the year in which the asset is brought into use (i.e. there is no apportionment), even if the asset was used for part of the year.

Royalties

Royalties incurred are a deductible expense in the determination of taxable income.

Interest

All interest incurred in the production of taxable income is deductible. There are special rules regulating the deduction of interest paid to offshore associated companies. Interest paid to finance the acquisition of movable capital assets does not form part of the cost of the assets for the purposes of any other allowance, but is deductible as and when incurred, provided that if the interest is calculated in respect of a period of more than 12 months then the interest is deemed to be incurred from day to day during the period in question.

Pre-production interest (i.e. interest incurred on any loan, advance or credit used for the acquisition, installation, erection or construction of an asset prior to being brought into use) is deductible in full in the year in which the relevant asset is brought into use for the purposes of trade.

Dividends

Dividends paid are not deductible.

Bad and doubtful debts

Bad debts may be deducted if the debts due to the taxpayer were previously included in income and are proved to the Revenue's satisfaction to be bad.

An allowance of 25% of total debts considered to be doubtful is usually allowed as a deduction. This must be added back to income the following year when a fresh allowance may be claimed.

Reserves and provisions

There is no deduction in respect of income carried to any reserve fund or capitalised in any way. The deduction of a reserve fund to meet contingent or anticipated liabilities, which have not actually been incurred, is prohibited. There is, however, a special allowance for future expenditure in certain circumstances.

Employees' and directors' remuneration and benefits

Employees' and directors' remuneration and benefits are generally deductible. In certain circumstances, remuneration, which is so grossly excessive that it could not be regarded in its total amount as producing income and has been awarded for some ulterior motive, may be disallowed. Factors to be considered are the relationship between employees and shareholders, value and nature of services, type of business, etc.

Specifically non-deductible expenses

The following types of expenditure are not deductible:

- expenditure that is recoverable under an insurance contract;
- any tax, duty, levy, interest or penalty imposed under the Income Tax Act, any additional tax imposed under the Value Added Tax Act, and any interest or penalty payable in consequence of any late payment under the Regional Services Act or any Act administered by the Commissioner for the South African Revenue Services;
- income carried to a reserve fund;
- expenses relating to income that is not subject to tax;
- expenses to the extent that they are not laid out or expended for the purposes of trade investments.

Related party transactions

Transactions considered abnormal or not at arm's length which have the effect of avoiding, reducing or postponing tax and which were entered into for such purpose may be brought within the ambit of the anti-avoidance legislation under the terms of which the Commissioner for the South African Revenue Service has broad powers to counter such avoidance.

Losses

Losses may be carried forward indefinitely or set-off against future years' taxable income. However, they may not be carried forward beyond any years during the whole of which no trade is carried on.

If a company with an assessed loss enters into an agreement or compromise with its creditors for the reduction of its liabilities, the company's assessed loss will be reduced by the amount of such reduction.

Anti-avoidance provisions exist to prevent the utilisation of tax losses where there has been a change in shareholding or an agreement affecting the company with an assessed loss, the sole or main purpose of which is to use the loss to avoid tax.

Corporate groups

There are no special rules relating to groups of companies. All companies are taxed individually and assessed losses may not be transferred between companies in a group.

Tax free mergers and disposals

The Income Tax Act makes provision for a moratorium on the payment of stamp duty, transfer duty and secondary tax on companies to facilitate the rationalisation of groups of companies listed on a licensed stock exchange. Companies with assessed losses do not qualify for the concessions and the schemes must be approved by the South African Revenue Service (SARS).

Liquidation/deregistration of companies and close corporations

Upon the liquidation of resident companies or close corporations, reserves of a revenue nature included in a liquidation dividend constitute a dividend (as defined) and are subject to STC if paid out of reserves earned in years of assessment ended after 31 March 1993. Reserves of a capital nature included in a liquidation dividend are not subject to STC. STC exemptions have, subject to certain provisions, been extended to dividends distributed in anticipation of liquidation and dividends distributed in the course of or in anticipation of deregistration.

Personal taxes

Tax year and filing requirements

The tax year runs from 1 March to the last day in February. Certain taxpayers, such as farmers, fishermen and diamond diggers, who have so elected, have a tax year ending 30 June.

Individuals, other than persons earning 'net remuneration' (as defined) not exceeding R 60,000 per annum, are required to submit annual income tax returns within 60 days of the last day in February or June each year. Requests for reasonable extensions of time are normally granted.

Taxes on income

Normal tax

Normal tax is charged on 'taxable income' defined at progressive block rates.

Standard income tax on employees (SITE)

SITE constitutes the final tax liability in respect of persons whose total income for the year consists of 'net remuneration' (as defined) not exceeding R60,000 per annum, in which case no tax return need be submitted. In all other cases SITE (which is not refundable) constitutes the minimum tax liability and will be allowed as a credit against normal tax assessed.

Sources of income

Employment income and directors' fees

Any amount derived from employment for services rendered or holding an office is included in gross income and subject to normal tax. Fringe benefits from employment are also included and special rules are laid down for the valuation of the cash equivalents of these benefits.

Limited exemptions apply on retirement, termination and retrenchment.

Business income

Income derived from carrying on a business, which is calculated in the same way as taxable income for a company, must be added to income from other sources to arrive at the total taxable income for the year. Financial statements are normally prepared on an annual basis.

Dividends

Dividends derived by an individual from a South African source are exempt from normal tax.

Interest

All interest received is included in income and is subject to normal tax. The first R 4,000 of interest derived in any year is exempt from tax, for taxpayers under 65 years of age, and R 5,000 for taxpayers over 65 years of age.

Rentals

Rentals received from letting fixed property are subject to income tax. Expenses incurred in earning such rentals are deductible.

Royalties

Royalties earned by an individual are generally subject to tax in the RSA. If such income is taxed in a foreign country, the foreign taxes paid may be deducted from the South African tax liability in respect of such royalties. In terms of certain double taxation agreements, royalties earned from certain foreign countries by a South African resident are not subject to tax in the RSA.

Social security benefits

Social welfare services in the RSA are funded by the proceeds of normal taxation and voluntary financial contributions by the public and include the following types of social security payments: Old Age Pension, War Veterans Pension, Pensions for the Blind, Disability Pension, Maintenance and Foster Care. Any benefit or allowance received in terms of the Unemployment Insurance Act is free of tax. Other benefits are subject to tax in the RSA.

Pensions and annuities

Pensions and annuities received from a former employer are generally subject to tax. Where less than two years of service in the ten years preceding the first pension payment were rendered in the RSA no part of the pension will be taxed in the RSA.

Pensions or annuities received from a fund in South Africa are also subject to tax. However, the capital element of a purchased annuity is exempt.

Exempt income

Certain amounts of income are entirely free of tax, the most significant being dividends received from a South African source. Up to R 30,000 of any amount received in respect of termination of employment (on retirement or retrenchment) is also exempt in certain circumstances. Lump sum benefits from Pension, Provident and Retirement Annuity

Funds are also tax free up to certain specified amounts, depending on retirement, death or resignation from the fund.

Investment income

A natural person ordinarily resident in the RSA will be required to include in taxable income all investment income earned from anywhere in the world. Such investment income will be deemed to have been earned from a source within the RSA.

Investment income includes any annuity, interest, rental, royalty or any passive income of a similar nature. Interest includes any other income which is subjected to the same treatment as income from money lent.

Certain exemptions and exclusions apply.

Expenses incurred in earning such income will be deemed to be for a trade carried on in the RSA, and will thus be deductible for purposes of determining taxable income.

Personal allowances and deductions

The following tax rebates deductible from tax payable are allowed:

Primary rebate	R 4,170
Additional rebate for persons over 65 years of age	R 3,000

Amounts deductible from income include:

- contributions (both current and in arrears) to pension and retirement annuity funds within defined limits;
- certain medical and disability expenses (dependent upon age and level of taxable income);
- entertainment, travel and subsistence allowances within defined limits;
- expenses incurred in the production of income derived from a trade carried on in the RSA.

Losses

Where an individual sustains a loss from business for a particular year, that loss may be set off against any other forms of income derived. If a loss still remains, it may be carried forward indefinitely to be set off against future years' taxable income. The need to continue trading in each year does not apply to individuals and any interruption of trade will not affect the balance of the assessed loss to be carried forward.

Special family rules

A husband and wife are taxed separately on all income which accrues to each of them, except in certain exceptional circumstances, and subject to special rules in the case of marriage in community of property. In the case of spouses married in community of property, income earned otherwise than from trade (such as rent and interest) is deemed to have accrued equally. Provisions exist to prevent the channelling of income from one spouse to the other for the purpose of reducing tax.

Income earned by minor children in their own right is taxed in their hands.

Income derived by a minor child from an asset donated by a parent is included in the income of such a parent.

Estate and gift taxes

Donations tax is payable at a flat rate of 25% on the value of all assets disposed of by way of donation or for an inadequate consideration. All natural persons are entitled to donate R 25,000 per tax year free of donations tax. Dispositions between spouses and donations to educational institutions are exempt from donations tax.

Estate duty is levied at a flat rate of 25% on the net value of an estate which exceeds one million Rand. In arriving at net value, specific deductions (inter alia, funeral and deathbed expenses, debts due, administration charges, charitable and other bequests and property left to a surviving spouse) are deductible.

Donations tax and estate duty will be reduced to 20% with effect from 1 October 2001.

Social security contributions

There is no statutory social security system. Employers must belong to compulsory indemnity funds such as unemployment insurance and accident insurance funds to which the employer must contribute. Welfare pensions, free legal clinics and free medical facilities are available to lower income groups and certain age groups.

Anti-avoidance measures

There are various specific anti-avoidance provisions designed to counter specific types of tax avoidance, such as ceding remuneration for services rendered, donations between spouses, donations to minor children, preference share financing and ceding the right to receive interest in exchange for dividends.

There is also a general anti-avoidance provision which gives the SARS the means to determine the liability for tax in the case of transactions or schemes entered into for the sole purpose of avoiding tax and which were carried out in an abnormal manner or which created abnormal obligations as tested between persons dealing at arm's length.

Rates of tax

The maximum marginal tax rate of 42% is reached at a taxable income of R 215,000.

Provincial and local taxes

There are no provincial and local taxes on income at present.

Tax credits

Employee's tax (comprising SITE and PAYE) deducted and provisional tax paid, must be set off against the normal tax liability arising for a particular year. Any credit remaining to the taxpayer's account after such set off must be refunded, unless such refund comprises SITE which is not refundable (see earlier; also refer to Foreign Tax Credits as previously discussed).

Payment of tax

Payroll deductions

Employee's tax (comprising SITE and PAYE) is deducted by the employer in respect of remuneration paid to employees. Such tax must be paid to the South African Revenue Service within seven days after the month end.

Prepayments

Provisional tax payments based on estimated taxable income for each year are made half-yearly. A final 'topping up' payment is made six months (seven months for taxpayers with February year ends) after the end of the tax year to avoid the payment of interest that might otherwise be payable in the case of an individual whose taxable income exceeds R 50,000 and whose original estimates have not met the full tax liability for a particular year. Certain taxpayers over the age of 65 are exempt from the payment of Provisional Tax on Taxable Income not exceeding R 80,000 per annum.

Other taxes

Regional services council levies

Two types of levies are payable, namely:

- regional Establishment Levy based on sales/income;
- regional Services Levy based on remuneration paid to employees (or drawings by sole traders or partners).

The rates vary between regions.

Stamp duty

Stamp duty is payable at laid down rates on specified classes of instruments, e.g. credit agreements, leases, shares, agreements or contracts, promissory notes, etc. There is no stamp duty on transactions that are subject to VAT.

Transfer duty

Transfer duty is levied on the transfer of ownership of fixed property at the following rates:

Individuals:

First R 70,000 of purchase consideration	1%
R 70,001 – R 250,000	5%
Thereafter	8%

Companies and Close Corporations and Inter Vivos Trusts:

On purchase consideration	10%

No transfer duty is payable on building stands costing not more than R 30, 000 and dwellings costing not more than R 70,000.

Capital gains tax

Capital gains tax will be introduced with effect from 1 October 2001. Some salient features of the proposals are:

- residents will be subject to the tax on the disposal of their assets held worldwide, while non-residents will be taxed on the disposal of certain assets in South Africa;
- only gains accruing after 1 October 2001 will be subject to the tax which will be levied on disposals or deemed disposals;
- the first R 10,000 of capital gain or loss realised by individuals per annum will be excluded. Certain exemptions will apply inter alia to primary residences, personal use assets, insurance and retirement benefits, assets of a small business disposed of for retirement, compensation for personal injury, lottery receipts, and foreign currency converted for personal use and gains arising on assets donated to certain public-benefit organisations;
- rollover relief will be provided for assets in certain circumstances, e.g. certain transfers between spouses or involuntary disposals;
- capital gains will be taxed with other income, a portion of the net capital gain being included in taxable income.

Value added tax (VAT)

VAT is a tax levied on the supply of goods and services by vendors in the course or furtherance of an enterprise.

Any person whose total value of taxable supplies exceeds R300,000 per annum must register for VAT. Persons with taxable supplies between R 20,000 and R 300,000 may register voluntarily.

There are currently two rates of VAT:

Standard rate	14%
Zero rate	0%

Zero rated supplies

Zero rated goods:

- goods which are exported;
- goods supplied in the course of repairing, renovating, modifying or treating any goods temporarily admitted into South Africa, provided that the goods supplied either become part of the other goods or are consumed in the repair process;
- goods supplied under a rental agreement for use exclusively in an export country;
- the supply of an enterprise or part thereof as a going concern

provided certain conditions are met;

- illuminating paraffin;
- petrol or crude oil which is subject to the fuel levy;
- supply of goods to a foreign branch of a South African company;
- certain foodstuffs;
- supply of gold to the Reserve Bank, Mint or a registered bank;
- farming inputs specified in Schedule 2 of the Act; these include animal feed, fertilizer, pesticide, dips, plants and seed.

Zero rated services:

- the transport of passengers or goods outside South Africa or from South Africa to an export country, or from an export country to South Africa;
- the transport of passengers within South Africa by aircraft as part of an international air journey;
- the supply of services to non-residents who are outside South Africa when the service is rendered (services in connection with land or improvements thereon are excluded);
- the supply of services to foreign-going ships;
- the transport of goods between places in South Africa supplied as part of international transport of passengers;
- the insuring or arranging of insurance or the arranging of the transport of passengers or goods internationally;
- the supply of services directly in connection with land or any improvement thereto in an export country;
- the supply of services in respect of movable property in an export country;
- the goods which are exempt from tax and are temporarily admitted into South Africa from an export country;
- the repair, maintenance, cleaning or reconditioning of a foreign-going ship or aircraft;
- the supply of services rendered to trains operated by non-residents;
- the supply of services rendered outside South Africa;
- the supply of rights such as patents, designs, trademarks, copyright or similar rights for use outside South Africa;

- the supply of services by welfare bodies to government and local authorities;
- the supply of services by a South African enterprise to a foreign branch;
- the supply of services to a public authority to the extent that the payment consists of a transfer payment.

Exempt supplies

As exempt supplies are not taxable supplies, the VAT on inputs which directly relates to those exempt supplies cannot be recovered from the South African Revenue Service, unless the value of the vendor's exempt supplies is less than 5% of the vendor's total supplies during a 12 month period.

Types of exempt supplies

Supply of certain financial services:

- premiums payable in respect of life policies and contributions to a pension, a provident retirement annuity, medical aid fund and compulsory charges included in the selling price of unit trusts;
- supply by an association not for gain of donated goods and services or where the association manufactures such goods, if at least 80% of the value of materials used consists of donated goods;
- supply of residential accommodation in a dwelling under a letting or hiring agreement, or where any employer permits his employee to occupy the accommodation as a fringe benefit for a period agreed upon by the supplier and the recipient;
- supply of leasehold land for existing dwellings or the erection of dwellings;
- sale or letting of land outside South Africa;
- supply of services to members of a sectional title, share block or old aged home scheme;
- supply of transport services to fare-paying passengers by road or rail;
- supply of educational and subordinate services by the State, Provincial Administration and institutions of a public character; subordinate services include any goods or services which are necessary and/or incidental to the supply of educational services (including board and lodging) where these are not supplied for a consideration other than the payment of school fees.

Skills development levy

Registration

It is compulsory for every business currently registered with the South African Revenue Service as an employer or whose payroll exceeds R 250,000 per annum to register.

Levies payable

The levy is payable monthly as follows:

- 1 April 2000 to 31 March 2001 – 0.5% of total remuneration;
- from 1 April 2001 – 1% of total remuneration.

Remuneration is defined in the fourth Schedule to the Income Tax Act and includes inter alia salaries, overtime, leave pay, bonuses, allowances, commissions and fees.

Certain important exclusions from remuneration are:

- any amount paid to a director of a private company or member of a close corporation;
- any amount paid to an independent contractor;
- any pension or allowance paid in terms of the Aged Persons Act, Blind Persons Act, Disability Grants Act and the Children's Act;
- reimbursements to employees for actual business expenses incurred;
- any annuity paid under an order of divorce or decree of judicial separation or under any agreement of separation.

Levies are payable on or before the seventh day after the end of the month for which the levy is due. Late payments incur a 10% penalty as well as interest at the prescribed rate, calculated on a daily basis.

Grants to employers

Grants of up to 50% of the levy paid are available to employers if certain requirements are met.

Taxation of non-residents

Non-resident shareholder's tax and non-resident tax on interest (NRST and NRTI)

No withholding tax is levied on dividend or interest payments made to non-residents.

Royalties and know-how fees

A withholding tax of 12% of the gross amount of royalties and know-how fees is deductible by the payer.

Other business losses may be off-set against the taxable portion of royalties.

The rate can be reduced in terms of certain double taxation agreements.

The entering into of agreements for royalties and other patents, trademarks, copyrights, designs, know-how and the like, requires the approval of the Department of Trade and Industry and Exchange control.

Interest

Interest earned after 2 June 1992 is tax-free. Interest earned after 1 April 1995 is exempt from tax provided that, in addition to being not ordinarily resident, the individual was also physically absent from the RSA for the period discussed earlier. The exemption does not apply to a natural person who was at any time resident in the RSA and carried on business in the RSA during the year in which the interest was received or accrued.

Other income

Fees, salaries, rent, share of profits, pensions etc. from South Africa are subject to South African normal tax.

Losses

Non-resident companies incurring tax losses in branches operating in the RSA may transfer such losses to a RSA subsidiary company subsequently formed to take over the business of the branch.

Special treatment for expatriates

In general, visitors from abroad who work temporarily in the RSA will be liable to tax on their earnings, even though they do not settle there. However, in terms of certain double taxation agreements such persons will not be liable to tax on their earnings in the RSA if the duration of their stay does not exceed 183 days in any year. Such earnings may nevertheless still be taxed in their country of residence.

Treatment of branches

Where a foreign company carries on business in the RSA through a branch operation (i.e. fixed place of business in the RSA), such a branch is regarded as a company for tax purposes but is taxed at the rate of 35% on its taxable income. This may be varied by double taxation agreements, where applicable, after tax profits are exempt from STC.

Other taxes

Treatment of partnerships

A partnership is not a legal entity distinct from the partners of whom it is composed, nor is it a taxable person for tax purposes.

The profits made by a partnership are allocated to the partners in accordance with their profit sharing ratios in terms of the partnership agreement. Such share is added to any other income derived by such partner in determining the total taxable income of that partner for a particular year.

Any income received by or accrued to the partnership is deemed to accrue to the partners in the profit sharing ratio on the same date on which it accrues to the partnership.

Trusts

At present the following rates of tax apply to other than Special Trusts:

R 0 – 100,000	32% of each R1
R 100,000 and over	R 32,000 + 42% of the amount over R 100,000

Trusts are not entitled to the primary rebate or the interest exemption.

The provisions in the Income Tax Act, whereby losses incurred by a trust could be transferred to beneficiaries (who could then set off such losses against their other taxable income) has been rescinded. However, such losses can be retained in the trust itself and be set off against future taxable income. This amendment applies to all trusts created from 11 March 1998, and to existing trusts from years of assessment commencing on or after 1 January 1999.

Special trusts

A special trust means a trust created solely for the benefit of a person who suffers from:

- any mental illness, as defined; or
- any serious physical disability;.

(where such illness or disability incapacitates such a person from earning sufficient income to maintain himself).

The Mental Health Act defines mental illness as meaning any disorder or disability of the mind and includes any mental disease and any arrested, incomplete development of the mind.

If the trust's income vests in the beneficiary, the income will be taxable in his hands at his rates subject to the applicable rebates. The income, which does not vest in a beneficiary, is taxed according to the table for natural persons but without the benefit of the rebate.

Customs and excise duties and import surcharges

In general, imported goods are subject to customs duty, varying at rates depending on the classification and valuation of the imported item.

Contra customs duty is levied, in addition to the ordinary customs duty, on items where a locally manufactured item is subject to excise duty.

Anti-dumping duties may be imposed on various items.

Excise duties are levied on certain specified locally manufactured goods, such as alcohol, tobacco, soft drinks and certain foodstuffs.

Doing business in South Africa

Southern Africa

Current developments in the sub-continent as a whole make the country a springboard for business dealings in the neighbouring territories in Southern Africa. Diplomatic ties have been established in every capital and relaxation in exchange control favour outward investment into the Southern African Development Community (SADC). It is the intention to implement complete free trade within the SADC by the year 2004. Over and above development schemes, various trade corridors are being planned and discussed. The primary focus of the RSA's policy is to develop telecommunications and energy infrastructures, economic structures and policies that will benefit the sub-continent as a whole. Zambia, Botswana, Angola, Zimbabwe, Malawi, Namibia and Mozambique have formed a regional grouping to attract international aid for development and are looking to the RSA for assistance. Trade between the RSA and these countries have increased dramatically in recent years. Most of the countries in the sub-continent have considerable natural resources, but it is difficult to compete in world markets due to the lack of economies of scale as well as the distances involved.

Business in the RSA can be conducted through various entities such as:

- sole proprietors;
- partnerships;
- trusts;
- close corporations;
- companies;
- branches.

There are no requirements for local residents and/or directors. However, a representative taxpayer who is a South African resident must be appointed.

Investment incentives

Small and medium enterprise development programme (SMEDP)

This programme is available to entities investing up to R100 million in qualifying assets. New and expansion projects in manufacturing, tourism, certain business services, information and communication, high value agricultural projects, agro-processing, recycling, biotechnology industries and cultural industries may be considered for the incentive.

Eligible projects qualify for a tax-free establishment grant (paid quarterly) in the first two years, calculated on the qualifying investments as follows:

South Africa

Investment R Million	*Assistance*	*R Million*
0 – 5	10% of each R1	
5 – 15	R 500,000 + 6% of the amount over	5
15 – 30	R 1,100,000 + 4% of the amount over	15
30 – 50	R 1,700,000 + 3% of the amount over	30
50 – 75	R 2,300,000 + 2% of the amount over	50
75 – 100	R 2,800,000 + 1% of the amount over	75

An additional grant for one year (third year) will be extended if the ratio between the labour cost and the value added is greater than 30%.

Skills support programme (SSP)

This programme is a three year cash grant to the value of 50% of the cost of training new staff for a new or expansion project. The grant is limited to 30% of the annual wage bill. The enterprise must have an approved training programme. Payment is on a performance basis. The programme also makes provision for a capital grant to acquire training equipment and course materials.

Small business development

The full cost of any investment in manufacturing assets made by a small business corporation, as defined in the Income Tax Act, may be deducted in the year in which the asset is brought into use by the taxpayer for the first time. This applies to assets brought into use for the first time on or after 1 April 2001.

Wage incentives

The National Treasury and SARS are developing an administrative and economically efficient wage tax mechanism for encouraging job creation and promoting employment in the formal sector.

Incentives for strategic investment projects

In 2000, the Department of Trade and Industry introduced a range of investment incentives. R 3 billion will be allocated over the next four years for incentives to encourage strategic investment projects. Qualifying projects will obtain an additional deduction of between 50% and 100% of the investment made.

Export incentives

The main scheme currently operated by the Department of Trade and

Industry (DTI) is the Export Marketing and Investment Assistance Scheme (EMIA). To qualify, the taxpayer must register as an exporter with the DTI.

Export marketing investment assistance

The EMIA scheme refers to certain marketing allowances involving the following:

Primary export market research

- 50% to 80% of the cost of an economy class return air ticket;
- subsistence allowance of R 800 per day for a maximum period of 15 days;
- cost of transporting samples up to R 1,000;
- 50% of the cost of car rental up to R 200 per day;
- designing and printing of export brochures and production of a video up to R 3,000 per annum;
- registration of products in an export market up to R 10,000 per annum;
- marching grant up to R 7,500 per annum for local and overseas marketing consultants.

Outward selling trade missions

- 50% to 80% of the cost of an economy class return air ticket;
- subsistence allowance of R 800 per day for a maximum period of 115 days;
- either 50% of the cost of car rental up to R 200 per day or 50% of the cost of minibus rental up to R 600 per day;
- cost of transporting samples up to R 1,000.

Inward buying trade mission

- One business class return air ticket from the point of departure of the mission member to the point of arrival in the RSA;
- business class air fares in respect of internal travel in the RSA;
- subsistence allowance of R 500 per day per mission member for a maximum period of 10 days;

- in the case of the company visiting an individual exporter, the contribution will be 50% of a business class air ticket and a daily subsistence allowance of R 500 for five days.

Exhibition assistance

- Limited to 80% of certain acceptable items, up to R 40,000. 'Certain acceptable items' are defined as rental of exhibition space and electrical costs, construction of stand excluding interior design, telephone installation excluding telephone calls and rental of essential furniture;
- up to R 10,000 including forwarding and clearing charges for the transport of samples;
- 70% or 80% of the cost of an economy class return air ticket;
- subsistence allowance of R 800 per day for the duration of the exhibition.

Assistance to specific industry sectors

- A matching grant of up to R 400,000 in the first year and R 200,000 in the second year of operation to establish and export council;
- financial assistance on a matching grant basis will be provided for the following:
  - ad hoc foreign trade exhibition schemes;
  - trade exhibitions in South Africa (50% of cost of rental and construction of stand up to R 7,500);
  - outward sale and inward buying missions on approval of DTI;
  - assistance for advertising in selected overseas markets up to R 25,000 per annum (on export brochures, videos and handbooks);
  - brochures up to R 3,000;
  - video production up to R 10,000 per annum;
  - handbooks up to R 20,000 per annum;
  - cost of an export marketing consultant up to R 25,000 per visit.

Inward investment missions

- One business class return air ticket from the point of departure of the mission member to the point of arrival in the RSA;

- business class air fares in respect of internal travel in the RSA;
- subsistence allowance of R 500 per day per mission member for a maximum period of ten days.

Outward investment recruitment missions

- 50% to 80% of the cost of an economy class return air ticket;
- subsistence allowance of R 800 per day for a maximum period of 15 days;
- either 50% of cost of car rental up to R 200 per day or 50% of the cost of minibus rental up to R 600 per day;
- cost of transporting samples up to a maximum of R 1,000.

Foreign direct investment research

- 50% to 80% of the cost of an economy class return air ticket;
- subsistence allowance of R 800 per day for a maximum period of 15 days;
- cost of transporting samples up to R 1,000;
- 50% of the cost of car rental up to R 200 per day;
- designing and printing costs of a project brochure or the making of a promotional video up to R 3,000;
- matching grant up to a maximum of R 7,500 for a local or overseas investment consultant.

The following criteria, inter alia, will be applied to applications for EMIA:

- past export performance of applicant;
- potential export performance;
- measure of export planning;
- type of product for export and local marketing performance;
- level of labour absorption, location of venture and technological requirements;
- industry in which the venture is planned.

Any assistance provided under the EMIA scheme is at the absolute discretion of the Director General of Trade and Industry whose decision will be final.

Other incentives

- Generalised Systems of Preferences in which the RSA exports are subject to certain conditions, allowed to enter various markets free of import duty or at reduced rates;
- customs and excise duty rebates and drawbacks in respect of imported or locally manufactured items which are exported;
- specific cash financial assistance schemes exist for exporters of certain products manufactured from locally sourced rolled or drawn primary steel where a minimum of 25% value is added;
- zero rating of VAT on export sales;
- from time to time schemes are introduced to promote the export of specific products through a system of duty credits similar to the concept of the Motor Industry Development Programme. Such a scheme is currently in operation in the textile, clothing and garment industry;
- low interest finance is available to certain industrialists who add at least one eight-hour shift that leads to new employment, are financially sound and does not lead to over gearing. No criteria are set for increases in production or sales, but a minimum working capital is required. Low interest rates will apply for the first three years of a maximum loan period of five years, with a maximum of R 40 million at low interest rates;
- finance is available to support the export of capital goods and services normally supplied as buyer credits direct to foreign buyers; the RSA content of 70% will result in 85% of the contract price being financed at a repayment period of two to ten years;
- financing for upgrading or expansion of fixed assets is available to textile, clothing, footwear and motor vehicle component manufacturers exposed to greater competition through import tariff reductions of at least 10%;
- stamp duties on bills of exchange, bills of entry and securities and surety ships have been removed with effect from 1 April 2001.

Tax treaties and withholding taxes

Royalties paid to non-resident individuals not carrying on business in the RSA and to companies having their effective place of management outside the RSA, are subject to a withholding tax at a rate of 12% unless covered by a double taxation agreement.

The following table illustrates the treaty rates currently in force:

	Royalties (%)	Notes		Royalties (%)	Notes
Algeria	10		Malawi	12	(1)
Australia	10		Malta	10	
Austria	0		Mauritius	0	
Belgium	0		Namibia	10	
Botswana	12	(9)	Netherlands	0	
Canada	10	(2)	Norway	0	
Croatia	5		Pakistan	10	
Cyprus	0		Peoples Republic of China	10	(10)
Czech Republic	10				
Denmark	0		Poland	10	
Egypt	12	(9)	Romania	12	(9)
Finland	0		Russian Federation	0	
France	12	(1)	Seychelles*	12	
Grenada*	12		Sierra Leone*	12	
Germany	12	(1)	Singapore	5	
Hungary	0		Slovak Republic	10	
India	10		Swaziland	12	(1)
Indonesia	10		Sweden	12	(1)
Iran	10		Switzerland	0	
Ireland	0		Thailand	12	(9)
Israel	12	(1) & (3)	Tunisia	10	
Italy	6		United Kingdom	12	(1)
Japan	10		USA	0	
Korea	10		Zambia	12	(1)
Lesotho	12		Zimbabwe	12	(1)
Luxembourg	0				

* Provisions of the double taxation agreement with the United Kingdom extended to these territories.

Notes

(1) If the royalty is subject to tax in the recipient's country of residence, there is no withholding tax.

(2) Rate reduced to 6% in respect of copyright royalties and other like payments in respect of any literary dramatic, musical or other artistic work or royalties for use of computer software, or for use of any patent or any industrial, commercial or scientific information (reduced rate does not apply to royalties in respect of films or videos or other means of reproduction in connection with rental/franchise agreements).

(3) As per note (1), with the exception of the use of cinematography or television film where withholding tax of 15% of the company tax rate applies.

(4) With the exception of Austria, Canada, Croatia, Czech Republic, Denmark, Finland, India, Ireland, Japan, Korea, Malta, Norway, Singapore, Sweden, UK and USA, there is no relief granted in respect of STC.

(5) Comprehensive agreements have been negotiated or renegotiated but not signed with Botswana, Bulgaria, Estonia, Ethiopia, Gabon, Germany, Kuwait, Latvia, Lithuania, Malawi, Malaysia, Morocco, Netherlands, New Zealand, Oman, Portugal, Spain, Swaziland, Tanzania, Turkey, Ukraine, United Arab Emirates, United Kingdom, Zambia, Zimbabwe.

(6) Comprehensive agreements, which have been ratified in South Africa, are with Greece, Nigeria and Uganda.

(7) Comprehensive agreements are being negotiated or renegotiated but have not been finalised with Bangladesh, Mozambique, Qatar and Sri Lanka.

(8) Limited sea and air transport agreements exist with Brazil, Greece, Portugal and Spain.

(9) The treaty provides that the rate may not exceed 15%.

(10) Withholding tax on payments for the use of, or right to use, any industrial, commercial or scientific equipment should be raised on 70% of the gross value of the payments.

Exchange control

Residents

Only authorised dealers may deal in foreign currency. Exchange control regulations affect residents of the RSA in that it restricts the movement of capital to other countries.

The RSA residents who emigrate are granted various allowances, subject to a tax clearance certificate being obtained from the South African Revenue Service. These include cash allowances comprising holiday travelling allowance and settling in allowance, an allowance for household and personal effects and a motor vehicle up to certain maximum values. The assets must have been owned for at least one year. Any remaining funds are 'blocked' and fall under the control of an authorised dealer. Income earned on blocked funds is remittable abroad. Blocked assets can be utilised to pay certain permissible expenses.

Immigrants

On arrival in the RSA, immigrants are required to declare to an authorised dealer whether they possess foreign assets (no details required) and give an undertaking that they will not place such foreign assets at the disposal of a third party RSA resident. Thereafter, for five years they may freely deal with their foreign assets and income without exchange control permission. During this five year period any assets introduced into RSA may be freely re-transferred abroad together with excess assets accumulated within RSA, provided such excesses are reasonable in relation to the immigrant's business or employment activities in RSA.

After five years the immigrant will be classified as a RSA resident and the normal exchange control rules would apply.

Inheritances

A non-resident beneficiary of a deceased estate of a person regarded as a South African resident at the time of death is entitled to the remittance of cash bequests without limitation.

- Inheritances of securities etc in the above circumstances will require the certificates to be endorsed non-resident (these can thereafter be sold and the proceeds are freely remittable).
- There are no limits or restrictions on the remittability of inheritances of South African assets of a deceased non-resident.
- Jewellery may be exported without restriction to a non-resident beneficiary.

Restrictions on local borrowings by non-residents

Non-residents may be limited in their local borrowing facilities by a formula dependent on the extent of the borrower's effective capital. Entities with foreign control or beneficial interest of 75% or more are affected persons. Such entities comprise companies, close corporations, foundations, trusts, partnerships or estates.

The permitted local borrowing formula is as follows:

$$100\% + \frac{(\text{RSA\% interest} \times 100\%)}{\text{Non-resident\% interest}} \times \text{effective capital}$$

The effective capital includes the aggregate of:

- issued ordinary share capital;
- share premium;
- non-distributable reserves, excluding unrealised reserves result-

ing from the revaluation of assets;

- distributable reserves;
- members' loans to the extent that local and foreign members' loans are in proportion to their holding in the entity;
- hardcore balance of inter-company balances with non-resident group members;
- deferred tax credit balance.

Local borrowings include the aggregate of:

- overdrafts;
- mortgage bonds;
- local acceptance credits;
- guarantees;
- instalment sale or lease liabilities;
- discounting;
- factoring;
- surety ship;
- buy backs;
- lease backs.

Foreign nationals temporarily working in the RSA

Special concessions are available for foreign nationals who work temporarily in the RSA on secondment to a local firm or who have been brought to the RSA on a contract basis.

Their status should be recorded by providing an authorised dealer with a copy of the letter from the employer confirming their contract arrangements and an undertaking that in respect of any foreign assets that they may have, these will not be made available to any other South African resident. When those formalities have been completed, they will be permitted:

- to conduct their banking on a resident basis;
- to deal freely with their foreign assets including any income earned thereon;
- to make transfers to their home country, reasonable in relation to their earnings in the RSA;

- on their permanent departure on conclusion of their contract, to transfer to their home country any savings accumulated in the RSA.

If the contract worker wished to introduce funds from abroad to purchase residential accommodation, this should be recorded with Exchange Control so that when the property is sold, the net proceeds will again be exportable.

Foreign investment in the RSA

- Non-residents enjoy unrestricted rights to invest in any South African listed or unlisted shares and gilts with the sale proceeds being fully remittable.
- Investment, through the introduction of loan capital, requires prior exchange control approval. Loans can be repatriated in their original foreign currency or in Rands. Interest is fully remittable at the appropriate rates applicable to the elected repatriation currency.
- Although there are no thin capitalisation exchange control constraints, the Receiver of Revenue may disallow interest paid on that portion of loan capital in excess of a loan (capital ratio of 3:1).
- After-tax profits and dividends are fully remittable – but subject to any restrictions imposed by exchange control in circumstances where local borrowings limits are exceeded.
- Exchange control will consider requests from South African companies/close corporations to remit funds to non-resident shareholders/members by way of loans in lieu of dividends/ distributions.

Trade transactions

A wide range of goods may be imported without a permit, but as a broad rule it is not permissible to mail payment for imports prior to shipment. Limited advance payments on capital goods will be allowed should the order otherwise be refused and such payment is normal in the trade concern. Forward exchange cover is available upon documentary proof of requirements regarding ascertained and firm commitments arising from approved commercial transactions.

Exporters must submit a declaration to an authorised dealer and as a broad rule settlement in full should be received within six months of shipment. The bank is required to ensure that this is done. Where longer terms of credit are required on capital goods, the rule can be varied within certain parameters or with exchange control permission.

Royalties

The entering into of agreements for royalties and other patents, trademarks, copyrights, designs, know-how and the like, requires the approval of the Department of Trade and Industry and Exchange Control.

Foreign transactions by residents

Investments – Individuals:	
Over 18 years of age	R 750,000
Participation in share incentive schemes	R 750,000 per employee of local subsidiary or branch of foreign parent company
Investments – Corporate entities:	
Investments	R 500 million per investment
Projects in African countries	R 750 million per project
Retention of export proceeds	Maximum of 180 days from date of rendering of service
Portfolio investments:	
Institutions	15% of total assets
Unit trust management companies	20% of total assets
Internet transactions	R 20,000 per transaction via credit/debit card
Payment for imports	R 50,000 per transaction on a cash order basis
Advance payment of imports of capital goods	Up to $^1/_3$ of ex-factory costs
Temporary residence abroad	Travel allowance and personal and household effects up to insured value of R 1 million

Spain

P.B. Auditores España, S.L.

Introduction

Since 1 January 1999 a new Law came into effect: the Non-Resident Income Tax Act (Law 41/98). This new law supported a change into the Spanish tax system, which separates into different Acts: the taxation of residents and non-residents.

As a result, this chapter will be divided into four parts:

- corporate taxes;
- personal taxes;
- non-resident income; and
- other taxes.

Corporate taxes

Introduction

The current Corporate Income Tax Act (Law 43/95) came into effect in 1996. It only regulates the income of resident companies.

The tax year for corporate income tax is the accounting reference period of the company. A tax year cannot exceed a period of 12 months.

Taxable entities

Resident companies are liable to corporate income tax on their worldwide income, including capital gains.

A company is resident in Spain for tax purposes under any of the following conditions:

- when it is incorporated in accordance with Spanish law;
- when its head office is within Spanish territory; or

- when its effective management centre is within Spanish territory.

Exemptions

- Public entities;
- the Bank of Spain and other official institutions; and
- social security institutions.

Taxable base

As a general principle, the taxable base is the profit of the company determined through accountancy rules and modified by the rules provided in the tax regulation.

Special provisions are provided for the following matters:

- depreciation of fixed assets;
- provisions for depreciation of other assets (bad debts, portfolio investments, etc.);
- accruals;
- non-monetary transactions;
- transactions between related parties;
- transfer of real estate (an inflation correction is available);
- change of residence;
- temporary imputation; and for
- thin capitalisation.

Related party transactions

Transactions between associated companies must be conducted on an arm's length basis.

Depreciation

Depreciation is allowed as follows:

- at rates and terms established by the tax regulations for various economic and industrial sectors (RD 537/1997); and
- under a depreciation plan specifically authorised by the tax office or any system subsequently agreed to by the tax office.

The following depreciation rates may be used as a general guide:

Asset	*Maximum rate (%)*	*Maximum period*
Industrial buildings	3-4	50-68 years
Plant and machinery	10-12	18-20 years
Tools	30-33	6-8 years

Small companies are allowed to accelerate their fiscal depreciation by 150%.

Free and accelerated depreciation is allowed, among other cases, in R&D assets.

Thin capitalisation

There is a debt-to-equity ratio of 3:1. Over this proportion any interest is considered a dividend.

Reinvestment of extraordinary profits

When the amount obtained from an assets transmission would be reinvested in new assets, the capital gain obtained from the transfer will be deferred.

The reintegration will be deferred by two ways:

- if the new asset is depreciable, the reintegration takes part during the depreciation; or
- if the new asset is undepreciable, the reintegration takes part during the next seven years after the period to invest (a year before or three years after the transmission).

Carry-forward of tax losses

If the taxable base is not enough to compensate the tax losses, it can be offset during the next ten years.

Tax rates

General rate: 35%.

Special rates are applicable to certain entities. Among others, the following rates are provided.

- 30% for small companies (those under €3 million of turnover);
- 25% for mutual institutions, associations, foundations etc;

- 20% for specially protected co-operatives;
- 10% for Foundations incorporated under L. 30/94;
- 1% for investment institutions;
- 0% for pension plans; and
- 40% for the hydrocarbons sector.

Deductions

Double taxation allowances

Internal

When dividends or similar amounts are included in the taxable base, a tax credit is available.

If the participation in the subsidiary is over 5% and the holding has been maintained for more than one year, the tax credit equals the amount received, multiplied by the tax rate.

If not, the tax credit is 50% of the amount received, multiplied by the tax rate.

The tax credit is also applicable in some transactions which might otherwise suffer double taxation. Among those transactions we must underline the transfer of shares. Under certain conditions the transfer of shares is liable to the tax credit calculated upon the increase of retained earnings during the period of holding.

If the tax quota is under the available tax credit, it can be applied during the next seven years.

International

Tax credits provided in the internal regulation are applicable only when its effect is better than an applicable Tax Treaty.

The general applicable tax credit follows the imputation system. Consequently, the deduction is the lower amount between the following:

- the amount effectively paid; or
- the tax quota that corresponds to the gross income received.

Taxes paid abroad must be included in the taxable base.

If the tax quota is under the available tax credit, the credit can be applied during the next seven years.

The exemption system is applicable to income obtained through permanent establishments. Consequently, when a foreign income has been included in the gross income it has to be subtracted from the taxable base.

Dividends and capital gains corresponding to foreign participated companies

Subject to certain conditions, dividends and capital gains corresponding to foreign participated companies are fully exempt from corporate tax. The main requirements are the following:

- 5% of participation, as minimum;
- participation acquired one year before;
- the participated company must have been subject to an income tax; and
- the income received cannot come from passive income.

When the exemption is not applicable, the imputation system (also subject to certain limitations) can be used. In this case, the deduction is the lower amount between the following:

- the corporate tax paid by the participated company; or
- the part of the tax quota that corresponds to the dividends received.

Deduction of investments abroad

Overseas investment is tax deductible (for the amount invested into the acquisition of the fixed capital of non-resident companies giving the majority of vote rights) if the following conditions are fulfilled:

- the non-resident companies must obtain active income;
- the activity of the non-resident company must be operated for the first time (i.e. not acquired from a third party); and
- the non-resident companies must be non-EU resident.

The maximum deductible is €3,005,605.22 if it exceeds 25% of the taxable base.

It should be noted that it is not a permanent deduction; it is only a deferral which unwinds during the following four years.

Bonus deductions from tax base

Income obtained in Ceuta and Melilla	50%
Income from book exports	99%
Profits from local public services	99%

Incentive tax credits

The Corporate Income Tax Law contains a system of tax deductions for certain investments and the creation of new employment. The annual Finance Law modifies the deductions and conditions each year.

The deductions available for 2001 are:

- 5% in book edition;
- 20% of any amount invested in Spanish audio-visual products;
- 5% in audio-visual production activities;
- 10% of any amount invested in environment protection;
- 25% for export companies:
  - the amount invested in the formation of permanent establishments or the acquisition of at least 25% of the capital of foreign companies or new foreign subsidiaries, provided that the activities of the permanent establishment or the foreign company or subsidiary are directly related to export activities of the Spanish taxpayer;
  - 25% of payments abroad for publicity with a projected beneficial period of more than one year, for the introduction of new products, for investigation and opening of new markets and for attendance at trade shows and fairs;
- 30/50% (+10%) in research and development activities;
- 10/15% in technological research;
- 10% of any amount invested in the promotion of the information and communication technologies;
- 10% on assets considered to be part of the national heritage; and
- 5% or 10 % for professional education and training of employees:
  - Pesetas 800,000 for an increase of one effective year of employment for disabled persons and employees more than 45 years old.

The deductions mentioned above are subject to an overall limit of 35% of the normal corporate income tax.

Other special tax allowances are granted to specific companies.

The tax deductions detailed in this paragraph are only available to resident companies and the Spanish permanent establishments of non-resident companies.

Payment terms

The corporate tax payment time is six months and 25 days after the closing of the corporate year.

It should be noted that resident companies and those non-resident companies which have a permanent establishment in Spain, are required to make payments on account of corporate income tax in April, October and December (during the first 20 days of each month). Each payment on account is calculated as follows:

- at 18% of the tax payable for the previous fiscal year; or
- at five-sevenths of the tax payable (applying normal tax rates) for the first 3, 9 or 11 months of the taxable period, deducting any amounts previously paid, plus any withholding tax.

Companies are required to decide which option to follow and to communicate their choice to the Tax Administration.

Special tax regimes

The following tax regimes are provided:

- agencies of economic interests;
- temporary union enterprises;
- capital risk entities and founds;
- collective investment institutions;
- fiscal transparency;
- groups of companies (consolidation);
- reorganisations: mergers, spin-offs, contributions of assets, and exchange of values;
- mining;
- hydrocarbons;
- small business: those under €3 million of turnover;
- contracts of leasing;

- foreign holdings (ETVE);
- entities partially exempted; and
- international tax transparency (CFC rules).

Territorial regulations

Companies established in Canary Islands enjoy special reductions and allowances.

The tax regulation of the Basque Country is partially governed by autonomous regulation. Some special regulations are provided for companies that totally or partially perform their activities in the said territory.

Personal taxes

Personal income tax (IRPF)

Taxable individuals

Taxpayers in Spain can be either individuals or family units (husband, wife and children who live at home).

Residents

Residence in Spain for tax purposes is determined according to the following rules:

- permanent presence in Spain for more than 183 days during a calendar year; temporary absences are included as presence in Spain unless the taxpayer can prove his residence for 183 days in another country for that calendar year;
- when the taxpayer has his base or the base for his economic or professional activities in Spain (bulk of economic interests); and
- unless he can prove the contrary, the Spanish tax authorities will presume that an individual has his or her residence in Spain when the spouse, not legally separated (and any under-age children) are resident in Spain.

An individual who is resident in Spain for tax purposes will be subject to income tax on his worldwide income.

Taxes on income

Withholding tax will be retained from most types of income that an individual can obtain or earn in Spain.

The amount of withholding tax suffered during a year will reduce the income tax payable and may be refunded should it exceed the tax payable.

Income tax is assessed on taxable income. Taxable income is the total amount of net income and net capital gains earned by the individual during the calendar year.

Sources of income

Remuneration in kind is subject to withholding tax and is included as taxable income according to the type of income from which it is derived.

Income earned from employment

This includes any kind of income derived directly or indirectly from dependant personal services.

Income earned from business activities

This includes income from industrial activities, farming, forestry and trade, where the individual owns, either wholly or in part, the business or the plant and where he or she holds the ownership directly and not through a corporate entity.

Income from professional or artistic activities

This includes any kind of income derived directly or indirectly from independant, professional or artistic work.

Income from an interest or holdings in any type of entity

Income obtained in this manner from entities resident in Spain must be included as part of the taxable income obtained from personal assets. The amount of income to be included as part of the taxable income is that which results from applying the following percentages to the income received:

Mutual assurance funds	125%
Collective investment funds	100%
All other income	140%

This system is also applicable to income imputed by means of domestic fiscal transparency (see below).

Once the taxpayer has calculated the total income tax payable, the excess income calculated as above (and any amounts withheld at source) may be deducted to arrive at the net tax payable.

Capital gains

Any profit derived from the transfer of rights or assets is considered to be a capital gain. The profit is generally taxable on the difference between disposal value and original acquisition cost.

Capital gains obtained in a period exceeding a year are subject to a flat rate of 18%. Only the acquisition value of immovable assets need be modified to correct the effect of inflation.

The coefficients to correct for inflation, depend on the acquisition year.

Year of acquisition	*Co-efficient*
1994 and prior	1.038
1995 (and 31 December 1994)	1.097
1996	1.059
1997	1.038
1998	1.018
1999	1.000

Assets acquired before 31 December 1994 receive a different tax treatment. The taxable profit for a disposal of immovable assets will be reduced by 11% for every year in which the right or asset has formed part of the taxpayer's wealth, commencing with the third year of ownership. When disposing of shares, the rate is 25% (if listed on the Stock Exchange). When disposing of other private shares or assets, the rate is 8%.

Income from rights or assets

This includes income derived from any right or asset not used in a business, trade or professional or artistic activity. The gross amount of dividends, interest, royalties, rentals and other such services is included as taxable income.

Taxation of fiscally transparent entities

Taxation of fiscally transparent entities is only applicable to resident individuals.

Both the taxable income and any deductions relating to an entity considered to be fiscally transparent are apportioned to the resident individuals in accordance with the interest or shareholding in the entity.

Non-residents who have an interest or hold shares in fiscally transparent entities will receive ordinary dividends.

Personal allowances and deductions

General rules

Personal minimum deductions have been introduced to cover normal expenses incurred by an individual. The table of deductions is as follows:

	Ptas.
General	550,000
Individual more than 65 years old	650,000
Disabled individual (33%–65%)	850,000
Disabled individuals (more than 65%)	1,150,000

Deductions depend on the source of the income. For income earned from employment, a deduction of between Ptas 375,000 and 500,000 is allowed, according to the income circumstance.

Deductions for children and others

For each single child under the age of 30 living with the taxpayer and having an annual income that does not exceed the minimum inter-professional salary granted by the state, the following allowances may be claimed:

First and second child	Ptas 200,000 each
Third child	Ptas 300,000
Additional children	Ptas 300,000 each

Irregular income

When income arises irregularly, or when regular but the production cycle exceeds two years, a general reduction of 30% is applicable, irrespective of the years in which it has been generated.

Capital gains or losses are taxed separately from other income and liable to a flat rate of 20% (17% for the State and 3% for Autonomous Communities). Capital losses can only be offset against capital gains and not against other kinds of income.

Losses

Losses can be offset against positive taxable income during the four subsequent years, and excess withholding tax for the year of loss is refundable.

Special family rules

Individuals can choose between being taxed individually or as a family. The option determines the application of different minimum vital deductions, although there is a single table of tax rates.

Tax rates

General rules

A proportion of personal income tax is paid to the State and a proportion is paid to the Autonomous Communities.

Taxable income is taxed as follows:

State

Taxable income (Ptas)	*Tax payable (Ptas)*	*Marginal income (Ptas)*	*Rate on margin (%)*
0	0	600,000	15.00
600,000	90,000	1,500,000	20.17
2,100,000	392,550	2,000,000	23.57
4,100,000	863,950	2,500,000	31.48
6,600,000	1,650,950	4,400,000	38.07
11,000,000	3,326,030	upward	39.60

Autonomous Communities

Taxable income (Ptas)	*Tax payable (Ptas)*	*Marginal income (Ptas)*	*Rate on margin (%)*
0	0	600,000	3,00
600,000	18,000	1,500,000	3.83
2,100,000	75,450	2,000,000	4.73
4,100,000	170,050	2,500,000	5.72
6,600,000	313,050	4,400,000	6.93
11,000,000	617,970	upward	8.40

Tax deductions

The following deductions may not be claimed by non-resident taxpayers, except when the income is obtained through a permanent establishment in Spain.

Residents may claim deductions from tax payable as follows.

Deductions for investments

- 15% of the amount paid for the acquisition of the principal residence (the costs of construction and restoration are also included if the residence is held by the taxpayer for a minimum of three years);
- 15% of the amount invested in the acquisition, conservation, repair, restoration, distribution and display of assets which are considered to be part of the national heritage, where those assets are held by the taxpayer for a minimum of three years.

Deductions for professionals and businessmen

- The same deductions and allowances enjoyed by companies are also granted to professionals and businessmen who are subject to tax under the general income tax regime.

Deduction for donations

- 20% of the donations to the State, or to other beneficial or cultural entities, of assets considered as part of the national heritage.
- 10% of the donations to the State, or to other beneficial or cultural entities.

Other deductions and allowances

- 40% or 25% of the amount of dividends received by the taxpayer from companies subject to Spanish corporation tax.
- Taxpayers resident in Ceuta and Melilla may enjoy a deduction of 50% on tax payable depending on the time of effective residency in those locations.

The amounts and limits applicable to tax deductions and allowances vary where the taxpayer is a family unit.

Autonomous Communities offer varying allowances and reliefs according to circumstance.

Tax payment

Amounts withheld at source

Tax withheld at source is deducted from the tax payable after taking into account all other deductions and allowances.

Prepayment

Businessmen and professionals must make quarterly payments of income tax on account.

Taxable period

The taxable period is the calendar year.

Filing requirements

Residents and non-residents are required to file a tax return.

Resident taxpayers may be exempt from filing a tax return if:

- their annual income from employment is less than Ptas 3,500,000;
- there is no business or professional income included in the annual income; or
- capital gains and income from rights or assets is less than Ptas 250,000.

Other taxes

Wealth tax

Wealth tax is levied progressively applying the following scale.

Taxable wealth (Ptas)	*Tax payable (Ptas)*	*Marginal wealth (Ptas)*	*Rate on margin (%)*
0	0	27,262,000	0.2
27,262,000	54,524	27,262,000	0.3
54,524,000	136,310	54,524,000	0.5
109,048,000	408,930	109,048,000	0.9
218,096,000	1,390,362	218,096,000	1.3
436,192,000	4,225,610	436,192,000	1.7
872,384,000	11,640,874	872,384,000	2.1
1,744,768,000	29,960,938	Forward	2.5

The first Ptas 17,300,000 of wealth are not subject to tax.

Shareholdings in private active companies are tax exempt if the taxpayer has a minimum 15% ownership of the company and his or her remuneration (in respect of employment as a director) is a substantial part of his income.

A number of personal allowances and deductions are granted for resident taxpayers.

Estate and gift tax

These taxes are levied on transfers on inheritance and on gifts. Rates are calculated on a progressive basis depending upon the value of the rights or assets transferred and the relationship between transferor and transferee. For the avoidance of international double taxation there are estate and gift tax treaties in force with France, Sweden and Greece.

Social security

Businesses and employees are obliged to contribute to the social security system. This system covers contingencies such as unemployment, accidents at work, sickness benefit, the guaranteed wage and the Professional Training Fund.

The employer's cost is 30.8% of the employee's gross wage. The employee's contribution is deducted by the employer from salary payments at the rate of approximately 6.4%.

Social security contributions are limited to certain maximum amounts depending on an employee's status.

Capital duty and transfer tax

Transfers of assets when the transaction is not subject to VAT are subject to this tax at varying rates (real estate 6%; goods 4%) and capital increases and decreases are taxed at 1%.

Value added tax

Since 1 January 1993, Spanish legislation has adopted the system of VAT common to EU countries and the rates are as follows:

Super Reduced	4%
Reduced	7%
Normal	16%

Real estate taxes

This is a tax on property and on the increase in value of urban real estate (known as*'Impuesto sobre el incremento del valor, de los terrenos'*).

In general, these are levied at various rates on most imported commodities in line with EU legislation.

Special taxes

Special taxes are levied on alcohol, alcoholic beverages, fuels, tobacco and insurance premiums.

Stamp duty

Stamp duty is levied on certain documentation.

Other local taxes

Other local taxes include business licence tax, motor vehicle tax and taxes on construction, installations and works.

Double tax relief

Foreign source income is taxed as a regular income for resident taxpayers (see under 'Corporate Tax').

Spanish income and corporate tax regulations allow credit for foreign tax suffered (subject to certain limits).

Non-resident income tax

Since 1999, there is a new legislation for non-residents in Spain: the Non-resident Income Tax Act (L. 41/98). This new tax is levied on the income obtained by non-residents in the Spanish territory. The only distinction in this legislation is the existence of a permanent establishment in the operations of non-resident persons in Spain.

Income obtained through permanent establishments

Non-resident persons (corporate or individuals) who operate in Spain through a permanent establishment are liable to corporate tax or individual tax on their income arising in Spain, including capital gains.

Income obtained without permanent establishment

General conditions

- The taxpayers are both individuals and corporate, without distinction;
- There is no tax year, the withholding tax system applies every time a new income is obtained;
- There is no possibility to offset gains and losses;
- International tax treaties are applicable;
- Non-residents must file a tax return every time they get income from Spanish territory (within four months after completion of a sale of real estate and within a month for other income after that income has been earned).

Non-residents may be required by the Spanish Tax Authorities to appoint a tax representative (a person or legal entity) domiciled in Spain to represent them before the Tax Authorities.

Taxable income

- 25% tax is charged on income from real estate property in Spain.
- Tax on real estate for non-resident companies is levied on real estate which is not related to a commercial, industrial or professional activity. The rate of tax is 3% of the rateable value of the real estate. It is possible to request an exemption from this tax by declaring the origin of the funds invested and the names of the ultimate beneficial owners of the foreign company.
- 18% on dividends, except in the case of EU members. Due to EU parent/subsidiary legislation, dividends paid from Spanish resident companies to EU resident companies suffer no withholding tax where the following requirements are fulfilled:
  - the EU parent company owns 25% or more of the subsidiary;
  - the shares are owned for at least 1 year;
  - the parent and subsidiary are subject to tax.

  Special exemptions are given for some types of income and capital gains arising from shares and Spanish bonds or securities.
- 18% on interests, except for members of the EU. The tax is withheld at a general rate of 18%. No withholding tax is levied on interest payments to the residents of other EU member states and distributions to parent companies resident in the EU are not

subject to withholding tax, provided that certain conditions are fulfilled. Treasury Bonds are tax-exempt.

- 25% on royalties.
- 35% on capital gains on assets situated in Spain. Non-resident individuals are subject to tax only on income and capital gains arising inside Spanish territory or paid by a person or entity resident in Spain, except when (in the latter case) the income is paid by a permanent establishment of that entity located outside Spain. When capital gains are realised in Spain by non-residents without a permanent establishment, the acquisition value is determined using the exchange rate at the date of disposal.
- 8% on public pensions.
- 25% on the remaining categories of income from Spanish sources.

The rates applying to the income of non-resident companies with no permanent establishment in Spain are limited by double taxation treaties.

The following table illustrates the rates currently in force in the selected treaty countries.

Country of residence	*Royalties (%)*	*Interest (%)*	*Dividends (%)*
Non-treaty countries	25	18	18
Selected treaty countries:	5	5	15/10 (a)
Austria			
Argentina	15/10 (c)	12,5	15710 (a)
Australia	10	10	15
Belgium (g)	5	15 (f)	15
Bolivia	15	15	10/15 (a)
Brazil	15/10 (c)	15/10 (b)	15
Bulgaria	0	0	5/15 (a)
Canada	0/10	15	15
Czech Republic	0/5 (c)	0	15/5 (a)
China	10	10	0
Cuba	5	10	5/15
Denmark (g)	6	10 (f)	15/10 (a)
Ecuador	10	5-10	15
Finland	5	10	15/10 (a)
France (g)	6	10 (f)	15/10 (a)
Germany (g)	5	10 (f)	15/10 (a)
Hungary	0	0	15/5 (a)
Italy (g)	4/8 (c)	12 (f)	15
India	20/10	15	15

Indonesia	10	10	15/10 (a)
Ireland	5	10	15
Israel	5/7	5/10	10
Japan	10	10	15/10 (a)
Korea	10	10	10/15 (a)
Luxembourg (g)	10	10 (f)	15/10 (a)
Mexico	10	15	5/15
Morocco	5/10 (c)	10	15/10 (a)
Netherlands (g)	6	10 (f)	15/10 (a)
Norway	5	10	15/10 (a)
Philippines	10/15/20	15/10	15/10 (a)
Poland	0/10 (c)	0	15/5 (a)
Portugal (g)	5	15 (f)	15/10 (a)
Romania	10	10	15/10 (a)
Russian Federation	0/5	10	18 (a)
Sweden	10	15	15/10 (a)
Switzerland	5	10	15/10 (a)
Thailand	15	10/15	10
Tunisia	10	5/10 (d)	15/5 (d)
United Kingdom (g)	10	12 (f)	15/10 (a)
USA (e)	5/8/10 (c)	10	15/10 (a)
URSS	5	0	18

Notes

(a) The reduced rate on dividends is applicable where the shareholder has a qualifying interest in the capital of the dividend-paying company. The capital share required varies from one agreement to the other.

(b) The reduced rate is applicable in those cases where interest is paid to financial entities on loans or credits for ten years or more which finance the acquisition of capital assets.

(c) The reduced rate is applicable in the case of royalties for the use of copyrights (including films).

(d) When the term of the loan is longer than seven years, the reduced rate is applicable.

(e) In force since 25 November 1990.

(f) At the present time, interest relating to personal property paid to residents from other EU members with no permanent establishment in a Spanish territory are not subject to any tax in Spain, in accordance with Spanish tax law.

(g) As a result of the implementation of the EU Parent Subsidiary Directive there is no withholding tax levied on distributions made to a parent company resident in an EU member state, provided that a substantial interest (i.e. 25% or more) has been held for at least 2 years.

Exchange control

Exchange control has been greatly relaxed since 1 February 1992 and an almost total liberalisation exists since 1999. Nevertheless, certain operations will still require verification from the Spanish authorities.

As a general rule, foreign investments in Spain and Spanish investments abroad are free from controls, although they may in certain cases be subject to prior verification by the Spanish Exchange Control Authorities (*'Dirección General de Transacciones Exteriores'*).

Sri Lanka

B R De Silva & Co.

Corporate taxes

Taxable entities

Resident companies

A company is considered resident if it is incorporated in Sri Lanka or if the control and management of its business is exercised there. Resident companies are taxable on income from all sources except dividends received from other resident companies.

Non-resident companies

A non-resident company is one which is controlled from abroad or which has its head office overseas. Such companies are taxed on income derived from or arising in Sri Lanka as well as on funds remitted out of Sri Lanka.

Taxes imposed

Taxes are payable on an estimated basis, calculated on the tax liability of the previous year, and the final tax must be paid within six months of the end of the year of assessment.

Rates of tax

Corporate tax rates are applicable to both resident and non-resident companies and are as follows:

Companies engaged in agriculture, fisheries, livestock, tourism & construction	15%
Export-oriented companies	15%
Listed companies (subject to spread of shareholding)	30%
Other companies	35%

Income subject to tax

All income arising in Sri Lanka or income deemed to arise under the taxing statutes is subject to tax.

Deductions

General rules

All outgoings and expenses incurred by a person in the production of income are deductible in arriving at statutory income.

Depreciation

For the purpose of claiming depreciation allowances, assets are broadly categorised as follows:

Plant, machinery, fixtures & equipment (including computer hardware and software)	50% on cost
Office furniture & commercial vehicles	25% on cost
Buildings constructed	6 $^2/_3$% on cost
Motor coach for transportation of employees	100% on cost

Non-deductible expenses

Entertainment, gifts and donations are not deductible and foreign travelling expenses are specifically disallowed except where such expenditure is incurred directly in relation to exports, earned foreign currency income or full-time staff training.

Special provisions – deductible expenses

Company formation expenses, research and development expenses and all expenses relating to plantations and animal husbandry (including capital expenditure on land development and cultivation) are deductible.

Investment incentives and special benefits

Tax concessions have been granted to both new and existing industries and services with the aim of promoting the diversification of Sri Lanka's export industries and to encourage investment in large-scale development projects, with a special emphasis on infrastructure.

The tax concessions granted are as follows:

- profits are exempt from income tax for specified periods or tax is levied at a preferential rate;

- dividends distributed are exempt from income tax or taxed at preferential rate in the hands of shareholders;
- exemption from import duty, excise duty on import of capital goods and raw materials;
- dividends paid to any person, including a non-resident, during the tax holiday period;
- capital gains arising on the sale of shares in quoted public companies and approved companies; and
- concessions on remittances of funds.

Tax exemptions have been granted under the following listed projects:

Project	*Tax Holiday*
Thrust industries engaged in exports (electronics, ceramic and glassware, rubber-based industries, engineering industries, approved pioneering industries)	5 to 20 years
Software development and training	5 to 8 years
Operating two-tier hospitals	10 years
Construction of housing units	7 to 10 years
Export of gems and jewellery	no specific time period
Sale of gold, gems and jewellery	no specific time period
Transport of workers from export processing zones	5 years
Regional operating headquarters managing offshore company	5 years
Textiles industry (exports)	5 years
Large-scale development projects (manufacture of cement, steel, textiles)	10 to 20 years
Provision of technical training	5 years
Provision of refrigerated transport or cold room storage or related services	5 years
Non-plantation agriculture and specified agricultural activities	10 years
Cultivation and export of fresh vegetables/ fruits	10 years
Agricultural marketing	5 years
Manufacture and export of apparel	5 years

Advance technology package

Tax concessions have been granted to newly formed and expanded undertakings which include animal husbandry, fisheries, tourism and community development projects.

The package was introduced to improve processing for manufacturing, upgrading quality, productivity and technical skills, with a better utilisation of raw material.

Concessions granted are as follows:

- a five year tax holiday on profits for newly formed companies and on incremental profits for companies with expanded undertakings;
- the exemption of distributed dividends from income tax in the hands of recipient shareholders; and
- the waiver of import duty on imports of plant and machinery.

In order to take advantage of the package, the following conditions must be met:

- a minimum employment for 50 persons within a specific period;
- the company should not be formed by splitting up or acquiring any business previously in existence;
- the qualifying activity should be carried out during the tax holiday period; and
- approval must be before 31 March 2002.

Losses	*Carry-forward period*
Agricultural losses	limited to 12 years
Other trade losses	limited to 7 years
Capital losses	no limit
Losses due to capital allowances	no limit

Personal taxes

Taxable individuals

Residents

If an individual is physically present in Sri Lanka for 183 days or more during any year of assessment, then he or she is deemed resident throughout that year of assessment.

A resident of Sri Lanka is taxed on income on a worldwide basis with relief for any foreign taxes paid.

Where an individual is resident for two or more consecutive years of assessment, then he is deemed resident until such time as he is absent from Sri Lanka for an unbroken period of 365 days and, when so absent, is deemed non-resident from the commencement of the year of assessment in which such absence begins.

Where an individual is present in Sri Lanka for a period (or periods) not exceeding an aggregate of 30 days and, but for such presence, would have been deemed non-resident, he will be treated as having spent that period outside Sri Lanka.

Non-residents

All non-residents are liable to Sri Lankan income tax on all income arising in Sri Lanka, with the exception of consultants working for the Government of Sri Lanka and other specified organisations.

Income arising in Sri Lanka includes income from:

- investments;
- services rendered in Sri Lanka;
- property in Sri Lanka;
- business transacted in Sri Lanka; and from
- royalties.

Taxes on income

Income taxes in Sri Lanka are levied by central government only.

Sources of income

Employment income

This includes all income derived from employment, such as salary, allowances, medical benefits, payments in respect of hotel bills, school fees, furnishing, other non-cash benefits etc., rent on residence provided, wages of employees provided and income tax paid on an employee's behalf.

Salary paid in Sri Lanka is exempt if a non-resident is employed by the United Nations Organisation (UNO) is under contract to the

Government of Sri Lanka or any other approved body or is engaged in certain tax exempt undertakings.

Expatriate taxation

A non-resident employed in Sri Lanka is liable to income tax at a concessionary rate of 15% for a period of five years from the date of commencement of his/her employment in Sri Lanka. Any income arising abroad during this period is exempt from income tax.

Business income

Business income is determined in the same way as for companies.

Capital gains

Any movement in the value of property is taken into account when taxing the capital gain on the disposal of a property and is calculated on a progressive scale (from 5% to 25%), depending on the number of years for which the property was owned. However, any capital gain arising from a change of ownership within two years will be subject to the normal rate of income tax.

The disposal of a property held for more than 25 years and acquired by way of purchase (by gift or inherited) is tax exempt.

Any capital gain arising on the sale of shares in a quoted public company (QPC) is exempt. Exempt assets are also assets of a personal nature, i.e. household effects, a motorcar or any other specific assets.

Capital losses can be set off against capital gains or carried forward to be set off against future capital gains. Capital losses cannot be set off against trading income.

Interest

All interest paid to taxable depositors by banks and financial institutions is subject to withholding tax of 10% and is subject to normal rates of tax in the computation of taxable income, with credit given for the withholding tax deducted.

Dividends

Any company, other than a quoted public company, is required to deduct 15% from gross dividends payable and remit such amount to the Commissioner General of Inland Revenue.

A withholding tax of 15% should be deducted by the quoted public company when dividends are paid to non-resident shareholders.

Any resident receiving such a net dividend is deemed to receive a gross dividend which includes the tax deducted at source, and is entitled to a tax credit of the withholding tax as well as advance company tax (ACT).

Dividend income for tax purposes = Gross Dividend + ACT

No ACT is payable in respect of non-resident shareholders.

Advance company tax (ACT)

ACT is payable when a resident company pays dividends to its resident shareholders. The rate of ACT varies, depending on the income tax rate of the company.

Exempt income

The following income is exempt:

- surrender value of a life insurance policy;
- terminal benefits of employment up to Rs.500,000;
- dividends received from exempt companies;
- income of a casual and non-recurring nature, including windfalls;
- from 1 January 1978, the first sale by an individual of a house used solely for residential purposes; and
- interest received from certain foreign currency bank accounts.

Tax-free allowances and deductions

For the years of assessment 1999/2000 & 2000/01, this is Rs.144,000.

Qualifying payments

Qualifying payment deduction is limited to the lower of one-third of the assessable income or Rs.25,000. A further Rs.25,000 is allowed in respect of premium paid on life and medical insurance. Qualifying payments are deductible from the assessable income and the entire investment can be deducted without any upper limit as a qualifying payment, if invested in specified projects.

Special family rules

There is no aggregating of income of members of a family other than aggregating the income of an unmarried child under 18 years with that of the parent.

Husband and wife are assessed separately.

Partnerships

Profits made by partnerships are allocated to the partners in accordance with the partnership agreement and are taxed in the partner's hands.

Rates of tax

Year of assessment 2000/01

On the first Rs.100,000 of the taxable income	10%
On the next Rs.100,000 of the taxable income	15%
On the next Rs.100,000 of the taxable income	25%
On the balance of the taxable income	35%

Payment of tax

Employment income

Taxes are deducted and remitted on a Pay-As-You-Earn (PAYE) basis and the employer is liable for any shortfall in remittance.

Interest/dividend income

Withholding taxes of 10% and 15% are deductible on interest and dividend income respectively, and credit is available for such deductions.

Taxes for any year of assessment are payable in four quarterly instalments. So, for the year commencing 1 April 2001 (Y/A 2001/02), taxes would be payable on 15 August 2001, 15 November 2001, 15 February 2002 and on 15 May 2002, with the final payment by 30 September 2002 incorporating any shortfall to avoid penalties.

Other taxes

Turnover tax

Turnover tax has been replaced with a goods and services tax, but still applies to financiers, moneylenders, bankers, ship owners and charterers.

Customs duty

Customs duty is charged on imports. The maximum tariff is 30%. Exemptions include the importation of gems and gold, computer software, telecommunication equipment, buses and coaches and any items related to the assembly thereof. Duty concessions are also available, subject to conditions in the binding, original information agreement (so the source of the goods is also relevant).

National security levy

National security levy is payable by importers, manufacturers, bankers, financiers and insurers at 6.5% and on imported capital goods at 0.5%. From 15 February 2000, businesses providing any services are also liable to national security levy at 6.5%. (exemptions are given for certain types of businesses).

Goods and services tax (GST)

GST is a consumption tax and is levied on the added value. Rates of GST are zero and 12.5%.

The following activities are zero-rated:

- export of goods;
- services relating to movable/immovable property outside Sri Lanka;
- services relating to repair of foreign ships or aircraft;
- services relating to goods imported to re-export;
- international transportation of goods or passengers; and
- services connected with the use outside Sri Lanka of intellectual property rights such as patents, copyright, trademarks, licences or other assets.

In the case of zero-rated activities, no output tax is payable, but input tax can be claimed as refund. In the case of tax-exempt activities no output tax is payable and no input tax is claimable.

Provincial taxes

Wholesale and retail are subject to sales tax at 1%, with the following exceptions:

Gems, gold and timber	5%
Jewellery and costume jewellery	10%

Excise duties are applicable to tobacco and alcohol and on various imported and manufactured goods.

Tax treaties and tax rates

Double taxation relief agreements are in force with the following countries (and rates of taxes are shown below):

Country	*Dividends (%)*	*Interest (%)*	*Royalties (%)*
Australia	15	10	10
Bangladesh	15	15	15
Belgium	15	10	10
Canada	15	15	10
Czech Republic	15	10	10
Denmark	15	10	10
Finland	15	10	10
France	15	10	10
Germany	15	10	10
India	15	10	10
Indonesia	15	15	15
Italy	15	10	10
Japan	–	–	0
Korea	10	10	10
Malaysia	15	10	10
Netherlands	10	10	10
Norway	15	10	10
Oman (limited agreement)	–	–	–
Pakistan	15	10	20
Poland	15	10	10
Romania	12.5	10	10
Singapore	15	10	15
Sweden	15	10	10
Switzerland	15	10	10
Thailand	15	10	15
United Kingdom	15	10	10

United Arab Emirates (limited agreement)	–	–	–
Yugoslavia	12.5	10	10
Mauritius	10/15	10	10
Nepal	–	–	–
Saudi Arabia	–	–	–

Detailed rules apply to certain reduced rates.

Countries to be ratified/under discussion are:

Austria
Bulgaria
Iran
Jordan
Kuwait
New Zealand
Philippines
Russia
Egypt
Cyprus
South Africa.

Sweden

Nexia Revision Stockholm

Corporate taxes

Taxable entities

Resident companies

Resident companies are liable to corporate tax on their worldwide income, including capital gains.

A company which is incorporated under Swedish Company law is considered to be a resident company.

Non-resident companies

Companies incorporated outside Sweden are taxed on income arising in Sweden if the company is deemed to have established a permanent place of business in Sweden. This would include such things as an office or factory providing evidence that the company is not trading in Sweden on a temporary basis. The concept of income includes capital gains on business assets and real property in Sweden.

Tax year and filing requirements

The tax year is the calendar year, but the financial year of a company may be 1 May to 30 April, 1 July to 30 June or 1 September to 31 August.

Company tax returns must be filed no later than 31 March in the subsequent year. It is possible to prolong the filing date until 15 June.

Taxes imposed

Companies are subject to national income tax.

Payments on account of corporate income tax are required, based on an estimate of income. Instalments based on this preliminary tax bill are payable every month, any additional payments on final computation are due 90 days after the company has received its notice of assessment. The tax authorities send out these notices sometime between September and December in the year of assessment.

Rates of tax

National income tax is calculated at a flat rate of 28%.

Income subject to tax

General rules

Corporate income tax is levied annually on the taxable income of the company. Taxable income is computed by adjusting net income: add disallowed cost items and subtract certain deductible items.

Income from all sources (business activities, capital investment, interest and capital gains) is aggregated to arrive at gross income. There is no separate tax on capital gains or any other source of income. An important feature of Swedish taxation is the connection between the annual accounts and the tax return. The annual accounts are used as an assessment base for the tax return and appropriations made in the books must correspond with the tax return, with certain exceptions as explained below (see 'Deductions – general rules').

This principle means that a Swedish income statement often consists of two parts, the first giving a true and fair result for the year and the second making adjustments and appropriations to show the taxable income.

Stock/inventory valuation

Stock must be valued in accordance with sound business practice, in most cases at the lower of cost or market value. The FIFO method must be used.

Capital gains and losses

Capital gains and losses are usually treated in the same way as other business income. The difference between the selling and the purchase price is a part of the taxable income.

Capital losses are deductible from any other income, with one exception: losses from the sale of shares and other securities that are held as portfolio investments are deductible only from capital gains made on the same type of assets.

Sweden

According to a Government proposal, capital gains from sale of shares will be tax-free under certain conditions. Capital gain from sales of shares in a company that is not listed on the stock exchange will be tax-free. If the shares are listed on a stock exchange, the company selling the shares must own more than 10% of the voting shares in the company, or show that the shareholding is for business purposes in order to get a tax-free capital gain. Furthermore, the company must hold the shares more than one year to achieve the tax-free status. Consequently capital losses will not be deductible in the above-mentioned situations. The proposed law is not applicable on sales of shell companies. Should the proposal will be legalised, the new law will come into force on 1 January 2002.

Dividends

Dividends paid are not deductible in arriving at taxable income. Dividends are normally subject to a withholding tax of 30% (or lower where prescribed by a tax treaty). Dividends paid by Swedish companies to non-resident companies will be exempted from Swedish withholding tax if the non-resident company holds at least 25% of the capital of the Swedish company. The non-resident company must also be subject to a tax in its country of residence similar to the taxation which Swedish companies are subject to, or it must be a company in the European Union fulfilling the EC Parent-Subsidiary Directive (90/435EEG).

Dividends received both from Swedish and foreign sources are taxed at the full corporate income tax rate. An exemption is available if participation exemption applies.

Dividends arising from investments in other companies, both Swedish and foreign, are exempt from corporate income tax in the hands of the recipient, provided the shareholding is at least 25% of the voting power and is not held as stock in trade.

Shareholders with holdings of less than 25% may be deemed to qualify in certain cases.

For holdings in foreign companies, there is a further requirement that the foreign company must be subject to a national profit tax in its own country similar to the Swedish tax provisions.

Deductions

General rules

All expenses directly related to business operations are generally allowed as deductions in arriving at a company's taxable profit.

As mentioned above, the results shown in the books of a Swedish company should be the same as the results shown in its tax return. The following differences may however arise between the profit in the books and the taxable profit:

- book depreciation on buildings or land improvements may not coincide with the depreciation for tax purposes;
- income tax is not an allowable expense;
- expenses for entertaining business contacts are allowed only up to specified limits;
- general provisions for bad debts are not allowed; and
- gifts, fines and membership subscriptions are not normally allowed.

Depreciation and amortisation

Machinery, equipment, patents and similar rights may be depreciated using one of two methods, the book depreciation method or the residual value method. The latter method is of minor interest to companies.

Book depreciation may be claimed to write down fixed assets (except buildings and land improvements) to the lower of the net book value of the assets arrived at on two different bases: a 20% straight-line method or a 30% declining balance method. The company may choose, at the end of each year, whichever basis is the most advantageous for that particular year.

When an asset is sold, or otherwise disposed of, the proceeds in excess of the tax written down value increase taxable income and vice versa.

Industrial buildings are normally depreciated by 4% per year, office buildings by 2% per year and land improvements by 5% per year.

Assets with an estimated useful life of less than three years may be written off in full in the year of purchase.

Assets with an acquisition cost, excluding VAT, of less than SEK 2,000 may be written off in full in the year of purchase.

For companies with gross sales over SEK 200, or with more than 200 employees, the limit is SEK 10,000.

The company can choose to charge less than the maximum allowable amount of depreciation in its accounts. For machines and equipment, only the amount actually charged can be claimed in the tax return.

Royalties

Royalties paid by a Swedish company for the right to use patents or similar rights are allowable deductions.

Interest

Interest paid by a Swedish company on borrowed capital is deductible for tax purposes.

Dividends

Dividends paid are not deductible.

Bad and doubtful debts

Debts should be valued on a specific basis. Write offs and provisions are deductible.

Reserves and provisions

The depreciation rules are the 30% declining balance method and the 20% straight-line method. The inventory may be valued at 97% of historical cost.

Employees' and directors' remuneration and benefits

Employees' and directors' remuneration and benefits are generally deductible.

Specifically non-deductible expenses

Gifts to business contacts above SEK 180 are not deductible. Costs that are related to entertainment of above SEK 90 per person are not deductible.

Investment incentives and special benefits

A company is entitled to defer taxation through allocation to untaxed reserves of an accrual accounting fund, where the reserve is limited to 25% of the annual income. The fund shall be cancelled to taxation not later than the sixth income year after allocation.

Related party transactions

Swedish tax law recognises the arm's length principle, and transactions between a Swedish legal entity (or similar) and a related party must be made at arm's length for tax purposes.

Losses

Losses can only be carried forward without time limitation. However, following a substantial change in the ownership of a company, the ability to carry the losses forward is limited to a maximum of 200% of the expense incurred by the owner to gain control of the company.

Corporate groups

Each company within a group of companies is taxed separately and there is no taxation at group level. It is, however, possible to relieve losses against profits within a group (i.e. group contributions). A group exists where more than 90% of the shares of a Swedish company are owned by a Swedish parent company.

Dividends from a holding of 25% or more are normally tax-free. In some cases, for shares held for business purposes, even a shareholding representing less than 25% can qualify for a tax-free dividend.

Restructuring of companies

Transactions below market value

The main rule for transactions below market value is that the seller will be taxed as if the transaction has taken place at market value, but there are certain exceptions from the main rule. Transactions below market value are allowed between parties that are taxable in Sweden. If the seller cannot give deductible group contributions to the buyer, the transaction needs to cover the seller's whole business or a line of business.

Exchange of shares

When a company or person, taxable in Sweden, sells shares to a company (whether Swedish or foreign) for a payment in shares, the seller can get a deferred taxation of the capital gain. The capital gain of the exchange will be calculated at the transfer, but the taxation of the gain will be deferred on request of the seller. A condition for deferment is that the acquiring company has to own more than 50% of the shares in the company (and these shares have to have been exchanged by the end of the year). The deferment will expire when the new shares are sold (or cease to exist) or when the seller ceases to be liable for tax in Sweden.

Group transfers of shares

If shares are transferred to a company within the same group, the taxation of the capital gain will be postponed on request of the seller. A 'group', for these purposes, is established if a parent company owns more than 50% of the voting shares in another company/companies. Taxation will be postponed until the shares are sold outside the group, or when the buying and the selling company are no longer part of the same group.

Tax-free mergers and disposals

Mergers can be tax exempt if certain conditions are met.

Liquidation of company

The funds distributed to a resident shareholder as a part of a liquidation procedure are taxed as a capital gain. Payments to non-resident shareholders are treated as dividends.

Capital taxes

Capital duty

There is no stamp duty on any contribution to the capital of a company.

Net worth tax

There is no net worth tax levied on companies.

Treatment of branches (branch profits tax)

The profits of foreign branches are treated as foreign source income.

There is no separate branch profit tax.

Personal taxes

Taxable individuals

The extent to which an individual's income is subject to Swedish tax depends on whether he is resident in Sweden.

Residents

Residence is determined 'according to circumstances'. Major factors are physical presence, having a home at one's disposal, location of family and centre of economic and social activities.

A person who leaves Sweden and returns within a year, without having been resident elsewhere, will be considered a resident of Sweden for the intervening period. A person who arrives in Sweden in the course of a year will be considered a resident from the date of arrival if it is his intention to stay. An individual who is resident in Sweden is subject to income tax on his worldwide income.

Non-residents

Non-residents are normally subject to income tax on income arising in Sweden but not on most interest and royalties. A wide network of double taxation agreements reduces the liabilities of non-residents.

Tax year and filing requirements

The taxable period is the calendar year.

Residents are not required to file a tax return if:

- they have received income from employment not exceeding SEK 8,784; and
- they have not received other income in excess of SEK 100.

In other cases, a return must be filed by 31 March or 2 May in the subsequent year. Residents who are not required to file a return may do so voluntarily if they expect a refund.

Non-residents are required to file a return if they have certain Swedish source income.

Taxes on income

Taxes on income comprise municipal tax and state tax.

Social security contributions are payable both by employers and employees.

Sources of income

Taxable income is derived from one or more of the following sources.

Employment income and directors' fees

Income from employment consists mainly of salaries, remuneration, pensions, taxable benefits, subsistence allowances and travel allowances.

In principle, all benefits are taxable and the ultimate taxation depends on what has been paid by the individual in comparison with the market value.

Certain deductions may be claimed. The main ones are:

- expenses for professional literature which is necessary in order to carry out the work, the additional costs incurred to keep an office in the home or, for some professions, tools and working clothes if the costs exceed SEK 1,000;
- expenses for travel costs to and from work are allowed if the costs exceed SEK 7,000; and
- superannuation premiums are allowed up to SEK 18,450 at present but not more than actual income, plus 5% of income between SEK 369,000 and 738,000.

Business income

Income from business conducted in the form of a partnership or a sole trader will be treated as business income.

Business income will, in principle, be the difference between sales and costs of goods sold or services rendered, labour costs, rents, and other expenditure directly related to business operations.

Deductions may also be claimed for:

- charges for social security;
- superannuation premiums, which are allowed to 35% of the income but not more than SEK 369 000; and
- income from royalties dependant on business carried out in Sweden – they will be taxed as business income.

Capital gains

Capital gains on owner-occupied homes are considered to be income from capital and are consequently taxed at 30%.

The main rule is that the taxable profit is computed as the difference between the sales price and the base cost. Apart from the original purchase price, the base cost may also include the costs of repairs during the last five years, provided that:

- the costs have increased the value of the house; and
- the costs exceed SEK 5,000 per year.

There are no such restrictions regarding the costs of rebuilding, or any extensions or similar improvements.

The taxable gain is limited to $^2/_3$ of the profit.

A profit on the sale of business real estate is taxed as income from capital unless the sale is regarded as a part of trading activity, although the taxable gain is limited to 90% of the profit.

Dividends

Dividends are taxed at 30%.

Interest

Interest is taxable in the hands of the recipient and interest income is subject to tax at 30%.

If the net difference between interest income (plus capital gains and interest costs plus capital losses) is a loss in excess of SEK 100,000, the excess amount is deductible, but only at 70% of the amount (a tax reduction of 70% x 30% = 21%).

Rentals

Rents received from letting real estate are subject to income tax. Deductions are allowed for expenses and depreciation.

If the real estate is a 'private home' the deduction is 20% of the rent plus SEK 4,000.

Royalties

Royalties are not subject to withholding tax. Royalties are taxed as income of a business activity subject to a deduction for expenses and depreciation of the costs of the rights.

Social security benefits

Social security benefits are taxable.

Pensions and annuities

A pension received from a former employer is taxed as income.

Foreign source income

Foreign source income may be exempt from Swedish tax provided a treaty applies. Generally, ordinary credit is used.

Personal allowances and deductions

Generally all personal allowances are deducted against a particular source of income or credits are given against tax payable. However, a statutory deduction called a base deduction is made by the authorities before calculating local income tax.

Losses

Where an individual sustains a loss from a business activity, he may offset it against future income from business activities.

Relief for capital losses is given at 21%.

Special family rules

Spouses are taxed separately for all income.

A condition for the separate taxation of income from business and agricultural property is that the individual must be actually working in the business or farm and not acting as a sleeping partner.

Wealth tax is calculated jointly.

The background for joint taxation is that the authorities want to prevent spouses from distributing wealth between them in order to obtain lower tax rates.

Rates of tax

The tax rates for 2001 are as follows (i.e. taxable income, assuming municipal tax is 31%):

Taxable income (SEK)	*Marginal tax rate*
Up to 271,500	31%
271,500 to 411,100	51%
Above 411,100	56%

Taxation of non-residents

Non-residents are taxed as follows:

- business income, if the business is carried out in Sweden;
- real property, where the property is situated in Sweden;
- royalties, where derived from business carried out in Sweden; and
- employment income (a final withholding tax of 25%).

Sweden has double taxation agreements with all its major trading partners and with many other countries throughout the world. The treaties generally deal with matters such as dividends, interest, licence fees and royalty fees.

Relief is given either by exempting the income from Swedish tax or, more usually, by crediting the tax paid in Sweden against the tax liability in the other country.

Expatriate tax

Sweden has introduced a tax relief for foreign experts, researchers, and other key persons who work in Sweden temporarily. According to the new rules only 75% of the salary is subject to tax and some benefits, e.g. removal costs, are tax-free. The tax relief is only for the first three years in Sweden. The intended length of the temporary work in Sweden is not allowed to exceed five years. Only foreign citizens can get the tax relief. To get a tax relief an application must be sent to a special research committee (*'forskarskattenämnden'*) within three months after the key person has started their work in Sweden.

Withholding taxes

No withholding tax is imposed on interest paid. Dividends are subject to a withholding tax of 30% in the absence of a double tax agreement. This rate is reduced by tax treaties for selected countries (as listed below).

Payment of tax

An employer is responsible for withholding preliminary taxes from employees in accordance with special tables showing rates depending on income. An employer must pay the tax withheld to the authorities one month in arrears, e.g. in March for tax withheld in February.

People doing business in the form of a partnership or as sole traders must pay their preliminary taxes themselves. The authorities issue a tax card based on a preliminary assessment or on the income of the previous year. This may be adjusted upon the request of the taxpayer if incorrect.

The authorities must agree the tax return not later than 30 November. After that date there may only be changes in the tax return in special cases.

The final tax bill is sent out no later than 15 December in an assessment year. Any balance in favour of the taxpayer is refunded immediately. Any balance in favour of the tax authorities must be paid the following year.

Prepayments

Payments on provisional assessments are spread over the tax year and made monthly.

Estate and gift taxes

Tax on inherited wealth is imposed at progressive rates on the net assets of the estate and is paid out of the estate before it is distributed to the beneficiaries.

The same rates of tax are payable on gifts. Any gift not exceeding SEK 10,000 is tax-free. An individual can make any number of tax-free gifts up to SEK 10,000 to different recipients during each year. Conversely, an individual can receive any number of gifts up to SEK 10,000 from different donors during the year. Gift tax is normally paid by the recipient, unless the donor accepts liability.

The rate of tax payable depends on the recipient's relationship to the donor or deceased.

Class 1: Mainly spouse, children, grandchildren and spouse to children. Under Swedish law a spouse is entitled to receive 50% of the estate regardless of the provisions in the will. This 50% is always tax-free. In addition, a spouse receives all the estate which is taxable to the extent it is in excess of SEK 280,000. A child of the deceased may receive SEK 70,000 tax-free. The remainder is taxed at progressive rates, starting at 10% on estates or gifts up to SEK 300,000 and rising to 30% on estates or gifts over SEK 600,000.

Class 2: Anyone not belonging to Class 1 or 3 is taxed at 10% on estates or gifts up to SEK 70,000, rising to 30% on estates or gifts over SEK 140,000.

Class 3: Mainly charitable trusts, churches and municipalities are charged at 10% on gifts of up to SEK 90,000, rising to 30% above SEK 170,000.

For the avoidance of international double taxation, there are certain estate and gift tax treaties in force.

Wealth tax

Wealth tax is charged as shown below. The tax is calculated on a taxpayer's net assets as at 31 December. This is the difference between his or her total taxable assets and total liabilities. The main taxable assets are real estate, bank balances, bonds, shares and claims, with an exception in the case of assets in close companies.

SEK	*Rate (%)*
Single	
Over 1,000,000	1.5
Married taxed jointly	
Over 1,500,000	1.5

Social security contributions

The cost of all social welfare is shared between the government, the employer and the employees. Self-employed individuals (partnerships and sole traders) must pay their own social insurance, although the cost is allowed as a tax deduction.

In 2001, people with income from employment or business income must pay 7% of that income up to SEK 304,200 as a pension charge. The cost is deductible when calculating income tax.

The cost to employers of statutory social insurance contributions is about 33% of their total bill for wages and salaries.

In addition to this, under collective agreements employers contribute to private insurance schemes. For wage earners the cost works out at about 6% and for salaried persons, about 12% of their total remuneration.

The various types of social insurance schemes – both statutory and private – can, therefore, be said to cost the employer approximately 39% of the total remuneration of wage earners and approximately 45% of the total remuneration of salaried persons.

Other taxes

Treatment of partnerships

Profits made by a partnership are allocated to the partners in accordance with their profit shares and taxed in the partners' hands.

VAT and sales taxes

VAT is levied on all commercial sales of goods other than the transfer of real estate. VAT is chargeable on all services other than those explicitly listed as exempt services.

VAT is chargeable at current rates of 6%, 12% and 25%. Most products and services are charged at 25%.

Stamp tax

An individual who acquires a real estate is subject to a stamp tax of 1.5% of the purchase price. The equivalent tax for legal persons is 3%.

Other taxes

Special duties are levied on motor fuels, tobaccos, spirits, wine and advertisements.

Exchange controls

Exchange controls basically consist of a notification requirement in respect of the movement of funds in excess of SEK 75,000 into and out of the country.

Tax treaties and withholding taxes

Under the majority of double taxation conventions concluded by Sweden, dividend tax rate is reduced or waived completely. The domestic rate is zero if the holding is at least 25% and the recipient is subject to taxation similar to that of Swedish companies (see sector dividends). There is no withholding tax on interest and royalties paid to non-residents. Withholding tax rates on dividends under selected tax treaties (and where applicable, under European Directives) which are currently in force are:

Country of residence	*Normal dividends*	*Specially reduced rate*	*Minimum participation requirements*
Non-treaty countries	30	–	–
Selected treaty countries:			
Australia	15	–	–
Austria	10	0	25
Belgium	15	0	25
Brazil	15	–	–
Canada	15	5	10
Czech Republic	10	0	25
Denmark	15	0	10
Finland	15	0	10
France	15	0	10
Germany	15	0	10
Greece	0	–	–
Hungary	15	5	25
India	10	–	–
Indonesia	15	10	25
Ireland	15	5/0	10/25
Italy	15	0	25
Japan	15	10	25
Korea	15	10	25
Luxembourg	15	0	10
Malaysia	0	–	–
Malta	15	0	10
Netherlands	15	0	25
New Zealand	15	–	–
Norway	15	0	10
Pakistan	30	15	25
Poland	15	5	25
Singapore	15	10	25
South Africa	15	7.5/0	25

Sweden

Spain	15	0	25
Switzerland	15	0	25
Thailand	30	20/15	25
Turkey	20	15	25
United Kingdom	5	0	10
United States	15	5	10

Switzerland

NSL Audit & Consulting Sàrl

Corporate taxes

Introduction

Switzerland has a federal system of government and as a consequence has no uniform system of taxation. The Confederation and the 26 cantons all have their own legislation for taxation as do the over 3,000 communities, although they mostly follow cantonal tax laws. Tax laws often require the approval of the electorate. While they are valid indefinitely, they are revised from time to time. For federal tax purposes and for turnover tax purposes, the new legislation has became effective on 1 January 1995.

Taxable entities

Resident companies

Resident companies are, in principle, subject to federal, cantonal and communal taxes on their worldwide income (including capital gains) and on capital. Companies are resident in Switzerland if they are registered or if their central management is situated there. It follows that a company registered abroad can be a resident company if it is managed from within Switzerland.

Non-resident companies

Non-resident companies are subject to all the above mentioned taxes on their income and assets attributable to a permanent establishment in Switzerland. Moreover, they are taxable on the net income and the net value of real estate situated in Switzerland, including capital gains realised thereon. The unlimited tax liability of a non-resident company applies as soon as the company is administered in Switzerland.

Taxes imposed

Due to the country's federal structure, taxes are levied by three different authorities: the federal government, the cantons and the municipalities. Basically there are two taxes: income tax and capital tax.

Rates of tax

Income tax

In Switzerland, companies are assessed to cantonal and communal taxes at rates varying considerably according to the taxing authority and together total 15% to 30%. The tax payable is obtained by multiplying the 'basic' tax by a factor (tax multiple) determined independently from time to time by the cantons or municipalities according to their financial requirements for the particular year. The multiple is expressed either as a percentage (e.g. cantonal tax = 120% of basic tax) or as a simple multiplier (e.g. cantonal tax = 1.2 × basic tax).

For federal tax purposes, companies are assessed at a proportional rate of 8.5% of income after tax; tax expense being tax deductible.

Capital tax

The cantonal rates vary from about 0.04% to 0.7%. The effective cantonal or municipal tax is derived as described under 'Income tax' above. No federal tax is levied.

Income and capital subject to tax

General rules

Taxes on companies' income and capital are assessed for the calendar year. The basis for income tax is the financial year ending during the tax year (mostly 31 December).

Income subject to tax

Income, for tax purposes, is calculated in accordance with generally accepted accounting principles and should include all income and expenses attributable to the business operations. Charges deemed to be excessive may be disallowed.

Stock/inventory rules

Stock and work-in-progress (inventory) are valued at the lower of cost or market value. As a concession, a reserve against unexpected decreases in value of stocks of merchandise may be set up in the books. This reserve is allowable for all taxes provided, except to the extent that they can be substantied.

Capital gains and losses

Capital gains normally form an integral part of the taxable income under the majority of cantonal tax laws and under direct federal tax law. However, some cantons levy a separate tax on capital gains realised on real property.

Capital gains are calculated by deduction from the proceeds of disposal, the sum of original cost, improvement costs and some incidental expenses such as commissions and fees. Capital losses can be deducted from capital gains or from net income, depending on the system of taxation. Exemption is available if the participation exemption applies (see 'Participation companies' below).

Dividends

Dividends received from both Swiss and foreign sources are fully taxable and exemption is available if the participation exemption applies (see 'Participation companies' below).

Capital subject to tax

All cantons and municipalities usually levy a tax on the capital base of the company, including statutory and taxable hidden reserves.

Deductions

General rules

A company normally can deduct expenses incurred in earning income. However, some costs are not deductible, in particular:

- costs which are not wholly or exclusively in connection with business purposes;
- depreciation which exceeds the prescribed rate.

Depreciation and amortisation

Depreciation of tangible and intangible fixed assets is allowed to the extent that it is commercially justified, either calculated on cost or on diminishing balance or net book value. The latter rates are generally twice those allowed on cost.

Switzerland

The following rates published by the conference of tax administrations may be regarded as a general guide:

	On cost (%)
Residential property*	1
Offices, shops, cinemas, theatre buildings*	2
Hotels and restaurants premises*	3
Factory and workshop buildings*	4
Railway sidings, water, gas and electricity mains, storage tanks	10
Office furniture and machines, workshop and storeroom equipment	12.5
Computer installations (hardware and software)	20
Goodwill, patents, licence rights	20
Machinery, equipment and vehicles (excluding motor cars)	15
Machinery and equipment used in more than one shift, automobiles	20
Machine tools, larger hand tools, hotel and restaurant, dishes, cutlery and linen	22.5

* Excluding land.

Royalties

Royalties are normally deductible in full. However, if related to royalty income received by a foreign controlled, privileged company (see 'Tax incentives' below) under a sub-licence agreement from abroad, no more than 80% can be transferred to a foreign licensor and only then if the underlying right is registered (50% if received from a sub-licensee in a treaty country).

Interest

All interest incurred in the production of income is deductible. However, for loans from shareholders or related parties, special periodically adjusted rates must be observed. Excess payments are considered to be a hidden distribution of profits and are therefore added back to the reported results. Moreover, they are subject to 35% withholding tax. The same rules are valid if insufficient interest is received on advances to shareholders and persons connected to them.

Dividends

Dividends paid are not deductible in arriving at taxable income. They are subject to a withholding tax of 35%. This tax is creditable or refundable for residents against their individual or corporate income tax. Recipients abroad may obtain relief under the appropriate double tax treaty, if any.

Provision for doubtful debts

Reasonable provision, based on collection experience or special risk, may be made for bad debts. In normal cases, it should not exceed 5% of the amounts outstanding at the year end, with respect to domestic receivables, and 10% as far as foreign receivables are concerned.

Tax expense

Federal, cantonal and communal taxes, whether paid or due, are considered deductible expenses for federal tax and for the taxes of the majority of the cantons.

Foreign source income

In the absence of a double tax treaty, Swiss unilateral provisions apply. Investment in income derived from immovable property and permanent establishments abroad are exempt from Swiss taxes. On the other hand, except under tax treaties, no credit is provided for foreign taxes. However, foreign income is included in total income for the purpose of determining the tax rate applicable to the remaining income.

Investment incentives and special benefits

Investment incentives

As the country is already highly industrialised, there are generally only very marginal investment incentives available. In some areas however – particularly where unemployment is high – special finance and tax incentives are granted for new industries creating jobs. The incentives granted depend largely on the amount invested and the number of jobs created, but can go up to a full tax exemption for ten years on direct taxes.

Tax incentives

In addition to tax privileges given to newly established companies during a maximum period of ten years, there are very significant modifications to the general tax rules for the following special purpose companies:

Participation companies

A participation company is a normal operating company which holds equity investments in other (domestic or foreign) companies.

To qualify for relief in respect of taxes on dividend income, a particular investment must normally represent at least 20% of the other company's capital or have a value of not less than CHF 2 million.

The income tax on net income of such a company is reduced in the proportion of earnings from the participation holdings to the other earnings or the proportion of the net earnings from such holdings to the entire taxable net income.

Capital gains realised on sale of participations of at least 20% and held for at least one year are also tax exempt for investments purchased after 1 January 1997. For investments held prior to this date, a special transitional treatment is applicable until 31 December 2006 whereby income is deferred until this date as long as the participation is not sold outside the same group of companies.

Holding companies

In cantonal law, holding companies are those whose main (in some cantons, exclusive) activity is the holding of (domestic or foreign) participations and investments. Since income tax would already have been levied on the distributing company and then again on the shareholder, it was agreed by nearly all cantons that the income of such holding companies should be totally exempt from income tax. Most cantons also grant a reduced rate of capital tax.

For federal tax purposes, the holding company is treated in the same way as a participation company. If the holding company derives income and capital gains only from participations and investments, then it is totally exempt from federal taxes on profits.

Domiciliary companies

Domiciliary companies, in general, are companies which have only their legal domicile in Switzerland but do not perform business activities in Switzerland and are controlled by foreigners. As distinguished from holding companies, this type of company may be involved in business activities far beyond that of holding investments, so long as those activities are performed abroad. In some cantons such companies enjoy certain tax concessions: they are granted partial exclusion of (or a reduced rate on) foreign source income, although income from domestic activities is fully taxable. These latter activities must normally not involve the purchase, storage or exhibition of goods in Switzerland. Some cantons, however, allow limited transactions of up to 20% within the country. Additionally, the cantons often reduce the rate of capital tax. However, apart from the participation exemption, domiciliary companies do not enjoy concessions with respect to the federal direct tax.

Auxiliary, mixed or administrative companies

If a domiciliary company cannot operate without office space or personnel of its own, in certain cantons a substitute has to be found, under certain conditions, by establishing so-called auxiliary, mixed or administrative companies. They solely, or almost exclusively, perform services or auxiliary functions.

Related party transactions

Transactions with affiliates normally come under rather close scrutiny by the tax inspectors. Those not deemed to be at arm's length are adjusted for income tax purposes and treated as disguised, subject to withholding tax as for dividends.

Losses

Business losses are fully deductible and may be carried forward, depending on the federal or cantonal tax law, for a maximum of seven years. No Swiss tax law allows loss carry-backs.

Corporate groups

There are no special rules relating to groups of companies. All companies are taxed individually and assessed losses may not be transferred between companies within a group.

Personal taxes

Taxable individuals

In Switzerland, the extent of an individual's tax liability depends on whether his affiliation to the tax levying community is based on a personal or purely economic relationship.

Switzerland

Unlimited tax liability

Unlimited tax liability applies to individuals who:

- have their place of residence in Switzerland;
- remain in Switzerland for a certain minimum period (e.g. for three or even only one month) and exercise an activity (i.e. trade, business or employment);
- remain in the country for a protracted period (e.g. more than three months) but are not engaged in gainful activity (i.e. trade, business or employment).

Residence is defined as the place where a person dwells with the intention of living permanently and which therefore provides the centre of his personal and economic interest. Unlimited tax liability does not extend to capital invested or income derived from business, permanent establishments and real estate located abroad.

Limited tax liability

This exists for individuals who do not fulfil the above mentioned conditions but:

- own a business enterprise;
- maintain a permanent establishment;
- own (or have the beneficial use of) real estate or possess limited rights in them;
- are creditors to a claim secured by way of mortgage pledge or real estate;
- carry out personal services for a consideration;
- (as members of the administration of domestic legal entities) draw attendance fees, compensation, director's fees or any other form of remuneration;
- are paid a pension out of Swiss public funds originating in former employment in the Swiss Civil Service.

Taxes on income

Individuals are mainly subject to income tax which is imposed by the Federal Government, the cantons and communities.

The total tax burden varies from canton to canton and from community to community, often considerably. The maximum income tax charges lie normally between 35% and 40%.

Sources of income

Employment income

This covers:

- all regular or casual income either from employment in the private or public sector;
- additional secondary income, e.g. bonuses, anniversary gifts, commissions, gratuities and other wages or salary related remuneration as well as allowances (whether in cash or in kind).

All expenses necessarily incurred to earn this gross employment income may be deducted, including:

- travel cost between place of home and place of business;
- additional cost of food and lodging away from home and shift work expenses;
- other employment related expenses, such as outlays for special clothing, professional literature and training.

Some of these deductions can only be claimed up to a limited amount.

Additionally, certain contributions to pension schemes (e.g. AHV, IV, EO, ALV – see 'Social Security' below) are fully deductible. On the other hand, only a limited reduced reduction is allowed at federal level and in most cantons for premiums to individual savings schemes.

Business income

This comprises:

- all regular and casual income from an independent profession and freelance income;
- income from a commercial or industrial enterprise or from agriculture or forestry.

Professionally and commercially justified costs may be deducted from gross income. These include especially:

- employer contributions to the state social security schemes (e.g. AHV, IV, EO, ALV);
- contributions to occupational pension schemes according to the BVG;

- contributions to pension funds under the condition that any improper use of such contributions is excluded;
- actual business losses carried forward for seven years in total (with respect to the direct federal tax), while the cantons have various rules.

Capital gains

Capital gains may arise from:

- the disposal of an asset;
- the liquidation of a legal entity.

The capital gain is the difference between the proceeds and the cost price or book value of an asset. The taxation of capital gains varies considerably under Swiss tax law. It depends on whether the asset disposed of is part of a business property or an individual's personal net wealth. Furthermore, capital gains of movable and immovable properties are to be distinguished.

As a rule, business capital gains on movable and immovable property form part of the business profits and are therefore subject to direct federal and cantonal taxes.

Private capital gains on movable property may be taxable depending on the cantonal legislation, although most cantons exempt it from taxes. However, there are cases especially at a federal level where such capital gains on immovable property are assessed in all cantons and mostly with a separate tax. At a federal level, such capital gains are not subject to income tax.

Capital gains can be compensated with capital losses and, in some cases, with operation losses.

Income from movable property

This includes inter alia:

- all types of interest income from whatever source;
- dividends and other open or hidden distributions, as well as liquidation proceeds;
- royalties;
- hiring out of movable property.

The following may be deducted from such income for federal, cantonal and communal tax purposes:

- costs incurred by a third party in administrating the property;
- foreign withholding taxes insofar as they cannot be reclaimed or credited against Swiss taxes.

Income from immovable property

This comprises especially:

- rental income derived from a tenancy or a lease;
- rental value of an owned flat or house either used by the taxpayer or held available for his use.

The following may be deducted from this income:

- maintenance costs;
- running costs, e.g. insurance premiums for third party liability, cleaning and lighting cost and caretaker expenses;
- administrative expenses charged by a third party;
- mortgage interest;
- immovable property taxes.

In many cases the cantons and communities, for simplicity, grant a lump sum amounting to a certain percentage of the rent.

Social security benefits

As social security contributions are deductible, the benefits are taxable.

Pensions and annuities

As said before, contributions under the BVG are tax deductible. On the other hand, the respective benefits are fully taxable for federal, cantonal and communal income taxes. However, if lump sum payments are made instead of, or in addition to, pensions, these payments will be taxed separately from other income. Tax will be calculated using the rate appropriate if a corresponding annuity was paid instead of a one-off amount. Similarly, lump sum payments paid by the employer at the termination of an employment relationship are taxed at the annuity rate, but not separately from other income.

At a cantonal level various tax methods exist. Some cantons have chosen the method used for the federal direct taxes, others tax lump sum payments separately in every instance, either at an annuity rate or at a special rate; other cantonal tax law provides for a reduction depending on the extent the taxpayer himself financed the contributions to the pension scheme.

A partial exemption applies to benefits under BVG which start to run before 1 January 1987 or become due before 31 December 2001 and are based on a contract concluded before 31 December 1986.

Exempt income

The following deserve a special mention:

- maintenance payments, particularly alimony and similar benefits from private or public funds (some cantons, however, tax this income);
- as a rule, capital payments to the insured party from life insurance contracts (at federal level only if such contracts are redeemable);
- gifts, estates, bequests which as a rule are subject to a special tax.

Personal allowances and deductions

To arrive at assessable income, additional lump sum allowances are deducted from the balance of gross income after the above deductions. These allowances are graded according to the personal circumstances of the taxpayer (single person, married couple, number of children and any other persons supported by the taxpayer).

Special family rules

It should be noted that income and net wealth of husband and wife living together are accumulated and jointly assessed at the correspondingly higher rate. As a result of a principal decision of the Federal High Court, most cantons were obliged to reduce the tax burden for married couples in comparison to couples living together who paid lower taxes. As a rule, this is achieved by a lower rate which provides a lower rate for married couples and for taxpayers living together with children (or other persons that are supported by the taxpayer), than for single persons.

The taxation of the family as a unit applies insofar as the income and net wealth of minor children are also taxed with the parents' income and net wealth. Separate taxation, as a rule, only applies to employment income.

Rates of tax

General

In Switzerland, individuals are assessed to income tax at progressive rates. The direct federal tax rates start for single people at 0.17% on a taxable income of CHF 14,900 rising to the highest rate of 11.5% on taxable income of CHF 603,000 and above. The resulting tax amount represents the final federal tax burden, whereas at cantonal level the tax calculated correspondingly represents (in most cases) a basic tax only.

The effective cantonal or municipal tax is obtained by multiplying the basic tax by a factor (tax multiple) determined independently from time to time by the cantons or municipalities according to their financial requirements for the particular year.

In most cantons and on a federal level, married people are assessed at a lower tax level.

The multiple is expressed either as a percentage (e.g. cantonal tax = 120% of basic tax) or as a simple multiplier (e.g. cantonal tax = 1.2 x basic tax).

Individuals, who are only liable to tax in Switzerland on a part of their income or net wealth, pay taxes at the marginal rates that would be applicable to their worldwide income and net wealth.

Tax credits

Under a majority of the existing double tax treaties, the non-refundable part of foreign withholding taxes can be credited against the income taxes of a Swiss resident by means of the so-called lump sum credit.

Payment of tax

Deduction at source

Individuals living abroad may also be subject to deduction of tax at source if they:

- draw attendance fees, director's fees or any other form of remuneration (e.g. as artists, athletes);
- earn income from debts secured by way of mortgage or pledge on real estate located in Switzerland.

This tax is levied by the cantons and varies, as a rule, between 6% and 35% (depending on the canton where the debtor has his residence or domicile, or where the real estate is located) and usually comprises the direct federal tax.

Under certain circumstances, tax at source is also levied on income from gainful employment of individuals who live and work in Switzerland but have no residence permit.

Prepayment

Taxes may be paid to most cantons and to the Federal Government before the official due dates. If that right is exercised, the tax levying bodies grant a discount.

Taxable period

Taxes are assessed for the calendar year. The basis for income tax in respect of business income, is (as a rule) the financial year.

In respect of other income, the basis is the same, i.e. the actual calendar year.

Three cantons apply (until 2003) the old system, which means that the basis for income tax is the average of the two previous calendar years.

Filing requirements

Income and wealth taxes are generally assessed by the cantonal and municipal tax administrations. They normally base their assessments on the taxpayer's return.

Estate and gift taxes

These are cantonal taxes; there are no such federal taxes and normally the communities are not empowered to levy taxes of this nature. The cantons levy an inheritance tax, which is normally also supplemented by a gift tax.

The tax liability falls on the heirs and the legatees. As a rule, the tax is levied in the canton in which the testator resided at the time of his death. The tax is levied on the accretion of wealth by virtue of the statutory right of inheritance or by virtue of dispositions mortis causa. In the case of gift tax, the recipient of the gift is liable for the tax after the gift has been made.

To avoid international double taxation there are certain estate and gift tax treaties in force.

Wealth taxes

Wealth taxes are only levied by the cantons and the communities and not by the Federal Government. They are calculated on the net wealth, i.e. all assets (real estate, business value, securities, receivables, deposits, surrender value of life and similar insurance policies, movable belongings in excess of normal household requirements), less any liabilities (mortgages, loans, advances).

Lump sum allowances are deducted from the net wealth.

Net wealth taxes are in general progressive. The basic taxes vary between 0.1% and 0.3%. The effective cantonal or municipal tax is derived as mentioned under 'Rates of tax'.

The taxable period is the calendar year. The taxable amount depends on whether the canton assesses tax annually or biennially (only three cantons assess biennially until 2003).

Social security

Switzerland recognises three ways of providing for old age, survivors and disability, which are interlinked. This is known as the three pillar system comprising the following:

Old-age and survivors insurance (AHV) and disability insurance (IV)

AHV: All persons who live in Switzerland or carry on a gainful activity there, irrespective of their nationality, as well as Swiss nationals working abroad for an employer whose registered office is in Switzerland, are subject to this insurance. The contributions currently amount to 8.4% and are shared equally by the employer and the employee as far as employed persons are concerned. For non-employed residents the rates are progressive and different.

It should be noted that AHV contributions are a fixed percentage of salary, irrespective of the level of income, but the pension is maximised on CHF 24,720 per year.

IV: This is closely related to the AHV and is a mandatory form of insurance for all those gainfully employed. The contributions amount to 1.4% wages. It is collected with the AHV and is likewise shared equally between the employer and the employee.

Occupational retirement, survivors and disability pension

This so-called second pillar is based on a federal Act (BVG) effective from 1985. Together with the AHV, it aims at providing to retired people with 60% of their last salary. Insured persons are all employees subject to AHV with annual earnings of between CHF 24,720 and CHF 74,160. Employer's contributions must at least match employee's contributions. All insured persons pay a contribution either independent of age or scaled by age group. In principle, self-employed persons may be insured on a voluntary basis.

Individual savings

These form the third pillar and consist of, for instance, investment in bank deposits, insurance policies and immovable properties. Recognised linked endowment assurance with an insurance company and linked savings with banks are privileged forms. Related contributions are tax deductible for those with an employee benefit plan up to CHF 5,933 and for others up to CHF 29,665.

When paid out, capital sums from recognised forms of linked savings are subject to income tax. However, at a federal level they are taxed separately from other income as capital sums from occupational pension schemes at the so-called annuity rate. The cantons have put out differing taxation rules analogous to benefits from occupational pension schemes.

Unemployment insurance (ALV)

Since 1977, there has been an obligation for all employees in Switzerland to insure against unemployment. The premium is currently 2% of the gross wage and is borne equally by the employer and employee. The assessment limit is at an income level of CHF 8,900 per month. Above, a 1% contribution is levied up to a maximum of CHF 20,250 per month. The contributions are also collected through the AHV organisation.

Wage compensation (EO)

A person suffering loss of earnings through compulsory military service is protected by the wage compensation order (EO). The insurance contribution amounts to 0.3% of income and is shared by the employer and the employee. The employer continues to pay the wage of the person providing military service and receives compensation up to a certain level through EO.

Accident insurance

According to revised federal law, effective from 1984, employees, including home workers, trainees and voluntary assistants as well as apprentices, must be insured. Persons engaged in a part-time job must be insured for this activity only if their earnings are subject to AHV. The premiums for the mandatory insurance of occupational accidents and illnesses are to be paid by the employer; those for the mandatory insurance of non-occupational accidents by the employee. Self-employed persons may insure themselves voluntarily.

Other taxes

Federal taxes

Stamp duty

The issue of Swiss share capital is subject to a 1% duty, which in the case of acquisition or mergers is reduced to the zero rate in relation to the foundation of small companies (with an initial capital up to CHF 250,000). A further stamp tax is due on the purchase, sale or exchange of Swiss and foreign securities by registered professional security dealers. The rate is 0.15% on securities of a Swiss issuer and 0.3% on securities of a foreign issuer.

Value Added Tax

The legislation for VAT has become effective from 1 January 1995. The VAT has replaced the turnover tax. Most goods and services within Switzerland are subject to 7.6% VAT. Certain essential goods of daily consumption are taxed at 2.4%. A zero rate applies to the export of goods and services.

Cantonal taxes

Tax on real estate

Many cantons and municipalities levy an annual tax on real estate which is based on the gross value without any deductions at rates between 0.05% and 0.3%.

Transfer tax

Is basically calculated on the purchase price, or, alternatively, the market or tax value. The rates normally range from 0.2% to 4%, although in special cases they can be set at a lower rate or not levied at all.

Motor cars

All cantons levy an annual tax on motorcars.

Church tax

The majority of cantons impose an annual church tax as a percentage of the basic cantonal tax at varying rates.

Exchange controls

Switzerland has no exchange controls.

Double tax relief

Corresponding with the internal law, international double tax relief is given by Switzerland through an exemption system. The elements of income and assets, which have been allocated for taxation to the other contracting state, by the treaty are exempted from Swiss taxes, subject to tax rate progression. This applies especially to ownership of real estate and permanent establishments abroad. Additional treaties concluded since 1965 provide for Swiss recipients of dividends, interest and royalties, a relief from Swiss federal, cantonal and communal taxes for withholding taxes that may be levied in the other country as the country of source.

Withholding taxes

The anticipatory tax is the only Swiss federal tax levied at source. It amounts to 35% and is applied to a large part of the revenues derived from Swiss capital investments, such as dividends paid by Swiss companies (including the distribution of the liquidation surplus and of pecuniary value to shareholders), interest on bonds (of a Swiss issuer) and bank deposits. Ordinary loan interest paid by debtors other than banks, as well as royalties paid by individuals or legal entities domiciled in Switzerland, are not subject to this tax. Recipients of dividends and interest who are domiciled in Switzerland may claim a refund of the tax if the related income and investments are included in their tax returns.

Companies domiciled, and individuals residing outside Switzerland, may not claim a refund of the tax unless (and to the extent that) this is provided for by the tax treaty concluded by Switzerland with the country of domicile or residence.

The following table illustrates rates of withholding tax currently in force. 'Qualifying companies' are those holding a prescribed minimum shareholding.

Country of residence	*Interest* (%)		*Dividends* (%)	
Non-treaty countries:	35		35	
		Normal dividends	*Special rate*	*Minimum holding*
Selected treaty countries:				
Australia	10	15	15	–
Austria	5	5	5	–
Belgium	10	15	10	25
Bulgaria	10	15	5	25
Canada	15	15	15	–
China	10	10	10	–
Denmark	0	0	0	–
Egypt	15	0	0	–
Finland	0	5	0	20
France	10	15	5	20
Germany	0	10	5	20
Great Britain	0	15	5	10
Greece	10	35	35	–
Hungary	10	10	10	–
Iceland	0	15	5	25
India	15	15	15	–
Indonesia	10	15	10	25
Ireland	0	15	15	25
Italy	12,5	15	15	–
Ivory Coast	15	15	15	–
Japan	10	15	10	25
Luxembourg	10	15	5/0	25
Malaysia	10	15	5	25
Mexico	15/10	15	5	25
Morocco	10	15	7	25
Netherlands	5	15	0	25
New Zealand	10	15	15	–
Norway	0	15	5	25
Pakistan	30/0	0	10/20	33 1/3
Poland	10	15	5	25
Portugal	10	15	10	25

Singapore	10	15	10	25
South Africa	10	7.5	7.5	–
South Korea	10	15	10	25
Spain	10	15	10	25
Sri Lanka	10/5	15	10	25
Sweden	5	15	0	25
Thailand	15/10	15	10	10
Trinidad & Tobago	10	20	10	10
USA	0	15	5	10

Non-treaty countries

Argentina, Bermuda, Brazil, Chile, Cyprus, Hong Kong, Jordan, Kuwait, Lebanon, Malta, Nigeria, Oman and Saudi Arabia.

Anti-avoidance measures

Swiss residents in receipt of income from abroad who request relief from foreign withholding tax through a double tax treaty must fulfil certain minimal requirements in accordance with the Misuse Decree of 1962. Otherwise, the application is considered unjustified or an abuse of the tax treaty.

The misuse measures may be summarized as follows:

- *capital structure*

  the Swiss company may not present the characteristics of 'thin capitalization' and must, therefore, have a reasonable capital structure; the ratio of interest-bearing debt to equity that is required for tax purposes should not exceed about 6:1;

- *interest rate limitation*

  the rate of interest paid on shareholder (or related party) loans shall not exceed the fair market rate; if there is no market, the rates indicated by the Federal tax administration apply;

- *expense limitation*

  tax deductible expenses, such as interest, royalties, management fees etc. paid to non-residents, may not exceed 50% of gross treaty favoured income; this limitation applies also to depreciation taken on property (tangible or intangible) acquired by non-residents;

- *redistribution requirement*

  the company is required to redistribute, in the form of a dividend, at least 25% of gross treaty favoured income.

Taiwan

Sun Rise CPAs & Co.

Introduction

There are 13 taxes levied in the Republic of China (ROC). Of these, seven are direct taxes and six are indirect taxes. They fall into three categories as follows:

National taxes

- customs duties (indirect);
- income tax, i.e. profit seeking enterprise income tax (direct);
- individual consolidated income tax (direct);
- mine concession tax (direct);
- enterprise income tax (direct);
- individual consolidated income tax (direct).

Provincial (city) taxes

- VAT business tax (indirect);
- stamp tax (indirect);
- vehicle licence tax (indirect).

Prefecture (municipal) taxes

- land tax, i.e. agricultural land tax, land value tax and land value increment tax (direct);
- house tax (direct);
- entertainment tax (indirect);
- deed tax (direct).

Each tax levied in the ROC is based on separate legislation. The research and planning of inland taxes and customs duties are the responsibility of the Taxation and Tariff Commission of the Ministry of Finance (MOF). The drafting, enactment and interpretation of inland tax code and the supervision of collection and administration of inland taxes are the responsibility of the Department of Taxation, MOF. The collection of taxes is the responsibility of the national tax administrations and local tax offices in various prefectures and municipalities.

The collection of customs duties is supervised by the Department of Customs Administration, Directorate General of Customs, MOF and all local customs offices respectively.

In order to encourage investment in the ROC, many tax benefits are accorded to profit seeking enterprises in general and to manufacturing enterprises in particular. Investors holding shares issued for the establishment or expansion of important enterprises or investing in equipment for automation and pollution control enjoy a credit against their income tax for four years. Also, companies can depreciate their R&D equipment, testing equipment and energy-saving equipment over two years.

Corporate taxes

The profit seeking enterprise income tax (business income tax) is imposed on the worldwide income of companies, sole proprietorships, partnerships and other forms of business organisations which have their head offices located in the ROC, and also imposed on the ROC sourced income of an enterprise which has no permanent establishment in the ROC. Income for tax purposes is computed according to the Generally Accepted Accounting Principles and adjusted for certain statutory provisions. The necessary and ordinary expenses of a profit seeking enterprise (a business) are deductible, provided they are adequately supported by documentation.

In addition, in order to create a better tax environment to encourage investment, the MOF has implemented an integration system to eliminate double taxation. The system integrates business income tax with individual income tax with effect from 1 January 1998.

Under the integration system, shareholders are allowed a tax credit of the business income tax paid on dividends against their individual income tax liability. In order to discourage businesses from retaining income (so as to benefit from the difference between the business income tax rate and individual income tax), a 10% surtax to undistributed net earnings is applied.

The aim of the reform is to achieve greater fairness and efficiency. The new system reduces the tax burden of taxpayers by deducting their business income tax from their individual income tax and reducing the highest marginal tax rate from 55% to 40%.

Taxable entities

Where the head office of a profit seeking enterprise is located in the ROC, the combined income of the entire enterprise both inside and outside the country is subject to business income tax. However, income tax paid to foreign governments on income derived outside the ROC may be claimed as a credit against the enterprise's total ROC income tax liability. The credit cannot exceed the ROC tax liability on such additional income.

Where the head office of a business is located outside the territory of the ROC, but has all or part of its permanent establishment in the ROC, business income tax is levied on that part of the business operating in the ROC unless otherwise provided in the income tax laws.

Where a profit seeking enterprise has no permanent establishment within the territory of the ROC but receives ROC sourced income, the tax payable is withheld at the source at a rate of 20% of the payment, there being no need to file a final return for settlement.

Registration and accounting

A profit seeking enterprise (business) is required to register with the tax office prior to the commencement of business, and is also required to register with the tax office within 15 days after: liquidation, a merger or demerger, transfer of ownership or a change of name, address, responsible personnel or nature of the business.

Where a business increases or decreases its capital, it must file an application for registration amendment within 15 days.

A business must keep sufficient and accurate accounts, vouchers and accounting records to calculate its total amount of business income. Accounting is on the accrual basis. With the approval of the tax office, non-corporate businesses may adopt a cash basis accounting system.

The tax year is the calendar year. However, a business may change the date of its fiscal year end with the approval of the tax authorities.

Tax rates

Taxable income (NT$)	*Tax rates*
0–50,000	Exempt.
50,001–100,000	15% of total taxable income, not exceeding 50% of that portion of taxable income over 50,000.
100,001 and above	25% on the excess.

Withholding tax

In addition to filing a final tax return, certain items of income received by a business are subject to a withholding tax (rates shown below). For businesses with no permanent establishment in Taiwan the withholding tax is final.

Type of income	*Profit seeking enterprise with a fixed place of business*	*Profit seeking enterprise with no fixed place of business*
Dividends distributed by companies and profits distributed by cooperatives.	–	(a) 25% (b) 20% if the investment was approved under the Statute for Investment by Foreign Nationals or the Statute for Investment by Overseas Chinese.
Commissions	10%	20%
Interest	(a) 10% (b) 20%, taxed separately from ordinary income, on interest from short-term commercial papers.	20%
Rental	10%	20%
Royalties	15%	20%

Awards or prizes from participation in contests, games or lotteries, etc.	(a) 15% if the amount exceeds NT$ 4,000 (b) 20%, to be taxed separately per item for government sponsored lottery receipts where greater than NT$ 2,000 per ticket.	(a) 20% (b) 20%, to be taxed separately per item for government sponsored lottery receipt below NT$ 2,000 per ticket.
Income from property transactions.	–	25% on the reported amount.
Income from international transportation, construction projects, furnishing of technical service and leasing of equipment by a foreign business, where a fixed rate of profit is approved by the MOF in accordance with Article 25 of the Income Tax Law.	–	25%
Foreign motion picture Enterprises in which income has been permitted to be calculated by a fixed rate according to Article 26 of the Income Tax Law.	–	20%
Other income.	–	20%

Expenses and losses

- Interest on capital that is paid from the distribution of profit shall not be listed as expense or loss.
- Interest payable on loans within a fiscal year is deductible as an expense of that year.

- Salaries of employees and workers that must be paid, regardless of a businesses profit or loss status, is treated as an expense.
- A reserve for pensions of no more that 4% of total salaries and wages paid in the year, or a reserve fund set up for pensions that is entirely separate from the business with a value of not more than 8% of the total salary and wages paid in the year, is deductible.
- All of those businesses which are subject to the application of the Labour Standards Law may, subject to approval from the local tax authority, set aside each year an amount not exceeding 15% of the total salaries and wages paid in that year as a retirement reserve fund and this appropriation is treated as an expense.
- Expenditure incurred in the expansion, replacement, improvement or repair of buildings, vessels, machinery, tools, apparatus, appliances and other equipment for use in business that results in an increase in value or efficiency that cannot be exhausted within two years is not treated as an expense or loss.
- Damages due to force majeure, to the extent they are covered by insurance, shall not be listed as expenses or losses.
- Contributions and donations made to officially register educational, cultural, public welfare and charitable organisations or associations are deductible, but cannot exceed 10% of the taxpayer's income. Contributions and donations made for assisting national defence, military morale or made to the government as well as those specially permitted by the MOF are fully deductible.
- Entertainment, meal and gift expenses (EMG) incurred through and directly related to the active conduct of business may be listed as expenses up to prescribed limits depending on the nature of the item.
- In addition to the limits listed in the table, for a business which engages in exporting and earns foreign exchange receipts, a special allowance of 2% of its total foreign exchange receipt settlement for the current year may be listed as expense.
- Losses not incurred in the course of operation of business or business related activities, household expenditure and any fines and surcharges for belated reporting, non-reporting, under estimation and belated payment as provided in various tax laws are not considered as expenses or losses.
- Losses incurred in the operation of business of prior years generally may not be included in the computation of the current year. However, a business which keeps a complete set of accounts, using the 'blue' returns or whose accounts are audited

by a CPA for both the loss year and the deduction reporting year, and which files its returns on time, may carry forward losses for five years.

Income subject to tax

As a principle, the income of a business is computed by subtracting costs, expenses, losses and taxes from the current year's total revenues to arrive at the amount of net income. Special rules of computation are provided by tax law for the income of international transportation companies, the foreign motion picture industry, and the construction industry that have their head offices outside the territory of the Republic of China.

Where a business has been in operation for less than one year, the amount of income for the actual period of operation is apportioned on an annual basis to a yearly income. Where the period of actual operation is less than one month, it is deemed to be one month.

Tax exempt organisations and institutions

- Income derived by educational, cultural, public welfare and charitable organisations or associations which are established and operated in conformity with the tax exemption criteria prescribed by the Executive Yuan are exempt from business income tax as are those of qualifying cooperatives and certain non-profit motive organisations.
- Income obtained from operation inside the territory of the ROC by a foreign enterprise engaged in international transportation may be exempt from taxation, provided that reciprocal treatment is accorded to an international transport enterprise of the ROC.

Tax exempt items

- Interest derived from loans offered to the government of the ROC or legal entities in the ROC by foreign governments or international economic development banking institutions, and interest derived from loans offered by a foreign financial institution to its branches or to other financial institutions in the ROC, is exempt from taxes.
- Interest derived from loans extended to legal entities in the ROC by foreign financial institutions approved by the MOF for financing important economic construction projects are exempt from taxes.
- Interest derived from 'favourable interest' export loans offered to

or guaranteed to legal entities of the ROC by specialist foreign government institutions and foreign financial institutions are exempt from taxes.

- Royalties paid to a foreign enterprise for use of its patent rights, trademarks and various kinds of specially licensed rights to introduce new production technology or new products, improve product quality, or reduce production costs (under the approval of the competent authority), as well as remuneration to foreign enterprises for technical services rendered in the construction of a factory for an important productive enterprise (again, as approved by competent authority), are exempt from taxes.
- Proceeds from land sales and income from property transactions disposed for the purpose of war stockpiling in accordance with government regulations are exempt from taxes.

Tax incentives

Instruments and equipment used exclusively for R&D, experimentation or quality inspection, as well as machinery and equipment involved in energy saving or alternative energy use, may be depreciated over two years.

Based on certain requirements for the adjustment of industrial structure and improvement of scale of operations and methods of production, depreciation of the machinery and equipment of specially designated industries may be accelerated by one half of their service lives as prescribed by regulations.

To promote the upgrading of industry, companies are allowed an investment tax credit of 5% to 20% on the costs of specified investments in the year, which may be deducted from business income tax payable in the same year. Any excessive investment tax credit may be carried forward for up to four years. This credit is limited to 50% of the income tax payable in each year except the last year. Investments qualified for the investment tax credit are those made in:

- equipment or technology to automate production;
- equipment or technology purchased to reclaim resources or control pollution;
- equipment or technology used for the reduction of greenhouse gas emission or the enhancement of energy efficiency;
- equipment or technology acquired for energy saving and recycling of industrial water.

As an incentive to balance the distribution of industries across various geographical areas, a company investing a certain amount of capital or employing a certain number of employees, in specific industries, in an underdeveloped area, or in an area with scant natural resources, is eligible for the investment tax credit of up to 20% of the total amount of investment. This may be deducted from the business income tax payable in the current year. Any excess investment tax credit may be carried forward for up to four years.

In order to encourage the establishment or expansion of important science and technology enterprises, important investment and venture capital investment businesses, and where the registered stocks subscribed or underwritten have been held for a period of three years or longer, profit seeking enterprise may credit up to 20% of the price paid for acquisition against business income tax payable in the current year an individual may credit up to 10% of the price paid for acquisition of such stock against the consolidated income tax payable in the then current year. However, in the case of investment in a venture capital investment business, the amount of investment that may be credited to tax payable may not exceed an amount based on the ratio of the amount of investment actually made to the total paid in capital. Any excess of investment tax credit may be carried forward for up to four years. This credit is limited to 50% of the income tax payable in each year, however, this limit does not apply to the last year.

An important science/technology based business or an important investment business conforming to the requirements set out above may, within two years of the commencement of shareholders' capital contributions, apply for (with shareholder approval) an investment incentive in the form of either an exemption from business income tax or a shareholders' investment credit against income tax payable. Once an option has been selected, no subsequent change is allowed. Where a company selects the tax exemption pursuant to the preceding paragraph, during the exemption period, the equipment shall still be depreciated according to the serviceable life of fixed assets as provided in the Income Tax Law.

A company investing overseas according to government policy, and with the approval of the competent authority, may deduct an allowance of up to 20% of its total overseas investments to cover actual investment losses. With exceptions specifically approved by the Executive Yuan, a company must, in order to benefit from this provision, have at least a 20% stake in the overseas enterprise.

Where a non-resident individual or a non-resident business, having been approved to make investment in the ROC under the Statute for Investment by Overseas Chinese or the Statute for Investment by

Foreign Nationals, receives dividends distributed by a company located in the ROC or profits distributed by a partnership in the ROC, the income tax payable by such individual or enterprise shall be withheld at the rate of 20% at the time of payment. The provisions provided in the Income Tax Law for filing final income tax return shall not apply.

A company may retain earnings up to the amount of its paid-in capital. An important productive enterprise designated as such by the government may retain its earnings up to twice its paid-in capital. If either limit is exceeded, the excess retained earnings in each year shall be free from the restrictions stated in the Income Tax Law after the levy of a 10% business income tax.

The appreciated value of a company's assets that result from its revaluation according to the Income Tax Law is not taxed as income.

Where the premiums on stocks issued by a company in accordance with company law is set as a reserve fund of the company, the account of such premiums shall be excluded from the taxable income for the year in which the premium has incurred.

Personal taxes

Introduction

Income tax consists of individual consolidated income tax (personal income tax) and profit seeking enterprise income tax (business income tax). Since 1 January 1998, the business income tax and personal income tax systems have been integrated to allow, under certain specified rules, the deduction of business income tax from individual income tax (described more fully under the section of Corporate Taxes above).

Individual consolidated income tax is levied on income derived from sources in the Republic of China (ROC) by ROC resident or non-resident individuals.

Individual consolidated income tax is levied on a calendar basis. Income received by taxpayers, their spouses, and qualified dependants claimed in tax returns is consolidated. However, the tax payable on the salary income of a spouse may be separately calculated.

Taxable individuals

Any individual who receives income from an ROC source shall report and pay income tax. Individual taxpayers are divided into two categories, i.e. resident and non-resident taxpayers. Aliens and overseas Chinese are categorised as either resident or non-resident for tax purposes.

A resident is required to prepare and submit an income tax return for the payment of tax. Collection of the tax from a non-resident is through withholding at source or by other procedures provided under income tax legislation.

Resident individuals

An individual is resident in the ROC for tax purposes, as follows:

- the individual is domiciled and ordinarily residing in the ROC;
- the individual is not domiciled but has resided in the ROC for 183 days or more in a tax year.

Non-resident individuals

A non-resident individual is one who does not meet the definition of a resident individual as described above.

Taxable income

Income derived from sources in the ROC comprises the following:

- dividends distributed by corporations registered under the ROC Company Law or by foreign companies authorised to operate in the ROC;
- profits distributed by cooperatives or partnerships in the ROC;
- remuneration for services rendered in the ROC, excluding that is paid by an employer outside the ROC to an individual not residing but staying in the ROC for no more than 90 days during a taxable year;
- interest received from all levels of government agencies, legal entities or resident individuals in the ROC;
- rental income from properties situated in the ROC;
- royalties received for the use of patents, trademarks, copyrights, confidential formulae and franchises utilised in the ROC;
- gains from sale of properties situated in the ROC;
- remuneration for services rendered by ROC government employees stationed abroad;

- profits derived from industry, commerce, farming, forestry, fishing pasturage and mining;
- awards or prizes received from participating in contests, games or lotteries in the ROC;
- any other income received in the ROC.

Exemptions and deductions

Personal allowances

Individual consolidated income tax is assessed on the taxpayer's gross consolidated income in a particular tax year, less exemptions and deductions as follows:

- taxpayers, their spouses and qualified dependants are each entitled to a personal allowance of NT$ 74,000 each (in 2000);
- the allowance for dependant lineal ascendants, e.g. parents, grandparents, etc., over 70 years of age is NT$ 110,000 (in 2000).

Standard deduction

The taxpayer may choose to take a standard deduction of NT$ 44,000 for a single person and NT$ 67,000 for a married couple filing a joint return (in 1998).

Itemised deductions

Taxpayers who do not take the standard deduction may claim itemised deductions as follows:

- contributions and donations are deductible up to 20% of gross consolidated income if given to officially registered educational, cultural, public welfare and charitable organisations or associations, and are fully deductible if given for the purpose of national defence or military morale, or given to the government;
- premiums for life insurance, labour insurance, government employee insurance and national health insurance for the taxpayer and the taxpayer's spouse and lineal dependants are deductible up to NT$ 24,000 per person;
- medical and childbirth expenses incurred by the taxpayer, the taxpayer's spouse and dependants and paid to public hospitals, specially contracted hospitals for civil service insurance, specially contracted hospitals or clinics for labour insurance or national health insurance, or those hospitals having complete and accurate accounting records as recognised by the MOF are

deductible, apart from that portion covered by an insurance payment;

- uncompensated losses from disaster;
- mortgage interest incurred and paid by taxpayers to financial institutions on loans acquired for the purpose of purchasing an owner occupied residence are deductible up to NT$ 300,000 per filing unit.

Special deductions

The taxpayer is entitled to the following special deductions irrespective of whether standard or itemised deductions have been made:

- against the gains from property transactions for any losses that were incurred from other property transactions for the same year;
- for wage income up to a maximum of NT$ 62,000 (in 2000);
- for savings and investment up to NT$ 270,000;
- NT$ 74,000 (in 2000) for disabled (handicapped) or mentally ill dependants;
- educational expenses up to NT$ 25,000.

Exemptions and deductions are adjusted in accordance to the consumer price index when it rises by more than 3% compared to the prior adjustment year.

Tax rates

Taxable income (NT$)		*Tax rates*
From	*To*	
0	370,000	6%
370,000	990,000	22,200 plus 13% of the portion in excess of 370,000
990,000	1,980,000	102,800 plus 21% of the portion in excess of 990,000
1,980,000	3,720,000	310,700 plus 30% of the portion in excess of 1,980,000
3,720,000	Upwards	832,700 plus 40% of the portion in excess of 3,720,000

Withholding tax

Type of income	*Rate for resident*	*Rate for non-resident*
Dividends distributed by companies and profits distributed by cooperatives.	—	(1) 0% (2) 20% if the investment was approved under the Statute for Investment by Foreign Nationals or the Statute for Investment by Overseas Chinese.
Profits paid to partners or to the owner of a sole proprietorship.		(1) 30% (2) 20% if the investment was approved under the Statute for Investment by Foreign Nationals or the Statute for Investment by Overseas Chinese.
Wages and salaries	10%, or withheld in accordance with the regulations governing the withholding of wages.	20%
Commission	10%	20%
Interest	(1) 10% (2) 20% on interest from short term commercial paper.	20%
Rental	10%	20%
Royalties	15%	20%
Income from professional practice.	10%	20%

Awards or prizes obtained from participating in contests, games or lotteries, etc.	(1) 15% (2) 20% (per ticket) for a prize over NT$2,000 received from lotteries sponsored by the government.	(1) 20% (2) 0% if received from lotteries sponsored by the government and below NT$2,000 per ticket.
Income from the payments for retirement, severance, etc.	6% to be taxed on the excess amounts prescribed by the Income Tax Law.	20% excess amounts prescribed by the Income Tax Law.
Other income.	—	20%

Tax incentives

- Where a patent right or copyright in computer software is legally obtained by a national of the ROC through registration of his creation or invention and provided or sold to a company for use in the ROC with the approval of the relevant competent authority, the royalties received from the company are excluded from the individual's consolidated income.
- Where a business which is approved under the relevant Statute to make investment in the ROC temporarily (i.e. for less than 183 days in aggregate in a given tax year) seconds its directors, managerial officers or technical personnel to the ROC to perform work (such as making investment, plant construction or market survey), salaries paid outside the ROC are not treated as income sourced in the ROC.
- Where a company reinvests its undistributed earnings or its employees invest their bonuses in designated enterprises (e.g. science, technology, investment, venture capital, R&D, energy saving, sanitary, etc), the value of the newly acquired registered stocks is not included in taxable consolidated income until such time as stocks are transferred.
- In order to encourage the establishment or expansion of designated enterprises, if the registered stocks subscribed or underwritten are held by the investors for a period exceeding three years, they may credit up to 10% of the acquisition price against income tax payable. However, in the case of investment in a venture capital investment enterprise, the amount that may be credited must not exceed an amount based on the ratio of the investment actually made to total paid in capital. Any excess investment tax credit may be carried forward for up to four years. The credit is limited to 50% of the income tax payable in each year, although the limit does not apply to the final year.

Other taxes

Customs duties

Import duty payable is based on the customs value of imported goods, or on quantity of imported goods as specified by Customs Import Tariff. Values are determined and calculated on the basis of their true transaction value. The customs authorities may adjust the value of goods declared according to reasonable values or estimated values based on production costs and expenses and may make reasonable investigations to determine the value of goods.

The ROC adopts the Harmonised Commodity Description and Coding System, with two sets of rates, one general and the other applying to goods imported from countries or areas which extend special reciprocal treatment to ROC commodities.

In addition to certain zero-rated imports, the following are exempt from customs import duty:

- personal effects and advertising materials and samples of no commercial value;
- certain machinery, equipment, instruments and apparatus used exclusively for R&D or examination and analysis, or energy conservation, waste recycling or manufacturing improvement, where not locally manufactured (as verified by the Ministry of Economic Affairs);
- machinery, equipment, raw materials, fuel and parts imported for processing by manufacturers located in export processing zones or a science based industrial park;
- a private organisation may be exempt from duty on imports of construction machinery and equipment (and their components and the specific transportation tools used in their implementation) where alternatives are not manufactured or supplied domestically.

Bonded warehouses and bonded factories may be established according to approval by Customs and conditions co-specified by the Ministry of Finance (MOF) and the Ministry of Economic Affairs, to enable the customs duty exempt re-export, or manufacture or process for re-export, of various raw materials or components.

Offset and refund of customs duties and commodity tax

Customs duties and commodity taxes payable on raw materials for use in manufacture of products for export may be recorded on account against guarantee at the time of importation and offset after exportation of the finished products, or where paid at importation a refund may be applied after exportation.

Special customs duties

In order to take account of extraordinary domestic and international economic situations to accommodate the supply of goods and to rationalise operations, the MOF can make an upward or downward adjustment of customs duties on imported goods within the range of 50% of the prescribed Tariff duty rates for a period not to exceed one year, as approved by the Executive Yuan. Upward adjustments may be applied in the following cases:

- where imported goods have directly or indirectly received a bounty or subsidy in production or shipment or export from the country of exportation or production, thereby causing injury to the industry of the ROC;
- where imported goods are 'dumped' at a price lower than the normal value of goods of the same kind; ('normal value' is the comparable selling price in the country of exportation or production in the ordinary course of trade, or the comparable exporting price of identical goods exported to a third country or a price reflecting the production cost of identical goods plus overheads in the country of production);
- where goods exported or conveyed from the ROC receive discriminatory treatment by an importing country which impairs the marketing position of the ROC, then goods imported from such country to the ROC may be liable to an appropriate retaliatory duty in addition to the customs duties leviable under the Customs Import Tariff.

Service charges for aids to navigation

Unless otherwise provided, any ship which navigates on the waters of a port authority of the ROC and enjoys the navigation buoys or beacons or harbour facilities of the ROC is subject to service charges for aids to navigation, payable by the shipping manager prior to departure of the ship from port, as follows:

Tonnage	*Tax rate*
Over 150 tons	NT$ 6.00 per ton
Under 150 tons	NTS$ 3.00 per ton

Business tax (VAT)

Any transaction involving goods or services within the territory of the ROC, including importation of goods, is subject to VAT.

A VAT liability is imposed on business suppliers of goods or services, consignees or holders of imported goods and recipients of services supplied by foreign enterprises or organisations with no permanent business establishment within the ROC, whose fiscal representative holds the status of a taxpayer.

Zero rating and non-credit exemption

Sales of goods or services are zero rated principally in connection with the export of goods and specified transportation.

The sales selected goods or services are exempted without credit for business tax previously paid, particularly the sale of land, welfare and educational services, and an extensive list of other specific exemptions.

Businesses	*Rates (%)*
(1) Enterprises involved in banking, insurance, trust investment, securities, short term commercial paper and pawnshops.	5% (1% on revenue from reinsurance premiums).
(2) Enterprises engaged in special beverage and food services:	
– nightclubs or restaurants providing entertainment;	15%
– saloons or tearooms, coffee shops and bars offering female companionship.	25%
(3) Traders in the wholesale agricultural market and small business supplying agricultural products.	0.1%
(4) Small businesses and other businesses excluded by the MOF from reporting their transactions.	1%
(5) Other business entities subject to VAT reporting.	5%–10%

Businesses falling into categories (1) to (4) above calculate their tax liability by gross receipts with no credit, while VAT businesses (5) calculate their tax liability by offsetting output tax against input tax.

Commodity tax

Commodity tax is levied on goods listed in the Statute for Commodity Tax, whether manufactured domestically or imported from abroad. Manufacturers are liable for commodity tax on those commodities which they produce locally. The consignees of taxable commodities from abroad also pay this tax.

The taxable value of locally manufactured commodities is calculated according to a formula.

The taxable value of imported commodities is the total of the value on which customs duties are assessed, the customs duties and harbour construction fees.

Eight classifications of commodities are taxed at the rates shown below.

Tax rates

Tobacco and wine	Currently suspended (sold under the monopoly system).
Rubber tyres	
– buses/trucks	10%
– other	15%
– man/animal powered/farming vehicles	exempt
Cement	Flat rates for various grades.
Beverages (soft drinks)	8%, 15%
Certain approved fruit/vegetable juices	exempt
Sheet glass	10%
Glass used in mold-making	exempt
Oil/gas	Flat rates for various grades.
Electric appliances	10%, 13%, 15%, 20%
Vehicles	
– cars	25%, 35%, 60% (engine capacity)
– trucks, buses	15%
– special purpose (including import for R&D) not used on public roads	exempt
– motorcycles	17% (3% where developmental)
– electric motorcycles	8.5%

Exemption and refund

Exempt commodities include raw materials (except flue-cured leaf tobaccos), export goods, exhibition-only goods and certain military use goods. Commodity tax may be refunded on export goods, raw materials used to manufacture export goods and certain goods not sellable or damaged.

Land taxes

Agricultural land tax

This tax has been suspended since 1987.

Land value tax

Land value tax is paid according to the value of land by the owner(s), lessee or public administrator. Two rates, standard (progressive) and privileged, are applied.

The standard rate ranges between 1% and 5.5% of an assigned value, based on average local land values. Land used in factories, mining or agriculture are exempt from tax.

Special privileged rates range from 0.2% and 1% and are accorded to various specified land uses including residential, government approved project and industry, and publicly owned land where the use is non-public.

There are many reductions and exemptions to land value tax, applying to both public and private land use and to passage between properties.

Land increment tax

A land value increment tax is payable where transfer of property establishes a new value for the land. Progressive rates are applied according to the increment ratio calculated by dividing total increased value against the value originally prescribed or reported in the previous transfer.

There are certain exemptions and refunds available according to the nature and purpose of the land transfer.

House tax

The taxpayer is a house owner or lessee (lien right owner). Houses and improvement costs form the tax base.

Tax rates

Classification	*Max. rate*	*Min. rate*	*Actual rates enforced*		*Education surcharge*
House with residential use	2%	1.38%	Taiwan Province	1.38%	–
			Taipei/ Kaohsiung Cities	1.38%	
House with business use	5%	3%	Taiwan Province	3%	30% of the house tax
			Taipei City	3%	1% of the house's current value
			Kaohsiung	3%	–
Houses for private hospitals, clinics, professional offices, and the premises of non-profit organisations.	2.5%	1.5%	Taiwan Province	2%	–
			Taipei City	2%	–
			Kaohsiung City	2%	–

Exemption and reduction

No house tax is levied on a number of specified public buildings, nor on private buildings used for educational, religions, certain non-profit making purposes or those valued below NT$ 100,000.

House tax is reduced by half on the following private houses:

- dwelling houses sold by the government to people at reduced prices;
- buildings owned by approved and registered factories for direct use in production;
- warehouses and houses used for testing purposes by farmers' associations;
- houses of which more than 30% but less than 50% of the floor

area has been destroyed, subject to reporting and investigation procedures.

Deed tax

Tax liability (at rates between 2.5% and 7.5% depending on the transaction) arises on buying and selling, establishing lessee (lien) rights, exchange, donation, partition and legal possession of real estate, excluding real estate already subject to land value increment tax.

Exemption and reduction

- Ownership of real estate acquired as a result of inheritance is exempt.
- Businesses specifically approved by the Ministry of Economic Affairs for rationalisation merger.
- The proceeds realised from a sale of land and plant in accordance with approved merger, where proceeds are wholly used to purchase new land and plant under the same plan.

Stamp duty

Stamp duty is payable on monetary receipts, deeds for the sale of movable property, certain contract agreements, certain deeds or sale contracts for real estate. As a principle, the person who executes contracts, deeds or receipts is subject to stamp tax levy. A number of exemptions exist for particular bodies or classes of transaction.

Securities transactions tax (STT)

Transactions involving bonds, shares, share certificates or corporate debentures and any other subscription securities approved by the government may be subject to STT. The tax is collected from the seller by the sales agent or broker, and is between 0.1% and 0.3% of the value of securities issued.

Government bonds, treasury bills and certain other securities are exempt from STT.

Estate and gift tax

Any estate inherited from an ROC resident national is subject to estate tax whether the property is located within or outside the ROC. Any estate inherited from a non-resident ROC national or foreigner is taxable on that portion which is located in the ROC. A number of exclusions and deductions exist.

Gifts made by ROC resident nationals are subject to gift tax irrespective of the location of the donated property. The gifts of non-resident ROC nationals or foreigners are subject to gift tax only where the donated property is located in the ROC. The donor is the taxpayer and the tax is assessed on prevailing values, but an extensive list of exclusions and deductions exists.

An annual exemption of NT$ 1,000,000 is available to each donor.

Tax rates – estate tax

Net estate NT$	*Rate %*
0 – 600,000	2
600,000 – 1,500,000	4
1,500,000 – 3,000,000	7
3,000,000 – 4,500,000	11
4,500,000 – 6,000,000	15
6,000,000 – 10,000,000	20
10,000,000 – 15,000,000	26
15,000,000 – 40,000,000	33
40,000,000 – 100,000,000	41
100,000,000 upwards	50

Gift tax

Net estate NT$	*Rate %*
0 – 600,000	4
600,000 – 1,500,000	6
1,700,000 – 2,800,000	9
2,800,000 – 3,900,000	12
3,900,000 – 5,000,000	16
5,000,000 – 7,200,000	21
7,200,000 – 14,000,000	27
14,000,000 – 29,000,000	34
29,000,000 – 45,000,000	42
45,000,000 upwards	50

Entertainment tax

Tax liability for entertainment tax arises on the value of tickets sold or fee collection by entertainment businesses that provide equipment or activities for entertainment, e.g. cinemas, occupational singing, story telling, dancing circus, magic and acrobatic shows, night club performance, competitions and contests involving skill and dance halls, billiard halls, bowling alleys, golf clubs, etc., where these are provided as a form of recreation for consumers. The taxpayer is the consumer and the tax collector the provider or sponsor.

Tax rates

The tax rates vary between 5% and 100% according to the nature of the entertainment.

Exemption

Various exemptions exist to include the provision of entertainment by educational, public welfare, charitable institutions organisations and specified approved foundations. Also exempt is entertainment where the proceeds are used for disaster relief or military morale purposes and where deductible expenses do not exceed 20% of the proceeds. Cultural and entertainment activities provided temporarily, exclusively and free of charge are also exempt.

Mine concession tax

A concession used for mining activity is subject to taxation. The mine owner is permitted to prospect or mine the mineral specified by certificate as well as other minerals incidental to the same deposit. The taxpayer is the mine owner or the lessee of a mine leased from the government.

Tax rates

Prospecting concession	NT$ 0.6 per acre per year
– beneath riverbed	NT$ 0.6 per metre per year
Mining concession	NT$ 1.8 per acre per year
– beneath riverbed	NT$ 1.8 per metre per year

Exemption and reduction

The mine concession tax can be deducted either from business tax or mineral product tax upon provision of the relevant tax receipt.

The mine concession tax is exempt for a period of inoperation (more than two months) due to industrial action or other major interruption.

Thailand

V.A.T. Accounting

Corporate taxes

Income tax is payable by legal entities based on their net profits. Incorporated firms operating in Thailand must pay corporate income tax at a rate of 30% on net profits. Foundations and associations engaged in any revenue seeking business, except for those designated as tax exempt organisations, pay income tax at a rate of 2% or 10% of gross business income, varying according to the type of activity by which that income is generated.

Taxable entities

All companies registered under the Thai Civil and Commercial Code are subject to tax as stipulated in the Revenue Code. Taxable entities include companies, public companies, registered ordinary partnerships, limited partnerships, foundations, associations and joint ventures.

Tax year and filing requirements

The tax year is the accounting year. Usually, an accounting year is 12 months. The first year after registration, or the year of liquidation of a business, may be less than 12 months. The closing date of every accounting year must be consistent, but an application to change may be granted by the Director General.

Companies, registered ordinary partnerships, limited partnerships and joint ventures must file tax returns twice yearly, i.e. a semi-annual income tax return and an annual income tax return, subject to detailed rules for first and last periods of account.

Semi-annual returns must be filed within two months from the end of the first six months of the accounting period, with payment of half of the corporate income tax due on the estimated net profit for the whole year.

An annual income tax return must be filed within 150 days from the closing date of the annual accounting year together with payment of the tax at a rate of 30% of net profit (adjusted in compliance with tax rules).

Income subject to tax

Corporate income tax is calculated in accordance with generally accepted accounting principles, as adjusted by the specific rules of income tax law, to arrive at chargeable income. All realised economic gains are deemed to be income, whether arising in the normal course of business or on capital gains or dividend receipts.

A Thai company is subject to tax on income derived from all sources within Thailand or abroad. Foreign companies not registered or not residing in Thailand are subject to tax only on income derived from sources within Thailand.

Income and expenses are calculated using an accruals basis.

Dividend receipts from a limited company organised under Thai law and mutual funds or a finance institution organised by a specific law of Thailand – for the purpose of lending money to promote agriculture, commerce or industry – are 50% exempt from tax. For listed companies and companies holding at least 25% of the total shares of the dividend paying company, dividends are 100% tax exempt. Such 50% and 100% tax exemptions, only provided for the relevant shares, are held at least three months prior to (and three months subsequent to) the dividends' receipt date.

Deductions and expenses

Generally, all expenses and outgoings (which are wholly and exclusively incurred in the production of income) are deductible, unless specifically prohibited. With expenses of a capital or personal nature, taxes paid on income and VAT are not deductible. Net losses can be carried forward for a maximum of five consecutive tax years.

Subject to certain conditions and restrictions, the following items are not deductible expenses:

- reserves (except reserves set aside for life or other insurance and certain provisions for bad debt or write-off);
- contribution to any fund (except provident funds under the Provident Fund Act);
- any private expenses, gifts or donations (except for a charitable donation designated by the Director-General of the Revenue Department, which may not exceed 2% of net profit, and except

for a sum paid for the purpose of education or athletics as designated by the Director-General of the Revenue Department for which deduction may also be made to the extent not exceeding 2% of net profit);

- excessive entertainment expenses not consistent with the Ministerial Regulations;
- capital expenditure (or expenditure incurred on addition, alteration, extension or improvement of property, other than repairs and maintenance);
- tax penalties and/or surcharges, fines, value-added tax and income tax;
- certain sums withdrawn from an investment fund;
- unreasonable amounts of salary paid to shareholders or partners/directors;
- artificial expenses or expenses which are not charged to the appropriate accounting period;
- interest on capital, reserves or funds of the company or registered partnership;
- any loss or damage recoverable under an insurance or indemnity contract or the net losses incurred in the preceding year (except net allowable losses brought forward from accounting periods no longer than five years preceding the current accounting period);
- expenses not related to the purpose of acquiring profits or the purpose of business activity;
- expenses not related to the business in Thailand;
- artificial prices paid for properties, or excessive expenses in connection with the purchase or sale of properties;
- loss due to devaluation of assets, except securities;
- any expenses paid to a recipient that cannot be proved or identified by the payer;
- any payment made out of profits at the end of an accounting period; and
- any additional, undeductible expenses notified by Royal Decree.

Remittance tax

Remittance tax is a withholding tax which applies to profits transferred, or deemed to be transferred, from a Thailand branch to its head office overseas at a rate of 10% of the amount to be remitted before tax. Remittance tax must be paid by the remitting office of the offshore company within seven days of the date of remittance.

Investment incentives

The Investment Promotion Act authorises the Board of Investment (BOI) to provide a number of incentives and privileges to selected enterprises.

The BOI confers two kinds of benefits, as follows:

- tax incentives in the form of tax holidays, tariff or import duty exemptions and dividends paid out of income – they are tax exempt; and
- non-tax privileges, such as permits to allow skilled foreign technicians or experts into Thailand to work on specific projects, and permits to acquire land normally unavailable to aliens.

There are three investment promotion zones throughout Thailand in line with the government policy of decentralisation from Bangkok. Promoted projects located in Zone 3 receive incentives greater than those available to the other two zones.

Zone 1 includes: Bangkok, Samut Prakan, Samut Sakhon, Nakhon Pathom, Nonta Buri and Pathum Thani.

Zone 2 includes: Samut Sonngkhram, Ratchaburi, Kanchanaburi, Suphanburi, Angthong, Ayutthaya, Saraburi, Nokhon Nayok, Chachoengsao and Chonburi.

Zone 3 includes: the remaining 61 provinces as well as the Laem Chabang industrial estates.

Taxes on investors in the stock exchange

Individual investors, including foreign individual investors, are exempt from taxation on capital gains from stock exchange securities trading.

However, foreign investors are subject to taxation as follows:

Type of Income	*Tax Rate*
Direct investment in stock exchange	tax-free
Capital gain for an individual	tax-free
Capital gain for a business	15% withholding
Dividend receipts for an individual	10% withholding

Dividend receipts for a business	10% withholding
Interest received by an individual	15% withholding
Interest received by a business	15% withholding

Income tax on gross receipts

Foreign companies, or registered partnerships, conducting international transportation business activity within Thailand while based in another country are subject to income tax on the relevant gross receipts.

For international passenger transportation, income tax is levied at a rate of 3% on fares, fees and other charges collected in Thailand.

For international goods transportation, income tax is levied at a rate of 3% on the freight, fees and other charges collected overseas, for transporting the goods from Thailand.

Payments to foreign companies

Payment made either from, or within, Thailand to those foreign companies not conducting business in Thailand are subject to income tax. The rate of tax applied depends on the type of payment being made. The tax must be withheld by the payer and remitted to the Revenue Department on behalf of the offshore company. The tax rates are based on a nature of income as follows:

Nature of Income	*Tax Rate (%)*
Interest on loans paid to banks, insurance companies and financial institutions.	15
Interest paid by the government or Thai financial institution legally permitted to lend money for the promotion of agriculture, commerce or industry.	Exempt
Other interest.	15
Dividends.	10
Rental payments.	15
Royalties from goodwill, copyright and other rights.	15
Professional fees (i.e., technical services, medical, architectural, engineering, fine arts, accounting, and legal).	15
Management fees.	15
Income derived from the post or office of employment, or service rendered.	15

Recipients from countries which have double taxation treaties are taxed by reference to such treaties.

Thailand has entered into double tax treaties with 40 countries and negotiations with a further three countries are underway.

Treaties to avoid double taxation

Thailand has treaty agreements to eliminate double taxation with the following countries:

Australia	Germany	Mauritius	South Africa
Austria	Hungary	Nepal	South Korea
Bangladesh	India	Netherlands	Spain
Belgium	Indonesia	New Zealand	Sri Lanka
Canada	Israel	Norway	Sweden
China	Italy	Pakistan	Switzerland
Czech Republic	Japan	Philippines	Udbaykistan
Denmark	Laos	Poland	United Kingdom
Finland	Luxembourg	Romania	USA
France	Malaysia	Singapore	Vietnam

Treaty negotiations are underway with Myanmar, the United Arab Emirates and Greece.

These treaties generally put the taxpayer in a more favorable position for Thai income tax than he would be in under the Revenue Code because they stipulate that profits will only be taxable if the taxpayer has a permanent establishment in Thailand.

Personal taxes

Each individual, resident or non-resident, who derives assessable income from employment or business in Thailand or has assets located in Thailand, is subject to personal income tax, whether such income is paid in or outside of Thailand. Exemptions are granted to certain persons, including UN officers, diplomats and certain visiting experts, under the terms of international and bilateral agreements.

Personal income tax is accounted on a cash basis.

Personal income tax on net annual income is at the following rates:

Amount in Baht	*Rate (%)*
1–50,000	0
50,001–100,000	5
100,001–500,000	10
500,001–1,000,000	20
1,000,001–4,000,000	30
4,000,001 or over	37

Individuals residing for 180 days or more in Thailand for any calendar year are subject to income tax on income from foreign sources if that income is brought into Thailand during the same taxable year (i.e. calendar year) that they are a resident.

Personal income taxes and tax returns must be filed prior to the end of March of the year following the year in which the income was earned.

A standard deduction of 40%, but not in excess of Baht 60,000, is permitted against income from employment or services rendered. Standard deductions ranging from 10% to 85% are allowed for other categories of income. In general, however, taxpayers may elect to itemise expenses in lieu of the standard legislated deductions.

The following annual personal allowances are permitted

	Baht
Personal allowance	30,000
Spouse allowance	30,000
Child allowance	15,000 per child to a maximum of three children
Education allowance	2,000 per child to a maximum of three children
Insurance allowance	Actual cost incurred to a maximum of 10,000
Provident fund allowance	Actual cost to a maximum of 300,000
Interest allowance (housing loans)	Actual cost to a maximum of 50,000
Contribution to Thai Social Security Fund	Actual cost
Charity and donation	Actual cost not exceeding 10% of net assessable income.

Other taxes

Value added tax

Value added tax (VAT) is collected from the sale of goods and services. A business which earns revenue in excess of Baht 1.2 million per annum, must apply for VAT registration as an operator. The operator is required to levy value added tax at a rate of 10% from the sale of goods and services (currently reduced to 7% until 1 October 2001, unless there is an extension of the reduction period). Exports are zero rated.

A VAT monthly tax return must be filed with the Revenue department by the fifteenth day of the following month.

The payment due is calculated by deducting input VAT from output VAT.

Where input tax exceeds output tax, the taxpayer is entitled to a tax credit or refund.

Specific business tax

Individuals or businesses that conduct the following business in Thailand must pay specific business tax.

- commercial banks and entities acting as a commercial bank (activities such as making loans);
- finance businesses, securities businesses and credit financing;
- life insurance;
- pawnshops;
- selling of immovable properties; or
- selling of securities in the stock exchange of Thailand.

Tax rates range from 0.1 to 3.0 %, according to the type of income.

The specific business tax return must be filed to the Revenue department by the 15th day of the following month.

Stamp duty

Stamp duty is levied on documentation such as loan agreements, services agreements, lease agreements, bills of lading, cheques, etc. Tax rates are specified under its tariffs.

Property tax

The owners of land and/or buildings in designated areas may be subject to property tax by the local government. Property tax is paid on an annual basis at a rate of 12.5% of the assessed assumed rental value of land and buildings.

Turkey

GYM Güreli Yeminli Mali Müşavirlik A.Ş.

Introduction

Resident companies are liable for corporation tax on their worldwide income in Turkey. A company is treated as resident if its legal or business headquarters are in Turkey.

Taxpayers are required to file tax returns after having determined their own tax obligations. The tax year is the calendar year, although companies and other businesses may have other year ends.

Corporate taxes

General

Income subject to corporate tax is based on several types of commercial earnings listed below (less losses, certain exemptions and deductions).

Taxable entities

Payers of this tax are the following corporations and institutions:

- joint stock corporations;
- limited liability corporations;
- joint stock limited partnerships;
- co-operatives;
- public economic institutions;
- economic enterprises belonging to associations and partnerships;
- joint ventures; and
- foreign entities which fit the above-mentioned cases.

There exists the classification of 'full liability' and 'limited liability' as for the taxation principle of the corporations. The distinguishing criterion among them is based on:

- the legal centre of the corporation; and
- the business centre of the corporation.

If either one of these centres is in Turkey, the corporation is considered within the status of 'full liability'. On the other hand, if neither are in Turkey, the entity will have the status of 'limited liability'.

Tax year and filing requirements

Although (in normal circumstances) the financial year is the calendar year, upon the demand of the taxpayer, the Ministry of Finance is entitled to fix special 12-month periods for the companies.

The tax return has to be filed within four months after the termination of the tax year. The corporate income tax is paid in three equal instalments: April, July and October.

Income subject to tax

Corporate income tax is imposed on corporate earnings composed of the following:

- commercial gains;
- agricultural gains;
- wages;
- gains from independent professions;
- revenue from immovable property;
- revenue from movable property; and
- revenues and earnings regardless of the sources from which they have been gained.

Rates of tax

Corporation tax shall be charged at the rate of 30% of the corporate revenue determined under the Corporate Tax Law. Those that are liable to pay corporation tax shall pay advance tax at the rate of 25% over their quarterly revenues (according to the principles set out in income tax law) on condition that the same be deducted from the corporation tax payable for the current taxable year. Advance tax is paid within 45 days after the end of the related quarter. However, 10% over the corporation tax shall be paid.

Dividends from corporations are subject to 16.5% withholding tax.

Deductions

General rules

Expenses directly or closely connected with the conduct of the business are wholly or partially tax deductible.

Among the allowable tax deductions are general expenses, social expenses, losses, damages and reimbursements, travelling expenses, property taxes, duties and fees, amortisation, issuing expenses of shares and bonds, establishment and structuring expenses, donations and previous years' losses.

Depreciation and amortisation

Various methods of depreciation and amortisation are permitted, provided that they are in accordance with generally accepted accounting principles and sound business practice. In determining the depreciation and amortisation rates of tangible and intangible fixed assets, the residual value and the useful life of the asset are taken into account.

As for the amortisation principles of an asset forming an economical and technical unity, either the straight line or the decreasing residuals methods are applicable.

Due to the annual inflation rate announced by the Government, the assets each year are re-evaluated.

Amortisation rates vary from one asset to another; from a maximum rate of 40% and a period of five years for the assets of a corporation keeping its account books on double entry principles, to a rate of 0% for unoccupied land and fields.

Bad and doubtful debts

Bad and doubtful debts are directly deducted from the income of the corporation, provided that their doubtfulness is documented according to the provisions of law.

Interest

In principle, all interest payments on loan stock and other debts of a company are considered to be business expenses and therefore tax deductible.

Turkey

Dividends

Dividends received by corporations are exempt from corporate tax.

Donations

Any kind of assets or money donated to public associations, municipalities, scientific research institutions, health institutions or foundations determined by the Council of Ministers are tax-deductible to a certain extent determined by law.

Taxes

With the exception of value added tax, taxes levied on business transactions (including real estate, stamp and municipal taxes) are deductible.

Formation and start-up costs

Expenses connected with the issue of shares and the establishment of a company are deductible.

Remuneration

Remuneration is deductible, but fees paid as a share of profits are regarded as non-deductible dividend distributions.

Foreign source income

Tax paid on income obtained abroad is deducted from the total tax levied in Turkey (tax credit), provided that the income has been taxed in the other country and ratified as so by the Turkish Embassies, Consulates or other relevant Turkish authorities in that country.

Foreign taxes suffered on foreign source income may be credited against Turkish tax. The total creditable tax may not exceed a sum calculated by applying the Turkish rate to the income.

Investment incentives and special benefits

Depending on the level of development, Turkey is divided into four different regions where the incentives in operation are applied differently – they are known as First Priority regions, Second Priority regions, Normal regions and Developed regions. Turkish tax legislation offers regional grants for investing in less developed areas.

Additionally, investments progressed in certain fields of industry and commerce, announced through regulations or decrees, are subject to various incentives established by the Council of Ministers, depending upon the sectors, geographic locations and export potentials of the projects.

The incentives include, tax reductions, several years of non-interest long or short term loans, customs exemption on machinery, equipment, raw materials, semi-finished goods and spare parts, investment allowances, other subsidised credits (such as 'Fund Sourced Credit'), tax, duties, and credit charges exemptions, reductions in social security premiums, compulsory savings and housing funds, energy incentives, VAT incentives and several others.

Investment allowances have been exempted from corporate tax, but are subject to 19.80% withholding tax.

Losses

If a loss arises, it may be carried forward against the income of the following five taxable years.

Corporate groups

Holding companies are subject to corporate tax at the same rate as single corporations.

In practice, the parent company and its subsidiaries issue separate balance sheets.

Profit distributed as a result of the operating activities of holding companies is subject to withholding tax, whereas participation exemption is, in effect, in the disbursement of the profits from the participations.

Tax-free mergers and disposals

In the case of mergers, only those revenues of the terminated company which have been gained up to the date of takeover shall be taxed and the profits arisen directly from a merger shall not be calculated and taxed provided the following requirements are satisfied and met:

- the terminated company and the absorbing company shall provide the tax office (which governs the terminated company) with a takeover declaration signed jointly by them within 15 days from the date of merger and shall attach the take over balance sheet to such a declaration; and

- the absorbing company shall undertake and warrant (by virtue of a covenant attached to the takeover declaration) that it shall pay for the tax debts of the terminated company, which have already accrued or shall accrue in the future, and that it shall fulfill the other obligations of the terminated company as well.

Liquidation of the corporation

In cases where the corporate body is liquidated, the liquidation gains shall also be subject to corporate income tax unless it qualifies for a tax-free merger.

Capital taxes

There is no capital tax or duty imposed in Turkey.

Treatment of branches (branch profits tax)

Profits of foreign branches are treated as foreign source income. Branches of foreign corporations in Turkey will be under limited liability provided that their centre of business is not in Turkey. They will, however, have to incorporate as soon as they are engaged in commercial activities in Turkey.

Taxation of non-resident entities

Only the revenues and gains obtained in Turkey by a limited liability entity are subject to corporate tax. These revenues and gains are as follows:

- the commercial gains obtained through the legal or business centres of the foreign entity in Turkey;
- wages obtained in Turkey;
- gains obtained from independent professions in Turkey;
- agricultural gains obtained in Turkey;
- revenues from immovable and movable properties obtained in Turkey; and
- other gains and revenues obtained in Turkey.

Personal taxes

Definition of income

Income is the gross total of all kinds of revenues and earnings gained by a real person during the course of a calendar year and used by that person for savings or spending purposes.

Income subject to tax

Income tax is imposed on seven main income factors, as follows:

Commercial gains

Gains received from trade, industry or service operations.

Agricultural gains

Gains received from agricultural activities such as farming, animal raising, fishing, etc.

Wages

Benefits of employees received from labour, which is based on labour relationship.

Gains from independent professions

Gains from the operations of independent professions such as those of medical doctors, lawyers, accountants, etc., which are operated and rendered independently and not as a result of a labour contract or a commercial activity.

Revenue from immovable property

These are merely the benefits collected on the lease of the immovable property. However, if the immovable property belongs to a business entity then the rent revenues will be considered as commercial revenues.

Revenue from movable property

The concept of movable capital merely covers stocks and bonds, and loans such as bank deposits or private loans. The benefits received as profit shares from corporations, or as interest, are classified as revenue from movable property, whereas the revenue from a movable property of a business entity is considered as commercial revenue.

Revenues and earnings regardless of the sources from which they have been gained

Incomes, which are not associated with the above 6 income elements, shall be taxed as other revenues and earnings.

Taxable individuals

The taxpayer for income tax purposes is every individual, either Turkish or foreigner, who attains a taxable income. The taxpayers are again grouped in two categories as:

- taxpayers of full liability; or
- taxpayers of limited liability.

Individuals in the first group are liable for all their income acquired in Turkey or abroad, whereas the ones in the latter group are liable only for their income attained within the boundaries of Turkey.

Citizens or foreigners who dwell in Turkey are categorised as having 'full liability' as well as the Turkish citizens dwelling abroad but whose work is attached to official or private bodies or institutions centralised in Turkey (Turkish citizens who have been taxed abroad where their work is, are not double taxed in Turkey). A taxpayer is deemed to dwell in Turkey if:

- his domicile is in Turkey; or
- he continuously resides in Turkey for more than six months per calendar year.

On the other hand, the following foreigners are not considered as having full liability, even if they stay in Turkey for more than six months per calendar year:

- business people, scientists, experts, officials, press members, students and patients who come to Turkey for a particular and temporary mission; or
- persons who are detained or who stay in Turkey due to their being arrested, convicted or being sick.

Individuals who do not qualify to be under full liability, but still acquire income in Turkey, are regarded as having a 'limited liability' status.

Tax year, filing requirements and returns

Annual return

The annual return is a yearly declaration of income. Except for income obtained from abroad, the following benefits are not subject to yearly declaration for unlimited liability income taxpayers:

- wages, which have been already subjected to withholding tax, received from an employer;
- wages received from more than one employer (wages gained during a calendar year shall be less than the half of the total amount of the first and second income segments of the income tariff as set forth in Article 103);
- revenue from movable properties (revenue gained during a calendar year shall be less than half of the total amount of the first and second income segments of the income tariff as set forth in Article 103);
- revenue from immovable properties (revenues gained during a calendar year shall be less than half of the total amount of the first and second income segments of the income tariff as set forth in Article 103);
- income gained by farmers not subjected to a real basis for taxation; and
- some portion of the revenues and gains which is exempted from tax.

The following benefits are not subject to yearly declaration for limited liability income taxpayers:

- wages, gains received from independent professions, movable and immovable property gains and dividends received from corporations which have been already subjected to withholding tax; or
- other revenues and gains.

If revenue is obtained only from immovable properties, then the annual return shall be submitted within the month of January and tax shall be paid in January, April and July.

If revenue is obtained only from commercial gains determined by the 'simple' method, the annual return shall be submitted within the month of February and tax shall be paid in February, May and August.

In other cases, the annual return shall be submitted within the month of March to the related tax office and tax shall be paid in March, June and September.

Individual return

An individual return of income tax is concerned only with persons of limited liability who are not obliged to submit annual returns and who acquire gains not subject to a withholding tax. Within the next 15 days after each of the specified transactions, the taxpayer of limited liability or his fiduciary has to submit an individual return and pay the tax by the end of the same term.

Withholding return

This return is submitted by employers or other persons who are assigned to withholding tax as they make income payments to the taxpayers.

Foreign source income

Turkish individuals under full liability, like Turkish corporations, are taxed on their worldwide income. They are granted credit for foreign taxes paid on foreign income, provided that such credit does not exceed the taxes they are to pay in Turkey.

Losses

Losses arising from a particular income subject to taxation are deducted from the other taxable income. If the losses are exceeding the total income, then they can be carried forward for a maximum period of five years against the income.

Rates of tax

After deductions and allowances, annual taxable income is charged at the progressive rates shown in Table 1.

In addition, as a contribution to fund payment, a surcharge of 10% of income tax is levied on the income declared in the tax return and a fiscal stamp duty of 0.60% is levied on gross wage earnings. Although in some respects allowances differ, the tax rates for residents and non-residents are the same.

Individual income tax rates

Band *(TL)*			*Rate* (%)
0	–	2,800,000,000	20
2,800,000,001	–	7,000,000,000	25
7,000,000,001	–	14,000,000,000	30
14,000,000,001	–	35,000,000,000	35
35,000,000,001	–	70,000,000,000	40
70,000,000,000	–	and above	45

Normally the tax bands are adjusted every year by a decree of the Council of Ministers, which is the compete authority.

Pension payments are exempt from income tax.

The wage earners, working at first and second-degree underdeveloped areas, are subject to gradually lower taxation rates on their incomes from salaries.

Provincial and local taxes

There is no provincial or local tax imposed on income.

Withholding taxes

Withholding taxes are applied for certain types of income of taxpayers under limited liability and for types of income which are not to be filed in the annual return.

Payroll deductions

Wage tax is deducted from wages and salaries by the employer and paid to the tax office. The amount deducted may be offset against the final income tax payable.

Other taxes

Municipal taxes

The following taxes are collected by local municipalities:

- real estate tax;
- announcement and advertisement tax;
- entertainment tax;

- fuel consumption tax;
- communication tax;
- electricity and gas consumption tax; and
- fire insurance tax.

Stamp tax

Commercial documents prepared in Turkey, and related to contracts, bills and business transactions are subject to stamp tax.

The documents prepared outside of Turkey, or prepared in Turkey by foreign embassies or consulates, are subject to stamp tax when presented to Turkish authorities or when transferred, endorsed or benefited from in Turkey.

Those liable to stamp tax are those who sign the classified documents or those who submit, transfer, endorse or benefit from the documents prepared outside of Turkey or by foreign embassies or consulates in Turkey.

Real estate tax

Real estate tax is comprised of two different taxes: building tax and land tax. This is a local tax based on the fair market value of the property and levied both on the owner and user.

As for the building tax, officially owned buildings, or those used by certain non-profit-making institutions are exempt from this tax. Tourist enterprises and buildings constructed on fairs and exhibition sites together with industrial establishments constructed in under-developed regions, are exempt from this tax for five years (the exemptions of the land tax are similar to those of the building tax).

Miscellaneous taxes

Various charges are levied as residence and registration fees.

Income receivable by banks is subject to a banking and insurance tax at a rate varying between 0.1% and 5%. Municipalities levy charges for business place permits and sanitary inspection rates depending on the type of business.

Inheritance and transfer tax

The taxpayer is the person receiving the goods and property in

Turkey. Turkish citizens who in this respect receive goods and property in foreign countries, are also taxpayers. However, foreigners who acquire goods and property abroad from a Turkish citizen are not subject to this tax.

In the case of inheritance, the inherited property is exempt from the tax, up to a certain limit.

The tax is initially assessed on the declared value of the inherited or received goods and property by the taxpayer. However, the declared value shall then be examined and if deemed necessary, re-evaluated by the tax administration as of day of death or donation.

The rate of inheritance and transfer tax ranges from 1% to 30%. Taxes are payable by the recipient, but spouses and children are each entitled to an inheritance tax exemption of TL 13,946,000,000-27,907,000,000

The tax may be paid in six equal instalments within three years of the assessment.

Tax treaties

The tax treaties contracted between Turkey and other selected countries, in order to avoid double taxation are listed below with details of withholding tax rates on dividends, interest and royalties pursuant to the treaties currently in force.

Country	*Normal Dividends (%)*	*Participation Dividends (%)*	*Interest (%)*	*Royalties (%)*
Austria	25-35	25	15	10
Belgium	15-20	10 in Turkey, 5 in Belgium		
Finland	15-20	25	15	10
France	15-20	10	15	10
Germany	15-20	10	15	10
Netherlands	15-20	10 in Turkey, 5 in Netherlands	10-15 & (Credits exceed 2 years)	10
Norway	25-30 in Turkey, 20-25 in Norway	25	15	10
Pakistan	10-15	25	10	10
South Korea	15-20	25	10-15 (Credits exceed 2 years)	
Sweden	15-20	25	15	10
United Kingdom	15-20	25	15	10

Other treaty countries

Jordan, Romania, Saudi Arabia, Tunisia and the Turkish Republic of Northern Cyprus.

Wealth tax

There is currently no wealth tax imposed in Turkey.

Social security contributions

Social security is compulsory both for employers and employees.

The Turkish social security system consists of:

- social security insurance;
- sickness insurance;
- work accidents insurance;
- occupational illness insurance;
- maternity insurance;
- death insurance;
- disability insurance; and
- senility insurance.

Unless the foreign wage earners notify Turkish authorities that they are insured abroad, they can automatically benefit from sickness, work accidents, occupational illness and maternity insurances and benefit from the others on request.

Employers' contributions vary, according to the field of industry, between 19.5% and 21.5% of the workers' salary. Foreign employers benefit from a similar kind of insurance system.

General funds

Employers and employees both contribute to the general funds.

Among others, the principal capital funds are the compulsory savings fund and the house ownership sponsoring fund.

Value added tax

Value added tax is levied on all goods and services supplied within the scope of commercial, industrial, agricultural and independent professional activities on the importation of goods and services. VAT is normally based on the price charged by the supplier for the delivery of goods or for rendering the service.

Most goods and services rendered within Turkey are subject to 17% VAT (this has been increased to 18% after 15 May 2001), however, certain essential goods and services are taxed at 8%. Luxury items, on the other hand, are taxed at 25% (and this has been increased to 26% after 15 May 2001). The term of the taxation is one calendar month.

The exemptions from VAT may be grouped as below:

- exemptions for exportation (refund of VAT);
- exemptions for delivery of transportation vehicles;
- exemptions for seaport and airport services;
- exemptions for the exploration of petroleum;
- exemptions for transit transportation;
- diplomatic exemptions; and
- exemptions for social and military purposes.

United Kingdom

Smith & Williamson

Corporate taxes

Taxable entities

Resident companies

A UK resident company is liable to corporation tax on its worldwide income and capital gains. A company is resident in the UK if it is incorporated in the UK or has its central management and control in the UK.

Non-resident companies

A non-resident company is liable to corporation tax on profits and capital gains arising as a result of a trade carried on in the UK through a branch or agency. Capital gains not attributable to the carrying on of a trade through a UK branch or agency are not taxable and other UK source income is subject to income tax, not corporation tax.

Tax year and filing requirements

The rate of corporation tax is set for each financial year that runs from 1 April to 31 March. If the company's accounting period ends on a date other than 31 March and the rate of tax changes for the financial years that the accounting period straddles, then the profits of the period are apportioned and charged at the appropriate rate of tax.

For accounting periods ending on or after 1 July 1999, a new system of Corporate Tax Self Assessment (CTSA) has been introduced under which companies are required to calculate their own tax bills and pay over the relevant tax or claim repayment from the Revenue. The Inspector has 12 months from the filing date for the tax return (which will still be 12 months from the end of the accounting period, or three months after the service of the return if later) in which to initiate enquiries. If the return is submitted late, there is a fixed penalty of £100 which is doubled if it is more than three months late. If the return is submitted more than 18 months after the end of the accounting period, there is an additional penalty of 10% of the unpaid tax, which becomes 20% if the return is more than two years late. The CTSA system is accompanied by enhanced Revenue powers to require documentation in relation to its enquiries, especially regarding transfer pricing and Controlled Foreign Company ('CFC') matters.

A major aspect of CTSA for larger companies is a new system for paying corporate tax by instalments. This also applies for accounting periods ending on or after 1 July 1999. Companies will only be subject to this system if they are 'large', others will continue to pay all their corporate tax nine months after the end of the accounting period as before. 'Large' for this purpose means that the profits for the accounting period (including capital gains) exceed £1.5 million. However, the £1.5 million limit has to be divided by the number of associated companies in the preceding accounting period plus one, so for example, where a company has two associated companies, the upper limit is divided by 3 to give a reduced upper limit of £500,000. If a company's total tax liability for a period is £5,000 or less, however, it will not be subject to instalment payments in that accounting period. There are additional rules that apply to rapidly growing companies.

If a company is 'large' as defined, it will (after the transitional period described below) have to pay its tax for a normal 12 month accounting period in four equal instalments. These will be due as follows:

- 6 months and 13 days after the start of the period;
- 9 months and 13 days after the start of the period;
- 13 days after the end of the period;
- 3 months and 14 days after the end of the period.

There are special rules for periods of less than 12 months.

There are special transitional rules to introduce the new system in increments over the four accounting periods ending on or after 1 July 1999 and before 1 July 2002 as follows:

Period ending on or after	*But before*	*Specified percentage of tax to be paid by instalments (% of total estimated liability)* (%)
1 July 1999	1 July 2000	60
1 July 2000	1 July 2001	72
1 July 2001	1 July 2002	88
1 July 2002		100

Any balance not paid by instalments (or repayment due from the Inland Revenue) is due nine months after the year end.

This will mean that the final tax payments under the present system will overlap with the first instalments under the new system. For example, a 'large' company with a 31 December accounting date will pay the whole of its 1998 tax on 1 October 1999 (the 'old' system), but will also have to pay the first instalment of its 1999 tax on 14 July 1999, the second on 14 October 1999, and so on, subject to the above transitional rules.

Interest will run on instalments which prove to be underpaid when the final tax bill is known and the Revenue will pay interest on instalments which prove to have been excessive. A major change is that interest paid by companies will be tax-deductible and interest received will be taxable. Penalties exist for companies which persistently and negligently under-estimate their instalment payments.

Advance corporation tax

Prior to 6 April 1999, companies were required to make an advance payment of corporation tax (ACT) whenever they paid a dividend or any other qualifying distribution. The rate of ACT was 25% of the net dividend and could be set off against the company's tax liability for the accounting period in which the dividend was paid, subject to a maximum offset of 20% of profits chargeable to corporation tax. Any excess ACT could be carried back up to six years or carried forward indefinitely by the relevant company, or surrendered to a 51% subsidiary (see definition below).

From 6 April 1999, Advance Corporation Tax (ACT) is abolished and dividends will no longer need to be accompanied by the payment of ACT to the Revenue. This is connected with the changes in the taxation of dividends in the hands of shareholders, which are covered later in the UK chapter.

Several complicated rules exist to deal with surplus ACT as at 5 April 1999. Surplus ACT is the ACT previously paid over on distributions which have not been used to offset the final corporation tax liability (and the situation is even more complex for groups of companies).

Rates of corporation tax

	Year ended 31 March 2001	*Year ended 31 March 2002*
Corporation tax (chargeable profits over £1,500,000)	30%	30%
Small companies rate (profits chargeable to CT up to £300,000)	20%	20%
Starting rate (profits chargeable up to £10,000)	10%	10%
Chargeable profits (between £10,000 and £50,000)	22.5%	22.5%
Chargeable profits between £10,000 and £50,000)	22.5%	22.5%
Effective marginal rate (chargeable profits between £300,000 and £1,500,000)	32.5%	32.5%

Profits subject to corporation tax

General rules

The profits chargeable to corporation tax are calculated by adding together income from the following sources:

Trading Profits	Schedule D Case I
Rental Income	Schedule A
Overseas Investment Income	Schedule D Case IV & V
Deposit Interest	Schedule D Case III
Capital Gains	

Deduction for certain categories of payments, such as patent royalties, are made from total profits and are allowable when actually paid.

Depreciation and amortisation

Depreciation and amortisation charged in the accounts are not allowable expenses for corporation tax and must be added back to the profits per the accounts. A company is entitled to capital allowances on certain qualifying items at varying rates.

General pool

Items of plant and machinery (not private motor cars) qualifying for the general pool will obtain an annual writing down allowance (WDA) of 25% of the pool on a reducing basis.

Expensive car pool

Cars costing over £12,000 must be recorded separately and the WDA is restricted to £3,000 per annum until the tax written down value falls below £12,000 when the WDA is 25% of the tax written down value of the car.

First year allowance

An initial enhanced allowance is available on qualifying plant and machinery if a company is classed as small or medium for accounting purposes. To be small or medium must satisfy two out of the following three criteria:

	Medium	*Small*
Turnover does not exceed	£11.2 million	£2.8 million
Assets do not exceed	£5.6 million	£1.4 million
No more than	250 employees	50 employees

If a company is part of a group, the limits are divided between the number of companies in the Group.

Qualifying plant and machinery purchased after 1 July 1988 will qualify for a 40% first year allowance.

For a small company only, certain plant and machinery purchased after 1 April 2000 (and before 31 March 2003) will qualify for a 100% first year allowance. This equipment must fall within the following broad categories:

- computers and associated equipment;
- third generation and wireless application protocol mobile phones; or
- software relating to the above.

On the disposal of plant and machinery, proceeds are deducted from the pool of expenditure subject to WDA and any excess is treated as a balancing charge subject to tax.

Industrial buildings allowances (IBAs)

The cost of qualifying buildings (not separate office or shop buildings) qualify for a 4% IBA on a straight-line basis on cost. Hotels and agricultural buildings are treated similarly.

On a second-hand building less than 25 years old, the purchase cost (or original cost if less) is allowed over the balance of the 25 years.

There are a number of detailed rules regarding IBAs which must be considered before any action is taken.

Capital gains and losses

Companies are liable to tax on gains arising from the disposal of 'chargeable assets'. The chargeable gain is calculated as follows:

Disposal proceeds			X
Less:	Original cost	X	
	Indexation on original cost	X	
	Improvement costs	X	
	Indexation on improvement costs	X	
		Y	(Y)
	Chargeable gain		Z

Indexation allowances cannot give rise to a capital loss and must be restricted accordingly.

Capital losses may be carried forward indefinitely and set against capital gains of future years but cannot be set against other sources of income.

Dividends

Dividends from UK companies are not charged to corporation tax (except for certain share dealing companies), but dividends from foreign companies are fully taxable with a credit for foreign withholding tax suffered. In some circumstances the corporate level taxation of the overseas dividend paying company is available as a credit in addition to the withholding tax credit.

Deductions

General rules

The starting point for the calculation of chargeable profits is the profits in the statutory accounts with adjustments for items specified in the tax legislation. The most common adjustments are in relation to the following:

- only expenditure incurred wholly and exclusively for the purpose of the trade is allowed;
- capital expenditure can only be deducted by way of capital allowances, if available;
- losses on the sale of buildings or investments can only be

deducted in arriving at trading profits if they are held as trading stock (otherwise they are treated as capital losses); and

- expenses such as patent royalties are not deductible on an accruals basis, but are allowed on the amount actually paid in the year (and are subject to a withholding tax regime at 22%).

Interest

Interest payable is deductible subject to detailed rules which govern payments to connected parties. The treatment of movements in the 'value' of the principal sum, as well as the effect of currency fluctuations on the loans, are all now taxable (with interest) under the general heading of 'loan relationships'.

Dividends

Dividends paid are not deductible.

Bad and doubtful debts

Specific bad and doubtful debts are allowable.

Reserves and provisions

General reserves and provisions are not allowable.

Employees' and directors' remuneration and benefits

The cost of remuneration and benefits are usually allowable.

Foreign source income

UK companies are liable to tax on all foreign income subject to relief for foreign taxes paid.

Dividends received from foreign companies are charged to corporation tax with a credit for foreign tax already deducted. There may also be relief for corporate taxes levied by the foreign country.

A UK company is subject to corporation tax on income from foreign branches and a UK company may set off branch losses against trading income from other sources. Foreign tax paid on branch profits is deductible from the UK tax liability subject to the limit of the UK tax on those profits.

Foreign withholding taxes on foreign income may be reduced, refunded or eliminated according to the provisions of relevant tax treaties.

Controlled foreign companies (CFCs)

The UK has rules which impute the profits of overseas subsidiaries back to the UK parent company where the subsidiary is established in a low tax jurisdiction. 'Low' is defined as less than 75% of the UK equivalent tax and detailed rules apply.

Investment incentives and special benefits

There are a number of reliefs available for UK resident individual investors in qualifying businesses. In some cases relief from income tax at the time shares are subscribed for can be available under the Enterprise Investment Scheme. Shares held for 3 years which qualify under this scheme are free from Capital Gains Tax on disposal.

Transfer pricing

The UK adopts an arm's length guideline for intra group trading where overseas affiliates are involved. Companies are required to 'self-assess' any transfer pricing adjustment where their accounting period ends after 1 July 1999. Penalties may apply for failure to do so or failure to maintain adequate records to justify arm's length prices.

Losses

Trading losses can be used in the following way:-

- set off against other chargeable profits (of any source) and capital gains in the year of the trading loss;
- carried back one year against total chargeable profits; or
- carried forward and offset against future trading profits from the same source.

There are anti-avoidance provisions in place that restrict the ability to carry forward losses in certain circumstances (normally associated with a change in ownership of the company and a change in the nature of the trading activity).

Capital losses can only be set against capital gains of the year or carried forward indefinitely to be offset against future capital gains arising on disposals made by the same company.

Corporate groups

75% group

Where there is a 75% (or more) equity relationship between two or more companies:

- trading losses can be utilised by any company in the group in the same year;
- chargeable assets can be transferred within the group at no gain and no loss; and
- interest can be paid without deducting basic rate tax.

Consortium

Losses can be surrendered in proportion to the respective share holdings.

Tax-free mergers and disposals

A number of reliefs are available on specified types of corporate reorganisation where corporation tax on chargeable gains would otherwise arise.

Liquidation of a company

Cash distributions received in the course of, and at the end of, a company liquidation are taxed in accordance with the capital gains rules outlined earlier. Any capital gain is taxable in the hands of the shareholders. Non-residents are not taxed on capital gains (except those arising on business assets), so liquidation proceeds paid to a foreign parent company will not be subject to capital gains tax.

Capital taxes

There is no capital duty and no tax on net worth.

Treatment of branches

Branches of foreign companies are charged to corporation tax in the same way as UK resident companies, except the small companies and starting rates of tax are not available. There is no branch profits tax, and no tax payable when profits are brought back to the UK.

Corporate incentives

Research and development tax credits

A tax credit of 150% of expenditure is available for certain companies on research and development expenditure. Detailed rules apply.

Corporate venturing scheme

Investments made in certain qualifying companies obtain a 20% tax deduction. Capital gains made on disposal can be deferred if they are reinvested in similar qualifying companies. Detailed rules apply.

Personal taxes

Taxable individuals

The extent to which an individual will be subject to UK tax is determined by his residence and domicile. He will be subject to UK income tax depending on whether he is resident and/or ordinarily resident and/or domiciled in the UK.

Residence

An individual will be resident in the UK for a tax year if he satisfies the following conditions:

- present in the UK for 183 days in a tax year (if this is satisfied the individual is normally resident from 6 April of the first tax year the criterion is satisfied); and
- present in the UK for an average of 91 days per tax year over four consecutive years (the individual will be resident from 6 April after the end of the fourth year, or earlier, if an intention to become resident is declared). For tax purposes, a tax year runs from 6 April to 5 April and the days of departure and arrival are not included in calculating the number of days present.

The exception to the above is that an individual who comes to the UK on a contract of employment spanning a whole tax year, or with an intention to stay for at least two years, will be resident from the day of arrival to the day of departure. An individual is not ordinarily resident until he has been in the UK for over three years, unless it is clear from the start that he intends to be in the UK for over three years.

United Kingdom

Domicile

An individual is domiciled in the country or state which can be regarded as 'home'. A domicile of origin is acquired at birth based on the individual's father's origin. This is retained unless the individual acquires a new domicile by choice, or unless the father's domicile changes during minority (i.e. until aged 16). To obtain a domicile of choice an individual must sever ties with his domicile of origin and settle in another country with the clear intention of making it his permanent home.

Liability to tax

- If an individual is a UK resident, ordinarily resident and domiciled, he is liable to UK income tax and capital gains tax on his worldwide income and assets.
- If an individual is UK resident, ordinarily resident but non-domiciled, he is liable to income tax and capital gains tax on income and gains arising in the UK, plus non-UK income and gains remitted to the UK.
- If an individual is non-UK resident, he is subject to income tax on certain income arising in the UK but not on capital gains, unless the gains arise on assets employed in a UK trade.

Tax year and filing requirements

The tax year which ended 5 April 2001 is referred to as 2000/2001. The Inland Revenue will issue tax returns to individuals in April for the tax year that has just ended. Self-assessment was introduced for tax years commencing on or after 6 April 1996 and the onus is now on the individual to notify the Inland Revenue of their liability to tax. Under self-assessment, a tax return must be filed by:

- 30 September for taxpayers who do not wish to calculate their liability to tax; and
- 31 January for taxpayers who calculate their own liability to tax.

Sources of income

Employment income

An employee who is resident, ordinarily resident and domiciled in the UK is taxed on worldwide earnings, regardless of where duties are performed.

An employee who is resident and ordinarily resident, but not domiciled in the UK, is subject to UK tax on income relating to duties performed wholly or partly in the UK. Income from duties performed exclusively outside the UK will only be subject to UK tax to the extent that these are remitted to the UK.

An employee who is resident, but not ordinarily resident and is not domiciled in the UK, is taxed on his emoluments for duties performed in the UK and any amounts remitted to the UK.

An employee who is non-resident in the UK is only taxed on emoluments for duties performed in the UK, subject to the operation of any relevant tax treaty.

The provision of a benefit-in-kind is taxable as remuneration.

Business income

For income tax purposes, trading profits are calculated in accordance with generally accepted accounting principles with tax adjustments similar to those outlined for corporation tax above.

If an individual incurs a loss in his trade, a claim can be made to offset the loss against other income in the year of loss. Any excess can be offset against other income of the previous year and the remainder is carried forward against profits of the same trade. Losses incurred in the first four years of a trade can be set against other income of the three years preceding the year the loss is made.

Capital allowances are given on the same basis as for companies (see corporate tax section).

Trading profits are based on the profits of the accounting period ending in the tax year, with special rules for the years of commencement and cessation.

Capital gains

Capital Gains Tax (CGT) is charged on capital gains arising on the disposal of assets. Capital gains on disposals before 5 April 1998 were calculated on the same basis as outlined in the company section above.

As from 5 April 1998, 'taper relief' was introduced for individuals and trusts to replace indexation. The rules are complex, but broadly, the relief operates by reducing the otherwise taxable gains by a percentage which increases the longer an asset is held, up to a maximum relief at ten years, as follows:

*Number of whole years in QHP**	*% of gain chargeable*	*Equivalent tax rate for 40% taxpayer*	*% of gain chargeable*	*Equivalent tax rate for 40% taxpayer*
1	87.5	35	100	40
2	75	30	100	40
3	50	20	95	38
4	25	10	90	36
5	25	10	85	34
6	25	10	80	32
7	25	10	75	30
8	25	10	70	28
9	25	10	65	26

Notes

**Qualifying holding period*

Under these rules, the QHP commences at the date of acquisition or (if later) at 6 April 1998. For assets which were held at 17 March 1998, an extra year of ownership is awarded for non-business assets.

If an asset was purchased before March 1982, the value at 31 March 1982 can be substituted for its true acquisition cost. If a capital loss arises in the year, it is set off against other capital gains of the year with any balance carried forward indefinitely to offset gains in subsequent years.

Gains on UK government securities and certain corporate bonds are exempt from CGT, as are tangible, moveable assets with a value of less than £6,000.

The first £7,500 (for 2000/01) of capital gains are exempt from CGT.

CGT may be deferred if the sale proceeds are re-invested in eligible shares in a qualifying trading company or in the holding company of a trading group.

An individual who is not resident and not ordinarily resident in the UK is only liable to CGT on assets held in the UK which are used in, or held for, the purpose of a trade carried on through a UK branch or agency. An individual who is resident, or ordinarily resident but non-domiciled in the UK, is only subject to CGT on gains arising on the disposal of assets situated outside the UK to the extent that the gains are remitted to the UK.

Dividends

6 April 1999 saw the start of a new system for taxing dividends

received from UK resident companies. The main features are as follows:

- advance Corporation Tax (ACT) was abolished from 6 April 1999;
- tax credits on UK dividends paid after 5 April 1999 will no longer be repayable to tax-exempt shareholders such as charities, or individuals whose income is below the personal tax threshold (£4,535); they have not been repayable to pension funds since 2 July 1997;
- however, there will still be a tax credit attached to dividends paid after 5 April 1999, which will be available to 'frank' or cover the income tax liabilities of individual shareholders who are resident in the UK and not taxable at the higher 40% rate the rate of tax credit will be reduced from the current one-quarter of the cash dividend to one-ninth – equivalent to 10% of the gross dividend; taxpayers whose income exceeds the lower and basic rate tax thresholds will have additional tax to pay on dividends;
- also from 6 April 1999, there are new rates of income tax for individual and trustee shareholders on UK dividends which, together with the reduced tax credit, will leave their post-tax income unchanged from that under the old system; trustees of Discretionary and Accumulation Trusts also have new rates applying which slightly reduce the tax payable on their dividend income provided it is not distributed to beneficiaries; individuals liable at the basic or lower tax rates and life interest trusts are chargeable at 10% and individual higher rate taxpayers at 32.5%; discretionary and Accumulation and Maintenance Trusts are charged at 25% (but the tax rate for such trusts on other types of income will remain at 34%).

These changes will mean that lower or basic rate taxpayers and life interest trusts will have no further tax to pay on receipt of a dividend, since the 10% tax rate will be matched by the new 10% tax credit.

Interest

Interest on most Government securities and interest from UK companies, including banks and building societies, is paid after deduction of investment rate income tax at 20% (2001/02). Individuals who do not expect to be liable to tax (and certain non-residents) may claim to have interest paid gross by banks and building societies if a declaration is made stating that they are resident in a country with which the UK has a double taxation agreement. A further payment is needed for higher rate taxpayers.

Interest is taxable in the year it is received, with credit given for the tax deducted.

If interest is received from overseas, credit is given for any foreign withholding tax deducted.

Rents

A UK resident individual is charged to tax on any rents received, less any expenses for repairs and other expenses incurred in renting the property. If a premium is paid for a lease of less than 50 years, a portion of the premium (depending on the lease) is taxed as rent.

Overseas landlords have basic rate tax withheld by tenants from payments of rent in connection with UK properties, subject to detailed rules. Exemptions are available in certain circumstances from the withholding regime, with the tax being collected at the normal times (see later).

Royalties

All royalties and copyrights are paid under deduction of tax at 21.1%, unless the rate is reduced for non-residents by a double tax treaty.

Social security benefits

Many benefits are exempt from income tax, but tax is charged on pensions, widow's pensions, sick, maternity and unemployment pay.

Pensions and annuities

Pensions received from a former employer are taxed as income. Most annuities are payable under deduction of tax and are treated as investment income. The capital element in a purchased life annuity is exempt from tax.

Foreign source income

Individuals who are resident and ordinarily resident but not domiciled in the UK (or Commonwealth or Irish citizens who are not ordinarily resident) are taxed on foreign investment income (except that derived from Ireland which is taxable as it arises) only to the extent that it is remitted to the UK.

Foreign business and professional income is not subject to the remittance basis, but is taxable in full as the principal place of business is deemed to be in the UK (being the place of residence of the individual).

Personal allowances and deductions

	2000/01 £	*2001/02* £
Personal allowance	4,385	4,535
Personal allowance for those aged 65-74	5,790	5,990
Personal allowance for those aged 75+	6,050	6,260
Married couple's allowance for those aged 65-74*	5,185	5,365
Married couple's allowance for those aged 75+*	5,255	5,435
Blind person's allowance	1,400	1,450

* These levels also apply to Additional Allowance and Widow's Bereavement Allowance.

Tax relief on all these is given as a tax credit of 10% of the amounts shown.

Married couples

Each spouse is a taxable individual and is responsible for filing his own income tax return.

Special treatment for expatriates

The only special rule is that if an individual is UK resident and non-domiciled, they will only be taxed on a remittance basis, however, careful tax planning is needed to ensure that an individual is not taxed on income arising before his arrival in the UK.

Charitable donations

Gift aid

An individual or company can make tax efficient gifts to charity under the gift aid scheme. Post 5 April 2000, no formal documents are required to make a charitable payment, but the individual must declare that it is in respect of gift aid. The payment is paid net of basic rate tax and the tax can be reclaimed by the charity. If the individual is a higher rate taxpayer, they will receive a further tax relief.

Deed of covenant

This is a legal document and ties the donor into making payments to charity for a period that must exceed three years. The payments are made net of basic rate tax which can be reclaimed by the charity, and further tax relief can be claimed by a higher rate taxpayer.

Rates of tax

	2000/01			2001/02		
10% lower rate	0	–	1,520	0	–	1,880
22% basic rate	1,521	–	28,400	1,881	–	29,400
40% higher rate*			28,400+			29,400+

* A special rate of 32.5% higher rate tax is introduced for dividend income of individuals for 1999/2000.

A 20% rate applies to non-dividend investment income (such as interest) below the basic rate limit.

Payment of tax

Payroll deductions

Income tax and social security contributions are deducted from wages and salaries of employed individuals under the Pay-As–You-Earn (PAYE) system.

Self-assessment

Any taxes due in excess of tax withheld at source must be paid directly to the Inland Revenue. Payments 'on account' will normally be made on 31 January and 31 July immediately after the end of the relevant tax year, based on the preceding year's tax liabilities. Any balancing payment is due on the following 31 January.

Inheritance tax

Inheritance Tax (IHT) is charged on the value of an individual's estate on death at 40% on amounts over £242,000 (2001/02). Individuals domiciled in the UK are chargeable on worldwide assets, while individuals domiciled outside the UK are chargeable only on assets situated in the UK. Place of residence is not relevant, except in the context of certain double tax agreements.

Lifetime gifts

Most lifetime gifts made by individuals will be potentially exempt from Inheritance Tax, becoming exempt if the donor survives seven years from the date the gift is made. If the donor dies within seven years, IHT will be charged on a reducing basis, depending on how many years they survived from the date of the gift. Potentially exempt transfers include gifts to individuals and certain trusts. Gifts to spouses are fully exempt, so long as the transferee spouse is domiciled in the UK.

Individuals can make lifetime gifts of £3,000 per annum which will be exempt from IHT. A lifetime gift over £3,000 which is a chargeable transfer (i.e. not potentially exempt) will be charged to IHT at 20% when the gift is made. If the donor dies within seven years, a further 20% tax will be due.

Wealth tax

There is no wealth tax

Social security contribution

For employment income, employees pay up to a maximum of 10% of salary for the year to 5 April 2001. The maximum contribution is £575 per week.

Employers pay 12.2% (with no maximum) for the year to 5 April 2001 (reducing to 11.9% for the following year. Special rules apply, depending on the status of the individuals pension planning arrangements

	2000/01	*2001/02*
Class 2 – self employed rate	£2 per week	£2 per week
Small earning exception	£3,825 per annum	£3,955 per annum
Class 3 – voluntary rate	£6.55 per week	£6.75 per week
Class 4 – self employed rate	7%	7%
Lower limit of profits	£4,385 per annum	£4,535 per annum
Upper limit of profits	£27,820 per annum	£29,900 per annum

Class 3 contributions can be paid by those going overseas who wish to maintain full entitlement to certain UK special security benefits.

Other taxes

Partnerships

Profits generated by a partnership are allocated to the partners according to their profit share and taxed in the partners' hands.

VAT and sales tax

Broadly, VAT is due on all supplies of goods and services supplied in the UK at the standard rate of 17.5%. However, a range of goods and services are exempted from VAT, including real property, finance and insurance, education, health and welfare.

United Kingdom

There are three rates of VAT in the UK. The standard rate is 17.5%, the reduced rate of 5% is applicable to domestic fuel and power, and the zero-rate which is applicable to a wide range of basic goods and services including new housing, food, domestic water and sewerage, books, transport, children's clothing and exports of goods and services. Unlike exemption, zero-rating allows VAT on related expenditure to be recovered.

Tax is usually calculated and paid quarterly on the difference between the tax charged on sales and the tax incurred on expenditure. However, businesses in a net repayment position may apply for monthly returns. Smaller businesses may take advantage of cash accounting and annual VAT returns, and there is a special 'flat rate' scheme available to farmers.

Any business making taxable supplies may register for VAT voluntarily. However, registration is compulsory if taxable income exceeds the registration limit, currently £54,000 per annum (from 1 April 2001). Businesses which make only zero-rated supplies may apply to be exempted from registration.

Stamp duty

Stamp duty is charged at various rates on the execution of documents. The rate on the transfer or sale of shares is 0.5% and real estate sales are on a sliding scale between 1% and 4%, depending on the value of the property transferred.

Tax treaties and withholding taxes

Income tax at 20% is withheld from interest, and at 22% from certain types of royalties, including copyright and design royalties, and from rents paid to non-residents. This tax (other than that on rents) is normally reduced or eliminated by double taxation treaties, of which the UK has over one hundred.

Selected Treaty countries:	*Royalties (%)*	*Interest (%)*
Australia	10	10
Austria	Nil(a)	Nil
Belgium	Nil	15
Canada	10	10
Cyprus	Nil	10
Denmark	Nil	Nil
France	Nil	Nil
Germany	Nil	Nil
Greece	Nil	Nil

Hungary	Nil	Nil
India	10-20	10
Indonesia	15	10
Ireland	Nil	Nil
Italy	8	10
Japan	10	10
Kenya	15	15
Korea	10	15(b)
Luxembourg	5	Nil
Malaysia	15	15
Malta	10	10
Mauritius	15	No limit
Netherlands	Nil	Nil
New Zealand	10	10
Nigeria	12.5	12.5
Norway	Nil	Nil
Pakistan	12.5	15
Poland	10	Exempt
Portugal	5	10
Singapore	15	15
South Africa	Nil	10
Spain	10	12
Sri Lanka	10	10
Sweden	Nil	Nil
Switzerland	Nil	Nil
Thailand	5-15	10-25
Turkey	10	15
USA	Nil	Nil

Notes

(a) The rate of withholding tax on royalties applies to royalties paid to a company controlling more than 50% of the payer. The rate for other corporate shareholders is nil.

(b) The rate of withholding tax is 10% for loans exceeding two years.

United States of America

Goldstein Golub Kessler LLP
American Express Tax and Business Services, Inc.
Altschuler, Melvoin and Glasser LLP
Cardona Irizarry Group
Chastang, Ferrell, Sims & Eiserman LLC
Harb, Levy & Weiland LLP
Hausser & Taylor LLP
Millward & Co. CPAs
Walpert & Wolpoff LLP
Ziner, Kennedy Lehan LLP

Introduction

In the United States not only the federal government, but also many of the states, counties and local municipalities impose taxes. The fundamental basis is self-assessment which requires annual filings by practically all entities and individuals. The discussion that follows is on federal taxes only.

Corporate taxes

Taxable entities

Resident companies – domestic corporations

Domestic corporations (corporations which are organised under the laws of any state or the District of Columbia) are liable for corporate income tax on their worldwide income including capital gains.

Non-resident companies – foreign corporations

Foreign corporations (corporations which are not domestic) are liable for corporate income tax on all income that is 'effectively connected' with the conduct of a US trade or business. Such income is taxable at the same rates as domestic corporations. Certain income which is not effectively connected but has a US source (such as interest, dividends, rents, etc.), is subject to a flat 30% tax unless reduced by a treaty. Foreign corporations are usually not taxed on capital gains from the disposal of non-business assets. However, any capital gain realised by a foreign corporation on the disposition of a US real property interest is treated as effectively connected with a US trade or business and fully taxed. A US real property interest includes the stock of a US corporation that is a, 'US real property holding corporation'.

Tax year and filing requirements

The tax year of a corporation can be any fixed 12 month period that ends on the last day of a month. Corporations can also elect what is known as the 52–53 week year. A 52–53 week year always ends on the same day of the week which falls closest to the last day of a calendar month.

Generally, a corporation can only change its tax year with the permission of the Internal Revenue Service. The tax return has to be filed within 2½ months after the year end (the calendar year end return is due 15 March). An extension can be obtained for an additional six months, but any tax due must be remitted by the original due date.

Taxes imposed

Taxes on income are imposed at the federal, state and local level. The federal corporate taxable income is usually the basis for state and local corporate income taxes. However, some states require adjustments to the federal base so that there may be little harmony between them.

Corporations must pay estimated income taxes on an instalment basis throughout the year usually based on the previous year's tax. An exception is made for large corporations (income of US$ 1,000,000 or more for any of the three immediately proceeding tax years) which must base their instalments on current year income. Additionally, a corporation cannot pay estimated tax payments based on last year's tax return if the prior tax year return was a short period tax year or if the prior year's tax return reflected a zero tax liability.

A very complex area in US tax law is the alternative minimum tax. This tax is imposed in order to ensure that profitable corporations do not escape income taxation by use of credits, preferences and deductions. An exception to the alternative minimum tax was added for small corporations. A small corporation is one in which the average annual gross receipts for the prior three year tax period do not exceed US$ 7.5 million. If the current year is the corporation's first tax year in existence, the corporation automatically qualifies as a small corporation exempt from the alternative minimum tax. If the alternative minimum tax is higher than the regular corporate tax in any given year, the alternative tax is paid. There is a credit mechanism by which a minimum tax credit is allowed against the regular corporate tax in subsequent years if the alternative minimum tax was caused by timing differences in recognition of income or deductions. The alternative minimum tax base starts with regular corporate taxable income to which certain adjustments and preferences are added or subtracted. Additionally, the taxpayer will have to calculate its adjusted current earnings, which will be incorporated into the alternative minimum tax calculation.

Personal holding company tax

In addition to regular corporate income tax, an additional tax of 39.6% is applied to undistributed personal holding company income (interest, dividends, certain rents, etc.). This tax only applies to 'closely held corporations'. A closely held corporation is defined as a corporation that, at any time during the last half of the taxable year, more than 50% in value of its outstanding stock is owned directly (or indirectly) by, or for not more than, five individuals.

Accumulated earnings tax

In addition to the regular corporate income tax, a tax of 39.6% is applied to the improperly accumulated earnings of a corporation. A corporation cannot be subject to both the personal holding company tax and the accumulated earnings tax. The purpose of the accumulated earnings tax is to ensure that the corporation does not accumulate earnings and profits rather than distributing them to the shareholders.

Rates of tax

Corporation income tax rates

Taxable income over US$	*Not over US$*	*Pay (US$)*	*% of excess*	*Of the amount over (US$)*
0	50,000	0	15	0
50,000	75,000	7,500	25	50,000
75,000	100,000	13,750	34	75,000
100,000	335,000	22,250	39	100,000
335,000	10,000,000	113,900	34	335,000
10,000,000	15,000,000	3,400,000	35	10,000,000
15,000,000	18,333,333	5,150,000	38	15,000,000
18,333,333		6,416,667	35	18,333,333

Taxable income of certain personal service corporations is taxed at a flat rate of 35%. The alternative minimum tax rate for corporations is 20%.

Income subject to tax

General rules

Income subject to tax is based on the gross income of the corporation less allowable deductions. Taxable income is determined by either the cash basis or accrual basis of accounting. The accrual basis must be used by corporations maintaining inventory (stock) and by certain large corporations. Certain personal service corporations may use the cash basis.

Stock/inventory valuation

Inventory valuation must conform to the accounting practice of the corporation's industry and it must clearly reflect income. The FIFO method may be used with the cost or the cost or market, whichever is the lower basis. The LIFO method is also permitted, but it may only be used with the cost basis. In addition, if a corporation uses the LIFO method for tax purposes, then it must use the LIFO method for financial reporting.

Also, for all manufacturers and certain wholesalers, certain period costs must be included in the valuation of inventory. This is known as the 'uniform capitalisation rule'.

Capital gains and losses

Capital gains are taxed at regular corporate rates up to 35%, which is the top corporate tax rate for ordinary income. The term 'capital assets' includes almost all property except inventories or other assets held for sale in the ordinary course of a trade or business, trade accounts receivable, depreciable business property and real property used in the business.

Gain is measured by the excess in value of property or cash received over the adjusted basis of the property surrendered. 'Basis' is usually the cost of the property, increased or decreased by adjustments provided by law. For example, basis is increased by the cost of capital improvements and decreased by depreciation (allowed or allowable). Capital losses are only deductible to the extent of capital gains. Capital losses in excess of capital gains in any taxable year may generally be carried back three years and carried forward five years. The carry-back of the capital loss is limited to an amount that does not cause, or increase, a net operating loss in the carry-back year.

Items of depreciable real or personal property used in a business are not capital assets, but a special rule allows a portion of the gain from their disposal to be treated as capital gains. Net losses from the disposal of depreciable real or personal property will be treated as ordinary losses.

Dividends

Dividends received by a corporation are generally taxable. A corporation is allowed a 'special deduction' for dividends received from a domestic corporation. The deductions are as follows.

- 70% of the dividend received from a corporation owned less than 20% by the recipient;
- 80% of the dividend received from a 20% or more owned corporation;
- 100% of the dividend received from members of the same affiliated group; and
- 100% of the dividends received by a small business investment company.

Dividends received from foreign sources are fully taxable by the US recipient, subject to available foreign tax credits. Dividends received by a domestic corporation from a 10% owned foreign corporation are subject to a special rule. The US corporation recipient is allowed a credit against the US tax for its portion of the tax paid by the foreign corporation. This is known as the Section 78 'gross-up'.

Dividends paid to foreign shareholders are subject to a 30% withholding tax or a lower rate provided by a tax treaty.

Deductions

General rules

Corporations, generally, may deduct from gross income the ordinary and necessary expenses of carrying on a trade or business that are paid or incurred during the tax year. Generally, if the cost benefits are more than one year they have to be capitalised and either depreciated or amortised.

Depreciation and amortisation

The cost of tangible property generally placed in service after 1986 is recovered using the Modified Accelerated Cost Recovery System which applies accelerated depreciation methods over 3, 5, 7, 10, 15 and 20 year periods. Examples of assets in the five year recovery period are cars, light trucks, property used in research and experimentation, typewriters, copiers and computers. The seven year recovery period of property includes furniture and fixtures and property not specifically included in the other categories.

Residential rental property is depreciated over a period of 27½ years using the straight-line method. Non-residential real property is depreciated over 39 years using the same method.

Depreciation is determined by applying a statutory percentage to the unrecovered cost of the property. Corporations may elect to depreciate an asset using the straight-line method (cost deducted in equal amounts over the life of the asset). Corporations can elect to expense immediately rather than capitalise the first US$ 20,000 for 2000 and US$ 24,000 for 2001 and 2002 of business property placed in service (reduced by the excess cost of such property over US$ 200,000, dollar for dollar). The use of accelerated depreciation is severely limited for luxury automobiles and other listed property placed in service after 18 June 1984. The accelerated depreciation is limited to the corporation's taxable income.

The capitalised cost of intangibles used in a trade or business or for the production of income is amortised, straight-line, over a 15 year period. Examples of such intangibles are goodwill, going concern value, covenants not to compete, customer lists and franchise or trademarks, etc.

Royalties

Royalty expenses are deductible as an ordinary and necessary expense, provided it is an arm's length transaction.

Interest

Interest paid or accrued on indebtedness, except for indebtedness that is directly or indirectly incurred to produce non-taxable income, is deductible. However, interest paid to a related foreign party is subject to special rules if the related foreign party is not engaged in a US trade or business and, therefore, not subject to mainstream US taxation. Interest paid to a US entity is also subject to these rules if a related foreign party guarantees the borrowings. Generally, if the debt-to-equity ratio of the payer exceeds 1.5:1, the interest expense can be subject to disallowance and carried forward. The disqualified interest may be carried forward to the next tax year. These 'earnings stripping' rules were enacted to prevent the thin capitalisation of US entities by foreign parties. Earnings stripping generally occurs when a foreign parent, not taxable in the US, loans money to its US sub and the sub deducts the interest paid on the loan owed to its parent.

Dividends

Dividends paid to shareholders are not deductible.

Bad and doubtful accounts

Generally, taxpayers must use the specific charge-off method to deduct business bad debts. Specific write-off is based on actual worthlessness of the receivable. Only small banks may use the reserve method.

Reserves and provisions

Generally US tax law does not permit a deduction for the establishment of a reserve.

Employees' and directors' remuneration and benefits

Generally employees' and directors' remuneration and benefits are deductible if they are deemed to be reasonable (especially in closely held corporations). Public corporations will not be able to deduct compensation paid to certain employees to the extent that the compensation exceeds US$ 1,000,000 per year, unless certain performance related guidelines are established and approved by the stockholders. Special deduction limits apply to reimbursed business meal and entertainment expenses.

Specifically non-deductible expenses

Business meals and entertainment expenses are only 50% deductible. Business gifts in excess of US$ 25 per year per recipient are not deductible. Certain club dues and political contributions are not deductible. Life insurance premiums, where the proceeds are payable to the corporation, are not deductible.

Foreign source income

US taxpayers are subject to tax on their worldwide income, including foreign source income. A foreign tax credit, subject to limitation, is available for any withholding tax assessed against the foreign source income. The US has very complex rules for the inclusion in dividend income of certain types of foreign source income for 10% US shareholders of a 'controlled foreign corporation' (CFC). A US shareholder must include his pro rata share of the CFC's subpart F income, plus earnings invested in US property.

Investment incentives and special benefits

Certain incentives and tax credits are provided in US tax law. Some of them are as follows.

DISC/ETI

If a corporation qualifies as a domestic international sales corporation (DISC), its shareholders can generally defer income attributable to US$10 million, or less, of qualified export receipts. However, these shareholders are subject to an interest charge on their deferred tax that reduces the benefits of the deferral. A foreign corporation that qualifies as a foreign sales corporation (FSC) will have a portion on its foreign trade income exempt from federal income tax at the corporate level.

Under Extraterritorial Income Exclusion Act 2000, a taxpayer may elect to exclude from gross income his/her sales of qualifying property for ultimate use outside the United States. Effectively, this exclusion can reduce federal taxes by more than 5%.

Credit for research and experimental expenses

A 20% credit is available for excess research expenditures for the taxable year over a weighted average of the taxpayer's yearly research expenditures during the base period. Only research and experimental expenditures paid or incurred in carrying on an existing or intended business qualify for the credit. The expenditures must be for qualifying research which excludes research conducted outside the US. Generally, the credit is not available for expenditures incurred after 30 June 1999 (subject to extension by legislation). Taxpayers may elect an alternative incremental research credit for tax years beginning after 30 June 1996. If a taxpayer elects the alternative incremental research credit for its first tax year beginning after 30 June 1996, such election is binding for all subsequent years. This credit is equal to an increasing percentage of qualified research expenses over a percentage of a base amount and is divided into three tiers, each of which provides for different percentages.

Work opportunity tax credit

A 40% credit of the first US$ 6,000 of wages per qualified person is available for employees hired before 1 July 1999 (a 35% credit is available for employees who began work after 30 September 1996 and before 1 January 2002). Qualified individuals generally consist of members of targeted groups with special employment needs.

Welfare-to-work credit

Employers who hire long term family assistance recipients after 31 December 1997 and before 31 December 2001 may claim a credit for 35% of up to US$ 10,000 of qualified first-year wages (US$ 3,500) and 50% of up to US$ 10,000 of second year wages (US$ 5,000) per qualified employee. If a welfare-to-work credit is allowed for wages paid to a worker for that year, that worker is not treated as a member of a targeted group that year for the purpose of the work opportunity tax credit.

Empowerment zone employment credit

Employers are entitled to a 20% credit on the first US$ 15,000 of wages paid to each employee who works in one of the 9 designated empowerment zones. Substantially all of the employee's services must be done in the zone of the employer's trade or business. Qualified zone wages do not include wages taken into account for the work opportunity credit.

Investment tax credit

The investment credit is one of the components of the general business credit. The investment credit includes the rehabilitation credit, the energy credit and the reforestation credit. The rehabilitation credit is available for the rehabilitation of buildings placed in service before 1936, or certified historic buildings. For buildings other than historic structures, rehabilitation expenditures include practically all interior and exterior expenditures as long as 50% or more of the existing external walls are retained. The energy and reforestation credits are based upon 10% of the basis of energy property and 'qualified timber property' respectively.

Credit for employer-provided childcare facilities

After 2001, employers are entitled to a tax credit for 25% of the expenses incurred in childcare facilities and 10% of the expenses for childcare resources and referral services. The maximum credit cannot exceed US$ 150,000 per year. The cost of depreciable property, along with any current operating cost deductions, must be reduced by the amount of the credit.

Additional credits

There are a number of tax credit incentives that target specific industry groups. Included among these are credits for: the development of certain medical drugs, the production of energy from certain low volume domestic sources, the use of alcohol fuels, the domestic application of enhanced oil recovery methods, making businesses more accessible to handicapped persons and for the use of gasoline and special fuels in certain business activities. In addition, many states and localities provide tax credits or grants if businesses locate and create jobs in specific areas that have a large number of unemployed people.

Related party transactions

Related party transactions are subject to a number of regulations. In order to ensure that related parties deal with each other on an arm's length basis, income, deductions and credits may be reallocated to prevent evasion of taxes or to reflect income more clearly. No deduction is allowed for losses from the sale or exchange of property between related parties. An accrual basis taxpayer is placed on the cash basis for purposes of deducting business interest and expenses paid to a related cash basis taxpayer. No deduction is allowed for an accrued expense by a US taxpayer to a related foreign party until the expense is paid.

Net operating losses (NOLs)

An NOL may be offset against the profits of the preceding two tax years (carry-back) and then carried forward to offset against the income of the following 20 taxable years (carry-forward). For NOLs arising in tax years before 6 August 1997, the carry-back period was three tax years and the carry-forward period 15 tax years. An election can be made to forego the carry-back and only carry forward the loss. Special carry-back and carry-forward periods apply in the case of specified liability losses – bad debt losses of commercial banks, real estate investment trust losses and NOLs generated by interest on debt used to fund 50% stock acquisitions or excess distributions. Note that the utilisation of an NOL is severely restricted if there is more than a 50% change in ownership of the corporation.

Corporate groups

A US parent corporation and its US subsidiaries (at least 80% owned) may elect to file a single consolidated return instead of separate returns. Some of the advantages of filing a consolidated return are:

- the ability to offset losses of one corporation (including capital losses) against the profits of another corporation;
- the avoidance of tax on inter-company distributions;
- the ability of the group to use the excess of one member's foreign tax credit over its limitation; and

- the deferral of income on inter-company transactions.

Once a consolidated return election has been made it cannot be broken without consent of the Internal Revenue Service.

To discourage the proliferation of corporations solely for the purpose of reducing taxes, corporations under common control that do not file consolidated returns must allocate various exemptions, exclusions and credit limitations among the members of the group. Not all states allow consolidated or combined tax return filings.

Tax-free mergers and disposal

There are several methods by which US corporations can be merged or acquired on a tax-free basis. Generally, in order to effectuate the tax-free transaction, there must be a business purpose, a continuation of control after the transaction and a continuation of the business. Tax avoidance cannot be one of the business reasons and the corporations must be solvent at the time of the transaction. If foreign corporations are involved in the transactions, a 'toll charge' may have to be paid in order to obtain tax-free status.

Generally, for distributions after 16 April 1997, if more than 50% interest in either the controlled or distributing corporation in a divisive reorganisation is acquired under a plan or arrangement, gain is recognised. A plan is presumed to exist if the acquisition takes place either two years before, or two years after, the distribution.

Liquidation of company

Under US tax law, if a corporation, which is not 80% owned by a corporate parent, makes liquidating distributions of appreciated assets (the fair market value exceeds the book value), the distribution is deemed a sale of the assets. A corporate tax is then due. The shareholder would then measure the value of the assets received on liquidation against his basis in the stock to determine gain or loss on liquidation. Thus, there can be a 'double tax' on a liquidation of the company.

A corporation that is 80% or more owned by another corporation will not recognise gain or loss on liquidating distributions to the parent and the parent will not recognise gain or loss on receipt of the liquidating distributions.

Capital taxes

The US does not impose any capital or net worth tax. However, many states and localities impose a corporate tax on capital or net worth.

Branch profit tax

The US imposes a 30% branch profit tax (unless reduced by treaty) on a foreign corporation's dividend equivalent amount. This is in addition to the regular corporate tax on the foreign corporation's 'effectively connected' income. The dividend equivalent amount is approximately the after-tax earnings that would have been distributed by the branch if it were a US subsidiary. In addition, interest paid by the branch is deemed to be paid by a US subsidiary. Thus, the interest is subject to normal US withholding rules.

Personal taxes

Taxable individuals

US citizens and resident aliens

With few exceptions, resident aliens are taxed in the same manner as US citizens. Resident aliens and US citizens are taxable on their worldwide income, including capital gains. Generally, an alien who is admitted as a permanent resident (i.e. who holds a 'green card'), or who meets the 'substantial presence test' is considered to be a US resident for tax purposes. The discussion under the heading 'US Taxation of Aliens' describes the US tax rules used to determine whether a non-US citizen is 'resident alien' in more detail.

Tax year and filing requirements

The federal tax return for a citizen, resident alien, or non-resident alien with compensation subject to withholding, is due on the fifteenth day of the fourth month following the end of the taxable year. All other non-resident aliens must file a return on the fifteenth day of the sixth month following the close of the taxable year.

The taxable year for individuals is usually the calendar year, unless a fiscal year is established. The US tax system is based on self-assessment, with taxpayers responsible to calculate their tax liability and file tax returns. Penalties and interest may be assessed for failure to file returns or pay taxes when due. Once filed, the government may select returns for audit and may assess additional tax as well as interest and penalties.

Taxes on income

Separate income taxes may be imposed at the federal, state and local levels. Federal income tax is calculated on 'taxable income', which is defined as gross income less allowable deductions and personal exemptions for the taxable year.

Many states and municipalities impose income taxes based on a variety of factors such as taxable income, gross income, wages, etc. Usually individuals are liable for state and local taxes in their place of domicile or residence as well as where business is transacted. However, some states or municipalities do not impose income taxes but levy real estate and/or personal property taxes. The rules regarding income subject to taxation as well (as tax rates) vary by state or jurisdiction. State and local taxes may be deductible in computing federal income tax.

Sources of income

Gross income includes compensation for services, net profits (losses) from trades and professions, gains (losses) derived from transactions in property, interest, dividends, rents, royalties, alimony, pensions and so on. Generally, income is taxable in the year received.

Employment income and directors' fees

In general, all compensation for personal services is taxable to the individual who performed the services. Compensation includes payments in cash as well as the fair market value of property or services received. Certain employee benefits are not included in income if incurred for the employer's benefit under a written plan that is non-discriminatory, e.g. accident and health premiums and pension and profit sharing plan contributions. Also, certain non-employee compensation for personal services, such as directors' fees, is taxable to the individual who performs the service.

Business income

Income from partnerships and 'S corporations' (certain domestic corporations with no more than 75 shareholders which are not subject to US corporate income tax) are included in the gross income of the individual partner/shareholder, whether or not the amounts are actually received. Only that portion of estate and trust income which is available to the beneficiary is taxable to the beneficiary. In the case of partnerships, S corporations, estates and trusts, the income generally retains its original character (i.e. dividend, capital gain, etc.).

Special rules postpone the deductibility of both partnership and S corporation losses to the extent that the taxpayer's accumulated losses exceed his/her 'at risk amount' in the partnership or S corporation. For this purpose, the at risk amount is the sum of:

- cash contributions to the activity;
- adjusted basis of property contributed to the activity; and
- amounts borrowed for use in the activity, with respect to which the owner has personal liability or has pledged property not used in the activity.

The amount at risk is generally increased or decreased each year by the taxpayer's share of income, losses and withdrawals from the activity and, in certain circumstances, a pro rata share of partnership liabilities or loans made to S corporations.

Additional limitations are imposed on the deductibility of losses relating to 'passive activities'. Usually, losses from passive activities may only offset income from passive activities and in most cases may not be used to offset salary, active business or portfolio incomes (interest, dividends, etc.). Generally, passive activities include:

- trade or business activities in which the taxpayer does not participate on a regular, continuous and substantial basis; and
- rental activities where payments are primarily for the use of tangible property (there are limited exceptions for individuals who devote full time to real estate activities).

Any disallowed passive activity losses are carried forward indefinitely and allowed in full against future passive income or when the taxpayer disposes of his entire interest in the activity in a taxable transaction.

Capital gains

Gains and losses from the sale or exchange of capital assets are subject to the regular income tax. The term 'capital assets' includes almost all property, whether or not connected with a trade or business, except inventories or other assets held for sale in the ordinary course of a trade or business (trade accounts receivable, depreciable business property and real property used in the business).

Gain is measured by the excess of property or cash received over the adjusted basis of the property surrendered. 'Basis' is usually the cost of the property, increased or decreased by adjustments provided by law. Basis is increased, for instance, by the cost of capital improvements and decreased by depreciation.

The tax on long term capital gain (gain from the sale or exchange of a capital asset held for more than 12 months) is limited to 20%. Short term capital gain is taxed at the same rates as ordinary income up to a maximum of 38.6% in 2001.

Up to US$ 3,000 of net capital losses are deductible against a taxpayer's other income. A net capital loss in excess of these limits may be carried forward indefinitely.

Items of depreciable real or personal property used in a business are not capital assets, but a special rule allows net gains from their disposal to be treated as capital gains. The preferential treatments may not be allowed to the extent that the gain merely recaptures part or all of the depreciation allowed against ordinary income in previous years. Recapture gain will be treated as ordinary income. Other depreciation taken is taxed on sale of the property at 25%. Net losses from the disposition of depreciable real or personal business property will be treated as ordinary losses.

Special rules permit reporting income over periods in which instalment payments are received. The gain with regard to each instalment is recognised in the proportion that gross profit from the sale bears to the contract price. This instalment method of reporting is not available for any publicly traded stock or security or for any recapture gain or for dealers in property.

Dividends

Dividends, whether in money or in property, are included in gross income in an amount equal to cash plus the fair market value of the property received.

Interest

Interest on most bonds issued by state and local governments and their subdivisions is not taxable (a state generally does not tax the interest paid on the bonds it issues, however, it may tax the interest on the bonds issued by other states). Most other interest is included in gross income.

Rentals and royalties

Rentals and royalties are included in gross income in the year received. Trade or business expenses attributable to property held for the production of rents or royalties are deductible.

Social security benefits

In all cases, 15% of social security benefits are exempt from income tax. The remaining 85% of such benefits may be subject to tax depending upon the income level of the recipient. Social security benefits are generally not taxable at the state and local level.

Pensions and annuities

Pensions received from a former employer are generally fully taxed at both the federal and state level. Annuities are tax-free to the extent that they do not exceed the amount paid for them out of previously taxed income.

Exempt income

Generally, income from the following sources is excluded from gross income:

- life insurance proceeds;
- interest on state and local obligations; and
- gifts and inheritances.

Foreign source income

Since every US citizen or resident alien is taxed on worldwide income, all foreign source income (with limited exceptions) is included in the gross income.

Deductions

Standard deduction

Individuals are generally allowed a standard deduction based on filing status (see its description under the 'rates of tax' section, below), or individuals may elect to reduce adjusted gross income by specific itemised deductions. Non-resident aliens cannot claim the standard deduction, but they may itemise. The standard deduction is as follows:

	2001 (US$) (estimated)	*2000 (US$)*
Joint return of married taxpayer	7,600	7,350
Head of household	6,650	6,450
Single	4,550	4,400
Married individuals filing separate returns	3,800	3,675

The standard deduction amounts are adjusted for inflation annually. Elderly and blind taxpayers get an additional standard deduction as follows:

	2001 (US$)	*2000 (US$)*
Married and surviving spouses	900	850
Heads of household and single	1,100	1,050

The following specific itemised deductions are allowed instead of the standard deduction amount.

Medical expenses

Medical expenses in excess of 7.5% of adjusted gross income.

Taxes

State and local income, personal property taxes and US and foreign real property taxes; foreign income taxes may be either deducted or credited against the tax liability.

Interest

Mortgage interest on amounts up to US$1 million borrowed to buy, improve or construct a first or second home; interest on up to US$100,000 in debt secured by a first or second home, which may be used for any purpose.

Investment interest expense, to the extent of net investment income. Investment income no longer includes capital gain income unless an election to forego the preferential rate on such gains is made by the taxpayer.

Personal (consumer loan) interest is no longer allowed as a deduction.

Interest attributable to carrying tax-exempt bonds is not allowed as a deduction.

Charitable contributions

Cash and property donations to US charities, subject to limitations based on a taxpayer's adjusted gross income, the type of charitable organisation, and the character of the donation. For example, cash contributions to public charities are limited to 50% of adjusted gross income. Contributions in excess of US$ 250 require a receipt.

Casualty and theft losses

Non-reimbursed casualty and theft losses, to the extent that they exceed 10% of adjusted gross income.

Miscellaneous deductions

Generally deductible only to the extent that they exceed 2% of adjusted gross income. They include:

- employment related expenses such as 'dues' to professional societies and unions, job seeking expenses and 50% of unreimbursed business meal and entertainment expenses; and
- expenses incurred in connection with the production of income, such as legal and accounting fees and fees paid to collect interest or dividends.

Taxpayers whose adjusted gross income exceeds a threshold amount are required to reduce the amount of allowable itemised deductions by 3% of the excess over the threshold amount. No reduction is required, however, in the case of deductions for medical expenses, investment interest and casualty or theft losses. The 2001 and 2000 thresholds are US$ 132,950 and US$ 128,950 respectively for married taxpayers filing jointly, and US$ 66,475 and US$ 64,475 for married filing separate taxpayers. However, the reduction may never be more than 80% of allowable deductions, excluding deductions for medical expenses, investment interest, and casualty or theft losses.

Personal exemption

A personal exemption of US$ 2,800 for 2000 and US$ 2,900 for 2001 (to be adjusted for inflation in later years) is allowed for the taxpayer, the spouse and each dependant.

The tax benefit of the personal exemption is phased-out for high-income taxpayers as the adjusted gross income of a taxpayer exceeds certain threshold amounts. The amount of allowable exemption is decreased by 2% for each US$ 2,500 (US$ 1,250 for married persons filing separate returns) in excess of the threshold. Threshold amounts are as follows:

	2001 *US$* *(estimated)*	*2000* *US$*
Joint returns	193,400	199,450
Head of household	161,150	166,200
Single taxpayers	128,950	132,950

Married, filing separate	96,700	99,725
Surviving spouse	193,400	199,400

Losses

Losses incurred in a trade or business, or in a transaction entered into for profit, may be used to offset an individual's other income. An unabsorbed net operating loss can be carried back two years and carried forward 20 years. Prior to 1998, losses could be carried back three years and forward 15 years.

Special family rules

The use of intra-family transfers of income-producing property to reduce income tax liability, by shifting income from the parent's high marginal tax rate to a child's generally lower tax rate, is greatly limited before the child reaches the age of 14. Instead, a child's net unearned income in excess of US$ 1,400 for 2000 and US$ 1,500 for 2001 is subject to tax at the top marginal tax rate of his or her parents. This provision applies to children who have not reached 14 before the close of the tax year and have either parent living at the close of such a year. The parent of a minor child under the age of 14 may elect to include the gross income of the child in excess of US$ 1,500 in his or her income for the year 2001.

Married taxpayers may elect to file individual income tax returns jointly or on a separate basis. In certain circumstances it can be advantageous for married taxpayers to file separately. Actual tax comparisons should be made using both joint and separate filing status to ascertain which method produces more favorable results. Considerations other than tax savings may enter into any decision to file joint versus separate returns. Some of the education tax credits (see below) are not available to married taxpayers who file separately.

Special treatment for US citizens or resident aliens abroad

A statutory exception exists for wages or self-employment income earned abroad up to US$ 76,000 for 2000 (US$ 78,000 for 2001 – thereafter US$ 80,000 each year). There is also a separate exclusion for qualified housing expenses that may be used in conjunction with the foreign earned income exclusion to reduce foreign earned income subject to US tax. Only the excess of the housing cost over a base amount (US$ 27.86 per day in 2000) is eligible to be excluded. In order to prevent double taxation, foreign taxes paid on any excess foreign source income may be creditable, dollar for dollar, against the US tax related to such income. The exclusions are determined separately for spouses and both spouses may claim the exclusions if each qualify (whether they are filing jointly or separately).

Rates of tax

General

There are four rate schedules:

- *single* – applies to unmarried individuals;
- *head of household* - applies to unmarried individuals who have a qualifying dependant residing in the taxpayer's household;
- *joint* – applies to married taxpayers who file one return combining income and deductions of both spouses; and
- *married filing separate* – applies to married taxpayers filing separate returns.

Single taxpayers

The rates for 2000 were as follows:

Taxable income (US$)	*Tax rate*
Not over 26,250	15% of taxable income
Over 26,250 but not over 63,550	3,937.50 plus 28% of the amount over 26,250
Over 63,550 but not over 132,600	14,381.50, plus 31% of the amount over 63,550
Over 132,600 but not over 288,350	35,787.00, plus 36% of the amount over 132,600
Over 288,350	91,857.00, plus 39.6% of the amount over 288,350

The rates for 2001 are as follows:

Taxable income (US$)	*Tax rate*
Not over 6,000	10% of taxable income
Over 6,000 but not over 25,750	600, plus 15% of excess over 6,000
Over 25,750 but not over 65,550	4,075.50, plus 27.5% of the excess over 27,050
Over 65,550 but not over 136,750	14,832.50, plus 30.5% of the excess over 65,550
Over 136,750 but not over 297,300	36,895.50, plus 35.5% of the excess over 136,750
Over 297,300	94,657.50, plus 39.1% of the excess over 297,300

United States of America

Married, filing jointly

The rates for 2000 were as follows:

Taxable income (US$)	*Tax rate*
Not over 43,850	15% of taxable income
Over 43,850 but not over 105,950	6,577.50, plus 28% of the excess over 43,850
Over 105,950 but not over 161,450	23,965.50, plus 31% of the excess over 105,950
Over 161,450 but not over 288,350	41,170.50, plus 36% of the excess over 161,450
Over 288,350	86,854.50, plus 39.6% of the excess over 288,350

The rates for 2001 are as follows:

Taxable income (US$)	*Tax rate*
Not over 12,000	10% of taxable income
Over 12,000 but not over 45,200	1,200, plus 15% of excess over 12,000
Over 45,200 but not over 109,250	6,780, plus 27.5% of the amount over 45,200
Over 109,250 but not over 166,450	24,714, plus 30.5% of the amount over 109,250
Over 166,450 but not over 297,300	42,446, plus 35.5% of the amount over 166,450
Over 297,300	89,552, plus 39.1% of the amount over 297,300

Notes

(a) Rates above 15% will be reduced by 0.52% in 2002, another 1% in 2004 and another 1% in 2006 (with the highest rate further reduced to 35% in 2006).

(b) The tables are adjusted annually for inflation.

(c) They are without regard to any alternative minimum tax and various credits against the tax liability.

An alternative minimum tax (AMT) is imposed if it exceeds the regular tax. The AMT is calculated on taxable income increased by tax preference items and adjusted with respect to certain itemised deductions claimed, with an exemption in 2001/04 of up to US$ 49,000 for individuals, depending on filing status.

If alternative minimum taxable income is between US$0 and US$ 175,000, the rate is 26%. If in excess of US$ 175,000, the tax rate imposed is 28%. Major tax preferences and adjustments include certain depreciation, intangible drilling costs, and excess percentage depletion. In computing the AMT, no deduction is allowed for any income taxes paid or miscellaneous itemised deductions.

Tax credits

Foreign tax credit

A credit is allowed for income taxes paid to foreign countries. The foreign tax credit is limited to the US tax imposed on foreign source income. Credits in excess of these limits may be carried back two years and carried forward five years.

Additional credits

Credits may be available to individual taxpayers who have dependant children under the age of 17. Other credits are available related to the adoption of children and still others are based on expenses incurred for certain educational expenses. However, all of these credits are subject to elimination if the adjusted gross income is above certain levels.

Payment of tax

Payroll deductions

Income and social taxes are withheld from employees' wages under a pay-as-you-go system. The balance of the tax liability is due on the original due date for filing the tax return. Penalties exist for underpayment of income taxes.

Estimated tax payments

Tax liabilities in excess of amounts withheld are payable on an estimated basis in instalments throughout the year in the form of estimated tax payments. These estimated payments are required on the fifteenth day of April, June, September and the following January for the calendar year taxpayers.

US taxation of aliens

Whether an individual is classified as a resident or non-resident, for US income tax purposes the classification will have a major impact on his tax liability. Non-US citizens who meet the definition of a US resident are taxed in the same manner as US citizens on a worldwide basis. Non-residents, however, are only taxed on income effectively connected with a US business and certain other income from US sources. In addition, non-residents are generally not subject to capital gains tax on the sale of US corporate stock and securities. Whether it is more advantageous to be taxed as a non-resident depends on the facts and circumstances of a given situation. Consideration must be given to the individual's global situation and how he or she is taxed in the home country. Individuals taxed as residents are eligible for a more favorable filing status (e.g. joint returns), and for more deductions, than non-residents are.

Resident alien defined

There are two objective tests to determine US residency for income tax purposes. An individual who meets either the 'green card' test or the 'substantial presence' test will be considered a resident alien. The green card test is satisfied by any individual who has been granted permanent residence status by the Immigration and Naturalization Service of the United States. Once residency is established under the green card test, this status will continue until the green card is rescinded or abandoned.

The alternative test to determine residency is the substantial presence test. This test is based on the time spent in the US. The test considers the days of presence in the US during the current year and the prior two years, and the test is applied on a year by year basis.

Under the substantial presence test, an alien individual is treated as a resident if he is physically present in the US for at least 31 days during the current year, and the sum of the days physically present in the US during the current year (plus one-third the number of days physically present in the US during the first preceding calendar year and plus one-sixth the number of days physically present in the US during the second preceding calendar year) equals or exceeds 183 days.

Various exceptions to the numerical substantial presence test are available for non-citizens. If an individual's 'tax home' is abroad and he is not in the US for 183 days or more during the current calendar year, the individual would not meet the substantial presence test under the 'closer connection' exception. That is, he has a closer connection to a foreign country during the year. Other exceptions are available to diplomats, teachers or trainees, students, persons unable to leave the US for medical reasons and to certain professional athletes.

Taxation of non-resident aliens

Tax year and filing requirements

The federal tax return for a citizen, resident alien or non-resident alien with compensation subject to withholding is due on the fifteenth day of the fourth month following the end of the taxable year. All other non-resident aliens must file a return on the fifteenth day of the sixth month following the close of the taxable year.

The taxable year for individuals is usually the calendar year unless a fiscal year is established. There are special rules for non-residents during the first and last years of residency. Taxpayers calculate their own tax liability and file tax returns subject to severe penalties for failure to do so. The government audits tax returns and may assess additional tax, as well as interest and penalties.

Non-resident aliens are limited with respect to filing status. A married non-resident alien must file using married separate filing tax rates, and a single non-resident alien must use single filing tax rates. In addition, a non-resident alien will not receive exemptions for his/her spouse or other dependants in the same manner as a US citizen or resident, and is only eligible to use certain itemised deductions to reduce taxable income. The standard deduction available to US citizens is not available to the non-resident alien.

Non-resident alien individuals are taxable in the same manner as US citizens on all income which is 'effectively connected' with the conduct of a US trade or business. Certain effectively connected income earned through a US or foreign partnership is subject to withholding tax at the rate of 39.6% for all non-resident alien partners.

The performance of personal services in the US is considered the conduct of a US trade or business, except in the case of a non-resident alien temporarily present in the US (90 days or less during the taxable year) who does not earn in excess of US$ 3,000 and is employed by a foreign entity. Trading in stocks or securities for one's own account does not constitute the conduct of a US trade or business. However, gain realised on the disposition of a US real property interest is considered to be income effectively connected with the conduct of a US trade or business. A real property interest includes real property located in the US and the stock of a US corporation that qualifies as a US real property holding corporation.

Certain income from US sources which is not effectively connected (e.g., certain interest, dividends, royalties, etc.) is subject to a flat 30% withholding tax, unless the rate is reduced by treaty provisions. Generally, capital gains are not taxable provided a non-resident alien is not present in the US for 183 or more days in the year the gain is realised. As stated above, capital gains from the sale of a US real property interest is subject to US tax.

Sources of income

A non-resident alien individual may have income from sources similar to a US citizen. Please refer to the section discussing various types of income taxable in the United States.

Taxes on income

Separate income taxes may be imposed at the federal, state and local levels. Federal income tax is calculated on 'taxable income', which is defined as gross income less allowable deductions and personal exemptions for the taxable year. Many states and municipalities impose income taxes based on a variety of factors such as taxable income, gross income, specific classes of income, wages or self-employment income, etc. Some states or municipalities do not impose income taxes but levy real estate and/or personal property taxes. Some others do not impose any taxes. Individuals are liable for state and local taxes in their place of domicile or residence as well as where business is transacted. Rates vary depending on where liability to file arises and on the method of taxation. State and local taxes are deductible in computing federal income tax.

As mentioned earlier, taxable income of a non-resident alien individual can be reduced by a limited number of itemised deductions. These include:

- charitable contributions;
- casualty and theft losses arising with regard to property located in the US; and
- other expenses related to a US trade or business including state and local income taxes, non-reimbursed business expenses and travel expenses such as the cost of lodging, meals (up to 50%) and transportation attributable to working temporarily away from home (determined by length of time away from one's principal place of business and not by the rules for determining resident alien status); travel expenses of members of the family are not deductible.

Also, as previously mentioned, a non-resident individual may only claim a tax exemption for himself. No exemption is allowed for his spouse or other dependants.

Income from services performed in the US may also be subject to social security tax. Many countries have implemented tax regimes that include a social security type tax such as national insurance or other similar systems. If an individual is contributing to the social security tax regime in a country other than the US, it is important to determine whether the individual is also liable to contribute to the US social security system. If the alien's home country has entered into a 'Totalisation Agreement' with the United States, and he does not intend to collect US social security upon his retirement, the individual may be able to obtain a 'Certificate of Coverage' from his home country. This certificate would indicate that he is covered by that country's national insurance, and he would, therefore, be exempt from contributing US social security tax on his US earnings.

Withholding taxes

The US requires taxes to be withheld at source on royalties, interest, dividends, proceeds from the sale of US real property, certain income allocations from partnerships (whether or not distributed), and certain other amounts paid to non-residents of the US. There is no withholding on interest qualifying as portfolio interest paid to non-resident aliens by US borrowers. Non-resident alien individuals who are employees of US companies are subject to the same wage withholding requirements as residents and citizens.

Departure of alien individuals

Individuals who remove themselves from the taxing authority of the United States either by relinquishing their green card or simply by having no taxable income or days of presence in the US, should be aware of certain special tax rules.

Individuals who have contributed to a US pension plan (or have paid US social security tax) will eventually receive income related to these contributions. At such time as the income is received, the individual must determine taxability in the US of these items. A review of any tax treaty between the US and the individual's country of residence at the time the income is received is also recommended.

Under Internal Revenue Code Section 877, the US implemented an expatriation tax in order to remove a perceived tax incentive for US persons to renounce their US citizenship. The provisions imposing this tax were expanded to include long term permanent residents. A long-term permanent resident is an individual who was a lawful permanent resident of the US for eight of the 15 years preceding termination of residency. This termination can include the abandonment of a green card. The expatriation tax on income applies for tax years ending within ten years of the date of the termination of residency.

These rules apply if the individual's average annual net income tax for the five years preceding the termination exceeds US$ 100,000 or if the individual's net worth at departure equals at least US$ 500,000 (these amounts are indexed for inflation).

If an individual is subject to the expatriation tax, the US retains the right to tax certain gains on stock and treat other income as US source income, which would otherwise be sourced to the individual's resident country.

The rules governing the expatriation tax and potentially taxable income are extremely complex. These rules must be carefully examined in the event exposure to this tax is at issue.

Estate and gift taxes

The US has a unified system of estate and gift taxation which is targeted for repeal in 2010. Until then, estates and gifts are taxed on a single graduated rate schedule with a maximum rate of 55% in 2001 and 50% in 2002 on transfers in excess of US$ 3,000,000. In 2001, a taxable transfer between US$ 10,000,000 and US$ 17,184,000 is subject to a 5% additional tax which phases out the benefit of the graduated rates and the unified credit. This additional 5% tax is eliminated as of 2002.

A tax is imposed on the donor of gifts with an aggregate fair market value in excess of US$ 10,000 per recipient per year. Through to 2009, an estate tax is imposed on the taxable estate, which is the fair market value of property transferred at death less certain allowable deductions plus lifetime taxable gifts. Gift taxes previously paid are credited against the estate tax.

Through to 2009, an unlimited deduction is available for property transferred to a US citizen spouse by gift or as part of the estate (the unlimited marital deduction is not available for property passing to a surviving spouse who is not a US citizen). Also, a unified credit is available against both gift and estate taxes. In 2000 and 2001, the unified credit was US$ 220,550 which is equivalent to a taxable property transfer of US$ 675,000. The taxable property transfer limit increases to US$ 1 million in 2002, US$ 1.5 million in 2004, US$ 2 million in 2006 and US$ 3.5 million in 2009. The entire estate tax is then repealed in 2010. However, the gift tax will remain in 2010 (at a maximum 35% rate). The exemption from gift taxes will rise to US$ 1 million after 2001 and will then remain at that level.

The states may impose separate estate, inheritance and/or gift taxes. State estate and inheritance taxes can be credited (subject to limitations) against the federal estate tax. Rates vary by state.

Non-resident aliens may be subject to US gift tax with regard to transfers of tangible property situated within the US and for US estate tax with regard to tangible and intangible property situated within the US. For decedents dying after 10 November 1988, the tax rates for non-resident aliens are the same as those applicable to US citizens and residents. A credit of US$ 13,000 is available to non-residents, which is equivalent to a taxable property transfer of US$ 60,000. Note that the US has negotiated several estate tax treaties that seek to avoid double taxation.

Transfers to resident alien spouses are not eligible for the unlimited marital deduction. Rather tax-free transfers of up to US$ 100,000 may be made to a resident alien spouse annually. At death, transfers to a resident alien spouse may be taxed unless set aside in a 'qualified domestic trust' for use by the living spouse, This concept was established in 1988 to assure that the assets transferred to the resident alien spouse, and not consumed during his or her lifetime, will eventually be subject to the US estate tax provisions.

Wealth tax

The US has no wealth tax.

Social security contribution

Any service performed in the US by an employee is subject to federal and state employment taxes (social security, unemployment, etc.).

The federal government requires that all workers and their companies contribute to the social security retirement plan. In 2000 the contribution is presently 6.20% of compensation up to US$ 76,200 (US$ 80,400 in 2001) for both employers and employees. The same tax for self-employed persons is 12.40% on self-employed income up to US$ 76,200. In addition, employers and employees each must contribute 1.45% and self-employed persons 2.9% of compensation/ earnings to Medicaid. Since 1994, the Medicaid contribution applies to all compensation with no maximum.

Treatment of partnerships

Partnerships are not subject to tax in the US. Rather, partnership items of income and deduction are apportioned and allocated among the partners. The partnership is a flow-through entity for tax purposes and each partner is subject to income tax on his distributive share of partnership income. There are special rules regarding the manner in which income and deductions may be allocated among the partners. In general, special allocations will be permitted if the allocations have substantial economic effect. All of the states have now adopted the concept of a limited liability company (LLC) which combines the pass-through taxation of the partnership with the limited liability protection of a corporation.

VAT and sales taxes

There is no national sales tax, but many states and municipalities have enacted their own sales tax on goods and services, subject to certain exemptions. Exemptions from the sales tax include goods and services purchased for resale, purchased by tax exempt institutions and purchased for use in the manufacturing process.

Other taxes

Federal taxes

Excise and stamp taxes

Applies to a limited range of goods and services including alcohol, tobacco, telephone and air transport.

Customs duties

Levied at various rates on most imported commodities; there are no export duties.

Property taxes

Imposed on real estate and various tangible and intangible property.

Transfer taxes

Imposed on real estate, securities, etc.

Severance taxes

Imposed on timber, minerals and other extractive sources.

Exchange control

The US has no exchange controls.

Tax treaties and withholding

The statutory withholding rate on US source interest, dividends, royalties, etc is 30%. Under most double tax conventions the rate is significantly reduced. Withholding tax rates under selected tax treaties are reflected in the table below. The table provides general withholding rates only. Many treaties have special rules and exceptions regarding withholding and the actual treaty article must be consulted. In addition, the US regularly renegotiates treaties.

Country of Residence	*Normal Dividends (%)*	*Participation Dividends (%)*	*Minimum Participation Dividends (%)*	*Interest (%)*	*Royalty (%)*
Non-treaty countries	30	–	–	30	30
Selected treaty countries					
Australia	15	15	–	10	10
Austria	15	5	10	0	0–10
Belgium	15	5	10	15	0
Canada	15	5	10	10	0–10
Cyprus	15	5	10	10	0
Denmark	15	5	95	0	0
Egypt	15	5	10	15	15
France	15	5	10	0	0–5
Germany	15	5	10	0	0
Greece	30	30	–	0	0–30
Hungary	15	5	10	0	0
India	25	15	10	15	10–15
Indonesia	15	10	25	10	10
Ireland	15	5	10	0	0
Israel	25	12.5	10	17.5	10–15
Italy	15	5	>50	15	5–10
Japan	15	10	10	10	10
Korea	15	10	10	12	10–15
Luxembourg*	15	5	50	0	0
Mexico	10	5	10	5–15	10
Netherlands	15	5	10	0	0
New Zealand	15	15	–	10	10
Norway	15	15	–	0	0
Pakistan	30	15	>50	30	0–30
Philippines	25	20	10	15	15
Poland	15	5	10	0	10
Portugal	15	10	25	10	10
Romania	10	10		10	10–15
Russia	10	5	10	0	0
Slovak Republic	15	5	10	0	0–10

South Africa	15	5	10	0	0
Spain	15	10	25	10	5–10
Sweden	15	5	10	0	0
Switzerland	15	5	10	0	0
Thailand	15	10	10	10–15	5–15
Trinidad & Tobago	30	30		30	0–30
Tunisia	20	14	25	15	15
Turkey	20	15	10	10–15	5–10
United Kingdom	15	5	10	0	0

* Not applicable to companies with tax-free status.

Other treaty countries

China, Finland, Iceland, Jamaica and Morocco.

Anti-avoidance measures

If a corporation, directly or indirectly, acquires control of another corporation to evade or avoid income tax by the use of the acquirer's losses, deductions or credits, then such use is prohibited.

In the international arena, the IRS will attack treaty shopping where the intent is to avoid US income taxes. The goal of government is to limit treaty benefits to residents of the two treaty countries. Many of the newer US bilateral treaties contain restrictive anti-treaty shopping clauses.

Uruguay

Normey – Peruzzo & Asociados

Introduction

The following is a summarised structure of the Uruguayan tax system.

Income tax

A tax on the earnings of the industrial, commercial, financial and farming sectors of the economy, made up of the following taxes:

IRIC (tax on the income of industry and commerce)

This is an annual tax on the income of Uruguayan source derived from industrial, commercial and any other similar activities, derived from activities developed, assets situated and rights economically used within the country.

The income subject to tax is the normal commercial income at entities and income derived from intellectual properties as follows:

- cessation of use;
- sale of trade marks;
- patents;
- industrial models or privileges (know-how);
- technical assistance given by non-resident individuals or enterprises and the dividends or profits credited or paid to non-resident individuals or enterprises.

Taxpayers subject to IRIC include partnerships with or without legal status, associations and foundations established to undertake taxable activities and those who obtain income from intellectual property as outlined above.

The tax is calculated on net income, after deducting the necessary expenses in order to obtain and preserve the gross income.

Exempt income

Income accruing to shipping or aircraft companies is exempt. If they are foreign companies there must be a reciprocity condition via a tax treaty for Uruguayan enterprises to secure exemption. Activities included in the IRA (farming products income tax) and those derived from holding shares of the National Corporation for Development are also exempt from IRIC.

In addition, the following entities are exempt of the IRIC:

- cultural;
- educational;
- sports institutions;
- not-for-profit societies;
- official institutions of foreign countries (subject to tax treaty reciprocity);
- income obtained by the National Corporation for Development and the income derived from enterprises whose sales do not surpass the amount established by the Executive Power yearly. Currently this amount is $ 330,000 of sales a year (US$ 27,000).

The rate of IRIC is fixed at 30% on net earnings.

IRA (farming income tax)

This is an annual tax on the income derived from the farming activity and its basic structure is similar to IRIC including the rate.

IMEBA (tax to the sale of farming goods)

1.5% to 2.5% on sales of farming products to taxpayers subject to IRIC, public institutions or direct exportations of farming products. It may be considered as a prepayment of the IRA and is an additional tax beyond the IRA.

Capital taxes

These are taxes on wealth and net 'Patrimony' (assets located in Uruguay) levied on all assets with special rules for financial institutions.

Patrimony taxes

An annual tax is levied on the value of assets situated, placed or economically used in Uruguay, on the difference between the assets and liabilities as adjusted for tax purposes.

Entities subject to this tax include individuals, families, inheritances, bank accounts, resident legal enterprises, non-resident enterprises and industrial and farming partnerships.

Non-taxable assets

Public debt bond shares of the National Corporation for Development, woods areas and citric plantations. The following assets are also exempt:

- deposits of individuals in bank institutions;
- public bonds;
- private bonds issued by enterprises and nominative bonds only when they are quoted on the Stock Exchange;
- farming real estate.

Allowable liabilities to offset against asset values in computing the taxable amount are those contracted with local suppliers of goods and services, local banks, with public institutions and those contracted with international credit institutions.

For individuals, families and undistributed inheritable estates of the deceased, there are progressive rates from 0.7% to 3.0%. For enterprises there is a fixed rate of 1.5%.

IMABA (tax on the assets of finance institutions)

Private banks, finance organizations, the BROU (Bank of the Republic of Uruguay) and the Mortgage Bank of Uruguay are taxed on assets including bank settlements, credits, long term assets and investments outside of the usual trading activity.

Rates

The rate is generally 1.5%. For credits to finance certain imports and exports, social credit, loans to public organisations and long term credits for bank guarantees, the rate is 0.75%. For public bonds the rate is 0%.

Personal taxes

Social security contributions

Individuals receiving wages as compensation for work and their employers are subject to this tax on wages received as compensation for personal services. The employer's contribution is 18.62% and the employee pays 20.12% on the wages earned.

Offshore companies

'Sociedades Anónimas Financieras de Inversión (SAFI)' offshore Co., established under Law No. 11073 of 24 June 1948 establishes a legal and tax system for offshore companies.

Legal system

The legal system of this kind of SAFI is similar to any other company in Uruguay, in that its by-laws are drawn up in a public or private legal document and require the approval of the Domestic Audit of the Nation, registration in the Public and General Register of Commerce, publication in the Official Newspaper and in another newspaper, its registration in the Merchants Register, and the certification in the books of Shareholders Assembly, Board of Directors and Accounting.

The shared capital may be represented by bearer or registered shares (the latter are exceptional) and in any currency (dollars generally).

At the end of the Fiscal Year, the SAFI must draw up its balance sheet, submit it for the approval of the Shareholders Assembly and introduce its tax affidavit to the Tax General Office (DGI).

Tax system

The tax system for SAFIs differs from common companies. SAFIs do not pay any taxes on profits. They pay an annual charge of 0.003% of their paid up capital subject to certain details of calculation.

SAFIs pay only this one tax in Uruguay. They are restricted from developing any kind of activity or from holding real estate within Uruguay.

Like many countries with an offshore company legislation they are broadly exempt from taxes provided their operations are outside the territory.

Other taxes

IVA (value added tax)

Entities who sell goods and services and who receive fees for personal services are charged to IVA on domestic consumption of goods and services within Uruguay and the importation of goods.

As with most taxes under this description, the charge is on the value added at each cycle of production, wholesale and retail and on the value agreed with the authorities on imported goods.

The rate is dependant on the nature of the goods and services and is between 14% and 23%. There is a prepayment of 5% and 3% when goods are imported.

IMESI (specific domestic indirect tax)

Manufacturers and importers of taxed goods are taxed on the sale of certain goods as set out below.

- alcohol 11%;
- spirits 85%;
- cosmetics 20%;
- tobacco and cigarettes 72%;
- some vehicles 22%;
- oils 35%;
- fuels (different rates from, a minimum of 7% for crude, to a maximum of 102% for superior i.e. 'green').

Venezuela

Cardona, Rodriguez y Asociados

Introduction

Taxation in Venezuela is applied at two different levels by national and municipal governments, including inheritance and donations tax, tobacco and alcoholic beverages.

The national taxes are based on income and are supervised and controlled by the Finance Ministry (*'Ministerio de Hacienda'*) through its tax department, Servicio Nacional Integrado de Administracion Tributaria (SENIAT). SENIAT also controls customs operations and collects taxes for every liable contributor. Municipal taxation is controlled by the municipal government (*'Alcaldias de Municipios'*) and varies between municipalities throughout Venezuela. A municipality is located within a single state and a state can have more than one municipality.

Each taxpayer is assigned an identification number by the Finance Ministry. This number applies for all taxes payable and must be printed on invoices, delivery notes, receipts, etc. An expense is not considered deductible unless the supporting invoice contains the appropriate identification number, otherwise considered non-deductible.

Tax payments are made using personalised slips prepared by the tax authorities. The tax liability lasts for over four years and the personal tax period runs from 1 January to 31 December. For corporate tax, the tax period is one year, but the start date may be varied. Where tax is overpaid, the taxpayer can make a formal claim to recover the balance. There are court procedures to resolve conflict between taxpayer and tax authority over the interpretation of tax laws, decrees or articles, culminating in a decision from the Justice Supreme Court.

Overpayments and underpayments are only offset against tax of the same nature.

Dividends

On 22 October 1999, the National Assembly approved a modification of the Income Tax Law published in the Official Gazette No. 5.390.

When a company approves dividends to be paid to its shareholders, those dividends will be taxable when larger than the declared earning (tax applies to the difference in declared earning and approved dividend).

Income tax

Income tax applies to the profits of industry, trade, financial services and equities. It must be declared and paid within three months of the fiscal year end. Because Venezuela has experienced high inflation during the last decade, the tax authorities have, since 1991, included in amendments to tax legislation an inflation adjustment system for all non-monetary assets and liabilities. The difference between adjusted values and historical values results in equity increasing or decreasing liable to tax or a deduction (see below).

Taxable income

Income is liable to tax on the availability principle. Venezuelan income is considered available when it is effectively paid. For example, income from leasing activities, professional services and salaries becomes available when the services are performed.

Deductions

The following main deductions may be made, with some restrictions:

- salaries and professional fees;
- interest charged on loans, where the interest and capital loaned is invested in the business;
- labour benefits included in employment legislation, as well as any other benefit given to employees;
- a reasonable percentage for depreciation and amortisation;
- reserves made by insurance companies in accordance with financial institutions legislation;
- leasing rents;
- insurance expenses;

- other necessary and reasonable expenses incurred in the course of the business.

Tax rates

Tax rates vary according to whether the taxpayer is a company or an individual. Mining corporations are taxed at rates different to those of other corporations.

Due to the high inflation rate in Venezuela, taxable income is measured by tax units (unidades tributarias) which are updated with reference to changes in the consumer prices index (IPC) published monthly by the Central Bank of Venezuela. At the time of writing, the tax unit is Bs 13,200,00.

Individuals are taxable over minimum earnings of 1,000 tax units during the fiscal period. Corporations must make a tax declaration regardless of their level of profit.

The rates for income tax are as follows:

Tariff No. 1 (applicable only to individuals):

Taxable income (tax units)	*Tax rate (%)*
Up to 1,000	6
1,000 – 1,500	9
1,500 – 2,000	12
2,000 – 2,500	16
2,500 – 3,000	20
3,000 – 4,000	24
4,000 – 6,000	29
6,000 and over	34

Tariff No. 2 (applicable to corporations, excluding mining companies):

Taxable income (tax units)	*Tax rate (%)*
Up to 2,000	15
2,000 – 3,000	22
3,000 and over	34

Tariff No. 3 (applicable to mining and similar companies):

- earnings from mining company royalties are taxed at a 60% proportional rate;
- earnings from mining companies are taxed at a 67.7% proportional rate.

Transfer pricing

A transfer pricing system was implemented since the last modification of the income tax law. This system applies for transactions between related parties.

There are four methods for calculating cost and deductions related to transactions made between related parts:

- *Resale price method*
  Consists in calculating average resale price of goods and services, after deducting non-conditional discounts, taxes, commissions and fees and the profit margin calculated on resale price.
- *Comparable uncontrolled price method*
  Consists in calculating average price of goods and services in the internal market or foreign countries in similar payment conditions.
- *Manufacturing cost method*
  Consists in calculating average manufacturing cost of goods and services caused in manufacturing country, adding export taxes paid in source country and profit margin calculated on determined cost.
- *Transactional operative profit method*
  For this method, the taxpayer should calculate his profit based on operations made for similar companies in similar operations and conditions.

Fiscal inflation adjustment

In 1992, income tax legislation implemented an inflation adjustment system which specifies that most companies are obliged to make an adjustment in accordance with changes in the consumer prices index (IPC) published by the Central Bank of Venezuela for all non-monetary assets and liabilities. The difference results in an equity increase or decrease liable to tax or available as a deduction. The initial adjustment of non-monetary assets is at a rate of 3%. For subsequent fiscal years the tariffs detailed above will apply.

Enterprise assets tax

In addition to income tax, taxpayers must pay 1% tax on the average amount of the adjusted assets less the inflation loss of all monetary assets. Payment of this tax is treated as an advance payment of income tax.

Value added tax

Venezuela adopted a VAT system on 1 June 1999. The applicable rate is 14.5% throughout Venezuela, except in the state of Nueva Espata, which does not apply. This tax was created to be a replacement of the Sales Taxes which existed since 1994 with a rate of 16.5%. Some exemptions apply, including educational services and processed foods, among others.

VAT is payable by the fifteenth day of each month. The taxpayer must keep records showing fiscal credits for purchasing and fiscal debit for sales. The difference between debits and credits must be declared and paid. Accrued fiscal credits can be used to offset output taxes in subsequent periods in order to reduce the amount to be paid.

Withholding taxes

Some payments are liable to withholding taxes, and they can be deductible only when withheld tax has been applied and paid. In order to determine whether an expense is liable to withhold tax, there is an Official Decree (Decreto 1.808) which shows all liable payments and the rate to be used. Withholding taxes are applied in different conditions, such as for a resident or non-resident taxpayer (which can be companies or persons).

Rates for withholding are from 3% until 34%, as well as tariff 2 (see earlier), which is also used.

International agreements and tax treaties

Venezuela has treaties with the following selected countries, for the avoidance of double taxation in income and maritime tax:

- The Netherlands
- United States of America
- United Kingdom
- Argentina
- Germany
- Italy
- Spain
- Portugal
- France
- Canada

- Chile
- Switzerland.

Nexia contacts by country

Argentina	Graciela Vallès *Estudio Giordano & Asociados*	*Telephone:* + 54 11 4381 0416 *Facsimile:* + 54 11 4383 5675 *Email:* graciela_valles@bga.com.ar
Australia	Peter Cowdroy *Lord & Brown*	*Telephone:* + 61 2 9251 6700 *Facsimile:* + 61 2 9251 6744 *Email:* pcowdroy@lordandbrown.com.au
Austria	Vinzenz Hamerle/Andreas Ehemoser/Sascha Noss *Hamerle & Partner Wirtschaftstreuhand GmbH*	*Telephone:* + 43 1 712 4114 *Facsimile:* + 43 1 712 4114 20 *Email:* office@hamerle-partner.at
Belgium	Edward van Rijswijck *Delvaux Fronville Servais et Associés*	*Telephone:* + 00 32 2 352 0520 *Facsimile:* + 00 32 2 353 0555 *Email:* claude.selvais@dfsa.be
Brazil	Ricardo Julio Rodil *Villas Rodil Auditores E Consultores*	*Telephone:* + 55 11 3846 7077 *Facsimile:* + 55 11 3846 0697 *Email:* rodil@nexia.com.br
Canada	Jonathan Bicher *Friedman & Friedman*	*Telephone:* + 1 514 731 7901 *Facsimile:* + 1 514 731 2923 *Email:* bicher@friedman.ca
Chile	David Barros/Alejandro Sierra *Humphreys & Cia.*	*Telephone:* + 56 2 223 4937 *Facsimile:* + 56 2 223 4937 *Email:* david.barros@humphreys.cl alejandro.sierra@humphreys.cl
China (Beijing)	Chen Xi *Beijing Xingye C.P.As*	*Telephone:* + 86 10 8425 5948 *Facsimile:* + 86 10 6428 5411 *Email:* xycpay@china.com
(Guangzhou)	David Sun *Guangzhou Xin Zhong Nan C.P.As*	*Telephone:* + 86 20 8354 9875 *Facsimile:* + 86 20 8354 9309 *Email:* aaa@gzcpa.com
(Shanghai)	Song Xin *Shanghai New Zhong Chung C.P.As*	*Telephone:* + 86 21 3210 0018 *Facsimile:* + 86 21 6272 6017 *Email:* shzccpa@online.sh.cn
Colombia	Juan José Améquita P. y Leyda A. Talero *Amézquita & Cia.*	*Telephone:* + 57 1 368 5407 *Facsimile:* + 57 1 368 5416 *Email:* amezqbog@col1.telecom.com.co
Cyprus	Petros Nacouzi *Nexia Poyiadjis*	*Telephone:* + 357 2 666 406 *Facsimile:* + 357 2 666 276 *Email:* nexia.nacouzi@cylink.com.cy

Country	Contact	Details
Czech Republic	Vladimir Královicek/Petra Pechova *Audit Plus s.r.o*	*Telephone:* + 420 2 22 78 2492 *Facsimile:* + 420 2 22 78 0435 *Email:* audit.plus@volny.cz
Denmark	Peter Viereck *Nexia Preben Larsen*	*Telephone:* + 45 701 29 900 *Facsimile:* + 45 701 29 940 *Email:* pwv@nexia.dk
Egypt	A Hamdi Abou Saada *Abou Saada & Partners*	*Telephone:* + 20 2 76 11 003 *Facsimile:* + 20 2 7611 009 *Email:* aspnexia@intouch.com
France	Jean Marcel Denis/Olivier Lelong *Auditeurs & Conseils Associés*	*Telephone:* + 33 1 47 66 77 88 *Facsimile:* + 33 1 47 66 77 80 *Email:* aca.paris@wanadoo.fr
Germany	Dr Norbert Neu *DHPG/BTR Rheinland GmbH*	*Telephone:* + 49 228 81 00 00 *Facsimile:* + 49 228 81 00 020 *Email:* n.neu@DHPG.de
Hong Kong	Selwyn Mar/Thomas Wong *Charles Mar Fan & Co.*	*Telephone:* + 852 2 520 0333 *Facsimile:* + 852 2 529 4347 *Email:* marfan@pobox.com
Hungary	Dr Péter Galambos/Dr Éva Somogyi/Judit Guth *Metrum Auditing Ltd*	*Telephone:* + 00 36 1 209 4922 *Facsimile:* + 00 36 1 209 4923 *Email:* metrum@metrum.hu
India	Shreedhar T Kunte & Farook M Kobla *Sharp & Tannan*	*Telephone:* + 91 22 204 77 22 *Facsimile:* + 91 22 204 59 63 *Email:* sharp@bom3.vsnl.net.in
Indonesia (Jakarta)	Johan Yoranouw *Johan, Malonda & Rekan*	*Telephone:* + 62 21 661 7115 *Facsimile:* + 62 21 669 6918 *Email:* jmmajkt@johanmalonda.com
(Surabaya)	J Malonda/Henry Supit *Johan, Malonda & Rekan*	*Telephone:* + 62 31 594 7939 *Facsimile:* + 62 31 593 8601 *Email:* jmsby@johanmalonda.com
(Medan)	Rosni Oendang *Johan, Malonda & Rekan*	*Telephone:* + 62 61 452 0350 *Facsimile:* + 62 61 457 1681 *Email:* jmmamdn@johanmalonda.com
Ireland	Dermot Troy/Robert Browne *Oliver Freaney and Company*	*Telephone:* + 353 1 614 2500 *Facsimile:* + 353 1 614 2555 *Email:* dtroy@ofc.ie/rbrowne@ofc.ie
Isle of Man	Nigel Rotheroe *Crossleys*	*Telephone:* + 44 1624 822 816 *Facsimile:* + 44 1624 824 570 *Email:* nrotheroe@crossleys.com
Israel	Israel Strauss *Strauss Lazer & Co.*	*Telephone:* + 972 3 623 7777 *Facsimile:* + 972 3 561 3824 *Email:* slcpa@strauss-lazar.co.il
	Ran Artzi *Haft & Ziv*	*Telephone:* + 972 3 6386 868 *Facsimile:* + 972 3 639 3727 *Email:* artzir@zivhaft.co.il

exia contacts by country

aly	Massimo Milan *Arietti & Partners*	*Telephone:* + 39 011 561 27 22 *Facsimile:* + 39 011 561 91 14 *Email:* massimo.milan@studioarietti.com
Japan	Akinaga Murayama *Sawamura & Co.*	*Telephone:* + 81 3 3269 8801 *Facsimile:* + 81 3 5261 2782 *Email:* murayama@nexia.gr.jp
Jersey	Michael Weston *Langtry International*	*Telephone:* + 44 1534 750 000 *Facsimile:* + 44 1534 750 075 *Email:* langtry@itl.net
Kenya	Beth Mwisywa *Carr Stanyer Gitau & Co.*	*Telephone:* + 254 2 338 092 *Facsimile:* + 254 2 338 095 *Email:* csg@insightkenya.com
Korea	Myung Chul Kim *Samduk Accounting Corporation*	*Telephone:* + 82 2 735 0241 *Facsimile:* + 82 2 730 9559 *Email:* cpamck@kicpa.or.kr
Lebanon	Farouk Addada *Usamah Tabbarah & Co.*	*Telephone:* + 961 1 75 1111 *Facsimile:* + 961 1 74 6749 *Email:* nexiab@terra.net.lb
Luxembourg	Nigel Hodges *Nexia International*	*Telephone:* + 44 207 487 4648 *Facsimile:* + 44 207 487 3484 *Email:* nhodges@nexia.com
Malawi	F S Sakyi/D Ngwira/J B Mchakama *Graham Carr*	*Telephone:* + 265 623 484 *Facsimile:* + 265 623 168 *Email:* grahamcarr@malawi.net
Malaysia	Nigel Hodges *Nexia International*	*Telephone:* + 44 207 487 4648 *Facsimile:* + 44 207 487 3484 *Email:* nhodges@nexia.com
Mauritius	Abdoul Sattar Hajee Abdoula *Hajee Abdoula & Ramtoola*	*Telephone:* + 230 212 9477 *Facsimile:* + 230 212 9473 *Email:* sattar@bow.intnet.mu
Mexico	Hector J. Garcia Martinez *Gossler, S.C.*	*Telephone:* + 52 8 347 35 75 *Facsimile:* + 52 8 348 98 87 *Email:* hgarcia@gossler.com.mx
Morocco	Mohamed Ouedghiri *Fiducia*	*Telephone:* + 212 22 36 43 77 *Facsimile:* + 212 22 36 48 25 *Email:* fidunex@casanet.net.ma
Netherlands	A C Krol *Horlings, Brouwer & Horlings Tax Consultants*	*Telephone:* + 31 20 670 6159 *Facsimile:* + 31 20 670 6205 *Email:* tkrol@hbh.nl
New Zealand	Nigel Hodges *Nexia International*	*Telephone:* + 44 207 487 4648 *Facsimile:* + 44 207 487 3484 *Email:* nhodges@nexia.com
Nigeria	Ernest Cukelu *Sulaimon & Co.*	*Telephone:* + 00 234 62 240 776 *Facsimile:* + 00 234 62 240 779 *Email:* sulcokd@skannet.com